Violence after War

Violence after War

Explaining Instability in Post-Conflict States

MICHAEL J. BOYLE

Johns Hopkins University Press
Baltimore

© 2014 Johns Hopkins University Press
All rights reserved. Published 2014
Printed in the United States of America on acid-free paper
2 4 6 8 9 7 5 3 1

Johns Hopkins University Press
2715 North Charles Street
Baltimore, Maryland 21218-4363
www.press.jhu.edu

Library of Congress Cataloging-in-Publication Data

Boyle, Michael J., 1976–
Violence after war : explaining instability in post-conflict states / Michael J. Boyle.
pages cm
Includes bibliographical references and index.
ISBN 978-1-4214-1257-3 (hardcover : alk. paper) — ISBN 978-1-4214-1258-0 (electronic) — ISBN 1-4214-1257-8 (hardcover : alk. paper) — ISBN 1-4214-1258-6 (electronic) 1. Political violence. 2. Peace-building. 3. Conflict management. 4. War. I. Title.
JC328.6.B686 2014
303.6—dc23   2013024544

A catalog record for this book is available from the British Library.

Special discounts are available for bulk purchases of this book. For more information, please contact Special Sales at 410-516-6936 or specialsales@press.jhu.edu.

Johns Hopkins University Press uses environmentally friendly book materials, including recycled text paper that is composed of at least 30 percent post-consumer waste, whenever possible.

CONTENTS

Acknowledgments *vii*
List of Abbreviations *xi*

1 The Challenge of Violence in Post-Conflict States   1

PART I   UNPACKING VIOLENCE AFTER WARS

2 Understanding Violence after Wars: *Concepts and Contexts*   23

3 Explaining Violence after Wars: *Patterns and Pathways*   45

PART II   FIVE CASE STUDIES OF POST-CONFLICT VIOLENCE

4 Bosnia-Herzegovina   99

5 Rwanda   143

6 Kosovo   175

7 East Timor   227

8 Iraq   257

PART III   PRODUCING PEACE AFTER WARS

9 Controlling Violence: *Implications and Policy Recommendations*   305

Notes   *323*
Bibliography   *383*
Index   *423*

ACKNOWLEDGMENTS

This book has been a long time in the making. It was developed out of my doctoral dissertation, "The Prevention and Management of Reprisal Violence in Post-Conflict States," at the Centre for International Studies at the University of Cambridge (2005). That dissertation was written in response to an internship that I completed in summer 2000 in the Office of the Special Advisor for Democracy in the Balkans in the U.S. Department of State. My job was to serve as a temporary replacement for the staff assistant who was in charge of Balkans-related matters and to ensure that the necessary papers (such as memorandums or talking points) were written and approved for use at the highest levels of government. As part of this job, I read news clippings and internal documents on the violence in Kosovo that continued after the war. I began to see the political ramifications of the hundreds of reprisal killings against Serbs and other minorities in the post-conflict period as they impeded efforts to build a functioning transitional government. I became fascinated with the contending explanations for post-conflict violence—whether it was revenge, crime, political violence, or some combination thereof—and decided to trace out the implications of these distinctions in my academic work.

I pursued this topic, in different forms and with different conceptualizations, in a master's thesis at Harvard and later in my doctoral dissertation at Cambridge. My supervisor for my master's thesis at the Kennedy School of Government, Monica Duffy Toft, provided the initial encouragement that I should pursue this topic. At Cambridge, my supervisor, Paul Cornish, was an unfailing source of advice, good humor, and encouragement and read dozens of drafts and wrote literally hundreds of reference letters for me. At Cambridge, I also thank many of the current and former staff at the Centre for International Studies, especially Tarak Barkawi, Wendy Cooke, Charles Jones, James Mayall, Mette Sangiovanni, Yezid Sayigh, Brendan Simms, Phillip Towle, and Marc Weller. I would also like to thank my friends in my Ph.D. cohort, who made those years so productive and enjoyable: Agnes Batory, Duncan Bell, William W. Burke-White, Susanna DiFelicitanio, Zaheer Kazmi, Maria Neophytou, Ricardo Soares de Oliveira, Casper Sylvest, and Anna Wishart. I am also grateful to many friends at Wolfson College, including Marie-Louise Daly, Varun Khanna, Ken Kwek, Anusha Mahalingam, Andres Melo, Mahesh Menon, Chris Neugebauer, Dervis Salih, Gregor Sutherland, and Karen Venetia Tiah.

This project ultimately became very different from its first drafts, but it would not have come to fruition without the fieldwork done in Kosovo (March–April 2002, March–April 2003), East Timor (May–June 2005), and Bosnia (May–June 2009). During fieldwork, I collected original statistics with the civilian police officers and officials and interviewed approximately one hundred people across the three cases. Many of the interviews were not cited in the final manuscript, but the conversations helped me to interpret the data more carefully. I am grateful to all of those I interviewed, both on and off the record, but I would particularly like to thank Karl Clark, Raffi Gregorian, Scott Korsnes, and Ambassador John Menzies for their kindness and logistical help in all three locations. I am also grateful to the United Nations for granting access to the Bosnia archives, and for those in the U.S. government who processed Freedom of Information Act (FOIA) requests for materials used in the case studies.

I was fortunate also to receive institutional support from a number of sources during the evolution of this project. In 2003–4, I was a Hamburg Fellow in Conflict Prevention at Stanford University and wrote up most of the challenging parts of the dissertation. I am grateful to the CISAC staff, particularly Lynn Eden, James Fearon, Scott Sagan, and Stephen Stedman, for their support and feedback on early draft chapters. At Stanford, I was also extraordinarily lucky to have Alexander L. George read drafts of my dissertation chapters and offer his wise advice on academic life in general. Some others played a key role, even if their involvement was brief. I owe a special debt to Charles Tilly, who took the time to meet me when I was a struggling Ph.D. student, to identify what I was doing wrong, and help me reframe the project.

In 2004–2005, I was a Fulbright fellow in the Department of International Relations at the Australian National University (ANU), where I finished my dissertation and worked on the East Timor chapter of this book. At the ANU, I was grateful for the advice and encouragement of Christian Reus-Smit, who sponsored my visit, and the rest of the faculty and graduate students. In 2005–2006, I was a postdoctoral fellow at the Belfer Center for Science and International Affairs (BSCIA), where I transformed this idea from a doctoral dissertation into an expanded book project. At Harvard, I am grateful to Graham Allison, Stanley Hoffman, Sean Lynn-Jones, Steven Miller, Steven Peter Rosen, Robert Rotberg, and Stephen Walt.

Throughout these years, many friends and colleagues have encouraged me, in ways big and small, or read pieces of this work at some point in its evolution. I would like to thank Max Abrahms, Marie Bescanon, Stephen Biddle, Nikolas Bizourias, Mia Bloom, Andre Broome, Fred Cocozzelli, Devon Curtis, Alexander Downes, Denise Garcia,

Rachel M. Gisselquist, Kelly M. Greenhill, Yee Kuang Heng, Bruce Hoffman, John Horgan, Michael C. Horowitz, Dominic Johnson, Joakim Kreutz, Anthony F. Lang, Marc Lantaigne, Peter Lehr, Orla Lynch, Kimberly Marten, Brad McAllister, Omar McDoom, Greg Mitrovich, Assaf Moghaddam, Tonya Putnam, Joel Quirk, Louise Richardson, Sebastian Rosato, Leonard Seabrooke, Todd Sechser, Rashmi Singh, Michael Smith, Jessica Stanton, Shogo Suzuki, Dominic Tierney, William Walker, Catherine Wilson, and Thomas J. Wright. All errors and omissions in the text are entirely my own.

While working on this project, I spent four years as a Lecturer in International Relations and Research Fellow at the Center for the Study of Terrorism and Political Violence (CSTPV) at the University of St. Andrews. During this period, this project received feedback and encouragement from many of my colleagues. A special debt of thanks is due to the inestimable Nick Rengger, for his advice and company on many late nights in the pub discussing this book and other things considerably less academic. I am also grateful to the former CSTPV Directors, Alex Schmid and Paul Wilkinson, both of whom were unfailingly generous with their time and advice on this project.

This project was completed with a generous grant from the Airey Neave Trust (2007–2009). Its support enabled me to do some additional fieldwork in New York and Sarajevo for the Bosnia chapter, to collect the primary documents used here, and to compile the cross-national dataset employed in chapter 3. I am grateful to Hannah Scott and the Trustees of the Airey Neave Trust for their support. Some of this work was done with the aid of highly capable undergraduate research assistants. I am grateful to Neil Best, Fiona Casling, Helene Pfeil, Caroline Sapp, and especially John Raines, whose work contributed immeasurably to the final project. I also worked with a number of excellent graduate students—Jeremy Kleidosty, Daniela Pisiou, and Sarah Whiteford—who aided with the more in-depth work of data collection in the case studies. In particular, I owe some special thanks to Torsten Michel, who cheerfully disagreed with the epistemological foundations of this project but was instrumental in seeing it through to completion. Many friends in St. Andrews also deserve special thanks for their involvement, especially Emma Buckley, Alison Careless, Faye Donnelly, Trudy Fraser, and John Morrison.

Since returning to my alma mater, La Salle University, in fall 2010, I have developed this project extensively with the encouragement and patience of my colleagues. I am very grateful to all of my colleagues, and former teachers, as well as to the generous support of the administration of the university. I particularly thank all of my colleagues in the political science department: Mary Ellen Balchunis, Michael R. Dillon, Miguel Glatzer, Kenneth L. Hill, Beth Paulin, and Edward Turzanski. A special debt of thanks is also due to William M. Sullivan, who first inspired me to think about an academic career, to John Grady, for his advice and encouragement through the Honors Program, and to Dr. Joseph Brogan, who was an unfailing supporter of my academic career, despite my ignoring his advice not to pursue a Ph.D.

Some of this material included here has been published in earlier articles, though all of it has been substantially revised, with only fragments of the published text and data replicated here. An early version of the theoretical argument, with some of the Kosovo and East Timor material, was published as "Explaining Strategic Violence after Wars," *Studies in Conflict and Terrorism*, 32:3 (March 2009), 209–236. The dissertation argument was summarized with some of the Kosovo data in "Revenge and Reprisal Violence in Kosovo," *Conflict, Security and Development* 10:2 (2010), 186–216 (available at www.tandfonline.com). Some of the arguments made in the Iraq chapter were employed, with different data, in "Bargaining, Fear and Denial: Explaining Violence against Civilians in Iraq, 2004–2007," *Terrorism and Political Violence* 21:2 (2009), 261–287.

At Johns Hopkins University Press, I am very grateful to both of the outstanding editors that I have worked with, the late Henry Tom and Suzanne Flinchbaugh, for their encouragement, patience, and support, and to all those involved in the production of the book. I am also grateful to the anonymous reviewer for constructive comments on the earlier draft and to Brian MacDonald for his copyediting assistance.

Too many friends to name have encouraged me throughout this process, but thanks are especially due to Brian Piech for his humor and good advice. A special debt of gratitude is due to Emma Jane Leonard, who provided the final push needed to get this project finished and made the past few years of my life among the happiest that I have had. This book is dedicated with love to my family: my parents, Teresa A. Boyle and the late John M. Boyle, and to my sister Susan M. Boyle.

ABBREVIATIONS

AAK	Alliance for the Future of Kosovo
ABRI	Angkatan Bersenjata Republik Indonesia (Indonesian military)
AFDL	Alliance of Democratic Forces for the Liberation of Congo-Zaire
ALA	Albanian Liberation Army
ALIR	Army for the Liberation of Rwanda
ANA/AKSh	Albanian National Army
AQI	Al Qaeda in Iraq
ARBiH	Army of Bosnia-Herzegovina
BiH	Bosnia and Herzegovina
BND	Bundesnachrichtendienst (Germany's intelligence service)
BSP	Border Service Project
CDR	Coalition for the Defense of the Republic
CENTCOM	Central Command
CIA	Central Intelligence Agency
CIVPOL	Civilian Police
CNRM	Conselho Nacional da Resistêncie Maubere
CNRT	Conselho Nacional de Reconstrução de Timor
COMKFOR	Commander of KFOR
CPA	Coalition Provisional Authority
CPD-RDTL	Committee for Popular Defense of Democratic Republic of East Timor
DDR	Demobilization, disarmament, and reintegration
DFAT	Department of Foreign Affairs and Trade (Australia)
DPA	Dayton Peace Accords
DRC	Democratic Republic of the Congo
ETTA	East Timor Transitional Administration
F-FDTL	Falintil-Forças de Defesa de Timor Leste
Falintil	Armed for Forces for the Liberation of East Timor

FAR	Rwandan Armed Forces (Forces Armées Rwandaises)
FARK	Armed Forces of the Republic of Kosovo
FRE	former regime elements
Fretilin	Revolutionary Front for an Independent East Timor
HDZ	Croatian Democratic Union
HRW	Human Rights Watch
HVO	Bosnian-Croat Army
IAC	Interim Administrative Council
IAI	Islamic Army of Iraq
ICG	International Crisis Group
ICITAP	International Criminal Investigative Training Assistance Program
ICTR	International Criminal Tribunal for Rwanda
ICTY	International Criminal Tribunal for Yugoslavia
IDP	internally displaced person
IEBL	Inter-Ethnic Boundary Line
IFOR	implementation force
IGC	Iraqi Governing Council
IIG	Iraqi Interim Government
INTERFET	International Force for East Timor
IOM	International Organization for Migration
IPTF	International Police Task Force
ISF	Iraqi security forces
JAM	Jaish al-Mahdi (Mahdi Army)
JIAS	Joint Interim Administrative Structure
JNA	Yugoslavian National Army
KDP	Kurdistan Democratic Party
KFOR	Kosovo Force
KLA	Kosovo Liberation Army
KM	Konvertibilna Marka (Bosnian currency)
KPC	Kosovo Protection Corps
KPS	Kosovo Police Service
KRG	Kurdistan Regional Government
KSF	Kosovo Security Force
KTC	Kosovo Transition Council
LDK	Democratic League of Kosovo
MONUC	United Nations Organization Mission in the Democratic Republic of the Congo
MRND	National Republican Movement for Development
MRP	Ministry of Public Order

MSF	Médecin sans Frontières
MTA	military technical agreement
MUP	Ministry of Interior Police
MUNJ	National Movement for Unity and Justice
NATO	North Atlantic Treaty Organization
NGO	nongovernmental organization
NLA	National Liberation Army
NRA	National Resistance Army
OHR	Office of the High Representative
OSCE	Organization for Security and Cooperation in Europe
PARMEHUTU	Party of the Hutu Emancipation Unit
PDK	Democratic Party of Kosovo
PIC	Peace Implementation Council
PISG	Provisional Institutions of Self-Governance
PKF	Peacekeeping Force
PL	Patriotic League
PNTL	Policia Nacional de Timor-Leste
POLRI	Indonesian national police
PPDK	Party for Democratic Progress of Kosovo
PU	Policia Ushtarake
PUK	Patriotic Union of Kurdistan
RANU	Rwandese Alliance for National Unity
RCD	Rally for Congolese Democracy
RDR	Rally for the Return of Refugees and Democracy to Rwanda
RPA	Rwandan Patriotic Army
RPF	Rwandan Patriotic Front
RPG	rocket-propelled grenade
RS	Republika Srpska
SBS	State Border Service
SCIRI	Supreme Council for the Islamic Revolution in Iraq
SDA	Party of Democratic Action
SDS	Serbian Democratic Party
SFOR	Stabilization Force
SHIK	Sherbimi Informativ I Kosoves (Kosovo Information Service)
SNC	Serbian National Council
SNSD	Alliance of Independent Social Democrats
SOI	Sons of Iraq
SP	Serbian Socialist Party
SPU	Special Police Units

SRSG	special representative of the UN secretary general
STOP	Special Trafficking Operations Program
TAL	Transitional Administrative Law
TMK	Trupat Mbrojtese te Kosoves (Albanian for KPC)
TNI	Tentara Nasional Indonesia (Indonesian military)
TWJ	al-Tawhid wal-Jihad
UCPMB	Liberation Army of Presevo, Medvedja, and Bujanovac
UCK	Ushtria Clirimtare E Kosoves (Albanian for KLA)
UIR	Rapid Response Unit
UN	United Nations
UNAMET	United Nations Mission in East Timor
UNAMIR	United Nations Assistance Mission to Rwanda
UNDOC	UN Office on Drugs and Crime
UNHCR	United Nations High Commissioner for Refugees
UNMIBH	UN Mission in Bosnia-Herzegovina
UNMIK	UN Mission in Kosovo
UNMISET	UN Mission of Support in East Timor
UNMIT	UN Integrated Mission in Timor Leste
UNOTIL	UN Office in East Timor
UNPOL	UN Police
UNSCR	UN Security Council Resolution
UNTAET	United Transitional Administration in East Timor
UPF	Border Patrol Unit
USAID	United States Agency for International Development
VJ	Yugoslav Army
VRS	Army of the Republika Srpska
WANRA	People's Resistance Unit
ZKZ	Zbulim-Kunderzbulim
ZOS	Zone of Separation

CHAPTER ONE

The Challenge of Violence in Post-Conflict States

All wars end, but they rarely end as predicted. The history of warfare is littered with accounts of leaders who have exhibited false optimism about how easy it will be to defeat an enemy in battle.[1] Wars expected to go on for years sometimes end in short order, while others expected to be quick fights descend into slow wars of attrition.[2] When a war ends, policy makers are often surprised to find that the post-conflict security environment is different from what they had envisioned. Armed conflicts that were supposed to have a bloody and chaotic aftermath sometimes end with a whimper, while others presumed to produce stable post-conflict environments turn out to be more violent than expected.[3] As the most recent war in Iraq illustrated, short and decisive wars can sometimes produce post-conflict environments bloodier than the war itself. Against the predictions of experts, some long-running and extremely violent wars, such as the civil war in Bosnia-Herzegovina (1991–1995), end with reprisals and criminal violence but without an organized violent attempt to restart the war. Far more than is recognized by those who start them, wars are a gamble and offer few guarantees about the nature of violence that will emerge in their wake.

The recent U.S. experiences in Iraq and Afghanistan provide vivid illustrations of how predictions about violence in the aftermath of wars can go very wrong. Concerned that the regime of Saddam Hussein might have weapons of mass destruction and be willing to offer these weapons to terrorist organizations, President George W. Bush authorized a plan to overthrow the Iraqi government in mid-2002.[4] During the invasion planning, the working assumption of the Bush administration was that the government could be toppled by U.S. and allied forces while leaving many of the state institutions intact.[5] On 25 February 2003, General Eric Shinseki publicly dissented from the view that few U.S. troops would be needed in the post-conflict period and told the Senate Armed Services Committee that the United States could require "something on the order of several hundred thousand soldiers" to contain the chaos that would follow the war.[6] Secretary of Defense Donald Rumsfeld was reportedly furious, and Bush administration officials moved quickly to downplay the number of

U.S. troops needed to occupy Iraq.[7] Only two days later, Deputy Secretary of Defense Paul Wolfowitz told the House of Representatives Budget Committee that "some of the higher-end predictions that we have been hearing recently, such as the notion that it will take several hundred thousand U.S. troops to provide stability in post-Saddam Iraq, are wildly off the mark. First, it's hard to conceive that it would take more forces to provide stability in post-Saddam Iraq than it would take to conduct the war itself and to secure the surrender of Saddam's security forces and his army. Hard to imagine."[8]

Nearly a decade after the invasion of Iraq in March 2003, it is clear that Shinseki's fears—and those of others who predicted high levels of violence following the overthrow of the Saddam Hussein regime—were well founded.[9] Senior members of the Bush administration believed that the overthrow of the Iraqi government would lead to a soft security environment with only residual violence against regime loyalists. In fact, the opposite occurred: after a lull of several months, an insurgency emerged and thousands more were killed in terrorist attacks, reprisals, criminal violence, and intersectarian bloodletting. While more than 7,356 Iraqis died in formal combat operations, more than 82,682 were killed in post-conflict violence over the next five years.[10] From a policy vantage point, managing the post-conflict environment proved more difficult than managing the war. By July 2008, five years after the formal declaration of victory in Iraq, 182,060 U.S. troops were in Iraq, roughly the same number that were present for the original invasion force.[11]

The assumption that things would go well in Iraq contrasts sharply with the widespread fear that the war in Afghanistan would be a quagmire from which the United States could never claim victory or extricate itself. When the United States launched its invasion of Afghanistan in October 2001, several influential commentators warned that the country was well known for being the "graveyard of empires" in which imperial powers such as Britain and the Soviet Union were bogged down for years fighting a vicious but resilient insurgency.[12] Within the United States, the war in Afghanistan reawoke memories of Vietnam, prompting a veteran journalist to remark that, "like an unwelcome spectre from an unhappy past, the ominous word 'quagmire' has begun to haunt conversations among government officials and students of foreign policy, both here and abroad."[13] One concern was that the overthrow of the Taliban might lead to a resumption of civil war or factional fighting among warlords now part of the Northern Alliance.[14] Others were concerned about the prospect of ethnic reprisals against Pashtun civilians for abuses committed by Pashtun forces in the Taliban.[15] Prospects for the war in Afghanistan were bleak, as many observers feared that the United States would find itself either in a long-running dirty war against the Taliban or in the midst of an endless war between the factions of the Northern Alliance.

Initially, the war in Afghanistan appeared to defy these expectations. The Taliban were expelled from Kabul by December 2001, and their apparent defeat was credited to a new approach to war fighting.[16] The war did not initially appear to be a quagmire, as predicted, but rather a sleek and high-technology operation that decimated the Taliban and capitalized on the on-the-ground fighting of the Northern Alliance.[17] Similarly, the first three years of the post-conflict period (2001–2004) went smoother than expected. There was relatively little direct violence in Afghanistan against U.S. forces or the Afghan security services.[18] A coalition government led by Hamid Karzai began to take shape, even if its governmental reach was limited. Human rights abuses, as well as criminal violence and corruption, were rampant in Afghanistan, but a civil war between the ethnic factions in Afghanistan did not occur. From 2001 to 2004, Afghanistan suffered from a kind of a violent and illiberal politics—one in which threats, intimidation, and gratuitous violence by political leaders, public officials, and ethnic warlords were common—but it did not have the high rates of strategic violence that normally characterizes insurgencies.[19]

Yet Afghanistan ultimately provided a case in point of how the nature of violence in post-conflict states can evolve over time, often in dangerous ways. In reality, the Taliban were never defeated; they continued limited operations from sanctuaries across the border in Pakistan. By 2005, they had restructured themselves, forging new alliances with warlords disaffected by the Karzai government.[20] As the government of Afghanistan struggled with poverty, corruption, and the opium trade, the Taliban metastasized from a small and weakened residual force into a more complex and lethal insurgency.[21] The fragile partnership of warlords within the Northern Alliance ruptured, as several reasserted de facto control over their home territories and turned on the government. Over the course of the occupation, the soft security environment of Afghanistan transformed into a hard security environment characterized by a full-blown insurgency, led by the Taliban but supported by an array of disaffected tribal and Islamist networks.[22] By the time that President Barack Obama had assumed office, the violence in supposedly post-conflict Afghanistan was so severe that the country was considered by NATO to be spinning "out of control."[23] Like Iraq, Afghanistan relapsed into full-fledged armed conflict several years into its post-conflict period. As was the case in Iraq, violence during the post-conflict period was markedly different from the violence during the war. In neither case did this relapse into armed conflict occur in the manner or timeline predicted before the war began.

Why do policy makers so often get it wrong when trying to predict security threats in post-conflict states? In neither of these cases can the failure be blamed on a lack of information or dissent within government. Firsthand accounts from key players in the Bush administration indicated that the United States received warning signs that its assumption of a favorable post-conflict environment in Iraq could be wrong.[24] In part, the explanation lies with several well-known psychological and organizational biases that can lead policy makers to misjudge threats. Within the study of the psychology of decision making, the two most obvious culprits are misperception and overconfidence. Policy makers can misperceive both the will and capability of their enemy, underestimating its desire to continue the fight beyond the formal end of the armed conflict.[25] Policy makers are often overconfident about the prospects for success in warfare; this psychological mechanism can lead to a systematic discounting of the potential negative consequences of their actions.[26] Alternatively, two organizational factors may be responsible for this failure to predict. First, there is the familiar problem of groupthink, in which those involved in collective decision making begin to systematically discount unwelcome alternatives to their preferred course of action.[27] Second, organizational pathologies among the uniformed military may make planners less willing to countenance the messy problems of violence after wars and more willing to focus on the neater problem of defeating the enemy's armed forces.[28] Together, these psychological and organizational factors can explain why U.S. officials found it so hard to imagine that the post-conflict environment of a chosen war (Iraq) would be difficult but so easy to believe that the aftermath of the war that they did not want (Afghanistan) would be disastrous.

Yet there is another, less-explored, reason why policy makers so often get it wrong: a failure to appreciate how the arrival of the post-conflict period reorders the incentives and organizational structures of the combatants, thus transforming the very nature of the violence that occurs within that state. When planning for an armed conflict and its aftermath, policy makers often assume continuity in the goals and strategies of the major actors as well as the targets and motives of violence. Their mental images of the war—particularly of who are the victims and perpetrators of violence, or the "good guys" and "bad guys"—tend to remain constant, despite the changes brought about by the termination of hostilities. As Iraq demonstrated, the post-conflict period can bring about entirely new categories of victims and perpetrators. While the war was conducted between the United States and its allies and the Iraqi government, much of the violence in its aftermath pitted U.S. and Iraqi forces against an array of Islamist insurgent groups and competing sectarian militias. Similarly, the categories of victims and perpetrators can be reversed if a peace settlement transfers power to a long-abused minority or disrupts an existing ethnic, religious, or political hierarchy.[29] In Iraq, the Baathist regime placed loyal Sunnis in dominant positions throughout the government and engaged in violent repression against Shi'a and Kurds. When the Baathist regime was overthrown, Shiite and Kurdish parties wound up as the backbone of the new government, leaving the Sunnis in a disadvantaged position. During the post-conflict period, tit-for-tat violence unfolded between Sunni and Shi'a communities, as well as between Sunni and Kurdish forces in the north of the country, some of which involved revenge for atrocities committed by the

Sunni-dominated Baathists during Saddam Hussein's rule. This dynamic—in which violence emerges after a reversal of fortune at the end of a long hated occupation—is not new. The end of German occupation in Europe brought about hundreds, if not thousands, of reprisals against collaborators and alleged collaborators, especially across Soviet-occupied Eastern Europe.[30] Similarly, after the surrender of the Japanese in East Asia, there was dozens of uprisings, including assassinations and reprisals, against Japanese soldiers and settlers in occupied countries.[31] In Malaya, nationalist insurgents killed five hundred Japanese and local police in the first two weeks of the post-conflict period, nearly the same number that they killed during the war.[32] Far more than participants can envision, the post-conflict period blurs the distinctions between the "good" victims and the "bad" perpetrators and produces unexpected shifts in the targets and perpetrators of violence, especially if the former victims take out rough justice on their oppressors.

Moreover, violence in post-conflict states unfolds for a range of complex, often evolving, motives that can be detached or indirectly related from the original rationale for the war. The peace settlement reorders the incentives of the local actors, leaving some interested in challenging the settlement through violence and others focused on preserving their gains.[33] Such a reordering of incentives can generate a scramble for power and resources by the existing actors, or fragment existing armed groups into a series of competing splinter factions.[34] In other words, the peace settlement can spur existing combatants to continue the fight, or it can generate a new array of smaller, often more hard-line, combatants willing to fight for their own purposes. Under the second scenario, the violence that occurs after wars will arise from bargaining conducted *across* and *within* these factions. Not only can such violence be unconnected or only indirectly related to the cause of the war itself, but it can also provide a space for opportunists to pursue a variety of personal or criminal vendettas, some of which will be detached from the fighting that preceded it.[35] In part because of these incentive shifts and organizational fractures, the violence of the post-conflict period will often appear as an inchoate mix of personal attacks, criminal violence, and political-strategic violence significantly different from the violence in the war that preceded it.

Violence in the Reconstruction (1865–1877)

As an example, consider the varied forms of violence that emerged in the post–Civil War American South. While the decisive defeat of the Confederate army appeared to offer the promise of freedom to the millions of black slaves, it did not offer them freedom from violence. Throughout the Reconstruction era (1865–1877) and afterward, freed slaves in the South were often brutally attacked by a wide range of actors, including former Confederate soldiers, Ku Klux Klan, state militias, criminal groups, former slaveholders and landlords, and ordinary citizens.[36] Many freed slaves were attacked to prevent them from voting or organizing for political action but also to ensure their compliance with the demands of their white employers or to stop them from opening businesses or building homes.[37] Freed slaves attempting to flee work on plantations were often beaten or killed as an example to others who would seek to exercise their rights after emancipation.[38] In some cases, freed slaves were brutalized for perceived violations of social mores, such as not demonstrating deference when encountering whites on the street.[39] Some attacks were also driven by petty grievances rather than any apparent political motive. Many white southerners attacks on black Union soldiers "seldom revealed any discernible motive other than resentment."[40]

Amid the violence devoted to separating the races and exercising social and political control over freed slaves was a significant amount of criminal violence. Gangs of criminals, often called regulators, "rode about the countryside whipping, hanging and murdering blacks, immune to capture by local authorities or federal soldiers."[41] Southern newspapers described much of the violence as a "crime wave," often produced by men who learned during the Civil War to settle disputes with violence.[42] Such an explanation was partially true but also self-serving. While some of the violence was purely criminal, attacks on freed slaves tended to increase dramatically when they attempted to vote; many of the atrocities against blacks betrayed clear organization and the involvement of militia groups that were composed of former Confederate soldiers, such as the Ku Klux Klan, the White Brotherhood, and the Knights of White Camellia.[43] Moreover, such violence was often tacitly approved by southern elites, who claimed either claimed no knowledge of the attacks or welcomed their results if not their methods. Indeed, many Klan leaders were from the respectable and professional families in southern towns and could hardly be written off as bandits or the criminal underclass.[44]

However, what is most striking about this violence is its variety, the extent to which attacks unfolded in different ways across space and time for myriad political, criminal, and personal reasons. Historians have also noted that it is not possible to reduce all of the violence in the post-conflict American South to political repression of freed slaves or efforts to block the political and social reforms in the Reconstruction.[45] Many targets of attacks appeared to be almost random, as freed slaves became victims through chance encounters and unfortunate timing. Many freed slaves were brutalized by angry southern whites whom they had never met. The sheer prevalence of violent attacks apparently driven by anger or rage has led historians to speculate that such random, expressive violence was "related to the peculiar psychological condition of a people frustrated and enraged by defeat in a long and painful civil war."[46] While there is no doubt that much of the violence against blacks was politically organized and condoned by southern elites, this strategic-political violence was intermixed with criminal depredations, "honour killings," score settling, and seemingly random violence driven by the anger, frustration, and despair of southern whites.[47]

While freed slaves were by far the most endangered during the Reconstruction period, they were not the only targets of violence. Supporters of the Union, Union soldiers garrisoned in southern towns, northern businessmen and travelers, and southern landlords or businessmen willing to deal fairly with freed slaves were also subject to violent attacks. Southern Republican Party officials, who were seen as the living embodiment of the Radical Reconstruction policies so hated by the South, were threatened and often fled as their offices were destroyed.[48] Northern politicians—so-called carpetbaggers involved in the administration of southern states—were threatened by criminal gangs and organized political groups such as the Ku Klux Klan in order to convince them to withdraw. In local elections, gangs and supporters of rival political factions engaged in tit-for-tat violence and coordinated attacks against southern politicians working with Washington—"scalawags"—were also common.[49] While motivated by the issues of race, not all of the violence corresponded to neat categories of victims and perpetrators; whites were also victims of violence, particularly if they were seen as being too sympathetic to the North or to the abolitionist cause. While the balance of the violence was disproportionately directed against blacks, newly freed slaves and black Union soldiers stationed in southern towns also committed offenses against white southerners.[50] Although the evidence is more fragmentary, it is also clear that some freed slaves engaged in retributive violence against southern whites, which in turn stoked fears that a black insurrection was forthcoming.[51] While it is clear that the central fault line of race remained the most important, new or rearranged categories of perpetrators and victims emerged in the multiplying forms of violence that accompanied the Reconstruction.

As this example demonstrates, violence in post-conflict states is varied and is often driven by personal grievances and criminal purposes as much as the central political fault lines of the conflict itself. But it also demonstrates that the chief political actors in the post-conflict period are often substantially different from those who were prominent during the war. During the Reconstruction, the defeated Confederate army demobilized and unfolded into militias, veteran's groups, criminal groups, and the Klan. Moreover, southern society itself had been transformed by the war, giving rise to a countermobilization of disaffected southern citizens, criminal elements, and opportunists, all of whom had their own reasons for acting violently. Introduced into this situation were northern transplants, including politicians, business leaders, and Union soldiers, as well as a host of southern collaborators with the government in Washington. The ensuing violence was not a replay of the Civil War but rather a new conflict, largely conducted at a subterranean fashion by new actors or by splinters from existing groups.

This example points to one of the reasons why policy makers often misunderstand the violence in post-conflict states: that the actors of the conflict themselves have changed or been transformed into less recognizable forms. Even more, these actors may no longer be fighting for goals related to the casus belli of the war itself. The post-conflict period can bring about shifts in the incentives and organizational structures of the chief combatants, leading them to engage in violence for reasons sometimes only peripherally related to the original conflict. Rather than mirroring the violence of the war, even highly strategic forms of violence in post-conflict states, are refracted through the political and organizational changes experienced by the combatants, producing an array of victims and perpetrators and a mix of violent acts different from what occurred during the war. The violence reflects their reordered priorities, their new estimation of their own bargaining strength, and the complex partnerships and rivalries that motivated their political behavior before and after the war itself. For all of these reasons, it is qualitatively different—in incidence, magnitude, type, and target—from the organized violence that preceded it.

The Puzzle

This book seeks to explain the complex mix of personal, criminal, and political violence that appears in post-conflict states. It starts with the assumption that no single logic can explain all incidents of violence because of the sheer variety of actors and motives for violent action present in post-conflict states. Chapter 2 proposes a conceptual approach, which disaggregates the complex mix of violence in post-conflict states into three broad categories: expressive violence (acts motivated by emotional reactions to loss or suffering), instrumental violence (acts directed at achieving criminal or personal gain), and strategic violence (acts designed to transform the balance of power and resources in a state). As the examples of violence during the Reconstruction period demonstrated, these three categories of violence are often intertwined, both conceptually and empirically, in post-conflict states.

Post-conflict states—seen here as a distinct category or class of states—are primed for all three categories of violence because of their common experience of armed conflict, though each case will feature its own unique mix of violent acts. Expressive violence (such as revenge killings) and instrumental violence (such as banditry and personal score settling) are particularly prevalent in societies where the wounds of the war run deep and the capacity of the government has been significantly diminished by the conflict.[52] Acts of strategic violence—such as assassinations, reprisals, insurgent attacks, and even acts of terrorism—are present in many, but not all, post-conflict states, if there are actors interested in challenging the peace settlement or in fighting over the division of the spoils. The complexity of violence in post-conflict states arises because these acts of strategic violence are interspersed, in varying degrees, within the waves of expressive and instrumental violence present in the society. The crime statistics of post-conflict states will reflect a mix of expressive, instrumental, and strategic acts, often aggregated and recorded as "murders," "arsons," and "assaults." Chapter 2 discusses how these different categories of violent activity relate to, and sometimes reinforce, one another in post-conflict environments. It also addresses an important but underexamined issue: How one can reliably determine whether an act, or set of acts, is strategic in an environment where information on motives is limited and the reasons for acting violently are many. In doing so, it aims to provide a textured account of the violence that occurs in post-conflict states, while also narrowing the analytic focus to the category of violence—strategic violence—most directly consequential for the peace settlement.

Like much of the scholarly literature, the predominant explanatory focus of this book is on strategic violence.[53] However, it relaxes the assumption that strategic violence is necessarily directed toward overturning the peace settlement or restarting the war. Rather, it argues for a broader conception of strategic violence, in which multiple actors can engage in violent bargaining with each other for a diverse range of purposes. As discussed in chapter 3, many instances of strategic violence are detached from an explicit or implicit challenge to the peace settlement; they reflect instead the ambitions and strengths of local actors, which are engaged in overlapping bargaining games with their rivals. In other words, the violence from the post-conflict state need not revolve around the "macro-cleavage" of the conflict, but can instead be understood as arising from local contests of strength between rival political factions.[54] Also, strategic violence is not necessarily directed against agents of the government or the state but can be conducted between ethnic, religious, and political communities, either in a tit-for-tat pattern or with one group victimizing civilians from the losing side of the conflict. This account of strategic violence also looks beyond the familiar forms of strategic violence, such as insurgent attacks and terrorism, and sheds light on the other, less noticed forms of strategic violence (e.g., assassinations, reprisals, acts of intimidation, and expulsions) that are prevalent in post-conflict states. Accordingly, it presents evidence of cases with low-intensity types of violence that have a cumulative effect of changing the balance of power and resources in the state while leaving the formal peace settlement intact. It also seeks to decouple the scholarly understanding of this violence from the study of spoiling and insurgencies and to produce a more complete account of the varying motives and forms of violence in post-conflict states.[55]

This portrayal of violence in post-conflict states differs from existing treatments of this subject in four ways. First, the predominant scholarly focus on violence in post-conflict states has been on cases (such as Iraq and Afghanistan) where the magnitude of the strategic violence is severe enough to restart the war.[56] Low-intensity strategic or criminal violence that falls below that threshold has been understudied, despite the fact that it can change the distribution of power or resources in the state. Only when violence rises to the level of an insurgency or a concerted attempt to "spoil" an existing peace settlement does it attract sustained scholarly attention.[57] By contrast, this book examines cases where low-intensity violence generates an unstable or dysfunctional peace but does not threaten the stability of the settlement itself. It also examines cases similar to the American South during Reconstruction in which violence is used to blunt efforts at political reconstruction and to change the effective terms of a peace settlement without resuming the conflict.

Second, the existing scholarly literature has focused on cases where the violence has led to a resumption of the war and offered a wide range of explanations for how outside actors can help to stop this from happening.[58] For the most part, casting the dependent variable as war resumption, rather than on the violence itself, is entirely appropriate: the resumption of the war is by far the most serious consequence of violence in a post-conflict state. However, much of this literature assumes that if war did not resume that the violence was negligible or epiphenomenal to the key issues that produced the conflict.[59] As chapter 3 demonstrates, this is itself due to an empirical underestimation of the actual extent of violence in post-conflict states. A closer look at violence in these cases reveals that there is substantial variety of violent acts, arising from diverse motives and practices, that are consequential for the peace even if they do not restart the war.[60] Such violence, conducted at low levels of intensity, can heighten tensions between ethnic and sectarian groups, undermine faith in a peace agreement, and produce a dysfunctional or illiberal peace. In this book, the dependent variable is not the resumption of the war but rather the violence itself; the analytic focus is on how changes in the incentives and organizational structure of local combatants generate unexpected variations in violence even in cases where the peace settlement remained intact.

Third, much of the existing literature tends to discount the local dynamics in play in the case in favor of an analysis which emphasizes the agency of external powers or peace builders.[61] This literature puts the onus for a successful peace agreement on the ability of external actors to bridge the gaps in trust between the actors or resolve the underlying source of contention.[62] It also suggests that violence is the result of a failure of external actors to achieve these tasks. Here the focus is on the local dynamics of each case, specifically the shifts in incentives and organizational fractures and realignments that occur in the post-conflict period that produce the violence. The case studies show that the external actors are largely reactive to the dynamics on the ground that produce the patterns of violence. In fact, many of these "custodians of peace" fail to grasp the reasons behind post-conflict violence because they are wedded to fixed images of good guys and bad guys that they developed during the war.[63]

Fourth, the narrative and historical literature that mentions violence in post-conflict states tends to treat each post-conflict state as a *sui generis* case, assuming that the violence is so idiosyncratic, case contingent, or driven by individual grievances and motives that comparative study would yield little insight. Only recently has work begun to appear that compares violence in multiple post-conflict states.[64] In this tradition, this book is an explicit effort to conduct a systematic comparative study of violence across a larger sample of recent post-conflict states. Its assumption is that this sample constitutes a unique class of states, marked by a distinct opportunity structure owing to their recent experience of armed conflict. This assumption does not mean that all post-conflict states are exactly alike or that violence within them is necessarily identical but that they share a set of characteristics that distinguishes them from other comparable classes of states, such as weak or failed states.

Using this conceptual framework as a starting point, this book aims to develop a theoretical framework that can explain the onset and variation in the levels of strategic violence in post-conflict states. It asks two related explanatory questions. First, why does strategic violence occur in some post-conflict states but not others? Second, why do some post-conflict states experience greater levels of strategic violence than others?

The Argument

The central argument of this book is that there are two causal pathways that can explain the onset of strategic violence in post-conflict states. The first pathway is called the *direct pathway*. Under this pathway, the existing combatants begin to employ strategic violence to spoil or renegotiate a peace settlement, to repress the losing side, or to expand the conflict to neighboring states as a way of achieving wider regional ambitions. Much of the existing literature focuses on this direct pathway, explaining violence after wars as an effort to spoil or disrupt the peace settlement in some way.[65] What distinguishes the direct pathway is the continuity of purpose with the violence during and following the conflict, as the perpetrators and victims largely remain the same and their motivations for employing violence are directly tied to those which motivated the original conflict. The distinguishing feature of the direct pathway is that the types and targets of the violence often remain the same as those during the war, and the violence revolves around the same fault lines in the society that motivated the war.

The second, and less explored, pathway to strategic violence is termed here the *indirect pathway*. Under the indirect pathway, former combatants find that they cannot enforce compliance with their factions or splinters over the terms of the peace settlement. As a result of their inability to exercise internal control over their ranks, the original combatant groups fragment into an array of splinter groups that begin to compete with one another for power and resources in post-conflict states. Under these conditions, strategic violence comes about through multiple and overlapping bargaining games between new and emergent claimants for power and resources.[66] In contrast to the direct pathway, which portrays the strategic violence as another iteration of the violence that occurred during the war, the indirect pathway portrays strategic violence as fundamentally different from what occurred during the conflict owing to the emergence of these new, highly localized bargaining contests between factions or splinter groups emerging from the ranks of the original combatants. The interaction between the decline of organizational cohesion among existing combatants and the incentives that new splinters or factions have to grab their own share of the power and resources produces shifts in the types and targets of violence often around new fault lines or cleavages in the society.

The indirect pathway focuses attention on the organizational challenges faced by combatants after wars, a factor sometimes overlooked in studies that treat the combatants—often portrayed stylistically as the "government" and "rebels"—as homogeneous actors that operate with the same cohesion and clarity of purpose as states.[67] Most wars today, however, are fought not between two equally organized and coherent militaries but by irregular armed groups and government forces that can lack cohesion, discipline, and strong leadership.[68] The onset of the post-conflict period produces a new set of political pressures on these heterogeneous armed groups, who find that they must comply with the settlement while maintaining organizational discipline and enforcing compliance with the settlement on factions within their ranks. The first issue that the leaders of armed groups face is whether to even sign the peace settlement. Peace settlements are not always signed sincerely as leaders of groups may sign agreements either to buy time to rearm and renew the fight or as a way of mollifying factions in their ranks.[69] Peace deals can be signed to the advantage of one faction or to throw another off balance. In other cases, mediation efforts by the UN or regional organizations may interrupt the conflict, forcing cease-fires on the participants before they are ready to accept the final terms of a peace settlement.[70] The tactical decision to sign a peace settlement, even if the leaders are dissatisfied with it, may lead to a surge in post-conflict violence if significant factions within their ranks are dissatisfied with it. Seen from this light, the mere existence of a peace settlement says little about the depth of support for it, and the level of support may vary significantly between the signatories and the rank and file of the armed group.

The second issue that armed actors face is enforcing compliance with the settlement. If significant portions of the rank and file of an armed group are dissatisfied with some or all of a peace settlement, they will have strong temptation to split off from the "parent" group and resume fighting on their own. Whether they have the capacity to do so depends on the level of internal control wielded by the group's leaders. Internal control is defined as the ability of the leadership of an organization to efficiently produce compliance by its members with the terms of an agreement. As chapter 3 argues, internal control varies significantly across government and rebel forces alike and is dependent on the original organizational endowments of the group, its resources, and leadership. As a rule, vertically organized or hierarchical groups, such as state-run militaries, exercise strong levels of internal control, whereas informal armed groups (such as militias or cellular resistance organizations) tend to exercise weaker levels of internal control. Yet internal control cannot be considered static, as armed groups can be hardened by fighting and emerge from a conflict more cohesive than they were at the outset. Similarly, the arrival of the post-conflict period produces its own series of pressures that can weaken internal control and generate organizational fractures within a formerly cohesive group.

Internal control is crucial to leaders of armed groups because it allows them to maintain organizational discipline and to control those who employ violence on their behalf. To maintain internal control, leaders of armed groups will distribute goods (such as profits, key resources, jobs, or political offices) to their factions and use sanctions and selective violence to punish those who defect or challenge their dominance. If internal control wanes and the distributional or patronage functions break down during the post-conflict period, splinter groups or factions will emerge and compete with each other through the use of strategic violence.[71] These overlapping bargaining games between existing and emerging claimants to power can generate local or regional microcosms of violent activity. This violent competition is often driven by local or factional politics more than the macro-cleavage of the conflict. For this reason, strategic violence in post-conflict states is not a replay of the violence during the war but rather reorders and transforms the fault lines of the conflict in a way that reflects the organizational and political changes that the combatants experienced following the settlement.

Cast more analytically, this conceptualization of the dilemmas that actors face when signing a peace settlement yields two key variables that will determine the pathway through which strategic violence emerges. The first is whether *support for the peace settlement* by all major actors in the post-conflict environment is present. The second is whether the degree of *internal control* wielded by the leaders of the key armed groups is high or low. The combination of these two variables yields four hypotheses about the incidence of strategic violence:

1. H_1: If all armed groups accept the settlement and have high levels of internal control, strategic violence should be absent or very low.
2. H_2: If all armed groups accept the settlement but at least one has low levels of internal control, strategic violence will be present as factional violence (the indirect pathway).

3. H_3: If some armed groups do not accept the settlement but all groups have high levels of internal control, strategic violence will be present as an attempt to spoil the settlement (the direct pathway).
4. H_4: If some armed groups do not accept the settlement and some groups also have low levels of internal control, strategic violence will be present as both spoiling and factional violence (the direct and indirect pathways).

In order to have little or no strategic violence, there must be high levels of support for the settlement, and armed groups must be capable of maintaining their control over their members. Especially in an age where the predominant form of conflict is internal or extrastate war, it is rare to find situations where armed actors fully accept the settlement and retain full control over their members.[72] As chapter 3 demonstrates, this fact accounts for the prevalence of strategic violence in many post-conflict states, including those in which the peace settlement remains formally intact.

These hypotheses also have clear implications for the types and targets of the violence. In cases where the direct pathway operates, the strategic violence will be similar to that of the war itself, reflecting the types and targets of violence that dominated the war. Under the direct pathway, strategic violence will revolve around the "macro-cleavage" that motivated the conflict. In cases where the indirect pathway is at work, the strategic violence will have a different set of types and targets of attack than the war itself. In these cases, strategic violence will revolve around a series of newer cleavages and fault lines in the society, including those that were nonexistent or latent during the conflict itself. In cases where both support for the settlement and internal control are low, both pathways will be in evidence. In these cases, such as Iraq (2003–2008), strategic violence will be particularly severe and will reflect a mix of attacks that constitute both a challenge to the peace settlement and the factional bargaining games that emerged in its aftermath.

The second major question addressed in this book concerns the variation in the levels of people killed by strategic violence in post-conflict states. The cross-national dataset presented in chapter 3 reveals a clear stratification in the levels of strategic violence, with some post-conflict environments recording relatively few deaths and others having hundreds or even thousands killed. As chapter 3 argues, the levels of strategic violence are jointly determined by the pathway through which the strategic violence emerges and by the opportunity structure present for violent action.[73] The opportunity structure operates like an intervening factor, amplifying or diminishing the effect of the pathways in generating the overall levels of strategic violence. In post-conflict states, this opportunity structure for violence is determined by three factors: the vulnerability of ethnic, political, or religious groups in the civilian population; the flexibility of the institutions of the government or transitional administration in the post-conflict state; and the ability and willingness of external forces or international peacekeepers to protect civilians and respond to the use of violence.[74] As the case studies show, the opportunity structure within post-conflict societies is highly dynamic, as groups in the civilian population can become more or less vulnerable on the basis of population movements and the emergence of new fault lines in the society. Similarly, the ability of the government or peacekeepers to accommodate new claimants to power and respond to violent challenges can change over time as they develop new capacities and change their mission orientation or structure. The use of strategic violence can also produce a dynamic of countermobilization as rival armed groups will emerge to oppose persistent patterns of victimization against one group. When this occurs, the countermobilization of opposed groups can itself change the opportunity structure of the post-conflict society, reordering the fault lines of the conflict and making increased levels of strategic violence and eventual escalation into full-fledged armed conflict more likely. In post-conflict societies, the level of strategic violence is jointly determined by the pathway through which the violence emerges and the opportunity structure in which these actors operate.

Methodology

This book employs a mixed-methods approach to test its hypotheses. It employs a dataset of fifty-two post-conflict states from the period 1989–2007 to explore variations in strategic violence across cases. It also reconstructs and interprets the violence in the five case studies (Bosnia, Rwanda, Kosovo, East Timor, and Iraq) through a range of data sources, including original statistics, newly compiled datasets, and documents derived from fieldwork, archival work, and witness and firsthand accounts from human rights organizations and secondary sources.

The cross-national dataset comprises cases in which an armed conflict has ended during the post–Cold War era (1989–2007).[75] The sample was selected among all wars (interstate war, civil war, and extrastate wars) for which a formal settlement came into effect between 1989 and 2007. The dataset records the total number of people killed from strategic violence for five years following the imposition of the settlement.[76] Whenever possible, the dataset notes the targets of attack and types of violence, which is significant if the targets appeared to be significantly different from those victimized during the war. The dataset also includes an ordinal ranking of the magnitude of strategic violence (mass, scattered, occasional, and residual), based on the number of people killed per year from strategic violence. This dataset represents the first collection of data on violence in post-conflict states, with several thousand acts of violence recorded and coded in it. Underlying the cross-national dataset are more than fifty datasets recording the violent acts in post-conflict states, with some having only one entry but with others recording more than one thousand violent acts in one case alone.[77]

In addition, for each of the case studies, this book uses a collection of original violence statistics, drawn from a variety of data sources: unpublished statistics from UN missions or local governmental authorities; a newly compiled dataset from newspaper sources tracking every reported violent act in that case during the five-year period; internal archival material from each UN mission, as well as documents requested from the United States government through the Freedom of Information Act (FOIA); and data drawn from a wide range of secondary sources. Most of the data included in the case studies come directly from the local governing authority (either the government or the UN) and are published for the first time here. For three of these cases (Bosnia, Kosovo, East Timor), this book takes advantage of unpublished statistics collected by the UN to portray the extent of the post-conflict violence. For Rwanda, the lack of a well-resourced UN mission following the genocide in 1994 makes statistical analysis more difficult. In this instance, the case study relies on a newly constructed dataset of violent acts (drawn from both international and local French-language sources), as well as narrative and investigate reports published at the time and subsequently. For Iraq, there has been an extensive effort by the U.S. military to collect data on violence, which have been published in many forms. This case study relies on unpublished statistics from CENTCOM released via a Freedom of Information Act (FOIA) request.

The data presented here constitute the most complete and textured account of violence in post-conflict states yet available. However, the data must be treated carefully, with due attention to the methodological limitations inherent in working with data in societies where crime-reporting is spotty, if it occurs at all. First, both types of violence data, from official crime statistics and newspaper sources, may suffer from underreporting.[78] This is not surprising because crime statistics may be underreported in states coming out of authoritarian rule or emerging from armed conflict.[79] Second, violence in some post-conflict states will be better reported than others owing to the attention they receive in the international press, while violence in cases such as long-running secessionist conflicts or civil wars in sub-Saharan Africa and Asia may be underreported. Third, some of the recorded violence in official statistics will not reflect the phenomenon of interest (i.e., strategic violence) but will instead provide totals of the different types of attacks, such as murders, arsons, and kidnappings. Aggregate indicators of violence will necessarily include attacks launched for personal and criminal purposes and may consequently give a misleading impression of the extent of strategic violence. Fourth, there are also concerns about the reliability of some of the original statistics. For example, fieldwork in Kosovo and East Timor produced statistics that were culled from original police reports, yet some of the original crime reports were not available because of the legal and ethical implications of handing over victim and witness reports for crimes in ongoing court cases.

To ensure that inferences drawn from the data are reliable, this book cross-checks data from a self-generated dataset of all acts of strategic violence reported in local and international newspapers. Most of the case studies employ two different sets of data: summary statistics drawn from official but often unpublished sources; and an event-level dataset of every act of strategic violence reported in the press in the post-conflict period, thus providing a snapshot of the types of violence present in each case.[80] There is no attempt to reconcile these statistics in the case studies, as the acts of strategic violence reported in newspapers are only a subset of the crime rates reported in the official statistics. The case studies will include detailed accounts of violent attacks in the case studies, including information on who was attacked, when the attack happened, and the types of weapon employed. As chapter 2 makes clear, the case studies attempt to provide a contextual portrayal of the violence, relocating the crime statistics back into their historical and cultural environment in order to make sense of the patterns present in the data.

Case Selection

The plausibility of the direct and indirect pathways is demonstrated by a comparison of five cases: Bosnia, Rwanda, Kosovo, East Timor, and Iraq. These cases were selected because of their values on the key variables of interest: acceptance of the peace settlement and internal control. The first case study examines the case of Bosnia-Herzegovina (1995–1999), in which a war that killed hundreds of thousands ended with an unusual pattern of strategic violence in its post-conflict period. Bosnia featured high numbers of nonlethal attacks, including harassment, intimidation, and expulsion but relatively few deaths from strategic violence compared to other similar cases. As chapter 4 argues, this pattern is due to ambivalence among nationalist Serbs and Croats about the terms of the peace produced by the Dayton Accords. While these parties were dissatisfied with not having achieved their own independent state and exclusive control over their territories, they were reluctant to explicitly spoil the settlement and endanger the political and economic rewards they achieved from remaining inside Dayton's complex federal structure. This strategic position provided them with incentives to carefully modulate the use of violence to apply pressure to international actors, while not risking their wartime gains. Chapter 5 examines another counterintuitive case, Rwanda (1994–1998), where the winning side—the Rwandan Patriotic Front (RPF), which captured full control over the government months after the long war that culminated in the genocide in 1994—began to use strategic vio-

TABLE 1.1.
Case Selection

Level of Internal Control	Fully Accept Settlement?	
	Yes	No
High	Little or no strategic violence No pathway —	Strategic violence Direct pathway Bosnia, Rwanda
Low	Strategic violence Indirect pathway Kosovo, East Timor	Strategic violence Direct and indirect pathway Iraq

lence against the losing side, ranging from the organizers of the genocide to the Hutu population inside and outside the country. This strategic violence came about not because the RPF lost control of its factions but because the highly organized RPF was not satisfied with its victory and made a decision to subdue the Hutu majority with intimidation and violence and to spread the war across the border into Zaire in pursuit of regional hegemony. Chapter 6 considers the case of Kosovo (1999–2004) as an example of the indirect pathway, where the apparent victory of the clan-based Kosovo Liberation Army (KLA) was undone by the emergence of rival Albanian splinter groups, often criminal and hypernationalist in orientation, which began to use violence against each other as well as minority communities in local bargaining games. Chapter 7 considers another case of the indirect pathway where the coalition of parties that won independence in East Timor (1999–2004), the CNRT, had little internal control and dissolved into competing factions and began to fight along regional lines in the post-conflict period. The final case study on Iraq (2003–2008) presents a case where both the direct and indirect pathways were operative, as former Baathists and Iraqi soldiers offered a determined resistance against U.S. forces (i.e., direct pathway), while an array of sectarian and Islamist militias fought among themselves for a greater share of the power and resources of the state (i.e., indirect pathway). The consequence of these interlocking struggles was a severe escalation in strategic violence across the post-conflict period, which left thousands dead and pushed Iraq into a civil war. In each of these cases, the pathways are only part of the story, as the opportunity structure for violence—either permissive or nonpermissive—varies across them. Table 1.1 indicates how the case studies illustrate the pathways identified here.

Because many of these cases are broadly similar in other respects, some focused, paired comparisons between them are possible.[81] Bosnia and Rwanda, for instance, have some common features: both were ethnic wars, had high casualties, and remained divided societies after the war. Kosovo and East Timor, though, share a different set of similar features: both were long-running secessionist conflicts in deeply divided societies, featured the direct combat involvement of an external power on behalf of a secessionist armed group, and had the imposition of a UN-led executive-authority peacekeeping mission, in which the UN with the cooperation of another external power assumed responsibility for restoring public order. While there are some important differences between these pairings—for instance, Bosnia featured three warring ethnic groups, whereas Rwanda featured two; Kosovo was an ethnic war, whereas East Timor was not—they are sufficiently similar to allow comparisons and to trace whether variables such as the support for the peace settlement and the internal control of the combatants can explain the variations in strategic violence between them. By contrast, Iraq is an outlier that does not feature the same original conditions as the other four cases. Only Iraq—which arose from the forcible overthrow of an existing regime by the United States and subsequent intersectarian conflict—cannot be compared directly to the other cases and is treated as a sui generis case here.

The Way Forward

The purpose of this chapter has been to lay out a general critique of the literature on violence after wars and make the case for developing a theory that explains the variation in violence in these cases. Chapter 2 develops a theoretical framework for understanding violence in post-conflict states and establishes criteria for identifying and analyzing strategic violence. Chapter 3 lays out the two pathways for strategic violence and illustrates the variation in strategic violence through a dataset of post-conflict states from 1989 to 2007. Chapters 4 through 8 present the case studies that demonstrate the utility of the pathways in explaining the onset of strategic violence, while also describing the opportunity structures that affected the overall levels of strategic violence. The concluding chapter highlights the key findings of the study and identifies the challenges that it poses for striking the delicate balance between order and justice in post-conflict states.

PART ONE

UNPACKING VIOLENCE
AFTER WARS

CHAPTER TWO

Understanding Violence after Wars
Concepts and Contexts

To understand why violence occurs after wars, one must begin by unpacking the concept of violence. As noted in chapter 1, violence in post-conflict states is driven by a diverse range of motives, from the highly personal (such as revenge killings) to the criminal and political. Some violent acts are driven by more than one purpose; in many post-conflict states, the personal desire for retribution and an array of criminal and political motives may overlap to make involvement in violence attractive to survivors of the war. To an international official or a peacekeeper arriving in a post-conflict state, the purposes behind the bewildering and complex set of violent transactions that they encounter can seem obscure or idiosyncratic. Particularly in cases of extreme violence like Iraq, an outside observer may conclude that the bloodletting may be driven by nihilism rather than any specific purpose.[1] This problem of understanding the varying forms of violence in post-conflict states is compounded by a lack of information: outsiders are rarely able to grasp the individual incentives and local dynamics that lie behind the attacks because they lack detailed knowledge about the politics and history of that town, region, or state.[2] This is even more the case if violence reflects highly specific local grievances and historical experiences, which may not mirror or even reflect the macro-narrative of the conflict.[3] Parsing out the truly strategic forms of violent activity from the multiple forms of criminal and personal violence evident in crime statistics is a difficult proposition in any case. Under the conditions of limited information so common in post-conflict states, understanding violence is a particular challenge, involving something akin to detective work, with only truncated or fragmentary evidence to guide the investigation.

The purpose of this chapter is to identify and propose remedies for the problems associated with understanding violent action under conditions of limited information. To some extent, its arguments are applicable to understanding violence in a wide range of cases beyond post-conflict states; the problems of detecting intention and of understanding opportunistic violence are common ones, particularly in cases where law enforcement capability is weak and information about the act is limited. Yet it is particularly important for this set of cases—in which violence unfolds in complex and often unexpected ways between new categories of perpetrators and victims—to think critically about how one assesses the strategic intent behind violence. The problem is also an empirical one: the evidence of strategic violence in post-conflict states will often be circumstantial or fragmentary, while the questions of interpretation—that is, who is responsible, and why—will be many. An observer may be aware that an unknown percentage of the violent acts in the post-conflict state are strategic or political in nature, but the available records provide only a glimpse into the motives behind the act. With some exceptions, most aggregate crime statistics detail the type of crime (such as murders, arsons, or assaults) but are silent on why the crime has occurred.[4] To make even a rough estimate of strategic violence, one would require some empirical markers or standards of evidence to make assessments and determine, even in relative terms, how much strategic violence is present in a case. The development of a theory that explains the onset and variation of strategic violence after wars—the focus of the next chapter—presupposes an understanding of violence that permits this subset of strategic violence to be analytically separated, even imperfectly, from the rest of the violent activity in the society.

This chapter is divided into four sections. The first section lays out the definition of violence used here and develops a typology of violent action, based on two key criteria: the intention of the act and victim selection. This typology identifies the violent acts as strategic within this study. Strategic violence is the focus of attention in the dataset of post-conflict states (1989–2007) and the subsequent case studies. The second section considers the epistemological problem of detecting intentions for violent action, which underlies the effort to separate strategic violence from other forms of violent behavior. It argues that tracing and analyzing the context and the patterns of violence over time and geographic space goes some way toward mitigating—but not fully solving—the problem of detecting the intention of violent activity under conditions of limited information. This approach does not solve all of the evidentiary problems involved in analyzing strategic violence—particularly because the lines of control over the violence are difficult to ascertain and verify—but it allows for a relative judgment about whether strategic violence has occurred and whether different cases have higher or lower levels of strategic violence. Identifying the empirical markers of strategic violence will also help in making some conditional or probabilistic attribution of responsibility for strategic violence in the case studies. The third section deals with the problem of opportunism and discusses how armed groups can subsidize or endorse violent actions by others for strategic gain, thus blurring the line between expressive and strategic violence. The fourth section examines the entangled relationship between political and criminal violence in post-conflict states.

The concluding section summarizes the implications of this approach for the study of strategic violence after wars.

Defining Violence

For the purposes of this study, the definition of violence will be restricted to acts that involve the exercise of physical force, or the threat thereof, to inflict injury or measurable harm to person or property.[5] This interpretation of violence—sometimes called the minimalist or observational definition because it is rooted in the observable application of physical force—focuses on the use of "material, measurable force" as the key indicator for determining what constitutes violence.[6] Some writers in this school of thought include threats as a form of violence, for a threat implies the "reserve capability and means of exercising physical power" even when no actual violence occurs.[7] This study includes verbal threats (such as intimidation) when accompanied by a specific threat of physical harm as within the definition of violence.

As portrayed here, there are three ideal-type categories of violent acts: expressive, instrumental, and strategic. These categories are differentiated by the nature of the intention behind the act. These categories of violence are designed to be useful heuristics in sorting through the complex mix of violence present in post-conflict states. However, they are not exclusive empirical categories, as there is some degree of overlap between them. While many acts of violence can be understood as solely expressive, instrumental, or strategic, an unknown percentage of violent acts will have more than one intention behind them. A small percentage of acts may even have all three categories of intention at work in producing the decision to attack. Moreover, these categories are difficult to test empirically because evidence of intention is often elusive.[8] Data on violence in post-conflict states is typically available only in the aggregate; the category of murders will include acts that should be properly assigned to each of these three categories. While all of these categories of violent acts are often simultaneously present in post-conflict states, they will be present in different degrees of magnitude. Some cases will have high levels of expressive violence (such as revenge killings) but low levels of strategic violence; other cases may have the opposite. Still others may have high rates of instrumental violence, such as denunciations and criminal violence, but no organized strategic forms of violence designed to challenge the settlement. What is of particular interest here is why some post-conflict states have higher levels of strategic violence than others. This is important because strategic violence, designed to transform the balance of power and resources in a state, is ultimately more threatening for the peace settlement and carries with it the risk of restarting the war.[9] To begin to understand why some cases have more or less strategic violence, one must start by identifying how this category of violence differs from other types of violence present in post-conflict states.

Expressive Violence

One of the most common distinctions in the study of violence is that between expressive and instrumental forms of violence.[10] Expressive acts of violence are motivated by emotions, such as anger, rage, or grief. The quintessential act of expressive violence is the revenge killing for betrayal, such as when a wife kills her husband for committing adultery. Such an act may be primarily motivated by the desire to convey a sentiment or emotion rather than by an instrumental calculation of what she may gain through committing the act. This does not mean, however, that it is an irrational act; perpetrators of expressive violence can exhibit significant evidence of instrumental rationality in selecting the modalities of the attack.[11] The end goal of the violence need not be senseless or nihilistic, though some forms of expressive violence can appear to the victims as such. The key criteria for expressive violence are that it is primarily motivated by the desire to satisfy some emotion and involves no necessary premeditation or instrumental purpose beyond harming the immediate target. In some cases, expressive violence can lead to material gain, though its primary impulse must be emotional reaction, rather than cool calculation of gain.

Expressive motivations no doubt play a significant role in explaining violence at the individual level.[12] Psychologists have long noted that strong emotions can play a role in motivating ordinary or interpersonal crime, particularly among family members and in tandem with the consumption of alcohol and other drugs.[13] Within armed conflict, ample anecdotal evidence indicates that expressive motives can shape both the incidence and the style of killing and scale of the brutality. Some of those fighting are motivated by sadism and the pleasure of fighting; other are reacting to considerations of social pressure and honor, yet wind up enjoying the thrill of power that sadism can bring.[14] Others resort to expressive violence opportunistically, giving in to emotions such as fear, anger, and resentment at moments only when the risk of being caught or penalized for doing so is low.

This type of opportunistic expressive violence is particularly apparent in post-conflict states. The end of an armed conflict often produces what might be called a "public security gap" where the government or interim political authorities have not asserted control over the territory and a chaotic environment prevails. The arrival of the post-conflict period reveals populations brutalized by their wartime experience and in many cases thirsty for revenge against those who harmed them. At the same time, many of the normal constraints on violent behavior—for example, the threat of police action or judicial sanction, even shame—have not yet been restored. The brief window of time following the end of an armed conflict tends to be extremely violent, as a mix of former fighters, returning refugees, and criminal opportunists unleash their anger and desire for revenge on an array of targets. This is particularly the case if political authority has collapsed in the state, allowing a significant period of time before the resort to violence will be effectively punished by the government.

It is difficult to generalize about the role of emotions at the collective level, because the mechanisms by which groups feel or register emotions is complex and hard to test empirically. But it is clear that at the collective level emotions can facilitate an individual's participation in violence, particularly as would-be perpetrators can more easily latch their personal grievances onto wider political causes in a group context.[15] This can be seen particularly in the important role that emotions such as fear, anger, and resentment play in fueling mob violence. Riots, for example, can involve a host of expressive violent acts as individuals swept up and subtly transformed in crowds use the cover provided by them to commit acts of brutality.[16] But riots can also reflect a kind of collective fury, which leads violent action by mobs to outstrip any possible instrumental purpose.[17] The phenomenon of deindividuation within mass movements—in other words, getting caught up in the crowd—tends to increase the prospects for anonymity among perpetrators and encourage expressive violence.[18] This phenomenon, according to Donald Horowitz, "also suggests the answer to a puzzle relating to participation in riots, for it means that ordinary people, rather than just aggressively disposed people, can be induced in the crowd setting to do things they would not do in other settings."[19] In post-conflict states, a similar dynamic often comes into play, as the return of refugees and large population movements can provide a kind of cover for a range of expressive violent actions such as riots and revenge killings.[20]

While it is clear that expressive violence occurs in post-conflict states, it is important not to overstate its importance or to attribute too much of the violence evident to raw or unbridled emotion. First, as Stathis Kalyvas has pointed out, this may confuse the cause of a violent action with how it is performed; many acts that are motivated by cool calculation appear as blind fury to the victims.[21] The descriptive details of violent action from the vantage point of the victim are not always a reliable indicator of expressive intent. Violent action can be conducted according to "scripts" that may make the act appear as expressive, when in fact it is instrumental and highly coordinated.[22] Second, like victims, perpetrators may find themselves drawn to interpretations of violent action that highlight the expressive motives.[23] Many perpetrators of violent action will claim expressive motivations—particularly that they were blinded by fury or grief—as a way of avoiding responsibility for their actions. Third, expressive motivations tend to be less empirically verifiable at the collective level; it is difficult to assert with certainty that a group—for example, refugees—are angry or vengeful, for there will almost always be variations in sentiments across that population that belie such a blanket description. Expressive violence occurs, and can influence crime patterns even at the aggregate level, but it is insufficient to point only to emotion to explain all of the variations in violence evident in post-conflict states.

Instrumental Violence

The second category of violent action, instrumental violence, is driven by a cool calculation of means and ends and is directed toward criminal, personal, or other nonpolitical goals. Instrumental violence can be conducted by individuals or groups seeking some form of personal advancement. As conceived here, instrumental violence includes all forms of directed action toward any personal or criminal (but nonpolitical) goal. Common forms of instrumental violence in post-conflict states include personal violence, denunciations, mafia or criminal violence, and some types of looting. Individuals who engage in denunciations of their business or personal rivals as being "collaborators" with the other side are acting instrumentally for personal gain.[24] Organized groups that use the chaos of post-conflict states to pursue avenues of criminal gain with limited risk of sanction from law enforcement are also acting instrumentally, and in some cases rationally, in response to incentives in their environment. Armed groups that use violence to victimize ethnic or religious groups that had a superior position in the social hierarchy of the state—and thus better access to jobs in the civil service, and other economic opportunities—are acting instrumentally as well.[25] Across all three of these examples—denunciations, criminal enterprise, and social opportunism—the purpose of the violence is criminal or personal and driven by a calculation of gain, rather than impelled by emotions or instinct. Instrumental violence is often highly rational, particularly as the perpetrators tend to pay careful attention to the costs and benefits of the action.[26] At the same time, instrumental violence can overlap with expressive violence, as some actions and patterns of behavior may have both expressive and instrumental dimensions.[27] As Roger D. Petersen has argued, emotions can serve as triggers for a range of instrumental violent attacks that would not have happened under other circumstances.[28]

In a recent study, Stathis Kalyvas illustrated that instrumental motives play a key role in explaining the patterns of violence in civil wars.[29] The social setting of armed conflict plays an important role in shaping the willingness of individuals to engage in violence, particularly if they believe that a climate of disorder protects them from retributive violence.[30] The result is an increased number of individuals who will choose to settle personal grievances, seek short-term advantage for their careers or their businesses, or act opportunistically for their own gain. The prevalence of violence arranged around what Kalyvas calls "local cleavages" explains why simple explanations relying on the chief fault line of the conflict cannot account for the ambiguous, often contingent and complex, patterns of violence that emerge within wars.[31] As the example of the violence in the Reconstruction demonstrated, a similar dynamic is in play in post-conflict states, with the violence often unfolding for personal and criminal reasons only tangentially related to the conflict itself. The choices made during wars to collaborate or resist, as well as the new categories of winners and losers brought about by the peace settlement, can create new petty grievances and incentives for instrumental violence that did not exist before the conflict began. The post-conflict period merely brings about new reasons for instrumental violence; the end of the war and the imposition of a peace settlement do not interrupt the fundamental logic of self-interest that drove instrumental violence during wartime.

Strategic Violence

In order to separate the high-impact forms of strategic violence that threaten the peace settlement from the forms of ordinary criminality present in post-conflict states, this book limits the understanding of instrumental violence to criminal or personal violence, and reserves what is commonly called "political violence" for the category of strategic violence.[32] While strategic violence could arguably be considered a subset of instrumental violence, defining it as a stand-alone category of violence improves analytic clarity by separating those events meant to directly change the balance of power and resources between political actors from those designed to strengthen criminal operations and settle personal grievances. The latter, while serious in their impact on the victims, are less likely to threaten the peace settlement or restart the war. While they remain theoretically distinct, empirically criminal and political enterprises are often entangled in post-conflict states, thus making a strict separation between strategic violence and instrumental violence difficult to obtain in practice.

Strategic violence is defined here as a violent act aimed at transforming the balance of power and resources within the state. As it is understood here, strategic violence includes all forms of political violence present in the case, as well as attacks launched without an explicit political program, provided that they have the object of transforming the balance of power and resources in the state. This is particularly important in post-conflict states, as some actors may avow that they have no political program or ideology but engage in strategic violence nonetheless. Common types of strategic violence include (1) targeted killings and assassinations, usually of prominent individuals or state officials; (2) riots and pogroms, in which local elites and angry mobs conspire to kill or expel parts of a perceived hostile population; (3) symbolic attacks, such as the destruction or desecration of religious sites or political symbols; (4) reprisals, defined here as the targeting of innocent civilians ostensibly in response to a previous act of violence; (5) insurgent attacks, directed at government targets or representatives of occupying forces; (6) terrorist attacks, designed to spread fear to an audience beyond the target; and (7) genocide or ethnic cleansing, which aim to expel or exterminate a group. There is no limit to the purposes that acts of strategic violence may be put to, with some attacks aimed at overturning the peace settlement while others are directed to entirely new purposes. When armed groups use strategic violence after wars, they typically direct that violence to several purposes at once.

Each post-conflict state will feature a unique array of acts of strategic violence, subject to the characteristics of the state. Dense urban areas, for example, are traditionally more prone to riots and pogroms; targeted killings and assassinations tend to follow occupations, in which the occupying forces created networks of collaborators among local officials and prominent elites.[33] While strategic attacks can appear random, the perpetrators are often highly selective in choosing targets and careful to use violence in the service of a distinct goal.[34] In this sense, strategic violence is politically instrumental and can be understood as a specific type or subset of instrumental violence.[35] The immediate goal of strategic violence can vary significantly and range from forcing groups to surrender territory or resources to degrading the opponent's offensive capacity or to signaling a willingness to fight. But the ultimate goal of strategic violence is to shift the balance of power and resources from one group or faction to another, either by explicitly challenging the existing political order or by changing facts on the ground to this effect.

Four observable indicators of attacks against specific groups have strategic intent. First, strategic attacks against these groups tend to be concentrated in high-value, resource-rich, or contested territories, where multiple parties have conflicting stakes on territory and resources. Second, these attacks tend to be directed in greater numbers against vulnerable groups, such as ethnic or religious minorities, or civilians from the losing side of a conflict. Third, strategic attacks often include an element of communication, either explicitly, with warnings by the perpetrators, or implicitly, through symbolic attacks like the desecration of religious sites.[36] Much of this communication is polyvalent, as the violent acts convey different messages to different groups.[37] Aside from terrorizing the target group, this message is also directed toward the perpetrator's self-ascribed constituency or "identification group."[38] Such violence can be used to "stimulate popular activism, bolster a group's base of support, jump-start the mobilization process, and help achieve a self-sustaining rate of organizational growth."[39] Carefully scripted strategic violence indicates that the armed group has the capability of inflicting pain on the enemy and of protecting its chosen constituency. This can improve its relative position in domestic bargaining against its more nonviolent rivals. Finally, strategic violence is often marked by more sophisticated tactics and weaponry than ordinary civilians typically use. Highly coordinated attacks involving grenades and other military-issue equipment are likely (but not conclusive) indicators of strategic intent in attacks against targeted groups.[40] These contextual details—where the attack happens, how it happens, and what weapons are involved—are essential to determining whether an act is strategic.

It is important not to overstate the number of "strategic attacks" in post-conflict states. Not every attack directed across the former battle lines qualifies as a strategic attack. Some of the violence that follows the collapse of political authority in a state is intracommunal, as members of each side try to enforce discipline on their members and to prevent defections.[41] Not all attacks that cross communal lines are necessarily strategic attacks. Street crime, for example, can be directed at a member of a target group but may be unrelated to the armed conflict. States emerging from civil wars are awash in criminal and personal violence, ranging from revenge attacks to score settling and even senseless gang killings. Particularly after an armed conflict, those on the losing side of a conflict are attractive targets for opportunistic violence, as they are vulnerable and may not be fully protected by the police and judiciary. Also, while strategic attacks tend to be highly organized, not all organized attacks are strategic, as criminal groups (such as organized crime gangs) can develop sophisticated, well-planned attacks that are similar to those executed by political organizations. The category of "strategic violence" applies only to a limited set of events: attacks on individuals or groups that demonstrate the clear intent of transforming the balance of power and resources in a contested area.[42] As an empirical matter, strategic violence is embedded in varying levels of expressive and instrumental violence and must be detected amid a range of violent acts conducted for other purposes.

The typology presented in table 2.1 classifies specific violent acts according to these three categories, as well as by the criteria by which victims are selected. Victims can be selected on two grounds: on individual grounds, the victim is selected for a specific reason relating to his or her prior behavior; on categorical grounds, the victim is selected on the basis of his or her membership in a targeted group rather than individual activity before or during the war.[43] The essential distinction between individual and categorical victimization is that the former targets individuals for what they have done, whereas the latter targets individuals for who they are.

The point of distinguishing between violent acts in this fashion is to illustrate that within the category of violence in post-conflict states lay a diverse range of acts, only some of which are designed to have a degree of political or strategic impact. The typology is merely a heuristic, and its categories are not airtight. Many violent acts will cut across categories, be motivated by multiple types of intentions, and be descriptively similar. Yet it is essential for analytic purposes to acknowledge the variety of intentions—personal, criminal, and political—that can generate acts that will be classified under categories such as *murder* or *arson*. This typology also points to the types of violent acts that will be of greatest consequence for the peace. Acts of stra-

TABLE 2.1.
A Typology of Violent Acts

	Expressive	Instrumental	Strategic
Victim Selection			
Individual	Revenge killings, rage killings	Personal violence, opportunistic violence, denunciations	Targeted killings, assassinations
Categorical	Mob violence, riots	Criminal or mafia violence, riots, collective opportunistic violence	Reprisals, insurgent attacks, ethnic cleansing, genocide, terrorism

tegic violence, particularly those waged on categorical grounds against whole ethnic, sectarian, or political groups are more likely to pose a substantial threat to the peace than those conducted for expressive purposes and waged on individual or discriminate grounds. Within the case studies, particular attention will be paid to evidence of violent activities here classified as strategic and categorical, with particular attention paid to the contextual details—such as the location, type of violent behavior, evidence of communication, and use of weapons—that mark it as this type of violence.

The Problem of Intention

At the heart of the descriptive difference between expressive, instrumental, and strategic types of violence lies the problem of intention. The term *strategic* implies intention, as it posits that actors are explicitly or implicitly attempting to change the balance of power and resources in a state.[44] Understanding the motives for another's actions has always been a difficult problem for social scientists. An extensive literature within philosophy suggests three reasons why motives are difficult for outside observers to ascertain.[45] The first is the problem of "other minds"—that is, that the outside observer can never be fully certain that the apparent or perceived motive behind a given act was in fact the actual motive.[46] A second problem involves mixed or multiple motives. With some violent acts, numerous motives for a given act may exist, with none having salience in any meaningful sense. In Kosovo, for example, many of the killings that took place in Pristina happened to those who lived in or occupied expensive houses in the affluent section of the city.[47] Those killed or expelled in revenge attacks in those parts of the city often had their residence claimed by the person who attacked them. At least two motives—revenge and greed—may have existed side-by-side in these attacks, with neither necessarily having precedence over the other. Finally, in some cases motives are unclear even to the person doing the act. Human beings are not rational machines; they are driven by emotions—desires, needs, fears, and impulses—and by subconscious preferences. The outside observer seeking to understand why X did Y must acknowledge not only that X may have had multiple motives for Y but that X's motives may be partially obscured to X.

These obstacles have led some scholars to conclude that human motivations remain ultimately unavailable to outside observers.[48] If this is the case, it follows that typologies of violent acts (such as the one presented here) should be constructed without reference to the intention lying behind the act. Some existing typologies of violence do not employ intention as a key criterion, focusing either on relational or causal mechanisms behind the act or on whether the acts are directed against individuals on the basis of their behavior or their membership in a specifically targeted group.[49] Yet while there are sound theoretical reasons for avoiding the difficulties that intention creates, excluding it entirely poses a serious limitation on the explanatory power of theories of the causes of violence. On one level, it violates basic descriptive accuracy because even apparently similar violent acts do not proceed mechanistically from similar causal processes. Some betray evidence of intention, and some do not. Consider, for example, the difference between uncoordinated brawls at soccer matches in Europe and coordinated clashes between union and non-union forces in a labor dispute. Both may be descriptively similar in the account of the actual violence, but they are very different in purpose and coordination. The latter may be organized by union leaders to gain leverage in negotiations and may have involved the designation of leaders to mobilize crowds and coordinate instigating events. In other words, the latter are organized and have an obvious purpose, while the former may be entirely uncoordinated and sporadic.[50] To classify these events as descriptively similar does not reflect the obvious organization and purpose behind the former act.

Second, aside from descriptive accuracy, any serious analysis of the purpose of violence requires an explicit statement of the evidentiary markers for detecting intent behind certain acts. The definition of strategic violence—as an act of violence directed at changing the balance of power and resources in a given polity—presupposes that the intention of a violent act can be detected. To say that an act is strategic, or that a group is behaving strategically, implies that it is possible to parse out and identify the intentions behind different types of violent action.[51] Without a theory of intention behind violent action, there is no way to separate expressive attacks, such as revenge killings, from strategic attacks, such as targeted killings, if they have similar descriptive details. In the absence of an account of motive or intention behind violent action, attacks conducted for a variety of (sometimes conflicting) reasons become analytically indistinguishable. Killings that were done for a variety of purposes would collapse into the general category of "murder" without further elaboration. To understand or explain the problem of targeted killings, for instance, and to determine whether these attacks are meant to threaten the peace, one must first have a theoretical position on one's ability to detect the purpose behind the action. To assert that certain violent acts are strategic without explaining how motive or intention can be derived is to sidestep some of the fundamental epistemological problems encountered in the study of violence.

Finally, a theory of intention would be needed by analysts and policy makers alike if they hoped to prevent or manage the kinds of strategic attacks that have a greater political impact and can threaten the peace. For example, if a peacekeeping force hopes to confront "spoilers," it will first have to confront the question of whether violent action in the society is strategic and, if so, how the intentions behind that violence are assessed.[52] Given the variety of violent acts that emerge in post-conflict states—political and criminal, episodic and regular, coordinated and uncoordinated—it becomes imperative both for analytic leverage and for the policy response to develop a theoretical account of how one can derive or assess intention behind patterns of violent acts.

In this book, the problem of intention is addressed by drawing a distinction between individual and collective intent. Without direct information on the nature of an individual act, or access to the perpetrator or witnesses for interrogation, it is impossible for the outside observer to identify the intention behind an individual act of violence. As a stand-alone event, an act of violence will partially remain a mystery, because the motives for violence are often idiosyncratic and driven by personal grievances and previous events unknown to the observer. Yet collective intent—that is, evidence that groups of people have been targeting other groups of people in a consistent manner across time and space—can be derived on the basis of the contextual details of the violence itself, particularly when seen amid a pattern of similar acts.[53]

This distinction between individual and collective intention has empirical implications. Consider the case of postwar violence in Afghanistan. An outside observer may not be able to understand what bundle of motives drove an individual Tajik refugee to burn down the home of a Pashtun in an ethnically contested region. The combination of potential motives—ethnic antipathy, personal hatred, or greed, among others—that led that individual Tajik to destroy that particular Pashtun's home will likely remain obscure to the outside observer unless he or she had access to the perpetrator and highly detailed knowledge of his circumstances. In many post-conflict states, such access is not possible for legal or ethical reasons. But seen as part of a pattern, the outside observer could begin to use contextual details (where, when, how) to infer the range of possible purposes behind similar acts of burning in a region. For instance, if the burning happened in an area where the Northern Alliance had been targeting its operations on pro-Taliban forces, and if the details of the burning—for example, it coordinated timing with similar attacks this evening—were similar to prior attacks, one may begin to infer a collective strategic intent behind a set of similar acts. Here the important details for deriving the intention of the act lies in the context—the location of the house, the time of the crime, the relevant details of the actual burning, repeated over time—rather than in the mind of an individual actor. Such inferences are validated only if the burning was done as an empirically verifiable pattern of violent activity, rather than as a stand-alone act.

It is important to stress what is within the realm of estimation and what is not. The intentions behind individual acts remain outside the reach of those who deal only with aggregate data and witness accounts. But collective intention behind an array of similar violent acts can be estimated if over time the patterns of violence—that is, repeated evidence that people chose to act violently in certain ways and in certain contexts—provide empirical weight to the claim that these events were not unique or unrelated but rather part of a collective effort to achieve a particular strategic goal. Put another way, the iteration of regular patterns of violence together with the regularly occurring contextual details of the crimes can reveal evidence of collective intent. For example, consider a case in which over a few weeks several homes owned by ethnic minorities burn every night in a specific region at approximately the same point in the evening. While the motives that drove the individual perpetrators of these burnings may remain at least partially obscure, the pattern of violence (who was targeted and how often) and the contextual details of the crime (method of arson, location, and timing) can, over time, suggest that the intention (of either an organized group or individuals acting on behalf of a group) of the repeated house burnings was to expel this group from the area. What is possible with this approach is not to ascertain the motive behind a particular house burning but to provide a preliminary answer to the question of why houses are being burned at all.

While this may seem like an abstract discussion, it should be borne in mind that drawing inferences of collective intention from contextual details is exactly what law enforcement and intelligence officials do. Broadly speaking, law enforcement officials look at three sources of data to draw inferences of intention behind criminal acts: the perpetrator's statement of responsibility, the victim's statement, and the contextual details of the crime.[54] The first step in any criminal analysis is to determine whether a perpetrator claimed responsibility. If no claim of responsibility is made, or if the claim is unreliable, details from the victim's statement become the key indicator of motive. In the United Kingdom, for example, the victim's statement is widely considered the key determinant for understanding the motives of violent crimes.[55] If the victim cannot provide a statement or if the statement is insufficient, law enforcement authorities then turn to the contextual details of the crime—location, timing, detail of crime—and, cross-referencing it with victim's and witnesses' accounts, make a judgment about criminal intent. In the FBI's method of analysis for deriving intention, these contextual details are considered just as important as the victim's statement.[56] In the analysis of post-conflict violence, the first two pieces of evidence—the statements of the perpetrator and the victim—are often unavailable for legal or ethical reasons. Given the conditions of limited information common in these cases, contextual details will be essential to understanding and analyzing the violence patterns. In UN-led police missions (like Bosnia, Kosovo, and East Timor) in post-conflict states, context is generally considered a reliable indicator of the intention behind violent crime.[57]

Whenever possible, this book attempts to use data on the motives and circumstances of the violence to infer the intention behind violent action, much in the way that law enforcement or intelligence officials would. However, in some cases where only aggregate-level data are available,[58] the method of inquiry involves the contextual mapping of the violent crime data onto the political landscape of the case. This approach—similar in many respects to intelligence analysis—involves compiling the available data on violent crime and sketching the patterns of crime over time, to detect patterns of violence that are congruent with the strategic objectives of armed groups present in the territory. This kind of contextual mapping of aggregate crime statistics to detect group intention provides little insight into the motive of stand-alone violent acts. It cannot tell why a certain refugee burned a particular house on a given night. Only by grafting crime statistics back onto their original context can it suggest why, over time, dozens of houses burned in similar ways. The distinction between individual and collective intention is important here: what is sought out of context is not the reasoning behind an individual act but the intention of armed groups in acting violently over a period of time. In other words, it shows only the congruence between the stated goals of these groups and the patterns of violent activity. No information about the motive of an individual violent act can be derived from this method, but a probabilistic, and carefully qualified, judgment about the intentions of armed groups operating can be made. This judgment about the collective intent of armed groups is limited by the evidence, as the connective tissue between the evidence of a strategic violence and the intentions of actors may be missing or anecdotal. The lines of control for the violence—who is behind what set of violence acts—is difficult to determine in many cases, and often must be inferred from qualitative evidence, such as witness statements, human rights reports, and other descriptive accounts. Each case study in this book discusses not only the patterns of violence that indicate some strategic intent but also the evidence from narrative accounts about who might be responsible.

This method—which focuses on the context and patterns of violent action to derive strategic intent—is imperfect and subject to error. At least four criticisms can be made of this approach. First, there is the problem of false positives. Without reliable information from perpetrators, victims, and witnesses, an unknown percentage of violent acts may be misclassified as strategic, when they are in fact driven by expressive or instrumental reasons. Second, there is a risk of an ecological inference problem, that is, where individual-level intentions are incorrectly inferred from aggregate-level data.[59] Here the issue of collective intention comes into play, for this analysis limits itself to probabilistic assessments of collective intent without delving into individual intentions behind specific attacks. Third, there is the familiar danger of inferring intention of an act from its effect. This is particularly problematic in post-conflict states. Population flight, for example, can be induced not only by strategic violence but also by high rates of expressive or instrumental violence; the cause and effect here might be confused, as population flight might cause the violence rather than vice versa. In cases like this, the effect of violence will provide no reliable guide to the intention of those behind it. Fourth, there is a problem of reporting bias. As noted in chapter 1, it is likely that violence is underreported in many post-conflict states, just as it is in many authoritarian and weak regimes. At the same time, however, acts of strategic violence may be overreported in the universe of violent acts, especially in mainstream media accounts.[60] This reporting bias may skew the sample in different ways, underestimating the levels of violence in some cases, while making it appear as if a greater percentage of the total violent acts is strategic in others. Moreover, the data may be skewed because actors will selectively spin the media and play up atrocities against their side in order to build up political support for their cause.[61]

To compensate for these difficulties, this book takes three steps. First, if possible, it checks inferences about the strategic nature of violence against multiple datasets for each case, often drawn from unpublished law enforcement or UN sources. For four of the five case studies, this book draws equally on data drawn from internal UN documents, government sources, and a new dataset drawn from media sources. In some instances, the data available are compiled directly from unpublished police reports. Second, this book relies on qualitative evidence (particularly accounts of the violence from international organizations, NGOs, and other secondary sources) to crosscheck its inferences for strategic violence. If the patterns of strategic violence are detected in the analysis of the crime data, they should be confirmed in the qualitative accounts as well. Such contextual information and local knowledge may help to mitigate the effects of the ecological inference problem, though it falls short of a resolution of the problem.[62] Third, for each case, it also tests inferences about the strategic orientation of the violence against the possible alternative explanations to ensure that its probabilistic judgments about the strategic nature of some attacks are grounded in the available evidence. Finally, the estimates of strategic intent produced are limited to groups—not individuals—on the basis of group-level crime data, and uncertainties and estimates of the intentions are clearly stated. This approach does not eliminate the problems of relying on intention for determining the purpose of violence, but it goes some way toward mitigating it.

The Opportunism Problem

In order for the distinction between expressive, instrumental, and strategic forms of violence to have heuristic value, it must come to terms with the problem of opportunism. The end of a war often leaves a society in chaos, with widespread criminality, population movements, and armed groups freely intermixing to generate an environment conducive to violence. In such environments, the law enforcement capability of the state is significantly weakened, thus creating a permissive security environment where crimes can be committed with impunity. The opportunities for violence, for settling scores, and for obtaining long-sought personal objectives multiply in chaotic post-conflict environments where violence is transactional and the costs to acting violently are low.[63] In post-conflict states, such freelance or opportunistic violence will be a nonnegligible part of the aggregate crime statistics, thus introducing more risk of potential error in assessing the levels of strategic violence.

Moreover, an environment rife with opportunistic violence is attractive for armed groups that wish to subsidize opportunistic violence for their own gain. Particularly in societies where long-running armed conflict has polarized politics and led civilians to turn on one another, there will be a significant number of people who wish to attack those on the "losing side" for either expressive reasons (such as revenge or hatred) or instrumental reasons (i.e., to settle scores or claim advantage in postwar business opportunities). With such a mass of potentially willing recruits, armed groups have an opportunity not only to settle scores but also to get others to do their dirty work for them. In effect, armed groups can encourage or lend indirect support to entirely apolitical attacks that have the cumulative effect of achieving their strategic objectives. In the language of economics, if expressive or instrumental attacks have positive externalities for an armed group, that group can subsidize them with variable levels of support, funding, and coordination up until the point they would no longer occur without their direct involvement. Behaving opportunistically by sponsoring violence allows armed groups to achieve their strategic objectives at lower cost and without the risks associated with committing the acts themselves.

This fact—that armed groups can endorse or subsidize opportunistic violence that helps them achieve their goal—poses a problem for the analysis of crime statistics. Apparent acts of expressive violence—such as revenge killings by refugees—may be encouraged or otherwise supported by armed groups in order to facilitate plans at reverse ethnic cleansing. For instance, evidence suggests that the Kosovo Liberation Army (KLA) lent support to revenge attacks by returning refugees against Serbs in order to expel them from Albanian-majority territory immediately after the war.[64] Similarly, instrumental violence, such as assassinations by criminal gangs, may be supported by armed groups for strategic effect. The levels of support offered for expressive and instrumental action by armed groups may be modest and subtle, therefore complicating efforts to detect it, particularly with aggregate data. At the same time, it is likely that opportunism plays a role in inflating crime statistics across all three categories of violence (expressive, instrumental, and strategic), although there is no reason to believe that it plays a greater role with strategic violence than with the other categories.

There is no perfect fix for dealing with opportunistic violence, particularly in the absence of richly detailed contextual details about the crime itself. For analytic clarity, it is important to stress that varying levels of sanction or support by the armed group can make opportunistic attacks look like well-organized strategic attacks. As the level of coordination and support increases, opportunistic attacks can increasingly resemble a classic strategic attack, with all of the telltale signs in terms of tactics employed and weapons used. As an empirical problem, this dynamic may artificially inflate the total number of strategic attacks present in the case studies. Opportunistic attacks will share a cluster of characteristics with the purely strategic forms of violence, making subsidized attacks hard to separate from direct acts of strategic violence in aggregate crime data. If conducted in sufficient numbers, these opportunistic attacks may also have the same cumulative effect as strategic violence. Hundreds of opportunistic but sanctioned attacks against minorities will have the same impact on the crime patterns and population movements as hundreds of organized and purely strategic attacks by armed groups. In both cases, the violent crime record will still show evidence of an increase in attacks against targeted groups and an increase in attacks that betray evidence of strategic intent.

The only approach that can mitigate the problem of opportunism lies in pairing an analysis of crime data with witness statements and contextual-level details about the violence in the narrative accounts of the attacks. Through a careful examination of the narrative accounts of the different types of attacks, the case studies will seek to detect the "lines of control" over violence, specifically the extent to which organized armed groups participated in attacks and directed them. While the challenges of assessing the lines of control are formidable especially under conditions of limited information, it is only by examining such narrative accounts in tandem with crime statistics that some estimation of the relative impact of opportunistic violence, as opposed to organized strategic violence, may be made. Within the case studies, the crime statistics are analyzed along with a range of contextual details—for example, the tactics and type of weapons used—to make a qualified assessment of strategic intent.

The Relationship between Political and Criminal Violence

One of the most noted factors within post-conflict states is the prevalence of criminal networks, operating in both the black and gray economy below the surface of the state. The relationship between these networks and political actors has been described in various ways ranging from "interdependent" and even "symbiotic."[65] To some extent, the entanglement between crime and politics is an outgrowth of the war itself. The use of force on a territory is often accompanied by the proliferation of criminal actors that support and often profit from the war effort.[66] To some extent, the development and deepening of criminal networks in warfare is driven by the demands of the war itself. In an environment marked by lack of resources, conducting an armed conflict is difficult in the absence of a regular supply of arms and other necessary materials. The demand for these items is soon matched by a host of criminal suppliers, which join the supply chain to enrich themselves through war. This demand can create some unusual bedfellows. In Bosnia, for instance, organized crime networks often collaborated across ethnic lines in order to supply arms and material to the warring militias.[67] One of the chief suppliers of oil to Belgrade during the sanctions was Albania, which turned a blind eye to the repression of its co-ethnics in Kosovo.[68] Both in wartime and afterward, the prospects for profit supersede ethnic or religious antagonisms and create cooperative relationships that run contrary to the so-called "macro-cleavage" of the conflict. Such is also the case with protection rackets, in which armed groups police their own territories and often demand fees for uninterrupted transit of goods.

Another reason why criminal networks are prevalent in post-conflict states has to do with the mobilization of combatants. While some participants in armed conflicts are involved because they have a strong preference for this kind of behavior (in Tilly's words, they are "violent specialists"), a significant portion of the recruits must be induced to join an armed group through some form of reward or coercion.[69] The production of these selective incentives has decisive effects on the organization of the group and its propensity to engage in indiscriminate violence.[70] The use of loot during wartime can create a predatory class of political-criminal actors, who by definition are specialists in the extraction of resources of a state for profit. The mobilization of followers through the use of loot as a reward for involvement in violent action also contributes to the normalization of violence as a means of settling routine transactions and can desensitize the noncombatant population to the use of violence.[71] In this sense, the mobilization and need to reward combatants creates lasting networks of political-criminal violent actors that are often sustained once the war has formally ended.

The wartime imposition of sanctions by external powers can also play a part in creating long-lasting criminal networks. As Peter Andreas has documented, the imposition of sanctions gives rise to a host of substitution effects, as normal market transactions are driven underground during the war period.[72] This has at least three effects. First, it creates a symbiosis between the state and organized crime, which proves hard to disentangle during the post-sanctions period. Corruption and resistance to reform come about in part because war often leaves a criminal class entrenched within the political class of the state.[73] Second, armed conflict creates a new class of criminal entrepreneurs, often highly skilled in the application of violence. These entrepreneurs diversify their holdings in the post-conflict period, expanding both geographically (especially with respect to cross-border or regional transactions) and across fields (from holdings in drugs, cigarettes, and human trafficking to other legal aspects of the normal economy).[74] Third, the imposition of sanctions shapes a social acceptance of smuggling and the so-called gray market, which in turn makes rooting out corruption and penalizing those who participate in the black or gray economy difficult. Thus, the roots of criminal networks within post-conflict states arise from both endogenous factors (the demands of irregular warfare and the need for mobilization) and exogenous factors (the imposition of sanctions by external actors).

Finally, opportunism plays a significant role in the deepening of criminal networks. During wartime, the group that profits most is the criminal class, which finds the relative impunity of wartime and the gradual normalization of violence conducive to its operations. This criminal class expands during the war, incorporating new, often opportunistic, actors who might otherwise have been diverted to other activities. As Abraham Lincoln famously remarked, in wartime "every foul bird comes abroad and every dirty reptile rises up."[75] Such opportunistic criminal violence can serve as both a facilitator and a cause of violence. As John Mueller has argued, the collapse of law enforcement not only leads to barbarism but can also fuel more violence by allowing drunken thugs to be transformed into nationalist warriors.[76] This criminalization of the violence is in part predicated on the weak law enforcement capacity of the state. Under these conditions, both types of criminality—the highly organized and coordinated networks and the opportunistic thugs let loose by the collapse of public order can—coexist and feed off one another to produce a criminalized environment once the war ends. This can act both as a facilitator for certain kinds of violence—such as internecine wars between rival criminal gangs—and as a cause of continuing violence into the post-conflict period.

These criminal networks do not disappear once the war ends. Some take advantage of their entrenched position to expand their operations across borders. The splinter groups that emerged from the KLA, for instance, have become essential links in the supply chain of heroin into Western Europe. In Guatemala, political-criminal networks organized around the counterinsurgency structures of the government have become involved in lucrative trade in illicit drugs across borders.[77] Others continue to fund their own operations through the extraction of loot and other natural resources, ensuring that their stranglehold on key natural resources (such as oil, diamonds, and minerals) remains intact once the peace is established. Other criminal networks expand into more petty crime, such as bank robbery. The former members of the Irish Republican Army (IRA) now involved in bank robbery are a case in point. Some ex-IRA members have become freelancers in violence and are now collaborating with their Colombian counterparts in the drug trade.[78] Yet these are the rule, not the exception. Especially in cases where law enforcement capacity remains weak and the social acceptance of violence is high, criminal networks can continue to operate and, in some cases, expand their operations in the post-conflict period.

Opportunistic criminal violence also remains a problem after wars, particularly in the immediate aftermath of the conflict. As evidenced by the widespread looting that occurred after the fall of Saddam Hussein's regime in 2003, the collapse of political authority in a state and a climate of impunity can lead ordinary civilians to engage in looting and petty forms of criminal theft. Looting occurs for a wide variety of reasons and is not always reducible to a strategic or political purpose.[79] Petty theft and misappropriation is often a consequence of the formal end of a conflict, particularly when a reversal of fortune occurs leaving a group vulnerable to predation. Such was the case with the Roma following the end of the war in Kosovo.[80] Because of their low social status and the blame they received for alleged collaboration with the Serbs, Roma were ideal targets of opportunity for both petty crime and more serious forms of brutality, including rape, assault, and expulsion.[81] Historically, such scapegoat groups have suffered disproportionately during wartime and also during periods of low law enforcement capacity, as in many post-conflict states.[82]

Finally, the kind of social reordering that happens as a function of wartime—in which new elites are created through their involvement in violent action, often for the "defense" of the nation—has a decisive political effect. These new elites are often neither purely criminal nor purely political actors but rather straddle the divide between politics and crime. In some cases, they harbor ambitions of going "legit" and becoming formal political actors. As chapter 6 discusses, this was the case with Hashim Thaci, a former KLA commander with long-noted ties to criminal networks in the Balkans, who created a political party and was elected as the prime minister of Kosovo. The question that many analysts asked was whether Thaci and other ex-members of the KLA were going into crime to support the politics or into politics to support their organized crime operations.[83] Even those political elites who came to power during periods of strife are often connected, either directly or indirectly, with organized crime. For instance, Milo Djukanovic, the former prime minister of Montenegro, was allegedly responsible for sustaining the illegal smuggling of cigarettes by criminal gangs into Western Europe.[84] In Iraq, various members of the Saddam

Hussein regime were tied into smuggling and fraud rackets often associated with the "oil for food" program. The experience of wartime often makes normal political actors accustomed to dealing with the devil in order to keep their states functioning and their political futures intact. Especially after long periods of armed conflict, the elites emerging from the war often are political-criminal actors, with varying levels of ties (either direct or indirect through their associates and subordinates) with criminal actors. Their entanglement varies over time; some actors have deep and even constitutive links with criminal actors, whereas others may have more of an incidental relationship.[85]

Like the opportunism problem, the entanglement of politics and crime in post-conflict states has some implications for the study of violence after wars. There can be no neat divide between political and criminal violence after wars; crimes may be motivated by both purposes simultaneously. Across cases, the entanglement of politics and crime affects both perpetrators and targets. Armed groups engaged in strategic violence are often also criminal groups, and separating which of their actions are "political" and which are "criminal" is often difficult to do in practice. In each of the case studies, almost all of the major armed groups have deep connections with criminal activities. While political actors may cease involvement in crime after the war, some often continue with this double life as political operators and criminal actors. Similarly, the targets of strategic forms of violence may have an overlapping political and criminal purpose: the assassination of a government minister, for instance, may both facilitate a bid to change the power and resources in a state and deepen an armed group's hold on criminal enterprises. Just as perpetrators have a double life as political and criminal actors, some victims doubtlessly have a similarly dual or complex identity, thus making the definitive classification of an act as purely political or criminal difficult to achieve.

As an empirical matter, the entanglement of politics and crime in post-conflict states poses some challenges for the outside observer. As argued earlier, the available contextual data on violent crime—where, when, and how—does not provide any insight into whether an individual violent act was motivated by politics or crime (or both). At the aggregate level, this interdependence means that a neat division between what counts as strategic and instrumental violence will be impossible to obtain. But at that level of analysis, it also does not mean that no strategic intent can be detected. In many post-conflict states, politics and crime work as mutually reinforcing drivers of violence, often to the same strategic effect. For instance, predatory violence based on both strategic gain and criminal advancement may be directed against the same target group, often on the losing side of the conflict. An analysis of the aggregate crime patterns can still yield evidence of collective strategic intent, even if an unknown percentage of those crimes is motivated by criminal and quasi-criminal purposes. The presence of criminal violence amid otherwise strategic acts becomes a kind of "noise" in the data but does not prevent the detection of intent for strategic violence.

Conclusion

The arguments of this chapter, though not exclusive to post-conflict states, are designed to deal specifically with the kind of theoretical and empirical problems associated with analyzing violence under conditions of limited information. The problem with analyzing strategic violence is that it is essentially a latent dependent variable. An official arriving in a post-conflict environment, for instance, knows that an unknown percentage of acts within the set of violent transactions in the society is strategic. To detect and analyze this subset of violent activity leads that person to confront a special set of theoretical and empirical problems. Even more so than in the analysis of crime patterns in developed states, the analysis of violence in post-conflict states involves a careful measurement of the data and evidence, with due attention to the natural limitations of the data. Particularly in cases where the outside observer has no direct access to victims, perpetrators, and witnesses of violent activities, it is important to have a clear theoretical conception not only of the types of violent action (expressive, instrumental, and strategic) but also of the conceptual problems (of opportunism and interdependent political-criminal violence) that require the exercise of caution and qualified judgment.

Despite the qualifications offered here, the analysis of violent crime in the context of limited information is not impossible. The best that can be done is to trace the crime patterns over time, while remaining sensitive to the geographic, historical, and cultural foundations of that violence. Such an approach cannot overcome the natural limitations of the data and their sources, but it can mitigate them. Acknowledging the problems identified here is essential for ensuring a proper understanding of strategic violence and showing sensitivity to the evidentiary problems associated with determining control and sponsorship of the attacks. The following chapter continues the theoretical discussion of post-conflict violence, but with a change in focus. Its purpose shifts from understanding the how strategic violence relates to the other types of violence present toward explaining its onset and variation during the post-conflict period.

CHAPTER THREE

Explaining Violence after Wars
Patterns and Pathways

As presented in chapter 1, strategic violence in post-conflict states can follow two broad patterns. In some post-conflict states, the combatants will continue to use strategic violence for reasons directly related to the war itself—as an attempt to spoil the peace settlement, to undermine its effective terms, or to achieve further gains from renewed fighting. In these cases, acts of strategic violence will revolve around the same cleavages or fault lines in the society that drove violence during the war, and the types and targets of violence will mirror those of the war. In other cases, strategic violence operates according to a logic that is local, contingent, and detached from the overarching rationale of the original conflict. In these cases, strategic violence is employed by new or newly emergent actors in the society, and there are unexpected shifts in the types and targets of violence from what occurred during the war. As a first step toward understanding why these two distinct patterns occur, chapter 2 unpacked the broad category of violence in post-conflict states into three constituent categories of violent activity (expressive, instrumental, and strategic) and addressed the methodological issues surrounding the interpretation of violence under conditions of limited information. As it suggested, despite the fact that strategic violence is enmeshed with opportunistic and criminal forms of violence in most post-conflict states, it can be empirically detected, however imperfectly, through a contextual analysis of crime statistics and of existing narrative and firsthand accounts of the attacks.

The purpose of this chapter is to explain (1) the onset of these two distinct patterns of strategic violence and (2) the variation in the levels of strategic violence across cases. The task of this chapter is both descriptive and analytical. At a descriptive level, it identifies how the experience of armed conflict transforms states and renders them more susceptible to strategic violence than comparable weak states. As understood here, post-conflict states are a distinct but ultimately transitory class of states whose features, particularly those derived from the recent experience of armed conflict, shape the violent bargaining that occurs within them. Those employing violence in post-conflict states do not operate in a vacuum; all those who bargain with violence do so within the context of a state that has recently undergone armed conflict, an experience that profoundly shapes the environment in which these actors operate. The contextual features of post-conflict states make them primed for strategic violence, and therefore more likely to experience it than weak states with similar political, economic, or demographic characteristics.

A second descriptive task is to illustrate the variation in strategic violence across post-conflict states. While all post-conflict states are primed for strategic violence, substantial variation exists in the observed levels of strategic violence across this class of states. Employing a dataset of fifty-two post-conflict states that emerged between 1989 and 2007, this chapter illustrates that variation by tracking deaths from acts of strategic violence for the five years following the establishment of a peace agreement. Across the sample, there is a clear stratification of strategic violence into four tiers (mass, scattered, occasional, and residual) based on the average number of people killed per year from strategic attacks. Using that framework, this chapter classifies post-conflict states into two broad types (hard or soft) depending on the severity of the strategic violence in that case. In hard environments, strategic violence will be a regular occurrence and pose a serious and public challenge to the stability of the post-conflict government or administration, while in soft environments strategic violence will be episodic and often obscured within the expressive and instrumental violence otherwise present in the society.

The analytic section of this chapter explains this variation in the onset and levels of strategic violence across post-conflict states in two ways. First, it identifies two pathways for the emergence of strategic violence in post-conflict states: direct and indirect. One of the key arguments here is that no single explanatory logic exists for strategic violence in post-conflict states; rather, two distinct pathways can produce this type of violence.[1] The explanatory powers of these pathways are limited to strategic violence and do not explain the onset of expressive or instrumental violence.[2] The *direct pathway* operates when the existing combatants do not accept the terms of the peace settlement and seek to contest it through violence. This contestation can take on many forms beyond overturning the peace settlement and resuming the war. In some cases, strategic violence will continue to occur as a sublimated conflict, operating beneath the surface of normal politics; in others, combatants may seek to extend the war beyond the borders of the state in pursuit of wider regional goals. The key feature of the direct pathway is that strategic violence in the post-conflict period is broadly similar to that of the war, with the types and targets of the violence mirroring that of the war. The direct pathway features the same actors, or a new organization adopting their political cause, and violence in the post-conflict state largely revolves around the original fault lines of the conflict. While strategic violence under the direct pathway is not an exact replica of the violence during the war, it is the direct descendant of that violence and aimed at renegotiating the central issues of that war.

By contrast, the *indirect pathway* focuses on the interaction between the local incentives that armed groups face and their organizational cohesion.[3] Under this pathway, strategic violence is driven by a dynamic and iterative process in which signatories must enforce compliance with the terms of the settlement over a period of time, while maintaining organizational discipline and rewarding factions within their ranks. Of key importance here is the level of internal control wielded by the leaders of the group, as manifested by the secure distribution of goods (such as political offices, jobs, or profits) to their factions and the corresponding ability to punish those who defect from the terms of the settlement.[4] The level of internal control is determined by several factors, including the original organizational endowments of the combatants, the resources at their disposal, and leadership, all of which can help the leaders of the armed group to buy off factions in their ranks and ensure compliance with the terms of the settlement.[5] If these distributional or patronage functions break down during the post-conflict period, they can fuel the rise of splinter groups, which will bargain with each other through the use of strategic violence. These overlapping bargaining games between existing and emerging claimants to power can generate regional microcosms of violent activity. This violent competition is often driven by local politics more than the macro-cleavage of the conflict, which in turn can produce unexpected shifts in the types and targets of attack. Under the indirect pathway, strategic violence is not a mirror image of the violence during the war but rather refracts the fault lines of the conflict through the prism of the organizational and political changes that the combatants experienced following the settlement.

The second analytical contribution of this chapter is to explain why some post-conflict states have higher or lower levels of strategic violence. As discussed in chapter 1, the pathways are only half of the story in explaining strategic violence. On their own, the pathways explain the nature and origins of the violence, but do not fully account for its severity, which is partially determined by the opportunity structure of the post-conflict state. In other words, the level of strategic violence in a post-conflict state is *jointly determined* by the pathways and the opportunity structure present. The opportunity structure is determined by: (1) the vulnerability of ethnic, political, or religious groups in the civilian population; (2) the flexibility of the institutions of the government or transitional administration; and (3) the ability and willingness of the external forces or international peacekeepers to protect civilians and respond to the use of violence. The opportunity structure exerts a mediating effect on the decisions of armed actors in the post-conflict state, amplifying or diminishing the overall levels of strategic violence. The opportunity structure can be permissive—that is, conducive to strategic violence—or nonpermissive depending on these factors. In this respect, the model for explaining violence after wars presented here accounts for both agency (pathways) and structure (opportunity structure). Each aspect of opportunity structure is capable of influencing the tactical decisions of those seeking to use violence, by providing targets of attack, by creating ways to buy off factions that might be inclined to freelance in violence, or by making certain types of attacks more or less costly. In the fluid environment of a post-conflict state, the opportunity structure for violence does not remain constant over time, as other actors (such as civilians, government officials, external actors, or peacekeepers) may respond to acts of strategic violence in ways that affect the opportunity structure. In some cases, the use of strategic violence against vulnerable groups will produce a countermobilization of new armed actors that will rally to the defense of their community. When widespread countermobilization occurs, the escalating levels of strategic violence raise the risk that the case will fully relapse into armed conflict instead of simply having a violent and occasionally unstable peace.

This chapter begins by defining what constitutes a post-conflict state. The second section then lays out the reasons why this class of states is more prone to violence than comparable weak states. The third section discusses the two broad types of post-conflict states (hard and soft), which are distinguished by the amount of strategic violence present in the case. The fourth section presents the data collected on violence in post-conflict states from multiple sources, identifying the stratification of violence into the tiers (mass, scattered, occasional, and residual) that make post-conflict environments hard or soft. The fifth section presents the pathways for the emergence of violence in post-conflict states, focusing attention on the two variables that drive them: support for the peace settlement and the level of internal control. The sixth section discusses the features of the opportunity structure in post-conflict states that together with the pathways determine the levels of strategic violence in the case. The final section identifies the implications of this model for the case studies.

Defining Post-Conflict States

A post-conflict state is a defined here by four conditions: (1) the state experienced an armed conflict between at least two parties; (2) the fighting for the war has been conducted on its territory; (3) there was an explicit and formal termination of the war; and (4) the peace settlement must last for at least one year.[6] While all of these conditions are necessary for post-conflict status, none is sufficient. Armed conflicts with variable levels of violence and temporary cease-fires do not qualify as post-conflict states. This means that some key cases (such as the Israeli-Palestinian crisis) do not qualify because agreements such as the Oslo Accords have fallen short of a formal settlement of the fundamental issues in the conflict. Similarly, nominal cease-fires do not produce post-conflict states.[7] For example, the multiple cease-fires conducted between the military junta in Myanmar and the ethnic rebel armies within its territory have not yet turned it into a post-conflict state. The criterion of ending the armed conflict for at least one year is designed to exclude cases in which a cease-fire halts the violence only temporarily, without a formal settlement of conflict.[8] Long-running secessionist conflicts, which often feature intermittent levels of violence, are excluded here. A mutually recognized settlement of the war is necessary for the designation of post-conflict status, even if parties relapse into war more than one year after. The dataset of post-conflict states presented here excludes these on-again, off-again conflicts, those where only a temporary cease-fire has been put in place and those where the conflict has relapsed within months of the settlement.[9]

A post-conflict state does not require a change in government or the imposition of a new political authority. If a government wins a civil war, for instance, it would still find itself in control of a post-conflict state. There does not need to be an explicit power-sharing agreement, or even implicit recognition of the underlying legitimacy of the opponent's claims, for a state to qualify as a post-conflict state.[10] Outright military victories, including those which produce a punitive or victor's peace, can still produce post-conflict states.[11] Similarly, regime change is not a necessary condition of a post-conflict state. Post-conflict states can have a wide range of governing authorities, including interim authorities (like a UN peacekeeping mission or a protectorate exercised by an external power) and transitional governments.[12] The dataset here includes cases where the UN and other regional actors are involved and cases in which they are not. Similarly, negotiated settlements that leave both combatants standing can also produce post-conflict states provided that there is a genuine settlement and a corresponding reduction in violence for at least one year. Unlike some of the existing literature on civil war terminations that consider military victories and negotiated settlements separately, this dataset includes a mix of both negotiated settlements and military victories and illustrates that the levels of post-conflict violence do not vary as much as widely assumed in the scholarly literature.[13]

Similarly, in contrast to much of the literature that treats interstate wars and intrastate wars as separate or mutually exclusive categories, this study suggests that interstate, intrastate, and extrastate conflicts can all produce post-conflict states.[14] More generally, it argues that, from the vantage point of understanding strategic violence, these categories may be unhelpful. The example of Iraq (2003–2008)—in which an interstate war created a post-conflict state rife with strategic violence, which later descended into civil war, which was partially populated by foreign and terrorist actors—illustrates that the neat divisions between interstate, intrastate, and extrastate conflicts can be overdrawn. Similarly, the line between domestic and international wars is also blurry. Many civil wars—such as the Spanish Civil War (1936–1939)—

start out as internecine struggles, but quickly develop an international dimension; more recent wars like Afghanistan (1979–2001) start as interstate wars but turn into intrastate wars over time.[15] The category of post-conflict states, as defined here, is an umbrella term for all states under which substantial armed conflict has occurred on the territory, irrespective of the type of war or its rationale.

The territoriality criterion has implications for case selection, as not all participants in a war will be designated a post-conflict state. For example, wars fought entirely in the commons (such as the open seas or air) are excluded here. More generally, this definition does not classify a state that fought a war entirely on another state's territory as a post-conflict state. This means that the designation of a post-conflict state is not always reciprocal (i.e., not all combatants are equally considered post-conflict states once a war is finished). In the Second World War, for example, only those states which experienced armed conflict or sustained organized violence on their territory would be considered post-conflict states. According to this definition, the United Kingdom, France, Germany, Japan, Russia, and arguably the United States would be post-conflict states after 1945, but Australia, Canada, and New Zealand would not.[16] The territorial criteria can mean that a state that initiates an attack on another's territory is not always considered a post-conflict state. For example, after 2003 war in Iraq, the United States would not be considered a post-conflict state, even though it was the instigator of the war, while Iraq would certainly qualify as such. Extrastate conflicts (such as those fought between a state and a terrorist group) can generate post-conflict environments, though the territorial criterion is necessary for both combatants to be designated post-conflict states. For instance, after the Israeli war against Hezbollah in Lebanon in 2006, Lebanon would be classified a post-conflict state, whereas Israel (which experienced limited rocket attacks and civilian casualties) would not.[17]

The designation of post-conflict status can also be complicated by the problem of overlapping wars, some of which may end at different times. Some states, such as the Democratic Republic of Congo, have multiple concurrent conflicts, but different wars on their territory may end at different times.[18] This can make it difficult to determine whether these states actually qualify for post-conflict status, for a case may have an active conflict in one region yet a post-conflict period in another. The fronts in many wars are so fluid, and marked by irregular actors, that drawing neat lines around wars and their combatants is often difficult to do in practice.[19] The multifaceted wars that have torn apart the Congo are a perfect example of this phenomenon, as the rebel groups fighting in different parts of that territory are sometimes allied and have common foreign sponsors. Moreover, such overlapping wars and post-conflict periods tend to be difficult to contain and slip into armed conflict relatively easily. This will be particularly apparent in the case study on violence in Rwanda (1994–1999) in chapter 5, in which the post-conflict violence in that country gradually transformed into an internationally sponsored civil war in the Congo. By 1998, when Rwandan forces were deeply enmeshed in the war in the Congo, it became questionable whether Rwanda was still a "post-conflict" state given its deep involvement in another war outside its territory and the extent of the cross-border incursions. Nevertheless, Rwanda will be studied in detail here because it demonstrates how even those actors which win outright military victory can employ strategic violence for a host of domestic and international policy goals.

A point of clarification on timing is necessary. Post-conflict status does not last indefinitely. While states can suffer from the lingering effects of armed conflict for years after a war, most of the immediate aftershocks of organized violence on the territory last only a short period of time after the end of hostilities.[20] Following an emerging convention of studies on the duration of peace, a state is classified as post-conflict for five years after the formal end of the conflict unless the war resumes before that time period has elapsed.[21] A state may be deemed post-conflict for less than five years if fighting has resumed and if battle casualties have resumed. States can lose their post-conflict status if another war breaks out, either between the same combatants or between a new array of actors.

In some cases, a formal end to the armed conflict may last more than a year but the conflict will quickly reemerge with a different array of actors. A good example of this is Iraq (2003–2008). This case, which will be discussed in detail in chapter 8, illustrates that post-conflict status is often transitory: Iraq was a post-conflict state in 2003 and into early 2004, slipped into civil war until late 2008, and returned to being a post-conflict state in 2009. Similarly, many notable post-conflict states—such as Afghanistan (2002), Rwanda (1995), and the Democratic Republic of Congo (2003–2006)—have relapsed into armed conflict only a few years into their five-year post-conflict periods, but often with different actors from those which dominated the war. While the dataset will include these cases only in their short post-conflict periods, the case studies on Rwanda and Iraq will trace the violence levels across the full five years to illustrate how violence in post-conflict states can gradually evolve into an entirely new armed conflict over time.

Are Post-Conflict States Different?

In many respects, post-conflict states share a lot of characteristics with weak states. In the majority of cases, post-conflict states are beset by poor governance, violent crime, economic problems such as unemployment and inflation, and poor infrastructure. In this respect, many post-conflict states resemble weak states whose control over their territory and ability to restrain the use of violence on their territory is more limited than the traditional Weberian notion of the state implies. There are some important exceptions: states that win decisive victories over weaker opponents, such as secessionist or revolutionary groups, can sometimes emerge stronger than they were before the war. A recent example of this might be Sri Lanka, which decisively defeated the LTTE (more commonly known as the Tamil Tigers) in 2009 and now engages in repression against Tamil sympathizers.[22] After its outright victory, Sri Lanka faces no significant secessionist movement and is arguably stronger than when it was fighting the Tamil Tigers.[23] Similarly, Egypt, which imprisoned and killed members of the al-Gama'a al-Islamiyya until they renounced violence in 1998, emerged stronger—at least over the short term—as its strategy of confrontation appeared to defeat the organization.[24] For the most part, however, post-conflict states are weaker than the normal states that suffer gaps in governance and capacity to establish order on their territory.

The fact that a state is a post-conflict state has implications for the ability of armed actors to employ strategic violence. Even in cases of outright victory, the experience of armed conflict subtly changes a state, reshaping the opportunity structure that actors face when engaging in violence. At the most basic level, the experience of armed conflict can magnify some of the social and political dysfunctions normally attendant to weak states, while producing an array of new reasons for acting violently that will affect the tactical calculations of armed actors. With some exceptions, the term *post-conflict* signifies not only that a state has ended a conflict but also that it has a particular set of distinguishing characteristics.[25] For many states, the experience of armed conflict is transformative, often reordering or destroying existing social relations and often changing governments that endure it in both obvious and subtle ways.[26] For this reason, states that have experienced substantial armed conflict on their territory share some characteristics that mark them out as a distinct class of states different from comparable other weak states. The social and political context of a post-conflict state—more specifically the experience of war—is relevant for the violence that occurs within it, providing new motives, targets, and opportunities for violent action not common in similar weak states. It is this context that renders them more susceptible to strategic violence than comparable weak states.

There are five ways in which the experience of armed conflict shapes post-conflict states and primes them for high levels of strategic violence. First, most post-conflict states do not have the basic capacity to meet their Weberian goal of reestablishing control over their territory.[27] The end of an armed conflict often convulses the society and fractures the government, producing a public security gap that lowers the cost of predatory or opportunistic violence. This public security gap is more marked if the interim government is in disarray or if the military or security services have been weakened or delegitimized by their wartime experience. Under these conditions, the post-conflict state can resemble an anarchic or semi-anarchic environment, which in turn creates facilitating conditions for many types of violence.[28] Such an obvious public security gap provides a boon for armed groups that wish to bargain with each other, as well as criminal actors and those seeking to settle personal scores. As the deterrent effect of law enforcement and judicial sanction wanes, the scramble for power among armed groups (and their factions) may intensify, leading to an increase in strategic violence as varying groups race against time to capture territory or resources before the government regains its footing. A prime example of this was the chaos that followed the U.S. invasion of Iraq, as most Iraqi government ministries and security forces lacked the ability to impose order on the country.[29] While Iraq is an extreme example, many post-conflict states feature a public security gap conducive to violence in the immediate aftermath of the war itself, and a process in which armed groups race to create facts on the ground before the government gets on its feet.

Second, post-conflict states often feature a traumatized population because of the societal costs of the war. The experience of armed conflict can leave a trail of death and destruction in its wake; the survivors are often brutalized by their wartime experience and thirsty for revenge against those who harmed them. It is not uncommon to find that the experience of armed conflict leaves thousands of refugees or internally displaced persons in refugee camps for years after the end of the war.[30] It can also produce disease and starvation on a large scale, thus extending the casualties associated with the conflict long after the conflict has ended.[31] War often results in the destruction of crops, homes, and physical infrastructure. As a result, some post-conflict states are closer to broken or failed states, where many of the basic institutions of public life (basic government services, utilities, social services) are nonexistent or dysfunctional. The visible reminders of the destruction of armed conflict tend to keep the suffering of the war fresh in the minds of those still living in the state and provide compelling motivations for violence in the post-conflict period. Especially in cases of intrastate conflict, those who harmed them may be their fellow citizens, thus creating a dangerous proximity between the perpetrators and victims of violence.

Additionally, the disposition of the population toward the government can lead to a social environment conducive to violence or resistance.[32] While in some cases the population may be relieved that the war is over and weary of additional fighting, others in the population may also no longer trust the government, leading to a sullen resentment against its agents or occasional acts of violent resistance.[33] In cases where the state was an agent of repression or violence, the population may refuse to cooperate with law enforcement authorities, thus making it difficult to pursue prosecutions for violent crimes. The problems resulting from this resistance to work with law enforcement are exacerbated in cases where armed conflict led to a deterioration of state capacity. In these cases, the institutions that pose a deterrent to criminals—police, judiciary, penal system—will often malfunction, thus creating a window of opportunity for those who would use violence to achieve their goals. The conjunction of an embittered population and a basic lack of coercive or deterrent capacity on the part of the state means that law enforcement officials often struggle to come to grips with violent crime with little help from the local population.

Third, post-conflict states often contain a number of actors with extensive experience in employing violence for political purposes. These actors, ranging from government forces to rebel groups, can be irregular and poorly trained. But their activity during war often provides them with essential skills of combat, command, and surveillance. Even weak and irregular rebel groups prone to criminal violence are hardened by their experience of combat, giving them tactical advantages in the contests for power and resources that follow the end of an armed conflict. Even more than weak states dominated by criminal or predatory violence, post-conflict states will contain actors (sometimes called "violent specialists") that are skilled at employing violence for collective purposes.[34] Additionally, post-conflict states often feature significant criminal networks that emerged during the wars, whose expertise and assets (such as weapons and cash) can be tapped by political actors for their own purposes.[35] As chapter 2 noted, many of the actors in post-conflict states operate at the intersection of politics and crime, and the networks that emerged during the war—for example, smuggling networks, or those used to finance rebel armies—do not wither away when the peace agreement is in place. They remain a valuable resource for those who wish to continue using violence in post-conflict states.

Fourth, armed conflict tends to reveal the preferences of the population because of its wartime behavior. Costly decisions—such as whether to collaborate with an occupying force or whether to support one political faction or another—tend to reveal the latent preferences of the individuals within the population, which were often unclear before the war began.[36] Armed conflict forces people to make hard choices, even in situations where they might prefer to sit on the fence. When the war ends, those on the losing side of the conflict are often attacked for their wartime choices by those on the winning side. This can be done with a lower risk of false positives in targeting because their latent preferences were revealed by their wartime behavior.[37] This is important because would-be perpetrators are often averse to accidentally killing people from their own side.[38] These revealed preferences can lower the risks attendant to violent action in the post-conflict period and make people more willing to act violently, especially against collaborators and others on the losing side. This dynamic was particularly apparent after the Spanish Civil War. Estimates of the number of Spanish Republicans killed in organized and sporadic violence ranged between 50,000 and 200,000 people.[39] Those arrested or killed were selected by a systematic government effort to penalize those whose wartime behavior revealed that they sided with the Republican cause, even if they were themselves responsible for no direct violence against Nationalist forces.[40] Similarly, there were dozens of assassinations and reprisals against those in France who had worked with the Nazi regime, which were unofficially tolerated by De Gaulle's government as a way of settling accounts.[41]

Fifth, the end of the war often brings about a reversal of fortune in power relations or hierarchies between social, ethnic, religious, and political groups that can leave previously dominant groups vulnerable to attack. When this occurs, groups that traditionally suffer from discrimination or political exclusion sometimes find themselves on the winning side and are, often for the first time, able to take out revenge against those who had harmed them.[42] This can lead to a proliferation of revenge killings and opportunistic violence, as excluded groups enact a kind of rough justice on those who they believe had kept them in an inferior position.[43] For example, thousands of ethnic Germans found themselves subject to reprisals and expulsions after the collapse of Nazi regime, often at the hands of those, such as Jews, Slavs and others, that Nazis had expelled, murdered, or treated brutally.[44] These attacks can continue for some time until the government reestablishes order, and relations between former warring communities can stabilize. This period following a social reversal of fortune also provides a window for strategic attacks, particularly those which can be embedded within waves of expressive and instrumental violence to obscure responsibility for the attacks.[45]

Types of Post-Conflict States

Despite these contextual similarities, there is no single type of post-conflict state. At the most basic descriptive level, post-conflict states vary significantly across several characteristics, most notably over whether the government remains in place, whether the country is partitioned, or whether a UN peacekeeping force has been put in place. They may also vary depending on whether the government has defeated a challenge and emerged victorious, or whether some peace settlement has been put in place with a challenger still standing. In terms of variations in the levels of violence, one can distinguish two main types of post-conflict states. Those cases with high levels of strategic violence, like Iraq (2003) and Afghanistan (2002), can be considered "hard" environments. In these cases, the scale of the violence goes beyond sheer brutality and lawlessness and is directed toward transforming the balance of power and resources between armed groups. This violence can be mass-scale and indiscriminate or more discriminate and tied to a subtle communicative intent and purpose. According to the terms of this study, environments with recurring mass-casualty violence (such as Iraq) and frequent yet low-casualty attacks between combatants (such as Lebanon, 1991–1995) would both be considered hard post-conflict environments.

Hard security environments in post-conflict states are dangerous because strategic acts of violence contain the embers that can reignite the conflict. When an armed group begins to employ violence for strategic purposes against its enemies, this violence can redraw the battle lines of the conflict or lead to the emergence of new factions willing to fight for their own purposes. Acts of strategic violence can also subtly challenge the credibility of a peace agreement and lead to a resumption of the war. The use of strategic violence is one of the biggest reasons why peace settlements, particularly those done through negotiation, are prone to failure.[46] This violence can gradually erode confidence in the settlement, producing a propitious environment for political opportunists to restart the war. But even when the war does not resume and the peace settlement remains intact, high rates of strategic violence can be dangerous. Such violence can produce a climate of fear for ethnic minorities, distort political outcomes by threatening elections, prevent the emergence of civil society, and undermine confidence in political leaders. The recurring incidence of acts of strategic violence can violate the effective terms of the peace settlement, or undermine the faith placed in it, even in cases where the war never formally resumes.

In extreme cases, the distinction between a hard post-conflict environment and a resumed armed conflict can be blurry. Consider again the case of Iraq. After the defeat of the Saddam Hussein regime, Iraq experienced a hard post-conflict environment in 2003, with escalating violence and growing lawlessness, from 2004 to 2005. By 2004, more than a thousand people a year were being killed in series of battles that met any reasonable definition of a civil war.[47] Similarly, supposedly "post-conflict" environments in the Democratic Republic of Congo and Rwanda had thousands killed in strategic violence, often by local militias supported by external powers.[48] The distinction between a hard post-conflict environment and the resumption of the war is difficult to determine in these cases. Iraq and Congo gradually slipped backed into armed conflict as the violence began to escalate, while Rwanda turned a long-running dirty war against Hutu militias into a cross-border war in the Great Lakes. These cases illustrate that post-conflict status—defined here as lasting five years following a formal armed conflict—is transitory, as states can become unstable or relapse into armed conflict if the casualties from strategic violence begin to mount.

Even when war does not resume, the high levels of strategic violence present in hard security environments may threaten the peace in other ways. Low-level and discriminate violence can lead to a slow bleeding process that gradually undermines the legitimacy of the peace settlement. This can resemble a subtle and often implicit form of "dirty bargaining," where a range of violent acts—from targeted assassinations to reprisals to other forms of highly coordinated attacks, such as bombings—are used to change the effective balance of power and resources even if the formal settlement remains intact.[49] This low-intensity violence (such as reprisals or targeted killings) can be part of a deliberate effort to effectively undermine a settlement or can arise from violent bargaining between the former combatants or newly emergent groups over smaller, more local contests over power and resources. Low-intensity violence is less studied than more spectacular forms of violence (such as terrorism), but it can pose an informal challenge to the settlement, especially if it changes the effective balance of power and resources within the state. This bargaining can be conducted with state actors or with peacekeeping forces, or alternatively between substate parties or new parties to the conflict.

Those environments with low levels of strategic violence are defined here as "soft" post-conflict environments. Soft environments are marked primarily by criminal or predatory violence, often decoupled from any attempt to challenge the legitimacy or power of the state. While it does not pose a direct threat to the government or peace settlement, expressive and instrumental violence can be severe in impact. For example, estimates of the number of people killed in the civil war in Guatemala (1960–1996) vary from 46,000 recorded deaths to more than 200,000 who have disappeared or been killed in fratricidal violence.[50] The post-conflict period (1996–2001) in Guatemala has also been extremely violent, with hundreds killed or "disappeared" by criminal and clandestine gangs. Low-level criminality and kidnapping remains rampant, and even despite its larger population (13.1 million), Guatemala remains one of the most violent states in the Americas, with between 5,000 and 6,000 people killed in murders each year.[51] In Guatemala, the violence is not an attempt by the former combatants to explicitly challenge the government or restart the conflict. The violence was driven by criminal gangs, some of which are composed of former paramilitaries, but many of which are composed of desperate and unemployed young men. A similar dynamic is also present in post-conflict El Salvador, which has been torn apart by gang violence, often conducted by the remnants of combatant groups, which have even begun to develop transnational links.[52] Both El Salvador and Guatemala are deeply violent societies but not ones in which organized political actors are agitating to restart the conflict. In other words, they are examples of "successful" peace settlements but remain highly violent societies. The predominantly instrumental and expressive nature of the violence distinguishes it from the hard post-conflict environments like Iraq, which are marked by the number and severity of acts of strategic violence and often an explicit attempt by armed actors to redraw the battle lines of the conflict.

Soft post-conflict environments feature significantly less strategic violence than hard post-conflict environments, and that violence is often not tied to restarting the war in any conventional sense. However, this does not say that they are free from strategic violence. As the case studies demonstrate, most soft post-conflict environments feature dozens of people killed per year, in assassinations, skirmishes with government forces, and reprisals. This violence is not merely epiphenomenal but in fact is often designed to change facts on the ground or to settle local disputes. It is a mistake to dismiss the strategic violence in soft post-conflict environments entirely, for it may be directed to political purposes and have an important effect, even if it never rises to the level of an insurgency or a renewed war. Across all post-conflict states, there is substantial variation in the levels of strategic violence, even among cases that are classified as hard and soft.

The Data

To determine the variation in violence and how many cases fall into the hard and soft categories, this chapter collects data on deaths from strategic violence in a sample of fifty-two post-conflict states whose conflicts ended during the period 1989–2007.[53] This dataset includes a mix of cases of international, internal, and extrastate wars, of wars fought over government or territory, and of cases with and without UN or external actor support.[54] It also includes wars that had long and short durations, as well as cases from all major geographic regions. Unlike other studies that focused exclusively on the outcomes of partitions or negotiated settlements, this sample includes cases where outright military victories by governments or rebel forces have occurred.[55] Based in part on criteria developed by the Uppsala Conflict Termination Dataset, this dataset selected cases where war was conducted on the territory of the state, a peace settlement was signed from 1989 to 2007, peace lasted for more than one year, and the casualties from war dropped to less than twenty-five deaths a year.[56] These stringent criteria are used to ensure that only terminated conflicts are included rather than cases with only cease-fires or temporary lulls in the fighting. To ensure that dataset captures major conflicts and excludes sporadic insurgencies or coups, the dataset includes only cases in which approximately one thousand people or more had been killed during the preceding war.[57] Because of these criteria, cases that had long-running wars with intermittent levels of violence were excluded.[58]

The data collection proceeded as follows. For each post-conflict state, the dataset records deaths from strategic violence for each of the five years, unless the case relapsed into war or the collection of the data extended beyond the cut-off year of 2009. The data were drawn from Nexus U.K. database searches of newspaper articles in major international papers and (whenever available) local papers.[59] The source datasets only record data on deaths from strategic violence and do not intentionally include deaths from expressive or instrumental violence.[60] Some of the source datasets have no acts of violence or only a few acts, while others have recorded over one thousand separate incidents.[61] The acts of strategic violence included in the dataset range from conventional attacks such as bombings, terrorist attacks, and assassinations to more unconventional acts, such as rioting and intercommunal violence and reprisals. The criteria for selecting an act to include were that a death must have occurred; and there must be some explicit evidence in the details of the attack that it was political or otherwise intended to alter the balance of power and resources in the state. As chapter

2 discusses, contextual details about the nature of the act, including the victims and perpetrators and the weapons used, were used to inform this classification. Deaths that were indirectly related to the war—such as deaths from disease and natural disaster and accidental deaths from land mines—were excluded. Table 3.1 lists the deaths from strategic violence for fifty-two post-conflict states.

This dataset represents the only cross-national study of violence in post-conflict states in which an explicit count of deaths from strategic violence is recorded for every year of the post-conflict period. This dataset does not include measures of expressive and instrumental attacks, which tended to be underreported, especially for cases where only major international newspaper and wire service reports were available. Strategic attacks that did not produce casualties are also excluded here. In some cases, this omission is significant; in Lebanon, for example, many of the tit-for-tat artillery volleys that occurred between the Southern Lebanese Army (SLA) and Hezbollah following the peace settlement with Israel in 1991 did not cause deaths but did make the situation highly unstable. Similarly, the case study on Bosnia (chapter 4) explores how nonlethal forms of strategic violence can have an important effect on the politics of the post-conflict state, even when the casualties from strategic violence remain low. Despite this qualification, this dataset is built on the presumption that the death toll from strategic violence is a reasonable proxy measure for assessing the overall severity of strategic violence in each post-conflict state.

The following section will consider variation along the eight dimensions: (1) incidence, (2) magnitude, (3) type, (4) target, (5) relapsed cases, (6) incidence of an insurgency, (7) geographic variation, and (8) temporal variation. Table 3.2 summarizes the descriptive characteristics of the cases in the dataset.

Most post-conflict states feature some level of strategic violence, but not all. In only one unusual case—Badme, Ethiopia (2001–2005)— was no strategic violence recorded across the five-year period. In three other cases—Congo Brazzaville (2000–2001), Kuwait (1992–1996), and Sri Lanka (2002)— fewer than ten deaths were reported in the post-conflict period. For the purposes of this analysis, these four may be considered negative cases, where the outcome of interest did not occur. What is striking about these four cases is that two of them—Congo Brazzaville (2000–2001) and Sri Lanka (1991–1995)—had no recorded strategic violence, yet the war resumed before the post-conflict period elapsed. Table 3.3 describes the circumstances of each of these cases.

As table 3.3 indicates, most of the cases where strategic violence occurred are marked by unusual conditions. Both Badme and Kuwait were atypical post-conflict territories in this dataset in that both emerged after interstate wars that ended with a decisive victory for one party. Both were effectively evacuated by the losing side in the aftermath of the war. The case of Badme is perhaps the most exceptional, as this

TABLE 3.1.
Post-Conflict States, 1989–2007

Entry No.	Territory	Start	End	Number of Deaths						
				Year 1	Year 2	Year 3	Year 4	Year 5	Total	Average
1	Afghanistan	2002	2002	828	—	—	—	—	828	828
2	Angola	1996	1997	166	568	—	—	—	734	367
3	Angola	2003	2007	12	66	20	0	0	98	20
4	Nagorno-Karabakh	1995	1999	84	0	11	8	0	103	21
5	Chitagong Hill Tracts, Bangladesh	1993	1997	14	1	6	64	6	91	18
6	Croatia	1995	1999	10	7	0	0	0	17	3
7	Bosnia	1995	1999	6	13	7	10	6	42	8
8	Serbia	1995	1999	127	6	16	50	828	1,027	205
9	Burundi	2007	2009	99	189	5			293	98
10	Cambodia	1999	2003	23	19	22	9	8	81	16
11	Chad	1995	1996	13	0	—	—	—	13	7
12	Chad	2003	2004	127	67	—	—	—	194	97
13	Congo Brazzaville	2000	2001	0	6	—	—	—	6	3
14	Cote D'Ivoire	2005	2009	155	76	17	18	0	266	53
15	Congo	2003	2006	2,661	847	682	348	—	4,538	1,135
16	Egypt	1999	2003	7	50	0	0	1	58	12
17	El Salvador	1992	1996	24	19	6	8	0	57	11
18	Badme, Ethiopia	2001	2005	0	0	0	0	0	0	0
19	Ethiopia	1991	1996	498	167	3	4	7	679	113
20	Abkhazia	1994	1998	33	24	42	8	53	160	32
21	Guatemala	1996	2000	10	1	1	0	3	15	3
22	Guinea	2002	2006	0	0	0	0	11	11	2
23	Guinea-Bissau	2000	2004	45	59	0	4	6	114	23
24	East Timor	1999	2004	278	31	1	3	9	322	54
25	Aceh	1992	1996	0	10	3	20	7	40	8
26	Aceh	2006	2009	8	13	12			33	8

#	Location								
27	Kuwait	1992	1996	3	2	3	1	1	10	2
28	Kurdistan, Iraq	1997	2001	3,465	462	330	89	7	4,353	871
29	Iraq	2003	2003	7,300	—	—	—	10	7,300	7,300
30	South Lebanon	2000	2004	10	16	19	15	10	70	14
31	South Lebanon	2007	2009	122	35	2	—	—	159	53
32	Lebanon	1991	1995	198	171	314	163	196	1,042	208
33	Liberia	1996	1999	248	8	3	0	—	259	65
34	Liberia	2004	2008	17	0	1	0	0	18	4
35	Western Sahara	1990	1994	0	19	0	0	0	19	4
36	Mozambique	1993	1997	4	30	145	9	0	188	38
37	Nepal	2007	2009	78	27	3	—	—	108	36
38	Nicaragua	1990	1994	92	37	7	146	47	329	66
39	Peru	2000	2004	40	9	30	24	1	104	21
40	Mindanau	1991	1992	179	268	—	—	—	447	224
41	Philippines	1996	1996	297	—	—	—	—	297	297
42	Philippines	2008	2009	318	133	—	—	—	451	226
43	Chechnya	1997	1998	24	28	—	—	—	52	26
44	Rwanda	1995	1995	3,345	—	—	—	—	3,345	3,345
45	Sierra Leone	2001	2005	80	2	0	0	0	82	16
46	Sri Lanka	1991	1995	1	0	0	0	—	1	0
47	Tamil Eelam	2002	2002	25	—	—	—	—	25	25
48	Tajikistan	1997	1997	77	—	—	—	—	77	77
49	Uganda	1992	1993	31	11	—	—	—	42	21
50	Northern Ireland	1999	2003	7	18	17	13	11	66	13
51	South Yemen	1995	1999	0	3	23	2	15	43	9
52	Kosovo	2000	2004	82	69	9	23	30	213	43
	Average			409.06	77.98	46.32	30.56	40.74	556	310.50

TABLE 3.2.
Descriptive Statistics

Conflicts ($N = 52$)	
Average Duration of Conflict	9.02 years
Average Battle Casualties from Conflict	41,844
Source of Dispute	
Territory	20
Nature of Government	32
High-Intensity Wars (>1,000 battle deaths per year)	38
Low-Intensity Wars (<1,000 battle deaths per year)	14
Types of Conflicts	
Extrastate Armed Conflict	1
Interstate	3
Internal	34
Internationalized Internal Conflicts	14
Post-Conflict Period	
Average Post-Conflict Period	3.92 years
Relapsed Cases	15
Types of Outcomes	
Negotiated Settlements	36
Military Victories	16
UN Peacekeeping Missions	29
No External Mission	23
Cases by Region	
Europe	8
Middle East	7
Asia	14
Africa	19
Americas	4

small town was a flashpoint that produced the Ethiopian-Eritrean war and could have plausibly been the site of strategic violence in the postwar period. Yet the town and surrounding territory was tightly controlled by the Ethiopian army throughout its post-conflict period, even though its legal status remained in dispute. Moreover, the fact that both parties agreed to refer its status to arbitration by the Ethiopian Eritrean Border Commission (EEBC) may have had a dampening effect on the possibility of violence.[62] In the case of the Persian Gulf War, an outright U.S. victory and the expulsion of Iraqi forces from Kuwait left the country largely free of strategic violence aside from periodic border clashes. Similarly, the gradual victory of the Sri Lankan government over the militant forces of the Janatha Vimukthi Peramuna (JVP), as well as the splintering of that movement and the decision of the JVP political wing to move into normal politics, effectively spelled the end of them as a military force.[63] Of all of the negative cases, the brief period of peace in Congo Brazzaville (2000–2001) is the most typical case of a post-conflict state. This case, however, should be understood as the calm before the storm, as Pastor Ntumi's forces—known as the Ninjas—resumed armed struggle after fighting on the side of the Cocoyes and Mouvement National

TABLE 3.3.
Negative Cases

Post-Conflict States	Year Conflict Begins	Year Conflict Ends	Types of Attacks	Targets	Death Toll	Explanation
Congo Brazzaville	2000	2001	Assassination	Political official	6	Congo Brazzaville had a brief period of peace following its civil war but the presidential election won by Sassou Nguesso in March 2002, as well as constitutional reforms, proved controversial. A rebellion by Pastor Ntumi in the Pool region of the country restarted the war later that year. Ntumi called off the rebellion in 2003 and agreed to disband his militia for a ministerial position in April 2007.
Badme, Ethiopia	2001	2005	None reported	None reported	0	The town of Badme was disputed between Ethiopia and Eritrea during their long-standing war. Under the Algiers Accord, both parties agreed to refer its final status to the Ethiopian Eritrean Border Commission (EEBC). The EEBC ruled in 2002 that the town belonged to Eritrea, but it remained under tight Ethiopian control, pending normalization of their relations. Periodic border flare-ups have occurred but no violence has been reported in the town.
Sri Lanka	1991	1995	Assassination	Political leader	1	Throughout this period, Sri Lanka remained in conflict with the LTTE, but its war against the Janatha Vimukthi Peramuna (JVP), a Marxist group, ended in 1990. The fatalities during this period are strictly limited to those linked to the JVP. The government defeated the JVP, and the organization became involved in normal politics.
Kuwait	1992	1996	Border clashes	Border guards, civilians	10	The end of the Persian Gulf war was a rout of Saddam Hussein's forces, which fled Kuwait entirely in January 1991. Most of the remaining violence revolved around flare-ups on the Iraqi border. Since the occupation of Kuwait was relatively short, there were fewer instances of reprisals than other occupations.

pour la Liberation du Congo (MNLC) during the war.[64] The decision to resume fighting was due largely to Ntumi's dissatisfaction with his share of the spoils, and his insurgency was ended by 2007 when he was awarded a ministerial position.[65]

Magnitude

Underlying the descriptive difference between hard and soft post-conflict states is variation in the amount of strategic violence present in the case. This can be described as the magnitude of the violence. Magnitude can be measured in different ways, but here it will be measured principally by mean and median death totals, both annually and across the post-conflict period. Table 3.4 identifies the means and medians for the entire sample, as well as a series of subsets within the sample.

In this sample, the mean was 556 casualties from strategic violence per post-conflict period, with a mean annual casualty rate of 311 people. Both means are higher, and suggest much more violence, than most of the conventional literature suggests, especially when the settlement remains intact.[66] It should be noted that these means are inflated owing to a small number of cases (such as Afghanistan, Rwanda, Congo, and Iraq) with extremely high levels of violence. These cases had violent, if short, post-conflict periods before they relapsed into armed conflict; their high levels of violence in their short post-conflict periods could skew the calculation of the mean. In particular, Iraq is an outlier: most post-conflict states are awash in a range of small acts of brutality and violence, ranging from petty theft to assault and murder, but none in the dataset rises to the extreme level of violence evident in that case.[67] To compensate for these outliers in inflating the average casualty totals, table 3.4 presents the means without including Iraq and lists the medians for the total and annual number of deaths from strategic violence. The median death toll was 101 people killed across the post-conflict period, with a median annual casualty rate of 24 deaths.

As Table 3.4 indicates, some characteristics of subgroups within the sample are associated with higher levels of strategic violence. Although the small sample size of the subgroups and the presence of outliers (such as Iraq) warns against drawing firm conclusions from these data, a comparative analysis of the medians of the subgroups is suggestive of some broad patterns.[68] Post-conflict states that emerged after wars over control of a government or ideology have a median total death toll of 114, almost twice the median total (66) of post-conflict states that emerged from wars fought over territory. More-intense wars are also associated with nearly double the level of casualties from strategic violence (median total, 111) in the post-conflict period as low intensity wars (median total, 62). Military victories are associated with slightly higher levels of strategic violence (median total, 114) compared to negotiated settlements (median total, 91).[69] Similarly, post-conflict states with UN peacekeeping missions

TABLE 3.4.
Measures of the Magnitude of Strategic Violence

	Number of Cases	Average Total Casualties	Median Total Casualties	Average Annual Casualties	Median Annual Casualties
Post-Conflict States					
All	52	556	101	311	24
All Excluding Iraq	51	424	98	174	23
Source of Dispute					
Government	31	698	114	468	38
Territory	21	347	66	79	18
Intensity of War					
High	38	606	111	385	34
Low	14	422	62	108	12
Types of Wars					
Extrastate	1	679	679	113	113
Interstate	3	2,437	10	2,434	2
Internal	34	281	81	77	21
International Internal	14	813	151	439	40
Outcomes					
Military Victory	17	1,093	114	757	23
Negotiated Settlement	35	295	91	94	25
Relapse?					
Yes	15	1,210	259	921	97
No	37	291	91	63	18
UN Mission?					
Yes	29	732	159	484	38
No	23	335	98	93	21

tend to have more violent post-conflict periods (median total, 159) than those without (median total, 98), though this may be due to the fact that peacekeeping missions are typically deployed to tough cases where violence is already more likely.[70] Post-conflict states that eventually relapse back into war are associated with higher median total casualties (259) than those which do not (91).

Table 3.5 identifies the high magnitude cases, both in absolute terms and in per capita terms (i.e., the risk of being a victim of strategic violence for every member of the population). The highest total casualty rate was Iraq (7,300 in one year), while the highest per capita casualty rate belonged to Rwanda (0.0558823480%), a rate that suggests that nearly one in every twenty people in the population was killed in the post-conflict period.[71] Both cases will be explored in subsequent case studies.

What the analysis of magnitudes in the dataset reveals is that the variation in violence in post-conflict states is significant. While 50 percent of the cases in the dataset have fewer than 100 casualties from strategic violence, 17.3 percent have more than 500 casualties from strategic violence across their post-conflict period. To break the

TABLE 3.5.
High Violence Cases, by Total Casualties and Casualties Per Capita

	Post-Conflict State	Year Conflict Begins	Year Conflict Ends	Total Killed
Total Casualties	Iraq	2003	2003	7,300
	Congo	2003	2006	4,538
	Kurdistan, Iraq	1997	2001	4,353
	Rwanda	1995	1995	3,345
	Lebanon	1991	1995	1,042
	Serbia	1995	1999	1,027
	Afghanistan	2002	2002	828
	Angola	1996	1997	734
	Ethiopia	1991	1996	679
	Philippines	2008	2009	451
Per Capita	Rwanda	1995	1995	0.0558823480%
	Iraq	2003	2003	0.0276168267%
	Lebanon	1991	1995	0.0054049708%
	Kurdistan, Iraq	1997	2001	0.0039496463%
	Angola	1996	1997	0.0032429261%
	Afghanistan	2002	2002	0.0029831624%
	Serbia	1995	1999	0.0026713244%
	Liberia	1996	1999	0.0026028372%
	Kosovo	2000	2004	0.0022421053%
	Congo	2003	2006	0.0019936684%

dataset down into tiers, an ordinal ranking scheme was developed, which classifies cases into one of four categories based on the numbers killed per year: mass-scale violence (more than 1,000 people killed per year), scattered violence (between 1,000 and 201 killed per year), occasional violence (between 200 and 26 people killed per year), and residual violence (25 or fewer people killed per year).[72] Both mass and scattered levels of strategic violence produce hard post-conflict environments, while occasional and residual levels of strategic violence can be considered soft environments. Table 3.6 identifies the totals for each, and whether these produced hard versus soft post-conflict environments.

The analysis of the magnitude of the strategic violence illustrates two important points. First, while many cases with high-magnitudes of violence involve relapsed wars, insurgencies, or renewed conflicts, not all cases of high-magnitude violence can be explained as renewed conflicts. In some highly violent cases, the peace has remained—at least formally—intact. Even excluding the three mass violence cases (Congo, Iraq, and Rwanda), there are seven "scattered violence" cases, with more than 200 killed per year in strategic violence, and fifteen occasional cases, with more than 25 people killed per year. In many of these cases, the level of strategic violence is striking because the peace settlement remains intact. In other words, many of these cases have a violent, unstable, or dysfunctional peace, with significant levels of killing

TABLE 3.6.
Ranking of Cases

Ranking of Violence	Numbers Killed per Year	Number of Cases	Type of Post-Conflict Environment	Number of Cases
Mass	>1,000	3	Hard	10
Scattered	200–1,000	7		
Occasional	<200	15	Soft	42
Residual	<25	27		

higher than most studies of conflict termination suggest. Second, this analysis proves that searching for explanations for this violence cannot be directed solely toward the high-magnitude cases but must also explain cases where low or intermediate levels of violence are present in the post-conflict period. A compelling theory that explains variation in strategic violence after wars must account for the different magnitudes of strategic violence that produce hard and soft post-conflict environments. Accordingly, the case studies in this book will examine one unusual residual case (Bosnia), as well as two cases of stable peace settlements that operate with an occasional level of strategic violence (Kosovo and East Timor).

Type

Substantial variation exists in the types of violent acts evident across cases. While it is impossible to capture the complexity of the types of violence present in each case, the dataset records the most common "types" of attacks evident. Table 3.7 indicates the percentage of cases in which that type of attack was common. Many post-conflict states end with violence that resembles that which occurred during the war itself, such as rebel attacks (73.08%), sporadic military action (50.00%), and border clashes (32.69%). In these cases, the best explanation is that the war has ended only nominally; for example, in Lebanon violence continued from 1991 to 1995, with repeated artillery attacks and ambushes that mirrored what happened in the war itself. In cases such as Angola (2003–2007) and Mozambique (1993–1997), much of the strategic violence that occurs in the post-conflict period arises from "mopping up" operations against rebels. Others end with a significant amount of reprisal violence (25%) and massacres (25%), often conducted by noncombatants and splinters against vulnerable groups in the population. In some cases, the violence is conducted along ethnic lines (34.62%), with riots also a common form of violent activity (34.62%). A larger number of cases featured lower-intensity types of violence such as shootings (94.23%), bombings (63.46%), and assassinations (57.69%), especially of prominent political figures. These cases reveal a shift in post-conflict states to more low-intensity attacks,

TABLE 3.7.
Common Types of Attacks

Type of Attack	Percentage of Cases
Shootings	94.23
Rebel Attacks	73.08
Bombings	63.46
Assassinations	57.69
Military Action	50.00
Ethnic Violence	34.62
Riots	34.62
Border Clashes	32.69
Reprisals	25.00
Massacres	25.00
Election Violence	19.23

closer in form to criminal activity than to war fighting. This portrayal of the proliferation of "ordinary" acts of violence in these cases suggests that strategic violence of the post-conflict period is not merely a continuation of the fighting that occurred during the war, as the nature of violence has shifted away from more conventional military attacks to politico-criminal depredations, often against civilians.

Finally, a comparison of these statistics with World Health Organization homicide statistics reveals that some cases feature relatively little evidence of strategic violence but ample evidence of expressive and instrumental violence, such as murder, kidnapping, assault, and theft. This was particularly apparent with several Latin American cases. For example, the murder rates in El Salvador were higher in the post-conflict period than they were in wartime, despite the fact that the civil war settlement has held.[73] During its post-conflict period, El Salvador experienced high rates of predatory violence—such as murder and kidnapping—but there was little evidence of a political strategy underlying the violence. The World Health Organization estimates that 9,528 murders happened in El Salvador during its post-conflict period (1992–1996), while only 57 deaths recorded from newspaper accounts could be clearly attributed to strategic violence.[74] Similarly, in Guatemala, the WHO estimates that 28,998 murders occurred in the post-conflict period (1996–2000), while only 15 deaths were reported from strategic violence. These cases illustrate the complex relationship between political and criminal violence, as it is well known that ex-paramilitary forces are engaged in criminal activity.[75] It is probable that many of the homicides reported to the WHO straddle the line between strategic and criminal forms of violence, thus making it difficult to draw reliable empirical estimates of how much strategic and instrumental violence is present. But these cases indicate that, even when the rates of strategic violence are negligible, and the peace settlement remains intact, the society can be highly violent and dangerous and imperil the lives of civilians but in a way that only occasional or residual strategic attacks do not. This survey of the crime statistics of post-conflict states reveals such substantial variation in the types of violent acts present—ranging from murder to kidnapping, assault, street crime, organized crime, targeted killings, reprisals, and insurgent attacks— that one must be careful not to equate the absence of strategic violence with a livable peace.

Target

There is a wide range of potential victims of violence in post-conflict states: political officials, peacekeepers, local criminal figures, and ordinary civilians. As argued in chapter 2, the predominant distinction for target selection is between individual targets—that is, those victimized on the basis of previous (often wartime) behavior—and categorical targets, who are singled out for attack on the basis of their membership in a particular ethnic, religious, or political group.[76] At the level of aggregate crime statistics, it is difficult to generalize about individual victimization, though this clearly occurs and will be reflected in the original crime statistics presented in the case studies. As for categorical victimization, two types emerged. First, victims were selected on the basis of their wartime behavior. The dataset records the most common types of victims present in the recorded events. This survey indicates that most cases have frequent attacks against government officials or representatives (82.69% of cases), rebels (76.92% of cases), and civilians (82.69% of cases). Second, victims were selected on the basis of ethnic or religious identity. In the dataset, more than one-third of cases (34.62%) features explicit evidence of ethnic or religious targeting of violence, usually against civilians, or violence involving rebel groups that represent a particular ethnic or religious constituency. Importantly, the individual datasets also indicate that in some cases new categories of victims arose, often for reasons only marginally related to the war. As chapter 7 shows, in East Timor those who were from the western part of the country—called loromonu, (westerners) in Tetum—came under attack in mid-2006 for their perceived collaboration with the Indonesian occupiers. Like the data on types of attacks, two targeting patterns emerge: one in which the principal targets of violence mirror the targets of violence from the war, and another in which the targets of violence in post-conflict states shift over time, producing new categories of victims and perpetrators.

Relapse

Fifteen of the fifty-four cases in the dataset experienced a relapse into war during the post-conflict period.[77] Table 3.8 identifies the relapsed cases and their levels of strategic violence. As a general rule, relapsed cases had higher levels of strategic violence

TABLE 3.8.
Relapsed Cases

Post-Conflict State	Post-Conflict Period	Year of Relapse	Deaths from Strategic Violence	Average Annual Deaths from Strategic Violence
Afghanistan	2002	2003	828	828
Angola	1996–1997	1998	734	367
Chad	1995–1996	1997	13	7
Chad	2003–2004	2005	194	97
Congo Brazzaville	2000–2001	2002	6	3
Congo	2003–2006	2007	4,538	1,135
Iraq	2003	2004	7,300	7,300
Liberia	1996–1999	2000	259	65
Mindanau	1991–1992	1993	447	224
Philippines	1996	1997	297	297
Chechnya	1997	1998	52	26
Rwanda	1995	1996	3,345	3,345
Tamil Eelam	2002	2003	25	25
Tajikistan	1997	1998	77	77
Uganda	1992–1993	1994	42	21

Note: The countries are ordered by their entry number from table 3.1.

than nonrelapsed cases. As table 3.4 revealed, relapsed cases had nearly five times the average total casualties from strategic violence (1,210) that nonrelapsed cases (291) did.[78] To some extent, this is not surprising: one would expect cases with high levels of strategic violence to be more likely to relapse. The question that arises is whether the strategic violence caused the relapse into armed conflict, or whether the relapse into armed conflict drove a gradual increase in the levels of strategic violence.[79] High levels of strategic violence may risk reigniting the conflict, but not all forms of strategic violence are directed toward overturning the settlement. Because this dataset measures strategic violence and relapse independently, it highlights cases with relatively high levels of strategic violence but no formal relapse.[80] Some cases do not relapse within their post-conflict period, yet have periodic conventional military engagements (i.e., periodic fighting between Israel and Hezbollah in South Lebanon, or between Turkish forces and the Kurdistan Workers' Party in Iraqi Kurdistan) that fall short of a formal relapse. Far more common, however, are violent post-conflict environments with stable peace settlements. Of the thirty-seven nonrelapsed cases, ten cases have more than 200 people killed from strategic violence across their post-conflict period.

Insurgencies

Within the dataset of fifty-two cases, nineteen cases have experienced insurgencies within the post-conflict period, according to a recent RAND study.[81] Table 3.9 lists all

TABLE 3.9.
Insurgencies

Post-Conflict State	Year Conflict Begins	Year Conflict Ends	Total Deaths	Average Annual Deaths
Afghanistan	2002	2002	828	828
Angola	1996	1997	734	367
Congo	2003	2006	4,538	1,135
Ethiopia	1991	1996	679	113
Aceh	1992	1996	40	8
Kurdistan, Iraq	1997	2001	4,353	871
Iraq	2003	2003	7,300	7,300
South Lebanon	2000	2004	70	14
South Lebanon	2007	2009	159	53
Lebanon	1991	1995	1,042	208
Liberia	1996	1999	259	65
Nepal	2007	2009	108	36
Mindanau	1991	1992	447	224
Philippines	1996	1996	297	297
Philippines	2008	2009	451	226
Chechnya	1997	1998	52	26
Rwanda	1995	1995	3,345	3,345
Tamil Eelam	2002	2002	25	25
South Yemen	1995	1999	43	9

Note: The countries are ordered by their entry number from table 3.1.

of the cases that experienced insurgencies in the post-conflict period. Not all insurgencies have led to a relapse of the war, as some states have managed to control the effects of a running insurgency without escalating into full-fledged wars. Predictably, cases that experience insurgencies have a much higher level of strategic violence. Cases with insurgencies had an average total casualty level in the post-conflict period of 1,304, with an average annual death toll of 797. Post-conflict states without insurgencies had an average total death toll of 126 deaths, with an annual toll of 31 deaths per year. Many of the cases that have high levels of strategic violence overlap with those cases where an insurgency is present, but this overlap is not perfect, and there are some cases with high levels of strategic violence and no definable insurgency.

Geographic Variation

Aside from the cross-case variation, there is also significant geographic variation within post-conflict states. Post-conflict states are not uniformly violent, as some regions are more violent than others. Such geographic variation does not always mirror the incidence of wartime violence; regions that were badly damaged during armed conflict often turn out to be strangely peaceful after the settlement is in place. The frontiers of violence can shift across time in response to political and social developments and population movements. For example, different provinces in Afghanistan became more or less violent over time, in response to efforts by NATO and Afghan forces to "hold" insurgent territory.[82] The center of gravity for the insurgency, for example, shifted between provinces in response to discrete initiatives. Just like a wildfire that can be controlled in one region while burning more fiercely elsewhere, high rates of violence can shift across geographic space in response to efforts by the state or UN peacekeepers to deter and respond to such acts. In the cross-national dataset, the evidence for most cases is not fine-grained enough to do a regional analysis or track within-case variation, but this contextual mapping of crime statistics on a regional basis will be done in some of the subsequent case studies.

Temporal Variation

In 55.7 percent of cases, the most violent year of the post-conflict period is the first year. Much of the violence within the first year comes out of the war itself, as the combatants conduct punitive raids on the other side, reprisals occur between civilians, and the last holdouts from the peace settlement are dealt with. Figure 3.1 illustrates that across the entire dataset of fifty-two cases that 74 percent of all deaths from strategic violence occur in the first year. The remaining years of the post-conflict period have lower levels of deaths from strategic violence. Despite this overall trend line, most cases exhibit some unique form of temporal variation, with the levels of violence tapering off in varying degrees throughout the rest of the post-conflict period.

The baseline level of violence in the post-conflict period is established by how violent the conflict is within its first year. Most cases feature a significant drop-off in levels of violence after the first year, but the baseline for the level of violence that they will experience is established in the first year. The only exceptions are cases in which the conflict resumes. In these cases, the level of strategic violence shows at least a slight increase throughout the years of the post-conflict period.

Pathways

What explains the onset and variation in strategic violence across post-conflict states? In the existing scholarly literature, no single theory explains why actors choose to employ strategic violence in post-conflict states. This is largely because the problem has often been framed differently. For example, of the many studies on the types of violent activity common in post-conflict states (such as riots to targeted assassinations to insurgent activity), none has considered what impact the context—the aftermath of a war—has on the patterns of violence.[83] Similarly, the substantial literature on the spoiling of peace processes and the duration of peace settlements defines the dependent variable in a different way from what is done here.[84] The spoiling litera-

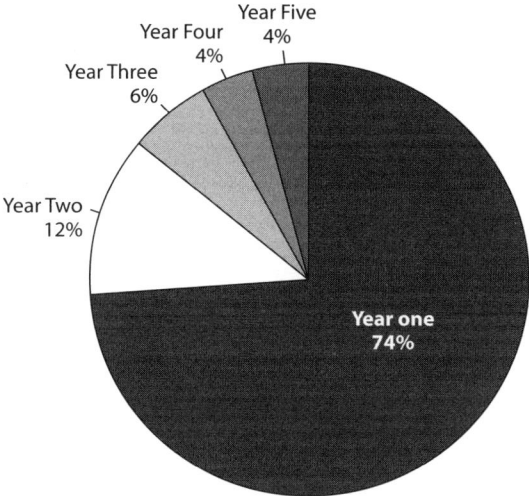

Figure 3.1. Total Deaths from Strategic Violence by Year.

ture frames the dependent variable as efforts, sometimes violent, sometimes not, to undermine a peace settlement, whereas the literature on civil war termination frames the dependent variable as a binary proposition (i.e., whether the war resumed or not).[85] Both sets of literature offer a more straightforward set of empirical questions to investigate, but both tend to underplay the extent to which strategic violence can be directed toward a range of diverse, often localized, purposes following armed conflict. Both also tend to discount violence that falls below a threshold that may endanger the peace, treating it as a residual or epiphenomenal form of criminal activity.[86] Many of these studies focus on violence as a symptom that may lead to a relapse into war, rather than analyze violence as a phenomenon in its own right.

This focus on the resumption of the war as the key dependent variable is for the most part appropriate: the resumption of war is by far the most dangerous consequence of strategic violence. But this approach has limitations. Framing the dependent variable in this way leads scholars to underestimate strategic violence that falls beneath the threshold and consequently to underplay the kinds of low-intensity brutality that can make a peace dysfunctional or unstable. In other words, this literature does not decouple the analysis of strategic violence from the stability of the settlement in a way that allows it to ask new questions about the proximate purposes of that violence.[87] Second, this framing of the dependent variable assumes a clear line between war and peace and underestimates the variation in post-conflict violence across cases of even ostensibly peaceful post-conflict states.[88] This approach cannot account for many cases where strategic violence occurs in the absence of an explicit challenge to the peace settlement. To remedy this, this book focuses attention on the strategic purpose of violence in three cases—Bosnia (chapter 4), Kosovo (chapter 6), and East Timor (chapter 7)—where the settlement remains largely intact. It also focuses attention on one case—Rwanda (chapter 5)—where the victor is the chief perpetrator of strategic violence in the post-conflict period.

In this book, the dependent variable is strategic violence itself, and the assumption is that even its most obviously strategic manifestations can be used for a wider variety of purposes beyond challenging the peace settlement. Such a conceptualization of violence—that it is broad in form and purpose, and not always reducible to the motives that led to the conflict—does not lend itself to a single causal explanation for violence in post-conflict states. No single cause or set of causes can explain all of the sources of such varied manifestations of violence; even if the focus was limited to strategic violence, the range of actors and contextual factors shaping violence is too wide to be depicted within a single causal pathway. For example, this book rejects as reductionist the assumption that actors in post-conflict states are solely interested in power or the dominance of their ethnic, religious, or political group. To assume this is to assume away part of the problem by treating ethnic, religious, or political groups as if they are monolithic and interested only in the dominance of their group. The reality is often messier. In many cases, the rebel armies unfolded into several smaller splinter groups, whose preferences were more fluid and more criminal than such accounts suggest. Rebel groups and their splinters often have new goals (sometimes political, sometimes criminal) that are not reducible to the dominance of one's own group. By focusing entirely on one fixed preference—domination of one's own constituency group—much of the rational choice literature underplays the potential for the emergence of new "latent spoilers" with entirely new, and often nonethnic, goals.[89] Moreover, there are some cases in which violence after wars was directed against political enemies, such as collaborators with the losing side, rather than ethnic identity. The targets for violence in post-conflict states can shift over time, rather than simply mirroring the victims and perpetrators within the war itself. Reductionist accounts of the motives of armed actors often fail to account for subtle and unpredicted shifts in perpetrators and victims of violence once the war is over.

As noted in the preceding analysis of the dataset, the evidence suggests that violence in post-conflict states sometimes mirrors wartime violence, but in other cases it is dramatically different. If there is more than one pattern evident in strategic violence in post-conflict states, it follows that there should be at least two pathways that can produce strategic violence. These pathways may be classified as direct and indirect, based on the extent to which they represent a continuation of the violence during the war and the extent to which the violence is directed at overturning the peace settlement or renegotiating its terms.

Direct Pathway

The starting point of much of the academic literature on violence after wars is that, if an actor is dissatisfied with the terms of a peace settlement, it may resort to violence to get a better deal. Within the scholarly literature, there are four bodies of work that often use this observation as their starting point. First, scholars of spoiling point to the extent to which armed groups are satisfied with the terms of the peace settlement as the explanation for their efforts to undermine the peace.[90] A related body of literature concerning the durability of peace settlements has linked its stability to the process by which it was reached (i.e., whether it comes after victory or through negotiation), to the sincerity of the combatants in signing the peace settlement, and to the extent to which external actors can overcome information and commitment problems to help the combatants reach credible bargains with one another in enforcing the terms of the peace.[91] When the peace settlement is not credible, or when armed actors wish to get a better bargain in the settlement, this literature suggests that armed groups will engage in acts of strategic violence as part of a spoiling strategy.[92]

Second, theorists of insurgency, for example, point to dissatisfaction with the terms of a peace settlement as one of the many reasons why insurgencies break out against governments or occupying powers.[93] To some extent, the connection between the incidence of strategic violence and insurgency is obvious; a "state of insurgency" is almost by definition an environment in which high levels of strategic violence are regularly employed, only with the objective of overthrowing a government or occupying power. There are also clear cases where rebel groups dissatisfied with a peace settlement have turned to insurgent attacks as a means of overturning the settlement. In Angola, for example, UNITA agreed to end its insurgency and join a coalition government as part of the Lusaka Accords in 1995, but violations of the cease-fire were common. It only took news that the Angolan government was continuing to stockpile arms and amassing its forces near UNITA-held territory to convince UNITA to resume its insurgency.[94] Similarly, in the Philippines, the New People's Army, the fighting wing of the Communist Party of the Philippines, ended its insurgency against the government in 1995, only to pick it back up again by 1997 with virtually the same organizational structure and goals.

Third, scholars who have studied the contagion effects of conflicts have pointed out how actors dissatisfied with a peace process may spread the conflict into neighboring countries by pursuing enemies across borders, by producing destabilizing refugee flows, or by expanding their war aims to include extending their political influence across the region.[95] As chapter 5 demonstrates, in Rwanda the victorious Rwandan Patriotic Front began to launch attacks across the international border against Hutu refugees in Zaire to consolidate their position and prevent a return of the genocidaires.[96] Despite the fact that the attacks crossed borders and generated the Great Lakes Crisis, the strategic violence that followed the Rwandan genocide revolved around the same ethnic divide as the conflict itself and could arguably be considered an extension of the conflict that motivated the genocide. This case shows clear evidence of strategic violence, but such violence is conducted by the winner and is not directed at overturning a peace settlement in the way that the spoiling literature typically suggests.[97]

Fourth, several scholars have pointed to peace settlements in which the winning side—often a government—uses methods of repression to destroy its opponents by imposing a harsh or punitive victor's peace.[98] Particularly in cases of clear military victory, winning parties may choose to destroy their former opponents and punish groups in the civilian population perceived as disloyal, as a way of consolidating their gains and preventing a recurrence of the conflict. For example, after the fall of the Taliban in Afghanistan in 2001, the victorious Northern Alliance forces (predominantly Uzbek, Tajik, and Hazara) conducted reprisal raids on Pashtuns to extend their control over their territories and to punish them for supporting their ethnic kin in the Taliban.[99] Similarly, as chapter 5 demonstrates, the Rwandan Patriotic Front used strategic violence to respond to a Hutu insurgency but also to punish parts of the civilian population that they saw as complicit in the genocide.

Together, these bodies of literature point to a *direct pathway* to strategic violence, in which combatants employ strategic violence as an explicit or implicit way of renegotiating the terms of the peace settlement. Each variant of this direct pathway begins with a rejection in whole or in part of the terms of the peace settlement by an existing combatant. This can happen for a variety of reasons: the actors may genuinely change their mind about an agreement, or they have been participating in the peace process as a stalling technique to allow them to begin to fight again at a later point.[100] The decision to sign a peace agreement is sometimes purely tactical, as leaders of groups sign an agreement without accepting its terms or desiring peace, particularly if they are under pressure from mediators or external actors to accept it. The leaders of armed groups are balancing two contending sets of negotiations: one across the table with their former enemies and also one with their own ranks, only some of whom may want to see the end of the conflict.[101] The decision to sign a peace settlement may be designed to mollify one of these factions or to throw one or more factions off balance by signing an agreement that works to their disadvantage. In some cases, the decision to sign a peace agreement may be motivated by a political calculation that suggests that the armed group will lose favor with a war-weary population unless it appears to seek peace.[102] The range of potential motives for signing an agreement is diverse, but the essential point is that a decision to sign an agreement can be a tactical move that conveys relatively little about the group's actual disposition toward its terms.

Moreover, some armed actors may also have a peace imposed on them by military victory or by international pressure to sign a negotiated agreement in order to stop the carnage.[103] In some cases, the interruption of the conflict and the imposition of a peace agreement before a "mutually hurting stalemate" is achieved may set the stage for violent challenges to the settlement once the post-conflict period begins.[104]

The terms of the peace settlement may be the source of dissatisfaction and the prompt for engaging in strategic violence for some armed actors. By their nature, peace settlements create winners and losers, rewarding those on the winning side with a greater share of the spoils of war.[105] As scholars have recognized, peace settlements draw boundaries, with some actors left "inside" the settlement and others excluded entirely.[106] The arrival of a peace settlement reorders the incentive structures of armed groups inside and outside the settlement. Those left outside the settlement may find that they have reasons to challenge the settlement to be included in its terms.[107] Those left inside may be more concerned about relative gains and wish to use violence to increase their share of the spoils. Even those nominally on board with the peace settlement may conclude during implementation that its terms do not give them or their allies enough of the spoils to be satisfied. This is particularly the case with heterogeneous armed groups that must satisfy not only the leading members of the armed groups but also the factions within their ranks, many of whom have goals that may not be perfectly aligned with those of the leadership.

Under the direct pathway, the dissatisfaction of the parties with the terms of the settlement can be either an absolute or a relative judgment—that is, parties can be dissatisfied either with the settlement as a whole or with their share of the spoils.[108] The essential feature of the direct pathway is that this dissatisfaction with the settlement is translated into strategic violence as the combatants resume the fight, often along similar lines to the war itself. This is done as a means of renegotiating the terms of the settlement, either to reject it entirely, to amend its provisions, or to gain additional strategic advantage not provided as part of the settlement. As conceived of here, each of these variants—spoiling, insurgency, expanded wars, and victor's peace—are in their own ways efforts at renegotiation of the peace settlement. Strategic violence is employed to challenge formal terms of the peace or to change its effective terms. It can also be used to seek goals left unfulfilled at the end of the war or to weaken or destroy an opponent left standing at the end of the war. Under the direct pathway, the strategic violence is a direct function of dissatisfaction with the peace settlement by the existing combatants.

What unites each of these variants is continuity of the violence, as the actors remain intact or nearly intact and they carry on the fight to achieve the goals of the original conflict. As a direct descendant of the violence during the war, strategic violence in the post-conflict period is then explainable on the basis of the fault lines (or macro-cleavage) of the conflict, while the types and targets of the violence mirror those which were employed during the war. As an empirical matter, strategic violence under the direct pathway will resemble the violence during the war, though there can be some minor changes to the actors and methods of attack if the peace settlement remains formally intact. The consequences of violence under the direct pathway are serious. When an existing combatant resorts to strategic violence to challenge a settlement, the peace settlement often collapses, leading to a relapse of the war and mobilization of the opposing party. This is particularly common in post-conflict environments after civil wars, as nearly 50 percent of all civil wars are relapsed post-conflict states.[109] The direct pathway—which assumes continuity between the actors, motives, and methods of the conflict and post-conflict period—provides a powerful first cut at explaining why some post-conflict societies relapse into armed conflict and why strategic violence in these cases so often mirrors that of the war.

Despite its many advantages, the direct pathway approach to violence cannot explain the variations in strategic violence after wars. The self-conscious focus of this approach—which sees strategic violence as evidence of an explicit challenge to the settlement by the combatants—is too narrow to explain strategic violence that operates according to a logic distinct from that which drove the war. While in some cases strategic violence is clearly aimed at challenging a peace settlement or renegotiating its terms, in others the violence is tied to more local or proximate goals, often unrelated or only indirectly related to the original rationale for the conflict. In some post-conflict states, strategic violence has little to do with the peace settlement and instead occurs for issues that are indirectly related to it. Much of the strategic violence in post-conflict states is directed to local bargaining games, often between claimants to power and resources that played only a marginal role in the conflict itself. Some of the violence is criminal in nature, designed to enrich actors and ensure exclusive access to key resources (such as smuggling routes or business enterprises) rather than challenge the settlement in any conventional way. In short, the assumption prevalent in the direct pathway—that strategic violence is an explicit form of renegotiation over the terms of the settlement—cannot capture the complexity of the local, contingent, and even idiosyncratic strategic violence evident in many cases.

Moreover, much of the literature focusing on the direct pathway tends to focus on strategic violence that is directed against the government, agents of the state, or custodians of peace (such as UN peacekeepers).[110] These are actors often seen as representative, or at least supportive, of the peace settlement; hence they can be attacked for supporting it. Yet in many cases, strategic violence is aimed at shifting the balance of power from one group to another—that is, tit-for-tat attacks between groups—without directly engaging the "custodians of the peace" or others who support the peace settlement. Many of the attacks directed at civilians fall into this category. For example, while some of the more egregious attacks against British military forces in Northern Ireland are clearly efforts to spoil the Good Friday agreement, much of the violence that has occurred since 1997 has been transactional and has been conducted as tit-for-tat attacks between remnants of the Catholic and Unionist sides vying over control of criminal interests and local political power.[111] Though it often borrows the language and iconography of the Northern Ireland conflict, this violence is not reducible to the simple division between Catholics and Protestants; its purpose is predominantly local and only indirectly related to the Good Friday Agreement. A broader conception of strategic violence—which does not require that it be directed against agents of the state or supporters of the peace—is needed to understand the complex patterns of attack apparent after wars.

There is no doubt that the direct pathway can explain why strategic violence occurs in some post-conflict states. However, it has limitations. Although it offers a compelling explanation for why war resumes and focuses due attention on the willingness of combatants to employ violence to get a better share of the spoils of the peace, it often underplays the emergence of new, often unrecognized actors that engage in violence for their own purposes.[112] It also does not account for the local, contingent, or evolving goals of the former combatants. The direct pathway tends to assume continuity between original wartime preferences of the combatants and their postwar behavior, often underplaying the ways that the post-conflict environment transforms their incentives and unravels the distinctions between victims and perpetrators that marked wartime activity. By contrast, the indirect pathway points to the enforcement problems and organizational pressures that armed groups face, while relaxing the assumption that strategic violence is always a referendum on the terms of the peace settlement.

Indirect Pathway

The indirect pathway to strategic violence moves beyond evaluating the disposition of the parties toward the settlement toward analyzing the problems that they encounter when enforcing the terms of the settlement. Much of the existing literature focuses attention on the problems involved in getting a combatant to sign an agreement and to credibly commit to delivering on its terms.[113] Yet credible commitment to the terms of the settlement is only the first step to a lasting peace. A peace agreement cannot be considered a singular event; most peace agreements are complex documents that involve implementation of costly terms or provisions over a number of years. The enforcement of the terms of a peace settlement does not occur once but rather involves a sequence of discrete decisions where the parties comply with the provisions of settlement and signal their acceptance of it repeatedly over the post-conflict period. This is particularly the case with negotiated settlements, which are often complex, multifaceted documents with dozens of provisions and confidence-building measures embedded with them. The enforcement of these provisions occurs over multiple years, sometimes without external monitoring or enforcement.[114] Seen from this vantage point, signing a peace agreement resembles a repeat-play decision where an actor must comply sequentially with its terms over time. For this reason, the ability of a party to deliver on the peace agreement and enforce its terms is often a paramount consideration in the negotiation process. One of the key reasons why peace settlements fail is due to the inability of the parties to enforce its terms.[115] If an armed actor believes that a party cannot enforce the terms, it may refuse to sign the agreement or defect from the agreement first in order to not leave itself in a disadvantageous position.

The extent to which an organization can enforce an agreement is dependent on the level of *internal control* that the organization wields over its members.[116] Internal control is defined as the ability of the leadership of an organization to efficiently produce compliance by its members with the terms of an agreement. The level of internal control for an armed group is dependent on three factors: the organizational endowments of the group, the resources available to the armed groups in the environment, and the type of leadership present for that group. First, the organizational endowments of the actor—whether, for example, the actor is a highly disciplined military group, a battle-hardened rebel group, or a coalition of preexisting tribes or clans—plays an essential role in its ability to exert internal control over prospective factions.[117] As a rule, complex, hierarchical armed groups have higher levels of internal control, whereas armed groups with diffuse organizational structures or cellular makeups have lower levels of internal control. Developed hierarchical organizations are generally marked by tight institutional or bureaucratic control over the behavior of its members, which fosters discipline among the rank and file and a culture of obedience to decisions of the leadership.[118] Hierarchical organizations also have information advantages and the ability to use violence discriminately against those who would freelance in violence for their own gain.[119] This advantage is due to the fact that hierarchical organizations have institutions (such as domestic intelligence or internal affairs bureaus) that provide the leadership with information on the rivalries, grievances, and ambitions in their ranks. The availability of this information allows these organizations to discriminately punish just those who use violence, while leaving others untouched. The absence of stark information asymmetries between leaders and the rank and file and the mechanisms for discipline and punishment inherent in complex, hierarchical organizations minimize the risk of backlash that indiscriminate punishment often generates.

By contrast, horizontal organizations have a very different set of organizational attributes that impact on their ability to reliably enforce the terms of a peace settlement and control the risks of defections in their own ranks. Horizontal organizations can vary: some are cellular organizations (such as terrorist groups) that are strongly motivated by an ideology or cause but have little formal contact with other members of the organization. Others have a greater degree of organizational infrastructure but are nevertheless composed of tribes, clans, or other preexisting social units that have separate, and sometimes conflicting, interests.[120] Others are even more diffuse, composed of little more than a loose collection of factions or militias, organized for the common purpose of rebellion but with little else to unite them. Whatever their form, horizontal organizations generally have a harder time enforcing peace agreements owing to the lower levels of internal control that they wield over their members. Without mechanisms of institutional control and a culture of obedience to the will of the leadership, these organizations are more susceptible to factionalism, particularly over the terms of the peace agreements that they sign.[121] Many of these organizations also lack coherent institutional mechanisms to monitor their ranks and record defections, thus leaving them with information asymmetries when violations of the terms of the peace settlement or freelancing in violence by factions occur. When an organization is diffuse, such as a collection of tribes or warlords, it will be harder for the nominal leadership of the organization to monitor the behavior of members and regulate it when it appears to jeopardize the gains from the peace settlement. These organizations also generally lack mechanisms (such as internal affairs units or intelligence services), which allow them to be capable of employing violence discriminately against those who violate the terms of the settlement. As a result, horizontal organizations face a higher risk of backlash when they use violence to discipline their members and protect the integrity of a peace settlement.

Second, the level of resources available to an armed group is a major driver of its ability to wield internal control over its members. Not all armed actors are equipped with the same level of resources, as some have access to deep sources of funding from their members, illicit trade, or foreign sponsors, whereas others are relatively cash strapped. Even government-run militaries are not always resource rich; some militaries in the developing world are not significantly better off in terms of resources than their rebel opponents. The military of the Democratic Republic of Congo (DRC), for example, has been marked by indiscipline, tribalism, and corruption and has crumbled in the face of rebel opponents at various points during its history.[122] The variation in the level of resources held by combatants is important because it influences the extent to which an actor can exercise patronage to ensure compliance with the peace settlement from those in its ranks.[123] For armed groups, a reserve of resources (such as jobs or profits from trade) is essential in shaping its ability to buy off key factions in its ranks, to make side payments to those contemplating noncompliance, and to build the institutional mechanisms needed to monitor compliance with the terms of the settlement by its members. While resources may have an ambiguous effect on conflict dynamics and may in some cases provide inadvertent incentives for predatory violence, they are essential for ensuring the internal control of a group in a fractious post-conflict environment.[124] Resource-rich groups will have to make fewer trade-offs in winning the loyalty of its members and ensuring compliance, whereas resource-strapped organizations will be less capable of employing patronage widely and will face hard choices when doing so. The resources needed to exercise patronage by the leaders become even more essential in fragmented environments with a large number of combatants or factions, as each can demand more for its loyalty and compliance with the terms of the settlement. One difficulty that the leaders of armed groups face in some post-conflict environments is that the international pressure to eliminate corruption and abide by the rule of law deprives them of the resources that they need to successfully use patronage with factions in their ranks.

Third, the nature of the leadership of an armed actor or military is a critical factor in its ability to exercise internal control. The leaderships of combatant groups (including both government forces and rebel organizations) can vary significantly. Some are conventional political or military leaders, who must produce selective incentives to motivate their followers and ensure compliance with the terms of the peace settlement. Some engage in predatory behavior, showing relatively little concern for the well-being of their followers.[125] In most cases, the leadership of the group exercises a relatively small effect in winning the loyalty of members and their compliance with the settlement, as this is driven more by the provision of selective incentives than anything else.[126] But for a select number of leaders—often those who are arising from dense clan or tribal structures or otherwise taking advantage of ethnic or nationalist sentiments—the nature of their leadership is an asset that allows them to exercise internal control without as many incentives needed. These leaders can rely on traditional authority based on clan loyalties (such as Ahmad Shah Massoud in Afghanistan) or can emerge by leading a liberation struggle (such as Nelson Mandela in South Africa). In rare circumstances, they may be what Max Weber famously described as charismatic leaders, who can exercise authority on the basis of their own exceptional abilities or insight.[127] Such leaders are exceedingly rare, but often find themselves at the forefront of social movements.[128] In post-conflict environments, these leaders are often capable of achieving the loyalty of their followers and their compliance with the settlement at lower cost than comparable leaders in other groups. As chapter 7 demonstrates, the charismatic leadership of Xanana Gusmao in East Timor was essential in keeping order and preventing strategic violence during the first two years of the post-conflict period, but his periodic withdrawal from political life occasioned a return to factional violence and an entirely new regional conflict within the country.

Internal control is relevant for peace processes before and after the peace settlement. At the most basic level, internal control is relevant before a negotiating process because it affects the likelihood that a peace agreement will be achieved in the first place. When an armed group has low levels of internal control, it will be seen as a weak bargaining partner, because the factionalism within its ranks makes the opposite side have less confidence that a peace settlement will stick. Some actors will refuse to negotiate with organizations that they believe to have low levels of internal control. For example, Israel has complained that a lack of internal control on the Palestinian side leaves it without a negotiating partner, thus rendering the peace process effectively dead.[129] When an armed group has high levels of internal control, the other side can reliably assume that it is capable of credibly committing to the peace settlement and enforcing its terms among its rank and file. For this reason, an assessment of internal control is highly important within negotiating dynamics, as the extent to which a party is seen as cohesive will shape how seriously the other side takes that party at the negotiating table and the extent to which each side can achieve concessions.[130]

While the impact of internal control has been addressed in the literature on negotiations and war termination, what has been less explored is the extent to which variations in the level of internal control—and the corresponding ability or inability to enforce the terms of the settlements—affects the prospects for violence in post-conflict states. In post-conflict states, the level of internal control is important because it affects not only the extent to which the armed group can enforce the terms of the peace settlement by credibly distributing the spoils of war and punishing those who defect from its terms but also the extent to which the armed group can manage its own demobilization and dissolution when the peace agreement requires it to do so. Internal control is important because it allows for the leaders to enforce the terms of the peace agreement through two types of activities: *distributional (or reward) activities*, in which the leaders of armed groups can fulfill the demands of their followers for political offices and the resources attached to the state; and *policing activities*, in which the leaders of armed groups can use discriminate, often low-intensity, violence to rein in troublemakers who may challenge the settlement.[131] If high levels of internal control are maintained following the war, the leadership of the winning side can make credible promises to divide territory and resources among its allies at a later point.[132] By pledging the delivery of power and resources to their rival power centers within their organization, leaders of winning combatant groups can consolidate their control and prevent the defection of their members from the peace settlement. Through the exercise of patronage, the leadership of armed groups can stop factional disputes from spiraling into open violence. This exercise of patronage and domestic reward is particularly important after ethnic or civil wars, in which the fighting forces are in some cases composed of multiple power centers—for example, loose alliances of powerful warlords—who will demand a share of power and resources after the war has finished.[133] When one group, or a stable coalition of groups, has won an acceptable share of the spoils from a war and can reliably distribute them, its prospective factions will have diminished incentives to use violence to strengthen their hand in local political contests.

Internal control is also relevant because it allows the leadership of the armed groups to retain the ability to monitor defection and conduct in-group policing.[134] Leaders of the combatant groups must have sufficient information on the loyalties of factions within its ranks, and the capacity to exert pressure and coercion against them, in order to prevent the emergence of splinters. The uncontrolled dissolution of an organization, and the corresponding emergence of new splinters or factions, is often sufficient to jeopardize the gains that the combatant made in the peace settlement.[135] These organizations must have the knowledge to identify factions and their goals reliably and the capacity to use discriminate punishment (and in some cases violence) to compel factions to obey the settlement without significant backlash.[136] If punishment is wielded indiscriminately against members of the group, affecting loyalists as well as those who actually sought to defect from the peace agreement, it may hasten the process of splintering that is so dangerous to their wartime gains.[137] In post-conflict states, the careful use of punishment to prevent defections can be difficult for two reasons. First, most peacekeeping operations exclusively reserve the right to use violence or force to the government or recognized international authorities, such as UN peacekeepers or government-backed police. This can mean that combatant groups may find that there is a political cost for reining in their factions if doing so involves the use of violence outside the confines of the law. Second, they must be skilled in using such punishment discriminately, to ensure that only those who would defect from peace settlement or engage in egregious criminal activities are sanctioned. Such careful and deliberate use of punishment or violence is difficult to achieve, particularly when the leadership of the group wants to "go legitimate" and engage in normal politics. As the discussion of the Kosovo Liberation Army (KLA) in chapter 6 illustrates, a rebel group's public face as a legitimate political actor and its private responsibility to rein in defectors within their ranks may be in tension in the post-conflict environment.

If an armed group or constellation of armed groups has a low level of internal control over its members and cannot fulfill these distributional and reward functions, a process of splintering will begin, as factions within its ranks will have little confidence that the peace will last or that they will receive their due share of the spoils of war. Under conditions of low internal control, armed groups will decay into an array of competing splinter groups, as former wartime allies begin to scramble to claim their share of the spoils and fight among themselves in local bargaining contests.[138] When these reward and policing mechanisms fail, an indirect pathway to strategic violence will emerge through the following five-stage process: (1) incentive shifts among factions within the original combatant groups; (2) organizational decay and the emergence of splinter groups; (3) the collapse or decline of the distributional and policing capacities of the parent armed group; (4) the gradual dissolution of the lines of control over violence, and (5) the reestablishment or reframing of targets, particularly among vulnerable communities in the population. The key dynamic here is one of control: if the leaders of the original combatant groups cannot navigate the organizational pressures that they face after the wars and efficiently enforce the terms of the settlement, the result will be a splintering of their movement and the emergence of multiple, sometimes overlapping violent bargaining games between existing or emergent factions. Such factionalism is perilous and will generate strategic violence through bargaining groups conducted across and within former armed groups, though the violence will be conducted for proximate and local purposes detached from the war itself.

Second, the level of internal control is paradoxically important in allowing the leadership of armed groups to manage their demobilization and transition into civilian life. The termination of a period of armed conflict through a peace settlement poses an almost existential challenge to the combatants: What do they do once the war has ended? While the international community often argues in favor of the rapid demobilization, disarmament, and reintegration (DDR) of combatants, the leaders of armed groups are often more concerned with dividing up the spoils of war and finding some way to maintain organizational discipline among the competing factions within their ranks.[139] While some armed groups are successfully demobilized and return to civilian life or normal politics, many armed groups descend into factional violence, as new splinter groups emerge and compete with one another through violent bargaining. The risks of factionalism for the leaders of armed groups are not trivial; excessive violence against civilians or the emergence of new peer competitors for power, for instance, may threaten their gains from the war. Just as the dilemmas of organizing rebellion preoccupies the leaders of armed conflicts before a war, the dilemma of managing their organizational dissolution—and in turn controlling the risks of predatory or intracommunal violence arising from factionalism—becomes one of their most important tasks in the post-conflict period.[140] Yet these armed groups face a paradox: to successfully and safely demobilize, they must retain just enough internal control that they control the risks of factionalism or splintering in order to ensure that their gains from the war are not jeopardized. As the case study on Bosnia shows, armed groups with high levels of internal control are often able to navigate this process and use their mechanisms of monitoring and enforcement to allow their members to have a successful entry into civilian life. By contrast, as the Kosovo and East Timor case studies will demonstrate, groups with naturally low levels of internal control often find that they cannot control the process of demobilization, and their attempts to do so—particularly under international pressure—may accelerate the process of organizational decay that produces splinters and higher levels of strategic violence. Contrary to accounts within the DDR literature that stress the need to demobilize the combatants and integrate them into civilian life at all costs, this account suggests that an uncontrolled demobilization is dangerous in the post-conflict period and that some groups may temporarily need to boost their level of internal control rather than fully demobilize in order to enforce the terms of the peace settlement.[141]

The indirect pathway may be summarized as follows. In cases where the combatants retain high levels of internal control, the original armed groups have a greater chance of rewarding domestic allies and conducting in-group policing to prevent factionalism. In these cases, rebel groups will maintain more of their organizational coherence, even as they become political parties or civilian defense forces, and the rates of strategic violence will be correspondingly lower. In cases of low internal control, former combatants will find themselves unable to reward powerful domestic allies or rein in their extremist wings. When this happens, these groups will fragment into several smaller groups, some of which will engage in violence for enrichment or to increase their power within internal and external bargaining games. When this process of organizational decay is underway and rebel groups splinter into small (often criminal) organizations, strategic violence will increase. Under these conditions, the environment of the post-conflict state will resemble a kind of mediated anarchy, in which the government or peacekeeping authority has only a residual ability to prevent, manage, and respond to the illegitimate use of violence in that territory. In this environment, a plethora of existing or newly emergent armed groups will engage in what might be thought of as "microcosms of violence," bargaining with one another for a range of local, criminal, or even idiosyncratic goals.

Once this process is underway, armed groups will have incentives to target weak or vulnerable groups (such as ethnic minorities) as a form of signaling of their capacity to harm and intent to destabilize the peace. Especially if they were on the "wrong side" of the war, these groups present an ideal target for opportunists within rebel organizations; attacking the vulnerable is a way to boost a local group's reputation for toughness; advertise its nationalist, ethnic, or sectarian credentials; and signal its willingness to fight in local power contests.[142] In other words, attacks against easy targets can be demonstrative and designed to send a signal to rivals more than it is to harm that group. Such demonstrative violence is particularly prevalent in highly factionalized environments. When these groups are intermixed in the population and vulnerable, leaders of organizations may find it hard to dissuade dissatisfied factions from employing violence against them as a powerful signal of their ability to fight. In other cases, gratuitous violence against civilians can be a hedging strategy: eliminating or expelling potentially dangerous groups is a sensible (if horrific) strategy if one cannot be certain whether the peace will last and these groups may prove disloyal. With no guarantee that the peace will last, factions within the armed group may find it safer to create new facts on the ground by expelling or victimizing civilians from hostile groups in case the war resumes. They may also turn to criminal activity, as a way of enriching themselves and preparing for a future round of war. This fragmentation of the armed group into a series of smaller groups, including some criminal or mafia groups, is cumulative; once it begins, it becomes harder to rein in those who would engage in freelance violence against targeted groups.[143] Because the peace remains fragile, commitment by the government or external actors will rarely be able to overcome their incentives to attack if such splintering begins to happen. Rather than an overt challenge to the settlement, what may emerge is a pattern of persistent low-intensity attacks as factions try to shore up their support and weaken their opponents.

The key difference with the indirect pathway is that the strategic violence occurs not because of dissatisfaction with the formal terms of the settlement but because armed groups gradually lose control over their factions and cannot enforce the terms of the peace settlement. Strategic violence emerges not because of a concerted effort to renegotiate the settlement but because the original combatants have found that their ability to reward or punish factions within their ranks has eroded over time. Here the problem is not one of dissatisfaction with its terms but rather a struggle to implement the terms of the peace amid intraorganizational disputes and rivalries. Any peace settlement involves many repeat-play decisions at different stages of the peace; an actor must decide whether to abide by some or all of the component aspects of the agreement at different points throughout the post-conflict period. If an actor has low levels of internal control and struggles with factions, it will gradually find that implementation will be more costly and that a splintering process—once it is underway—will be difficult to stop. This gradual collapse of internal control produces a shift in incentives among factions in their ranks and elsewhere in the wider society, as the context of a post-conflict state provides new, often tempting opportunities for violence. The diminished capacity of the original armed group to control these factions through either reward or punishment produces a blurring in the lines of control over violence, as the original group competes with its splinters in often highly localized political contests. This produces a reframing of targets of the violence, often by drawing new or newly salient political cleavages around which the rivalries are conducted. It can also lead to spirals of countermobilization, as former enemies begin to prepare themselves to bargain with violence in the post-conflict period. The net effect of these changes, occasioned by shifts in the incentives and organizational structures of combatants, determines whether strategic violence will take place in a post-conflict state and explains why that violence is qualitatively different in magnitude, type, and target from that which preceded it.

Together, the direct and indirect pathways point to a complex chain of events that can explain strategic violence in post-conflict states. The direct pathway points to a process in which the combatants employ violence to renegotiate the settlement in order to get a better deal from the government or external authorities. The indirect pathway points to mechanisms in which the combatants cannot reward or police their factions and, as a result, unfold into multiple groups that engage in violent bargaining with each other. Under the direct pathway, the strategic violence will at least echo the grievances and fault lines of the conflict; under the indirect pathway, it will take on often unexpected forms and variations in magnitude and type. It is important to stress that these two pathways are not mutually exclusive or independent. It is possible for one or more parties to defect from a peace settlement while also decomposing into factions, thus allowing the direct and indirect pathway to produce strategic violence in the same case. When the direct and indirect pathways combine and are operative within the same case, the levels of strategic violence are often correspondingly higher than when one pathway is present. In these cases, strategic violence arising through the direct and indirect pathways will feed off of each other, weakening the settlement and producing a highly violent post-conflict environment. When strategic violence is produced simultaneously through the direct and indirect pathways, the levels of violence escalate rapidly, and the case often plunges back into war, as will be evident in the case study of post-conflict Iraq (chapter 8).

Table 3.10 formalizes the discussion of the preceding two pathways by focusing attention on two variables: the disposition toward the settlement; and the levels of internal control wielded by the group. It identifies which conjunction of these pathways will produce the onset of strategic violence. In three of the four logical possibilities, the onset of strategic violence is predicted. This prediction for the widespread onset of strategic violence is borne out by the fact that only four of the fifty-two post-conflict states sampled here featured negligible strategic violence.

TABLE 3.10.
Pathways

Level of Internal Control	Accept Settlement?	
	Yes	No
High	Little or no strategic violence No pathway	Strategic violence Direct pathway
Low	Strategic violence Indirect pathway	Strategic violence Direct and indirect pathways

These pathways produce four hypotheses about the incidence of strategic violence across cases.

1. H_1: If all armed groups accept the settlement and have high levels of internal control, strategic violence should be absent or very low.
2. H_2: If all armed groups accept the settlement but at least one has low levels of internal control, strategic violence will be present as factional violence (the indirect pathway).
3. H_3: If some armed groups do not accept the settlement but all groups have high levels of internal control, strategic violence will be present as an attempt to spoil the settlement (the direct pathway).
4. H_4: If some armed groups do not accept the settlement and some groups also have low levels of internal control, strategic violence will be present as both spoiling and factional violence (the direct and indirect pathways).

These hypotheses are difficult to test with cross-national data, since the pathways and the observable indicators of the onset of violence—such as the disposition toward the settlement or the organizational pressures that groups face—are hard to measure at the aggregate level. Moreover, pathways can change over the post-conflict period, so that a snapshot of how the violence occurs in a single year might give a misleading picture of its nature. The extent to which the disposition toward the settlement and the organizational cohesion of the group can change over time and affect the levels of strategic violence will be explored in detail in the case studies. For this reason, the dynamics of the pathways will be demonstrated through detailed case studies, rather than cross-national analysis.

Nevertheless, to determine whether its broad predictions of this model are borne out across the sample of post-conflict states, a separate coding for the pathway in operation in each case was developed on the basis of the newspaper accounts underlying the cross-national dataset and the narrative descriptions of violence in the annual Human Rights Reports produced by the U.S. State Department for each year of the post-conflict period.[144] Each case was coded for whether the data and narrative accounts revealed (1) no discernible pattern of violence; (2) violence directed between the former combatants, with a continuity of types and targets (direct pathway); (3) violence directed between factions of the former combatants, with a shift in the types and targets of attack (indirect pathway); or (4) violence operating both between the combatants and between newly emergent factions (both pathways).

This comparative analysis of the pathways and the levels of violence reveals a broad correlation between the pathways in operation and the levels of violence and largely confirms the preceding hypotheses (table 3.11). Most (65.6%) of the cases with only residual levels of violence had no discernible pathway, while two of the three cases

TABLE 3.11.
Pathways and Levels of Violence

	None	Direct	Indirect	Both	Total
Residual	17	3	5	1	26
Occasional	1	2	9	4	16
Scattered	0	4	2	1	7
Mass	0	1	0	2	3
Total	18	10	16	8	52

(66%) with mass levels of violence—both Congo and Iraq—featured both pathways at work. Both the direct and indirect pathways were capable of producing occasional or scattered levels of strategic violence, with the direct pathway slightly more linked to scattered (or higher levels) of violence (57%) and the indirect pathway slightly more linked to occasional levels of violence (56%). Both pathways appear to be capable of producing moderate levels of violence. Identifying the pathways alone can explain 69 percent of the expected levels of strategic violence across the dataset.[145] While the pathways provide a powerful first cut at explaining the levels of violence, they are incomplete on their own and cannot fully explain the levels of variation in strategic violence in post-conflict states. This is because the pathways address only the motivation for action, leaving the other half of the story—the opportunity structure for the armed groups to act violently—underspecified.

Opportunity Structure

The levels of strategic violence in post-conflict states are jointly determined by the pathways and the opportunity structure of the state. An opportunity structure is a cluster of features in the external environment that shape the possibility for collective action and the ability of actors to make political claims.[146] Within the literature on contentious politics, an opportunity structure has been largely defined in terms of the characteristics of the regime that enable or constrict claimants from making certain types of demands.[147] The conceptualization of an opportunity structure is broader here, constituting not just the institutions of the government but also the unique features of the post-conflict state that amplify or diminish the ability of actors to use violence. The opportunity structure of post-conflict states acts as an intervening factor that mediates the ability of actors to use violence. Not all environments for violence are equally propitious for the perpetrator. An armed group operating in a chaotic and fragmented environment (e.g., post-conflict Iraq) may be relatively unconstrained in its use of strategic violence, while another actor facing a more restrictive opportunity structure (e.g., a post-conflict state with a significant peacekeeping force) will have to tread more carefully. It follows that two equally motivated armed groups operating along the same pathway may produce different levels of strategic violence depending on the environment in which they operate. The opportunity structure of some post-conflict state will enable some actors to use strategic violence to achieve their goals, whereas in others it will act as a check on their ambitions and reduce the overall levels of strategic violence. In post-conflict states, the opportunity structure is determined by: (1) the vulnerability of ethnic, political, or religious groups in the civilian population; (2) the flexibility of the institutions of the government or transitional administration in the post-conflict state; and (3) the ability and willingness of external forces or international peacekeepers to protect civilians and respond to the use of violence.

The first major aspect of the opportunity structure is the vulnerability of groups in the population. In many post-conflict states, the fighting has produced population shifts that have left minority groups in vulnerable positions in which they are unable to defend themselves. Scholars have long noted that proximity of former opponents shapes the opportunities for conducting attacks against targeted groups.[148] If the targeted group is not reachable for attack, because it is either geographically concentrated or separated by natural geographic barriers—for example, mountains or waterways—this will obviously reduce the opportunities for attacking it. Trapped islands of ethnic or sectarian groups are particularly vulnerable to depredations in civil and ethnic wars.[149] If targeted groups are geographically concentrated in a region with defensible borders, they will be less likely to experience strategic violence.[150] Such vulnerable groups must be clearly identifiable in the population. This identification can be based on outward appearance, language, or culture or by revealed preferences based on wartime behavior.[151] Moreover, minority groups in post-conflict environments that have few prospects for external rescue and little chance of an independent livelihood are most vulnerable. The sheer presence of these groups—and the low costs of attacking owing to their availability and limited prospects for self-defense—makes them a "pull factor" for factions or splinter groups contemplating a return to violence. In this way, their presence can hasten the process of splintering and the emergence of strategic violence in some post-conflict states. Yet the vulnerability of groups is not static, as groups may become more or less vulnerable depending on population movements within the post-conflict state. If, for example, refugees flee from one area where they are subject to attack to a region surrounded by their ethnic or religious kin, they will reduce their vulnerability and the prospects for strategic violence.

The second major component of the opportunity structure for violence in post-conflict states concerns the flexibility of the institutions of the settlement. As Samuel Huntington observed, flexible, adaptive institutions that are capable of accommodating new claimants to power are an important part of managing social conflict and ensuring social stability.[152] As noted, some post-conflict states lack institutions to channel these claimants to power more effectively because of the damage wrought by the war. But another, less-explored problem of post-conflict states is that interim institutions formed in the aftermath tend to ossify, as actors begin to develop vested interests in those institutions and become resistant to change.[153] The rigidity of these post-conflict institutions—ranging from political institutions to the military, police, and civil service—can fuel discontent among newly emergent factions and provide a fresh incentive for violence. In some cases, these rigid institutions can accentuate conflict and reify ethnic divisions rather than diminish them.[154] By contrast, flexible institutions can act as a release valve for political pressure from discontented factions and others excluded from the settlement. While elections can produce their own incentives for violence, regular elections at all levels of government can help to accommodate new claimants to power and mitigate social conflict in some cases.[155] An example of this dynamic is presented in the case study on Bosnia (chapter 4), where the unwieldy federal structure created by the Dayton Accords ultimately acted as a check on strategic violence by providing opportunities for would-be spoilers, including some nationalist leaders and parties, to play a role inside government. By contrast, the inflexibility of the security institutions (such as the police and military) accentuated the latent social and regional divisions in the society and spurred a renewed conflict in East Timor (chapter 7).

A third, and highly important, dimension of the opportunity structure for strategic violence in post-conflict states has to do with the presence and capabilities of peacekeeping and policing forces provided by the UN or external actors. A growing body of evidence suggests that peacekeeping missions are effective in reducing the overall levels of violence and ensuring stability in post-conflict states under certain conditions.[156] But the mere presence of peacekeepers and police officers is not sufficient to deter violent actions. What is crucial is the extent to which peacekeepers and police officers can cover the territory effectively and monitor the use of violence by the parties. By one estimate, this requires approximately twenty peacekeepers or police officers per one thousand persons in the population.[157] This ratio is rarely achieved, with only the most well-resourced post-conflict states such as Bosnia (22.6) and Kosovo (23.6) approaching that threshold.[158] In these cases where peacekeepers and police are deployed in sufficient numbers to cover the territory and population of the state, they can be effective in deterring strategic violence and otherwise reducing the freedom of activity for spoilers and new claimants to power. However, in cases where they are too few or strapped for resources to provide this level of coverage, their impact will be marginal. Just as important is the training and type of peacekeepers and officers present.[159] Without a sufficient range of capabilities, such as intelligence and policing, even a well-resourced peacekeeping force will be unable to keep the peace. Many UN peacekeepers, for example, are poorly trained and lack some key capabilities needed for functioning effectively in a hard post-conflict environment.[160] Finally, peacekeeping forces must also have a mandate that allows the use of force and engage in the kind of tasks necessary to reestablish order.[161] Overly restrictive mission mandates and definitions that preclude the use of force often render peacekeeping forces less than the sum of their parts.[162] The inadequacies in planning for the U.S. invasion in Iraq (chapter 8) illustrated that even a highly capable military force can sacrifice momentum and squander the chances of sustaining a soft post-conflict environment if it is slow to exercise policing functions or has an unclear mandate.

It is important to stress that all of these dimensions of the opportunity structure in post-conflict states are not static. The opportunity structure can shift within the post-conflict period in response to events in the politics of the state, thus making it more or less costly to use violence. Moreover, the behavior of the actors in the society and their use of strategic violence can also affect the opportunity structure, thus transforming it. For example, if an armed group engages in regular attacks on a minority group and produces population shifts as the group flees to protect itself, this will reduce the vulnerability of the group and make attacks more costly. Similarly, the departure of peacekeeping forces can affect the tactical calculations and make the use of strategic violence more attractive, whereas a change in mandate allowing peacekeepers to respond forcefully to violations of the settlement can be a deterrent. The dynamic aspects of the opportunity structure can be captured through tracing their impact on the levels of strategic violence over time, which is done in the case studies.

Countermobilization

One of the greatest dangers of the use of strategic violence in post-conflict states is that it will kick off a spiral of strategic violence as victimized groups mobilize for self-protection. Once the combatants have resumed the conflict along the same lines (direct pathway) or violence has begun to emerge among splinter groups or factions of the original combatant group (indirect pathway), a countermobilization of opposing forces can occur, either from the ranks of the former combatants or from the rest of the population.[163] In other words, the post-conflict situation is not static; unless the opposing side is crippled by its defeat in war, the violent behavior of one set of actors will occasion an opposite reaction of some kind from its former enemies, especially if its activity appears to risk restarting the war. The logic of the security dilemma will apply once significant levels of strategic violence are employed in a post-conflict setting, as vulnerable groups in the population will seek protection from those who might harm them.[164] Post-conflict states can then return to an anarchy reminiscent of the war, or even worse, as spirals of violence lead civilians to pledge their loyalties to armed groups and criminal gangs to protect themselves from future attack.[165] Perhaps the clearest example of this dynamic occurred within Iraq, as the emergence of Baathist-sponsored insurgent forces late in 2003 produced a countervailing mobilization of sectarian militias and Islamist groups over time.

The consequence of this countermobilization of actors is twofold. First, it may lead to the gradual criminalization of violence over time, as the security dilemma tends to reinforce predatory behavior.[166] This predatory behavior can lead groups to strike first, fearing that failing to do so will lead to others striking first or a loss in the spoils of the conflict, but it can also produce an environment conducive to criminal behavior.[167] This may account for why so many post-conflict environments are crime ridden and feature attacks that cut across the political and criminal worlds. Second, the countermobilization of opposing forces in reaction to strategic violence may further undermine the internal control of existing armed groups. The extent to which a group can control its potential factions or splinter groups is not a constant but rather varies over time, subject to exogenous or endogenous political and economic shocks and to the incidence of strategic violence. If internal control is undermined by strategic violence in the post-conflict period, and the countermobilization of former enemy groups is apparent, armed groups may reconsider their support for the peace settlement. Further, additional splintering of rebel groups and strategic violence can ensue as factions begin to believe that their leaders no longer are in control or have the capacity to punish them, thus producing a cascade effect of additional mobilization of splinters or factions and countermobilization of opposed groups. Conversely, if strategic violence is punished effectively by the leaders of combatant groups, they can increase their hold on the key resources, police their extremist factions, and mitigate the pressures of countermobilization of their former enemies. In short, the process is iterative, as countermobilization can produce strategic violence that corrodes internal control or provides an opportunity for armed groups to signal their support for the peace settlement. The process is also cumulative, creating both virtuous and vicious circles that can lead to the gradual escalation of strategic violence or its deescalation, depending on how effective groups are in wielding control over the factions amid evidence of a countermobilization of the opposite side. A gradual decrease in internal control or increase in target vulnerability can create new forms of political polarization or kick off a spiral of tit-for-tat escalation between armed groups, thus setting a new foundation for war.

Conclusion

The purpose of this chapter is both descriptive and analytical. First, it aims to survey the existing empirical evidence and demonstrate that there is variation in the incidence of strategic violence in post-conflict states. Using a newly created dataset on deaths from strategic violence in post-conflict states, it classifies that variation in four categories (mass, scattered, occasional, or residual). In most cases, massive violence in post-conflict states occurred in cases of relapsed wars, long-running insurgencies against an existing government, or wars that spilled across borders. That these were hard post-conflict environments, with significant levels of strategic violence, is not surprising. But this chapter demonstrates that even apparently stable peace settlements often feature much higher levels of strategic violence than commonly assumed. Soft post-conflict environments, marked by predominantly criminal and instrumental violence, nevertheless feature occasional or scattered magnitudes of scattered violence. This is a puzzle because such strategic violence has occurred even in cases where the peace settlement has been considered successful and no explicit challenge to the peace is present.

Second, this chapter aims to explain this puzzle by sketching out two pathways—direct and indirect—which explain how strategic violence can emerge in post-conflict states. It envisions that strategic violence can emerge either as an effort at renegotiating the terms of the peace, often along the same lines as the war (direct pathway), or through the emergence of highly localized bargaining games fought by factions within the former combatant groups (indirect pathway). This means that the production of strategic violence is subject to equifinality, as high levels of violence can emerge through the efforts at renegotiation conducted either by the combatants or by their splinter groups. The levels of strategic violence are jointly determined by the pathways operative in the case, as well as the unique features of the opportunity structure for violence.

In each of the subsequent case studies—Bosnia (1995–2000), Rwanda (1994–1999), Kosovo (1999–2004), East Timor (1999–2004), and Iraq (2003–2008)—this model for understanding strategic violence will be put to the test. Each case study will answer the following questions. First, is there evidence of strategic violence present amid the expressive and instrumental violence also in the case? Second, at what level of magnitude (residual, occasional, scattered, or mass) does the strategic violence occur? Third, does the violence mirror that which occurred during the war, or has there been a shift in the type and target of the attacks? Fourth, through which pathway, if any, did the strategic violence occur? Fifth, what features of the opportunity structure, if any, affected the levels of strategic violence in this case?

PART TWO

FIVE CASE STUDIES
OF POST-CONFLICT VIOLENCE

CHAPTER FOUR

Bosnia-Herzegovina

The civil war in Bosnia-Herzegovina (1991–1995) was famously described by U.S. secretary of state Warren Christopher as "the problem from hell" because of its complexity and apparent intractability.[1] The war was not a symmetrical civil war between two evenly matched sides, but rather a multisided conflict fought by combinations of conventional forces, local militias, and irregular forces representing, or claiming to represent, different ethnic groups.[2] Once Slovenia and Croatia declared independence in 1991, the slow-motion destruction of the multiethnic state of Yugoslavia began, as the Yugoslav army, dominated by Serb-led units, and Croatian regular forces launched operations to protect their ethnic kin.[3] The war not only was a top-down affair launched by state actors but also involved the mobilization of local militias and criminal forces that emerged to organize the protection of vulnerable civilians, among other less noble goals. The violence in the civil war was directed primarily against civilians, as all three sides (Bosnian Muslim, Croat, and Serb) killed and expelled civilians in order to "cleanse" territory and produce homogeneous pockets of their ethnic kin. The war produced some of the worst violence seen in Europe since the end of the Second World War. While the precise numbers are in dispute, an estimated 80,000 to 100,000 people were killed, and between 900,000 and 1.2 million people became refugees, excluding 1.3 to 1.5 million people who were internally displaced.[4] By some estimates, nearly half of the population of Bosnia was uprooted by the conflict.[5]

The peace accord that ended the Bosnian civil war—the General Framework for Peace in Bosnia and Herzegovina, but more commonly known as the Dayton Peace Accords (DPA)—forced all of the sides to accept a cease-fire and to relocate their political demands within the context of a multilayered federal state. From the outset there were serious doubts that the peace settlement would last. Between 1991 and 1994, there had been eight efforts to broker a negotiated settlement between the parties, including most notably the Vance-Owen plan, but each had failed.[6] The Dayton Accords were signed under duress, as all of the parties found themselves under intense diplomatic pressure from the United States and leading European states to put an end to the fighting. Among the most intransigent were the Bosnian Serbs, who did not take negotiations seriously until NATO began to use air strikes to reverse their territorial advances. The Dayton Accords did not resolve the fundamental issues that drove the conflict, such as the ethnic antagonisms and pervasive insecurity of small pockets of ethnic minorities. Instead, it conceded the point, creating a government composed of two distinct ethnic entities: the Federation of Bosnia-Herzegovina, composed of Bosnian Muslims and Croats; and the Republika Srpska (RS), composed of Bosnian Serbs. While formally linked together in a single state, each entity maintained control over taxation, education, and local administration.[7] Although it ended the civil war, the Dayton Accords left many final status issues—such as the status of contested cities like Brcko and Mostar, as well as the constitution of the police and army—unresolved over the short term. The agreement was marked by internal contradictions, as it "stabilized the lines of confrontation and derived political rights from them; on the other hand, it aspired to override these divisions both from above—in its joint institutions—and from below, in provisions for return."[8] Even Richard Holbrooke, the American diplomat most responsible for the Dayton Accords, admitted that it was a flawed agreement, particularly in that it left two standing armies (Serbian and Muslim-Croat) and did not immediately disarm the parties.[9]

In many respects, the post-conflict period was marked by failure. Bosnia effectively became a ward of the international community, as NATO enforced the peace on all of the parties, and a range of organizations, led by the UN, OSCE, and OHR, tried to build the institutions for democracy in a deeply divided society. According to one estimate in 2009, Bosnia had received nearly $14 billion in reconstruction aid right after the war, and "by the end of 1996, 17 different foreign governments, 18 UN agencies, 27 intergovernmental organizations, and about 200 nongovernmental organizations (NGOs)—not to mention tens of thousands of troops from across the globe—were involved in reconstruction efforts."[10] Yet the massive international effort to rebuild Bosnia never managed to overcome the ethnic chauvinism that drove the civil war. Nationalist parties were triumphant in the first rounds of post-conflict elections. On all sides, political parties resorted to fearmongering and exaggerating the threat of renewed war as a way of generating support among the traumatized population. Similarly, each of the major nationalist parties obstructed international efforts to rebuild a multiethnic Bosnia, and even minimal levels of cooperation in government between the three sides proved difficult to achieve. Years after the fighting stopped, Bosnia's politics remains entangled in the ethnic divisions that generated the war, and the goal of producing a unified and multiethnic country seems a distant, if not impossible, goal.

Yet despite its many problems, the federal state produced by the Dayton Accords has remained in place for nearly twenty years, and the peace—however dysfunctional

—has held. Underlying this stability has been the surprising fact that deaths from strategic violence have been low compared to other post-conflict states. According to the criteria identified in chapter 3, Bosnia experienced residual levels of strategic violence (42 deaths) during its post-conflict period (1995–1999). Its death toll was nowhere near comparable to cases in the Balkans, such as Kosovo (213 killed over a five-year period) or Serbia (1,027 killed over a five-year period).[11] Compared to a similar contemporary case—the ethnic civil war in Rwanda, which generated 3,345 casualties in its first post-conflict year alone and more than 8,439 casualties between 1995 and 1999—Bosnia was an unexpectedly soft post-conflict environment, with no organized attempt to restart the war or widespread factional violence. This soft post-conflict environment was particularly surprising given the severity and duration of the war, which led many experts to predict that it would have a bloody aftermath.[12] At the same time, Bosnia was not fully peaceful: there were recurring riots over ethnic minority returns and clear and regular patterns of assault and harassment against those who returned. The flare-ups of violence were not random, and the extent to which they followed international efforts to force interethnic cooperation suggests some level of organization or control of the violence. These attacks occurred along the geographic fault lines between two ethnic communities and often generated spirals of tit-for-tat riots and assaults between extremists on each side, but the number of deaths associated with violent episodes was low. In Bosnia, strategic violence largely consisted of nonlethal forms of intimidation and harassment, but it appeared to be choreographed in ways designed not to overtly spoil the settlement or to destroy the state that was created through the Dayton Accords.

What explains this unusual pattern of violence in Bosnia? In many respects, the observable patterns of strategic violence in Bosnia reflect the direct pathway, as many of the attacks resembled a continuation of the fighting during the war, though at a lower level of intensity and with some effort to obscure the responsibility of the attackers. The predominant type of strategic violence during this period—attacks on minority returnees—revolved around the ethnic fault lines that animated the war. The victims of attack, largely civilians located in pockets of territory away from their ethnic kin, were the same types of victims that were prevalent in the war. The actors remained the same: nationalist parties that commanded much of the killing in the war continued to fight over the same issues (ethnic dominance and political power) that motivated them before and during the war, although their often bitter confrontations were mostly at the political level. While strategic attacks occurred, they were conducted with observable limits. There were no concerted attempts to change the territorial balance between the parties or any sustained attempt to spoil the Dayton Accords through campaigns of insurgent attacks on NATO or representatives of other international organizations. Yet while the leading wartime combatants shied away from explicitly or openly using strategic violence against NATO or each other, they were regularly implicated in attacks on refugees, often through proxy forces or their loyalists in highly contested regions.[13] The most serious strategic violence in this case took the form of clandestine attacks designed by armed groups affiliated with the Croatian and Serbian nationalist parties to deter or expel minority returnees and to harass those that remained. Strategic violence emerged through the direct pathway and revolved around the ethnic fault lines of the war, but it was directed more toward subverting the multiethnic commitments of the Dayton Accords rather than openly spoiling it.

By contrast, high levels of strategic violence did not occur via the indirect pathway in the post-conflict period. The relative absence of factional violence is surprising because a wide range of irregular actors—such as local defense militias, paramilitary groups, and criminal organizations—participated in the war and could have fought among themselves for greater shares of the spoils of war. Some of the rank-and-file members of these organizations were dissatisfied with the Dayton Accords and could have established splinters or factions designed to "resist" the imposition of the Dayton agreement. Especially in an environment rife with criminal violence, it would have been tempting for hard-line nationalist factions to continue to kill and expel in the post-conflict period, if only to get a greater share of the spoils of war for themselves. Yet, for the most part, they turned to organized crime and did not publicly challenge the dominance or even the rapaciousness of the leading nationalist parties inside government. Even their involvement in organized crime was marked by relatively little overt factional violence.[14]

This chapter argues that strategic violence emerged via the direct pathway, but not the indirect pathway, and produced few casualties for three reasons: (1) the major nationalist parties were dissatisfied with the Dayton Accords because its commitment to multiethnicity threatened their exclusive control over territories where their ethnic group was in the majority; (2) their dissatisfaction was mitigated by the desire to take advantage of the extensive spoils of war provided to them under the terms of the agreement; and (3) the high levels of internal control that leaders of nationalist parties wielded over their rank and file allowed them to exercise a policy of domestic rewards in the form of patronage and to prevent widespread factional violence. Consistent with the predictions of the theory discussed in chapter 3, this conjunction of partial dissatisfaction with the terms of the Dayton Accords and moderate to high levels of internal control over the ranks of the former combatants produced strategic attacks via the direct pathway in the post-conflict period. The low levels of deaths, however, are in part due to the fact that the perpetrators—largely the Serbian and Croatian nationalist parties, through their proxy forces—circumscribed their use of strategic violence to nonlethal attacks to avoid risking their wartime gains. In other words, while the perpetrators were content to "keep the pot boiling" by periodically authorizing or endorsing strategic attacks on returnees, they sought to avoid causing too many deaths because they did not want to sacrifice what they had gained under the Dayton Accords.

The casualties from strategic violence in Bosnia were also lower than expected because of the distinct features of the opportunity structure—specifically, the limited vulnerability of the ethnic communities due to the success of the ethnic cleansing campaigns during the war, the flexible and open institutions that the Dayton Accords created, and the extensive NATO peacekeeping and UN policing effort—that made the country particularly inhospitable to the use of strategic violence. While the role of Bosnia's changed demography and the influence of NATO peacekeepers in depressing the levels of overall violence are widely acknowledged, the flexibility of Dayton's institutions has exerted an underappreciated but significant dampening effect on the levels of strategic violence.[15] Although the multilayered structure of the Dayton Accords produced dysfunctional politics, it also allowed hard-line nationalist factions to install their loyalists within different levels of government (e.g., domestic reward). Contrary to the literature that highlights only the flaws of Dayton, this chapter argues that the virtue of this particular peace settlement was that its almost byzantine complexity, its federal structure, and decentralized administration kept most of the major parties inside the settlement and gave them an ability to buy off, and rein in, latent factions within their own ranks. The result was that comparatively low levels of factional violence came about as a function of a flawed, but flexible and open, peace settlement that rewarded ethnic antagonisms and left a dysfunctional government in its wake.

This chapter is organized into five sections: (1) a brief description of the inherent contradictions in the Dayton Accords, with special reference to how the structure of the state produced by this agreement multiplied the opportunities for those inside it to engage in patronage and buy off factions in their ranks; (2) a history of the consequences of the Dayton Accords in the post-conflict period (1995–1999), which shows that the major nationalist parties were dissatisfied with the terms of Dayton yet nevertheless exploited it for rent seeking and patronage; (3) an analysis of the levels of internal control wielded by the major parties to the conflict that provided them with the organizational resources needed to carefully modulate the use of violence in the post-conflict period; (4) a presentation of data on violence patterns in post-conflict Bosnia, drawing from archival material and unpublished statistics collected by the UN and International Police Task Force (IPTF), which demonstrates how nonlethal strategic attacks were supported by some of the nationalist parties; and (5) an explanation for the patterns and levels of strategic violence, with a focus on why two of the major nationalist parties used proxy forces for strategic attacks on returnees and on how the opportunity structure had a dampening effect on the levels of strategic violence in this case.

Dayton Accords

The civil war in Bosnia-Herzegovina destroyed the multiethnic mosaic of Bosnian society and left much of the population deeply traumatized in its wake. In many respects, Bosnia was the quintessential broken and divided post-conflict state, with weak or nonexistent governance in many of its regions and the wounds of war readily apparent. The death toll had left thousands of broken families struggling to recover, and mass graves littered the country. Many of the perpetrators of the worst atrocities—such as noted war criminals Radovan Karadzic and Ratko Mladic, among others—remained at-large. Many of the people displaced during the course of the fighting remained in areas far from their original homes.[16] Perhaps the most dramatic change brought about by the war was in the demographic and ethnic makeup of the country. The ethnic cleansing of minority groups had unmixed the population and produced ethnically homogeneous pockets of territory throughout the country.[17] Some formerly multiethnic regions had only one ethnic group when the war finished; others were divided between a majority ethnic group and a small besieged minority. For many ethnic groups, parts of Bosnia occupied by other groups were effective "no go" areas because the chances of being attacked or expelled were high.

The Dayton Accords reflected considerable ambivalence about this state of affairs.[18] The Constitution of Bosnia states its formal commitment to "sovereignty, territorial integrity, and political independence of Bosnia and Herzegovina" (Annex 4, Preamble), but in practice it acknowledges and confirms the effective ethnic division of the country. For example, it preserves the territorial integrity of the country by linking two distinct entities, the Federation of Bosnia-Herzegovina (in practice, a Bosniak-Croat Federation) and the Serb-dominated Republika Srpska (RS), together in a weak federal structure. The two entities were separated by the Inter-Ethnic Boundary Line (IEBL), which was demilitarized and monitored by NATO's Implementation Force (originally called IFOR, later the Stabilization Force or SFOR). This was further strengthened by a Zone of Separation (ZOS), a two-kilometer buffer zone along the IEBL where IFOR/SFOR troops have been deployed to ensure the compliance of the parties.[19] This arrangement codifies the existing territorial division of the country, a 51-to-49 percentage territorial split, in favor of the Federation.[20] Because this division of the territory gave more to the Serbs than they had before the war, some critics have argued that the Dayton Accords effectively rewarded ethnic cleansing.[21] The Dayton Accords did not challenge the existing division of the armed forces, as the armed forces of the country consisted of separate forces for the Federation and for the RS. Although there were efforts to get these bodies to coordinate their activities, no joint military exercises were held between Federation and RS forces until 2001.[22]

While acknowledging and even reifying the ethnic divisions in Bosnia, the Dayton Accords indicated a sometimes contradictory preference for a return to multiethnicity. Under the agreement, the parties were obliged to provide a "safe and secure environment for all people living in their jurisdictions."[23] They were also required to provide for the highest level of respect for human rights and to create an environment in which citizens could vote for their preferences without fear or threat of violence. The Dayton Accords included strong provisions allowing refugees to return to their prewar homes (domicile return) and to be compensated for lost property.[24] They also obliged all levels of government, including the entities, cantons, and municipal levels of government, to cooperate with the UNHCR in facilitating the return of refugees. With these webs of cooperation, the goal was to slowly re-create a functioning, multiethnic state over time, rather than to codify the divisions of the country. As the architect of the Dayton Accords, Richard Holbrooke, put it, "Dayton was not the creation of two different countries inside Bosnia. It's one country with the rights of refugees to return, open roads, free elections, a single central government and a merger of two hostile forces, the Serbs and the Croats and Muslims. . . . This is going to be one country. If it isn't, then we have failed."[25] While the Dayton Accords aspired to create a unified Bosnia, the government created by it subtly acknowledges that years of mistrust and ethnic hatred would make a more centralized state unpalatable to the parties and devolves and layers power across various levels of government to alleviate these concerns.[26]

The structure of the government created by Dayton is also premised on allocating seats and voting preferences to ethnic groups. One of the key elements of the Dayton Accords was the recognition of the political rights of Bosnian Muslims, Croats, and Serbs as "constituent peoples."[27] At the national level, the constitution grants each of these three ethnic groups preferential rights in the House of Peoples, splitting its fifteen seats equally among them. In the House of Representatives, the constitution does not specify ethnic quotas but insists that two-thirds be elected from the territory of the Federation and one-third from the RS. Especially in the House of Peoples, these ethnic preferences have produced political deadlock by effectively granting veto power to each of the constituent peoples. In the House of Peoples, if a group declares that a piece of legislation is a "vital interest," the legislation must receive a majority of votes from each ethnic group.[28] As Sumantra Bose has pointed out, the result is that the Bosnia and Herzegovina (BiH) parliament has "been largely a talking shop since 1996, often immobilized by disagreements and sheer incompetence."[29] At the national and entity level, this ethnic quota system "breeds corruption, weakens political moderates, and stunts economic growth," and it has created "a spoils system that has led to extensive patronage networks, corruption and inefficiencies."[30] It has also sustained a culture of patronage in Bosnia, in which offices and positions in key government agencies are allocated on the basis of belonging to an ethnic group, rather than qualifications or talent.

The decentralized nature of the Bosnian state initially meant that more power is vested at the entity level (Federation and RS) than it is at the federal level. The Dayton Accords created a series of federal institutions, such as a joint presidency (with a representative from each ethnic group), and the distinctive features of a state, such as a bicameral legislature, constitutional court, and council of ministers. Under the constitution agreed to in Article 4 of the Dayton Accords, the federal government is in charge of foreign policy, monetary policy, immigration and refugee policy, and interentity criminal law enforcement.[31] In practice, much of the power in the country has remained at the entity level. The Constitution leaves any residual powers not explicitly given to the federal government of Bosnia to the entities (Constitution, 3.1.a) and permits them to form parallel relationships with neighboring countries.

Each of the entities has responded to this remit in power in different ways. The RS is a more centralized entity and asserts a wide range of powers, including the ability to have independent relationships with other states. It does not enshrine proportional representation of ethnic communities in the legislature and allocates fewer powers to the municipal level. In the RS, the local mayors and officials of municipalities are directly elected by local voters.[32] The Federation is more complex, for it operates "like a mini-Bosnia, explicitly constituted in order to balance the interests and office of the Bosnian Croats and Bosniacs whom it governed."[33] The Federation had its own preferential ethnic allocation system for seats in its House of Peoples.[34] The Federation is composed of ten cantons, including five dominated by Bosnian Muslims and five dominated by Croats, each of which enjoyed the power to tax and control its own police and judiciary.[35] More than just an administrative unit of the federal government, the cantons were vested with substantial powers that made the key positions within them sought after in local elections. Each canton was composed of municipalities, each of which had its own reserved powers and elected offices.

The openness and flexibility of the structures built in the Dayton Accords provided multiple opportunities for parties and factions within existing parties to be represented at some level of government. While the presidency of BiH and of the RS was elected on a majority basis, most of the other electoral opportunities at the different levels of government—including the House of Representatives at the national and federation levels, the National Assembly of the RS, and most municipal and cantonal elections—used proportional representation. This use of proportional representation allowed most political parties, as well as independents and coalitions of smaller parties, to claim seats inside government.[36] In many cases, the threshold for gaining a seat was relatively low, thus expanding the number of parties and coalitions that found themselves in government and, by extension, inside a structure created by the Dayton Accords. For example, the threshold for municipal elections in 1997 was as low as 1.43 percent of all votes cast for some of the larger municipal assemblies.[37] While the government produced by Dayton was inefficient and prone to deadlock, it was remarkably open to participation by a wide array of parties across the different levels of government. Moreover, it was flexible in that the multiple rounds of elections at all levels of government provided regular opportunities for new claimants, or factions within existing parties, to have a fresh chance to enter into the legislature at some level of government if they were denied entry in a previous election.

One consequence of this decentralized structure was to multiply the opportunities for participation and domestic reward by the different parties amid the multiple levels of government. The layered structure of the government in Bosnia has led to a proliferation of ministers, many of whom use positions in the civil service, police, and military to reward their loyalists. According to an estimate by Boris Divjak and Michael Pugh, the Federation had 160 ministers across its ten cantons.[38] In part, this was due to the fact that each canton had its own parliament and ministries. The cantons were divided even further into 142 *obstinas* or municipalities, each of which had layer of political and administrative positions.[39] Even at the municipal level, many of the jobs available were patronage positions and thus were the gift of the dominant party at that level of government. The consequence of this extensive use of domestic reward is that Bosnia has sustained an extraordinarily bloated public sector since the end of the war, with ministers having overlapping mandates, and often contradicting each other, across the levels of government.[40] In the Federation alone, the number of public officials in senior and administrative positions in government was estimated to be fifty thousand.[41] In the early days of the post-conflict period, there were also fourteen separate police forces in the Federation alone.[42] The entities and cantons also were responsible for their own budgets and had autonomy in raising revenue, which multiplied the number of administrative jobs available for patronage and also provided opportunities for rent-seeking behavior.[43] By one recent estimate, the public sector—especially salaries for government officials—constituted 50 percent of the Bosnia's gross domestic product.[44] While this structure was hugely inefficient, it allowed the extensive use of domestic reward to buy off factions within wartime parties with jobs inside government, which helps to account for the absence of factional violence in the post-conflict period.

To manage some of the internal contradictions of Dayton, a wide range of international organizations was involved in keeping the peace in Bosnia. The scale of this involvement was unprecedented. The most important contribution was from NATO, which fielded sixty thousand troops as part of the Implementation Force (IFOR), later renamed the Stabilization Force (SFOR). IFOR was given a broad mandate, from separating the parties and ensuring no infractions of the peace settlement occurred to preventing and monitoring any interference with the movement of civilian populations, refugees, and displaced persons. Policing functions were granted to the UN-led International Police Task Force (IPTF), while the OSCE was charged with managing the elections at all levels of government in Bosnia. The UNHCR was charged with handling the massive task of organizing the return of refugees. Regional organizations such as the Council of Europe were also involved, and international financial institutions (such as the World Bank) played a key role in reestablishing Bosnia's economy. Moreover, many international organizations were named as interim members of Bosnian institutions.[45] The coordination of these organizations was given to the Office of the High Representative (OHR), which was in theory the final civilian authority for resolving disputes among the various organizations active in Bosnia. The OHR was in turn accountable to the Peace Implementation Council (PIC), a collection of key governments and international organizations involved in funding and supporting Bosnian reconstruction.[46] In effect, the Dayton Accords left Bosnia as a ward of a collection of international organizations ostensibly representing the international community, while these organizations insisted that Bosnia was a multiethnic democracy with substantial local ownership.[47]

Post-Conflict Period (1995–1999)

The post-conflict period in Bosnia was marked by increasing international involvement to manage the inherent contradictions of the Dayton Accords. The initial deployment of IFOR was relatively smooth, with none of the parties officially breaking the settlement or attacking incoming NATO forces. However, the first commander of IFOR, Admiral Leighton Smith, adopted a minimalist approach to law and order and refused to engage in some policing tasks, such as preventing the evacuation of Serbs from Sarajevo and arresting war criminals.[48] As the year went on, Bosnian Serb hard-liners attempted to test the resolve of NATO forces, and confrontations over the control of police stations by Bosnian Serb hard-liners regularly occurred.[49] Bosnian Serb military officers were also posing as police in order to remain armed. Meanwhile, accused war criminals such as Karadzic were also in open defiance of NATO and were appearing in public to drum up local support. On the civilian side, the first steps toward implementing the Dayton Accords were unsteady. The first high representative, Carl Bildt, had few resources beyond his own cell phone and relatively little enforcement capability.[50] Many of the leading international organizations in Bosnia arrived shortly after the Dayton Accords were formalized but did not have the capacity to undertake significant work, and coordination among them was difficult.[51] By late 1996, it was clear that, although the military had stabilized the situation, the civilian reconstruction of Bosnia would take far longer than the architects of Dayton had hoped.

The first set of elections in Bosnia on 14 September 1996, was marked by irregularities and outright fraud.[52] Thousands failed to vote because they did not want to cross into the "no-go" zones to their original homes to place their vote, while ethnic intimidation and harassment were common.[53] OSCE officials had expressed concern before the election that, if not properly conducted, the result would be the "pseudo-democratic legitimization of extreme nationalist power structures."[54] To their dismay, the leading nationalist parties—the Bosnian Muslim Party of Democratic Action (SDA), the Croatian Democratic Union (HDZ), and Serbian Democratic Party (SDS)—emerged victorious, leaving in power many of the same figures who had led ethnic cleansing campaigns during the war. Each of the leading nationalist parties assumed a role in the joint presidency, with Bosnian Muslim wartime leader Alija Izetbegović holding the most votes and assuming the duty as chairman.[55] The other members of the joint presidency were Momcilo Krajisnik (SDS) and Kresimir Zubak (HDZ). In the Federation, the nationalists held sway, with the SDA winning 56 percent of the seats and HDZ winning 26 percent of the seats in the House of Representatives, while the SDA held 54 percent of the seats and the HDZ 21 percent of the seats in the Federation Canton Assemblies. Similarly, in the RS, the SDS held 54 percent of the seats in the National Assembly.[56] The early elections had rewarded some of the most unsavory figures in the wartime politics of Bosnia with seats in the new government, but it also kept them inside the settlement, giving them a stake in the government and a reason not to challenge it from the outside through strategic violence.

While this result may have kept the peace, the political costs of including these actors inside the settlement were substantial. Throughout the election and afterward, these parties portrayed themselves as the defenders of their ethnic kin, especially in the RS, where much of the Bosnian Serb political leadership still claimed that their entity had been incorporated into Bosnia against their will.[57] While the Dayton Accords aimed to alleviate ethnic tensions through enforced, institutionalized cooperation over time, the incentives facing the nationalist parties often encouraged a different type of behavior. Rather than cooperating, most of the nationalist parties played the ethnic card to burnish the credentials for the next election, while the government remained deeply dysfunctional.[58] One typical approach was to grandstand against the sins of the Dayton Accords and threaten to leave the government or demand revisions of its terms. For the most part, such grandstanding was cheap talk, as even the most ardent nationalist parties flirted with spoiling the Dayton settlement but refrained from acting in ways that might cut themselves off from the benefits that remaining inside the settlement yielded. Most of the nationalist parties reached the same conclusion: that obstructionism yielded short-term political gains in a highly polarized environment, while cooperating with the OHR, UN, or other international authorities would be portrayed by their enemies as a betrayal of the nationalist cause. Although the country was not dismembered or partitioned, as many had feared during the war, Bosnia emerged from the war a deeply divided society whose electoral politics was marked by the same ethnic antagonisms that had fueled the conflict.[59] The result was governmental paralysis and drift, as the nationalist parties focused their attention on capturing a share of the spoils rather than building the capacity of the government.

With the government mired in deadlock, the nationalist parties turned inward and began to exercise domestic reward to their loyalists. The vast exercise of patronage in Bosnia was possible because of the size and complexity of the government, which multiplied the positions available for those inside government to give out to their loyalists. After the elections, nationalist parties had access to positions at the federal, entity, cantonal, and municipal levels of government and could even appoint officials to private enterprises.[60] According to an independent study of corruption in Bosnia, the Dayton Accords were a crucial source of these patronage networks, as they provided the political parties "control over all means necessary to run a well organized criminal economy," allowing them exclusive control over "state assets, licensing, housing policy (an issue that is of exceptional importance in BiH), appointments to public offices and to management and executive functions of state owned companies, privatization processes, tax collection, public utilities, customs, the security."[61] The result of Dayton's open and flexible structure was that the parties in power became increasingly predatory, scrambling to divide up jobs, government contracts, and other spoils of war among themselves, while the stalemate in government prevailed. Each of the nationalist parties gave the key clans or families behind their wartime success ministerial jobs or other patronage-based positions. The SDA, for example, operated with a strict clan-based hierarchy and divided the spoils among clans that were loyal to Izetbegović.[62] Many of these clan members were rewarded with key ministerial or ambassadorial positions in government during the post-conflict period.[63] The onset of privatization in Bosnia provided an opportunity for predatory elites linked to the SDA and other ruling parties to capture lucrative businesses, such as hotels, casinos, construction enterprises, and telecommunications contracts.[64] The Croatian HDZ was deeply involved in similar corruption, skimming nearly a third of the 650 million Deutschmarks given by the Croatian government for the support of wartime veterans and civilians and diverting most of the funds into the pockets of its loyalists.[65] The HDZ even created 120 front companies to facilitate this massive corruption.[66] In the RS, the SDS behaved in a similar fashion, exerting a stranglehold on the local government and insisting its loyalists be appointed to government jobs as "independent experts" even when it was out of power.[67] Figures from moderate parties, such as Milorad Dodik from the Alliance of Independent Social Democrats (SNSD), were under suspicion of corruption, particularly in offering nontransparent contracts worth millions of euros to their allies.[68] Substantial fraud was also associated with the customs duties in the RS, and much of the proceeds went back into the pockets of those connected to the SDS.[69] In neither the Federation nor the RS was this exercise of domestic reward monitored or regulated in any way. All of the nationalist parties initially retained control over the parallel police and intelligence structures established during the war, and even when they were later transferred to the central government, much of the existing personnel—and their loyalties—rolled over into the new police and intelligence services.

This exercise of domestic reward to prospective factions continued apace for the first two years, but two political problems occupied the attention of the OHR and its international partners. The first was that the Bosnian Serb SDS party remained loyal to the war criminals Karadzic and Mladic, who remained at large and under the protection of elements within the SDS. The second was that the SDS and, to a lesser extent, the HDZ behaved in an obstructionist manner, blocking initiatives and stymieing progress on civilian reconstruction.[70] Although the Bosnian Muslim SDA remained broadly cooperative with OHR, both of the other nationalist parties continued to publicly condemn the OHR's plans and grandstand against the Dayton Accords. Neither wanted to accept the multiethnic provisions of the Dayton Accords, and both periodically organized attacks on refugees in areas where minority returns threatened their hold on power. Under Momcilo Krajisnik, the RS operated like an independent state, rejecting efforts to integrate the Bosnian Serbs into the joint institutions provided by Dayton. The HDZ was less obvious in its opposition to Dayton, but it quietly made plans for the creation of a third entity, which would effectively be an autonomous quasi state of Herceg-Bosnia in the western part of the country. In different ways, both parties demonstrated their dissatisfaction with part of the Dayton settlement, subverting its terms and challenging any efforts to reintroduce multiethnic politics while enjoying the benefits of being inside the settlement.

A second round of elections was conducted for all of the levels of Bosnian government and the first joint institutions in November 1997. Most of the nationalist parties continued to grandstand against the peace brought by the Dayton Accords and engaged in fearmongering to win votes. In the words of High Representative Carlos Westendorp, all of the nationalist parties were behaving "like animals who cling to their turf."[71] Reviewing the election, the International Crisis Group remarked that "it is no exaggeration to state that to date [the government institutions] have failed to function, that every issue has been viewed in zero-sum terms, and that almost all 'breakthroughs' have required disproportionate, indeed often ridiculous, amounts of time, effort and concessions on the part of the international community."[72] Although there was some progress—most notably when the SDS lost control of the parliament of the RS in November 1997 and Dodik from the SNSD was appointed as prime minister—the implementation of the Dayton Accords remained stalled.[73] According to an estimate by the International Crisis Group, in the 1997 municipal elections nationalist parties controlled 129 of the 136 municipalities that their ethnic group had controlled militarily.[74] These municipal elections were also marked by voting irregularities and gerrymandering of where individuals could vote, which in turn entrenched ethnic divisions. Yet despite the repeated obstructionism and inflammatory rhetoric about the illegitimacy of the Dayton structures, the SDA, HDZ, and SDS all bitterly fought for positions in the government in order to continue to funnel jobs and profits to their loyalists.

Frustrated with the pace of change, governments and donors that were involved in the PIC met in Bonn in December 1997 and agreed upon a package of reforms to strengthen the powers of the OHR. The Bonn powers allowed the OHR to decide the time and location of meetings, to enact interim measures when the Bosnian representatives could not agree on policy, and to fire or remove obstructionist officials at all levels of government.[75] Perhaps more importantly, the OHR also received the power to set benchmarks for improving governance and other social services. The representatives in Bonn also called on NATO, the IPTF and OSCE to extend their mandates indefinitely. The increased powers granted to the OHR in Bonn led Westendorp and his successor, Wolfgang Petritsch, to becoming increasingly assertive in imposing rules on the parties. Over the course of his tenure in office, Westendorp imposed forty-five decisions and laws on the parties. Petritsch went even further and fired twenty-two Bosnian officials in one day, on 29 November 1999.[76] Most of these decisions were met with howls of protest, particularly from officials within the RS, yet none of the leading parties left the Dayton structures because they were reluctant to sacrifice their gains in post-conflict Bosnia. There was a degree of cynicism in these protests as well, as OHR decisions to remove uncooperative officials often helped to police the troublemakers within the ranks of nationalist parties, while allowing their leaders to condemn the OHR's actions for political gain.

Despite this international pressure, a further set of presidential and parliamentary elections in 12–13 September 12–13 1998, did not move Bosnia toward acceptance of multiethnic democracy. By this point, according to the International Crisis Group, "it became obvious that OSCE was not acting as the impartial international referee envisioned by DPA. Rather, it was actively involved in the international community's efforts to unseat the SDA, HDZ and the Serb nationalist block, most notably the SDS and SRS."[77] But when the votes were counted, the record for nationalist parties was mixed, as the major nationalist parties, such as Croatian HDZ and Serbian SDS, had lost some ground but nevertheless had strong showings. In the RS, hard-liner Nikola Poplasen of the ultranationalist Radical Party (SRS) defeated the pro-Western candidate Biljana Plavsic.[78] The presidency was divided between Izetbegović (SDS), Zivko Radisic (Serbian Socialist Party (SP)), and the hard-liner Ante Jelavic (HDZ). Three elections had not moved Bosnia toward becoming a unified and genuinely multiethnic state but rather had left the nationalist parties in charge of government, which continued to divide the spoils among themselves. By 1998, three separate telecommunications networks remained in the country, and the common currency (the Bosnian convertible mark, KM) was openly rejected in Serbian and Croatian regions.[79] The Serbian and Croatian movement toward hard-liners within the Dayton structures did not alter or reverse the scale of the patronage present, as the predatory behavior of elites was a constant no matter which party they represented.

Despite the gradual emergence of weak moderate and nominally multiethnic parties in the 1998 elections, Bosnia remained in the grip of nationalist parties after the post-conflict period drew to a close. In October 1999, the OSCE banned the SRS and its candidates from participating in future elections.[80] The next elections in April 2000 showed only mixed results from this approach. While Bosnian Muslims began to support a wider range of parties beyond the SDA, the SDS remained dominant in Serbia, while participation rates in Croatian regions was low, which indicated displeasure with the HDZ. Because of the results, Serb nationalists in the SDS were forced into a coalition with the more moderate Serb Mladen Ivanic (Party of Democratic Progress), who served as prime minister for the RS from 2001 to 2003. In March 2001, the OHR took the controversial step of dismissing Ante Jelavic from the joint presidency for promising an independence referendum for the Croatian regions within the Federation.[81] The OHR and others also ramped up the pressure placed on the political leadership of the Bosnian Serbs to expel accused war criminals from the ranks of their parties. In December 2001, the SDS bowed to this pressure and expelled Karadzic and all other indicted war criminals, though they remained in hiding for years afterward.[82] None of these decisions moderated the influence of ultranationalist forces that remained powerful in the RS and elsewhere.

During the post-conflict period (1995–1999) and afterward, Bosnia had not returned to war, and its government remained intact, but it also remained a ward of the international community and was heavily dependent on foreign aid and assistance for survival. Moreover, its democratic legitimacy was stage-managed by a range of international organizations, especially the OHR and OSCE. In particular, the broad powers given to OHR—which had ultimately dismissed sixty-six officials under Wolfgang Petritsch and passed a series of controversial laws that were imposed over the objections of nationalist parties—were increasingly generating frustration and resentment among Bosnians of all ethnic groups.[83] Despite international encouragement for moderates in Bosnia's elections, nationalist parties remained entrenched in the government, and multiple rounds of elections had not tamed them or curbed their largely predatory behavior. Their inflammatory rhetoric and activity indicated their dissatisfaction with the terms of the Dayton settlement, even as they cynically exploited the gains that came from it.

The Enduring Internal Control of the Nationalist Parties

Aside from the openness and flexibility of Dayton's institutions and the patronage that they permitted, the second factor that contributed to the relative absence of casualties from factional violence was the high levels of internal control that the leading nationalist players—SDA, HDZ, and SDS—had over the factions in their ranks. Unlike many other civil wars, where rebel armies are composed of loose coalitions of factions under weak centralized control, the Bosnian civil war was predominantly fought by hierarchically controlled militaries, supplemented with a range of irregular (and not as well-controlled) actors, such as Arkan's Tigers, many of whom took directions from the military high command. Although much has been made of the predatory behavior of the gangs of thugs that did some of the fighting, the majority of the violence during the war was conducted by regular units and was directed toward capturing or defending territory where their ethnic kin was located.[84] Even the ethnic cleansing of villages and towns, which did involve the participation of local civilians, did not occur without coordination and direction by regular military forces, which often took control of the territory before the expulsions began.[85] Although there were high levels of criminality and opportunism mixed in the wartime violence, the Bosnian war was conducted mainly as "soldiers versus civilians," in contrast to the vast levels of intercommunal killing that characterized other wars like Rwanda.[86] As Stathis Kalyvas and Nicholas Sambanis have noted, most civilians sat outside the conflict and their participation in violence consisted of denunciations and giving information to existing military units, rather than killing on their own.[87] Only at the end of the war, when the suffering of civilians had become so apparent, did significant groups of civilians join in the fighting, often in order to seek revenge or to pursue vendettas.[88]

The high levels of internal control wielded by the major combatants during and after the war were also due to the presence of trained military officers in each of the major three sides and the links that they had to the militaries of external states. Many of the participants were former career officers of the Yugoslavian National Army (JNA) or home guards and reservists who had been trained by the JNA.[89] Some of the most fearsome wartime paramilitary organizations were trained by the JNA and acted in a semiofficial capacity on its behalf. The JNA, for example, trained the militias loyal to the SDS and an array of other Bosnian Serb paramilitary organizations.[90] Some of the paramilitary organizations that fought alongside the Bosnian Serb Military (VRS) were composed mainly of former JNA members and were highly dependent on arms and orders from Belgrade.[91] Similarly, the Croatian military had deep links with the local Croat forces doing much of the fighting in Bosnia, and many Croatian officers served with HVO units during the war. Even the Bosnian Muslim self-defense units were populated by veterans of the JNA, who had defected to serve their cause.

The high levels of internal control that the combatants had in the post-conflict period were also due to the organizational structures that survived the collapse of the Yugoslav military. None of the three major sides started from scratch in building an organization to fight the war. On the Serbian side, the dissolution of the Yugoslav army (JNA) in 1992 effectively divided the force into two forces, the new Yugoslav Army (VJ) and the Bosnian Serb Military. The VRS was not an entirely new army, and retained much of the organizational structure in place under the JNA. It was under the control of Belgrade, even to the extent of not being able to fire at a target unless it received approval.[92] The salaries of VRS officials were also paid directly by Belgrade until after Dayton was signed.[93] Similarly, in Croatia, the HDZ party organized its own military force (HVO) for the war in Bosnia, which was composed of former Croatian army members and drew on supplies from Zagreb, although some Croatian paramilitary organizations operated with less formal control from the HDZ command.[94] Even the Bosnian army (ARBiH), which was created out of territorial defense units and the Patriotic League (PL), as well as units from the JNA, was not a force created from scratch.[95] The nearly 100,000 members of the Patriotic League (PL) that formed its core had received military training and were organized into fighting formations even before the war began.[96] Even though it was divided by internal disagreements in its early days, the ARBiH retained its organizational integrity and fought as a coherent army, especially after it partnered with the HVO and received training and equipment from the United States.[97] While much of the violence in Bosnian civil war was brutal and predatory, most of the major actors were not a loose collection of factions, even if they were allied with politico-criminal armed groups that had less organizational discipline than a normal army. The fact that these organizations were sponsored by external states (in the case of Yugoslavia and Croatia) and were composed as regular forces were, with normal command and control structures, created an infrastructure and coherent leadership for each of the major national forces that did not disappear when the war ended.

Because of the original organizational endowments of the major combatants, the levels of internal control for each side remained high at the onset of the post-conflict period. The military leadership did not suddenly lose the organizational ability to monitor the thousands of demobilized soldiers and to stop them from engaging in factional violence. Rather, the wartime leaders ordered their forces to accept the cease-fire and to work with NATO forces as they regained control of the country. Although some sporadic resistance occurred, most of the fighting units obeyed the commands of their leaders and did not interfere with NATO's operations in the country. But this high level of internal control lasted in the post-conflict period because the provisions of the Dayton Accords left the military, police, and intelligence structures built by each of the wartime parties intact. The Dayton Accords confirmed the existence of each of the three standing military forces and required them to downsize to fifty-five thousand soldiers for the joint Federation and fifty-six thousand for the RS.[98] Unlike cases (such as Iraq), where the entire army was demobilized or formally abolished, the armies that fought the war continued to exist, although in a reduced form, in the post-conflict period. The armies survived because the "strategy implicit in the Dayton Accords was to allow the ethnically-defined, wartime regimes to consolidate their separate spheres of influence."[99] As a result, unlike many other similar rebel forces, these armed actors did not dissolve into competing factions. The ARBiH and HVO were nominally merged into a single Bosnian army, but in practice they remained under distinct command structures, with different training routines, and even wearing different uniforms, until 2005.[100] The territorial control of both units was never challenged; despite belonging to a common military, the HVO exclusively controlled 20 percent of the territory of Bosnia on its own until its integration.[101] The VRS remained the most independent of the three armies and jealously guarded the territory of the RS, permitting no more than token HVO or ARBiH presence, for the first years of the post-conflict period. The VRS also remained under control of the SDS and the military infrastructure in the RS, rather than integrating with the rest of the Federation forces. Similarly, the police services of each of the ethnic sides remained intact and independent, and all were deeply resistant to integration for years after Dayton was signed.[102] The Bosnian Muslim and Croat forces were merged into cantonal and Federation level police, but the RS police service remain functionally independent today. Despite nominal steps toward integration, each of the police services remained highly politicized and responsive to the demands of the nationalist parties, and cooperation across entities was rare for the first years of the post-conflict period.[103]

In part because the Dayton Accords left them intact, the military and police forces in the Federation and the RS never dissolved into competing factions in the post-conflict period. For the military and the police across all of the ethnic sides, the command structure and organizational endowments of these forces carried over into the post-conflict period, which allowed the leadership to monitor their ranks, to punish defections, and to ensure that there was little or no factional violence. Moreover, despite IPTF monitoring, the nationalist parties retained some level of internal control over the military and the police, which allowed them to block investigations, to ensure noncompliance with the demands of Dayton that were contrary to their political agenda, and to turn a blind eye when strategic violence was used. Examples of such behavior recur throughout the narrative accounts of attacks on refugees, and in some cases there is evidence linking agents of the SDS and HDZ directly to attacks.[104] In some cases, the nationalist parties were even able to command those inside the military and the police to use strategic violence on their behalf, often in a way that allowed them to preserve plausible deniability. Their involvement was often apparent in riots, where hundreds of demobilized and unemployed soldiers would often appear, presumably at the bidding of local political figures, to protest minority returns or steps toward integration. The informal structures of coordination and control established during the war proved durable in the post-conflict period and were selectively employed by those in power to ensure that minority returns did not succeed in regions where they sought exclusive control.

Another striking aspect of the Bosnia case compared to other cases (such as Kosovo and Iraq) where the demobilization of forces was uncontrolled has been the extent to which ex-soldiers outside the ranks of the military and police did not engage in factional violence. Approximately 300,000 of the 400,000 total forces in the country demobilized immediately, and many simply returned home where they were welcomed as heroes for their service in war.[105] Many soldiers found themselves unemployed and struggling to feed their families, which led to the introduction of World Bank programs from 1996 to 1999 to assist ex-soldiers in continuing to survive in the decimated economy.[106] Some former soldiers became diverted into the illegal economy and to organized crime. Despite the fact that the absence of effective institutions meant that the demobilization process was chaotic, and that the process of registering combatants was inadequate, there was no evidence of substantial factions within the armies refusing to demobilize or resisting the Dayton Accords on their own. While limited evidence exists of ex-fighters engaging in violence through organized crime, widespread factional violence did not occur, and for the most part former soldiers remained loyal to the military structures and nationalist parties that they had defended during the war. This was in part due to the fact that ex-soldiers received pensions and disability benefits from the local and regional governments and enjoyed privileges, including exemption from tax, for years after the war.[107] Such generous benefits helped the nationalist parties retain the loyalties of former soldiers long after the war had ended. Beyond loyalty, however, there is anecdotal evidence that veterans' associations outside the structures of the army and police helped to preserve internal control and ensure that their members remained responsive to the demands of the nationalist parties.[108] The involvement of veterans in attacks on returnees and periodic riots indicated not only the nationalist sympathies that they held but also, in some cases, that their loyalties were still attached to these organizations and the political figures who supported them. The residual organizational structures present, and the culture of loyalty to the nationalist parties that were prominent during the war, meant that these nationalist parties were selectively able to call upon the veterans for participation in acts of strategic violence in the post-conflict period.

Violence in the Post-Conflict Period

In Bosnia, there was a wide range of factors—popular discontent with the Dayton Peace Accords, persistent ethnic antagonisms, early elections that led to nationalist victories, political deadlock, corruption, high unemployment, and onerous levels of international involvement in managing the democratic process—that should have produced the ideal conditions for a return to strategic violence. Even in the Federation, the level of support for Dayton was low; a poll in January 1997 revealed that 68 percent of Bosnian Muslims and 82 percent of Bosnian Croats believed the war would resume in a few years.[109] Contrary to expectations, Bosnia featured significantly fewer attacks than NATO and other international officials had feared. This is not to say that it was nonviolent: Bosnia had low levels of expressive violence (such as revenge killings) but high levels of instrumental violence (especially organized crime, sexual trafficking, and corruption) throughout its post-conflict period. In terms of strategic violence, post-conflict Bosnia would be classified as a soft environment with only residual violence, as only 42 deaths were recorded from 1995 to 1999 (an average 8.40 deaths per year). For a war that killed approximately 100,000 people and devastated nearly 66.58 percent of the housing stock in the country, this result is surprising as it puts Bosnia at a per capita rate of victimization in the bottom half of the post-conflict states surveyed in chapter 3.[110] As noted, however, Bosnia featured a significant amount of nonlethal strategic violence designed to harass and intimidate so-called minority returns (refugee returns to regions where they are in the minority) and to influence voting in elections. During its post-conflict period, Bosnia also had an "uncivil" society, where threats and intimidation against minority groups and efforts to prevent their return to their prewar homes were common. Much of the threat of strategic violence was latent, with a hostile atmosphere perpetuated by armed groups and gangs of civilians in order to prevent minorities from returning to their original homes. There were also sporadic confrontations between NATO and the still-operating paramilitary and special police forces associated with the combatants in the first year of the post-conflict period. Although these attacks were designed to undermine the effective terms of the peace, there was no explicit attempt to overturn the Dayton Accords, and strategic violence never transformed into an organized insurgency against the interim government, the OHR, or NATO.[111]

There are no publicly available data on crime in Bosnia from 1995 to 1997, but unpublished statistics collected by the IPTF task force for the second half of the post-conflict period give a snapshot of the scale of the criminal activity in Bosnia for the second half of the post-conflict period. Table 4.1 indicates the total numbers of crimes by type and percentage by entity and region from July 1998 to June 2001. It is important to note that for some categories of crimes—for example, murders, assaults, and kidnapping—no data on motive are available.[112] These incidents might arise from criminal or ethnic motives, or some combination thereof.

The data indicate that crime is nearly evenly distributed between the Federation (51%) and the RS (49%). For a population of 4.3 million, most of the violent crime statistics would be considered at normal level. For example, the total number of murders (184) and kidnapping attempts (83) is consistent with other countries in the Balkans with a similar population size and demographic profile.[113] For most of the measures of crime, including sexual assaults and property crime (like breaking and entering, robbery, and theft), the incidences are spread evenly across the Federation and the RS, and no discernible regional differences are evident. However, analysis of a second set of crime statistics often associated with nonlethal harassment of minorities indicates higher-than-expected levels of violence (table 4.2). For example, Bosnia recorded 1,191 assaults, 986 incidents of harassment and intimidation, 138 incidents where free movement was interrupted, and 4,675 evictions across a two-year period. Particularly notable as tactics that indicate strategic violence are the levels of explosions (1,060) and sniper fire (78) over this nearly two-year period. As with violent crime, the evidence suggests that such tactics of harassment, intimidation, and expulsion were nearly evenly distributed across the country, with only slightly higher overall crime evident in Tuzla, Sarajevo, and Brcko than the other regions. Moreover, these data are suggestive of the extent to which IPTF and SFOR forces participated in the demilitarization of Bosnian society, as they removed 87 checkpoints and conducted 1,070 weapons inspections. The evidence suggests that two dynamics were at play: a gradual demilitarization of Bosnian society from the remnants of the war and the emergence of new campaigns of nonlethal harassment, intimidation, and expulsion against vulnerable minorities.

As a more specific measure of the strategic violence in post-conflict Bosnia, data were collected on acts of strategic violence from newspaper accounts of violent activity in the post-conflict period. It is important to stress that these data differ from those already given on three grounds: (1) they include only acts of strategic violence, which by definition are a subset of overall levels of violence in a society; (2) newspaper sources are subject to selection bias and tend to report on strategic violence more consistently than they do expressive or instrumental forms of violence; and (3) acts of strategic violence that cause casualties are more likely to be reported than nonlethal forms of harassment and intimidation. The determination of whether to include a violent act in this dataset was made on the basis of an assessment of the contextual details surrounding the act, specifically the type of targets, perpetrators (if known),

TABLE 4.1.
IPTF Crime Statistics with Percentages by Region and Area, July 1998–June 2001

Type of Crime	Total Number	Federation n (%)	RS n (%)	Tuzla %	Brcko %	Sarajevo %	Banja Luka %	Mostar %	Bihac %	Doboj %
Assault/Injury	1,191	687 (58%)	504 (42%)	16	12	17	14	10	15	16
Assault/Sexual	267	184 (69%)	83 (31%)	16	12	17	14	10	15	16
Breaking/Entering	647	348 (54%)	299 (46%)	25	16	8	7	6	15	23
Damage/Criminal	580	280 (48%)	300 (52%)	20	6	14	10	12	20	18
Drugs/Dealing/Possession	144	92 (64%)	55 (36%)	15	0	19	14	26	15	10
Forgery	364	299 (82%)	65 (18%)	12	4	64	3	5	6	6
Fraud	118	54 (46%)	64 (54%)	15	31	18	6	8	8	14
Kidnapping	83	43 (52%)	40 (48%)	32	11	25	8	5	6	13
Murder	184	100 (54%)	84 (46%)	20	4	14	14	11	22	15
Murder/Attempted	214	142 (66%)	72 (34%)	18	4	9	24	8	21	16
Robbery	247	137 (55%)	110 (45%)	20	11	13	15	4	15	22
Robbery/Attempted	105	78 (74%)	27 (26%)	11	8	66	4	1	5	5
Robbery/Weapons Possession	204	109 (53%)	95 (47%)	15	16	9	16	6	14	24
Smuggling	90	38 (42%)	52 (58%)	19	6	13	1	39	16	6
Theft	1,364	744 (55%)	610 (45%)	21	11	9	10	11	20	18
Theft/Attempted	115	57 (50%)	58 (50%)	30	5	6	10	15	15	19
All Crimes	33,266	17,045 (51%)	16,221 (49%)	15	6	14	17	10	12	26

TABLE 4.2.
IPTF Common Strategic Attacks with Percentages by Region and Area

Type of Crime	Total Incidents	Federation n (%)	RS n (%)	Tuzla %	Brcko %	Sarajevo %	Banja Luka %	Mostar %	Bihac %	Doboj %
Arson	396	230 (58%)	166 (42%)	19	3	5	12	10	36	15
Eviction	4,675	2,238 (52%)	2,437 (48%)	11	1	11	16	3	4	54
Exhumation	229	136 (59%)	93 (41%)	14	0	35	8	3	31	9
Explosion	1,060	554 (52%)	4,506 (48%)	12	5	17	22	12	16	16
Expulsion	12	5 (42%)	7 (58%)	17	17	25	8	25	0	8
Free Movement	138	95 (69%)	43 (31%)	1	2	14	7	3	71	2
Harassment/Intimidation	986	478 (48%)	508 (52%)	12	12	12	11	10	24	19
Looting	56	37 (66%)	19 (34%)	45	4	13	2	4	23	9
Sniper	78	27 (35%)	51 (65%)	23	22	12	9	6	14	14
Weapons/Inspection	1,070	595 (56%)	475 (44%)	23	0	12	14	16	14	21
Checkpoints	87	23 (41%)	65 (59%)	16	6	15	24	7	17	15
Detention/Illegal	47	30 (64%)	17 (36%)	15	1	19	14	26	15	10
Hijacking	24	13 (54%)	11 (46%)	17	25	4	0	42	4	8
All Crimes	33,266	17,045 (51%)	16,221 (49%)	15	6	14	17	10	12	26

and weapons involved. Table 4.3 presents data from these sources on acts of strategic violence for the post-conflict period (1995–1999) and subsequently.

Although this represents a nonrepresentative sample of the overall levels of violence in Bosnia, table 4.3 does suggest that much of the reported strategic violence in post-conflict Bosnia was nonlethal. From 1995 to 1999, there were 199 reported events of strategic violence, yet only 42 casualties. The number of wounded was significantly higher, with more than 199 wounded across the five-year period. Some of those wounded and killed came from repeated arson attacks (14 reported from 1995 to 1999) and bombings (63 reported). Of particular interest from the vantage point of strategic violence is the extent to which the events appeared as part of a pattern. Of the total acts reported over this period, 49 (24%) were coded as reprisals (i.e., acts clearly linked in retaliation to a previous act of violence). An even greater number (77, or 39%) were coded as being part of a pattern of attacks (i.e., when dozens of houses burn down in the same region every night). Together with the IPTF statistics from 1998 to 2001, the evidence of strategic violence indicates regular and observable patterns of strategic violence against minorities, particularly involving arson, explosions, evictions, and harassment and intimidation, but relatively few deaths relative to the number of attacks.

A survey of the qualitative and narrative accounts of violence in the post-conflict period suggests seven main types of violence: revenge attacks; riots; opportunistic violence; criminal violence; scattered attacks on NATO and Bosnian government officials; postwar ethnic cleansing; and violence against returnees. Each of these is considered in turn to determine their relative impact on producing significant levels of nonlethal strategic violence. The following focuses particularly on the varying types of expressive and instrumental forms of violence present in this case, which set the backdrop for the use of strategic violence against minorities and returning refugees.

Revenge Violence

Although the precise number of murders, assaults, and arsons attributable to revenge are not available, it is clear that sporadic acts of revenge violence occurred in the immediate post-conflict period, often in areas where NATO or the local police had not established control. In Mostar, for example, eighteen people were found murdered on its west (Muslim) side right after the war, but the Bosnian Croat police refused to pursue an investigation.[114] Some of the violence was clearly punitive and gratuitous: for example, in the Serb-controlled suburbs of Sarajevo, sixteen Muslim men were abducted and tortured over a ten-day period.[115] In some cases, these attacks were traditional revenge attacks, as those who lost loved ones in the war sought out their enemies for vengeance, but in others, individuals were killed for accidentally crossing

TABLE 4.3.
Strategic Violence in Bosnia, 1995–2001

Year	Events	Casualty	Wounded	Bombings	Kidnappings	Arsons	Expulsions	Reprisals	Patterns
1995	16	6	4	4	1	2	0	2	6
1996	80	13	82	23	2	6	0	10	26
1997	56	7	80	24	0	3	2	23	27
1998	26	10	22	5	0	9	0	5	13
1999	21	6	11	7	0	2	0	9	5
2000	11	5	10	2	0	0	0	2	4
2001	9	0	73	3	0	1	0	1	4

into the wrong territory. For example, in August 1996, some Bosnian Muslims found working farms on Serbian land were killed or beaten, and the bridge that allowed Muslims to cross to Serb-held territory was destroyed.[116] Some of the revenge violence came about through tit-for-tat patterns of killings between communities. When members of the elite Muslim Black Swan paramilitary unit disappeared, ten gunmen ambushed a Serbian vehicle, shooting a sixty-year-old woman. In response, Bosnian Muslim government police also began detaining Serbian men, some of whom were reported to have been shot.[117] Some of the revenge violence also occurred within ethnic communities, as the nationalist parties sought revenge against their political opponents. For example, those who did not support the SDA or fought on the Bosnian Serb side found themselves persecuted and threatened in the Una Sana canton.[118]

Yet, given the extent of the mass mobilization during the war, the presence of war criminals throughout the country, and the extent to which homes and lives had been destroyed, the level of revenge violence in Bosnia was relatively low. A U.S. AID study in 2005 found that revenge violence was significantly lower than expected in part because of a widespread sense of war weariness and exhaustion among much of the public.[119] To some extent, this absence of revenge was driven by the opportunity structure, particularly the lack of geographic proximity between ethnic groups. The mass displacement of the population had the effect of producing ethnically homogeneous strips of territory, which featured relatively few, often besieged, minorities. When the war ended, many of these scattered pockets of minorities moved to areas where their ethnic group was in the majority. By one estimate, eighty thousand Bosnians moved to areas where their group was in the majority in the immediate aftermath of the Dayton Accords.[120] Revenge violence did occur throughout post-conflict Bosnia, but the forcible separation of the population into monoethnic territories had a dampening effect on the overall incidence of revenge violence.

Riots

One of the recurring types of expressive violence in post-conflict Bosnia was rioting. Riots tended to occur when Bosnians sought to gain control over their prewar homes, when SFOR forces assumed control over a city or town, or when territory was transferred from one group to another. In some cases, the riots were apparently spontaneous and driven by angry crowds of civilians who engaged in severe intercommunal attacks. For example, gangs of Bosnian Serbs threw rocks at busloads of Croats seeking to return to their prewar homes in Modrica in April 1996.[121] In Brcko, mobs of Bosnian Serbs attacked American peacekeepers with firebombs and clubs when they arrived to hand over control of a police station from Karadzic's allies to Bosnian Serb moderates.[122] In the village of Gajevi in the RS, a mob of two hundred

Serbs ambushed Muslim refugees with rocks and destroyed their building materials to prevent them from rebuilding their homes.[123] Riots also flared when the city of Mostar was being divided into Bosnian Muslim and Croat sections and individuals entered the "wrong" part of the city.[124]

In some cases, there was evidence of organization to the riots, which reflected the degree of internal control that local nationalist figures had over their followers. Some cases clearly indicated that the rioting was orchestrated or amplified by local figures for their political gain. For example, in Serb-held Doboj, more than one thousand Bosnian Serbs charged NATO troops and threw rocks at them when Bosnian Muslims came back to see their wartime homes in 1996.[125] There were allegations that the assault was organized by Doboj's mayor, and local radio stations had broadcast an appeal by Bosnian Serb leaders to go to the edge of the town to prevent Muslims from entering. Similarly, a violent mob of 250 Serbs attacked a convoy of Bosnian Muslim women when they visited the site of a former detention camp in an attack that SFOR officials said was orchestrated by the Bosnian Serb political leadership in Prejidor in May 1996.[126] Among the most serious incidents was in April 1998, when Croat extremists shot two elderly Serbs who had returned to reclaim their homes. Their bodies were found in their burning homes, to the apparent indifference of the Croat local police. In response, a crowd of hundreds of angry Serbs blocked Croats from attending Mass at the local Catholic Church.[127] Days later, a crowd of fifteen hundred Croats attacked the municipal offices, beat the mayor nearly to death, and assaulted IPTF staff. The investigation following the incident suggested that Croat soldiers were involved in the crowd and that Serb-owned homes had been destroyed and burned in a systematic and nonrandom fashion.[128]

Opportunistic Violence

In the immediate aftermath of the war, there was also a series of attacks that could have been explained by revenge, opportunism, or some combination thereof. In the RS, for example, non-Serbs were forced to flee the territory and reported assaults, harassment, and the arson of their homes by gangs of Serbian thugs.[129] In the villages surrounding Teslic in the RS, more than two hundred non-Serbs fled their homes after the Dayton Accords were signed to avoid "serious and protracted" harassment, including beatings, stone-throwing, threats, and verbal harassment by local Serbs who wanted their homes.[130] Some violent attacks were neighbor on neighbor, with Bosnian Serbs harassing and expelling their longtime neighbors, in some cases using beatings, thefts, and grenade attacks to force Muslims to flee. In these attacks, angry Serb crowds would taunt and threaten the refugees, but also seize their homes when they fled, which raises questions about the priority of motives that generated the attack. A similar dynamic was reported in the Federation, as Serbs in the neighborhoods surrounding Sarajevo were also expelled to the apparent indifference of the Federation police. By one estimate, the IPTF estimated four hundred reports of abuse against Bosnian Serbs in the area around Sarajevo in the first eight months of the post-conflict period.[131] Bosnian Serbs reported that their homes and valuable property were seized by Bosnian Muslims in the assault, while the Federation police acknowledged the theft but acted as if it was inevitable. Many attacks on minorities in post-conflict Bosnia are extremely difficult to parse for a motive, because the mass mobilization of the war and the scale of the death and destruction created so many perpetrators and victims on both sides. Much of the violence was categorical: those who were seizing homes and property in the post-conflict period were victims of violence but not necessarily victims of those they now attacked. There was also some evidence of former soldiers running markets in confiscated houses by seizing them from their original owners and selling them to their ethnic kin for a small profit.[132]

Criminal Violence

One consequence of the civil war in Bosnia was the development of powerful criminal networks that continued to operate in the post-conflict period. As Peter Andreas has documented, the war reordered Bosnian society in significant ways and produced powerful criminal networks that had profited off of events like the siege of Sarajevo.[133] These criminal networks were enmeshed with those of armed groups, creating a seamless web of politico-criminal actors that used the war to their own advantage.[134] The post-conflict period did not stop their activities but facilitated it in new ways. Many of the political allies of the new criminal elite were now in government, and a wartime amnesty bill—which extended to siphoning off humanitarian aid, illegal commerce, and tax evasion—allowed criminal elites to present themselves as legitimate businessmen.[135] The decentralized nature of the state created in the Dayton Accords multiplied the opportunities for corruption, as officials at all levels of government could reward their allies with contracts or block investigations into their activities.[136] The carve-up of state-owned enterprises also proved to be a boon for organized crime, as powerful mafia figures sought concessions from the government and paid bribes to ensure that they happened. One Bosnian official involved in telecommunications efforts remarked that "bribes are flowing in here like water."[137] The incompetence and corruption of the local police and the unwillingness of SFOR to engage in policing activities meant that organized crime networks faced few obstacles to continuing their involvement in the black and gray economies after the war. As a result, the illegal and semilegal economies boomed during the post-conflict period, as criminal networks engaged in illegal commerce (such as trade in cigarettes, alcohol, and pirated CDs and DVDs), money laundering, fraud, and tax evasion. By one estimate, nearly 50 percent of Bosnia's gross domestic product in 1999 was generated by this underground economy.[138] By 2001, the Bosnian economy was operating at only 50 percent of its prewar capacity.[139]

The significant level of criminal activities was more than just a nuisance. Most international officials argued that the ongoing criminal activity and the corruption that supported it was enfeebling the Bosnian state and strengthening nationalist networks hostile to the goals of the Dayton Peace Accords. A confidential OHR report in 2000 summarized the problem:

> That corruption and organized crime is rampant in BiH is well known. To a certain extent it is the expected consequence of a transition economy. But to an alarming extent the patterns of corruption and crime clearly demonstrate intricate networks designed to illegally finance nationalist parties and factions, protect war criminals and line the pockets of individuals. . . . The schemes that today support the nationalist factions involve a range of illegal activities including illegal trafficking, smuggling, fraud, money laundering, tax evasion, illegal land allocation and privatization. They are supported by networks of corruption at every level—political, police, judiciary and business. High level politicians, entity ministries, mayors, and public companies are used to generate, protect and channel funds gained through illegal activities. The damage to BiH includes corruption at every level, perpetration of ethnic nationalism and separatism, a business environment inhospitable to legitimate enterprise or foreign investment, blockage of much needed reform, and hundreds of millions of KM of lost government revenues.[140]

Because the Federation and RS retained rights over local law enforcement and customs duties, international support for law enforcement tended to be concentrated on the entity level, which left the capacity of the central government underdeveloped. Criminals soon focused on exploiting this fact, often engaging in illegal commerce in the Zone of Separation that lay between the entities.[141] Owing to a lack of internal police capacity, criminals were free to sell smuggled goods openly on street corners and in marketplaces, making such transactions almost normal.[142] The development of a State Border Service (SBS) went some way to correcting the porosity of the borders, though this did not have an effect until 2000–2001.

Nationalist parties of all sides profited from criminal transactions and corruption. In the RS, allies of Radovan Karadzic in the SDS used the profits from the illegal land allocation, tax evasion, and timber trading to fund their activities and to divert reconstruction funds to their own ends.[143] Such corruption and criminal activity were often strongly predatory even on one's own side; the OHR estimated that the HDZ spun a "complex web of fraud" through Croatian banks in Bosnia to support itself at the expense of people it claimed to protect.¹⁴⁴ These criminal networks divided the spoils of state-owned enterprises and blocked efforts at privatization, which in turn slowed economic growth substantially and left much of the population in poverty.¹⁴⁵ By 1999, an estimated $1 billion in humanitarian and reconstruction aid had been stolen or diverted from its original purpose.¹⁴⁶ Moreover, crime and corruption had a corrosive effect on the level of support that the population had for the Bosnian government. A World Bank survey revealed that 60 percent of respondents believed that corruption was a serious problem in Bosnia and that perception of dishonesty was pervasive at all levels of government.¹⁴⁷

Most of the ordinary crime in post-conflict Bosnia was not explicitly violent and involved activities—such as selling black market goods, fraud, corruption, and tax evasion—that do not produce significant levels of casualties.¹⁴⁸ But crimes that brought in significant profits—such as the drug trade, car theft rings, and human and sex trafficking—produced some well-armed gangs that did use violence to protect their interests. For example, in Mostar, rival gangs divided the city and controlled trade in their sectors, extracting customs fees and bribes. In 1996, they killed at least twenty different people for being "uncooperative."¹⁴⁹ In Sarajevo, mafia shootouts and executions occurred regularly, and Sarajevo gang members were widely believed to be behind the car bomb death of Bosnian deputy police minister Jozo Leutar in March 1998.¹⁵⁰ Bosnia remains a key conduit point for the transfer of narcotics into Europe, with an estimated $20 billion dollars per year earned as drugs move through checkpoints in the Federation and RS, with police officials paid to look the other way.¹⁵¹ Protection rackets in post-conflict Bosnia often required shopowners to spend $200 to $300 a month to buy off powerful local gangsters, who meted out violence to those who failed to pay.¹⁵² By some estimates, organized crime and smuggling amounts to $250 million in lost state revenue each year.¹⁵³

The most serious dimensions of crime within Bosnia involved human trafficking. Bosnia became a key conduit point for the illegal transit of individuals into Europe, which was often done by paying off organized crime networks to secure safe passage. This trade in human beings emerged during the war, as Sarajevo's airport was a conduit point for smuggling goods and foreign volunteers into the country. These networks remained in place, as migrants from the Middle East, Asia, and elsewhere would come to Sarajevo and disappear, only to head across the border into Croatia and onto Western Europe.¹⁵⁴ An internal report submitted to the UN secretary general provides a glimpse of the scale of the human trafficking: "Between January 1 and October 26, 2000, 24,850 foreign nationals from 8 different countries, but principally from Iran (11,264) and Turkey (12,052), have entered BiH through Sarajevo airport but only 5,488 citizens of the same countries have departed via the Airport, leaving 19,362 unaccounted for. In the same period, the Croatian police have returned 2,578 persons from those same countries to Bosnia and Herzegovina."[155] The introduction of the State Border Service (SBS) in 2000–2001 and a visa regime interrupted the overall levels of human trafficking, but it remained a serious problem. In 2001, the UN Mission in Sarajevo estimated that approximately 50,000 migrants made it into Western Europe through Bosnia.[156] Much of this trafficking occurred without overt violence, though the mafia gangs that ran it would engage in violence if someone failed to pay for transit or if they could extract extortion money from their families to ensure safe passage.[157] Among the most dangerous routes for human trafficking was across the Adriatic. Smugglers often crammed refugees in rubber dinghies with high-speed motors for shipment into Italy; if given chase by Italian officials, refugees were thrown overboard to fight for their lives to allow the smugglers to escape.[158]

Another serious and violent criminal enterprise in Bosnia was sex trafficking. Throughout the post-conflict period, women from Bosnia and a range of countries—most notably Moldova, Romania, and Ukraine—were lured into the country with the promise of safe passage into Europe and then forced into the sex trade in bars and brothels throughout the country.[159] SFOR soldiers and employees of the many international organizations and NGOs in Bosnia were major customers of the sex trade and bore some responsibility for its expansion in numbers across the post-conflict period.[160] The sex trade was not always explicitly violent, although it was premised on the threat of violence if the women did not comply with the demands of their bosses or clients. Moreover, organizers of the sex trade would use violence (especially assaults, including sexual assaults) against women who rebelled against their poor treatment. From 1999 to 2002, the International Organization for Migration (IOM) and the UN rescued more than two hundred women from the sex trade.[161] Yet the scale of the problem became apparent only when the UN Mission in Bosnia-Herzegovina (UNMIBH) implemented the Special Trafficking Operations Program (STOP) program, which conducted raids on suspected brothels and rescued women who were often kept against their will. The STOP program rescued 257 women and resulted in 98 convictions between 2001 and 2002. But it also came under criticism for being ineffective (particularly as the freed women often disappeared back into the sex industry), liable to corruption, and run by the same IPTF officers who were clients of the brothels.[162]

Post-Dayton Attacks on NATO/IPTF and Civilian Targets

Beyond the expressive and instrumental forms of violence present in this case, three types of strategic violence were also evident in post-conflict Bosnia. The first was periodic attacks on NATO and IPTF forces, as well as attempts to test the peace by firing on civilian targets in the aftermath of the Dayton Accords. While SFOR met no significant resistance, once the UN mission in Bosnia had begun, a series of attacks on NATO forces in the first year of the mission constituted an attempt to test the resolve of NATO forces. For example, periodic shooting attacks against NATO helicopters often led to forced landings.[163] In the immediate aftermath of Dayton, sniper fire was regularly used against the streetcars in Sarajevo in an attempt to test the nerve of those implementing the peace agreement.[164] Grenade attacks were used both on streetcars and on NATO vehicles.[165] Especially for divided cities such as Sarajevo and Mostar, mortar attacks and periodic sniper fire were used against civilian targets by armed groups on both sides.[166] NATO forces also found themselves victims of sniper fire from civilian locations, though tracing the source of the attacks was difficult.[167] As late as July 1996, Bosnian Serb forces were threatening to shoot down U.S. helicopters.[168] However, by 1997, such overt challenges to NATO had stopped, and strategic violence came about more through a dirty war against refugees and other minorities rather than direct assaults against NATO or representatives of the Bosnian government.

Postwar Ethnic Cleansing

While some of the expulsions in post-conflict Bosnia were led by angry mobs of civilians, there is significant evidence that some of these attacks were planned by armed groups that were consolidating their own gains or destroying territory that would be turned over to another group. For example, as the Dayton Accords were in the final stages, riots erupted in Mrkonjić Grad and Sipovo, where members of the Bosnian Croat forces burned and looted houses that would go back to Serb control once the Dayton Accords took effect. More than twenty houses a day were burned while the UN looked helplessly on.[169] A report from Human Rights Watch details how the parties continued to employ ethnic cleansing and other forms of brutality to consolidate their hold on territory:

> Minorities remaining in majority areas throughout the region still fear they will be forced from their homes, despite the Dayton Agreement—or perhaps because of it. On January 25, in the village of Majdan, near the town of Mrkonjić Grad, Croat troops arrived with twenty trucks and began the forced relocation of hundreds of Croat civilians to the town of Glamof. Majdan is slated to come under Bosnian Serb control under the Dayton Agreement. The forced displacement and political resettlement of civilians, in this case conducted by soldiers of their own ethnic group, is only one example of the kind of abuses civilians have continued to experience despite the Dayton accords. In Sanski Most, Bosnian government authorities recently held Serb civilians, some of them elderly, for exchange. In Banja Luka, hundreds of men remain in forced labor or are otherwise unaccounted for.[170]

Some efforts to consolidate ethnic cleansing were opportunistic. For example, in February 1997 Bosnian Croat police took advantage of visits by Bosnian Muslims to their side of the city to block their return and reinforce the division of the city.[171]

In other cases, armed groups forcibly removed their own ethnic groups to produce defensible territory and to protect them from violence at the hands of their enemies. One of the most egregious examples of this phenomenon occurred with the Serbs of Sarajevo. Bosnian Serb forces were concerned that Serbian civilians in the neighborhoods surrounding Sarajevo would be targeted for reprisals after the siege of Sarajevo, which had killed an estimated 10,500 Bosnian Muslims during the war.[172] According to Holbrooke, shortly before these suburbs were transferred to Federation control in February 1996, the Bosnian Serb leadership in Pale ordered the Serbs of Sarajevo to burn down their own apartments and flee the city, even to the point of providing instructions on how to do it properly.[173] The Bosnian-Croat government in the Federation sent mixed messages to the Serbian population, particularly about whether they would receive amnesty for offenses in the war.[174] The Serbs of Sarajevo were also bombarded with propaganda from the Bosnian Serb leadership and prompted by gangs of young Serbs who threatened them with death if they did not leave.[175] Gojko Klickovic, head of the Bosnian Serb resettlement office, declared that the goal was not to leave a single Serb in Muslim-held territory.[176] The entire process dissolved into chaos as Serbian irregulars forced their ethnic kin at gunpoint from their homes to resettle them in Serb-controlled territory.[177] Their homes were later torched and ransacked by gangs of Bosnian Muslims before the local police could arrive.[178] An estimated fifty thousand Serbs fled the Sarajevo suburbs for areas of Bosnian Serb control.[179] What makes this case striking is the extent to which there was collusion between nationalists with apparently very different goals, for "in a pattern that would become more blatant over the year, the Bosniac leadership wanted no minorities in Sarajevo, and the Serb leadership had strategic interests in a wholesale Serb flight to populate areas in the Serb republic still considered insecure and vulnerable to assault, such as the strategic town of Brcko whose status remained undecided."[180] IFOR refused to do anything about the expulsions and arsons and eventually even gave it support for buses to transfer evacuees out of Sarajevo.[181]

Attacks against Returnees

The most common form of strategic violence in post-conflict Bosnia involved attacks on returning refugees, particularly those from minority groups. When the war ended, the scale of the refugee problems was immense, with nearly half of the country living as refugees in other countries or internally displaced persons within Bosnia. Under the stewardship of the UNHCR, but with substantial input from the UN and other

TABLE 4.4.
Returning Refugees and Internally Displaced Persons (IDPs) in Bosnia

	1996	1997	1998	1999	2000	Total
Bosnia Herzegovina						
Refugees						
Bosniak	76,385	74,756	78,589	18,440	7,633	255,803
Croatian	3,144	33,568	23,187	6,299	4,834	71,032
Serbian	8,477	11,136	6,765	6,332	5,303	38,013
Other	33	820	1,459	579	837	3,728
Total	88,039	120,280	110,000	31,650	18,607	368,576
IDPs						
Bosniak	101,402	39,447	15,806	24,907	36,944	218,506
Croatian	505	10,191	4,325	6,760	7,779	29,560
Serbian	62,792	8,452	9,139	11,315	14,175	105,873
Other	42	205	300	403	449	1,399
Total	164,741	58,295	29,750	43,385	59,347	355,338
Federation						
Refugees						
Bosniak	76,385	74,552	77,310	17,359	4,815	250,421
Croatian	3,144	33,495	22,930	5,960	3,498	69,027
Serbian	552	2,849	4,307	4,370	5,164	17,242
Other	33	754	1,453	491	569	3,300
Total	80,114	111,650	106,000	28,180	14,046	339,900
IDPs						
Bosniak	101,266	38,821	9,041	14,320	9,638	173,086
Croatian	447	10,163	4,040	5,747	6,660	27,057
Serbian	1,179	3,971	6,059	9,649	13,811	34,669
Other	21	205	300	219	172	917
Total	102,913	53,160	19,440	29,935	30,281	235,729
Republic Srpska						
Refugees						
Bosniak	0	204	1,279	1,081	2,818	5,382
Croatian	0	73	257	339	1,336	2,005
Serbian	7,925	8,287	2,458	1,962	139	20,771
Other	0	66	6	88	268	428
Total	7,925	8,630	4,000	3,470	4,561	28,586
IDPs						
Bosniak	136	626	6,765	10,587	22,461	40,575
Croatian	58	28	285	1,013	456	1,840
Serbian	61,613	4,481	3,080	1,666	362	71,202
Other	21	0	0	184	277	482
Total	61,828	5,135	10,130	13,450	23,556	114,099

organizations, a massive effort to encourage refugees to return home was undertaken. In 1996–1997 returns were slow, but by December 2000 a total of 723,914 refugees and internally displaced persons had returned.[182] Table 4.4 details the total refugee returns to Bosnia during the post-conflict period.[183]

The returns were not evenly distributed, with fewer returns and internally displaced persons (IDPs) to the Republika Srpska than to the Federation. On balance, almost five times as many refugees and IDPs returned home in the Federation (total returns: 575,719) compared to the RS (total returns: 142,685). Of particular concern to the UNHCR was the level of minority returns. In the Federation, a total of 51,911 Serb refugees and IDPs returned (9% of the total returns), whereas in the RS 49,882 Bosniaks and Croats returned (35% of the total returns). To have more than 718,404 returns completed by the end of 2000—out of a total displaced population of 2.2 million (32.6%)—is an impressive accomplishment, but the ethnic division of the country was in some respects consolidated by the postwar population movements. Many refugees, particularly Serbs and Croats, chose to remain in Serbia or Croatia rather than come back to ethnically mixed areas within Bosnia. Some of these reported returns were "ghost returns," where individuals come back to an area to reclaim their house and sell it to buy a new house where they will be located close to their ethnic kin.[184]

The UNHCR embarked on various programs designed to encourage refugee returns, particularly minority returns, with some success by the end of 2006.[185] Among these were programs designed to rebuild shelters in target areas, as well as the Open Cities initiatives that provided incentives for municipalities to welcome back minority returnees.[186] In many respects, these international organizations were deeply involved in the process, providing security for returnees, piloting programs to make a sustainable livelihood, and resolving disputes about property ownership and the displacement of those who seized the wartime homes of refugees and IDPs. This process was made more difficult by nationalist politicians, who often found ways to obstruct the return of refugees by impeding the application of Bosnia's property laws to cases of destroyed houses, and by the paucity of reconstruction funds especially at the end of the post-conflict period.[187] The reasons why individuals choose not to return are complex; a range of factors beyond security and ethnic antagonisms often affected their decision making.[188] Some refugees and IDPs were displaced to cities and preferred to stay there for better employment prospects; others were deeply concerned about the quality of health, social protection, and education facilities in towns controlled by other ethnic groups.[189] Moreover, some refugees and IDPs found that they were resented in their hometowns for having presumably escaped the impact of the war to an easier life elsewhere, which created an unwelcoming climate for their return.

One of the biggest reasons for the slow return of minority groups to their homes was the threat of strategic violence. Refugees were often attacked by mobs when they came back to reclaim their homes and often found that local police either refused to protect them or were complicit in the attack.[190] The IPTF statistics give some sense of the scale of this violence but do not specify whether these acts were directed against minority returnees. Table 4.5, drawn from UNMIBH archives, gives a snapshot of minority related offenses in post-conflict Bosnia from 2000 to 2002. It is important to

TABLE 4.5.
Minority-Related Incidents, January 2000–March 2002

	Incidents by Targets of Attack				
	All	Bosniak	Croatian	Serbian	Other
Location of Attack					
Total RS	229	207	21	0	1
Federation	113	41	9	62	1
Brcko	16	12	2	2	0
Total	358	260	32	64	2

stress that not all incidents reported here constitute violent acts, and that even verbal harassment or intimidation can count as an incident within this set of data.

The data suggest that most incidents were directed against Bosnian Muslims and that the number of incidents was significantly higher in the RS than in the Federation. This is particularly striking because the number of returns to the RS during 1995–1999 was lower than those to the Federation, which suggests that the heightened threat of violence may have deterred returnees to the RS and that those who returned faced a higher risk of abuse. An internal SFOR estimate found that a Bosniak returnee to Bikeljina or Prijedor was ten times more likely to be the victim of a violent crime (defined as bombing, rape, stoning, assault, arson, or murder) than a local Serb.[191]

Narrative accounts of harassment and attacks against minorities provide a clearer picture of the kind of violence present in this case. Types of attacks on minority returnees varied in tactics and approach substantially. Some involved harassment and forced expulsions by mobs. For example, in April 1996 mobs of Serbs attacked three hundred Croatian refugees who had come to see their homes, causing injuries and their retreat.[192] In August 1997, approximately seven hundred families that returned to Croat-controlled town of Jajce were threatened by mobs and expelled in a single weekend.[193] But even in cases like these, the extent to which some of the nationalist parties controlled the violence became clear. A subsequent IPTF investigation found that the mobs had been organized by officials associated with the HDZ party and that the local police response had been "wholly inadequate and in some instances deliberately negligent."[194] In some cases, it was less clear that the nationalist parties controlled the violence than that they informed their loyalists in the police to turn a blind eye. In Mostar, there were more than seventy attacks against Muslim refugees in one year, with attacks ranging from confrontations by angry mobs to rockets fired into or near the homes of refugees.[195] In some cases, such attacks set off tit-for-tat mob violence, with rival gangs attacking each other in reprisal for previous events. In Mahala, Serbian and Muslim crowds attacked each other for several days in August 1996, trapping IFOR and IPTF forces between them.[196] In some cases, returnees were prevented by organized mobs from moving by assaults on convoys or vehicles with stones or bottles. In May 1996, buses of Bosnian women aiming to visit villages near Prijedor were attacked by mobs of angry Serbs.[197] In August 1996, the same happened as Serbs coming to visit their homes in Gorazde were attacked by Bosnian Muslims.[198] This tactic of attacking IFOR-guided convoys and buses continued throughout the post-conflict period.[199] As late as 2002, a bus carrying seventy Serb returnees was stoned as it approached Gorazde.[200]

In other cases, harassment of minorities occurred via arson attacks, which were in turn not pursued by local police complicit in the attacks. For example, on 11 March 1997, prefabricated houses for returnees were burned in Gajevi, and a subsequent UN investigation found four local police officers complicit in the attack. Similarly, on 2–3 May 1997, twenty-five homes owned by Serbs were set on fire and another twenty-five were primed for burning in the village of Mokronoge, near Drvar, in order to interrupt the return of Bosnian Serbs to a Croat-held area.[201] Two police officers were later relieved of their duties for turning a blind eye to the attacks. Coordinated bombings were also used in some cases to force refugees to flee. For example, in Tuzla, crowds of angry Serbs attacked prefabricated houses left available for refugees with petrol bombs to destroy them and prevent returns three times in the same year.[202]

Some tactics of the violence also clearly indicate its strategic nature and the desire of the perpetrators to send a message of threat to returnees. In rare cases, mortar attacks were used to terrify refugees and force them to flee from their homes en masse.[203] Grenades have regularly been used against the homes of Bosniaks and Croats in the RS. In one case, a Bosniak returnee in Banja Luka was attacked five times since 1999.[204] In Suhaca in the RS, Serbs threatened to cut the throats of returnees and launched grenades and rockets against their homes in May 1999.[205] In the village of Kula (RS), a series of six grenades was fired at villages and automobiles of returnees, and stray mines were placed near their homes.[206] In a two-week period in October 1996, there were seventy explosions near the homes of returnees, many of involving landmines moved and rigged for detonation. IFOR officials believed that the use of landmines was suggestive of "some kind of military involvement."[207] Symbolic attacks on religious targets such as churches and mosques were also periodically used to remind returnees that they were not welcome in their prewar homes. Bombs were often placed near rebuilt churches or mosques to signal that members of a religious community were no longer welcome.[208] A series of twenty-three landmines was also placed underneath a bridge along the motorcade route of Pope John Paul II when he visited Bosnia in April 1997.[209] Attacks on minorities declined after the post-conflict period elapsed, with 277 return-related incidents in 2003 (only 38 of which were violent) and 135 reported in 2004. Yet some of the signaling with the violence continued, with more than 34 incidents targeting religious sites in the first half of 2004.[210]

Explanations

Throughout its post-conflict period, Bosnia experienced a complex mix of expressive violence (such as revenge killings and riots), instrumental violence (such as violence associated with the drug trade or human trafficking), and strategic violence (such as postwar ethnic cleansing, attacks on SFOR/IPTF forces, and attacks on minority returns). As discussed in chapter 2, all three categories of violence were intermixed in the crime statistics, which makes parsing out the exact number of each kind of attack present in the case difficult. The evidence derived from the crime statistics and the contextual details of attacks in narrative accounts suggests the following general conclusions: (1) expressive violence was variable, with relatively few revenge attacks but occasional riots that produced many injured but few deaths; (2) instrumental violence was concentrated in cities and towns and was more often associated with drug crime and human trafficking than more mundane types of street crime and corruption; and (3) strategic violence was largely nonlethal and revolved around postwar ethnic cleansing and attacks against minority returns.

With the exception of the occasional attacks against SFOR and IPTF forces, much of the strategic violence was directed along ethnic lines, as proxy groups linked to nationalist parties tried to deter minority returns to regions that had become monoethnic during the war. In rare cases, such as the expulsion of the Serbs from Sarajevo, these proxy groups—sometimes with the support of official forces, such as the police—expelled their own people from vulnerable locations in order to create defensible pockets of territory in case war would resume. Consistent with the prediction of the direct pathway, these attacks revolved around the fault lines that drove the war and involved the same types of victims, largely civilians from ethnic minority groups. While some attacks on returnees emerged spontaneously from angry mobs of citizens, many of these attacks betrayed evidence of organization and planning in their timing and tactics. The responsibility for these attacks is often difficult to trace, as shadowy proxy forces often linked to the nationalist parties would be allegedly behind them, but hard evidence for the lines of control between them was difficult to obtain. What is clear is the correlation between the location of these attacks with the interests of the SDS and HDZ. Resentful of the commitment to a multiethnic society made in Dayton, the SDS and HDZ sought to obstruct international efforts to encourage minority returns in areas controlled by a single ethnic group in the hopes of preserving the territorial gains that they made during the war. Their behavior was also political, as neither party could maintain its grip on power if other ethnic groups moved into "its" regions and began voting in elections. The clear coordination of violent attacks and the appearance of SDS- and HDZ-linked plainclothes police and former soldiers in mobs that attacked returnees testify to the extent to which the nationalist parties would direct, sponsor, or endorse violence consistent with their strategic goals. Similarly, the extent to which the nationalist parties appeared to be able to turn the violence on and off when needed was an indication of the degree of control that they had over it.

Among the most unusual aspects of the patterns of strategic violence in Bosnia were the relatively low rates of lethality given the number of attacks. According to figures compiled from newspaper sources in table 4.3, only 42 people were killed in acts of strategic violence out of a nonrepresentative sample of 199 incidents (21%).[211] The IPTF statistics in table 4.1 suggest that over a two-year period (July 1998–June 2001), Bosnia experienced nearly one arson every other day (396), nearly 6.4 evictions per day (4,765), and more than an explosion (1,060) and an act of harassment or intimidation (986) per day. But the murder rates were comparatively low (184 murders over the same period) especially given that only a subset of these murders came from strategic violence. Based solely on casualty rates relative to other post-conflict states, Bosnia would be classified as having only residual strategic violence.[212]

At least three general explanations rooted in the opportunity structure might explain why deaths from strategic violence were significantly lower in this case than other comparable cases. First, the enforced ethnic division of the country during the war reduced the vulnerability of the population by pushing it into defensible borders and therefore impeding ethnic violence.[213] One of the consequences of the population transfers during the war was to produce relatively homogeneous pockets of territory that were politically controlled by a single ethnic group, often with a negligible number of minorities present. This ethnic division of the population reduced the vulnerability of the groups and made it more costly to attack one another. Unlike prewar Bosnia, where communities of Serbs, Croats, and Muslims coexisted across the country, post-conflict Bosnia was effectively partitioned, which meant that there were fewer pockets of ethnic minorities vulnerable to attack. Where ethnic groups were intermixed or where fault lines between them were present, strategic violence did occur more frequently. Most of the strategic violence in post-conflict Bosnia revolved around international efforts to undo these borders by fostering minority returns. Yet the overall levels of strategic violence were low because the Dayton Accords implicitly accepted the consequences of ethnic cleansing and because most of the country consisted of monoethnic regions.

Second, the intervention of sixty thousand IFOR/SFOR troops and a UN-backed IPTF mission changed the strategic calculations of the actors and made attacks more costly.[214] Even those dissatisfied with Dayton, such as the SDS leadership in Republika Srpska, realized that attempts to challenge the terms of the peace settlement were unlikely to succeed with such a substantial international presence in the country. Given an estimated population of 2.6 million people, the SFOR deployment was effectively 1 peacekeeper for every 22.6 people in the country, above the threshold for what is considered a well-resourced stability operation.[215] Particularly important was a decision by SFOR to adopt a more proactive role in civilian implementation of Dayton, including protecting the return of the refugees.[216] The size and scope of the international mission and SFOR's gradual adoption of a policing model effectively placed a lid on discontent with Dayton, keeping the resentment bubbling beneath the surface but preventing it from spilling into an outright attempt to destroy the Dayton Accords.

Third, the flexible and open institutions produced by the Dayton Accords produced a dysfunctional politics in Bosnia, but it allowed for most of the prospective factions to be inside the settlement or bought off by patronage. The overlapping governance structures within this state—federal, entity, and cantonal or municipal levels—multiplied the resources available to the nationalist parties (such as offices and patronage appointments) and allowed them to reward their allies with key positions inside government. At the local level, the Dayton structures effectively created offices that were turned over to powerful wartime officials and local commanders. The parties also stacked the police with their own loyalists and, in many cases (particularly the RS, but to a lesser extent the Federation), rewarded those who fought in the war with police and military appointments in the post-conflict period. The deep patronage networks extending into the police were reflected in local police complicity in many of the attacks against minority returns, either through the agitation of undercover police officers in leading attacks or through their willingness to turn a blind eye to attacks that were occurring in their midst.[217] In December 1996, the UN estimated that 70 percent of the human rights violations in Bosnia were committed by the police.[218] The high levels of political control over the police, and their corresponding unwillingness to pursue investigations over attacks on minorities, is one of the reasons why the OHR began to gradually assert more control over the local police in the post-conflict period, though in many respects nationalist control over the police survived.[219] Given this nonpermissive opportunity structure, it is hardly surprising that overall casualties from violence were low.

At the same time, the IPTF data and narrative accounts suggest that there was a high number of nonlethal strategic attacks, often in response to events such as attempts to return expelled groups to their homes. This regular pattern of frequent acts of strategic violence with low casualties, suggests that these actions constituted a repertoire of violent acts designed to signal resistance to the terms of Dayton without causing the kinds of casualties that might reignite the conflict or cause a severe counterreaction from SFOR and IPTF.[220] In other words, the nonlethal nature of the frequent violent attacks was calibrated to signal displeasure with efforts to force multiethnic governance back on Bosnian society and to block efforts to undermine the hold of nationalist parties over their respective territories. It was not designed to "spoil" the settlement in the traditional way that this is understood. Clandestine attacks (such as arsons and threats) were used in tandem with more noticeable forms of violence (such as explosions) in order to produce a climate of fear and deter minorities from returning to their wartime homes. Even the protest events, such as the riots that often occurred when minorities returned to the prewar homes, appeared to be conducted in an almost choreographed way, where the crowds would throw stones and bottles at returnees and swarm SFOR and IPTF officials present at the scene, but rarely cause direct casualties.[221] There was a particular kind of restraint to the use of strategic violence in this case, because with some exceptions it appeared to be tailored not to cause the kind of casualties that would precipitate a crisis or a threat to Dayton.

Why was strategic violence in post-conflict Bosnia circumscribed in this way? Following the logic of the direct pathway, the source of this careful use of strategic violence lies in the levels of dissatisfaction that the parties had with the settlement. Here the answer is mixed: each of the key nationalist parties—the SDA (Bosnian Muslims), SDS (Serbs), and HDZ (Croats)—accepted the territorial gains of Dayton and wished to consolidate its political position in the new state. In the cases of the SDS and HDZ, both were arguably in possession of more territory after the war than they had before the war. Each of these parties had also strengthened its political position during the war, for "the Bosnian war was a form of primitive accumulation, and political parties like the SDS were vehicles for capital accumulation through coercion and institutionalized kleptocracy."[222] They had amassed considerable political power by appearing as the defenders of their ethnic kin and wished to retain the preeminent status in Bosnian politics. Despite hopes that the Dayton Accords would produce a multiparty democracy, with cleavages other than ethnicity, the nationalist parties were the immediate benefactors of the peace settlement. The first round of elections installed each of these parties within government and consolidated their control over their territory and the resources within. Subsequent elections effectively ratified their stranglehold on power and strengthened their trajectory toward becoming semiauthoritarian parties that ruthlessly used patronage networks to enhance their position.[223] For this reason, they were unwilling to engage in violence directly and openly spoil the settlement if doing so risked their wartime gains.

Yet at least two of the nationalist parties—the SDS and HDZ—were dissatisfied with the multiethnic commitments of Dayton and had a common interest in blocking international efforts to introduce minority returns and allow minorities to vote in the territory of their prewar homes. These parties did not wish to destroy Dayton or upset the fundamental balance of the power, but they were irrevocably opposed to any minority returns or political arrangement that would jeopardize their hold on power. In other words, they wished to undermine the terms of Dayton that called for refugee returns and the free movement of people, while effectively consolidating their gains under the agreement. This ambivalence about Dayton produced a kind of choreographed strategic violence around minority returns, which signaled displeasure with international efforts to produce a multiethnic society without causing the kind of casualties that might endanger their position. Seen from this light, the fact that Bosnia had few casualties but many incidents of harassment, intimidation, and low-grade violence is not surprising. The violence was not an attempt to "spoil" Dayton or restart the war but rather to renegotiate its terms in ways that blocked any of its provisions that threatened their control over their regions. The theatrics of violence evident in this case—specifically the repertoires of protest and contestation around minority returns—were designed more to create a climate of fear and intimidation than to kill many civilians.

Among the most difficult issues with strategic violence in post-conflict Bosnia is in attributing attacks to the elements within the SDS and HDZ. Not all attacks were organized by them; some were locally generated by angry mobs or opportunistic local politicians. But others were directly orchestrated by the nationalist parties, either through their own agents or through proxy forces.[224] For example, a Human Rights Watch report in 1996 found evidence that underground paramilitary organizations under the direct control by the SDS, and supported by the Ministry of Internal Affairs, local police, and RS military units, were leading operations to murder, kill, and expel minorities and eliminate their political opponents in Doboj and Tesli regions.[225] Similarly, in extensive riots against refugees in Drvar, off-duty Croat police loyal to the HDZ led the mobs and organized the violence to ensure that Serbs could not return to the region. Many of the tactics were coordinated: warnings against resettlements of minorities and encouragements to Croats to move to strategically valuable areas would be paired to regular patterns of intimidation and harassment, as well as arsons and other nonlethal attacks. The International Crisis Group concluded that the HDZ had an unofficial policy of organizing attacks on minorities and promoting strategic resettlement of Croat refugees into areas where it sought to consolidate its control.[226] Many of the apparently spontaneous attacks conducted by mobs of civilians were encouraged or endorsed by Serbian and Croatian nationalist parties, which recognized that a hostile environment would deter even more returnees. In the words of one SFOR commander, many of the attacks were mob led but "the seeds of hatred fell on fertile ground."[227] Even the SDS leadership in the RS—which regularly decried the occupation of NATO and threatened to secede and join Serbia—rarely openly used strategic violence, preferring instead to coordinate with paramilitary groups and clandestine actors to expel minorities from its territory. Partially dissatisfied with how the war ended, the Serbian and Croatian nationalist parties were trying to strike a balance between supporting efforts to block minority returns without jeopardizing the resources and patronage networks that they had built as a result of Dayton.

For its part, the SDA was broadly supportive of the Dayton Accords and largely supported the return of Bosniak refugees to Serbian and Croatian regions. But it conducted its own quiet campaigns of violence and intimidation against its political opponents to protect its gains in the post-conflict period. For example, former Bosnian prime minister Haris Silajdzic was hit over the head with an iron by SDA supporters in northwestern Bosnia.[228] There was also regular tension between the SDA and supporters of the Fikret Admic, who had concentrated power in Bihac and allied himself with the Bosnian Serbs during the war. The Bosnian Intelligence agency (AID) pursued and harassed the followers of Admic "by systematically arresting, beating and threatening those perceived to support him."[229] Senior AID officials were later arrested for having information on the deaths of Croatian refugees but also on the assassinations of Bosnian Muslim officials after the war.[230] Similar allegations were also made against the SDS and HDZ parties.[231]

Aside from occasional examples of rivalries turning violent, factional violence was not widespread in the post-conflict period. The absence of violence via the indirect pathway was not inevitable: the nationalist parties wished to renegotiate the multiethnic commitments of Dayton through carefully controlled strategic violence, but that policy provided no guarantee that they would be able to stop dissatisfied factions from within their ranks from going even further in their attacks and risking a renewed civil war. If they lost control over the factions within their own ranks, these factions could have fought among themselves and increased the levels of strategic violence. To avoid the emergence of factional violence, they would need to have the resources to engage in domestic rewards and ingroup policing with the factions—comprising military units, irregular militias, and criminal gangs—that fought on their sides during the war. As noted, the structure of the government, with its opportunities for participation and patronage, enabled them to engage in a program of domestic rewards to keep their factions on the sidelines. Yet other factors—including the original organizational endowments of the combatants as hierarchically organized militaries and the survival of their own military and police forces after Dayton—also helped the nationalist parties retain internal control and forestall the emergence of widespread factional violence. In many respects, the nature of the war affected the nature of the peace. Because the Bosnian civil war was fought by regular armies with substantial internal control, post-conflict Bosnia did not see the kind of vicious factional fighting present in other cases. Aided by high levels of internal control over the military and police and by vestigial loyalty among the demobilized soldiers, the nationalist parties were able to preserve moderate levels of internal control and buy off the factions within their ranks. This retention of internal control, produced in part by Dayton's provisions to leave the ethnic forces intact and in control of territory, allowed these parties to strike a fine line between challenging Dayton's commitment to multiethnicity and consolidating their gains under its terms.

Conclusion

One of the great ironies of the Dayton Peace Accords is that it produced a dysfunctional government and an illiberal peace, but at the same time it provided the means by which its principal signatories could control the means of violence. The nationalist victories in the early elections had the effect of reinforcing obstructionist behavior (especially by the SDS and HDZ) and producing an exclusionary, hypernationalist politics. This was always the danger, for even Richard Holbrooke acknowledged that the elections might be free and fair and nevertheless award power to the "racists, fascists, separatists, who are publicly opposed to [peace and reintegration]."[232] But the elections also invested these illiberal nationalist parties in the peace in post-Dayton Bosnia, curbed their dissatisfaction with Dayton, and gave them the incentives and opportunities through the multilayered Bosnian state to circumscribe the use of violence. As a result, strategic violence in post-conflict Bosnia was carefully controlled, as the SDS and HDZ coordinated and supported nonlethal attacks on minorities that would not jeopardize their gains in the Dayton Accords. As evidenced by the degree to which post-conflict violence operated along the ethnic fault lines of the war, the strategic violence reflected the direct pathway, although it was more a form of violent subversion through proxies than an attempt by the parties to destroy the state built by the Dayton Accords. This choreographed form of violence had serious consequences for the victims but never reached the level of brutality and political consequence evident in other post-conflict states. Against expectations, the strategic violence in post-conflict Bosnia did not fully reignite the war or spread across borders. As the following chapter on Rwanda will show, these devastating consequences can flow from the unfettered use of strategic violence via the direct pathway.

CHAPTER FIVE

Rwanda

The genocide in Rwanda from April to June 1994 is one of the most horrifying events of the late twentieth century. Over a period of one hundred days, approximately 800,000 people were killed by the Hutu ultranationalist regime, which seized power after President Juvenal Habyarimana was killed in a plane crash on 6 April 1994.[1] The victims were predominantly Tutsi civilians but also prominent opposition political figures and Hutu intellectuals and moderates, as well as the poor, disabled, and sick. The slaughter was deeply personal: neighbors killed neighbors in small villages and towns across the country, and many civilians stood by as their friends and neighbors were hunted and killed by Hutu militias and gangs of unemployed youth. To the outside world, the genocide in Rwanda appeared as a Hobbesian nightmare with thousands engaged in intercommunal violence that appeared to defy explanation.[2] The reality was very different: much of the killing was organized and precise, and although the genocide did mobilize thousands of Hutus, it was not a spontaneous outbreak of bloodletting.[3] As Gérard Prunier has argued, the genocide in Rwanda was a product of years of indoctrination, where the moral prohibition on killing had been overcome by the "the mental and emotional lubricant of ideology."[4] The increasingly authoritarian nature of the Rwandan state, political polarization, competition over land rights, and years of racial and cultural animosity combined to create an environment conducive to the Hutu-led genocide.[5]

Most scholarly accounts highlight how the breakdown in the implementation of the Arusha Accords—the peace process between the Habyarimana government and the Tutsi guerrilla group, the Rwandan Patriotic Front (RPF)—unleashed an almost unstoppable chain of events that produced the genocide.[6] This reading effectively treats the violence as an artifact of a peace process that was either mismanaged by international negotiators or pursued in bad faith by the parties. Yet these accounts overstate the extent to which international malfeasance created the conditions for the genocide. This was a local genocide, driven by ethnic tensions and extremist ideologies cultivated by political parties long before the event.[7] While Belgium, France, and the UN played a role in supporting the Hutu-led regime or prolonging the Arusha process, there had been a gradual escalation of internal violence by the Hutu extremists and Tutsi rebels for years before the genocide. Even the genocide itself was presaged by outbursts of intercommunal rioting and ethnic massacres in 1992 and 1993.[8] Rather than being a discontinuous event in Rwanda's history, the genocide should be seen in context as an extreme point in an increasingly desperate competition between Hutu and Tutsi hard-liners over the control of the Rwandan state. Moreover, that struggle did not end with the genocide. The capture of the Hutu stronghold Gisenyi by the RPF on 18 July 1994, brought an end to the genocide, but the RPF used strategic violence throughout the post-conflict period as a way of enforcing social control and solidifying its grip on power. In this hard post-conflict environment, the RPF and mobs of Tutsis would have been expected to exact harsh retribution on the remaining Hutus. But the RPF was not satisfied simply to control Rwanda, and within two years RPF forces moved across the border into Zaire to crush those who had caused the genocide. This intervention, and the ensuing panicked movements of the refugees under attack, had a cascade effect, accelerating the demise of the Mobutu regime, metastasizing the existing ethnic divisions in the Kivu provinces, and touching off a wider regional war for control of the Congo. In part because most of the outside world viewed Tutsis as victims in the genocide, key regional players such as the United States and France averted their eyes to the use of strategic violence by the RPF in post-conflict Rwanda. The result was an explosion of post-conflict strategic violence in Rwanda that produced almost unimaginable consequences for the wider region.

This chapter examines the nature of the violence in post-conflict Rwanda (1994–1999). Its goal is not to exonerate the Hutu genocidaires or to draw a false equivalence between what they did and what the RPF did in the post-conflict period. Nor will it be drawn into the so-called double genocide hypothesis, which held that both groups sought to exterminate the other, with nearly equal levels of violence.[9] The crimes committed by the Hutu regime operated on a scale and demonstrated a level of organization that far exceeded the response by the RPF; moreover, there is no evidence that RPF aimed to conduct an equivalent genocide or to kill a comparable number of Hutu refugees in the post-conflict period. But the mass-scale strategic violence conducted by the RPF is significant nonetheless because it demonstrates that the so-called winners of wars can be dissatisfied with the peace and continue killing well after their enemy is defeated. In this case, the RPF won an outright victory over the Hutu forces that led the genocide, but its leaders gradually expanded their wartime goals after surviving the genocide. They sought to annihilate the Hutu forces that produced the genocide, even if that meant expanding the war across the border into Zaire, and gradually enlarged their ambitions to building a sphere of influence in Central Africa. What began as a counterinsurgency campaign became a regional conflict, as the RPF regime entangled its desires for revenge against the Hutu forces that led the genocide and for protection against Hutu cross-border attacks with its hope to become the key geopolitical player in the region. Seen from this light, the RPF was not satisfied with the terms of the peace settlement, even though it was an outright victory that left it in control of Rwanda, and eventually deployed its forces in a clandestine way across borders for new, more expansive goals than it ended the war with. At the same time, the RPF did not unravel in the post-conflict period and maintained its high levels of internal control in the post-conflict period. As a consequence, factional violence was rare. Consistent with the predictions of the theory presented in chapter 3, this conjunction of dissatisfaction with the terms of the settlement and high levels of internal control produced strategic violence through the direct pathway in Rwanda. As predicted, the types and targets of strategic attacks operated along the same ethnic fault lines in the post-genocide period, although the victims had now become the perpetrators of the killings and expulsions.[10]

This chapter is organized into five sections: (1) a history of the post-conflict period, with particular attention to how the opportunity structure was highly conducive to strategic violence and to the increasing levels of dissatisfaction within the RPF over the terms of its victory; (2) an organizational analysis of the RPF throughout this period, demonstrating its high level of internal control over its members and its ability to employ violence discriminately; (3) a presentation of newly collected data on strategic violence from newspaper sources during this period; (4) an assessment of the degree of responsibility born by the RPF for violence during this period; and (5) an explanation of how the RPF extended its use of violence via the direct pathway to broaden its war aims by invading and dismembering Zaire (and later the Democratic Republic of the Congo).

Post-Conflict Rwanda (1994–1999)

The country that the RPF controlled following the genocide was chaotic and traumatized. The evidence of the genocide was everywhere, with bodies strewn about in towns and villages and survivors still in shock. The surviving Tutsi population was scattered, with many living in the bush or hiding with family or friends to escape the remaining Hutu gangs that still roamed the country. Many of these survivors—called *bapfuye buhagazi* (translated as the "walking dead")—roamed the country and were viewed suspiciously as potential collaborators by the Tutsi refugees who flooded back into the country.[11] In many respects, Rwanda was an even more broken postconflict state than Bosnia. Approximately 150,000 homes had been destroyed, and nearly 300,000 children were without parents.[12] Throughout the country, social and economic life was almost entirely disrupted. Much of the country's infrastructure was destroyed, and normal commerce had come to a halt.[13] The former regime had taken almost everything in the treasury, including gold from the national bank.[14] The country had only a few underfunded and underequipped medical facilities, many of which were overwhelmed with patients. The judicial system was not functioning, and its few remaining agents were overwhelmed with the scale of the task in front of them, especially given that as many as half a million Hutu—roughly 10 percent of the population—had taken part in the genocide.[15] By early 1998, 135,000 Hutus languished in jail awaiting trial for crimes in the genocide.[16] Moreover, roughly half of the population of Rwanda had been uprooted. Between the genocide and the population movements produced in fear of the RPF reprisals, nearly 1.7 million people had fled the country and nearly 1.3 million were internally displaced.[17] The refugees dispersed into multiple countries, including Zaire (especially in the Goma and Bukavu regions), Tanzania, and Burundi. Many of the refugees were Hutu civilians who fled in advance of RPF troop movements to escape the attacks, but a significant number of the remaining army of the Hutu regime, the Forces Armées Rwandaises (FAR), and Interahamwe blended in amid the civilians and escaped into the refugee camps outside the country.

All of these conditions would have been ideal for strategic violence, yet three specific features of the opportunity structure rendered this case especially likely to have a large number of attacks. First, there was a high level of vulnerability for the civilian population on both sides. While the genocide had produced some ethnic unmixing of the population similar to Bosnia, it did not have the same effect of leaving fully homogeneous pockets of territory in control of one ethnic group. In part because of the high population density in Rwanda, the Hutu and Tutsi populations remained in close proximity to each other and were still intermixed in small towns and villages. Especially as refugees returned, each was vulnerable to attack by the other group. The Hutus, for example, often fled reprisals from Tutsi civilians and the RPF. Second, Rwanda remained an extremely polarized environment, and the RPF-led transitional government was neither resource rich nor open and flexible for new claimants to power. The surviving Hutu population knew that the consequence of losing the war was an RPF government that was likely to at least exclude it from political power and to form a rigid, Tutsi-controlled government with only token participation by Hutus. The Hutu population, composing most of the population, faced an indefinite future being governed by a hostile minority group that would exclude it from key positions in government.[18] Third, when the French-led Operation Turquoise departed in August 1994, no peacekeeping international mission was present in Rwanda. The absence of peacekeeping forces and the fact that many local police were implicated in the genocide meant that there were few deterrents during the breakdown of law and order after the FAR defeat, and a climate of impunity for killings prevailed. All of these features of the opportunity structure made Rwanda an almost ideal environment for the use of strategic violence.

The initial transitional government established by the RPF in July 1994 followed the broad outlines of the Arusha Accords, though it outlawed those Hutu parties (such as MRND and CDR) that were behind the genocide.[19] By initial appearances, the government was more democratic and sympathetic to the political demands of Hutus than many initially suspected. Existing opposition parties (Hutu, Tutsi, and non-ethnic) were permitted to operate, and a prominent Hutu, Faustin Twagiramungu, was appointed prime minister. Opposition parties, including some small Hutu-led parties, were permitted in the unity government (dubbed the Broad Based Government of National Unity) and were given seats in the Transitional National Assembly. But some significant changes to the Arusha framework immediately suggested that the RPF was not willing to cede power in the new Rwanda. Ministerial positions in the government reserved for the MRND were allocated to the RPF, thus giving it effective control over some of the most important functions of government. The RPF assumed control of the presidency and appointed Pasteur Bizimungu as president. The RPF also named General Paul Kagame, military commander of the RPF, as vice president.[20] These subtle changes were designed to consolidate the RPF's control over the rebuilding process and were broadly supported by international donors, many of whom felt guilty over abandoning Rwanda during the genocide.

One of the immediate problems faced by the new RPF regime was the explosion of revenge killings against Hutus remaining in the country. The exact numbers of people killed were impossible to obtain, and estimates varied significantly from 5,000 or 10,000 to as high as 100,000.[21] Kagame and the RPF leadership officially condemned revenge killings and called for national reconciliation, but it remained unclear how much control they exercised over the newer RPF recruits in the immediate aftermath of the genocide. Some RPF officials have later admitted that there was a "certain tolerance" for these attacks.[22] Trials of military officers who had committed revenge killings did occur, but these trials were typically conducted only when the motive of the killing was instrumental (i.e., seizing a victim's land or property).[23] The revenge killings were difficult to trace back to the RPF leadership in part because so many new Tutsi volunteers had joined the ranks of the RPF at the end of the genocide that telling who was, and was not, taking orders from its leaders when engaged in revenge killing was difficult. Moreover, the genocide had created a social environment conducive to killing, which itself produced waves of opportunistic violence in the post-conflict period. Amid these high levels of expressive and opportunistic violence were allegations of direct involvement by the RPF in revenge killings, as well as evidence that the RPF endorsed or sponsored revenge killings during this period, though this was denied by the RPF leadership during this period.

The primary security concern of the new government was the refugee camps in Zaire. Although the RPF had won control over Rwanda, its Hutu foes had escaped and still posed a threat. By August 1994, the surviving elements of the FAR and Interahamwe had moved into the camps across the border in Zaire and begun to reorganize. By some estimates, nearly twenty thousand to fifty thousand ex-FAR units and between ten thousand and fifty thousand Interahamwe members escaped into the camps in Zaire.[24] The remnants of the Hutu power regime were now slow in remobilizing and even managed to get its radio stations—with the same broadcasts that advanced the genocide—operating by August 1994. The MRND political leadership renamed itself the Rally for the Return of Refugees and Democracy to Rwanda (RDR), a political party that officially called for a comprehensive solution to the conflict in the Great Lakes and the repatriation of the refugees.[25] A second, more extremist organization of former FAR units, Interahamwe, and new recruits also formed, calling itself the Army for the Liberation of Rwanda (ALIR). The ALIR began to exercise tight control over the refugee camps, using them as a base of recruits, resource and tax extraction, and protection. A former CDR official remarked that "even if the RPF has won a military victory it will not have the power. It has only the bullets and we have the population."[26] Among the most important tools of social control was propaganda, as ex-FAR forces would terrorize Hutu civilians in the camps, convincing them that they would be slaughtered if they returned to Rwanda.[27] These organizations also funneled weapons through Zaire to rearm and begin limited incursions into Rwanda. The UNHCR was aware that genocidaires were in the camps but was reluctant to identify and remove them, in part because of the fear these surviving elements would begin to target humanitarian workers in the camps.[28] The ex-FAR units began by stealing cattle and engaging in petty banditry but by mid-1995 moved toward direct engagement of RPA units.

As the Rwandan government began to consolidate, the UNAMIR mandate was expanded in May 1994 to include the protection of refugees and survivors, the provision of humanitarian aid, and national reconciliation. UNAMIR officers were also asked to support the newly created International Criminal Tribunal for Rwanda (ICTR) as it began to prosecute those involved with the genocide.[29] Yet the Rwandan government was skeptical of the value of the UNAMIR after experiencing its passivity during the genocide. From its vantage point, the offer of $600 million in bilateral and multilateral reconstruction aid in January 1995 was more important than justice.[30] The RPF-led government also benefited from the creation of a "Friends of New Rwanda" collection of countries, including the United States, United Kingdom, and the Netherlands. Reyntjens has argued that "these countries are not burdened by much knowledge of Rwanda or the region, and driven by an acute guilt syndrome after the genocide, they reasoned in terms of 'good guys' and 'bad guys,' the RPF naturally being the 'good guys.'"[31] The Kigali government was particularly irritated by calls to broaden its basis of support to include Hutus from the diaspora within Zaire and elsewhere, noting that most of the Hutu moderates had been killed in the genocide.[32] The RPF government was also enraged by the inability of the UNHCR to prevent cross-border incursions and control the growth of Hutu militias in the camps. The RPF particularly blamed the UNHCR and NGOs that supported refugees for providing a safe haven and legal sanctuary for the genocidaires, who continually attacked Rwanda.[33] The dynamic of international involvement with the new Rwandan government was paradoxical: as international organizations, NGOs, and states became more invested in Rwanda's fate in a way that they had failed to do during the genocide, the Rwandan government became more disenchanted with their advice and less willing to take their demands seriously.

In 1995, the RPF government was growing increasingly anxious about security threats emanating from the refugee camps and began operations to clear out the IDP camps in the southern part of the country. The IDP camps were reduced from 600,000 to 160,000 by April 1995 through a combination of forced repatriation and intimidation.[34] Among the most notorious incidents during this time was the RPF's destruction of the Kibeho camp near the border of Tanzania, which involved the massacre of between 2,000 and 4,000 people under the eyes of UNAMIR troops.[35] After the massacre, the RPF denied that the victims had fled out of terror but instead insisted that they were "unwilling to face the reality of the genocide."[36] By late September 1996, amid escalating attacks by the ex-FAR, the Rwandan government signaled to its international partners that it was determined to destroy the refugee camps in Zaire that had been incubating the threat from Hutu power extremists.[37] Using the pretense of a rebellion by the Banyamulenge (a small Tutsi group of Rwandan origin that had been in Zaire for one hundred years) and oppression by the Mobutu's government, the RPF launched an assault on Zaire in October 1996 in an attempt to clear the camps of the genocidaires and former FAR elements in South Kivu.[38] Here Rwanda was playing a complex game: supporting a rebel movement protesting mistreatment of ethnic groups in Zaire but also seeking to destroy those elements in the former Hutu regime that had participated in the genocide. It also claimed that many of the refugees had been held against their will in Zaire by former members of the FAR and would be glad to come home to Rwanda. Large numbers of refugees did return to Rwanda, but the cumulative effect of this invasion was also to scatter the refugees in multiple directions, including deeper into Zaire. The RPF tried to force many of them back toward Rwanda where they would be repatriated (and better controlled than they were in Zaire). Hundreds of thousands of refugees still remained in Zaire by early 1997, but most were deprived of the humanitarian aid and social structure provided by the refugee camps. They were repeatedly attacked and harassed by advancing RPF forces and pushed deeper into Zaire, where thousands disappeared or were killed. One estimate by Médecin sans Frontières (MSF) held that at least thirteen thousand refugees had been killed in the RPF invasion.[39]

One of the ironies of this invasion was that although it was portrayed as a decisive end to the security threat emanating from the camps, it was anything but. Although the camps were cleared of some of the Hutu forces, the invasion accelerated the collapse of the Mobutu regime in Zaire and set the stage for a wider regional conflict. There is evidence that this was in part Rwanda's goal, as it supported a local Congolese rebel group, the Alliance of Democratic Forces for the Liberation of Congo-Zaire (AFDL), led by Laurent Désiré Kabila, in its efforts to overthrow the Mobutu regime. In an interview with the *Washington Post* in July 1997, Kagame admitted that the RPF regime had been training for three years for this operation and took advantage of the Banyamulenge rebellion to destroy the camps and topple the Mobutu regime.[40] Under Kagame's orders, the RPF dispatched weapons and agents across the border with instructions to local Congolese forces to prepare for war. Kagame acknowledged that Rwanda's actions in Zaire precipitated the regional crisis, saying that "there are not many people who thought that Mobutu was very weak. They thought of Mobutu as a big monster who wouldn't be defeated, with his big hat and his big stick. They thought little Rwanda and big Zaire. . . . Only when we started did they look at the map and see the possibilities."[41] With the support of Rwanda, Burundi, and Uganda, the AFDL—with substantial elements of the RPF fighting within its ranks—was successful in overthrowing the decrepit Mobutu regime by May 1997 but only at the cost of its own legitimacy. Kabila captured Kinshasa, and the country was renamed the Democratic Republic of the Congo (DRC). But the AFDL was soon criticized internally as a puppet of its foreign masters and as a representative of minority Tutsi interests in the Congo. The legitimacy of the AFDL was not helped by the boasts by the RPF general secretary Denis Polisi that Rwanda had become the "master player" in the Great Lakes region.[42]

The RPF invasion of the Zaire/DRC also had a blowback effect within Rwanda itself and made an already hard post-conflict environment even worse. Throughout 1996, Rwanda had experienced an escalation of human rights abuses, particularly extrajudicial killings of alleged genocidaires and opposition figures. The RPF's decision to reimport the refugees into the country enhanced the strength of the Hutu insurgency against its rule. The counterinsurgency efforts by the Rwandan Patriotic Army (RPA, the new name for the RPF military once it became an official state-run military) killed an estimated six thousand people, including many civilians, in the northwest of the country.[43] Particularly in Ruhengeri and Gisenyi regions, the RPF cordoned off areas of the country and conducted search and destroy missions against former FAR elements, who responded by slaughtering unarmed civilians. The violence escalated in the second half of the 1997, with an estimated ten thousand people killed between October 1997 and January 1998. As Reyntjens pointed out, the civilians "faced a murderous dilemma: if suspected of assisting the rebels, they were killed by the RPA; if they refused to collaborate with them, they became their target."[44] This dilemma was made even more stark because the RPF assumed collective responsibility for civilians in ALIR or insurgent-controlled zones, saying that "if civilians had been killed, they were accomplices, persons who sympathized with these armed men."[45]

On the domestic front, the Rwandan government began to shed some of the power-sharing principles of the Arusha Accords during 1996–1997 and become more authoritarian. By late 1995, most of the prominent Hutus in the cabinet had resigned and alleged that the RPF leadership was the real power behind a superficial coalition government and was using threats, intimidation, and abuse of power to silence dissent.[46] This was particularly important because Hutu represented roughly 84 percent of the population, while Tutsi represented only 15 percent of the country, making the new government effectively a minority regime.[47] This population balance was crucial for the RPF, which knew that it could not win a free and fair election if the Hutu populated voted along ethnic lines. While Hutus remained within the Rwandan government, there was a gradual process by which Tutsis—and in particular RPF loyalists—assumed a greater share of the key positions in government. As a result, the democratic development of Rwanda also began to resemble a kind of managed semi-democracy, where one party—the RPF—monopolizes the key positions, controls the political process, and permits only token participation by opposition parties.[48] A calculation by Reyntjens found that by 2000 "out of a total of 169 of the most important office holders 135 (or about 80%) were RPF/RPA and 119 (or about 70%) were Tutsi."[49] Similarly, 80 percent of the mayors and university staff were Tutsis, which reinforced the perception—despite RPF protestations to the contrary—that the RPF-led government was ethnic in nature, allowing a Tutsi minority to rule over a Hutu majority. In this respect, the RPF tried to bolster its already high levels of internal control by doling out patronage appointments (e.g., domestic reward), which helped it control its internal factions and send a warning to those Tutsis and Hutus who dared to challenge its hold on power.

More defections from the RPF's ranks followed in 2000–2001, including some prominent RPF leaders and Tutsi genocide survivors, many of whom felt discriminated against by the RPF leadership. As Helen Hintjens has argued, a political gap emerged between the Tutsi survivors of the genocide and the RPF leadership, many of whom spent much of the war in exile in Uganda and elsewhere. The assertion of control by the RPF is infused with what Robin Cohen has termed "diasporic nationalism," in which a core of diaspora elites—here the RPF leadership that emerged in Uganda—uses its victimization as a recurring myth, to monopolize social and political discourse and silence dissent, even among the victims of the event it commemorated.[50] Part of this myth that the RPF tried to perpetuate was a denial of ethnicity as a motivating factor in the violence. The RPF's founding myth was that ethnic divisions were created after colonization as a way of sowing division among Rwandans and that these ethnic divisions were neither real nor important for contemporary Rwandan politics. The RPF even banned the terms Hutu, Tutsi, and Twa from official discourse after 1995. Such an enforced silence had some advantages: it masked what was essentially a Tutsi-led stranglehold on the state and proscribed the kind of ethnic language that would be needed to point that out. The RPF further silenced dissent by describing its opponents as preaching "divisionism," when they critiqued either the role of the RPF or the dominance of the Tutsi in Rwanda's social and political life. The effect was that by late 1996 Rwanda became politically claustrophobic, with activists, media figures, and civil society leaders reporting harassment and intimidation by authorities and fleeing in greater numbers. By the end of 1997, an estimated one hundred people—often critics of the RPF regime—"disappeared" from Kigali each month.[51] This was culminated with an extension in 1999 of the so-called transition period that effectively left the RPF in control of the state until 2003.[52]

As the RPF consolidated its semiauthoritarian control over the Rwandan government, it faced new problems with the DRC. The RPF was successful in putting down much of the domestic insurgency in the northwest, leading to a modest improvement in the human rights record of the country in 1999–2000, but the operation in the former Zaire was spinning out of control. The RPF had formally ended its operation in the Congo in September 1997, but in reality its forces continued to patrol North and South Kivu in the Congo.[53] The Rwandan government struck a cooperative agreement with the AFDL, now in charge of the government in Kinshasa, and made plans for joint operations against the remaining Interahamwe forces. But the closeness between the AFDL and Rwanda and Uganda created problems for Kabila, who increasingly looked like a puppet of his foreign backers. In July 1998, Kabila ordered all foreign forces (including Rwanda) to leave the DRC. Threatened with losing its hard-won sphere of influence in the DRC, the RPF threw its support behind another rebel group, entitled the Rassemblement Congolais pour la Démocratie (RCD), to challenge Kabila.[54] Another RPF-backed rebellion emerged in Kivu, Goma, and other eastern regions and RPF forces backed the RCD rebels as they pushed toward Kinshasa. However, several African states, including Angola and Zimbabwe, intervened to back Kabila and repel the invasion. The war in the Congo became a pickup game, as Chad, Libya, and Sudan also entered the conflict. In part because of its strong Tutsi nationalist agenda and desire for regional dominance, Rwanda experienced some important alliance realignments, as it began to feud with its traditional ally Uganda and sections of the Banyamulenge. Even its own rebel army, the RCD fractured into two competing armies, RCD-ML and RCD-Goma, with Rwanda allied mainly to the latter. The UN tried to enforce a cease fire and deployed a twenty-thousand-strong peacekeeping force (dubbed MONUC) in late 2000, but to no avail.[55] But the war—described by U.S. assistant secretary of state Susan Rice as Africa's "first world war"—would rage on for nearly a decade, producing 5.4 million dead by the end of the decade.[56]

The RPF in Post-Genocide Rwanda

How did the RPF—a guerrilla force representing the minority of a relatively small and poor country—manage to expand its reach into Zaire given the condition of Rwanda after the genocide ended? While most rebel groups fracture and squabble over the spoils of war, the RPF consolidated its domestic political position, pursued its enemies ruthlessly, and expanded its influence through proxy forces into the DRC. Much of the explanation for the RPF's track record in post-conflict Rwanda is due to its original organizational endowment. Unlike some other African guerrilla groups, the RPF was not a loose coalition of factions, but rather a well-equipped, highly organized military machine with substantial battle experience. As a result, it exercised a high level of internal control over its members. While other guerrilla organizations featured multiple contenders for its leadership position, the RPF had a stable cadre of political leaders, led by the charismatic Paul Kagame, which held a tight grip on power and used a combination of rewards and threats to prevent alternative power centers from emerging within its ranks. As a rebel group fighting for national liberation, the RPF is an unusual outlier in terms of its unity of purpose, its organizational cohesion, and its ability to prevent dissidents from forming alternative power centers within its ranks.

The origin of the RPF lies in the emergence of a refugee rights organization for those displaced during the upheaval in the Mouvement Démocratique Republicain Parmehutu (MDR-Parmehutu) rebellion and the subsequent reprisals by Hutu forces. Between 1959 and 1964, after the MDR forces seized control of the country, between fifty thousand and seventy thousand Tutsi fled Rwanda for Uganda.[57] The Tutsi refugee flow continued into Rwanda for a few years, which dropped the total number of Tutsi in Rwanda itself to only 9 percent.[58] These refugees were discriminated against within Uganda, as they were denied citizenship and economic opportunities under the rule of Idi Amin. By 1979 these refugees formed an organization, the Rwandese Alliance for National Unity (RANU) in Kampala. This organization was relatively small, numbering only approximately one hundred members, but it was dedicated to the eventual return of the refugees to Rwanda.[59] The strategy employed by RANU was two tiered, with a series of autonomous cultural and social organizations that championed the cause of the refugees as a front and an underground, clandestine structure devoted to furthering the political ambitions of the Rwandan refugees.[60] The actual content of these ambitions remained murky in part because of the ambivalence of its members over whether to pursue rights for Rwandan Tutsi refugees in Uganda or to push for a return to Rwanda. Officially, RANU adopted a Marxist-themed ideology that called for the abolition of the monarchy and the creation of a socialist state in Rwanda, though it had few plans to make this goal a reality.[61] But RANU functioned effectively as a front movement for the cause of Rwandan Tutsi exiles and those within their ranks who would soon become enmeshed into Uganda's politics.

In 1971 Idi Amin launched a coup d'etat in Uganda and overthrew his former ally, President Milton Obote. Desperate to consolidate his rule, Amin was willing to support any faction that would defend his rule against rebel invasions, including the normally marginalized Rwandan Tutsi refugees.[62] A few Tutsi refugees supported Amin's regime by taking posts in the army and police. But a much greater number of Rwandan Tutsi would pay a bitter price for the decision of these few when Tanzania, with the support of rebel forces led by Obote and Yoweri Museveni, invaded to overthrow Amin's government in 1979.[63] After Amin was overthrown, dozens of Tutsi civilians were attacked in reprisal for the decision of the few Tutsis to back Amin. By 1980, Obote and Museveni's alliance had fallen apart and Museveni retreated to the bush to lead his National Resistance Army (NRA) in an effort to overthrow the new Obote regime. Obote attacked the Rwandan Tutsi refugees for their support of Amin and for being in league with the NRA, and accused them of being cousins of the Banyankole, Museveni's ethnic group.[64] The Ugandan government began to seize their land and cattle and dismiss them from government service, leaving the stateless Rwandan Tutsi with few advocates other than RANU.[65] By 1982–1983, the Ugandan regime had undertaken dozens of attacks against Tutsi refugees and displaced between twenty thousand and forty thousand refugees.[66]

These attacks transformed the nature of the RANU movement in profound ways. By the mid-1980s, RANU began to take steps to reorganize its structure, consolidate its ranks, and broaden its basis of political support. It developed a wide range of international contacts with other African rebel groups and with Eastern bloc countries.[67] At this point, RANU began to move away from its Marxist ideology. The RANU Congress adopted a series of more nationalist policies that stressed the unity of the people, the need for a return of the refugees, and the desire for a return to the rule of law. RANU decentralized its leadership structure in its engagement with its diaspora, allowing its regional chairman to take the initiative for fundraising while remaining responsible to the new RPF centralized leadership structure.[68] By 1986, it had fully transformed itself from a refugee return movement into the semiofficial representative body for the Rwandan Tutsi refugee community and a voice for Rwandan

Tutsi interests in the NRA. It renamed itself the Rwandan Patriotic Front (RPF) in 1987.

While the RPF reorganized and became more coherent, it also increasingly became the front organization for the Rwandan Tutsis who had joined the NRA's insurgency against the Obote regime. With the tacit support of RANU's leadership, some Tutsi refugees began to join the NRA's ranks and fight to overthrow the Obote regime. Among the first Rwandan Tutsi recruits were Fred Rwigyema and Paul Kagame, both of whom had spent much of their lives in exile in Uganda.[69] Hostility toward Tutsi refugees within Uganda drove many young men towards the NRA. By the time of the final assault on Kampala in January 1986, three thousand of fourteen thousand soldiers of the NRA were Rwandan Tutsis.[70] The overthrow of Obote had a dramatic effect on the ranks of the NRA, which drew confidence from its success against a vastly more powerful government. One RPF commander remarked that "if the NRA could liberate Uganda, the RPF began to ask why it could not do the same in Rwanda."[71]

Once Museveni had assumed power in Uganda, the number of Rwandan Tutsi refugees in the army increased to fourteen thousand soldiers, with a significant number (including Kagame) in the officer corps.[72] While the attention of the RPF's leaders now turned back to Rwanda, they were prevented by Museveni from openly organizing for invasion.[73] Instead, the RPF-affiliated soldiers within the NRA began acting as an army within an army, strengthening their ties with their Rwandan kinsmen in the ranks and making plans for an invasion of Rwanda. This clandestine effort contributed to the overall organizational coherence of the NRA. Fearing infiltration of the NRA by Rwandan government spies, the RPF leadership established a small, secret cell to plan how the invasion would take place. The plans, developed over a three-year period, would require the rank and file members of the RPF to desert their posts in the Ugandan army upon receipt of an order from the leadership.[74] A parallel command structure within the NRA was established, and most members of the RPF knew only a few other members to prevent word of the plans from leaking.[75] They were so successful at this effort that "members of the NRA recall awakening on the morning of 1 October, only to find that large numbers of their ranks, most of whom they thought were Ugandans, had seemingly vanished overnight."[76] The RPF expected one thousand deserting troops to join the invasion force in 1990, but had four thousand with an additional five thousand volunteers appearing along the way. This core force of well-trained and experienced fighters was commanded by RPF officers, such as Kagame and Rwigyema. Although critics have suggested the Museveni must have known about the invasion of Rwanda before it happened, the evidence suggests that he was taken by surprise, particularly by its speed.[77]

The initial RPF invasion of Rwanda was a disaster, as the RPF forces were turned back by FAR forces after a few quick battles and retreated back into Uganda to regroup. Rwigyema and other senior Tutsi commanders were killed in this raid, leaving Kagame as the chief leader of the organization.[78] However, even during this period in the wilderness, the RPF was not a loose, weak, or disorganized force. The RPF had prepared for a protracted struggle; it had stored food and even planted crops in neighboring countries for an extended period of resupplying.[79] Visitors to the RPF's camps found that the RPF had a comparatively well-educated force, with trained professionals, including doctors, engineers, and lawyers, in its ranks.[80] It operated a radio station and an organized process for repairing vehicles and weapons.[81] The RPF managed to translate its resources—including both troops and funds of nearly $1 million a year from the diaspora—into strategic advantages as it became a trained and experienced force.[82] Unlike many other comparable organizations, the RPF did not have substantial problems with freelancing in violence by its members, as the leadership exercised firm discipline over the rank and file throughout this period. Because of high levels of internal control, disputes over leadership were also nonexistent, as Kagame was acknowledged widely as the leader of the organization by the end of 1990. In the build-up to the war itself, the RPF carefully executed a two-tiered strategy where it negotiated with the Habyarimana regime but also prepared for war. It increased the number of covert operational cells operating throughout the country from 36 in 1990 to 146 by the time that the invasion began in March–April 1994.[83] On the eve of the invasion, U.S. intelligence officials estimated that the RPF had 13,000 troops, including 4,500 in Kigali, and sophisticated weapons such as air defense guns, mortars, and SA-7 man-portable missiles.[84] In part because of its organization and persistence, the RPF had become the first Rwandan exile movement to be recognized by the Habyarimana regime.[85]

Even as the invasion and genocide produced new pressures on the organization, its levels of internal control did not diminish. At the onset of the genocide, a secret U.S intelligence assessment suggested that the RPF had "better command" than the government forces.[86] Amid the mass killing of fellow Tutsis, the RPF did not lose sight of its objectives and advanced into the country to seize strategically valuable territory.[87] It organized a complex military strategy that involved sweeping from RPF-held territories in the north to surround the capital, while its battalion based in Kigali would distract the FAR.[88] As the war dragged on, there was some evidence of indiscipline in the RPF ranks, as RPF members killed Hutus that they blamed for the genocide, but the RPF leadership attributed this to the new recruits who joined as the genocide happened rather than to its core force. Through the capture of Kigali, the RPF managed to remain a coherent fighting force, with significant levels of internal control, even as thousands of its fellow Tutsis were massacred around it.[89]

In the post-conflict period, the RPF managed to translate its high levels of internal control in military operations into political discipline through the exercise of mechanisms of domestic reward and ingroup policing. Despite initially establishing a broad-based government with seats held for moderate Hutus and political opponents, the RPF never conceded the key levers of power and reserved for itself the key positions of state. Most of the key decisions were made by Kagame and his allies in the cabinet, while token offices with little power were left for the RPF's rivals, thus preserving the patina of a broad-based government. Internal decisions within the RPF were conducted by a "Council of Colonels," largely composed of Tutsi who had served in Uganda; in military affairs, the judgment of senior officers held considerable sway.[90] As René Lemarchand has argued, Rwanda is now a "thinly veiled military ethnocracy" in which decisions are taken by the Tutsi elite, not by the nominal political establishment.[91] Under the control of the RPF, the Rwandan state "reasserted itself vigorously" as the government established courts, reestablished internal administration structures, and collected tax revenue.[92] While elections were permitted, the RPF controlled the National Electoral Commission and used its political influence to back candidates in the elections.[93] As more dissenters left the Rwandan government and even the RPF, the leadership circle narrowed to Kagame and his close associates, which allowed them to exercise even more control over the levers of power in the state. The result was that the RPF military and political structures, which were always closely linked, became nearly inseparable, as Kagame appointed all of his key allies to important positions in the government, which effectively produced a concentration of Ugandan refugees at the center of government. As Wm. Cyrus Reed has pointed out:

> While the RPF maintained virtually no civilian administrative structures, nearly all of the skilled manpower now available in Rwanda has come from the exiled community which gave birth to the movement. By fusing its military and political wings, the RPF successfully avoided the internal fissures which plagued similar organizations elsewhere in Africa. By developing a clear political line within the military, the RPF was able to sustain morale, and to impose strict internal discipline. Thus, separating the military and the state from the party has proved to be difficult at best.[94]

The stranglehold that the RPF had on the government of Rwanda was also a result of the substantial internal security and intelligence apparatus that was run by RPF loyalists. The value of good intelligence was never underestimated by Kagame, who had served as acting head of military intelligence in the NRA before the invasion.[95] Under the direction of the RPF, Rwanda became "an emerging police state," as press and civil society organizations were monitored and harassed, and as movements, particularly of dissidents, were watched by internal security forces.[96] Unlike many other comparable groups, which struggle to reward and police their internal factions in the post-conflict, the RPF exercised an almost stifling level of control on those in its ranks and those who might challenge it. As a result, there was little if any factional violence within the RPF, although its leaders were ruthless in repressing those who left the organization or who dared to challenge it from the outside.

The high levels of internal control exercised by the RPF have been advanced by two additional factors distinct from its organizational endowments as a highly disciplined guerrilla force. First, the RPF has insisted that it is not an ethnic force but rather represents all Rwandans, including Hutus. While this claim is manifestly untrue in practice, it is politically useful to deny the role of ethnicity in politics, for doing so obscures the gradual Tutsification of the state and the RPF's control over key offices.[97] Accusations that the RPF is constructing an ethnically based authoritarian regime are met with accusations that the critic is preaching "divisionism" and insinuations that the critic is in league with Hutu extremists. Second, the RPF has consistently employed the threat of armed conflict to justify a perpetual state of emergency in Rwanda and provide a rationale for its control. Guerrilla assaults from the ex-FAR units are seen as proof that the crisis in Rwanda has not passed, so normal politics—which would inevitably involve multiparty elections that the RPF may not win—cannot start again. Moreover, the war in the Congo, for which the RPF is partially responsible, has also been deployed as a way to bolster the RPF's power. As the Rwandan government forces pushed deeper into the former Congo, they encountered stiff resistance from local Hutu militias and their backers, which deepened their sense of crisis and produced a continuing rationale for the RPF's tight control over the party, the government, and the society at large.

Violence in Rwanda (1994–1999)

The question of the RPF's control over its ranks is central to the evaluation of the violence that occurred in the post-conflict period. The official explanation of the Rwandan Government is that the violence was due to revenge killings by Tutsi returnees and new RPF recruits but that there was no systematic use of strategic violence by the RPF in post-conflict Rwanda. In other words, the violence was a result of a few "bad apples," of freelancing individuals, or rogue RPF units, but it did not represent official RPF policy. Given the strong history of organizational cohesion of the RPF and its capacity to exercise internal control, such arguments must be treated with skepticism. Critics have alleged that the strategic violence was much more widespread and systematic than was acknowledged at the time, and that the RPF used the cover provided by these expressive attacks to pursue its political enemies and to collectively punish Hutus whom it blamed for the genocide. What makes this case particularly complicated is that the strategic violence was embedded in genuine waves of expressive violence (such as revenge killings), criminal attacks, and opportunistic violence after the war. Parsing out the strategic attacks amid scattered Hutu resistance, as well as dozens of revenge killings, atrocities against Hutu refugees, and criminal and opportunistic violence occurring throughout the country, is a difficult task. Even the post-genocide arrests were distorted by this opportunistic violence, as "hapless hangers-on, victims of property quarrels, cuckolded husbands and common criminals" were denounced and thrown in jail for involvement in the genocide.[98] Moreover, at least some of the strategic violence evident in this case was transactional, as the RPF (now renamed the Rwandan Patriotic Army) responded to Hutu guerrilla attacks with counterattacks and reprisals. Post-conflict Rwanda hosted a complex web of violent interactions, with strategic violence being used in at least two directions against domestic enemies and Hutu irredentist forces in Zaire.

How many Hutus were killed in the immediate aftermath of the genocide is not known, but estimates have ranged from 10,000 to 100,000 people killed.[99] Other estimates have put the total around 30,000, but most believe that even this represents a fraction of the real violence. No official crime statistics from the Rwandan government or the UNAMIR mission have ever been released. Violence was so underreported in part because of what Prunier calls "corpse confusion," where the bodies of genocide victims and those killed in the post-conflict period were thrown together in pits and sometimes burned.[100] There was also some evidence that the RPF coordinated a corpse disposal process in order not to attract attention.[101] Such practices made detailed forensic work on the murders discovered in the post-conflict period particularly difficult as it was often hard to tell when a victim was killed, by whom, and whether the victim was Hutu or Tutsi. Moreover, the RPF often closed off regions that featured current military operations to independent experts and journalists, which meant that it was difficult or impossible to fathom who was responsible for killings in those regions.[102]

In the absence of official crime statistics, it is difficult to assess how much of the violence is attributable to the RPF, to Hutu militias, or to other actors operating in Rwandan society. In lieu of official statistics, figure 5.1 collects data on deaths from strategic violence from newspaper sources from 1994 to 1999. As noted in chapter 3, the "hard" post-conflict period in Rwanda officially lasted only one year (1995), before it lapsed back into armed conflict. In this chapter, data are presented for 1994–1999, though this time period certainly captures some of the violence from the border wars and counterinsurgency campaign against the FAR. This case illustrates the difficulty of drawing a line between post-conflict violence and the violence that occurs within a war. Most of the violent attacks recorded here are within Rwanda itself, though some attacks that spilled across the border into Zaire, Uganda and Burundi are included if they have a clear link to the Rwandan conflict. Attacks are reported as strategic if there is a concerted effort to change the balance of power and resources in their ex-

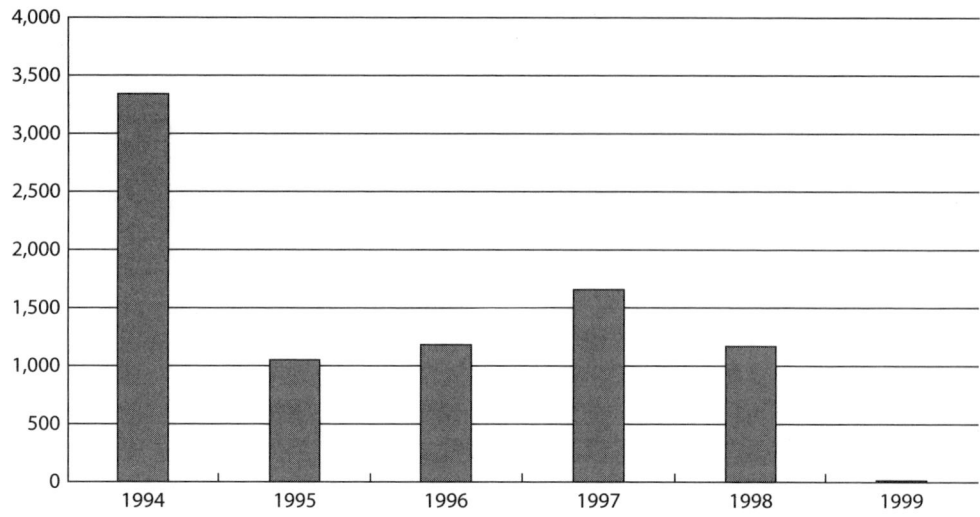

Figure 5.1. Deaths from Strategic Violence in Rwanda, 1994–1999.

ecution or if a political motive is apparent. Some attacks here are borderline strategic attacks where revenge and the desire for strategic gain have overlapped to facilitate involvement in violence. Figure 5.1 summarizes the total deaths from strategic violence throughout this period and indicates two main waves of violence: (1) revenge and RPF-led killings in the immediate aftermath of the genocide from June–December 1994; and (2) a second wave of additional killings that increased from 1996 to July 1998.[103]

Rwanda experienced 3,345 casualties in 1995 alone and 8,439 casualties from strategic violence across the period 1995–1999. From 1995 to 1998, Rwanda had more than 1,000 killed per year, which means that it experienced mass-level violence. Both of these figures reflect only what was reported in the newspapers, which is a significant underestimation of the actual level of violence. As table 5.1 indicates, the ethnic identity of victims and perpetrators of most incidents was unavailable for approximately half of the cases reported in each year.

Over this period of time, Hutus were the victims of 33.5 percent of all reported events, while Tutsis were victims in 14.6 percent of cases. Across both ethnic groups, 81.8 percent of all reported victims were coded as civilians. Many reports of events in newspapers also did not have an alleged perpetrator; of those that did, though, 38.3 percent reported Hutu perpetrators (often militias in cross-border attacks) and 22.1 percent reported Tutsi perpetrators (including RPF and civilians).

Descriptive data on the strategic attacks during this period indicate that the violence was predominantly done via low-technology implements, including machetes and small-arms fire and occasionally bombings. Partially as a result, the casualty rates

TABLE 5.1.
Descriptive Characteristics of Reported Strategic Attacks in Rwanda, 1994–1999, n (%)

	Total Incidents	Hutu Victims	Tutsi Victims	Hutu Perpetrators	Tutsi Perpetrators	Civilians
1994	8	2 (25.00)	2 (25.00)	4 (50.00)	2 (25.00)	6 (75.00)
1995	23	15 (65.22)	2 (8.70)	7 (30.43)	7 (30.43)	19 (82.61)
1996	73	24 (32.88)	2 (2.74)	3 (4.11)	23 (31.51)	57 (78.08)
1997	30	5 (16.67)	7 (23.33)	18 (60.00)	3 (10.00)	27 (90.00)
1998	49	15 (30.61)	14 (28.57)	38 (77.55)	6 (12.24)	40 (81.63)
1999	2	1 (50.00)	0 (0.00)	1 (50.00)	0 (0.00)	1 (50.00)

for attacks (both killed and wounded) were substantial, with one attack often producing large numbers of casualties and refugees. The average attack during this period wounded 7.3 people and killed 45.7 people. Table 5.2 provides descriptive data on the numbers wounded and killed per attack as well as tactical details.

Of all attacks, 48.1 percent were mass-casualty attacks, which produced more than 10 people killed per incident. Bombings were comparatively rare (14.6%) and kidnappings (0.01%) and arsons (5.9%) were also relatively rare. Most of the violence was conducted with guns, knives, machetes, grenades, and other manual implements, such as hoes or axes. This low-intensity struggle was waged in two directions, with former FAR forces and RPF forces both launching assaults on each other's ethnic group. The strategic attacks evident in Rwanda itself from 1994 to 1999 can be grouped into four main categories: (1) reprisals against those associated with the genocide; (2) raids by the former FAR forces into Rwandan territory; (3) attacks against refugee camps; and (4) assassinations of prominent regime critics.

Reprisals

Immediately following the genocide, there were dozens of reprisals against supporters of the Hutu government. Much of this violence reflected the fault lines of the war and could arguably be considered an extension of it. According to Amnesty International, members of the RPF conducted dozens of "disappearances" of prisoners who were later found executed and sometimes tortured.[104] During the war itself, the RPF killed "hundreds—possibly thousands"—of unarmed civilians as it seized control of territory in its march to Kigali.[105] Separating what were revenge (expressive) attacks and reprisals (strategic) attacks is particularly difficulty here. As RPF forces uncovered evidence of the systematic genocide of the previous government, its own forces resorted to indiscriminate revenge, and Tutsi sympathizers also joined in on the killing.[106] After the RPF captured Kigali, reprisals were common particularly in southeastern Rwanda.[107] Dozens of bodies were found dumped in the Akagera River, in an eerie

TABLE 5.2.
Descriptive Details on Attacks

	Incidents	Wounded	Mean Casualty	Mass Casualty	Bombing	Kidnapping	Arsons	Number Burned	Expulsions
1994	8	17	3,345	4	3	1	0	0	0
1995	23	186	1,053	12	2	0	0	0	2
1996	73	341	1,183	24	15	1	4	2	10
1997	30	338	1,670	19	3	0	3	3	2
1998	49	480	1,188	28	4	2	4	4	1
1999	2	1	27	2	0	1	0	0	0

reminder of the killing during the genocide.[108] Many of the bodies were found with their hands bound via kandoya, or three-piece tying, and their heads were smashed in with blunt instruments.[109] Those suspected of killing RPF supporters were also targeted by RPF forces for extrajudicial killing.[110]

Disappearances of former Interahamwe members were common as well, with numerous reports that they were buried in mass graves.[111] Reyntjens argues that from April to September 1994 the violence was a mix of genuine revenge killings and "programmed terror killings" but that after a brief period of calm the reprisals continued against anyone associated with the Hutu nationalist movements, the genocidaires, and opponents of the RPF.[112] What marked the reprisal killings during this period was the categorical nature of the victims: all Hutus, as well as Tutsis who stayed behind and survived the genocide, were under suspicion by the most aggressive elements within the RPF.[113] The reprisals continued throughout the post-conflict period, as the RPF responded to incursions by ex-FAR rebels with increasingly indiscriminate violence against anyone who might be seen as aiding their cause. In April 1995, RPF forces rounded up and shot seventeen Hutu men in reprisal after an attack by unidentified gunmen.[114] An increase in reprisals through 1996 was tied to increased cordon-and-sweep operations against Hutu rebels, as civilians were often summarily executed for allegedly supporting the Hutu insurgency, but human rights groups began to accuse the RPA of engaging in collective punishment of Hutu civilians living in areas where the rebels were present. Between April and July 1996, approximately 650 Hutus were killed in these collective operations.[115] In December 1997 alone, Amnesty International reported that the RPA had killed hundreds of Hutu civilians in large-scale reprisals after ex-FAR rebels had butchered 300 Tutsi Congolese refugees.[116] The RPF did punish some of its members for killing and other forms of indiscipline, but it did not do so for reprisals against combatants. It tended to reserve punishment (including public execution) for petty crimes and opportunistic killings.[117] Evidence suggests that these reprisals only increased in late 1997; one estimate suggests that as many as 10,000 people were killed at the hands of the RPA between October 1997 and January 1998.[118]

Raids by Ex-FAR Guerrilla Forces

The ex-FAR forces that escaped across the borders in Rwanda did not surrender their hopes of retaking the country. Throughout the post-conflict period, armed incursions by ex-FAR rebels occurred and left hundreds of civilians dead in scorched-earth operations that seemed to some RPF officials as a continuation of the genocide. These attacks very clearly reflected the direct pathway, as former members of the FAR continued to fight the RPF for the same reasons—political power and ethnic hatred—that produced the genocide. Ex-FAR rebels would throw grenades at buses and massacre civilians in regular raids in the country.[119] In early 1996, the Rwandan government estimated that nearly one thousand infiltrators were arrested by RPF forces.[120] The cumulative goal of the ex-FAR raids was to make parts of Rwanda ungovernable, as the rebels "assassinated local officials, laid ambushes on the roads, massacred scores of Tutsi civilians in their homes and attacked jails, freeing hundreds of Hutu men who were awaiting trial on genocide charges."[121] Ex-FAR rebels would ambush Rwandan government forces and conduct massacres as well.[122] The body counts from FAR raids would be substantial; one raid in the northwest led to fifty-eight civilians being hacked to death with farming tools.[123] In some cases, the violence was more discriminate and attacks were used to punish those who had refused to join Hutu rebel groups.[124] In some cases, the ex-FAR wished to punish civilians for seeking protection from the RPF. One attack in May 1998 led to ninety-four civilians being killed with machetes for seeking help from the local Tutsi force.[125]

One common tactic was prison raids, in which ex-FAR rebels would assault a prison to free its comrades accused of genocide. In May 1996, three separate prison raids freed more than fifty inmates but led to the deaths of many more.[126] These prison raids—some of which could free several hundred prisoners in each successful attack—were used to replenish the ranks of the ex-FAR forces.[127] One prison raid conducted in conjunction with the assassination of local officials and the burning of administrative offices freed five hundred prisoners.[128] However, significant numbers of prisoners were often killed in the attacks. One botched raid in November 1997 left more than eighty prisoners dead near Ruhengeri.[129] In response, RPF forces would often cordon off an area in order to destroy the ex-FAR rebels and their sympathizers, which in turn led to an increase in civilian deaths. In one set of raids after the residents of the town of Giciye had been massacred in July 1996, RPF forces rounded up more than three thousand men for questioning, while RPF soldiers killed approximately ninety-nine for resisting. A similar sweep in August 1996 rounded up ten thousand men and killed between fifty and one hundred men.[130] Civilians often assisted RPF efforts, denouncing people as "infiltrators" and subjecting them to summary execution.[131] One uprising by civilians killed twenty-seven Hutu rebels who had regularly raided villages in Rushasha commune.[132] By late 1997, such ex-FAR raids were extending deep into Rwanda, into central regions of the country and closer to Kigali.[133] One consequence of these attacks was to internationalize the crisis, as RPF forces invaded Zaire to destroy the camps supporting Hutu militias, while their army traded fire across the borders.[134]

Attacks against Refugee Camps

Among the most common tactics during this period were attacks on refugee camps. Almost all parties were guilty of attacks on refugees. Former FAR guerrillas now located in camps in Burundi, Tanzania, and Zaire would regularly launch attacks against Tutsi refugees in camps in Rwanda itself to terrify the civilians and deepen its sense of crisis.[135] The effect of the insecurity generated by these attacks was to paralyze political progress and make reconciliation impossible.[136] The Hutu refugees in neighboring countries were held under ex-FAR rebel control, and refugees were threatened with violence if they returned. For the ex-FAR elements, the refugee camps were an essential military sanctuary and their base of political support; for this reason, they regularly told Hutus in the camps that to return to Rwanda was to submit oneself to slaughter.[137] Violence became localized, as Tutsis and Hutus in neighboring countries were drawn into this bitter dynamic. Ex-FAR forces attacked local Tutsis in Zaire, who in turn fled toward Rwanda for safety.[138] In Burundi, army officers (who were largely Tutsi) attacked Hutu refugees, who fled back toward Rwanda for fear of being massacred.[139] Kagame accused ex-FAR forces of seeking to conduct ethnic cleansing of Tutsis in neighboring countries in order to secure territory to launch assaults on Rwanda.[140]

Such violence also continued within Rwanda itself. One massacre of Tutsi refugees (many of whom had fled Zaire) left more than 272 people killed as the entire camp was burned down.[141] The ex-FAR forces would often attack camps in Rwanda near the border with other countries and massacre Tutsis, especially genocide survivors. The RPF would respond with countermeasures, many of which involved operations that cordoned off areas and destroyed any insurgents. Some of these operations also involved the deaths of Hutu civilians. One RPF sweep of the Gisenyi region in northwestern Rwanda led to the deaths of 62 people.[142] A similar sweep operation that killed 100 people in July 1996 was criticized by UNHCR officials for leading to the deaths of unarmed civilians.[143] Many of the attacks followed a tit-for-tat pattern, with massacres of Hutu refugees being met with massacres of Tutsis. For example, in August 1997, 148 Tutsi refugees—some of whom had come to Rwanda from Zaire—were killed by Rwandan Hutu rebels in an attack in a refugee camp near Gisenyi. Yet only weeks before this attack aid workers discovered the bodies of nearly 120 Hutu refugees in mass graves.[144]

This dynamic—with ex-FAR rebels attacking refugees, and RPF officials retaliating with indiscriminate violence—left many refugees in the crossfire and increased the number of civilian deaths. Thousands of refugees were caught between the combatants and fled into the hinterlands of Rwanda, Zaire, and neighboring countries, where disease and starvation killed even more.[145] Between April and December 1997, for example, one unofficial estimate produced by the UN Human Rights monitors suggested that six thousand people had been killed while caught between these contending forces.[146] Eventually, the RPF sought to close refugee and IDP camps that proved to be a target for Hutu extremist attacks and a source of their logistical support. In one attempt to clear a camp in Kibeho in April 1995, between two thousand and four thousand refugees were slaughtered by a rogue RPF unit determined not to leave any space outside its control that could host genocidaires.[147]

Assassinations

In post-conflict Rwanda, many critics of the government—including journalists, local officials, and more high-ranking political figures—were assassinated. Some attacks were directed against local government officials designed to stop them from rebuilding the country. For example, in a period of a few weeks in February and March 1996, three local Tutsi officials were assassinated in areas near the border with Zaire.[148] Assassinations would often come in waves with multiple government officials and prosecutors being ambushed with small arms fire in a series of incidents, often connected as part of a pattern.[149] Judges and prosecutors of genocide cases were particularly at risk of assassination.[150] Ex-FAR rebels also hunted down and killed witnesses to the genocide in order to protect themselves from prosecution.[151] One of the unspoken stories of post-conflict Rwanda was how witnesses and survivors of the genocide were hunted down and killed to prevent them from testifying about their experiences to the ICTR or local *gacaca* courts. In May 1996 alone, 17 genocide survivors were killed throughout the country.[152] One attack in June 1996 killed 15 genocide survivors in one refugee camp.[153] Between January and October 1996, 122 Tutsi genocide survivors were killed by Hutu extremists to prevent them from testifying.[154]

Some journalists who reported on RPF atrocities were also assaulted or killed to force their silence.[155] On 29 January 1995, a gang of armed men assaulted Edouard Mutsinzi, a journalist critical of the government, and bludgeoned him nearly to death.[156] In other cases, the assassinations were conducted against foreign aid workers in order to make operating in the camps more difficult.[157] The ex-FAR rebels often killed any Hutus that they saw as collaborating with the RPF. Pierre Clever Rwangabo, a former Hutu guerrilla who served as a minister in the first RPF-sponsored "broad-based government" was assassinated by a gang of Hutu militants in March 1995.[158] Former FAR officers and local Hutu political leaders would also be killed by Hutu extremists for collaborating with the RPF regime.[159] Finally, political dissidents were also killed, allegedly by the RPF regime. The most famous case was that of Seth Sendashonga, who survived one attempted assassination in Nairobi in February 1996 before being killed on 16 May 1998 in a coordinated assault.[160] Sendashonga, who had resigned from the government in protest over the killings of Hutus, believed that his killers were RPF operatives designed to stop his efforts to oppose, and potentially overthrow, the RPF regime.[161] Many more, however, reported threats of violence and intimidation and fled the country for Europe or elsewhere in fear of their lives.

Efforts to Assess RPF Responsibility

The extent of RPF control over some types of strategic violence—particularly the reprisals that characterized the immediate post-conflict period—remained debatable. There is no doubt that the RPF was responsible for assaults against Hutu rebels in the country and killed civilians in the cross-fire. Similarly, there is no doubt that Rwanda deployed its forces in Zaire to flush out these rebels and were responsible for violence that led to the death of thousands of refugees.[162] Both have been admitted by the RPF directly. What remains unclear is whether sustained strategic violence against Hutus represented a concerted policy by the RPF leadership. There are clear alternatives here: it could be a policy of simply not asking questions or subtly endorsing violence by its members. Alternatively, it could be that disgruntled RPF officers were operating on their own against the RPF's official policy. Experienced observers at the time saw the problem as one of RPF indiscipline, where individual RPF soldiers went berserk or where commanders lost control of their units in the midst of the genocide.[163] The difficulty became one of corroborating evidence: many UN and NGO officials saw relatively little evidence of widespread RPF massacres, but most were also kept away by the RPF from active conflict zones. Unfortunately, the chaotic and highly violent environment did not lend itself to allowing independent experts to find precise numbers of people killed or to determine responsibility for these killings. Most reports simply note that there is ongoing "insecurity" without attributing its source.[164] The sources of this insecurity were complex: ordinary civilians engaged in revenge killings and score settling amidst the criminal and strategic violence after the RPF's victory. Nevertheless, there were three notable efforts to determine the extent of RPF control over the violence, including the controversial Gersony report, as well as important narrative reports from Human Rights Watch and Amnesty International, each of which concluded that there were incomplete but significant levels of RPF control over the killings in Rwanda during this period.

Gersony Report

The first major effort to assess the sources of violence was conducted by a UNHCR-sponsored Emergency Repatriation Team, led by Robert Gersony. Gersony's team visited 41 of Rwanda's 145 communes during a five-week period in August–September 1994, and conducted hundreds of interviews within Rwanda and neighboring camps in Burundi, Tanzania, and Zaire. Gersony's report estimated that between twenty-five thousand and forty-five thousand had been killed by the RPF after the war, particularly in the northwest and Kibungo.[165] His estimate suggested that nearly five thousand people were being killed by month from April to August 1994. As Allison Des Forges noted, Gersony began his mission with sympathy to the RPF and was impressed that its orders were followed out down the chain of command with remarkable precision.[166] But the analysis of his team found widespread patterns of arrests and disappearances, as well as RPF massacres of Hutu civilians in the south and southeast of the country.[167] His findings were confirmed by other UNCHR officials operating in the country, as well as independent sources in the refugee camps or elsewhere in the country.

The Gersony report was never formally released.[168] A written summary of Gersony's findings in an oral presentation that he gave to the UNHCR's Commission on Experts on 11 October 1994 was leaked years later and contains some indication of his chief arguments.[169] The report found that significant areas of Butare, Kibungo, and southeast Kigali regions were the scene of "systematic and sustained killing and persecution of the civilian Hutu population by the RPA."[170] The Gersony summary indicated that the violence occurred in regions without significant resistance from Hutu rebels and that victims included women, children, and the elderly. Among the most common tactics would be scheduling a "meeting" where Hutu civilians would be called to a common area for information on food delivery or peace and security problems, only to be attacked with sustained gunfire, grenades, and manual weapons.[171] This tactic was to some extent a continuation of violence patterns within the genocide, as the RPF used this tactic against Hutu civilians during the genocide itself to cleanse areas of Hutu refugees.[172] RPF soldiers conducted to house-to house hunts for Hutu civilians and pursued hidden populations (such as those displaced or turned into refugees) with coordinated attacks with gunfire and manual weapons. According to Gersony, some refugees were lured back with a promise of reconciliation or peace, only to be killed when they returned to their home villages.[173] Asylum seekers and the elderly were also ambushed and killed. The Gersony team concluded that there was "an unmistakeable pattern of systematic RPA conduct of such actions."[174] Moreover, such violence was clearly categorical as "the great majority of these killings had apparently not been motivated by any suspicion whatsoever of personal participation by victims in the massacres of the Tutsis in April 1994."[175] According to Gersony, much of the targeting was by pure chance, and there was little evidence of vetting to establish complicity in prior attacks. Further details were revealed in an unclassified memorandum by U.S. diplomat George E. Moose, which noted that victims were killed with hoes, axes, machetes, and gunfire and that men between the ages of eighteen and forty were particularly targeted. Moose reports that the Gersony report estimates that the RPA was responsible for 95 percent of the killing.[176] The U.S. memorandum notes that its strategy is not to "get out in front" of this story, for fear of endangering U.S. personnel and NGOs working in the country. The United States would later change its strategy and dispatch Under Secretary of State for Global Affairs Tim Wirth to attack Gersony's methodology and suggest that the entire report was tainted by planted evidence as the result of a Hutu conspiracy.[177]

The findings of the Gersony report generated a hostile response by the Rwandan government and significant controversy within the UN. According to a released UN cable discussing Gersony's presentation of findings, the Rwandan government objected to Gersony's contention that such systematic killing could only be the result of a "plan implemented at the highest echelons of the government" with two arguments: (1) that it would not be possible for the government to massacre thirty thousand people without the world noticing; and (2) the RPA would not conduct killings with hoes, clubs, and machetes. The Rwandan government admitted that revenge killings were common during this period, especially in areas where the UN and NGOs were underrepresented but denied that this was its policy. The view of senior UNAMIR official Shaharyar Kahn was that the accounts of RPF killings could not be reconciled with the RPF's public efforts to encourage Hutus to remain and seek reconciliation and that field visits to Gisenyi and elsewhere did not confirm Gersony's findings. Kofi Annan's conclusion was that "the report, 'if there was in fact a written report,' should now be referred to as information which would be investigated and that, meanwhile, it should stay in the folder as a public airing would be sensationalizing findings and conclusions that had not been checked and/or verified."[178] Yet neither the Rwandan government nor the UN Commission of Experts on Human Rights did more than a superficial visit to the country, which produced no conclusive verification of the findings. Annan also emphasized to Rwandan officials that, while the killings should stop, the UN would do its best to minimize attention paid to Gersony's evidence.[179] UNAMIR noted that the effect of the report was to have "queered the pitch" for the UN Agencies operating in Rwanda, which left the UN engaging in a damage limitation exercise.[180] As Des Forges reported, when a representative of the special rapporteur on Rwanda for the Human Rights Commission sought a copy from the UNHCR, he received the following reply: "We wish to inform you that the 'Gersony Report' does not exist."[181]

Other Narrative Reports

Two additional narrative reports written at the time point to some level of RPF involvement in the strategic violence against Hutus after the genocide. The first report of RPF killings in the aftermath of the genocide was produced by Amnesty International in October 1994. The report noted that it had received reports of deliberate and arbitrary killings, extrajudicial executions, and disappearances of Hutu seen as sympathetic to the government by the RPA. There was evidence of torture (including kandoya) and of a permissive environment that allowed RPF sympathizers to kill with impunity.[182] Amnesty International cautioned that it was unclear whether these human rights abuses were ordered or condoned by senior RPF officials but said it was incumbent upon them to stop the killings.[183] It also noted that the UNHCR had received dozens of testimonies to the effect that the RPA was conducting campaigns of killing, but evidence was difficult to verify, in part because of the extent to which the RPF controlled the movements of independent experts.[184]

Second, in her landmark work on the Rwandan genocide, Alison Des Forges details how the RPF regularly engaged in the killing of noncombatants throughout the genocide as a matter of policy. According to her account, Kagame admitted as much in a 27 July 1994 radio address in which he remarked that "harmful elements were hidden in bushes and banana plantations. Therefore a cleaning was necessary, especially to separate the innocent people with the killers."[185] As Des Forges's report indicates, the tactics employed during the genocide and in the months following are broadly similar, including massacres at public meetings and summary executions. There were also some accusations that the RPF sought new recruits to conduct a massacre of civilians in a stadium in Kigali.[186] Some attacks were discriminate, with efforts by RPF soldiers to identify the victim's identity, reputation, party allegiance, and behavior, while others were entirely indiscriminate. In her view, revenge alone could not account for the scale of violence evident in Rwanda after the war, and that members of the RPF high command must have been aware. Des Forges notes that "these killings were too wide-spread, systematic, and involved a large number of participants and victims. They were too many and too much alike to have been unconnected crimes executed by individual soldiers or low ranking officers. Given the disciplined nature of the RPF forces, and the extent of communications up and down the hierarchy, commanders of this army must have known of and at least tolerated these practices."[187]

Explanations

Why would the RPF—now victorious and in charge of the levers of power in Rwanda—continue to use strategic violence in the post-conflict period? One simple explanation for its willingness to continue to use strategic violence is that from its vantage point the crisis in Rwanda did not pass at the end of the genocide. Much of what drove the RPF to engage in violence was its pervasive sense of insecurity. The fact that the ex-FAR had escaped the country almost intact across the border in Zaire meant that the war was not truly over for the RPF. The transfer of the genocidaire regime across the border to Zaire merely prolonged the crisis, resetting its terms and internationalizing what had been an internal war. The Hutu extremists in the ex-FAR regime were not content to simply wait for a better day, but almost upon arrival were determined to destabilize the regime by whatever means necessary. Hundreds of small-scale attacks—including massacres, prison breaks, and assassinations—continued throughout the post-conflict period, especially in the northern and western regions, all of which generated a sense of crisis that worked to the advantage of the RPF regime. The mounting casualties among both Tutsis and Hutus, and the regular infiltration by Hutu extremists across the border, would provide any government in the RPF's position with a compelling rationale for continuing the fight. The cross-border strategic violence is attributable to the direct pathway, as the RPF forces continued to fight the same ethnic struggle that produced the genocide in the post-conflict period. Accordingly, the types and targets of the violence in the post-conflict period were similar to that which occurred during the war.

But explaining the strategic violence only as a function of the cross-border war between the ex-FAR and RPF overlooks two important ways in which the RPF expanded its war aims in the post-conflict period. On a fundamental level, the RPF was not satisfied with its victory because it faced a long-term future where it governed over a restless and angry Hutu majority that would be sympathetic to the ex-FAR rebels across the border. One consequence of the victory won by the RPF was to whet its appetite for absolute control over social and political life in Rwanda. Once in government, the RPF gradually consolidated its control of the country via institutions like the Department of Military Intelligence (DMI) and the local cadres of the RPF (abakada).[188] The situation, as Reyntjens describes it, is that, "in an emerging police state, the press and civil society were put under increasing control, party political activities were prohibited, mail was opened, telephones and other communications were monitored and movements inside and abroad were carefully watched."[189] In many respects, Rwanda returned to its status quo ante as an extraordinarily powerful, highly bureaucratic state with authoritarian tendencies and a stifling presence in the lives of its citizens. As has been noted, the RPF's decision for a government of national unity masked a concerted effort on its part to consolidate its power by rewarding key allies with posts in the government (e.g., domestic reward). The government was superficially broad-based, but the actual decisions were controlled by the RPF military leadership, which often served as the power behind the throne in important decisions. In practice, however, this allowed the RPF to practice ingroup policing to ensure that its high levels of internal control did not fray once the actual practice of governing began. Its ability to impose discipline on its members means that the RPF was one of the few African guerrilla groups that translated its organizational endowments before the war into political success afterward. Its high levels of internal control also explain why in contrast to other African rebel groups there was relatively little factional violence in the post-conflict period.

The RPF also used violence selectively against its domestic opponents (including many Tutsis, who fled under threat of their lives) but also against the Hutu majority, which was distrusted by the Kagame leadership for its complicity in the genocide. As a government representing a minority ethnic group, the RPF regime was confronted by a large and impoverished Hutu majority that was a potential fifth column for the ex-FAR insurgents operating across the border. The use of strategic violence in post-conflict Rwanda became a mechanism that reinforced its level of control over the population, as arrests and attacks on Hutu civilians—especially those seen as involved with or complicit in the genocide—became important for disciplining behavior and imposing social control on the discontented Hutu population. The RPF adopted the position that attacks would be used only against "bad people," presumably those who collaborated with the genocidaires. In practice, many Tutsis and members of the RPF used the accusation of collaboration with the genocidaires to secure economic advantage or settle personal grievances.[190] But this created a culture of impunity that led not only to thousands of Hutu deaths but also a general atmosphere of repression that left much of the remaining population afraid to speak up. The abakada arrested thousands of people, only some of whom were responsible for genocide, so that by August 1995 nearly eighty thousand people were in jail.[191] The direct killings of Hutu civilians by the RPF, the news of atrocities in RPF-closed zones of military activities, and the indiscriminate reprisals against Hutu villages combined to enforce RPF domination over large swathes of Rwandan society. Beyond simply repelling the ex-FAR attacks, strategic violence was instrumental in consolidating the RPF's increasingly authoritarian hold on Rwandan society. Kagame himself said in January 1998 that "we don't have to kill them all. It is enough to beat them hard enough so that they don't bite, that all dogs remain sitting."[192]

Even after Rwanda achieved an unprecedented level of control over the government, the RPF was not content merely to consolidate its hold over Rwanda. At a fundamental level, it was not satisfied even with outright victory and an almost stifling level of control over social and political life in the country. Over time, the reprisals against Hutu civilians and domestic dissidents culminated in the expansion of its war aims to include establishing a regional sphere of influence among its neighboring states. To a substantial degree, this was driven by the real security threat emanating from the refugee camps in Zaire. No government, no matter how fair-minded or restrained, could have ignored the growing spate of insurgent attacks within Rwanda itself by elements with the ex-FAR government. But significant evidence suggests that the RPF-led government saw its post-conflict period as an opportunity to dismember Zaire, which it blamed for supporting the genocidaires, for being unwilling or unable to shut down the genocidaire refugee camps, and for being an ally of the RPF's enemy, France.[193] The RPF made no secret of its ambitions of "break[ing] the abscess" of the swollen Hutu refugee camps in Zaire and warned several key players, including the United States, before doing so.[194] One advantage of doing so was clearly economic: the Kagame regime would also gain access to Congo's vast mineral resources by overthrowing or crippling its government.[195] The RPF infiltrated Zaire with military units as early as July 1996 and proceeded to use clearing the refugee camps as an excuse for inciting rebellion against the Mobutu regime.[196] The RPF began to train Banyamulenge rebels in northwest Burundi, and it embedded its own forces among the Banyamulenge rebels in South Kivu to incite rebellion.[197] With the RPF as its motivator and guiding force, the Banyamulenge rebellion conquered South Kivu and spread to North Kivu in October–November 1996, with RPF units gradually capturing control over Zairean territory and forcing the flight of the refugees back to Rwanda, where they could be monitored and controlled. Despite frequent reports of RPF involvement in the attack, and collusion with Uganda and Burundi, the RPF regime denied any responsibility for the "uprising" and presented itself as a victim of continuing assaults by the genocidaire regime in exile. Kagame himself praised the RPF's control over information in the escalating crisis in Zaire, saying that "we used communication and information warfare better than anyone. We found a new way of doing things."[198]

While Kagame was doubtlessly correct, there is some evidence to suggest that the RPF misjudged the risk of backlash, and particularly countermobilization of opposing forces, from their military operations in Zaire. The RPF's operation assumed that under the pretext of an ethnic rebellion that Zaire could be dismembered and that local allies backed by Rwanda and Uganda could be installed without significant difficulty. Underlying this assumption was the view that the Mobutu state—weakened, corrupt, and highly inefficient—would remain inert as Rwanda carved out a sphere of influence in Zairean territory near its border. But the extension of the Hutu-Tutsi struggle into Zaire redrew the fault lines of its politics, as so-called native Congolese forces turned on the Banyamulenge as rebels and called for their slaughter.[199] The RPF's backing of AFDL, led by Laurent Kabila, in the First Congo War was successful in overthrowing the Mobutu regime. But Rwanda could not control its client, and Kabila's determination to put distance between himself and Kigali again reset the terms of the Congolese crisis. It also produced an international countermobilization of forces against Rwandan domination of the Congo, as Kabila found new allies in Namibia, Sudan, Angola, Chad, and other countries. While the fault line of the Rwandan genocide remained salient, and was even transferred into the Second Congolese War, the expansion of the RPF's war aims into regional domination produced a countermobilization that dragged much of central Africa into a vicious war.

Conclusion

Throughout its post-conflict period, strategic violence in Rwanda was marked by its severity (i.e., much of the violence operating at mass levels of magnitude) and its continuity with the violence that occurred during the war. While much of the world's attention drifted away from Rwanda after the genocide, the RPF continued to employ strategic violence throughout the post-conflict period. The data collected here record more than eight thousand deaths from strategic violence, far higher than most other comparable cases, but even this is a substantial underestimation of the actual levels of killing. Some of this strategic violence was a response to guerrilla incursions by the ex-FAR; some of it was employed against Hutu refugees who collaborated with the ex-FAR or appeared sympathetic to its goals. Much of it was categorical, as Tutsi civilians and RPF forces selected Hutus as victims on the basis of their ethnic identity rather than on their individual behavior or choices. The strategic violence was embedded among waves of expressive and instrumental killings, as denunciations for crime, petty grievances, and personal rivalries became intertwined with responsibility for genocidal acts to widen the scope of killing and destruction. But the terms of the war remained the same despite the conflict nominally ending with the RPF capture of the country in July 1994. Throughout the post-conflict period, the majority of the violence revolved around the same ethnic fault line between Hutu and Tutsi that produced the genocide. Indeed, one could argue that the violence in the post-conflict period was merely an extension of the dirty war between the Hutus and Tutsis that was conducted prior to, and throughout, the genocide in 1994.

The continuity of the violence around its ethnic fault lines and the continuing prominence of actors that came to power before the war itself (including elements of the FAR and RPF) indicate that Rwanda's strategic violence in its post-conflict period can be explained through the direct pathway. But it also demonstrates how even victorious parties can employ strategic violence after wars to settle old scores or to expand their war aims to include regional dominance. While much of the existing literature focuses on how those who lose out in wars use violence to spoil peace processes, Rwanda is an unusual case where the victor expanded its war aims to include regional dominance once the war ended.[200] The experience of Rwanda suggests that post-conflict strategic violence can occur even when one side achieves a nearly complete victory. As the RPF demonstrated, a well-organized and disciplined victorious party may be able to control its factions through the mechanisms of ingroup policing and domestic reward but still decide that the spoils of war are not enough. Moreover, this case demonstrates that international responses to such activity can be stymied by fixed perceptions of "good guys" and "bad guys." In this case, the United States, France, Belgium, and other key players in that region were so paralyzed by their own guilt over the genocide, and wedded to the notion of the RPF as the "good guys" who brought an end to the genocide, that they looked the other way as the RPF became more authoritarian, violent, and fixated on achieving regional hegemony.[201] Their fear of drawing a false moral equivalence between the genocidaires and the RPF enabled Kagame to expand his reach into the Congo and drew much of the continent into a war unprecedented in its scope and brutality.

CHAPTER SIX

Kosovo

Seen in retrospect, NATO's war in Kosovo (24 March–11 June 1999) was the high-water mark of the series of humanitarian interventions that dominated debates over foreign policy during the 1990s.[1] Reacting in part to their legacy of inaction over Bosnia, the United States, United Kingdom, France, and other members of the NATO alliance deployed diplomatic pressure, air strikes, and the threat of ground troops to force the Yugoslav government of Slobodan Milošević to stop its campaign of expulsions against the ethnic Albanian population in Kosovo. The Yugoslav security forces, which had fought an increasingly bloody counterinsurgency campaign against the secessionist Kosovo Liberation Army (KLA) throughout the 1990s, began in April 1999 to kill and expel hundreds of thousands of Albanians from the province as part of a scorched-earth operation. Their objectives were multiple: to destroy the KLA as a fighting force, to expel the ethnic Albanian population to the surrounding states, and to reassert Serbian control over the province. The conflict took seventy-eight days of bombing and diplomatic pressure before Milošević agreed to withdraw his forces from the province and allow the return of the refugees.

When the war ended, many observers assumed that Kosovo would have a soft post-conflict environment, similar to Bosnia, with revenge attacks, sporadic resistance by Yugoslav forces, and flare-ups around the return of refugees. But within weeks, it became clear that Kosovo's violence was of a different hue from that of Bosnia. Unlike Bosnia, where strategic violence remained at the residual level and revolved mainly around the return of refugees, strategic violence in Kosovo occurred at the occasional level, and featured a regular stream of coordinated attacks against Serbs and other minorities. On some level, post-conflict Kosovo remained stable: the war never resumed, and attacks against NATO or UN officials were rare. Yet underneath its apparent stability was a near-constant drumbeat of strategic attacks against the Serb, Roma, and other minority communities scattered throughout the country, as well as growing factional violence between rival Albanian groups. As a result, despite the fact that Kosovo has approximately half the population of Bosnia, more deaths from strategic violence occurred in Kosovo (213) than in Bosnia (42) across a comparable five-year post-conflict period.[2]

In part, Kosovo was more violent than Bosnia because of its more permissive opportunity structure for violence, particularly in the first year of the post-conflict period. In Bosnia, the armies associated with the nationalist parties remained intact and coordinated with NATO commanders over control of the territory as the peacekeeping mission took shape. In Kosovo, by contrast, there was no agreed-upon interlocutor for NATO forces, and the province collapsed into near anarchy as the Serbian police forces withdrew. The withdrawal of the Yugoslav armed forces from Kosovo's territory left a security vacuum that was to be filled by the NATO Kosovo Force (KFOR) and the Civilian Police (CIVPOL) associated with the UN Mission in Kosovo (UNMIK).[3] In practice, however, both organizations were beset by staffing and logistical delays that made them slow to arrive. The result was a grave public security gap. By late June 1999, no one watched Kosovo's borders or patrolled its streets, its prisons were left unguarded, and most of the basic functions of the local government (e.g., electricity, water, and sanitation) were left unattended. What had been among the most heavily policed areas of Europe during the 1990s had become one of the most lawless territories in the world.

This chaotic situation was compounded by political upheavals and population movements. Following the war, the Serbian community experienced a sharp reversal of fortune. While constituting approximately 10 percent of the prewar population of the province, Serbs had long enjoyed the protection and privileges of the Serb-dominated Yugoslav government. With the withdrawal of Yugoslav troops and the collapse of the political institutions, Serbs found themselves under fire as a distrusted minority in an Albanian-dominated Kosovo.[4] Their position became more precarious when rival shadow governments composed of different sets of ethnic Albanian nationalists emerged. Both self-proclaimed governments were dominated by those who had fought for independence and whose vision of Kosovo's future marginalized, or even excluded, Serbs and other minority groups. Fearing their future in a state governed by a hostile ethnic Albanian majority, approximately 150,000 Kosovo Serbs fled northwards to Serbia or Serb-majority regions for protection. Hundreds of thousands of Albanian refugees also returned to the country en masse.[5] International relief organizations were overwhelmed by the volume of people on the move. Among the most vulnerable at this point were the Serbs and other minorities (including Roma, Ashkali, Gorani, Egyptians, and Turks) who remained scattered in small pockets of territory throughout the province. In the first months of the post-conflict period, these minority enclaves were not protected by police or peacekeepers and had few resources to resist attack by ex-KLA forces. All of these factors—a lack of policing capacity, inflexible and illegitimate institutions in the grips of one ethnic group, and high levels of vulnerability for the remaining Serbs seen as being on the wrong side of the war—produced a permissive opportunity structure that allowed strategic violence to flourish in the first year of the post-conflict period.

The first wave of violence in Kosovo (June 1999–December 2000) reflected the initial anarchy of the post-conflict period. In this wave, there were very high levels of expressive violence, such as assaults, arsons, and riots, from survivors and returning refugees. In particular, there were frequent reports of revenge killings, some according to the traditional Albanian cultural codes, and vendettas between families and organized crime gangs.[6] Instrumental violence, particularly petty crime, such as theft and seizure of property, and score settling by organized crime networks, was also rampant. Porous borders opened up new opportunities for the sophisticated organized crime networks that had developed during the war. What was criminal and was political became nearly impossible to determine: reports of intra-Albanian factional violence became interwoven with stories of criminal gangs settling scores through killings, arsons, and assaults. Seeing an opportunity to expand their businesses, rival criminal gangs used murder and intimidation to exert their control over regional smuggling routes and black market businesses. Many of the deaths reported in the first year of the post-conflict period were attributable to these expressive or instrumental purposes. Yet many strategic attacks were also embedded amid the hundreds of revenge killings, riots, and criminal attacks that dominated the first wave of violence. Allegations of KLA-led reprisal attacks against Serb and Roma civilians began to mount, as KLA forces seized control of towns and villages, while hundreds of arsons burned members of these minority communities out of their homes. More than four hundred Serbs, Roma, and dissident Albanians were "disappeared" into a network of secret KLA prisons throughout the country.[7] There were daily reports of KLA units harassing and expelling Serb and Roma civilians from Albanian-majority towns and villages. According to Human Rights Watch, the "most serious" incidents of violence against Serbs and Roma were attributable to the KLA, and some evidence exists that KLA members took advantage of the chaos to eliminate their rivals and strengthen their hands for future political contests.[8]

The second wave of violence, during the rest of the post-conflict period (January 2000–December 2004), featured significant reductions in the number of attacks and the deaths associated with them. In part, this decline in violence was due to significant changes in the opportunity structure. By early 2000, most of NATO's peacekeeping force—some fifty thousand troops for a relatively small province—had arrived, and thousands of UNMIK CIVPOL forces were on the streets.[9] This initial wave of revenge killings and expulsions displaced thousands to Serb-majority regions and produced an ethnic partition of Kosovo, which reduced the vulnerability of Kosovo Serbs to attack. Yet, despite the opportunity structure becoming less permissive by

2001, all three categories of violence (expressive, instrumental, and strategic) continued, though at a reduced, often covert, level. Criminal violence, particularly threats and intimidation against civilians who refused to pay bribes and protection money for their businesses, remained a part of everyday life in Kosovo. Intermixed with the flourishing of organized crime in this wave were dozens of carefully coordinated strategic attacks against Serbs who remained vulnerable in Albanian-majority regions. Yet the real change in this period was the explosion of factional violence between the remnants of the KLA. Underneath the surface of Kosovo's official politics emerged a violent struggle between loyalists of main Albanian political parties, many of which were frustrated by the diplomatic deadlock over granting Kosovo's independence. This factional struggle overlapped with the sporadic assaults, harassment, and intimidation of Serbs and other minority groups, producing a blended pattern of violence from the direct and indirect pathways in the second wave.

The question that preoccupied KFOR and UNMIK authorities during the first wave of violence was the extent to which attacks on Serbs were tied to a KLA-led effort to expel minorities from the province or whether they were revenge attacks for atrocities during the war. The confused end of the war—in which the KLA nominally won the conflict, but independence for Kosovo was postponed indefinitely by the terms of UN Security Council Resolution 1244—left many within its ranks dissatisfied with the terms of the peace settlement.[10] But the final status of Kosovo was not set in stone. Under the terms of UNSCR 1244, what happened to Kosovo—whether it would be independent, autonomous, or remain part of Serbia—was left to be negotiated with Belgrade at a later, unspecified point. This uncertainty over the future of the province and dissatisfaction with the terms of the peace settlement among some hard-line KLA members provided a relatively straightforward incentive for strategic violence. So long as Serbs remained in Kosovo after the war, Belgrade had a powerful argument to resist the full independence of Kosovo and to insist on retaining some control over territories where they remained in significant numbers. In other words, the presence of Serbs in Kosovo provided a bargaining chip for Belgrade. For the KLA, the presence of Serbs constituted a stumbling block in the way of outright independence and full ethnic Albanian control of the political institutions. One risk was that the presence of minorities in Kosovo would lead to an internationally backed compromise solution, such as a power-sharing arrangement, which would either give the ethnic Albanians less than full independence or offer the Kosovo Serbs a greater say in the government in Kosovo than their population numbers might suggest.[11] Given this situation, some elements within the KLA believed they had a reason to fight a dirty, covert war against the Serbs as a way of subtly challenging the commitment to multiethnicity made in the terms of UNSCR 1244 (i.e., direct pathway). By victimizing Serb and Roma civilians and forcing them to flee, they would create "facts on the ground" that would make a multiethnic Kosovo impossible and produce an irreversible momentum for independence. If that failed, they would at least weaken Belgrade's rationale for keeping control over Kosovo and reduce the number—and political strength—of Serbs in Kosovo.

Yet while some of the violence was clearly an attempt to refight the war, not all of the strategic violence evident in Kosovo is explainable by the direct pathway. During the second wave of violence, a growing portion of the strategic attacks occurred via the indirect pathway, as factions within the former KLA clashed over the division of power and resources. What drove much of this violence was the organizational decomposition of the KLA into rival political parties, as well as an array of splinter groups and criminal gangs. As part of these organizations, ex-KLA members used strategic violence to bargain with each other in local power contests. The variety and wide geographic range of the attacks, coupled with the evident inability of the former KLA leadership to control the violence through domestic reward and ingroup policing, suggest that this strategic violence came about through the collapse of its internal control and the emergence of regional bargaining games conducted between competing splinter groups. As a result, microcosms of violence in each region were detached from or only indirectly related to Kosovo's official politics. These regional contests reflected a set of fault lines and targets different from the ethnic fault line that was dominant in the war. In the second wave, the empirical manifestations of this dynamic included a growing number of assassination attempts against party loyalists, journalists, and dissidents, as well as unfolding border conflicts launched by ex-KLA forces in Serbia and Macedonia.

This chapter examines the regional variation in violent crime in Kosovo during the period 1999–2004. The first section covers the major events in the post-war period (1999–2004) and afterward. The second addresses the internal control of the KLA and its organizational decomposition into splinter factions. The third section reviews the unpublished UNMIK summary data and event-level data on violence during the 1999–2004 period to show the decline in overall rates of crime from the first to the second wave as the public security gap closed and the ethnic partition of the population became entrenched. The fourth section reviews the most common types of strategic violence across both waves, highlighting the shift toward factional violence among ex-KLA groups during the second wave. The fifth section assesses the culpability of the KLA leadership for this violence. The conclusion reviews the patterns of violence and explains why a significant portion of the strategic violence in the latter half of the post-conflict period must be explained by the indirect pathway.

The Post-Conflict Period (1999–2004)

The war in Kosovo was a relatively short one, as NATO forces bombed targets in Kosovo and Serbia to force the Yugoslav government to withdraw its troops and to allow the return of the ethnic Albanian refugees.[12] The scale of the suffering and refugee problem was striking, given the relative brevity of the war. From March–June 1999, 863,000 civilians were forced out of Kosovo and 590,000 were internally displaced.[13] By the end of June 1999, 90 percent of the population of Kosovo had been driven from its homes.[14] Between the beginning of the Serb military offensive on 20 March and the end of the war on 12 June, approximately 10,500 Albanians were killed.[15] Estimates of the Serb casualties ranged from 1,000 to 5,000 military casualties and from 500 to 1,500 civilian casualties.[16] Under threat of invasion by ground troops and under increasing domestic pressure because of the damage done to his country by over 38,400 NATO sorties, Milošević bowed to diplomatic pressure and agreed to withdraw Yugoslav forces from Kosovo on 3 June 1999.[17]

After negotiating the details of a military technical agreement (MTA) for the deployment of its troops in Kosovo, NATO ended its bombing campaign of Yugoslavia on 10 June 1999. On 12 June, the UN Security Council passed Resolution 1244, which authorized NATO troops to enter Kosovo under "Operation Joint Guardian." UNSCR 1244 did not, however, settle the final status of Kosovo but instead jointly affirmed the sovereignty and territorial integrity of the Federal Republic of Yugoslavia and the need for "substantial and meaningful self-administration for Kosovo."[18] NATO's Kosovo Force (KFOR) met with negligible Serb resistance upon entry into Kosovo as most Serb security units and paramilitaries had withdrawn in the time allocated by the MTA.[19] However, as Serb security forces and thousands of civilians fled to Serbia, two rival self-proclaimed governments declared themselves in control of Kosovo. The first, the Government of the Republic of Kosova, was based on the preexisting parallel structures that had sustained the Albanian population through Milošević's repression in the 1990s.[20] It was led by Ibrahim Rugova of the Democratic League of Kosovo (LDK). The second and more powerful Provisional Government of Kosova, headed by Hashim Thaçi, was effectively the political wing of the KLA.[21] By the end of the summer, the unauthorized KLA-backed provisional government had assumed control over much of the territory and set up provisional government structures in twenty-seven of its twenty-nine provinces. As these shadow governments vied for control of the province, a wave of violence—ranging from property theft to murder—occurred "under the nose" of KFOR peacekeepers.[22] Through the end of July 1999, KFOR stood alone in maintaining order amid spasms of revenge killings and massive refugee flows and in placating the self-declared rival governments because neither the UN nor the OSCE was able to deploy a substantial field presence on short notice. This was particularly apparent in the divided city of Mitrovica, which was partitioned into a Serbian north and Albanian south in the early days of the post-conflict period.[23]

On 8 August 1999, the first international police units arrived in Kosovo and began to patrol Pristina. Three months later, only 1,400 of the mandated 3,200 police had arrived in Kosovo.[24] While the international security forces were understaffed and the security situation remained chaotic, more than 808,913 of the estimated 848,100 war refugees returned to their homes by November 1999 in what was described as the "biggest refugee return in modern history and also the quickest role reversal."[25] Kosovo was convulsed with internal population movements, as approximately 150,000 Serbs fled northward, often into Serbia proper, for fear of reprisal attacks from the returning Kosovo Albanians.[26] The pervasive insecurity of the Serbs and other minorities and a lack of job opportunities in an Albanian-dominated Kosovo also acted as drivers of population movements. By early November 1999, the prewar population of Serbs had been reduced by approximately 50 percent.[27] The Serbs who remained were largely concentrated in Mitrovica region and enclaves like Gracanica, Orahovac, Strpce, and Novo Brdo.[28]

Among the first objectives of the UNMIK administration was to demobilize the shadow governments and disarm the combatants. Under an agreement with NATO, the ten-thousand-strong KLA agreed to disarm and demobilize, while a significant number (five thousand) would be transformed into an emergency response and reconstruction force called the Kosovo Protection Corps (KPC).[29] On 20 September 1999, the KLA was officially demilitarized. Under the leadership of Dr. Bernard Kouchner, UNMIK attempted to meet the emergency needs of the population and undertook a host of longer-term projects, including setting up a new judicial system, repairing physical infrastructure, restoring postal services, rebuilding roads and factories, and establishing central banking and financial authorities. Operating under an unprecedented level of international administration, Kosovo became a ward of the United Nations. At the same time, the UN was anxious to incorporate Albanian and Serb political parties into the interim government. UNMIK established a Joint Interim Administrative Structure (JIAS), which provided a framework for sharing duties in the provisional administration with a broad cross section of Kosovo society, and a Kosovo Transition Council (KTC), which was an executive committee of all the leading political figures in the province.[30] However, until April 2000, the Serb National Council, led by Bishop Artemije, refused to participate in the Interim Administrative Council (IAC) because of KFOR's and UNMIK's alleged failures in protecting the Serb community from ongoing attacks.[31]

On 28 October 2000, municipal elections were held in Kosovo and representatives were elected from all but the predominantly Serb districts. The special representative of the UN secretary general (SRSG), Hans Haekkerup, appointed Serb representatives for the Kosovo Assembly for the boycotting districts.³² In early November, Milošević was deposed from power in the Federal Republic of Yugoslavia and a new government, led by Vojislav Koštunica, assumed power. On 17 November 2001, with the blessing of Koštunica, province-wide elections were held to fill seats in a new Kosovo Assembly and to set up a UN-backed government entitled the Provisional Institutions of Self-Governance (PISG).³³ In February 2002, a new power-sharing government, headed by President Ibrahim Rugova of the LDK and Prime Minister Bajram Rexhepi of the PDK, was established, leaving the Albanian-dominated PISG with effective control over all aspects of governance except security and justice, which remained under the exclusive control of KFOR and UNMIK. Yet the PISG was not a fully independent set of governmental structures, as PISG department heads were paired with an international counterpart, often part of UNMIK, who had to approve all key decisions.

The removal of Milošević did not put an end to the ethnic tension that had roiled Kosovo for the previous decade. The institutions of the PISG were viewed suspiciously by both sides, and Kosovo remained ethnically divided and polarized between its Albanian majority and its Serbian minority. While the first wave of revenge killings subsided in mid-2000, violence against Serbs and Roma continued, leaving many Serbs convinced that the international community was leaving them to their fate at the hands of the ex-KLA units and Albanian extremist groups. Between 2002 and 2004, the overall rates of violence declined, but attacks on Serbs and other targeted groups remained high, despite their dwindling numbers. Some of the more gruesome attacks during this period—for example, a Serb couple and their son being hacked to death and burned in their home in Oblic in June 2003 or Serb children being gunned down with AK-47s near Gorazdevac in August 2003—caused hundreds of Kosovo Serbs to rally in the streets, urging KFOR and UNMIK to do more to protect them. In some cases, it also led to retaliatory assaults on Kosovo Albanians in neighboring villages.³⁴ Aided by nationalist politicians within Serbia, local Serbian National Council (SNC) politicians such as Oliver Ivanovic advocated a rejectionist policy that minimized Serb cooperation with UNMIK and with Albanian-dominated PISG. Serb rejectionism was facilitated by the countermobilization of parallel Serb nationalist structures, particularly in the judiciary in Serb-dominated regions, as well as by informal Serbian militias such as the so-called Bridge Watchers of Mitrovica.³⁵ Ironically, just as the LDK had established parallel judiciary and taxation systems for its shadow state under Serbian rule, Serb nationalist parties established parallel systems as a basis for rejecting Albanian rule over Kosovo.

In late 2003, the political deadlock between Albanians and Serbs began to break. Under pressure from the U.S. and European governments to avoid having an open-ended and expensive presence in Kosovo, the UN began to signal that independence for Kosovo might be on the table, provided that the Albanian population respected the human rights of the Serbian minority. This policy—often described as "standards before status" was countered immediately by Belgrade, which insisted on high levels of "cultural autonomy" for the Serbian population in Kosovo. Under UN pressure, the conditions for final status talks were laid out in December 2003.[36]

Progress toward a negotiated solution in Kosovo was interrupted by a series of ethnic riots in March 2004. The proximate cause of the riots was the drowning death of two Albanian children from Caber village, allegedly by Serbs, who had chased the boys into the Ibar River.[37] The riots—in which ultimately nineteen people were killed and nine hundred were injured—were the culmination of escalating ethnic tension, but it was also partially organized by KLA veterans' associations and hard-line Albanian nationalist groups. From 17 to 19 March 2004, UNMIK police recorded thirty-three major riots, involving an estimated fifty-one thousand participants.[38] More than seven hundred homes were damaged or destroyed, along with ten public buildings, thirty Serbian Orthodox churches, and two monasteries.[39] Approximately forty-five hundred people—mostly Serbs, Roma, and other targeted groups—were displaced from their homes. Among the injured were sixty-one KFOR soldiers, sixty-five UNMIK CIVPOL officers, and fifty-eight Kosovo Police Service (KPS) officers. More than one hundred UNMIK vehicles were burned or damaged.[40] Originating early on 17 March in flashpoints like Mitrovica and the Serb enclave Caglavica in Pristina region, mob attacks spread like wildfire across the province. Within hours, angry mobs burned UN cars and attacked Serbian residences in previously peaceful neighborhoods of Pristina while hundreds of protesters chanted "UCK, UCK" outside UNMIK headquarters.[41] Attacks came in many forms, including stone throwing, stabbing, small arms and sniper fire, torching cars (including CIVPOL cars and KFOR Armored Personnel Carriers), arson with petrol bombs or explosives, and even hand-to-hand fighting. No ethnic group emerged unscathed from the attacks, though the most of the victims were Serbs, Roma, and Ashkali.[42] In the words of one KFOR official, the fighting between the ethnic groups had devolved into an almost "medieval battle."[43]

The rioting undermined the modest steps taken toward political tolerance in Kosovo. In October 2004, the LDK party won 47 seats in a 120-seat parliament, but the election was boycotted by Serbs. In December 2004, the parliament reelected Ibrahim Rugova as president and former KLA commander Ramush Haradinaj as prime minister. The election was immediately controversial: Haradinaj was indicted by the International Criminal Tribunal for Yugoslavia (ICTY) in March 2005, on charges that he participated in atrocities in 1998.[44] He submitted himself to ICTY immediately and was put on trial in 2007. When he was found not guilty in April 2008,

Haradinaj resumed control of his Alliance for the Future of Kosovo (AAK) party.[45] Interethnic violence continued to afflict Kosovo in 2005, and evidence mounted that prolonging a decision on final status was untenable. Now even "internationals" came under fire: the UN, OSCE, and the Kosovo Parliament were bombed in July 2005. In October 2006, voters in Serbia approved a new constitution, which reaffirmed that Kosovo remained an "integral part" of its country.

In February 2007, the UN moved toward achieving a settlement on final status, as Special Envoy Martti Ahtisaari unveiled a plan for internationally supervised independence.[46] The Serbian backlash was immediate, and the promise of independence was dropped from the UN proposal at Russian insistence. As negotiations over the Ahtisaari plan stalled, it became increasingly apparent that the pro-independence supporters in Kosovo would no longer wait for an internationally acceptable solution. Former KLA leader Hashim Thaçi was elected as prime minister of Kosovo in elections in November 2007 on a promise of full independence for the province. Kosovo declared its independence on 17 February 2008, a decision that in turn led to rioting in Mitrovica and an immediate Serbian rejection of the declaration. Both the Albanian-dominated government of Kosovo and Serbia still claim de jure control over the province.

The Dissolution of the KLA

The Kosovo Liberation Army (KLA) was founded in 1993 and gradually coalesced from competing, often squabbling, groups, into a guerrilla army by late 1996.[47] The KLA always had weak internal control, and it never managed to transcend its origins as an alliance of factions and develop the organizational attributes of a normal guerrilla army. Formed by Kosovo Albanian expatriates in Germany and Switzerland in the mid-1990s, the core of the KLA was small in number, combining highly personalized leadership with a strategy of propaganda and fundraising abroad. Ibrahim Rugova, the head of the LDK and the leader of the Albanian parallel governance structures, even denied the existence of a KLA until after the Dayton Accords.[48] The first-known KLA casualty from an attack on a police station in western Kosovo was Adrian Krasniqi, who died in October 1997.[49] The repression of the Albanian population, and the seeming futility of Rugova's nonviolent approach, fueled the KLA movement and swelled its ranks from mid-1995 onward with additional fighters and money.[50] During the war, estimates of the KLA's strength varied, though KLA commander Agim Çeku claimed that he had twelve thousand men under arms in Kosovo and eight thousand training in Albania.[51] The hardened core of the KLA—that is, those trained to fight and highly committed to the cause—was probably far less than the estimates produced by the KLA during the war, possibly numbering only a few thousand fighters.

In terms of its organizational endowments, the KLA never possessed the internal control of other guerrilla armies like the Viet Cong. Resembling an "association of clans," the KLA was based more on individual loyalty, and some of the lower-level operatives had no allegiance to KLA leader Hashim Thaçi or any members of the KLA high command.[52] The KLA was also divided along regional lines, with local KLA commanders (based in each municipality) recruiting young men as impromptu self-defense units against attacking Yugoslav Army (VJ) and Ministry of Interior Police (MUP) forces.[53] The KLA occasionally enmeshed these new recruits in with bands of more experienced fighters for operational reasons, but in many villages the KLA forces were little more than local militia. Many nominal KLA members were little more than local farmers and workers who fought for the cause of independence on a part-time basis but never subscribed to the larger political programs of its leaders. Albanians from the rural areas of northern Albania were also frequent recruits to the KLA, even though they had relatively little military experience. In part because it was an inchoate alliance drawn from several factions, the wartime KLA rarely worked in a coherent, organized way; at best, the various units in the KLA pursued broadly similar goals with limited coordination. This was particularly the case for the three chief political factions within the KLA, including that of Hashim Thaçi, Ramush Haradinaj, and Rustem Mustafa (widely known as Commander Remi), who agreed on little but the need for ending Serbian rule in Kosovo.[54] Nonetheless, they could be effective in cooperating for common purposes, such as opposing the counterinsurgency efforts of the VJ and MUP or more generally making Kosovo ungovernable.

In terms of military capabilities, the KLA had relatively few hard assets even during the height of its power. While the KLA had an extensive network of logistics bases and smuggling routes in Kosovo, Albania, and Croatia, it relied mainly on small arms, such as AK-47s and grenades, for its hit-and-run attacks on VJ and MUP forces. Before the war, there were estimates that the KLA had roughly thirty thousand automatic weapons, which were purchased on the black market after Albanian military arsenals were looted during its 1997 economic collapse.[55] Though it made extensive efforts to purchase German antitank weapons, heavy machine guns, sniper rifles, and rocket-propelled grenades, the KLA had only limited success.[56] By the end of the war, it had not acquired substantial amounts of heavy artillery and had no tanks or armored personnel carriers.[57] The KLA's greatest asset was its funding from the diaspora: it drew funds from local tax levies, the Kosovo Albanian diaspora, Albanian nationalists, Islamic charities and NGOs, and from organized crime.[58] Because much of its funding was done in secret, there is no comprehensive estimate of how many small arms were purchased. During the post-conflict period, some observers suspected that arms caches littered throughout the province were left in waiting in the event that international authorities did not accede to the KLA's demands for independence.

Such fears were not entirely unfounded: KFOR regularly discovered caches of small arms in KLA-linked houses in Kosovo, especially in the period immediate following demilitarization.[59] Officially, however, the KLA turned over its limited heavy artillery to KFOR, and kept only 30 percent of its small machine guns and an unknown quantity of explosives after the 21 June agreement took effect.[60]

Once the war ended, the policy dilemma that occupied UN and NATO authorities was how to dismantle the KLA while keeping the peace. The MTA abolished the KLA's provisional government and attempted to co-opt some of the KLA's membership into the political and law enforcement structures of postwar Kosovo, while returning others to civilian life. The understanding of Thaçi and KFOR commander General Sir Michael Jackson was that KLA members would have three options for employment in postwar Kosovo: (1) involvement in a newly formed political party, the Party for Democratic Progress of Kosovo (PPDK, later shortened to PDK); (2) employment in the newly formed Kosovo Police Service (KPS); or (3) employment in the Kosovo Protection Corps (KPC), a national guard–like organization devoted to civil emergencies.[61] Yet not all of the KLA members found official employment within the KPC and KPS. Many rank-and-file KLA members returned to civilian life but often found relatively poor job prospects given the shattered economy. Some former KLA volunteers also formed "veterans' associations" to petition the UN and PISG for pensions and medical aid as war heroes. Other former KLA members joined splinter organizations—some hard-line organizations committed to the independence cause, some linked to regional or national political figures, and some criminal gangs operating at the intersection of the black and gray economies—that emerged out of the network of clans that made up the wartime KLA.

The former KLA leadership tried to capitalize on its role during the war and capture political power by transforming itself into a legitimate political party. Yet the ability of Thaçi and others to enforce the terms of the settlement across their diffuse membership and win elections was complicated by the low levels of internal control that the KLA leadership traditionally had. Shortly after the war, the PDK publicly promised that it would find a place for all of those who fought in the war against Yugoslavia in the "new" Kosovo. Yet the postwar PDK lacked the means to hire and employ all those who claimed to be KLA war veterans, especially given that many KLA members were members of local militia who joined the war in 1998–1999. No more than four thousand jobs in the KPC, and several thousand more in the KPS, were available for patronage. The PDK did not have the resources or latitude to employ domestic rewards as widely as necessary to keep the wartime KLA together.

Even if that had not been the case, the alliance of factions that formed the basis of the wartime KLA began to fray because of the behavior of its leadership and the constraints imposed by international partners. First, the PDK began to seize almost all of the initial positions for Hashim Thaçi's allies, which in turn alienated other factions in its ranks. Once the post-conflict period arrived, Thaçi immediately attempted to fill the Political Directorate of the PDK with his loyalists, such as Azem Syla, Thaçi's uncle (aka the "Big Uncle") and a noted arms smuggler for the KLA; Xhavit Haliti, the logistics and finance chief for the KLA and another reputed arms smuggler; Jakup Krasniqi; and Sokol Bashota, the former director of the information directorate of the KLA.[62] According to the International Crisis Group, the new PDK was less of a popular movement than a "new kind of nomenklatura, which is exclusive and hard to join."[63] Also, unconfirmed reports claimed that Thaçi and his allies ordered the executions and purges of their enemies within the ranks of the KLA in order to consolidate their power in the PDK.[64] What was once a collection of various, often feuding, Kosovo Albanian nationalist factions before the war gave birth to a political party controlled almost entirely by Thaçi and his loyalists, mainly from the Drenica region. Other regions of the country, including traditional KLA strongholds like Prizren, were underrepresented in the new PDK. Though the PDK was widely seen to be the successor of the KLA in the post-conflict period, the reality was different: the PDK represented only Thaçi's own loyalists, rather than the disparate factions that made up the wartime KLA. Those left outside Thaçi's orbit—and left outside of the key positions of the PDK—became disaffected with his leadership and eager to involve themselves in a range of other activities.

Second, the KLA's already tenuous levels of internal control weakened further because the PDK did not have the capacity to employ domestic rewards effectively against all of those disaffected by its hold on power. UNSCR 1244 and the abolition of the KLA's provisional government dashed the hopes of outright victory held by the KLA and left the PDK as merely one political party among many, not a government-in-waiting. Moreover, it did not win the first rounds of elections in the post-conflict period. In the first municipal elections in 2000, the PDK faced tough electoral competition because of the popularity of the LDK and Ibrahim Rugova. The LDK captured 58 percent of the vote, compared to 27.3 percent for the PDK.[65] In the first Kosovo Assembly elections in 2001, the LDK captured 45.65 percent of the vote, compared to the PDK's 25.70 percent.[66] In the first UN-backed provisional government (2002–2004), the PDK was forced to share power with the LDK, which enjoyed international favor owing to its use of nonviolence in the days leading up to the war. The KLA may have won the war, but it faced real challenges in winning elections in the immediate post-conflict period.

Given that the PDK was now a legitimate party, operating in political institutions under supervision from UNMIK and the OSCE, it could not broker bargains with its members that were wholly unacceptable to these actors. The result was that the PDK could not use domestic rewards too widely—for example, offering business concessions or key positions in government to many in its ranks—without attracting unwanted attention or allegations of corruption. Efforts by Thaçi to reward members of his closest inner circle—many of whom were deeply involved in organized crime and had poor human rights records—were widely condemned by leaders of UNMIK, NATO, and local NGOs as evidence of nepotism or outright corruption. The PDK was then doubly constrained in employing domestic rewards: first, by its position sharing power in a provisional government; and second, by the strong pressure applied by external actors not to engage in excessive patronage within its own ranks. The result was that the PDK became a legitimate actor in Kosovo's politics but only by shedding many of its members and accepting limits on its ability to openly reward its factions.

As a result of these constraints, much of the KLA's ranks unfolded into an array of contending political and criminal factions, only some of which were aligned with the goals of the PDK. The PDK, while nominally the "face" of the KLA, became detached from much of the rank and file of the organization. While some ex-KLA members simply returned to civilian life, others became employed in the KPC, drifted into the orbit of organized crime gangs, or joined splinters from the KLA. Some of these KLA successor organizations—including "veterans' associations" and some groups linked to secessionist movements in the southern Serbia and Macedonia—believed that the PDK leadership had betrayed their cause by accepting anything less than outright independence from UNMIK. The following organizations, some legitimate and some illegitimate, were among the most important of those composed of dissatisfied ex-KLA members during the post-conflict period.

Alliance for the Future of Kosovo

Among the most important parties that emerged from the KLA was the Alliance for the Future of Kosovo (AAK). In 2000, Ramush Haradinaj, who initially served as deputy commander of the KLA, resigned from the KPC and in April 2001 founded his own party, the AAK, to challenge Thaçi's preeminence and claim his part of the legacy of the KLA. The AAK formed originally as an alliance of minor parties but soon became the chief opposition to the dominance of the LDK and PDK in Kosovo's politics. In practice, the ranks of the AAK included many ex-KLA who had not been allied to Thaçi. There was a strong regional divide between the PDK and AAK as well; the PDK was based around Thaçi's allies in the Drenica region, while the AAK commanded significant loyalty in the Dukagjini region and elsewhere. The AAK attempted to build bridges with the Serbian community and was more moderate than the PDK, but it consistently placed below both the LDK and PDK in elections. Under pressure from the PDK, the AAK and the LDK were forced into a coalition by mid-2004 and have remained cooperative since. Haradinaj, who became prime minister in 2004, has remained a controversial figure in Kosovo's politics, especially after he was indicted by the ICTY for alleged war crimes.[67] The AAK also has deep ties within the KPC, due in part to Haradinaj's status as a KLA war hero. No evidence exists that the AAK has directly participated in violence, and in its capacity as opposition, the AAK has called for an investigation of the KLA's intelligence services and other shadow structures underneath the state for their involvement in strategic violence against the Serbs and Roma.[68]

Kosovo Protection Corps

When the MTA over the KLA's dissolution was negotiated, its leadership won some key concessions, including that its regional command structure remained intact within the new Kosovo Protection Corps (KPC). The KPC was designed to be a civilian defense organization, charged with tasks such as disaster response, humanitarian relief, and demining. KPC members were forbidden from engaging in military activity or law enforcement tasks. Of the 5,000 positions in the initial formulation of the KPC, 4,552 KLA soldiers were appointed to the organization.[69] While General Sir Michael Jackson was successful at winning KLA agreement to transfer command of ex-KLA units to the command of the commander of KFOR (COMKFOR) and to turn over KLA heavy weapons to NATO under a phased disarmament scheme, the KLA retained the rights to have small weapons for bodyguards, to keep its brigade structure in place, and to use its insignia for the KPC uniforms.[70] Even the name of the Kosovo Protection Corps in Albanian, Trupat Mbrojtese te Kosoves, or TMK, was a concession to the KLA because employing the word *mbrojtese* (which in Albanian can mean either protection or defense) allowed the KLA to claim that it had not surrendered its ambition to be the future army of Kosovo.[71] Nonetheless, the creation of the KPC helped to siphon off some of the most skilled fighters from the KLA's ranks and direct them toward civilian reconstruction tasks. According to senior American diplomats involved in the negotiations, the agreement to create the KPC was designed to "defang the rebels who considered themselves victorious and the army of Kosovo"[72] and to "keep an eye on [the KLA]."[73]

Throughout the post-conflict period, the KPC was a thorny political issue because Kosovo Serb leaders argued that the KPC was merely an army-in-waiting for an independent Kosovo. This later turned out to be largely correct, for much of the membership of the KPC was transferred into the new Kosovo Security Force (KSF) once independence was declared.[74] Beyond that basic point, the KPC was controversial because its members engaged in freelance illegal activities, such as collecting taxes and protection money from businesses around Kosovo.[75] Some of its members have been accused of being involved in organized crime networks throughout the country.

KPC members have also been accused of participating in the armed campaigns of secessionist groups in Macedonia and southern Serbia. In 2001, twenty-two KPC officers, including four generals, were suspended for supporting these guerrilla movements and declared a danger to U.S. national security in an executive order signed by President George W. Bush.[76] While there is no hard evidence of an institutional link between the KPC and the shadow structures beneath the state, some KPC officers have been arrested by the police for involvement in organized crime, theft, torture, kidnapping, and assassinations of political figures during the post-conflict period.[77]

Armed Forces of the Republic of Kosovo

The growing assertiveness of the KLA before the 1999 conflict also spawned a smaller rival armed faction, the so-called Armed Forces of the Republic of Kosovo (FARK), funded and led by Bujar Bukosi, a former prime minister in the parallel government run by Rugova in the prewar period.[78] The FARK was designed to be the army of the LDK, yet during the war it joined forces temporarily with the KLA to fight for independence.[79] The relationship between the FARK and the KLA was uneasy and sometimes spilled over into open rivalry and violence. In September 1998, the FARK minister of defense, Colonel Ahmet Krasniqi, was gunned down in Tirana only days after a KLA communiqué warned that "one day these kind of people will pay for the damage they have caused our nation."[80] After the war, it attempted to back the LDK's gambit at a provisional government and came into conflict with the KLA's own forces. During the first wave of violence, there were sporadic reports of KLA-FARK factional violence, although some of these attacks were driven by personal rather than political vendettas.[81] The FARK was officially abolished with the LDK and PDK provisional governments, but ex-FARK members have continued to operate in the postwar period, in some cases on their own and in some cases with sanction from elements of the KLA. The lines of command are particularly blurry, for "all FARK soldiers now refer to themselves as KLA members, but they are by no means under KLA control."[82] Members of the KLA—including Daut Haradinaj, the brother of Ramush—have also been accused of torturing and murdering ex-FARK officers, though their trial was interrupted by the murder of the witnesses.[83] This has led to a series of "politically coloured" executions of former FARK members in western Kosovo.[84]

Albanian National Army/Albanian Liberation Army/ National Liberation Army

Another armed group to emerge from the ashes of the KLA is the Albanian National Army (ANA/AKSh). Dates of the origin of the ANA are unclear, but most observers agree that it formed between 1999 and 2001. Composed of ex-KLA members as well as pro-independence clans and criminal elements, the ANA is a pan-Albanian movement with interests in encouraging the Albanian-led insurgency in Macedonia, as well as extensive criminal contacts.[85] The ANA comprises several hundred, often masked fighters who operate in northern Kosovo near areas of Serb control and conduct their own informal patrols.[86] The ANA was widely believed to be behind a bombing on a railway in a Serb-majority region of Kosovo in 2003 and was condemned by UNMIK SRSG Michael Steiner as a terrorist organization in 2003.[87] The chief suspect in this attack was a current KPC officer who was claimed by the AKSh as its "soldier."[88] The principal threat, in the eyes of the ANA, is the prospect of a partitioning of Kosovo into Albanian and Serbian territories; accordingly it challenged the LDK and PDK to declare independence or else it would enact its own plan for seizing power.[89] While its ability to launch such a coordinated coup d'etat is doubtful, its antipathy toward multiethnic rule in Kosovo makes it a prime suspect for attacks on Serbs, particularly in northern Kosovo.

A successor group, called the Albanian Liberation Army (ALA), emerged in early 2005 with ambitions of pushing for independence through renewed violence. It engaged in several bomb attacks against UNMIK and government sites in Pristina, though its political program remained underdeveloped.[90] Some critics alleged that these organizations committed to pan-Albanian political unity are phantom armies, with no more than a few hundred members and negligible presence outside of their home regions.[91] In Macedonia, an organization calling itself the National Liberation Army (NLA) also operated, allegedly with the support of KLA members, but it remains unclear how distinct it was from these other organizations.[92]

Former KLA Agencies

Another consequence of the collapse of internal control in the KLA is that its former constituent agencies—including the secret police, paramilitaries, and intelligence units—were under less central control than they were during the war. Their growing autonomy makes it unclear whether high-ranking PDK officials would have the information or capability needed to effectively control them or conduct ingroup policing against them. This was particularly problematic when dealing with three KLA organizations that allegedly continued to operate into the postwar period but without clear lines of control from the PDK: the Policia Ushtarake (PU), the Sherbimi Informativ I Kosoves (Kosovo Information Service, or SHIK), and Zbulim-Kunderzbulim (ZKZ).

The PU was the military police organization of the KLA and, as such, had responsibility for maintaining order within Kosovo. While the PU forces were abolished by

UNMIK and KFOR, they were rumored to continue to function on various fronts, ranging from directing traffic and controlling crowds to demanding "voluntary contributions" from local businesses to support the KLA's local governments. Some of the PU activities in Kosovo were benign, such as managing the evictions of Kosovo Albanians from claimed flats or houses to make room for those left homeless, who would not have survived the harsh winter of 1999–2000.[93] However, the PU is also allegedly involved in extortions from businesses, the burning of Serb homes, and the expropriation of flats and businesses from Serb owners.[94] Among the most alarming rumors about the PU is that it calls in Kosovo Albanian citizens for "informative talks," designed to convince them to end their opposition to PDK activities. Such efforts carry echoes of the famous KLA tactic of abductions of Serbs and Albanian collaborators for the purposes of torture and intimidation.[95] Finally, according to U.S. KFOR intelligence, the PU has ongoing ties to some individuals within the PDK Political Directorate. In fall 1999, one of Thaçi's closest advisers, Beqir Krasniqi, was discovered to have lists naming eighty PU officers in his car, months after the organization was officially outlawed by UNMIK.[96]

The SHIK is also alleged to be functioning in postwar Kosovo, perhaps outside the control of the PDK Political Directorate. Allegedly linked to the Albanian intelligence service, the SHIK was controlled by a senior ex-KLA member, Kadri Veseli, otherwise known as Luli or Number 7.[97] In an interview in *Zeri* published in January 2000, Veseli explained that the chief function of the SHIK was to combat the Serbian secret service operating in Kosovo and to counter organized crime.[98] Veseli alluded to ongoing KLA control of SHIK activities by saying that the SHIK "is not an executive organ and so does not have executive competencies. Our duty is to gather information."[99] This statement implies that the SHIK is located within some remnant of the original KLA executive body that continues to operate in the post-conflict period. The extent to which the SHIK continues to operate, at the behest of Thaçi and the PDK leadership or on behalf of some other group, remains a highly controversial issue in Kosovo.[100] By some accounts, the SHIK was formally disbanded in 2008, but it remains unclear whether this was genuine or simply an attempt to deflect attention from its activities.[101] Some regional commanders of the SHIK were co-opted by organized crime networks as well.[102] As will be discussed, political opponents of the PDK, particularly those in the LDK, have reported that the SHIK has continued to use threats and intimidation, as well as murder, to stop them from contesting the PDK's bid for power and resources.

The ZKZ is the counter-intelligence unit of the KLA. During the war, its commanders reported directly to the KLA general staff, led by Thaçi.[103] At the end of the war, the ZKZ was subsumed under the KPC, and intelligence units were placed under the KPC general staff and regional commands. While the KPC does not officially include an intelligence service, the general staff retains an "information department," which was headed in 1999 by Fadil Kodra, a former ZKZ officer.[104] The International Crisis Group suspected that parts of the ZKZ continued to function in the postwar period because it "would be a major sacrifice on the part of the ex-KLA to give up a network already in place."[105] Some parts of the ZKZ have reportedly been turned over to SHIK while some critics have suggested that parts of the ZKZ have ties to the LDK.[106]

Regional KLA Units

Initially, silence greeted violence against Serbs and Roma in the postwar period as ex-KLA members refused to condemn attacks that were motivated by "revenge." Eventually this gave way to protests over the violence and calls for "restraint" among the PDK and LDK alike. As the violence mounted and began to jeopardize the claim for Kosovo's independence, members of the former KLA attempted to shift blame more explicitly onto rogue KLA units or other extremist elements. From 2001 onward, Thaçi claimed that these rogue elements within Kosovo's society—perhaps comprising a shifting combination of groups already identified—have stolen KLA uniforms and weaponry and claimed that they were the KLA in order to throw blame on the PDK and to discredit it.[107] Attacks on Serbs and Roma in which the assailants identified themselves as coming from the KLA do seem particularly suspicious, as there is little reason for the PDK to endorse such public displays of violence and intimidation while competing in internationally monitored elections. There are also cases (e.g., in Prizren immediately after the war) where those wearing the uniform were identified by strong northern Albanian dialects and accents, a detail that suggests that they may be among the five thousand to eight thousand Albanians recruited during the war, but perhaps operating in the ANA or outside KLA structures.

By 2003–2004, it became clear that many of these apparently "rogue" KLA members were regionally based and often engaged in violence for their own purposes. One prominent example was the Dukagjini ex-KLA members loyal to Ramush Haradinaj in Pec, who were responsible for a string of attacks in 2004–2005.[108] While small in number, these regional KLA units had high levels of organizational cohesion and significant numbers of weapons on hand, which could be mobilized quickly.[109] Some of them have declared themselves "liberation armies" and engaged in highway robbery.[110] The PDK has expressed concern about these regional units and, on occasion, has turned over suspected ex-KLA members to KFOR and UNMIK for arrest.[111] Some of these alleged KLA units may have been linked to the LDK or the FARK, while some might be attached to former KLA regional commanders operating outside of Thaçi's authority. All of these examples suggest that the leadership of the KLA—predominantly in the PDK but also located in the KPC—was unable to control all of the KLA units that emerged from their ranks in the post-conflict period.

Veterans' Associations

One significant development in post-conflict Kosovo was the emergence of "veterans' associations" as a substantial political force. After senior KLA commanders took roles in the PDK, AAK, or KPC, many rank-and-file KLA members began to form these associations to lobby for pensions and other benefits. A key problem facing Kosovo's leadership was that the number of so-called veterans'—40,000 by one estimate—is double the number of fighters that the KLA had in 1999.[112] This problem led to several government initiatives to verify service in the KLA and ensure that benefits were reaching the right people. Frustrated with a lack of pensions and benefits, these veterans' associations became politicized quickly, often pressing the government on the need to take a hard line with both Belgrade and UNMIK on the need for independence. In 2007, with the talks on independence stalled, the KLA veterans' associations made a thinly veiled threat: "We the veterans of the KLA war will be forced to act as KLA soldiers to fulfil the oath of our national heroes."[113] Other KLA veterans' associations tied in with regional political figures have made threats of unrest and violence over the arrest of prominent KLA commanders for war crimes.[114] These "veterans' associations" have been linked to violence, particularly the March 2004 riots, as well as to ongoing attacks against Serbs and other minorities.[115] In many respects, they are deeply embedded in the growing factional divides among Albanians that marked Kosovo's politics after the first two years of the post-conflict period.

Ministry of Public Order

Some evidence indicates that the KLA postwar governing structures continued to operate even after the KLA had formally disbanded its provisional government. This was particularly the case with the Ministry of Public Order (MRP). The MRP began as part of the KLA-backed provisional government, but after it was abolished, it became a shadowy organization composed of former KLA rebels and some members of the PU. In the aftermath of the war, the MRP emerged as an organization that confiscated property and demanded protection money from local Albanian businesses.[116] In effect, the MRP continued to operate as a splinter group, separate from the formal KPC or PDK structures, and tried to fill the power vacuum that emerged after the KLA officially disbanded. According to KFOR intelligence, the MRP had established various "commissions"—for evictions, illegal taxation, and other operations.[117] Through its Commission for Evidence of Social and Private Property, the MRP became involved in contesting property that lay unclaimed after the war. The MRP had established local officials in charge of each municipality and, according to U.S. military sources, "intimidated, threatened, assaulted—and sometimes allegedly killed—anyone who questioned their rule."[118] The MRP also allegedly had links to the PU and the ZKZ, which it used to track opponents and those who would cut into its lucrative illegal businesses. While much of the activities of the MRP were in the shadows, there were several public reports of black cars following KFOR and UNMIK patrols and then being discovered later at makeshift MRP regional stations.[119] The outlines of the organization became clear only when the U.S. KFOR began to develop "blood lists" of known MRP malefactors and connected the dots between those linked to the MRP.[120] The goals of the MRP remain unclear but the chief conclusion of the U.S. military was that ethnic hatreds were deliberately stoked by the MRP command, for it realized that a "multiethnic state threatened their grip on power."[121] Like the ex-KLA units that ran protection rackets on Albanian businesses based on intimidation and violence, some activities of the MRP proved to be outside the capacity of the now-legitimate PDK leadership and the KPC to control or punish, even though it originated from within its ranks.

Liberation Army of Presevo, Medvedja, and Bujanovac (UCPMB)

In early 2000, ethnic Albanian guerrillas with the support of KLA networks in Serbia proper began to organize under the banner of the Liberation Army of Presevo, Medvedja, and Bujanovac (UCPMB).[122] The objective was to challenge the Serbian government in the Albanian-dominated Presevo Valley, in the hopes that this region would be allowed to break off from Serbia and join a newly independent Kosovo. Their ambitions reignited fears that the KLA would resume its call for a "Greater Albania," comprising Albania, Kosovo, and parts of Macedonia and Serbia. The insurgency gradually gained strength throughout 2000 and was supported by some ex-KLA units.[123] The UCMPB was an outgrowth of KLA structures: former KLA members (and some members of the KPC) participated directly in the fighting, and the insurgency was sustained in part by the same smuggling routes that once facilitated the KLA.[124] UCMPB fighters drew directly on the support of the regional KLA "veterans' associations" that formed to lobby for compensation from the provisional government. While appealing for an end to the violence, the PDK leadership was not able to control the violence, despite being explicitly told by the United States that the insurgency jeopardized the case for Kosovo's independence.[125] Despite calls by Thaçi to stop the violence and to solve the problems through the democratic process, the insurgency raged on unabated.[126] Only when NATO intervened to broker the Konulj Agreement between the Serbian government and UCMPB did the insurgency stop.[127]

TABLE 6.1.
Official Organizations or Splinters from the KLA's Ranks

Official Organizations	Ex-KLA Units (abolished but possibly still operating)	Criminal/Informal/Rival Organizations
PDK	PU	FARK
AAK	ZKZ	ANA
KPC	SHIK	MRP
Veterans' Associations	Rogue/regional KLA units	UCPMB
		Organized crime
		Clans

Table 6.1 lists the organizations that have emerged from the ashes of the KLA. These organizations were widely believed to have survived in some form in the post-conflict era, though evidence of their specific involvement in attacks against Serbs and Roma is hard to obtain. Some of these organizations have overlapping members. Others are hostile to one another and have fierce rivalries. All of these organizations have links with criminal organizations that have their own alliances and rivalries.

Coupled with the traditional clan networks of Albanian society and criminal-mafia organizations, these organizations were widely believed to constitute a shadow structure beneath the state in Kosovo. These organizations do not have a single voice or purpose but instead often operate at cross purposes, each hoping to extend its control over the resources of the state. Together, they form a web of interlocking bargaining relationships that operate underneath the surface of Kosovo's official politics. While some of the hard-line elements of these organizations are attempting to carry on the KLA's struggle against the Serbs, often in a covert or sublimated form, many others are engaged in factional violence that is disconnected from or only marginally related to Kosovo's ethnic fault line. As these groups proliferated, especially after 2001, there was a stark increase in factional and predatory violence, such as assassinations and acts of intimidation, which occurred without explanation or apparent motive, throughout the country. The violent bargaining that occurred in post-conflict Kosovo gradually changed and occurred across a range of new fault lines—regional, local, ideological, even personal—that emerged during the post-conflict period.

First Wave: June 1999–December 2000

The immediate aftermath of the war in Kosovo produced a near-anarchic environment with the thousands of refugees flooding back in the country and the emergence of Albanian nationalist shadow governments vying for control over the state. Given the permissive opportunity structure, it is hardly surprising that expressive violence—particularly revenge attacks and riots—was common in the first wave. Thousands of returning refugees sought vengeance on those who had harmed them or remained complicit during their expulsion, often expelling them from their homes, stealing their possessions, and in some cases murdering them. At least some of the apparent revenge violence was categorical, as some Albanian refugees killed or looted from anyone belonging to an ethnic group blamed for wartime atrocities.[128] Similarly, many Roma and other minorities were denounced and victimized for "collaborating" with VJ or MUP forces, even when this was not the case.[129] Some of this violence was opportunistically encouraged or endorsed by returning KLA units that saw political advantages in the expulsion and murder of the Serbs. Instrumental violence—particularly associated with mafia-based score settling, criminal attacks, and the seizure of Serb-owned property, including private homes—also was rampant during this period. Many of the criminal networks in drugs and stolen goods that remain in place today took root during the chaotic aftermath of the war. Individuals and businesses often had to pay "protection money" to groups calling themselves the KLA to survive. Many of the evictions in Pristina and other cities, for example, occurred during this time, as Serbs were forced at gunpoint to leave highly valued properties.[130]

Amid this "rising tide of violence and crime" across Kosovo, strategic violence was increasingly prevalent and politically consequential.[131] Small-scale massacres of Serb, Roma, and other minorities became widespread, especially in the small cities and the regions, such as Pec and Prizren, hard-hit by the VJ and MUP during the war. Within four months, the OSCE had reported 348 murders, 116 kidnappings, 1,070 lootings, and 1,106 cases of arson.[132] Within five months, KFOR had recorded more than 400 murders, nearly evenly split between Albanian (36.25%) and Serb (33.8%) victims.[133] Unpublished UN data on violence give some indication on the extent of the strategic violence—particularly targeted killings, kidnappings, reprisals, and acts of intimidation—which were employed during the first wave of violence (table 6.2). UNMIK breaks its crime records into two categories: violent and nonviolent. Violent crime includes: murder, attempted murder, kidnapping, attempted kidnapping, rape and attempted rape, aggravated assault, abduction, arson, robbery, intimidation, and grenade attacks. Nonviolent crime ranges from car theft to traffic violations but also includes evictions, one of the crimes implicated in "strategic sales"—that is, the forced transfer or sale of property from Serbs to Albanians at below-market rates.[134]

A gradual decrease in violent crime between 1999 and 2000 was followed by a steep decline in 2001, as the first wave of violence subsided. The murder (672), kidnapping (427), and arson (1839) totals for 1999–2000 are high for the population of Kosovo (1.5 million). Compared with Northern Ireland, a European country with an experience of conflict and a similar population (1.68 million), Kosovo's overall reported crime rate is not extraordinary, but the severity of some of its violent crimes is striking.[135] Consider the differences between the two countries in six different types of violent

TABLE 6.2.
Violent Crimes in Kosovo, 1999–2001

	1999	2000	2001	Total
Murder	427	245	118	790
Attempted Murder		275	225	500
Kidnapping	237	190	175	602
Attempted Kidnapping		108	91	199
Rape/Attempted Rape		115	133	248
Assault		365	N/A	365
Arson	1,316	523	218	2,057
Robbery		582	521	1,103
Eviction		654	N/A	N/A
Intimidation		2,402	N/A	N/A
Grenade Attacks		N/A	N/A	N/A

Source: Unpublished UNMIK crime data

Note: An important limitation to this dataset is that it does not include crimes recorded by KFOR. The 1999 totals are a best-guess joint attempt by KFOR and UNMIK officials to estimate the number of crimes committed. This gap in the data was in part created because UNMIK did not have investigative authority between the period of 12 June 1999 and 8 August 1999. During this period, KFOR alone was responsible for law and order because the UN CIVPOL. KFOR classified its operations and has not released even summary datasets to the public. Thus there are two windows where the dataset here is insufficient: (1) crimes that took place before either KFOR or UNMIK were able to enter a region (thus it excludes some of the slash-and-burn tactics of the VJ before June 12, 1999); and (2) crimes recorded only by KFOR when it arrived in a region before UNMIK arrived (12 June 1999–8 August 1999), which remained classified.

crime in 2000 presented in table 6.3. For certain crimes like aggravated assault and rape or attempted rape, Kosovo and Northern Ireland are more or less equal. But for other crimes, particularly some types of crimes most commonly associated with strategic violence, the crime rates are very different. Kosovo's murder and attempted murder totals far exceed Northern Ireland's totals for the same year. While Northern Ireland had no reported cases of arson that year, Kosovo had 523 reported cases. Also, almost four times as many reported cases of intimidation (2,402) occurred in Kosovo as in Northern Ireland (624). These inordinately high numbers of arsons (523) and other nonlethal violent crimes are consistent with the thousands of reported attacks against Serbs and Roma as refugees flooded back into the country.[136] Moreover, there is some evidence that even these statistics are underreported. A confidential UNMIK report estimated 4,089 assaults, 3,508 acts of intimidation, 790 evictions, and 909 grenade attacks on businesses or homes between August 1999 and February 2001.[137]

There is little hard evidence available on the motives behind this violence. For the first nine months of the mission in Kosovo, CIVPOL kept no records on the motive of crimes in its database. When it began to record motives in March 2000, CIVPOL adopted the FBI's motive classification scheme and created six classes of motives: anger, domestic, political, unknown, ethnic, and personal gain (table 6.4). Initially,

TABLE 6.3.
Comparison of Violent Crimes in Kosovo
and Northern Ireland, 2000

	Kosovo	Northern Ireland
Murder	245	44
Attempted Murder	275	124
Aggravated Assault	365	411
Rape / Attempted Rape	115	232
Arson	523	0
Intimidation	2,402	624

Source: UNMIK crime statistics and UK Home Office internal documents.

TABLE 6.4.
Motive Records for UNMIK Crime Data

	2000	2001	2002	January–March 2003
Anger	18	1,072	4,780	781
Domestic	5	302	937	216
Political	1	43	86	45
Unknown	173	14,293	62,097	11,387
Ethnic	1	66	176	30
Personal Gain	395	5,218	17,779	3,376
Political and Ethnic	2	109	262	75
Total Crimes	596	20,994	85,855	15,835

Source: Unpublished UNMIK database.

most CIVPOL officers recorded either "unknown" or "personal gain" for most crimes that they encountered. In the first full year of motive records (2001), 20,994 crimes were logged in, with 14,293 listed as "unknown" and 5,218 listed as "personal gain."[138] Only 66 ethnic crimes and 43 political crimes were recorded, although the number of recorded ethnic and political crimes steadily rose over the next two years as CIVPOL officers became more acquainted with the classification scheme.[139]

Throughout the duration of its mission, UNMIK CIVPOL has not released detailed information on the ethnicity of victims of violent crime. There are no publicly available data on the ethnicity of the victims between 1999 and 2001 except for murder and kidnapping (tables 6.5 and 6.6).[140] What these percentages reveal is the extent to which Serbs and other minorities were disproportionately victimized in post-conflict Kosovo relative to their population numbers. In 1999, Serbs—who constituted less than 10 percent of the population—experienced 34 percent of the murders and 23 percent of the kidnappings. Other minorities—including the Roma, Ashkali, Gora, Bosniaks, and Turks, together approximately 3 percent of the population—experienced 26 percent of the murders and 20 percent of the kidnappings. By late 2000, the rates of victimization had decreased, with Serbs facing 22.3 percent of the murders and 10.5

TABLE 6.5.
Murders in Kosovo, %

	1999	2000	2001
Albanian Victims	40	59.7	68
Serbian Victims	34	22.3	22
Other Victims	26	17.9	10

Sources: Unpublished UNMIK crime data.

TABLE 6.6.
Kidnapping in Kosovo, %

	1999	2000	2001
Albanian Victims	57	67.5	63
Serbian Victims	23	10.5	15
Other Victims	20	22	22

Sources: Unpublished UNMIK crime data.

percent of the kidnappings. Other minorities faced 17.9 percent of the murders and 22 percent of the kidnappings.[141]

Analyzing the location of the incidence of violent crimes—in effect, determining whether these crimes occurred in regions where targeted groups were most at risk—provides additional insight into how Serbs and other minorities were particularly targeted in 1999 and 2000 (table 6.7 and 6.8). The first wave of violence—comprising high levels of murder, arson, assaults, and property theft—affected each region differently. Pec was in the path of a large number of refugees returning from Albania and had more than double the number of murders (123) as any other comparably sized Albanian-majority region.[142] Perhaps not surprisingly, Pec also had a high incidence of looting (236). Prizren, the southern province directly in the path of the refugee returns from Macedonia, had a particularly high rate of arson (151 homes burned). Much of the violence in Pec and Prizren is attributable to revenge as these regions were also among the most badly damaged during the war. According to a European Commission damage assessment conducted in July 1999, 77.14 percent of all homes in Pec were damaged during the war, with 49.33 percent of all homes razed to the ground. Prizren experienced less severe and more uneven devastation, but nevertheless had 51.12 percent of all homes damaged in some way during the war.[143] The witness reports of atrocities in Pec and Prizren suggest that returning Albanian refugees sought to kill those who harmed them and destroy their homes, often with the encouragement of the KLA. There were regular reports of direct KLA involvement in murders and expulsions at the time, and many of the arsons in Prizren were apparently coordinated, with several Serb-owned homes burned down at one time.[144] As table 6.7 points out, Gnjilane remained violent, with 175 cases of looting and 117 cases of arson, but was

TABLE 6.7.
Crimes by Region, 1999

	Pristina	Pec	Mitrovica	Prizren	Gnjilane	Total
Murder	198	123	43	61	58	483
Kidnapping	55	27	15	48	33	178
Assault						0
Looting	510	236	28	180	175	1,129
Attempted Murder						0
Attempted Kidnapping						0
Rape / Attempted Rape						0
Arson	521	123	334	151	117	1,246
Intimidation						0
Violent Crimes Total	1,284	509	420	440	383	3,036
Overall Crimes Total	13,700	4,800	5,000	5,800	6,000	35,300

Sources: Unpublished UNMIK crime data.

TABLE 6.8.
Crimes by Region, 2000

	Pristina	Pec	Mitrovica	Prizren	Gnjilane	Total
Murder	74	61	32	30	49	246
Kidnapping	62	23	19	29	58	191
Assault	98	98	49	69	95	409
Looting	3	3	0	16	0	22
Attempted Murder	81	49	33	49	62	274
Attempted Kidnapping	23	10	15	22	37	107
Rape / Attempted Rape	32	7	23	21	32	115
Arson	160	72	62	73	156	523
Intimidation	828	404	344	419	407	2,402
Robbery	173	128	88	101	95	585
Burglary	1,642	532	531	823	822	4,350
Eviction	301	15	303	22	13	654
Drug Related Crime	55	14	12	18	45	144
Violent Crimes Total	3,532	1,416	1,511	1,692	1,871	10,022
Overall Crimes Total	9,287	3,467	3,363	4,230	4,612	24,959

Source: Unpublished UNMIK crime data.

comparatively less violent than Pec or Prizren in 1999. Owing in part to its large population, Pristina featured the most murders (198), lootings (510), and arsons (521) in 1999, though on a per capita basis this level of violence was less severe than that of Pec or Prizren.

One of the consequences of this flourishing of strategic violence was the ethnic partition of the province. In 1999, the U.S. State Department produced the following estimate of the population by region: Pristina (453,000), Gnjilane (305,000), Prizren (290,000), Pec (277,000), and Mitrovica (232,000), for a total population of 1.5 million.[145] According to the OSCE, Serbs and other minorities constituted approximately 39 percent of Pristina, 26 percent of Gnjilane, 10 percent of Pec, 15 percent of

Prizren, and 37 percent of Mitrovica in 1999.[146] The war and the first wave of strategic violence afterward had dramatic effects on the population, bringing thousands of refugees back into the country and moving those who remained to regions controlled by their ethnic kin. By 2000, the population had increased to approximately 2.1 million people owing to the return of Albanian war refugees and expatriates. Yet the relative percentage of Serbs and other minorities in most regions had decreased, as more Serbs fled the country amid a growing Albanian population. By 2000, Serbs and other minorities constituted only 12 percent of Pristina, 18 percent of Gnjilane, 5.1 percent of Pec, 10 percent of Prizren, and 54 percent of Mitrovica.[147] Throughout the first wave, kidnappings and arsons occurred at high rates in regions where minorities were concentrated. After the initial population movements emptied Pec and Prizren of their minority populations, the small Serb community in Gnjilane became the most significant minority population center outside Mitrovica. What is striking is that Gnjilane remained violent in 2000, even as other Albanian regions became more peaceful. By 2000, Gnjilane had nearly as many arsons (156) and kidnappings (58) as Pristina, despite the fact that the latter was significantly larger in population. This may have been part of a concerted campaign of harassment and intimidation to make that population flee, as ethnic kin in Pec and Prizren had done. By 2000, the Mitrovica region was the only region in which Serbs and other minorities were in greater numbers than they were during the war. Outside the Mitrovica region, Serbs and other minorities were concentrated in geographically disparate enclaves in Albanian-majority regions.[148]

By 2001, the cumulative effect of the strategic violence in the first wave could be seen in the further departure of the Serbian population from Albanian-majority regions. By the end of that year, the Serb population had fallen to 0.346 percent in Pec and to 0.39 percent in Prizren. Both were effectively emptied of their Serb population while a few "other minorities" remained.[149] The other Albanian-majority region has similar experiences of ethnic partition, but retained a greater percentage of its Serb population. By 2001, the Serb population had fallen to 9.69 percent of Pristina, while remaining at the same level in Gnjilane. The effect was most dramatic in cities: the relocation of rural Albanians to Pristina itself doubled the city's prewar population but left it with almost no Serbs except for those scattered in surrounding villages. In all of these regions, their crime rates dropped when they became more monoethnic and the vulnerability of Serbs, Roma, and other minorities decreased, though Pec was still considered the "Wild West" of Kosovo because of substantial factional and gangland violence.

In the northernmost region of the country, Mitrovica, the reverse dynamic happened. Between 1999 and mid-2000, the Serb population of Mitrovica jumped nearly 18 percent from 36.43 percent to 53.68 percent.[150] Much of this population movement was accompanied by strategic violence. During the collapse of the Yugoslav political institutions, Serbs fled to the north half of Mitrovica while Albanians fled to the south, and both groups burned their homes, or were burned out of them, at this time. Mitrovica had low murder and assault totals but high levels of arsons (334 in 1999) and evictions (in 2000) because of its bloody partition in 1999–2000. By mid-2000, the ethnic population transfer was complete: most Serbs lived apart from the Kosovo Albanians, either north of the Ibar River or in the heavily guarded Srbica and Vucitrn municipalities. One consequence of this partition was less violence during the second wave: fewer opportunities for interethnic contact and reduced vulnerability for Serbs exerted a gradual dampening effect on the levels of strategic violence after the first wave subsided. At the same time, there were regular confrontations between Serbian armed groups, such as the "Bridge Watchers" who patrolled the bridge separating the northern and southern halves of the city, and Albanian crowds, allegedly organized by the KLA or its descendants, in 1999 and 2000. These confrontations had a coordinated and often symbolic dimension, as both sides attempted to intimidate the population in the other half of the city.[151] For these reasons, as well as the deep penetration of criminal gangs on both sides, Mitrovica remained a dangerous flashpoint for the French KFOR troops stationed there.[152]

Second Wave: January 2001–December 2004

After the first wave of revenge killings and instrumental attacks subsided in late 2000, and the Serb population had relocated northward toward Serbia, a second wave of strategic violence struck throughout Kosovo. This wave was of significantly reduced in magnitude and scope, yet it had serious political consequences. This violence took on one of two forms: periodic attacks against Serbs and other minorities, which culminated in the March 2004 riots, and escalating gang warfare between Albanian political factions.

Relatively few UNMIK data on violence during this period are publicly available. As table 6.2 reveals, there are some data on murder (118), kidnapping (175), arson (218), and robbery (521) for 2001. Each of these totals is lower, sometimes significantly so, from those recorded the previous year after the first wave of violence had subsided. As tables 6.5 and 6.6 reveal, there were more Albanian victims of murder (68%) and kidnapping (63%) in 2001, though this could be due to the reduced vulnerability of the Serb community, the influx of Albanians into the population from other countries, or an increase in factional violence. No official data for 2002–2004 exist, and no tallies for the ethnicity of perpetrators or victims are available.

To compensate for absence of official UNMIK statistics for 2002–2004, the following analysis employs uses a new dataset of 375 violent incidents from 13 June 1999

TABLE 6.9.
Violent Crime in Kosovo by Region, 1999–2004

	1999	2000	2001	2002	2003	2004	Total
Southern	18	25	21	6	8	4	82
Eastern	11	12	10	0	2	2	37
Central	32	37	15	3	10	15	112
Northern	7	36	28	8	9	11	99
Western	4	15	1	8	12	5	45
Total	72	125	75	25	41	37	375

Source: Kosovo dataset, compiled from wire or newspaper reports.

to 31 December 2004 to describe the characteristics of strategic violence during the second wave (table 6.9). The events reported here are from major news sources and represent only a portion of the overall violence present in the society.[153] As expected, the event-level data—only a subset of the total number of crimes committed during this period—suggest a gradual decrease in strategic violence between 1999 and 2004, as the total number of violent events per year drops from 125 in 2000 (the first full-year of reporting) to 37 by 2004.

According to these data, the two regions with the most violence are the most populous central region, Pristina (29.8% of all attacks) and divided north, Mitrovica (26.5%). The three remaining Albanian-majority regions had fewer recorded acts of strategic violence, but a closer analysis shows the two distinct patterns of attack evident in the second wave. In Gnjilane, attacks against Serbs continued at a level that belied their numbers in the population, with arsons and intimidation remaining common tactics.[154] In Pec and Prizren, factional violence, especially between PDK and LDK loyalists, became increasingly common. According to the International Crisis Group, factional violence was almost part of the political culture in Pec, as "wartime rivalry between the KLA and the LDK-loyal Armed Forces of the Republic of Kosovo (FARK), the region's particularly poor law enforcement, a continuing contest for ownership of the organized crime and smuggling business, and the socially-ingrained tradition of blood feuds have combined to produce a post-war stream of killings with political colouring."[155]

Across all regions, Serbs remained at greater risk of strategic violence throughout the entire post-conflict period (table 6.10). While it is important not to draw too many inferences from small-sample data, table 6.10 gives some indication of the nature of violence during 1999–2004. More than 68 percent of attacks were directed against civilian targets. Despite their relatively small number (approximately 10% of the population) and a location in less vulnerable pockets around the society, Serbs remained more likely to be attacked (52.80% of all attacks) than Albanians (21.87). Most attacks were launched by unknown assailants (63.20%) or by Albanians (28.80%),

TABLE 6.10.
Number (%) of Victims and Perpetrators, 1999–2004

	1999	2000	2001	2002	2003	2004	Total
Albanian Victims	12 (16.67)	30 (24.00)	14 (18.67)	7 (28.00)	9 (21.95)	10 (27.03)	82 (21.87)
Serb Victims	47 (65.28)	66 (52.80)	39 (52.00)	12 (48.00)	18 (43.90)	16 (43.24)	198 (52.80)
Other Victims	15 (20.83)	35 (28.00)	23 (30.67)	8 (32.00)	14 (34.15)	7 (18.92)	102 (27.20)
Civilian Victims	65 (90.28)	85 (68.00)	39 (52.00)	16 (64.00)	28 (68.29)	22 (59.46)	255 (68.00)
Albanian Perpetrators	31 (43.06)	32 (25.60)	24 (32.00)	5 (20.00)	8 (19.51)	8 (21.62)	108 (28.80)
Serb Perpetrators	5 (6.94)	11 (8.80)	6 (8.00)	1 (4.00)	2 (4.88)	2 (5.41)	27 (7.20)
Unknown Perpetrators	36 (50.00)	84 (67.20)	45 (60.00)	20 (80.00)	31 (75.61)	21 (56.76)	237 (63.20)

Source: Kosovo dataset, compiled from wire or newspaper reports.

TABLE 6.11.
Descriptive Statistics on Violence by Category, 1999–2004

	1999	2000	2001	2002	2003	2004	Total
Wounded	19	14	9	2	7	281	332
Casualty	71	82	69	9	23	30	284
Bombings	6	12	6	6	7	1	38
Kidnappings	2	0	1	0	0	0	3
Arsons	2	4	2	0	1	3	12
Expulsions	0	1	0	0	0	1	2

Source: Kosovo dataset, compiled from wire or newspaper reports.

TABLE 6.12.
Tactics and Weaponry in Attacks, 1999–2004

	1999	2000	2001	2002	2003	2004	Total
Shooting	36	66	37	7	18	12	176
Grenades/Bombs	16	28	14	12	17	5	92
Mortar/RPG	6	10	9	2	0	0	27
Other	4	21	5	5	6	13	54

Source: Kosovo dataset, compiled from wire or newspaper reports.

though some of this trend could be due to overreporting of interethnic violence. Direct attacks against KFOR and UNMIK were comparatively rare, though they did happen more frequently in 2003–2004.[156]

According to this sample, strategic violence in Kosovo was dominated by low-casualty attacks, often with gunfire or small arms. In the 375 incidences of violence recorded from 13 June 1999 to 31 December 2004, 284 people were killed, and 332 were wounded (table 6.11). If we exclude some of the borderline attacks at the end of the war in June 1999, and focus only on the five full years of the post-conflict period (2000–2004), there are 213 casualties and 315 wounded in 303 incidents, though most of these are from the March 2004 riots.[157] Only 2 of the attacks during this period killed more than 10 people; the majority of attacks killed less than 1 person per attack. Bombings (38) were comparatively frequent, constituting 10 percent of all attacks during this period.[158] Arson, kidnapping, and expulsions are clearly underreported in this sample, which is evident when these totals are contrasted with the actual incidence of these crimes in 2001 in tables 6.6 and 6.7.

Nearly half (46.9%) of the reported attacks in this sample (1999–2004) involved shooting or sniper fire, 24.5 percent of all attacks involved grenades, and 7.2 percent involve mortars (table 6.12). For all types of violence, there was a clear peak in the number of attacks in 2000, but violence declined thereafter. The following section reviews some of the most common types of violence across the two waves and tracks the shift toward intra-Albanian factional violence during the second wave.

Types of Violence

Throughout both waves, the following types of strategic violence were the most prevalent: (1) revenge and reprisal attacks; (2) sniper fire; (3) grenades, mortar, and bomb attacks; (4) assassinations; (5) riots; (6) arsons; (7) kidnappings; (8) harassment and intimidation; (9) demonstrative violence; and (10) church bombings.

Revenge and Reprisal Attacks

During the first wave of violence, many of the deaths from violent action came about from revenge attacks by returning Albanian refugees. Those who arrived in Kosovo at the end of the war report seeing the arsons of dozens of Serb- and Roma-owned homes in a single night. During the coordinated arsons in Prizren, one Albanian told a journalist that "we want to burn them all . . . we want to take revenge for what they did to our houses."[159] Others reported that returning Albanian refugees set alight dozens of homes in an almost carnival-like atmosphere, with people "dancing in the streets, drinking coffee and wine while the houses burn."[160] There were regular reports of massacres of Serb civilians by returning refugees.[161] The massacre of fourteen Serbian farmers in Gracko on 23 July 1999 was the incident with the largest single loss of life in the post-conflict period, but there was no clear evidence of KLA involvement.[162] Some incidents were senseless: a sixty-two-year-old university professor was dragged from his car and shot to death by rampaging crowds in Pristina on Albanian Flag Day, while four others were killed elsewhere in the city.[163] Similarly, an ethnic Albanian gunman opened fire on a family in Pristina in May 2000, killing three Serbs, including a four-year-old child.[164] Some of the revenge killings were done against those who had worked with Yugoslav authorities or collaborated with VJ or MUP forces. In other cases, the revenge was categorical, as any Serb or Roma—including the elderly, weak, infirm, and others who could not defend themselves—was selected as an easy target for retribution. In one egregious example of this, a family of four Bosnian Muslims, including a seventy-year-old woman, was gunned down by ethnic Albanians.[165] Gruesome attacks against elderly Serbs in enclaves in a majority region became a pattern. In December 2000, an elderly couple was dragged from their home, had their throats cut by ethnic Albanians, and were left in the streets to die.[166] Another elderly couple was founded axed to death outside Kamenica in February 2001.[167] An elderly Serb couple and their son were axed to death while their house was set ablaze in June 2003.[168]

Amid this chaos, significant evidence exists that members of the KLA "rode the wave" of revenge attacks and employed reprisals designed to settle scores and force evictions of Serbs and Roma. Armed gangs calling themselves the KLA marched into towns and executed Serbs, often at point-blank range.[169] For example, in Belo Polje village, in Pec region, three ethnic Serb men, alleged to be members of a Serb paramilitary gang, were shot between the eyes at point-blank range by self-proclaimed KLA members on 19 July 1999. Witnesses told Human Rights Watch that ten uniformed KLA soldiers entered the village in broad daylight and executed the men on the street in front of their homes, in clear view of the rest of the population.[170] In some cases, KLA members appeared at the doorstep of Serbian civilians, demanded that they turn over protection money, and killed them if they refused.[171] In others, KLA members pulled fleeing Serbs from refugee columns and executed them on the spot.[172] As late as 2001, there were assassinations of Serbs alleged to be part of paramilitary gangs in central Pristina.[173] A general pattern that lasted throughout 2003–2004 was that Serbs returning to visit their prewar homes were shot or bombed by ethnic Albanians, who were determined to prevent a return to multiethnicity.[174]

Many of these reprisal attacks were described as revenge attacks in newspaper accounts but were conducted on categorical grounds and betrayed clear evidence of strategic intent. Stylistic details of some attacks appeared to point to KLA involvement. For example, some attackers often had KLA insignias on their uniforms or identified themselves as KLA. Albanian nationalist and KLA-related graffiti was also found on the walls of burned homes and churches. As noted, one of the key open questions is whether these self-identified KLA are genuinely from the organization or its more extreme offshoots, or whether such obvious self-identification is a ruse designed to obscure responsibility for the attacks and throw blame onto the PDK. Ultimately, what was revenge and reprisal was difficult to determine, because both types of violence were empirically intertwined in the crime patterns, especially in the immediate aftermath of the war.

Sniper Fire

Sniper fire was often employed against the ethnic communities to terrify the population and encourage it to flee. Throughout this period, seemingly random sniper attacks in Serb or Roma settlements were used to intimidate their populations and to encourage them to flee toward Serbia or Serb-majority regions. One common tactic was that Serbs would be victims of drive-by shootings, almost at random.[175] Most of the drive-by shootings were of Serb, Roma, and other minority civilians.[176] In a few isolated cases, snipers took aim at Kosovo Serb politicians.[177] In most cases, the sniper fire was inaccurate and missed the target, but in a few cases it was precise and deadly. In August 2002, a single sniper shooting at Serbian woodcutters pinned down arriving KFOR troops for two hours in Pec before the sniper was finally captured.[178] On some occasions, such as the Mitrovica riots in February 2000 and border flare-ups with UNPMB and other smaller groups, sniper fire was directed against KFOR troops, with lethal accuracy.[179]

Snipers would often target convoys of Serbs traveling either between enclaves or to Serbia. On 13 February 2001, the twice-weekly KFOR-escorted convoy of buses carrying Serbs from Strpce to Serbia came under highly accurate sniper fire, resulting in one death and several injuries. This sniper attack was effective in intimidating the Serbian population, which relied on buses to Serbia proper for basic living needs. Convoys of Serbs traveling to Serbia would be fired on by unknown gunmen, often wounding or killing their passengers.[180] Some examples of sniper attacks betrayed clear military training and skill, and coordination that would be beyond the ability of those conscripts who fought in the war. In Gnjilane in 2000, after KFOR established escorts for Serbs to go to the market, four Serb vehicles were fired upon on the road from Kamenica to Gnjilane in a matter of a few hours, resulting in the death of four Serbs and the injury of four more.[181] What is significant about this attack is that it could not be entirely unplanned; to select a target, track it, and achieve that level of death and injury betrays clear evidence of military training. Sniper attacks against KFOR-guarded convoys began to occur less frequently after 2001.

Grenade, Mortar, and Bomb Attacks

One of the clearest indicators of strategic violence in Kosovo was the frequent use of explosives against civilian targets. In the newspaper-generated dataset of strategic attacks from 1999 to 2004, there were ninety-two grenade attacks and twenty-seven attacks involving mortars or rocket-propelled grenades. During the first wave of violence, most of these grenade and mortar attacks were used against Serb or Roma targets. Some grenade attacks were cruel and almost random: in August 2000, a grenade was tossed onto a basketball court, injuring ten Serbian children.[182] A car bomb in December 2002 in central Pristina injured twenty-nine people, with no apparent motive.[183] But in other cases the targets were more carefully selected. On 13 July 1999, there were reports that Albanians had tied up family members in several Serb homes and then threw grenades into the building.[184] Grenades were also regularly thrown into Serb-owned businesses, such as bars and restaurants, and were sometimes followed by gunfire.[185] Some of these attacks were done with petrol bombs that had the advantage of burning the house down, even if no one was killed.[186] One tactic that was common was to throw grenades into marketplaces in order to maximize the number of deaths.[187] In some cases, mortars were used against Serb homes and businesses, even when they were under KFOR protection, or at cars carrying Serbian passengers.[188] In other cases, grenades and mortars were used against buses, particularly from Serb regions, to kill passengers but also to make social and economic life impossible.[189]

Coordinated grenade attacks were also frequently used throughout the post-conflict period. In the town of Petrovce, for example, twelve coordinated explosions occurred on one morning in September 1999.[190] Following the incident, a KLA uniform was found in the sweep of the area, but it was unclear if it was related to the attack. Similarly, four Albanian men were arrested after nine mortar shells were fired within a few minutes of each other into Pasanje, in southeastern Kosovo.[191] In Mitrovica, there were coordinated grenade attacks on refugee registration locations in the Serb-held northern half of the city in March 2000.[192] During the first wave, grenades were particularly directed against Serbian targets and to amplify population flight. On 18 December 1999, a series of grenade attacks on Serb and Roma enclaves in Orahovac killed one Serb and injured several others. Only the local Serb community interpreted the attacks as a signal to leave. By December 29, forty-six Serbs, most of them elderly and children, demanded that KFOR escort them out of the town.[193] Another example could be seen in Vitina region. By early July 1999, seven thousand Serbs remained in this area, split between five mixed villages and three Serb-only villages. By this point, the OSCE reported that "increased KFOR protection is urgently required in the above-mentioned mixed villages where the remaining Serb (and Roma) population have recently been the victims of killings and assault and are on the verge of being forcibly displaced."[194] Just at the moment that the Serb community was considering fleeing Vitina, a grenade exploded in front of a Serb shop in Vitina city center, wounding thirty people and triggering a rash of departures by Serb families.[195] These grenade attacks were a force multiplier, designed to amplify population movements that might otherwise have slowed or not occurred. Similarly, booby-traps were often used against Roma homes and villages to convince the residents to flee.[196] In 2002–2003, there was a spate of bomb attacks against unoccupied houses, which were due to be filled with returnees.[197] The use of coordinated grenade attacks gradually tapered off in late 2003, but in Gnjilane the remaining Serb community continued to be victimized by these attacks through 2004.[198]

Grenades were often used in tandem with other attacks to terrify vulnerable communities, especially during the first wave of violence. For instance, KFOR reported an upsurge in grenade attacks on Serb homes between 5 and 10 July 1999, coupled with eighty-one arson attacks, thirty-six lootings of homes, one kidnapping, and four missing persons cases, most of which occurred in the mixed villages.[199] The types of bombs used sometimes betrayed military training and a degree of organization to the violence.[200] On 2 February 2000, an antitank rocket was fired on a UN bus traveling between two Serb villages.[201] These antitank rocket and RPG attacks became a semiregular event, sometimes causing significant casualties. On 16 February 2001, the lead bus of a KFOR-escorted Serb convoy (called the Nis Express) was destroyed by a remote-controlled bomb near Podujevo, resulting in eleven deaths and forty injuries.[202] Having received advanced warning of the attack, KFOR conducted a search of the route in advance of the convoy and failed to discover the bomb. The bomb involved 100–200 kilograms of explosives and was detonated from nearly one-half mile away.[203] At a minimum, someone with military training was responsible for this attack, though the timing involved in monitoring KFOR's movements in order to place the bomb after the sweep occurred suggests military involvement.[204] Mortars and RPGs were also used against ordinary civilian targets. For example, in Klokat, mortars were fired into a Serb village on 17 August 1999, killing two and wounding six.[205] On 19 October 1999, five rocket propelled grenades were simultaneously launched on the Serb houses in Mogila, in Vitina municipality.[206] In other cases, landmines were deliberately set to kill Serb civilians, in attacks that betrayed clear military training.[207] Especially in Mitrovica, Serbs would respond with grenade attacks on Albanian homes and shops, often causing deaths and injuries.[208]

Over time, however, grenades came to be used for attacks between Albanian factions as well. In July 2000, Ramush Haradinaj and his brother Daut were seriously injured in an bombing on their car shortly after they formed the AAK.[209] In the lead-up to the elections, grenades were thrown at the party offices of various minority parties in Pristina and the LDK offices in Malisevo.[210] In December 2002, a car bomb killed an LDK activist and former KLA member in a clear assassination attempt.[211] In some cases, grenade attacks were used as a warning to UNMIK after arrests of prominent KLA members over war crimes. Shortly after noted KLA commander Rustem Mustafa was convicted of war crimes in July 2003, there were bomb attacks against the CIVPOL stations and the judiciary.[212]

Assassinations

One of the most common tactics in post-conflict Kosovo was assassinations. In the first wave, many of the assassinations were almost random targets of opportunity, but the timing of the attacks suggested some organization to the violence. For instance, between 12 and 17 January 2000, a wave of thirteen murders occurred across all the Albanian-majority regions, including the execution of a family of four Muslim Slavs in Prizren, the four murders of Kosovo Serbs in Pasanje, three Kosovo Serbs murdered in Gnjilane, and a double murder in Djakovica.[213] The sudden nature of these attacks, and their geographic scope, suggests that an organized armed group paced this series of assassinations to apply pressure on targeted groups to leave. In some cases, the attacks were conducted by people wearing KLA uniforms, though it remained unclear whether they were sanctioned by the leadership or by one of its offshoots.[214] Political assassinations against moderate Serbs also occurred. Josif Vasic, a medical doctor and representative of the Kosovo Serbs, was assassinated in Gnjilane by unknown assailants in early 2000.[215] Serbs working for UNMIK were sometimes shot and killed by unknown assailants.[216] A powerful bomb destroyed the home of top Yugoslav representative to Kosovo in a botched assassination attempt in November 2000 and was followed by another bombing on the same offices in April 2001.[217] Kosovo politicians who called for links with Yugoslavia were also targeted.[218]

Despite rumors that dozens of assassinations of FARK members occurred in late 1999, the earliest recorded assassination among the Albanian community was of Besim Mala, a former KLA fighter and high-ranking KPC official, who was gunned down in a restaurant in Pristina in April 2000.[219] Soon these assassinations became more common, especially of former KLA officials who had played a significant role during the war but fell out with Thaçi or other powerbrokers in the PDK or testified against their allies in trials.[220] Similarly, in mid-2000 there were reported assassinations against LDK officials, allegedly by the KLA. For example, a senior member of the LDK, Alil Dreshaj, was shot by men wearing KLA badges who broke into his house in June 2000.[221] Shootings and kidnappings of LDK officials continued throughout 2000, especially after some KPC members were found shot dead, presumably through factional violence.[222] In some cases, there were coordinated bombing attacks of LDK candidates for the municipal election in October 2000.[223] Shortly after the elections in November, there was a wave of shootings and a bomb attack against LDK candidates who were successful in the election.[224] Another LDK council was shot by masked gunmen only weeks after the elections.[225] A few weeks later, the top adviser to Ibrahim Rugova was also gunned down.[226] In October 2001, there occurred a bombing of the LDK main in Suva Reka, arson of LDK offices in Viti, and reported assassination attempts against LDK officials, activists, and sympathetic journalists.[227] There was even an assassination attempt of an LDK official shortly after the inaugural meeting of the Kosovo Assembly.[228] By the end of 2001, a marked shift was apparent in the types of assassinations and their targets, away from Serbs and toward party loyalists of the LDK.

By 2002, the intensifying factional competition between the PDK and the LDK led to a rash of assassination attempts against LDK and AAK officials. In January 2002, a LDK assembly member was shot dead on his doorstep in Pec.[229] A member of the KPC close to Haradinaj was bombed in his home in the southwest of the country in 2002.[230] In August 2002, a rocket attack on a restaurant in Pec injured eight people, including some prominent LDK operatives.[231] After the LDK was successful in the October 2002 elections, three people, including a senior LDK official, were killed.[232] In September 2003, Ramiz Murici, a close associate of Rugova, was seriously wounded in a car bomb attack, which was the third assassination attempt against him in the post-conflict period.[233] Rugova's own home was bombed in March 2004, though he escaped unharmed.[234] The violence against LDK figures never stopped, even as others were targeted. AAK officials were also subject to assassination attempts.[235] Journalists looking into official misconduct and corruption were also targeted in drive-by shootings, as were businessmen involved in tendering major contracts with the government.[236] It was during this period that the shift in the nature of strategic violence from attacks on Serbs and other minorities to attacks between intra-Albanian political violence became apparent.

In 2003, these assassinations of political figures continued, but there was also growing evidence of gang warfare in the west of the country, much of it with a distinctly political hue. In January 2003, three former KLA members were shot in western Kosovo in a gang-style killing. One of the dead, former KLA fighter Tahir Zemaj, was a prosecution witness in a trial of former KLA members accused of killing members of the FARK after the war.[237] Three months later, another witness at the same trial was killed by gunmen spraying the car with bullets.[238] In September 2003, another bomb attack on a witness in the same trial was reported.[239] Reports of criminal violence in western Kosovo grew considerably, but distinguishing what was criminal and political was extremely difficult to do.[240] KPS officers, including former KLA fighters, were assassinated as well by unknown gunmen, but it remained unclear what the motives behind the attacks were.[241] Similarly, KPS patrols in northern Kosovo were occasionally ambushed following the riots in March 2004, but it was unclear how much this was driven by ethnic antipathy.[242]

The question of who was responsible for the assassinations has become a controversial one in Kosovo. In 2003, an LDK official pointed the finger of blame at the PDK and AAK, saying that the "communists in Dukagjin and Drenica" were responsible for the attacks.[243] The language of this accusation hints at the extent to which regional fault lines, rather than ethnicity, became salient in the post-conflict period. The PDK has denied that it is responsible and claimed that it had received death threats as well.[244] Over time, much of the suspicion has settled on the SHIK. One former SHIK member, Nazim Bllaca, alleged that SHIK killed 450 people, mostly political opponents from the LDK and other groups, following the war.[245] A leaked report by the EU's rule of law mission, EULEX, suggested that the SHIK was responsible for a PDK-directed campaign of assassination between 1999 and 2001, with some attacks occurring as late as 2003, mostly against LDK activists.[246] Yet there has been no hard evidence of SHIK or PDK control over the violence, and it is likely that many of the competing splinter groups from the ranks of the KLA played at least some role in the violence.

Riots

The most serious incident of rioting in post-conflict Kosovo was the March 2004 riots, which left nineteen dead and hundreds injured. Aside from this major event, rioting was a common occurrence in Kosovo, though it did not generally have the severity and geographic spread that the March 2004 riots demonstrated. Especially during the first wave of attacks, riots were common at flashpoint cities like Mitrovica, often producing clashes that lasted days and caused significant casualties. In February 2000, riots broke out in Mitrovica after grenades were rolled into Serbian cafés, wounding twenty, and two Albanians were killed in response by Serbian gangs. Five more people were killed in these riots, described by a UNMIK spokesperson as a "terrifying and appalling increase in multi-ethnic violence."[247] The result was an increase in tit-for-tat violence, which left three more Albanians killed in drive-by shootings and executions.[248] As crowds attacked French KFOR for failing to protect them, more than sixteen peacekeepers were injured by the mobs.[249] Within a week, more than nine hundred Albanians had fled their homes in northern Mitrovica for fear of additional attacks.[250] Some riots in Mitrovica emerged as a result of street altercations between individuals from both ethnic groups, but in that combustible environment large-scale rioting could result from even a small spark.[251] Others spun out of control after altercations between KFOR and an array of protesters.[252] For example, riots emerged because attempted arrests by KFOR forces were met with hostility and violence in some villages.[253] French KFOR forces were often injured, sometimes seriously, while breaking up crowds that had formed on either side of the Ibar River.[254] Throughout the country, riots emerged after grenade and bomb attacks, as angry civilians started stopping and assaulting anyone from the ethnic group that they suspected of attacking them.[255] For example, after the Nis Express bombing in February 2001, riots broke out in Serb enclaves in Pristina. Yet at least some riots betrayed evidence of strategic planning. For example, after fifty elderly Serbs were brought back to Pec in 1999, more than six hundred Albanians suddenly came together and rioted with stones and Molotov cocktails.[256] As was the case in Bosnia, these semispontaneous riots occurred throughout the post-conflict period whenever refugee returns of minority groups were attempted.

Kidnapping

One recurring tactic throughout this period of time was kidnapping. The prevalence of kidnapping in Kosovo is an important contextual feature of this case, as it was used more often here than in any other case study except Iraq. Kidnapping is underreported in the sample from 1999 to 2004, but (as table 6.2 indicates) at least 602 kidnappings were recorded between 1999 and 2001. Members of the KLA were noted to have abducted hundreds of people, including Albanian dissidents, journalists, and LDK activists, and tortured them in secret prisons.[257] In the immediate aftermath of the war, KLA units commandeered abandoned police stations as detention centers. According to Human Rights Watch, other locations, such as homes, garages, and barns, were also used as detention centers once KFOR assumed control.[258] One common tactic for self-proclaimed KLA units was to abduct Serbs and Roma from villages, beat them severely, and return them to their village with a warning to leave.[259] In some cases, the KLA told Serbs that the country belonged to the KLA.[260] The KLA would often beat detainees and sexually abuse them, but also sometimes seek out information on their wartime behavior in order to decide how to dispose of them.[261] In many villages, Serb and Roma men were abducted, detained, and beaten, but often released days later. Because kidnapping is so effective in communicating a message, it was often used to encourage members of a minority group to flee. For example, on 14 June 1999, four uniformed KLA members abducted a Serb couple from Lutogllava, near Prizren. They were taken to a barn in the nearby village of Grejkoc, and self-described KLA officers beat the male severely. After several days, they were freed, in part because the KLA claimed to have received favorable information about them from their Albanian neighbors. But the KLA officers sent them with a warning: "Go to Serbia. Go to Milošević—never come back."[262]

Abductions and beatings had three advantages for those hoping to expel Serbs from Albanian-majority regions. First, the victim not only survived but "got the message" and then spread it to his or her coethnic kin. Second, since the victim was returned without lethal injuries, the violence rarely drew the attention of KFOR and UNMIK, which were consumed with dealing with murders and other more violent crimes. Third, the victim had a strong incentive not to report the incident to police for fear of an escalation, possibly including death. Human Rights Watch is unequivocal about the strategic purpose of the abduction and notes that "the intent behind many of the killings and abductions that have occurred in the province since early June appears to be the expulsion of Kosovo's Serb and Roma population rather than a desire for revenge alone."[263] In other words, kidnapping was part of a strategy to accelerate the pace of Serb and Roma expulsion from the province.

Border Incidents

Especially in 2000–2001, there were regular incidents along the buffer zone that separated Serbia's administrative border with Kosovo. Most of these involved armed attacks by organized groups that emerged out of the ashes of the KLA. The earliest reported border incident occurred in November 1999.[264] By early 2000, there were clashes between Yugoslav police and what were described as "Albanian terrorists" who had crossed the border to operate in southern Serbia.[265] By spring 2000, the self-proclaimed UCPMB forces were allegedly using automatic weapon fire against police patrols and ambulances in southern Serbia.[266] Another tactic was to fire mortar rounds against Serbian police targets within Serbia from villages in Kosovo, which would often wound police officers.[267] By the end of 2000, there were regular skirmishes, and shots taken against Serb police and KFOR, in the buffer zone separating Kosovo from Serbia.[268] By early 2001, the skirmishes had taken on a more serious tone, with multiple Yugoslav soldiers being wounded in each incident and UCPMB insurgents being killed.[269] In April 2001, several Russian peacekeepers were killed by a sniper in the buffer zone separating Kosovo from Serbia.[270] Joint U.S.-Russian KFOR patrols were periodically under sniper fire.[271] Sustained attacks on Serb police stations in villages led to the use of bombs and heavy fighting.[272] Some of the UCPMB members resorted to kidnapping as well.[273] Eventually, UCPMB members began to use an array of weapons, including "heavy fire from mortars, recoilless rifles, rocket launchers and machine guns" against Serbian police stations.[274] By August 2001, there were a reported 68 dead and 150 wounded on both sides of the conflict.[275] In 2003, attacks in Serbia began to take a different character, as ANA forces joined the fight and began to attack police stations.[276]

In March 2001, there were additional skirmishes, with Albanian rebels reported on the border with Macedonia.[277] This led to the exchange of fire with U.S. KFOR, as well as engagements with Macedonian soldiers.[278] A shadowy group called the National Liberation Army, allegedly linked with the KLA, began engaging Macedonian police on a semiregular basis.[279] Macedonian forces allegedly responded with shelling across the border into Kosovo, though the government was careful to downplay the attacks.[280] British KFOR troops were wounded and killed along this border as well.[281] In one incident in April 2001, eight Macedonia soldiers were ambushed and killed through machine gun fire and bombs.[282]

Demonstrative Violence

Some of the violence against Serbs and other minorities could be described as demonstrative. Its purpose was complex: in some cases, the attacks were used to intimidate Serbs and other minorities to flee, while in other cases it was done to signal the capacity of the KLA or its splinters to KFOR and other international actors. In some cases, the theatrics of the violence were indicative of this purpose, such as when crowds would suddenly appear when refugees would return. In October 1999, for example, nearly fifteen hundred Albanians gathered in a coordinated ambush on a UN convoy transporting Serb civilians from Kosovo to Montenegro.[283] This occurred after warnings from the KLA and others to KFOR and UNMIK that refugee returns should not be undertaken. Coordinated arsons were also used in Gnjlane and elsewhere to terrify Serbs and Roma in the population and to send a message to KFOR. For example, as KFOR forces attempted to establish control over the contested Istok municipality, three Roma families were burned to death in their homes in coordinated arson attacks in Dubrava village.[284] In some cases, arson attacks were increased near KFOR checkpoints to demonstrate KFOR's inability to protect the Serb community. In Slovinje village, in the Lipljan municipality, Serb and Roma houses were burned to the ground only three hundred yards from a KFOR checkpoint in a series of coordinated attacks in July 1999.[285]

Similarly, some of the more gruesome murders were designed to send a message to the Serbs, or to organizations like KFOR and UNMIK. For example, on 9 July 1999, a Serb male was decapitated in the town market during the midday shopping period in Lipljan.[286] His body was left in the market as a warning to Serbs, and possibly to those in UNMIK who would seek to restore multiethnic governance to Kosovo. Shortly after the Lipljan decapitation, four grenade attacks of Serb stores occurred, all in the space of one hour, each attack at a regular fifteen-minute interval. Those behind the grenade attacks knew that coordinated and timed attacks would send the limited KFOR forces scrambling back and forth across the town, in a clear demonstration of their inability to establish control over this contested space. Sometimes abductions and murders were also used to send a message to KFOR. In November 2000, four Ashkali (Albanian-speaking Roma) males returned to Dasovec, in the Srbica municipality in central Kosovo. Only days after refusing KFOR protection, the men were found dead, lying on the ground outside their tent. Amnesty International argued that, "whether or not the killer's prime intention was to send a message that returnees were in danger and not welcome, that is what they did."[287]

In a few cases, the violence included an element of what Charles Tilly called polyvalent communication, defined as "the individual or collective presentation of gestures simultaneously to two or more audiences in ways that code differently with those audiences."[288] In Kosovo, some attacks sent different messages to Albanians and Serbs about the likelihood that they will become victims of violent crime. Because polyvalent signals are a function of communicative contexts familiar only to "insiders" to the culture, evidence of this kind of communication is scattered throughout firsthand accounts of the attacks.[289] Only in exceptional cases are outsiders to the culture witness to the direct communication of a polyvalent message. One such incident occurred to a Human Rights Watch team in June 1999:

> In Vitomirica, which housed a Serb majority population prior to the conflict, there had clearly been considerable arson and looting of Serb homes. Houses with "Alba-

nian house" written on the side were left untouched, while other houses had clothing and detritus strewn about in the front lawns and doors left open. Some Serbs homes were being occupied by Albanian returnees. One man told Human Rights Watch, "We are occupying Serb houses because they burned ours."[290]

There are other examples in which demonstrative acts of strategic violence sent differently coded messages to the ethnic communities. For example, Oblic municipality had a Serb population of approximately nine thousand people in July 1999, almost all concentrated in four villages (Babin Most, Plementina, Crkvena Vodica, and Milosevo). In early July 1999, a Serb was shot dead on his doorstep in Oblic village, which in turn triggered a fresh wave of reprisal attacks against Serbs and a population flight of Serbs. The Albanian population did not "read" an apparently random attack as a signal of a threat to itself.

Church Bombings

Church burnings and detonations also continued in force in Pristina and Gnjilane, and against isolated communities elsewhere.[291] In the immediate aftermath of the war, numerous church burnings and detonations occurred, especially in regions with high refugee returns like Pec. In some cases, this was because Serbian refugees had fled to Orthodox churches for protection, making them an attractive target for remnants of the KLA. In September 1999, for example, two antitank rockets were fired into the Pec Patriarchate, which housed Serbs expelled from their homes or seeking shelter.[292] Yet these targeted and symbolic attacks in contested regions continued unabated throughout 2000 and 2001. On 14 January 2000, the Orthodox church in Cernica, Gnjilane, was badly damaged in a bomb attack shortly after KFOR withdrew its static guard.[293] In June 2000, nine mortars were fired at five-second intervals at an Orthodox monastery in Decani.[294] Some of these attacks were devastating: a nighttime bombing of a church in Pomazetin destroyed the entire structure and sent its staff fleeing in July 2000.[295] Less than a year later, in February 2001, Orthodox churches were attacked in Jornji Livoc and Draganac, and mortar rounds were fired into the Orthodox cemetery at Orahovac.[296] Another Serb cemetery in Staro Gracko was bombed in August 2001. On 17 November 2001, an explosion completely destroyed Saint Basil of Ostrog Church in Ljubova, an attack that came on the heels of three blasts that badly damaged the All Serbian Saints Church in Durakovac.[297] Hand grenades were then tossed into the Orthodox Church in Pristina on 22 December 2001.[298] All of these churches had KFOR protection, in the form of either static guard or regular patrols. Nonetheless, the bombing attacks continued as two churches were destroyed as late as November 2002.[299] Religious leaders were also not immune to attacks. For example, on 12 July 1999, a Serbian Orthodox priest and two seminary students were caught in a drive-by shooting near the mixed village of Klokot.[300] Such attacks on religious sites and clergy were designed to reinforce the message that the Serbian community, and the markers of its culture and faith, were not welcome in post-conflict Kosovo.

Was the KLA Responsible?

As noted, one of the key questions that UNMIK officials wrestled with was the extent to which the KLA—or some splinter from its ranks—was responsible for the strategic violence evident in the post-conflict period. This is not an easy determination to make. Determining the lines of control for certain attacks—that is, connecting a certain faction or splinter group with a specific act of violence—is particularly difficult. Separating who did what always is difficult in a society in which politics, crime, and personal rivalry intermix as freely as it does in Kosovo. No hard evidence exists that the top leadership of the KLA was directly behind the violence, but a widespread suspicion among KFOR and UNMIK officials held that remnants of the original KLA were secretly directing, sponsoring, or endorsing attacks consistent with its goal of securing independence. Many observers pointed to the categorical nature of the violence as evidence that that it was part of a plan to expel the remaining Serbs and Roma from the province. A senior U.S. official remarked that the attacks were directed at "targets of opportunity—elderly people, buses of people shopping . . . especially in places which were not effectively protected" and that "it was directed at some level—we could never tell what level, or pin it to the top level. Some of it was politically motivated but a lot of it was encouraged by mid-level KLA."[301] What remained unclear was whether the midlevel KLA was working at the behest of the top PDK leadership or for any of the splinter groups that operated like a shadow structure beneath the state. An early report of the OSCE found that ethnic Albanian fighters were responsible for the violence and that the armed groups seemed "to operate in an organized fashion and have some form of hierarchy, command and control."[302] In its first full report on attacks on minorities, the OSCE remarked that "it would appear that there is an orchestrated campaign, or campaigns organized by, as yet, unidentified elements whose aim was to terrorize minority populations, destabilize the province and prevent democratization and peaceful co-existence."[303] In its report, Human Rights pointed to the gap between identifying ex-KLA units as responsible and pinning responsibility on the ex-KLA members in the PDK:

> Although a desire for revenge and retaliation provides some of the explanation for violence, especially in the case of arson and looting of property, Human Rights Watch research suggests that a great deal of the violence is politically motivated;

namely, the removal from Kosovo of non-ethnic Albanians in order to better justify an independent state. There is also clear evidence that some KLA units were responsible for violence against minorities beginning in the summer of 1999, and continuing throughout 2000 and early 2001. Human Rights Watch has no evidence, however, of a coordinated policy to this end of the political and military leadership of the former KLA, which has made public statements condemning attacks against minorities.[304]

The sophistication of the violence made the blanket condemnations and disavowal of knowledge about the source of the attacks offered by Thaçi and the PDK leadership seem suspicious to many observers. This was particularly the case because "in such a small territory and close-knit society as Kosovo, it seems inconceivable that the KLA with its intelligence services and influence in every corner of life does not know at least in some cases who the culprits actually are."[305] Intelligence agencies were particularly suspicious of the PDK's connections with a dense network of criminal organizations throughout Kosovo. In a secret assessment leaked to the press, the German intelligence service (Bundesnachrichtendienst, or BND) commented that "the key players (including Haliti, Haradinaj, and Thaçi) were intimately involved in interlinkages between politics, business, and organized crime structures in Kosovo."[306] Subsequent reports have alleged that Thaçi was deeply involved in criminal activities, such as organ trafficking, in as late as 2003–2004.[307] Another assessment alleged that Thaçi had also exerted "violent control" over the heroin trade.[308] Yet many of these allegations have never been substantiated with hard evidence, and no charges have been filed against Thaçi for these crimes.

On one level, the extent to which the top PDK leadership was interdependent with criminal networks suggests that it would have at least knowledge of their activities and an ability to influence members through ingroup policing. The record of Thaçi and his allies in destroying their rivals and in ruthlessly enforcing order during the war suggests that at least some of the former KLA's activities in the post-conflict period might remain under his control.[309] One leaked but unverified KFOR report suggested that Thaçi had personally overseen "assassinations, detentions, beatings and interrogations" during and after the war.[310] In the post-conflict period, there were moments in which Thaçi and his allies clearly tried to reign in the activities of those in their ranks. Senior KLA officials would even hand over known criminals, sometimes from within their ranks, to KFOR.[311] Yet there was clearly a general preference to keep KFOR "out of the loop" in its enforcement of the peace settlement. Some of the KLA's efforts to conduct ingroup policing was done illegally. Periodic reports claimed that KLA or SHIK was conducting "clean-up" operations against ambitious former KLA commanders and officials linked to the FARK and other informal structures. One unconfirmed and classified BND report links Thaçi to at least eleven contract murders through a hit man named Afrimi.[312] Yet it is probably an overstatement to suggest that Thaçi and his allies could control or reign in all of the splinters that emerged from the ranks of the KLA. His efforts at ingroup policing are likely to be incomplete owing to the fact that they would have to be conducted with some degree of plausible deniability. It is also likely that the PDK would have incomplete information about the activities of the dozens of small armed groups and "phantom armies" now operating in Kosovo.

Beyond this point, three further difficulties are associated with assigning all of the blame for all of the strategic attacks to Thaçi and the PDK. First, because the KLA had formally disbanded, it was difficult to blame an organization that did not formally exist for strategic violence in post-conflict period. Even if some structures of the KLA continued to exist in the postwar period, the lines of control and accountability from the PDK to these units were blurred. Second, it was widely acknowledged that many of these organizations engaged in disinformation campaigns designed to cast blame on their rivals for attacks conducted by their members. Many Serb victims, for example, reported that attacks by actors who claimed to be the KLA or to wear KLA insignias, but had doubts that the attackers were really KLA, or spoke with accents different from those widely used in Kosovo. In a world in which an individual may be simultaneously a veteran of the KLA, a member of a KLA splinter organization, and an organized crime gang, tracing the lines of control for violence is incredibly difficult. Third, these allegations hinge not just on intention—that is, did elements of the former KLA wish harm against some or all Serbs?—but also on capability of the PDK leadership to act coherently, to enforce the terms of the peace settlement, and to control the splinter groups of the former KLA. The PDK could not reward all of the factions within its ranks because the LDK consistently won the elections in the interim period and forced the PDK into coalition governments, most of which were under international supervision. Even with a network of criminal enforcers and SHIK at its disposal, the PDK would have been unable to effectively punish all of the rogue units from within its ranks, in part because of information problems over what they were doing and in part because such punishment activities—especially if they were conducted outside the law—were forbidden by their international partners.

In other words, the KLA is likely only partially responsible for the violence in the post-conflict period. Strictly speaking, the KLA did not exist in the post-conflict period because the organization had devolved from an inchoate guerrilla force into a panoply of armed groups competing with each other and pursuing private agendas underneath the surface of Kosovo's politics. Perhaps the most important fact when assessing its culpability was that its organizational decomposition was incomplete. The PDK had become detached from many of the successor organizations to the KLA, and its leadership probably had only partial or incomplete control over troublemakers in its ranks. The splinter groups emerging from the KLA—as well as the factions operating within recognized organizations like the KPC—were tied loosely to the PDK core, but only some were responsive to the demands of the PDK leadership. Many others operated entirely independently, without concern for the political future of the PDK or even the original wartime goals of the KLA. This means that two apparently contradictory claims might simultaneously be true: (1) the "KLA" might be behind the attacks on Serbs and Roma in post-conflict Kosovo; and (2) the PDK and the key notable leaders of the KLA were not wholly responsible, or fully in control, of all of the strategic attacks.

This fact—that the PDK appeared not to be fully in control of violence against Serbs and other target groups, even when it appeared to jeopardize Kosovo's chances at independence—became apparent at various junctures during the post-conflict period. Through the period 2001–2003, there were instances in which gratuitous attacks on Serbs and Roma appeared to set back Kosovo's hopes for independence, to the clear displeasure of Thaçi and some of the PDK leadership. Perhaps the most notable examples in which the leadership of the ex-KLA appeared to lose control of events were the March 2004 riots, which left hundreds injured and harmed interethnic relations considerably. Observers are unanimous that these riots were planned, most likely by rogue ex-KLA units. On March 22, a Serbian Ministry of Interior (MUP) report concluded that "the manner [in which] the violence and the terror of armed Albanian extremists were realized, simultaneously conducted in the enclaves populated by Serbs, their mass number and the logistics, indicate that the action was organized and coordinated from one center."[313] The next day, on a visit to see the damage in Oblic, SRSG Harri Holkeri offered a similar assessment and condemned the violence as part of a premeditated strategy, "one huge plan for Kosovo" by extremists.[314] UN secretary general Kofi Annan later stated that "the onslaught led by Kosovo Albanian extremists against the Serb, Roma and Ashkali communities of Kosovo was an organized, widespread, and targeted campaign."[315] NATO secretary general Jaap de Hoop Scheffer said that the violence was "orchestrated and organized by extremist factions in the Albanian community."[316] Rumors of unknown extremists groups traveling by bus from KLA strongholds like Drenica to join riots in Pristina and Mitrovica swirled around Kosovo in the days after the attacks.[317] Observers also pointed out that the targets of the attacks did not appear to be random. For example, a string of Serb settlements straddling the north-south railway lines was particularly hard hit while less strategically valuable Serb villages in Lipljan were left untouched.[318] The nearly synchronized appearance of mobs at high-profile locations on 18 March suggested to some a design to overwhelm the resource-strapped KFOR and CIVPOL forces.[319] By late March, the political leadership of KFOR and UNMIK and some Albanian leaders had come to the conclusion that an organized group must have exercised at least partial command and control over the attacks.[320]

All of this suggests that elements of the 'KLA' might have been responsible for the March riots. But what is striking about this incident is that the rioting—which clearly involved Albanian nationalist groups frustrated with independence, veterans' associations, and criminal groups—appeared to be beyond the control of the PDK top leadership once it began. According to Human Rights Watch's report, KLA veterans' associations took the initial steps in stoking ethnic tensions and managed to spread protests in every major city in a matter of hours.[321] Yet these protests were not pro-PDK as much as anti-UNMIK. Much of the language of this protest revolved around blasting the UN and those who worked with the organization, which placed the PDK and LDK in a difficult position given their positions within UNMIK-endorsed political institutions. Accordingly, their initial response was weak, as both parties appeared to sympathize with the rioters. Yet after days of rioting and a widespread perception that the violence was getting out of control, both Prime Minister Bajram Rexhepi and PDK leader Hashim Thaçi had to go on television to appeal to the Albanian people for restraint. Rexhepi even went to confront crowds personally in Caglavica and Mitrovica, in order to prevent the riots from getting out of control, though he was not successful in stopping them in Mitrovica.[322] The fact that the leaders of the former KLA had to make a personalized appeal to end such highly coordinated violence suggests that the top echelon of its leadership was not fully in control of the violent activity coming from its formerly affiliated groups. In its extensive report on the riots, Human Rights Watch concluded that it was organized, but not by the PDK:

> Yet while the majority of the ethnic Albanian rioters probably came to join the protests spontaneously, there is little doubt that some ethnic Albanian extremist elements worked to organize and accelerate the violence. As with the 1998–99 actions against Serb and Yugoslav forces by KLA, most of these extremist elements organized on the local rather than the regional level, and their affiliations varied from town to town. Some were radical members of ethnic Albanian political parties, others had belonged to the KLA, and some were members of fringe groups such as the shadowy "Albanian National Army" whose initials (AKSh, Armata Kombetare Shqiptare) were often found spraypainted at the sites of rioting.[323]

Because the KLA's bid for independence was interrupted by the terms of UNSCR 1244 and its organization dissolved into competing splinter groups, its leadership—predominantly Thaçi and the Political Directorate of the PDK—could not maintain discipline on all of its members, especially those dissatisfied with the peace settlement. Its position within internationally monitored democratic structures limited its ability to reward the competing factions or police their rogue units. The emergence of regional power structures among the KPC leadership, of KLA veterans' organizations, and of political competitors like the AAK testifies to the KLA's inability to keep its wartime coalition together through domestic rewards. The KLA may have won the war, but it devolved into a series of competing pro-independence groups, some political, some criminal, and some in between. The failure of the PDK to control the riots, which were encouraged by shadowy politico-criminal organizations from within its ranks, suggests that it lacked the ability to effectively conduct ingroup policing once it could not guarantee its followers independence. A fear of what trouble the KLA successor groups could bring may explain why Thaçi was so concerned to get in front of the issue of independence during the parliamentary elections in 2007.

Conclusion

The sources of strategic violence in the post-conflict period were many: the failure of the KLA to enforce the terms of the settlement, its dissolution into competing splinter organizations, uncontrolled population movements, and the vulnerability of the Serb population all combined to create a permissive opportunity structure for the use of violence. While most of the strategic violence is explainable by the direct pathway in the first wave, the patterns of violence during the second wave are best explained by the indirect pathway. The splintering of the KLA into smaller rogue KLA units and factions, most of which could no longer be rewarded or policed by a factionalized PDK, produced fierce competition among them for resources and political support. Some of these organizations engaged in gang violence against other Albanian groups and conducted assassinations of anyone—such as loyalists of other political parties, journalists, and dissidents—of anyone who dared to challenge them. Others carried on a dirty war against Serb civilians and Roma "collaborators" for their atrocities during the war. Still others sought to expand the war into neighboring countries or to get rich by seizing control of key smuggling routes or organized crime networks. Together, these ex-KLA units operated like a shadow structure beneath the state. Their violent bargaining for electoral and criminal advantage drove much of the strategic violence during the second wave.

The empirical patterns of violence are complex and differentiated between the two waves. In the first wave of violence, some of the attacks were overt attempts to refight the war against the Serbs, by either murdering them or forcing them to leave. The surviving KLA, and many of its splinter organizations, tried to operate under the radar of Kosovo's formal politics by embedding highly coordinated strategic attacks designed to intimidate or expel Serbs amid the expressive and instrumental killings that accompanied the return of the refugees. The reprisals and targeted assassinations employed by these ex-KLA units were designed to amplify the political effects of the revenge violence that occurred as Yugoslav rule ended. These attacks constituted a continuation of the dirty war waged between Albanian hard-liners and their perceived

Serbian enemies that has raged since the early 1990s and reflected the same ethnic fault lines, and types and targets of violence, seen during the war in 1999.

The second wave of violence brought about a significant increase in intra-Albanian factional violence. Some of this violence had both strategic and instrumental purposes, as competition for smuggling routes and regional dominance in organized crime overlapped with the political ambitions of regional leaders from within the KLA. But the growing levels of the Albanian-on-Albanian violence was itself a form of strategic violence in that its purpose was to alter the balance of power and resources among key political factions. This could be seen in the rash of assassinations, especially against LDK and AAK officials and loyalists, as well as periodic attacks on dissidents and journalists. While some of these attacks served the interests of the PDK and may have been directed by them, there is evidence that the activities of some groups—such as the veterans' associations, and Albanian nationalist groups— were beyond the grasp of the PDK. Much of their activities resembled gangland violence over the spoils of war. Similarly, the efforts of UCPMB and other Albanian nationalist groups to spread the war across borders reflects the decomposition of the wartime KLA and the emergence of regional bargaining games between their successors. In this second wave, the violence became highly localized and took a different character for each region. Consistent with the prediction of the indirect pathway, the collapse of the KLA and the proliferation of these small, often criminalized ex-KLA units in the postwar period were correlated with an increase in strategic violence along different fault lines than the dominant one during the war.

Yet the patterns of violence during the second wave were unusually complex, because there is some evidence that these Albanian splinter groups, such as the MRP but also some Albanian nationalist groups, attacked Serbs and Roma as a way of outbidding each other for popular support. In an environment where the Albanian majority was increasingly frustrated with the stalled independence bid, attacking Serbs and other minorities became an easy way for contenders in regional power games to advertise their nationalist credentials and to outbid each other for public support. The vulnerability of Serbs, particularly in small pockets of territory in Albanian-majority regions, made them easy targets for demonstrative violence in which a splinter group demonstrated its capacity to use violence to KFOR, UNMIK, or other rival groups operating in their environment by killing and expelling Serbs. The result was an increase in gratuitous attacks against Serbs and other minorities, particularly by groups like the MRP, the KLA veterans' associations, and the shadowy Albanian nationalist groups, which culminated in the March 2004 riots. These demonstrative attacks against Serbs and other minorities also allowed armed groups to signal the strength (electoral and otherwise) of the perpetrators against their peer competitors and to increase their share of the criminal market, often by eliminating Serbian rivals. While the precise authorship of individual attacks is hard to identify, the violence against Serbs and other minorities in the second wave served a dual purpose: to kill and expel Serbs in order to weaken Belgrade's hand in negotiations over independence (i.e., direct pathway), but also to use Serbs and other minorities as easy victims for demonstrative violence designed to showcase the capabilities of ex-KLA splinters in regional bargaining games (i.e., indirect pathway).

The dissolution of the KLA into an array of competing, quasi-criminal organizations left some groups attacking Serbs and other minorities as a way of advancing the cause of independence but others using them as ideal, even easy, targets for their own reasons. The indirect pathway helps to explain why attacks continued during the second wave of violence even after they had produced a strong backlash among UNMIK and other international actors and seriously jeopardized the cause of independence. The efforts of the PDK leadership to "go legitimate" detached it from the movement that it started and left it unable to rein in attacks against Serbs and other minorities when (as in the March 2004 riots) things got out of hand. The following chapter examines a case in which the indirect pathway is also in play. In East Timor, the victorious coalition, the Conselho Nacional de Reconstrução de Timor (CNRT), gradually tore itself apart through its inability to reward all of those who fought on the winning side.

CHAPTER SEVEN

East Timor

One of the most vicious and long-running wars of independence during the twentieth century was waged by the people of East Timor. This small island nation, with a population of about 1 million people, was invaded and occupied by Indonesia in December 1975, just as it appeared to gain its independence from its European colonial master, Portugal. For the next twenty-four years, the Indonesian military (ABRI/TNI) was ruthless in its efforts to destroy the East Timorese independence movement, led predominantly by the Marxist guerrilla group Fretilin.[1] No conclusive tally of the number of East Timorese killed during the long Indonesian occupation exists, but estimates have ranged from 33,000 to more than 200,000 killed.[2] While some prominent exiled East Timorese struggled to keep the plight of their people on the international agenda, East Timor—known also as Timor Leste in Portuguese—was effectively abandoned by much of the international community until the Indonesian government unexpectedly agreed to a UN-backed referendum on the status of the country in 1999. This decision set the stage for a dramatic vote for independence, followed by a brutal crackdown by Indonesian army units and an Australian-led UN peace enforcement mission to help East Timor restore security and build a functioning state.

The security situation in East Timor, which followed the withdrawal of Indonesian military forces after the crackdown in 1999, was marked by two distinct phases: (1) the immediate post-conflict period (1999–2002), in which relatively little strategic violence occurred but crime increased gradually; and (2) the post 2003-era, in which the factions of the former pro-independence forces realigned as competitors inside and outside the government, leading to violent bargaining between factions, riots, and a second Australian-led intervention. Through tracing this within-case temporal variation, including the post-conflict period and some events afterward, this case demonstrates that the ability of the original combatants to maintain internal control over their factions inside and outside their ranks is essential to preventing high levels of strategic violence from emerging via the indirect pathway. In the first two years of the post-conflict period, an umbrella group including all of the pro-independence factions in East Timor (the Conselho Nacional de Reconstrução de Timor, or CNRT) was able to maintain internal control over potential factions, using a combination of patronage (through the provision of jobs in government), pensions, the charismatic leadership and influence of Xanana Gusmao, and subtle coercion to keep the most violent factions from undermining the peace. Because of their success in domestic rewards and ingroup policing, East Timor became a relatively soft post-conflict environment, marked by only occasional bursts of strategic violence. By 2002, this unity government began to suffer from resource constraints, internal rivalries, and corruption, which undermined its ability to strike these complex bargains. Because of these pressures, the pro-independence coalition began to decay and fracture, as the main political players tried to establish their own power bases in the military and police forces. As this happened, an array of militias, security forces loyal to different political players, and veterans' associations began to generate unrest, and strategic violence began to escalate. This violence was not directed against Indonesians, or even those Timorese loyal to Indonesia, but rather emerged along an entirely new east-west regional divide, which was exploited by local political players for their own purposes. In this respect, East Timor represents a compelling test of the indirect pathway, as the violence in its post-conflict period was a product of local bargaining games between factions of the victors to the long struggle for independence.

Post-Conflict Period (1999–2004)

From 1975 to 1999, the Indonesian military fought a brutal counterinsurgency campaign against the Marxist pro-independence party of East Timor, Frente Revolutionaria de Timor-Leste Independente (Fretilin), and specifically its armed wing, Falintil (Forcas Armada de Liberacao Nacional de Timor-Leste).[3] Under the leadership of Xanana Gusmao, Falintil fled to the mountainous interior of the country after the Indonesian invasion and conducted a "people's war, " while ABRI forces and their militias, largely drawn from the East Timorese population, repressed any pro-independence activity and established a network of local administrators across East Timor's thirteen districts. By the early 1990s, East Timor's hopes for independence were dim, as Falintil was outmatched and outgunned by Indonesian military and their local allies. With the Falintil forces low in numbers and morale, the pro-independence movement pressed its case in the international arena, lobbying the United Nations and sympathetic states (especially nearby Australia and Portugal, its former colonial master) to encourage Indonesia to allow a vote to allow the East Timorese people to decide how they would be governed.[4] Despite UN-sponsored peace talks in the late 1990s, Indonesia insisted that "integration" of East Timor as its twenty-seventh province was nonnegotiable, and there was little hope of a referendum that might allow the people of East Timor to exercise their abrogated right to self-determination.[5]

The situation began to change rapidly following the overthrow of President Suharto of Indonesia in May 1998.[6] His successor, President B. J. Habibie, was more open to granting wide-ranging autonomy to East Timor, though the reasons for this policy shift remain unclear.[7] On 23 December 1998, Prime Minister John Howard of Australia wrote to Habibie to suggest a review mechanism to consult the East Timorese about the plans to grant self-determination.[8] Habibie reluctantly agreed, though it remains unclear whether he was really swayed by the Australian suggestion.[9] One possibility is that he believed that the Timorese population would vote in favor of continuing its association with Indonesia, therefore settling the matter once and for all.

After some delay because of concerns about security and the mechanics of UN administration, the vote was held on 30 August 1999. Indonesian intelligence units and pro-independence East Timorese militia units were active in the period running up to the election, threatening those who campaigned in favor of independence and using selective acts of violence to manipulate the vote. But their efforts were unsuccessful. On 4 September 1999, the UN announced the results of the vote: 21.5 percent of the population accepted Indonesia's offer to remain as an autonomous province and 78.5 percent rejected it in favor of independence.[10] Even before the results of the vote were announced, TNI forces and pro-Indonesia militias went on a rampage in Dili, killing pro-independence supporters and seriously damaging some of the infrastructure.[11] During this period, more than 271,545 people were expelled over the border into West Timor, 70–80 percent of the business district in Dili was destroyed, and nearly 50 percent of homes in the capital were burned.[12] Approximately 1,500 people were killed, largely by rampaging mobs of TNI-backed militias.[13]

The patterns of violence indicated a concerted and direct attempt to launch a scorched-earth campaign to intimidate and expel the population. Much of the violence was launched by these local militias, but it was not uncoordinated or targeted randomly. This spasm of violence was coordinated by the TNI but often directly conducted by Timorese militias and intelligence units. The Indonesian military had built a web of pro-independence militias throughout its occupation and had offered training to local East Timorese on the condition that they swore allegiance to East Timor. These militias—called WANRA (popular resistance) groups—were formed in each local kingdom (*bupati*) and comprised an estimated eleven hundred soldiers, most of whom were trained, equipped, and supervised by the TNI.[14] In the post-referendum period, the militias were the principal agents of the violence, but received advice and leadership from the TNI, particularly the Kopassus unit (TNI's Special Forces Command). An investigation into the violence after the ballot was announced revealed an "unbroken connection" between the TNI and its militia partners, as well as high levels of sophistication in the selection of targets.[15]

Exactly why the TNI and militia forces decided to lay waste to much of East Timor after the status of the country had already been decided by the vote is still the subject of considerable dispute. The official explanation of the Indonesian armed forces is that its military had little or no role in the post-referendum violence and the murders were a result of fighting between pro-autonomy and pro-integration forces.[16] Others have argued that Indonesia was trying to cast doubts on the legitimacy of the vote by creating such disorder that the result would be nullified, thereby creating conditions for a new referendum, which pro-autonomy forces might win.[17] Some have attributed it to the internal politics of the Habibie regime or to a lack of control on the part of the commander of the Indonesian armed forces, General Wiranto, over the local militias that his army had trained.[18] Others have said that the violence was driven by the shock and rage of the TNI and militia forces, or that the outburst of murder and arson was a manifestation of the cultural tradition of amok, in which individuals or groups engaged in blind, frenzied violence in response to a slight.[19] An independent commission later found that the militias operated with the direct support with senior Kopassus officers, who were determined to head off the chances of losing East Timor, but it remains unclear the extent to which Jakarta controlled their actions.[20]

The actual behavior of Indonesian forces was to some extent puzzling: not only was there a concerted attempt to destroy the infrastructure of the province and kill pro-independence supporters, but the TNI organized forcibly deported 270,000 East Timorese into camps in West Timor.[21] This was a deliberate policy; throughout the rampage, trucks roamed through population centers warning people to flee to West Timor or they would be killed.[22] It remains unclear whether they believed that many of these deportees—concentrated largely, though not exclusively, in the western part of the country—were perceived by the TNI to be loyal to Indonesia. Some have suggested that the Indonesians, having expected the vote to turn in their favor, automatically began to remove parts of the population allegedly in favor of continued integration to protect them from reprisals from Falintil forces.[23] There is some evidence that the TNI planned to move the pro-integration supporters out of the country for fear of reprisals from pro-independence forces like Falintil if East Timor won independence. The UN was aware of these plans, but believed them to be contingency operations in the event of an outbreak of violence, not a deliberate plan of action.[24]

In the eyes of Falintil, however, the goal of the TNI and its militias was clear: to draw out Falintil forces and reopen the conflict on more favorable terms. An escalation of violence between the TNI and the remnants of Falintil might lead to the invalidation of the vote. Placing its bets that the results of the referendum would hold, Falintil held back. During the attacks on the pro-independence supporters in the population and the massive displacement of the population, most of the Falintil forces—totaling about 670 soldiers, with an extensive network of supporters throughout the island—were remarkably restrained in their response.[25] Despite a few threats to leave their UN-mandated canton areas, most Falintil never even picked up a gun.[26]

To some extent, this restraint was due to the calculation of the leadership. While some of the Falintil rank and file wanted to confront the TNI forces and local militias laying waste to East Timor, the leadership was concerned that an open resumption of armed conflict with the TNI would lend credibility to Indonesian claims that East Timor was sliding back into civil war. Gusmao and others recognized that this was the same pretext that Indonesia used to justify its last invasion; moreover, an escalation of violence might lead to the invalidation of the vote or to the reentry of massive numbers of Indonesian forces into East Timor merely to "stabilize" the country. Recognizing this danger, Gusmao implored the Falintil military commander, Taur Matan Ruak, to remain in the cantons or risk losing any chance of an armed intervention by the international community.[27] In effect, he was able to police his own forces to prevent them from taking defensive actions that might backfire. His charismatic appeal and the perception that Indonesia might have finally overplayed its hand convinced the pro-independence factions to act with restraint in the hopes of an international intervention.

Falintil's strategic calculations later proved correct. The public display of violence by militias led to outrage in Australia, Portugal, and the UN and in turn increased pressure on the Indonesian government to permit an international armed intervention. Eventually, under pressure from Australia and the threat of sanctions from the United States, Habibie relented and agreed to permit an Australian-led intervention force, INTERFET, into the territory.[28] INTERFET—authorized by the UN, and composed of troops from Australia, New Zealand, Thailand, and other countries—had a mission to restore peace and security and facilitate humanitarian assistance.[29] When INTERFET arrived in the territory on 20 September, they discovered that up to 80 percent of the buildings in Dili had been razed.[30] Later assessments revealed that nearly 500,000 people had been displaced, some to the mountainous regions, and up to 80 percent of the population would require some kind of food assistance.[31] Incoming Australian troops found bodies left in the street, and patrols of TNI and militia forces kept the atmosphere tense.[32] INTERFET had been charged to uphold the results of the UN ballot, but it discovered that most of the UN mission's buildings had been burned to the ground.[33] A small staff of UN officials remained during the Indonesian attack, often protecting refugees, but had no mandate or resources to restore order.[34] There were some sporadic violent encounters with departing TNI forces and local militias, but INTERFET was successful in establishing control over the territory by late October 1999.³⁵ Of particular concern was the border with Indonesia, where INTERFET faced a danger from militias slipping across the border to terrorize villagers.³⁶ Numbering ninety-four hundred troops, INTERFET functioned more as a police force, with the objective of establishing public order to allow the delivery of humanitarian aid and the repatriation of displaced persons.³⁷ It was transitioned into a multinational peacekeeping force in February 2000.³⁸ This was to some extent a cosmetic change, as 70 percent of the newly renamed Peacekeeping Force (PKF) comprised INTERFET forces that simply changed their title and formal command to the UN.³⁹

In tandem with INTERFET's successful operation, the UN established an assistance mission, the United Nations Mission in East Timor (UNAMET), to guide the fledgling state to independence.⁴⁰ On 22 October 1999, Gusmao returned to the country from captivity in Indonesia to rapturous applause from crowds. A successor mission, the United Nations Transitional Administration in East Timor (UNTAET) took over from UNAMET in October 1999, but many of the administrative staff were slow to arrive.⁴¹ In light of the destruction that followed, the UN found itself as the "de jure government of a broken country."⁴² Organized into three pillars, focusing on security, humanitarian emergency and rehabilitation, and governance and public administration, the UN set up provisional offices and began to try to restore normal life to the country. Though the mission included a civilian police (UNPOL) deployment, police officers were slow to arrive, with only 480 of the mandated 1,640 officers in country by February 2000.⁴³ Under the leadership of UN Special Representative Sergio Vieira de Mello, the governance and public administration responsibilities were transferred to local hands, thus establishing an East Timor Transitional Administration (ETTA) in July 2000.⁴⁴ This process of Timorization was designed to respond to critics who likened the rule of the UN in East Timor to that of a "pre-constitutional monarch in sovereign kingdom."⁴⁵ Having almost unprecedented authority over a state-in-waiting, the UN was criticized for brushing aside the demands of the CNRT, for centralizing control over administrations, and for favoring highly paid international technocrats over local representatives.⁴⁶

To some extent, this discontent with the UN reflected dissatisfaction with the its ability to drastically improve the condition of the East Timorese economy and infrastructure, which has been badly damaged by years of neglect and occupation. Early indicators of social and political development indicated the severity of the problems facing East Timor. By 2003, 46 percent of the population did not have adequate food, while 43 percent of the population was illiterate;⁴⁷ approximately 11 percent of all children born died before they were five;⁴⁸ and 63 percent of the population lived on less than two U.S. dollars a day in 2001.⁴⁹ East Timor lacked a functioning legal system or judiciary, most of which had been run by Indonesia before the referendum. Also, a lack of widespread education in professional fields (such as law or medicine) meant that few people could be called into service when the rebuilding began.[50] Few roads were in place outside of Dili, and unemployment ranged as high as 80 percent in some parts of the country. In the absence of a functioning currency, East Timor adopted the U.S. dollar as its currency.

Aware of the concerns over marginalizing Timorese voices in the country, Vieira de Mello authorized elections for an eighty-eight-member Constituent Assembly on 30 August 2002. The Constituent Assembly would replace the ETTA as a democratically elected body, though it would remain under the auspices of the Special Representative of the Secretary General (SRSG).[51] The CNRT dissolved itself to allow its various members to participate in the elections; in those elections, Fretilin won fifty-five seats. A Council of Ministers, led by Chief Minister Mari Alkatiri, served to advise the UN administration as it prepared for independence. On 22 March 2002, a new constitution for East Timor was approved, providing for a unitary government with both a president and a prime minister.[52] On 14 April 2002, East Timor had its first presidential election, with Gusmao winning an overwhelming victory (82% of the vote). East Timor was formally awarded its independence in May 2002, after three years of administration by the UN.

The first years of independence for East Timor were largely without significant strategic violence, making it a soft post-conflict environment. To some extent, this is surprising because the opportunity structure was largely permissive. There was a severe public security gap after Indonesian forces withdrew, as INTERFET took a few months to fully restore order. Throughout the island, collaborators with the Indonesian security forces remained unprotected in their home villages. These years were also marked by increasing evidence of political dysfunction, rising crime, and debilitating personal rivalries. The government was divided between President Gusmao, who commanded the loyalty of his Falintil units and still remained a symbol of the resistance, and a Fretilin-dominated Constituent Assembly led by Alkatiri. Their relationship, strained by ideological differences, was not perfect, but they managed to work together until 2002–2003. Still mired in poverty, East Timor began to explore offshore drilling for oil in the Timor Sea but shared the revenue with Australia, whose companies were essential for its exploitation.[53]

One of the most important decisions during this period concerned the composition of the military and police forces of East Timor. Many Falintil veterans felt excluded from the decision taken by the UN, PKF, ETTA, and the CNRT, and approximately 700 Falintil fighters returned to their homes, often to face unemployment and poverty.[54] In July 2000, Gusmao acknowledged that many of these forces were "almost in a state of revolt."[55] Vieira de Mello commissioned a study from King's College, London, to determine what military, if any, East Timor should have.[56] Facing stark fiscal constraints, the Transitional Cabinet of East Timor approved plans for a small force of three thousand soldiers, including only fifteen hundred regular forces.[57] In practice, this meant that many Falintil veterans could not be integrated into the military and would be left unemployed. The new East Timor Defense Force—also called the Falintil-Forças de Defesa de Timor Leste (F-FDTL)—came into being in March 2001. The first 650 members were selected from the ex-Falintil ranks to form the first battalion. This selection exacerbated tensions—political and regional—already latent in Timorese society and set the stage for violence to come.

In 2005, Indonesian president Susilo Bambang Yudhoyono made a symbolic visit to East Timor to reestablish normalized relations and to sign a border agreement.[58] On 20 May 2005, a further UN support mission for East Timor—entitled the UN Mission of Support in East Timor (UNMISET)—officially came to an end, and the UN presence was downsized even further to become a UN Office in East Timor (UNOTIL).[59] Yet there were signs of trouble in the horizon in East Timor. The departure of the UN forces placed significant strain to the Timorese economy, as shops, restaurants, and services catering to international staff began to go out of business. A series of antigovernment protests—ostensibly over the role of religious education in schools, but in practice exhibiting discontent with the Alkatiri government—occurred in April 2005, threatening the stability of the government.[60]

The most serious crisis that East Timor faced occurred just after its post-conflict period lapsed. In January 2006, Falintil veterans started a protest outside the National Parliament concerning their exclusion from the F-FDTL. Their complaints were based on regional prejudice: that westerners (*loromonu*) were being discriminated against in terms of promotions and other employment benefits within the F-FDTL, and that Falintil veterans from the western regions were excluded from the F-FDTL.[61] The veterans maintained that the F-FDTL tended to show preference to easterners (*lorosae*) in hiring and promotion in the mistaken belief that they had fought harder in the resistance.[62] By March 2006, nearly six hundred protesters were present and were refusing to leave the grounds of the National Parliament. General Taur Matan Ruak, former Falintil commander and leader of the F-FDTL, ordered all of the protesting soldiers to withdraw. Prime Minister Alkatiri supported the decision, but Gusmao, who had met with the protestors, did not.[63] On 24 April, the protests turned into a violent demonstration against the Alkatiri government, with hundreds of youths from the surrounding areas involved.[64] The F-FDTL were called out to put down the protests led by their comrades, but violence ensued, leading to the deaths of at least two protestors.[65] Strategic violence rippled across the city, and nearly one hundred houses were destroyed.[66] On 23 May, a rogue F-FDTL officer allied with the rebels ambushed an F-DTL patrol on the outskirts of Dili, leading to two more deaths.[67] A collection of rebel soldiers, Timorese police, and civilians attacked an F-FDTL headquarters, setting off a series of confrontations between the F-FDTL and the police (Policia Nacional de Timor-Leste, or PNTL). On 25 May 2006, F-FDTL forces assaulted the police headquarters. A UN-backed cease-fire was organized but did not hold, as PNTL forces departing the headquarters were shot by F-FDTL forces. Ten police officers were killed and thirty were injured in the ensuing violence, leading to even more protests and reprisals.[68]

Concerned that the violence was escalating out of control, the Alkatiri government called for Australian assistance, and a second Australian peacekeeping mission began. Blaming Fretilin for the crisis, Gusmao called on Alkatiri to resign and, in a dramatic bit of brinkmanship, threatened to resign the presidency unless he did so.[69] This put Alkatiri in a difficult position, for Gusmao's popularity led to an outcry that Alkatiri step aside so Gusmao could remain in office. On 26 June 2006, Alkatiri resigned, leaving former foreign minister Jose Ramos-Horta as premier. A new UN mission, the UN Integrated Mission in Timor Leste (UNMIT), was authorized by UN Security Council Resolution 1704 on 25 August 2006.[70] Up to 37 people had been killed, and 150,000 displaced, during the 2006 unrest.[71]

East Timor remained unstable throughout the rest of that year. In the 2007 parliamentary elections, the situation worsened. On 30 June 2007, Fretilin captured a bare majority of the seats available in the parliament (twenty-one seats) but was unable to form a government. Under the leadership of Alkatiri, Fretilin reluctantly accepted a coalition government with three other parties, including the newly reformed CNRT, led by Gusmao. Under the terms of the arrangement, Gusmao became prime minister, and Fretilin had a diminished role inside government, with Alkatiri having no formal ministerial position.[72] In Dili, Viqueque, and Baucau, hundreds of houses were burned by angry mobs loyal to Fretilin, upset that it surrendered leadership of the government in the compromise deal.[73] Running as an independent, Jose Ramo Horta was elected as president with a substantial share (69% of the vote), though he remained backed by Gusmao. Just as it had in 2002, the government remained divided, with Fretilin a restless force within it.

In February 2008, a rebel army officer—Alfredo Reinado—shot Ramos-Horta in the stomach in an assassination attempt; a similar attack was launched on Gusmao, who escaped unharmed.[74] Reinado was killed in the attack, and a state of emergency was declared in East Timor.[75] Fearing continuing unrest, Ramos-Horta—who survived the attack and returned to East Timor after two months of recuperation abroad—requested that the UN extend its stay in East Timor. In March 2010, a Timorese court convicted sixteen rebels of the attempted assassination of Ramos-Horta, though the president commuted their sentences and offered a pardon in an effort at national reconciliation.[76]

Factionalism in Post-Independence East Timor

In the immediate aftermath of the violence surrounding in the 1999 referendum, observers remarked that the chances for success in East Timor were perhaps better than other comparable post-conflict states, in spite of the permissive opportunity structure for violence. In 2000, the journalist James Traub remarked that in some ways "East Timor is almost ideally suited to the new generation of peacekeeping mission. There is no dictator determined to cling to power, and the country has a political culture that survived a quarter-century of Indonesian dominion."[77] The TNI-backed militias withdrew from most of the territory, and Indonesia appeared reconciled to granting East Timor independence. The years of resistance to Indonesian rule had established a cadre of well-recognized leaders who would presumably take the reins of the fledgling state. The CNRT—the nationalist umbrella group for independence—had been successful even before the 1999 referendum in uniting the various parties in their resistance to Indonesian occupation.[78] Its presence appeared to suggest that the Timorese people would have a unified national organization serving as their mouthpiece, which is rare among often bitterly divided post-conflict states. Moreover, there was no substantial opposition to those within the Fretilin and former Fretilin ranks who wished to see East Timor emerge as an independent, democratic state. The traditional leadership of the pro-independence movement, located inside and outside Fretilin, was a small group of people who had known each other for decades.[79] For this reason, enforcement of the peace settlement should have been relatively straightforward. As Traub concluded, "the country is peaceful and unified, and although that will change as the after-glow of the independence struggle wears off, there is no inherent impediment to a democratic future."[80]

The chief reason why this peaceful future did not emerge in East Timor was that the pro-independence coalition in East Timor—briefly united under CNRT—fractured into competing groups, divided by genuine political differences and petty personal rivalries. Far from having a unified body for voicing their concerns, the Timorese population watched their leaders turn on each other, co-opting the newly functioning security forces—including the F-FDTL and PNTL—for their own aims. To some extent, this was inevitable, because the CNRT was merely an umbrella group, composed of disparate groups and former rivals, and even during its most unified period never functioned as a coherent political party. For a while, the top constellation of leaders within the CNRT and Fretilin—including Gusmao, Alkatiri, Ramos-Horta, Tuar Matan Ruak, and Roque Rodriguez—were able to strike compromises and control latent rivals through a combination of domestic rewards and ingroup policing. But each step in implementing the peace agreement made these compromises harder to strike.

Costly decisions, such as whom to include within the ranks of the F-FDTL, and how to handle the recruitment of the police, undermined the fragile consensus that kept the pro-independence groups united during the first years of the post-conflict period. Combined with a series of exogenous pressures—including growing poverty and unemployment, corruption, and political deadlock that gradually undermined confidence in the government—the political leadership turned on each other, generating new grievances and rivalries. Their political competition rendered two key institutions—the F-FDTL and PNTL—inflexible and exclusive of those whose political loyalties were unknown or misaligned with the leading players in the CNRT. The ultimate consequence was to multiply the internal and external challenges to those who held power in Dili.

The origins of the decay of the pro-independence coalition in the post-conflict period lie in the ideological and personal rivalries that occurred in Fretilin in the 1980s. The first split was predominantly ideological. Meeting in exile in 1977, the Central Committee of Fretilin—under the leadership of Mari Alkatiri—reaffirmed Marxist-Leninism as the guiding ideology, against the wishes of Xavier de Amaral, the head of Fretilin, who believed that nationalism should be the source of the resistance. Subsequently, a purge of Fretilin was held, expelling de Amaral and others who did not subscribe to a doctrinaire interpretation of Marxism.[81] This was a break from what was called Mauberism (from *mau bere*, or "my brother"), an ideology created by Ramos-Horta emphasizing the brotherhood of the Timorese people.[82] Gusmao, never fully as ideological as Alkatiri and others on the Central Committee, concluded that the resistance struggle must be broadened beyond Fretilin and its revolutionary ideology. In 1983, he founded the Conselho Nacional da Resistêncie Maubere (CNRM) and tried to bring all of the various factions, including student groups, clandestine groups, Fretilin and others under a single organization for the negotiations with Indonesia.[83] His political philosophy was increasingly nationalist, rather than revolutionary, leading him to distance himself from the Fretilin high command. In practice, the formation of the CNRT was also an effort to dissociate the independence movement from the hard-liners within Fretilin and to strip the pro-independence cause of the Marxist language that had undermined its case internationally.[84] Gusmao formally left the Fretilin in 1987, but other members of the Fretilin high command remained committed to the ideological struggle and resented his decision. Crucially, however, Falintil remained loyal to Gusmao, thus separating the guerrilla army of the independence movement from the party that ostensibly controlled it.[85]

These moves by Gusmao were resented by Alkatiri and the rest of the Fretilin Central Committee. As Dennis Shoesmith has argued,

> Alkatiri, while formally accepting multi-party democracy, believes that the party he founded has been from its "founding moment" in 1974 the true representative of

the Timorese people and their quest for social justice. In practice, the Fretilin view fits within a dominant party system where opposition Parties compete for power in a regular elections, but a single majority party retains Government. It is doubtful that the Fretilin leadership could ever accept as legitimate a government formed by their political opponents on the right.[86]

Gusmao declared that Falintil, under his exclusive command, would refuse to allow Fretilin to install a revolutionary Marxist regime in East Timor. This was a risky decision, for some Falintil remained loyal to the Central Committee and attempted a coup against Gusmao in 1984.[87] During the mid-1980s, the ranks of Falintil were also purged, leaving two main groups of Timorese leaders: those loyal to Alkatiri and the Fretilin base, and those loyal to Gusmao and Falintil.[88] By 1987, Gusmao accused the Central Committee of Fretilin of "political infantilism" and fully removed Falintil from its control.[89]

The hostilities between the groups were briefly put aside in 1998, when Gusmao invited Fretilin to join the newly expanded (and renamed) CNRT (National Council of Timorese Resistance). The relationship remained an uneasy one, for Fretilin by sheer numbers constituted a bare majority of CNRT but had no control over Falintil, which unlike the Fretilin Central Committee still remained in East Timor. But as the UN negotiations seemed to gain speed, and Indonesia appeared willing to allow a referendum, the pro-independence groups were willing to put their differences aside, if only temporarily. After Alkatiri and others in the Fretilin command returned to East Timor following the 1999 vote, they left the CNRT.[90] By the time of the first election in 2001, Fretilin remained the party with the strongest name recognition, but Gusmao—who was the most charismatic and popular figure in the country—was elected president. The result was that the first government of East Timor was divided, between Gusmao and his loyalists and a Fretilin-dominated government and ministries.

The initial post-conflict period reflected a concerted attempt by Gusmao, Alkatiri, and the Fretilin government to bring in all of the relevant factions into the government, often offering them ministerial positions in order to control them. The mechanisms of domestic reward and ingroup policing were clearly evident during this period. Ramos-Horta was named foreign minister, Roque Rodriguez was named defense minister, and Falintil leader Taur Matan Ruak was named head of the F-FDTL by the Alkatiri government. Rogerio Lobato, a powerful Falintil officer, organized a demonstration of his supporters in May 2002, leading Alkatiri to offer him the position of minister for the interior, on the grounds that he was less of a threat inside government than out.[91] The inadvertent effect of this appointment was that Lobato gained control over the police force, which allowed him a separate power base for future exploitation. But the evidence of appointments, and subtle pressure placed on challengers like Lobato, suggests that the mechanisms of domestic rewards and ingroup policing were clearly successful until late 2002. The first government of East Timor included all of the major players of the first generation of pro-independence leadership in the country, no matter their position on the Fretilin-Falintil split. It was also aided by the fact that Gusmao remained enormously popular and could use his widespread appeal to encourage the restraint of those who would challenge the peace.

Yet this unstable compromise, underwritten by a set of political bargains and Gusmao's personal appeal, could not last forever. The tactical alliances within the Alkatiri government could not eliminate the underlying personal antipathies, as relations soured between Gusmao, Alkatiri, and their respective loyalists by 2003–2004. The issue that did most to divide them concerned the composition of the military (F-FDTL) and police (PNTL) forces. The initial 650 Falintil members selected for the first battalion of the F-FDTL came predominantly from the ranks of those most loyal to Gusmao. According to Edward Rees, a "sizeable minority" of the remaining 1,300 former Falintil excluded from this new force had an "acrimonious relationship with Gusmao and the FDTL high command from as early as 1981."[92] These excluded Falintil veterans soon began to organize petitions against the government, calling for their inclusion within the ranks of the F-FDTL. The second battalion, based outside Dili, was eventually filled with new recruits, but claims of discrimination continued. As predicted by the indirect pathway, this factionalism produced a shift in fault lines in the post-conflict period. In particular, the complaints began to revolve around a new regional divide, with ex-Falintil complaining that the ranks of the F-FTDL were filled with those from the east (*lorosae*), the region where most of the fighting occurred and Falintil was strongest, at the expense of those from the west (*loromonu*).[93] It did not help that the selection process for the F-FDTL was not transparent, and age limits for new recruits meant that many who served for Falintil were no longer eligible for employment. As James Scambray has argued, the issue was "not just about money but about people wanting symbolic recognition for their contributions to independence."[94]

This discontent presented an ideal opportunity for opportunists to develop their own power base. As early as 2001, Lobato had promised those Falintil veterans concerned about exclusion from the relatively small F-FDTL that he would create a "new concept" for them.[95] Such an opportunity came when the process for the selection of the police (PNTL) went awry. The PNTL selection process, begun in 2001, included more than three hundred East Timorese Police Force (POLRI) members, some of whom had worked in senior positions for the Indonesian government.[96] This enraged some ex-Falintil members and led to sporadic attacks on police posts.[97] Once operating as minister of the interior, Lobato made good on this promise of a new concept, filling the ranks of the police (PNTL) with his own loyalists.[98] Some of these elite units, such as the Rapid Response Unit (UIR) and Border Patrol Unit (UPF), had paramilitary functions and were designed to boost his power vis-à-vis the FDTL.[99] The F-FDTL viewed the creation of these units as an infringement of their role, exacerbating tensions between the military and the police.[100]

By 2004, the security forces were divided internally, but also against one another. The F-FDTL was divided by claims of regional bias; some of the units remained loyal to Gusmao, while other units were sympathetic to the claims of discrimination offered by veterans' associations and the petitioner groups. The PNTL was also seen to be close to Alkatiri, and rumors were rife that he had ordered PNTL units to use violence to eliminate his political enemies.[101] In practice, many of the elite PNTL officers were alleged to be more loyal to Lobato than to Alkatiri or the government itself.[102] In this environment, the riots in 2006—and the subsequent reactions of the F-FDTL and the PNTL against one another—became a catalytic event. The fissures long present within the security forces came out into the open, as F-FDTL and PNTL forces turned on one another during the crisis, with several battles occurring directly between them.[103] This crisis weakened the authority of the government and had a contagion effect, as more and more groups emerged to challenge the authority of the government. It accelerated the process of splintering, producing a range of new groups and giving rise to a new host of political-criminal organizations through countermobilization. Among the most important of these political-criminal factions that emerged by 2006 are:

- *Association of Ex-Combatants 1975*: These ex-Falintil fighters, often marginalized within the F-FDTL, appealed for more aggressive efforts to hire and promote *loromonu* (westerners). Often called "The Petitioners," their cause was later championed by former minister for the interior, Rogerio Lobato, once he was dismissed from government.[104]
- *Reinado's F-FDTL Faction*: Major Alfredo Reinado, who had served in Falintil and the F-FDTL, deserted in 2006 to support the "Petitioners" who were excluded from the first two battalions of F-FDTL. With strong support in the mountains of Maubisse, Reinado organized ambushes of F-FDTL soldiers and ordered the assassinations of Gusmao and Ramos-Horta.[105] He was killed during the assassination attempt in 2008.
- *Committee for Popular Defense of Democratic Republic of East Timor (CPD-RDTL)*. This dissenting organization, which separated from the Fretilin movement in the 1980s, sees itself as the true heir to the original proclamation of 1975. It rejects the UN presence, the current iteration of Fretilin, the new democratic elections, and the government of East Timor.[106] They regularly use

violence and attempt to intimidate villagers in the countryside to gain their support.[107] Based mainly in Viqueque and Baucau, they have a deep antipathy toward Gusmao and the CNRT.[108]

- *Sagrada Familia*: This small organization of ex-Falintil members, led by Cornelio Gama (also known as Eli Fohorai-Boot or Elle Sette),[109] is a western-region organization, composed of Falintil members who were excluded from the F-FDTL. Elle Sette was eventually removed from the Falintil ranks for misconduct.[110] The organization is rumored to have nearly five thousand members.[111]
- *Orsnaco (Organisasun Resisrencia Social Nacional Cooperativa)*: Little is known of this organization, which is an umbrella group that claims to represent all of the clandestine organizations that were active in resisting Indonesian occupation.[112] It is based in Manufahi and has an estimated "couple of thousand" supporters, mainly from the youth and unemployed.[113]
- *National Movement for Unity and Justice (MUNJ)*: This small group, based in the west of the country, claims to be an association of legal and civic groups, but it was allegedly behind violent riots in 2006–2007.[114]
- *Colimau 2000*: A small antigovernment organization active in many of the western parts of the country, this group is led by Gastão Salsinha, a former ally of Reinado.[115] It has a quasi-religious orientation, with animist beliefs. According to a survey of their members, Colimau 2000 members believe that fallen independence fighters will come alive again.[116] They have a long history of resistance and played a role in fighting the Indonesian occupation, though their members are poorly trained and illiterate.
- *Isolados (Individuals)*: These groups are often small guerrilla organizations, active locally and loyal to individual gangs. One former guerrilla leader, Samb Sembilan, in western Bobonaro, operates as an *isolado*.[117]
- *Martial arts gangs*: One of the most widespread problems in East Timor is gang related unemployment. Some estimates suggest that there are fifteen to twenty martial arts groups operating in East Timor, with a membership ranging from twenty thousand to ninety thousand people.[118]
- *Criminal and mystical gangs*. Several small organizations have also emerged in the post-conflict period. Some exhibit cultlike behavior and mystical orientations, while others are common street gangs.[119]

Many of these organizations are small; most are quasi-criminal. There is also considerable overlap between the organizations that are criminal and political, with some organizations being little more than a leader and a few local followers. However, one extensive survey puts their numbers at as high as 107 separate, small groups.[120] Their emergence has radically transformed politics within East Timor and has driven most of the strategic violence during this period. As the indirect pathway would suggest, a failure of the existing Timorese leadership to effectively reward and police factions beyond 2002 led to the proliferation of factions and splinter groups and the gradual escalation of strategic violence. Similarly, as the indirect pathway would suggest, violence in the post-conflict period does not reflect the central fault line of the original conflict but rather the local objectives and rivalries of these organizations themselves.

Violence in the Post-Conflict Period

East Timor represents a compelling case of within-case variation on the levels of violence. Its initial post-conflict period (1999–2002) featured low levels of strategic violence but rising levels of expressive and instrumental forms of violence. In 2003–2004, there was growing evidence of politicized crime and civil unrest. Once the post-conflict period ended, strategic violence escalated over the next four years (2005–2009), as a new generation of political-criminal organizations emerged to protest the decisions of government. Strategic violence during this period reflected not only their attempts to attack agents of the state (such as the F-FDTL and PNTL) but also to bargain with and outbid one another. As a result, evidence of strategic violence in the second period is greater than in the first. As the indirect pathway suggests, the emergence of these rebellious splinter groups corresponded to the failure of the government to successfully employ mechanisms of domestic reward and ingroup policing against these emerging factions. During this period, each stage of the indirect pathway was evident: (1) incentive shifts among factions within the original combatant groups; (2) organizational decay and the emergence of splinter groups; (3) the collapse or decline of the distributional and policing capacities of the parent armed group; (4) the gradual dissolution of the lines of control over violence; and (5) the reestablishment or reframing of targets, particularly among vulnerable communities in the population.

Post-Conflict Period (1999–2004)

The initial post-conflict period in East Timor was remarkably peaceful in light of what had happened to the country and the permissive opportunity structure for violence. Hundreds of thousands of people had been killed in a twenty-year occupation by Indonesian forces; much of Dili had been burned to the ground in the days following the UN vote. In addition to 1,000 deaths and the 271,545 forcibly expelled over the border into West Timor, the militia's activities forced approximately 200,000 people to flee to the mountains.[121] The Indonesian population of East Timor—many of whom worked in the local government, schools, and other social services—fled or were evacuated by departing TNI forces. The scale of the brutality in East Timor could have given an impetus to violent action, including especially revenge killings. One survey reported that 97 percent of respondents indicated that they had experienced some kind of traumatic event during the occupation, and 34 percent were characterized as having post-traumatic stress disorder.[122] Poverty and unemployment were rampant, and there was little or no effective governance, especially the weeks before the UN managed to establish its new mission. The absence of political institutions and police created a public security gap that could have been exploited by political factions or criminal gangs, leaving those who worked for Indonesia or participation in WANRA vulnerable to reprisal attacks from Falintil and other actors.

Yet, despite this favorable opportunity structure for violence, levels of strategic violence in East Timor were remarkably low in the first year of the post-conflict period. The worst political violence occurred in the eastern regions of the country, including Viqueque and Baucau, but these disputes were pacified by the personal intervention of Gusmao and other leaders.[123] Clashes between rival political parties and tribes were relatively few, even during elections.[124] Until 2002, this stability persisted. The selection of members of the ETTA and the first elections of 2002 were largely nonviolent and served as a reminder that "East Timor's cruel experiences with foreign intervention in the previous sixty years had had a unifying effect."[125] Given the widespread destruction wrought by the TNI-backed militias, the crime rate for East Timor was low given the population size, and expressive forms of violence such as revenge killings were rare. In the words of one observer, "the Timorese actually seem to be less angry than they have a right to be—making them very unusual victims."[126]

The most serious violent activity at this time were directed against the East Timorese refugees trapped over the border in West Timor, specifically in the Kupang and the Atumbua regions.[127] They were effectively kept as hostages by pro-Indonesian militia members, who used a combination of intimidation, violence, and misinformation to convince Timorese that they would be killed if they returned and demanded "protection money" from them.[128] These pro-Indonesian militias intimidated and victimized East Timorese refugees trapped over the border in West Timor and periodically launched violent incursions against civilians in the western districts of East Timor.[129] There were also isolated murders of returning militia members from West Timor and rare anecdotal accounts of severe beatings and expulsions.[130] UNHCR staff members who were responsible for humanitarian care and refugee returns were not immune to attacks, and after some effort resorted to a "snatch and grab" operation in order to return East Timorese refugees to their homes. Though it sporadically cooperated with UNHCR, Indonesia did little to confront the predatory militia members who remained intermingled with the seventy thousand refugees still trapped over the border. Little or no attempt

TABLE 7.1.
PNTL Crime Statistics, 2003

Violent Crime	Total Offenses	Percentage of Total Crime
Murder	13	0.7
Attempted Murder	51	2.7
Arson	34	1.8
Domestic Violence	426	22.2
Physical Assault	1,095	56.9
Suicides	5	0.3
Attempted Suicides	3	0.2
Child Abuse	4	0.2
Intimidation/Threats	244	12.7
Kidnap/Abductions	13	0.7
Robberies	35	1.8
Total	1,923	

was made by the Indonesian officials to capture or prosecute those involved in serious crimes during this period.[131] After most of refugees returned in 2001, slightly more violence occurred, as those responsible for leading militias gradually returned to the country. But killings and other lethal forms of strategic violence remained rare.[132]

What did begin to change from 1999 to 2002 were the levels of instrumental violence, particularly crime and domestic violence.[133] Deaths from strategic violence remained relatively rare, but rising levels of crime, particularly directed against UN and other international staff, became serious problem. A declassified U.S. government cable noted that "criminal elements roam freely at night and are known to target foreign mission facilities and affluent residential areas for burglary."[134] The crime rates increased dramatically, with 88 incidents of crime reported in January 2000 but 357 reported in December of the same year.[135] Much of this violence was reported as due to squatters and unemployed young men, especially in Dili. Observers also noted that weapons such as machetes and clubs were being used more frequently, but firearms use was less common.[136] Domestic violence, particularly against women, remained a serious problem within Timorese culture and accounted for some of the assaults during this period.[137]

No systematic data on violent crime are available for the period 2000–2002.[138] But by 2003–2004, crime levels increased substantially. Internal PNTL crime statistics for 2003–2004 reveal increases in the rates of physical assault and domestic violence but low levels of strategic violence (see table 7.1).[139] As these statistics make clear, violent crime in East Timor in 2003 consisted mainly of domestic violence and physical assault. Of the assaults, only a small portion could be considered revenge attacks or score settling; for the most parts, the assaults were part and parcel of violent interactions from crime, traffic accidents, or brawls among the gangs of young

TABLE 7.2.
Violent Crime, 2004

Violent Crime	Total Offenses	Percentage of Total Crime
Murder	36	2.6
Attempted Murder	13	0.94
Arson	21	1.52
Domestic Violence	250	18.05
Physical Assault	844	60.94
Suicides	25	1.81
Attempted Suicides	1	0.07
Child Abuse	8	0.58
Intimidation/Threats	167	12.06
Kidnap/Abductions	12	0.87
Robberies	8	0.58
Total	1,385	

men who would commonly fight for sport.[140] Threats and intimidation were also common (12.7% of the total), often made to UN officials and militia members and between civilians. Murder and attempted murder were comparatively rare.

Additional statistics reveal that 115 sexual-related crimes (including rape, sexual assault, and abuse of minors) were reported.[141] More than 280 crimes were committed against international staff, mostly burglaries and thefts.[142] The crime statistics do suggest that there was mounting evidence of a threat to public safety (total 128 crimes), including disorderly behavior, fighting, and stone throwing. More than 42 sets of explosives were also discovered during 2003.[143] But by this period, the politicization of the security services began to have some effect, as PNTL officers were accused of an increasing number of violations of human rights. In 2003, 158 cases of human rights violations were reported, 48 of which involved PNTL officials. By October 2004, 152 cases had been reported, with 54 cases involving PNTL officers.[144] According to a U.S. government cable, such human rights violations against the PNTL typically involved "brutality, the excessive use of force, assaults on civilians not in custody, illegal searches, sexual assaults, pistol whippings, extortion and bribery."[145]

By the end of 2004, there was some evidence that crime rates had decreased, though strategic violence remained low.[146] Internal PNTL statistics report a drop in violent crime in East Timor, from 1,923 in 2003 to 1,385 in 2004 (table 7.2).[147] As was the case in 2003, rape (16 incidents) and sexual assault (40 incidents) remained comparatively rare. Crimes against public safety also declined to 52 from 128, with fewer reports of discovered weapons (8 found) and explosives (1 found) than the previous year.[148] The majority of violent activity remained nonlethal, though the murder total nearly tripled from the previous year. Intimidation also remained relatively high, roughly 12 percent of all violent crimes reported.

The 2004 publication of crime data is also the first with regional totals, which

TABLE 7.3.
Violent Crime by Region

Region	Total Violent Offenses	Population	Violent Crimes per Capita
Aileu	23	36,889	0.00062349
Ainaro	32	53,629	0.00059669
Baucau	77	104,571	0.00073634
Bobonaro	150	82,385	0.00182072
Covalima	28	55,941	0.00050053
Dili	683	167,777	0.00407088
Ermera	75	103,169	0.00072696
Lautem	59	57,453	0.00102693
Liquica	102	55,058	0.00185259
Manufahi	14	44,235	0.00031649
Manatuto	38	38,580	0.00098497
Oecussi	31	58,521	0.00052972
Viqueque	73	66,434	0.00109883

Source: PNTL Crime Statistics, Sub-Divisional Counts, Census Timor Leste, 2004.

indicate that regional variations in violence were not stark. This is important because one of the arguments made by Petitioners was that western regions were facing high levels of violence from returning militias and PNTL human rights violations. For the most part, the evidence does not support this claim. The most populous regions had the highest levels of violence, and only slightly higher than average levels of violence were reported in western regions, such as Bobonaro and Liquicia.

A more precise measure of strategic violence was collected through a new dataset of thirty-nine reported acts of violence from 30 August 1999 to 31 December 2004 (table 7.4). The data were collected from major newspaper accounts, often in major international newspapers and news wires. Because newspapers are selective about what crimes they report on, this dataset may not report or include every act of strategic violence. It is important to emphasize that these crime statistics focus only on strategic violence, not on expressive or instrumental violence, so they represent only a subset of the violent acts presented previously.

The strategic violence during this period can be divided into three categories: (1) clashes with TNI, Timorese militias, and civilians in the immediate aftermath of the war (thirteen incidents); (2) clashes between militia members and UN peacekeepers (ten incidents); and (3) clashes between youth or criminal groups (ten incidents). The majority of the casualties from strategic violence (279 of 323 deaths) came from incidents in the immediate aftermath of the cease-fire, where TNI forces and Timorese militias continued to kill and expel much of the rest of the population. The trend line indicates a gradual decrease in violence from 1999 onward, as the number of events of strategic violence declined each year.[149] Relatively few events during this period counted as "mass-casualty" attacks (meaning more than ten people killed in the

TABLE 7.4.
Characteristics of Strategic Violence,
1999–2004

Events Involving TNI	3
Events Involving Civilians	24
Events Involving UN/INTERFET	12
Events Involving Militia	15
Reprisals	19
Patterns of Violence	24
Total Events	39
Mass Casualty Attacks (<10 killed)	6
Kidnappings	2
Arsons	8
Houses Burned	58
Shootings	19
Rioting	9
Total Killed	323
Total Wounded	115
Total Expelled	2

incident). Much of the violence after September 1999 stems from clashes between UN peacekeepers and militias, with semiregular clashes reported between pro-Indonesian groups and those patrolling the border with East Timor. Rioting and gang violence was also common, with riots in December 2002 leading to the deaths of three people. The evidence shows that assaults on refugees were particularly common, as was the attempts by criminal gangs to terrorize those living in the border villages.

Despite these events, East Timor remained considerably less violent than Kosovo, even though both were classified as having occasional levels of violence, based on the annual number of casualties from strategic violence. In contrast to Kosovo, there was no steady pattern of attacks where Timorese armed groups sought to victimize those on the "losing side" of the war. Some observers in East Timor attributed the lack of recurring strategic violence during 1999–2004 to the absence of an identifiable target group in the population. In the words of one senior UNPOL officer in East Timor, "most of the bad guys had fled to West Timor."[150] The departure of the Indonesian population—which was largely involved in the administration of the province, education, healthcare and trade—left only the people of East Timor present in the country. One could then argue that the low level of strategic violence was due to the absence of vulnerable targets in the population.

Yet this argument underplays the extent to which the roots of the occupation ran deep in East Timor. Over that twenty-five-year period, the TNI had constructed a large network of locally based militias to keep control over the territory, to gather information, and to punish those supporting the independence movement.[151] Each of the thirteen districts of East Timor had its own militia, led by a commander who was chosen by the TNI command. In some districts, multiple militias would work semi-independently, but most of the evidence suggests that they were under the command of the local leader (*bupati*). The militia consisted largely of ethnic East Timorese who had trained with the TNI (and in particular Kopassus, the military-intelligence unit of the TNI) and had developed sympathies for the Indonesian occupation. The two largest militia groups, Halilintar (based in Bobonaro) and Aitarak (based in Dili) were commanded by leaders who had been linked directly to the TNI or Kopassus.[152] Beyond the estimated thirteen thousand to twenty thousand militia members lay an extensive network of collaborators and informers, including most of the local *bupati*. Further, the western districts of East Timor—comprising Suai, Maliana, Ainara, and Ermera—were widely perceived to be sympathetic to Indonesia or the pro-autonomy side. These districts were also rumored to be willing to secede and join West Timor to remain part of Indonesia, a fact that may explain some of the mysterious population transfers during the scorched-earth operation.[153] In sum, there remained a sizable and identifiable "target group" in the population after most of the Indonesian forces had departed: the militia members and their collaborators and supporters, especially in the western districts of the country.

Moreover, there would not have been a problem of identification in recognizing who had sided with Indonesia and might be an attractive target in the post-conflict period. Much of the violence was local, with individuals in villages supporting the TNI and its militias in their hometowns. These individuals could have been easily recognized as bearing principal responsibility for the death and destruction that followed the referendum. While isolated reports claimed that the TNI directly participated in attacks on pro-independence supporters, its leadership appears to have concluded that the best strategy for maintaining plausible deniability would be to subcontract the violence to so-called self-defense units (WANRA) in the villages, which in reality were the militia.[154] According to defectors, the TNI-militia strategy was for the local militias to "liquidate all the senior pro-independence people—and their parents, sons, daughters and grandchildren. If they sought shelter in the churches . . . kill them all, even the priests and nuns."[155] These activities reflected discriminate targeting and depended upon reliable information on the loyalties of the population. The main wave of violence in September 1999 reflected this decision, as "many pro-independence supporters were singled out for summary execution while the systematically executed *pembumihangusan*, or scorched earth operation, was in progress."[156] This policy varied in intensity, concentrating more on the western districts, Covalima and Bobonaro.[157] In sum, a significant part of the surviving population in East Timor, and those who returned to the country after the intervention of INTERFET, could have reliably located the militia members and their supporters. Moreover, with a sizable pro-autonomy population in the west, and thirteen former militia scattered around the country in a permissive security environment, they would also have ample opportunity to find potential victims.

In contrast to Kosovo, where Serbs, Roma, and other minorities were attacked by the remnants of the KLA, East Timor witnessed members of Falintil actually intervene to stop violence against former militia members and returning refugees. To be clear, those on the losing side did experience some violence; there were scattered murders of those returning militias and a few anecdotal accounts of severe beatings and expulsions.[158] Yet no large-scale campaign of strategic violence occurred for two reasons. First, the lack of violence can be explained by the initial level of internal control that the pro-independence coalition, including both CNRT and Fretilin, wielded over those in the rank and file who had spent years fighting for independence. Despite fears that Falintil would seek revenge against militia members, there was no evidence of Falintil involvement in the attacks; quite to the contrary, Falintil members held meetings with militia leaders to ensure that the return of militia members—particularly those press-ganged into service—was conducted in an orderly and peaceable fashion.[159] Under the direct orders of Gusmao, Falintil soldiers incorporated into the local police also worked with UNHCR to facilitate the return, and reconciliation, of ex-militia members into their home communities.[160] Combined with UN efforts to manage the returns of militia members, and the application of traditional local justice and community reconciliation procedures (called *lisan*), the return of militia members was more peaceful than might have been expected.[161]

Second, the pro-independence groups were successfully able to wield the mechanisms of domestic reward and ingroup policing to control the risks of factionalism and keep levels of strategic violence low. The fact that the CNRT and Fretilin had won an internationally backed guarantee of independence initially allowed the leadership to make credible commitments about the division of power and resources in the state, at least in the first two years of the post-conflict period. Initially elected with 82 percent of the vote, Gusmao had few formal powers but significant informal powers and substantial popular support as the charismatic symbol of the resistance. More importantly, since Gusmao commanded loyalty among the Falintil rank and file, local political players could be certain that they would be rewarded during their service under his reign. For its part, Fretilin "gave itself a stranglehold on the state" by assigning most of the key cabinet positions to party members.[162] Having no other serious rival for state capture, Gusmao and Alkatiri rewarded powerful political personalities like Roque Rodriguez, Francisco Gutteres, and Rogerio Lobato with key government posts, even if their relations with some of these players were strained.[163] Those who commanded significant loyalty within the Falintil rank and file found themselves rewarded with government posts following independence.[164] The initial government was a "big tent" government, with virtually every actor who could command a following—and make trouble—inside the government rather than out. Whatever their political differences, the leadership of the first government of East Timor was able to deploy domestic rewards to prevent the emergence of factions that would exacerbate local and regional tensions and produce higher levels of strategic violence.

Aftermath (2004–2008)

What led to the resumption of strategic violence in East Timor was the gradual erosion of the CNRT's hold on the state. This process began in 2002, shortly after East Timor won its independence, when the CNRT was dissolved and elections forced Gusmao and his traditional rival Alkatiri to cooperate within the same government. At this point, the long-simmering political tensions in the CNRT came to the surface and the traditional pro-independence leadership found it more difficult to get its way with restive, somewhat dissatisfied, factions in their ranks. The first major riots in East Timor occurred on 4 December 2002 when the arrest of a student prompted mass-scale rioting throughout Dili.[165] Two were killed and eighty-eight arrested in the attacks, which involved burning down the house of Prime Minister Alkatiri. Some of the violence was due a lack of professionalism with the police. A UN report later found that twenty-two Special Police Units (SPU) and nine PNTL officers discharged their weapons against a largely unarmed crowd.[166] It was immediately in question whether a political motivation was behind the violence, with many pointing to Lobato as the source of the attack.[167] The riots followed Gusmao's demand on November 28 for Lobato's resignation, and Ramos-Horta argued that the violence was due to "political manipulation."[168] An Independent Parliamentary Commission also concluded that "a third party took advantage of the demonstration to challenge the existence of the Government."[169]

While Lobato's forced resignation superficially appeared to end the crisis, factionalism only increased without him inside government. Now outside of government, Lobato took up the cause of the Petitioners groups to lead repeated protests against the government. By 2003, allegations of corruption mounted, particularly against the Prime Minister Mari Alkatiri, and the former leaders of the pro-independence movement split into factions.[170] As the central government fractured, these former Falintil commanders began to exert more control, particularly in the western regions of the country that had been susceptible to militia incursion. For example, Cornelio Gama turned on his former allies in government and began to build a power base through the Sagrada Familia in Baucau. Some evidence suggests that his forces were behind much of the violence in 2002. Despite several offers by the government to bring him

TABLE 7.5.
Characteristics of Strategic Violence,
2004–April 2008

Events Involving TNI	1
Events Involving Civilians	19
Events Involving UN/INTERFET	5
Events Involving Militia	23
Reprisals	13
Patterns of Violence	10
Total Events	30
Mass Casualty Attacks (<10 killed)	0
Kidnappings	1
Arsons	9
Houses Burned	279
Shootings	8
Rioting	19
Total Killed	59
Total Wounded	147
Total Expelled	1

into the fold, Gama refused and began to talk openly of a new civil war.[171] It was at this point that similar groups like CPD-RDTL, largely based in the western districts, began to emerge, multiply, and pose a challenge to the government. Longtime Fretilin leaders, including Gusmao and Jose Ramos-Horta, found themselves unable to rein in newly ambitious former allies such as Lobato, now the champion of the Petitioners, and Gama. Other ambitious political figures emerged, such as ex-guerrilla Francisco Gutteres (also known as Lu'Olo), and they began to assert themselves and run against members of the pro-independence elite in elections. In effect, factionalism increased as domestic reward and ingroup policing became even more costly and difficult to sustain, as the government split between Gusmao and his Fretilin rivals and became further hobbled by factionalism within Fretilin.

As internal control over these factions waned, strategic violence against targeted groups—ranging from alleged Indonesian collaborators and those in the east, perceived loyal to Gusmao—increased. While no official PNTL data have been released for this period, data collected from major newspapers on strategic violence for the period 2004–April 2008 do give some indication of a shift in strategic violence toward rioting, arsons and militia-led violent action (table 7.5). By some measures, the strategic violence reported during this period is less significant than that of the previous period. There are fewer reported incidents of strategic violence, and fewer acts of violence are reprisals for previous acts of violence or are clearly part of a pattern of violent activities. Mass-casualty attacks are also lower than the previous time period. Casualties are slightly higher for this period (fifty-nine killed versus forty-four killed, if the 1999–2004 excludes data of killings in the immediate aftermath of the attack). Although fewer incidents of arson occurred, more homes burned as a result of the arson attacks, with 215 homes burned in one set of riots in August 2007.

But two measures of violence indicate a decrease in security in this period. First, riots increased significantly during this period (nineteen recorded). They tended to be nonlethal but caused substantial property damage, often through arson. Many of the riots involved violent acts alongside the public disorder, including shootings, firefights with security forces, and expulsions. Second, acts of violence directly involving militia members increased (twenty-three recorded). Many of the riots, for example, involved ex-soldiers, off-duty police, and other political-criminal gangs responding to events in East Timor's politics.

What changed during this period to produce these shifts in the nature of violence? A comparison between the two periods clearly indicates a shift from sporadic confrontations with UN peacekeepers and violence over refugees in 1999–2004 to semiregular riots and militia-led violence in 2004–2008. In other words, the strategic violence shifted from being externally focused (against UN peacekeepers or Indonesian-backed militia members) to internally focused, against local factions from within the ranks of the former Falintil. Consistent with the indirect pathway, the emergence of multiple splinters and factions can explain several dimensions of this shift. From 2002 onward, the ability of the CNRT or Fretilin to exercise internal control over its faction declined because of corruption, poverty, and deadlock in government. The effect was to produce and encourage factions within Fretilin (e.g., those concerning Lobato and Gutteres) as well as a range of new splinter organizations, such as the Sagra da Familia and CPD-RDTL. Despite the fact that many of these organizations shared grievances against the government, their incentives had shifted toward consolidation of power in their home districts, often in the western part of the country. The result was that the violence was directed against the government in some instances, while in others it more closely resembled gang warfare. Eleven of the thirty incidents during this period were described in the newspapers as gang warfare. These smaller splinter groups were concerned with local bargaining games and often struggled to outbid each another for their share of the population's support. Their violent activities were directed against one another as often as they were directed against the government.

As predicted under the indirect pathway, one of the inadvertent effects of the splintering was to redraw the battle lines of the conflict, in this case along regional lines. By 2003–2004, the Petitioners groups among the former Falintil ranks accused the government of systematically discriminating against *loromonu* (westerners) because they were perceived to be more sympathetic to the Indonesians.[172] In February 2005, the first wave of the Petitioners groups of Falintil veterans emerged, complaining directly to Gusmao about discrimination in promotions based on their regional identity.[173] In major riots in April and May 2005, there were frequent rumors concerning religious education—that shadowy organizations were hijacking the protests to their own ends.[174] By 2005, it was clear that a new range of organizations, often organized along regional lines, had begun to threaten not only the state but also the political viability of the first generation of leadership.

While East Timor was traditionally divided into ethnic groups and clans, the development and salience of this particular cleavage in East Timor was new. As a Report of the United Nations Special Commission concluded, there was "no modern history of concerted political violence between easterners and westerners as unified and opposing groups."[175] As late as 2006, a UNDP project report stated that "there is no sectarianism, tribalism, secessionism, or external threats; the population is, relatively speaking, ethnically and religiously homogeneous."[176] Yet once activated this cleavage became powerful and provided an opportunity for groups like the CPD-RDTL to exploit it for their own advantage. Latent social stereotypes—about who was more dynamic and committed to independence (easterners) and who was more willing to accommodate Indonesia (westerners) once again came to the fore.[177] Moreover, this regional divide was linked to membership in the police service, with the F-FDTL presumed to be dominated by easterners, while the PNTL was alleged to be dominated by westerners. The effect was that both institutions were not only opposed to one another but also divided internally between their western and eastern members.[178] This is one of the reasons that the violence in 2006 was so puzzling to outside observers: rather than revolving around the chief division of the conflict (pro-independence or pro-Indonesia), the violence in the post-conflict period revolved around a regional cleavage that had been largely dormant during the war. As the indirect pathway would suggest, there was a corresponding shift in the types and targets of violence from what had occurred in the war. During the latter period, gang warfare erupted in regions largely untouched by the war, while the parts of F-FDTL and PNTL turned on each other during periods of crisis.

The effect of the emergence of these factions and the increasing salience of the regional divide can be seen in the 2006 riots. By February 2006, 593 petitioners had assembled in Dili with claims of discrimination in promotion and hiring against westerners, as well as a range of petty grievances such as insults and snubs. While Gusmao met with the petitioners and offered to form a commission to review their complaints, the protests continued, with some petitioners refusing to meet the government-sponsored investigators. Frustrated with this stalemate, Taur Matan Ruak dismissed the officers, with the blessing of Alkatiri.[179] Gusmao protested the decision and called on Ruak to reverse the decision. According to the International Crisis Group, the effect was to make Gusmao appear to be backing the complaints of westerners, which led to riots throughout Dili. Seventeen houses were burned down, and Alkatiri exploited the crisis, arguing that only Fretilin could reestablish order.[180]

The effect of this incident in February–March 2006 was to exacerbate splits within the first generation of pro-independence leaders, with many of the existing leadership angry with Gusmao for backing the protesters. But this crisis had three additional effects. First, it exacerbated tensions between the F-FDTL and the PNTL, leading to tense standoffs between the two. Second, it created a sense of momentum for the second-generation splinter groups, which began to join into the crisis almost as members in a "pick up" game.[181] On April 24, the group of sacked soldiers called the Petitioners began to stage demonstrations outside the Parliament. As James Scambray has detailed, the protests were effectively organized by two newer, relatively small, western militia groups, the National Movement for Unity and Justice (MUNJ) and Colimau 2000.[182] These organizations claimed wide involvement of CPD-RDTL members, though evidence for this is unclear. But in many cases membership of groups overlapped; many MUNJ members and Petitioners, for example, were also members of Sagrada Familia.[183] Third, it turned Gusmao from an enormously popular national figure into a controversial one, which undercut his ability to use his charismatic appeal to rein in potential factions. As the second generation of East Timor's leaders came to the fore, Gusmao was increasingly sidelined and struggled to conduct ingroup policing, especially as the crisis grew in scope.

On April 28, the riots turned violent, leading to the deaths of two people. At this point, much of the violence looked intracommunal, as roving gangs of youth attacked one another. But there was a method in the madness: both eastern and western small political-criminal groups took up the cause of the Petitioners and conducted attacks against one another for local gain. While many of these small organizations were linked to political parties, "not all of the violence was committed by organized, identifiable gangs. Either spontaneously incited by rumors or organized by networks of middlemen linked to political figures, vigilante mobs were drawn from all sectors of society, organized off the street by youth groups, MAGS [Military Armed Groups], the unemployed and criminal elements. There was also money to be earned in violence."[184] Much of the violence reflected regional divides, with western youths attacking the houses of the easterners, only to find themselves confronted by F-FDTL forces dominated by easterners.[185] The official death toll from the crisis in April was five killed, but more than one hundred houses had been destroyed.[186]

The crisis as pick-up game continued on May 3, when Major Alfredo Reinado, head of the military police of the F-FDTL, deserted his post and joined those protesting the government. Though he claimed to be appalled at the shooting of westerners, Reinado saw an opportunity to brand himself as the spokesmen of the westerners.[187] On May 23, he ambushed F-FDTL soldiers, killing one and wounding seven. Confronted by escalating lawlessness, Fretilin forces resorted to arming Sagrada Familia forces, while pro-Lobato PNTL units mobilized to destroy their political enemies.[188] Some organizations saw this as an opportunity for countermobilization: Colimau 2000 leader Osorio Mau Lequi incited his followers to violence against easterners, while martial arts groups linked to rival political parties began to conduct "ethnic cleansing" of easterners from highly valued parts of Dili.[189] Some of the violence in this period, however, reflected rivalries between these groups; among the buildings destroyed in Dili was the headquarters of the CPD-RDTL.[190] Tensions escalated between the security services, with shots being fired between different camps within the East Timorese Army (F-FDTL) and the police (PNTL).[191] On 25 May, F-FDTL forces assaulted PNTL headquarters, resulting in the deaths of ten officers. As fighting spread across the city, the PNTL effectively disintegrated.[192] The subsequent violence involved opportunistic attacks against vulnerable civilian groups (e.g., those in regions perceived to be loyal to Indonesia, or those living in wealthy and pro-Falintil areas of Dili). After six months of crisis, two thousand homes had burned to the ground and 140,000 people had fled to the districts or to an internally displaced persons camp in Dili.[193]

The end of the crisis—in which Alkatiri resigned and an Australian-led UN peacekeeping force was called in—reflected a reversal of power for the traditional elite. The traditional leadership blamed each other for the crisis. For example, Gusmao had laid the blame for the violence on Fretilin and condemned the "Fretilin parliament that bred contempt, nepotism, corruption and arrogance" and whose behavior encouraged the revolt.[194] Newly elected President Ramos-Horta was forced into consultations with these political-criminal groups in order to keep the peace in East Timor, but absent significant security sector reform he struggled to reward or police some of those responsible for some of the violence. In the end, he was shot by Reinado's faction, in an attack that led to Reinado's death and spurred even more rioting and violence in East Timor. As CNRT and Fretilin's internal control over the state had diminished, their ability to reward domestic stakeholders or punish extremists had also diminished, while strategic violence has become ever more a function of local bargaining and outbidding processes between their loyalists within the F-FDTL and PNTL, splinters of the ranks of these services, and those in the former Falintil ranks determined to remake politics in East Timor.

Conclusion

The case of East Timor represents a compelling within-case test of the pathways proposed in chapter 3. During its most of post-conflict period, East Timor was a reasonably soft post-conflict environment, despite having an opportunity structure favorable to civil unrest and strategic violence. Compared to Kosovo, it experienced relatively few strategic attacks against those on the losing side of the conflict, and across the entire post-conflict period it registered only occasional levels of strategic violence. Yet like Kosovo the winning side of the conflict—here the CNRT coalition, composed of disparate, often rival organizations—was unable to manage its dissolution effectively, leading to a decline in internal control and a proliferation of small, politico-criminal organizations determined to seek their own ends. As the indirect pathway suggests, this process of dissolution is cumulative: as the combatants fracture and new groups emerge, additional groups will countermobilize to meet them, thus redrawing the lines of contestation within the state. In this case, this process was accelerated by CNRT and Fretilin's diminishing ability to strike bargains and conduct policing to keep potential factions inside the government as the conflict continued. When this happens, new fault lines in the society will emerge, and violence will be conducted along these lines, with different sets of targets and perpetrators. In East Timor, the emergence of a regional divide between westerners and easterners fits this pattern, and explains why violence at the end of the post-conflict period—and especially after— did not mirror the violence that occurred in the long struggle for independence. The next case, Iraq (2003–2008), focuses on a case where the emergence of factions in the post-conflict period not only reordered the politics of the society but generated an unanticipated sectarian civil war.

CHAPTER EIGHT

Iraq

The U.S. invasion of Iraq in March 2003 stands as one of the most controversial foreign policy decisions of the past decade. The official rationale of the Bush administration was that the overthrow the regime of Saddam Hussein was necessary so Iraq could not pass along nuclear, chemical, or biological materials to terrorist organizations.[1] Following the devastating September 11 attacks on New York and Washington, President Bush argued that the U.S. could not tolerate a hostile regime having weapons of mass destruction if there was even a small risk that they would pass this material to terrorist organizations such as al Qaeda.[2] Throughout 2002–2003, senior Bush administration officials developed an invasion plan that assumed both that the regime could be decapitated while the essential functions of the governance remained in place. Their plan envisioned an invasion force of approximately 150,000 U.S. and allied troops and was based on the assumption that significant numbers of Iraqi security forces would be willing to switch sides and support the U.S.-led occupation, thus allowing the United States to deploy a smaller number of troops than might otherwise have been needed.[3] U.S. military officials did anticipate that the post-conflict period in Iraq would have some inherent risks, including that of a humanitarian disaster and refugee crisis in surrounding countries.[4] But senior Bush administration officials believed that the security environment would be soft, with only episodic criminal violence rather than a sustained insurgency against the United States and its allies.[5] None of the leading administration officials anticipated that the U.S. invasion would unleash a maelstrom of sectarian bloodletting and terrorism in post-conflict Iraq. Vice President Dick Cheney, for example, confidently predicted the United States would be greeted by Iraqis as liberators.[6] As President Bush revealed later, he was convinced that Iraqis would be grateful to the United States for overthrowing a tyrant who had killed and tortured thousands of people.[7]

Today, it is widely acknowledged that many of the assumptions behind the Bush administration's war strategy were incorrect. The overthrow of the Saddam Hussein regime was relatively swift, but many of the institutions of the state—weakened by corruption, cronyism, and incompetence due to years of neglect and UN sanctions—collapsed once U.S. troops had captured Baghdad. The result was an anarchic environment, rife with criminal activity and intrapersonal violence, which gradually spiraled into an organized insurgency against U.S. troops. What had happened in the early days of the occupation was crucial. Without clear instructions about how to respond to the disorder, U.S. troops largely stood by as looting and violence spread across Iraq. Since they were slow to fill the vacuum that emerged after Saddam Hussein was gone, an array of different groups—sectarian groups, ex-Baathists, Islamists, and criminal gangs—took their place. This development significantly reordered Iraqi politics, creating a space for actors long excluded from the political process. As these groups began to seek their goals—some involving sectarian or local political agendas (i.e., indirect pathway), others constituting a wholesale rejection of the U.S. occupation and provisional Iraqi government (i.e., direct pathway)—there was a countermobilization of other political and criminal actors with opposing agendas. The result was the emergence of complex and multifaceted bargaining games between a range of actors—some factions or splinters of older organizations, some entirely new, and some like al Qaeda in Iraq (AQI) not entirely indigenous—that sought to capture for themselves the spoils of war.

These transactions produced a mass level of strategic violence throughout the post-conflict period. The levels of strategic violence in post-conflict Iraq are striking for various reasons. First, the sheer scale of the violence in the "post-conflict" period—82,682 Iraqi civilians were killed from 2003 to 2008, according to the CENTCOM-collected data employed here—is far greater than any other case considered here.[8] Second, the violence in Iraq was notable because it often lacked organized fronts and more closely resembled large-scale gang warfare than a conventional conflict.[9] Third, the patterns of strategic violence featured clear geographic and temporal variation. While the overall trajectory of events in Iraq was toward increasing strategic violence from 2003 to late 2007, it is important to note that the country was not uniformly violent. There were pockets of territory in Iraq, particularly in Kurdish regions, where almost no strategic violence occurred. Similarly, some regions were violent at one period, but not at others. Moreover, strategic violence in Iraq occurred at different magnitudes in each region at different points during the post-conflict period. The province of Anbar, for example, was a hotbed of the insurgency in 2003 but became significantly less violent as the Awakening movements emerged across the country. The nationwide trend indicated a steady increase in strategic violence from 2003 to 2007, and a decline at the beginning of 2008, but the type and nature of violence was highly localized and not always explainable by simple sectarian or ethnic divides.[10]

In the most general terms, the post-conflict period in Iraq can be broken down into two periods of time: the immediate post-conflict period (2003–2006), in which strategic violence gradually increased amid high levels of expressive and instrumental violence; and the post al-Askari mosque bombing period (2006–2008), in which strategic violence skyrocketed and a full-fledged sectarian civil war began. During the former period, there had been a steady increase in strategic violence by a wide variety of armed groups from varying sectarian, ethnic, tribal, and political factions, often in response to precipitant acts like mass-casualty bombings.[11] Much of the violence during this period could be explained by the direct pathway, as Baathists insurgents and an array of other actors turned their fire on the United States to force its withdrawal from the country. Despite the fact that the United States won an outright military victory in Iraq, there was deep dissatisfaction about the outcome of the war among many in the Iraqi military and the patronage networks associated with Saddam Hussein, which led to a gradual increase in insurgent attacks on U.S. forces. But the pivot point at which the nature of the strategic violence in post-conflict Iraq changed was the bombing of the al-Askari mosque in February 2006. This event was significant not just because of the death toll in that particular attack but because of the outraged reaction across Iraq and mobilization of sectarian militias that later engulfed the Sunni and Shi'a regions of Iraq in waves of sectarian killings and expulsions, primarily directed against civilians.[12] In this attack, the devastation of the gold-domed mosque was followed by reprisals that ripped apart the mixed neighborhoods near Baghdad; sectarian cleansing campaigns spread to other cities as well, as Shiite militias forced Sunnis (who were blamed for the attack) to flee to Sunni-dominated regions. The levels of strategic violence, particularly sectarian killings, were by several orders of magnitude more severe after this bombing than they were for the period building up to this event. As the indirect pathway would suggest, much of this strategic violence was driven by complex, localized bargaining games, as the number of Sunni and Shiite armed actors multiplied and competed with each other for power and resources.

The levels of strategic violence in the post–February 2006 period in Iraq are so extreme that Iraq from 2006 to 2008 should arguably be classified as a sectarian civil war, rather than a hard post-conflict environment. In 2007, James D. Fearon noted that Iraq would have already been the ninth most deadly civil war since 1945 in terms of annual casualties.[13] If the standard of one thousand annual casualties from violence was applied to this case, Iraq would have been classified a civil war even earlier, by June 2004.[14] Even by the standards of civil wars, Iraq in the post–February 2006 period would have been a particularly bloody one, with in excess of one thousand civilians killed per month. For this reason, Iraq is less clearly a post-conflict state than the others considered in this book and is therefore not directly comparable to them.

Despite the fact that Iraq is in many ways different from the other case studies in this book, it is important to consider this case in depth for several reasons. First, Iraq is an example of what happens if a hard post-conflict environment is left to fester, with strategic violence gradually escalating to the point of producing a civil war. It demonstrates the perils of underplaying the impact of strategic violence, as the United States and its allies denied that Iraq was experiencing serious levels of strategic violence or an insurgency for the first two years of the occupation.[15] At the same time, they also underestimated the role of jihadi groups like al Qaeda in Iraq (AQI) in stroking sectarian hatreds and provoking the civil war.[16] Second, the heterogeneous character of the violence in Iraq demonstrates how the various categories of violence employed here—expressive, instrumental, and strategic—can be intermixed to the point of sometimes obscuring the rising levels, and political significance, of strategic violence in post-conflict states. In Iraq, the violence was so complex and multifaceted, that parsing out the strategic types of violence from the personal and criminal was particularly difficult. Third, as is argued here, Iraq is a hybrid case, with evidence of both the direct and indirect pathway, as well as a countermobilization of opposed actors. As this chapter makes clear, there were multiple drivers of the conflict, but among the most important was the dissolution of the Iraqi security forces in May 2003. This decision left many of those involved in the Iraqi military and police with few employment prospects and allowed them to seed the nascent insurgency with their talents, training, and weapons. It also made U.S. and Iraqi efforts to exercise domestic rewards or ingroup policing on emerging factions even more costly and difficult. The insurgency—driven by a hard core of Baathist rejectionists and an array of sectarian militias—multiplied in number and strength as more of these factions joined the insurgency. This later produced a countermobilization of groups, especially Islamist groups, with significant levels of violence being driven by bargaining and outbidding within and across these groups. In some respects, this case is the most complex, for it includes elements of the direct pathway (i.e., Baathists fighting to expel the United States), indirect pathway (i.e., militias and gangs emerging from the ranks of the Iraqi army and police and elsewhere) and a countermobilization of former marginalized actors (including Shi'a sectarian forces and Islamists), all operating in a permissive opportunity structure for violence. Finally, the proliferation of violent actors created an environment conducive to criminal activity, leading to a virtual market in kidnapping and murder and the expansion of gang warfare across much of Iraq. For all of these reasons, the ensuing strategic violence that emerged in the hard post-conflict environment was multiple in form and purpose, and in many respects differed from what occurred during the war. Especially after 2006, much of the strategic violence in Iraq was closer to gang warfare and reflected fault lines—especially sectarian and ethnic divides—very different from what had motivated the war.

This chapter proceeds in four sections. The first section will discuss the post-conflict period in detail, focusing particularly on the decision to dismiss large parts of the Iraqi security forces and the origins of the insurgency against U.S. forces. The second section reviews what is called the "insurgency" and shows how the aftermath of decomposition of the Baathist forces led to the proliferation of violent actors in Iraq during the post-conflict period. The third section draws on unpublished CENTCOM data on violence in Iraq, including data on attacks by time period and region, to illustrate that there were two overlapping wars in Iraq: an insurgency against U.S. forces (i.e., direct pathway) and an array of sectarian gangland contests driven more by local agendas than an overarching political cause.[17] The fourth section focuses on countermobilization and explains how the proliferation of actors bargaining in local political contexts significantly raised the levels of strategic violence to the point of producing a sectarian civil war.

The Iraq War and Post-Conflict Period (2003–2008)

The aftermath of the September 11, 2001, attacks in the United States dramatically changed the U.S. attitude towards Saddam Hussein and his intransigence on developing a nuclear weapons program.[18] As early as September 2001, senior Bush administration officials discussed attacks against Iraq as part of the war on terror.[19] By early 2002, the Bush Administration began to make a public case for forcing Iraq to surrender its weapons programs so that it could not transfer nuclear, chemical, or biological materials to terrorist organizations such as al Qaeda. In the words of President Bush, the United States could not afford to wait for "the final proof—the smoking gun—that could come in the form of a mushroom cloud."[20] After the invasion, it would become clear that an extensive weapons program was not present and that Saddam Hussein had been carrying on a complicated bluff to keep his rivals off balance.[21] In 2002, under intense pressure from the United States, Iraq allowed weapons inspectors back into the country, but senior Bush administration officials continued to make the case that Iraq was being evasive with the weapons inspectors. This public case for war—designed to build international support through UN Security Council resolution 1441 and to demonstrate to the American people that regime change was ultimately necessary—was only partially effective.[22] Across the world, opposition to the war in Iraq remained intense. Some European states, for example, insisted that the UN must issue a second resolution authorizing the U.S. operation against Saddam Hussein for the invasion to be considered legitimate. But U.S. efforts to convince the American public of the necessity of war were successful. By the eve of the war, the public case by the Bush administration had convinced nearly 55 percent of Americans to support war with Iraq.[23]

On 19 March 2003, the United States and its coalition partners launched their attack on Iraq. Throughout the previous year, the United States had deployed 140,000 troops to neighboring countries, along with substantial contributions from Britain and Australia and smaller deployments from other countries.[24] Against this force were arrayed approximately 500,000 Iraqi forces, including the elite Republican Guard. The war was relatively swift, as American forces had capitalized on their technological superiority and speed to devastate Iraqi military units and convince others to surrender.[25] Speed was achieved at the cost of staying power, however, as the United States fielded far fewer troops than was needed to occupy the country over the longer term.[26] By 9 April 2003, Baghdad had fallen to U.S. troops. Saddam Hussein went into hiding and remained at large for six months, but was eventually captured by U.S. troops in December 2003.[27] On 1 May 2003, President Bush announced the formal end of combat operations in Iraq, behind a banner that announced "Mission Accomplished."

The post-conflict period did not have an auspicious start. Immediately after the fall of Baghdad, looting erupted in cities across the country. Nearly every ministerial building was stripped bare, and hotels, palaces, hospitals, and other key facilities were targeted, vandalized and often burned down. Baghdad's police force, numbering some forty thousand officers under normal circumstances, almost entirely disappeared.[28] Those few officers who remained operated without instructions, and in some cases faced looters in possession of AK-47s and even rocket-propelled grenades.[29] On the ground, U.S. soldiers had no immediate orders for how to handle public disorder, so many units stood by while others intervened into the chaos. While some of the violence and looting was spontaneous, there was also some evidence of premeditation and planning. According to Ali A. Allawi:

> The scale, method and focus of the looting and destruction betrayed the existence of considerable organization and premeditation. The systematic theft and targeted destruction could not have been only the work of mobs of wild looters who seized or burnt whatever was at hand. . . . It subsequently became established that more targeted and purposeful looting was organized by insiders, either from former ministries or former security agencies.[30]

Despite this evidence, senior U.S. officials initially insisted that there was no evidence of organized resistance or command and control for the activities, and that much of the violence could be attributed to instrumental (especially criminal) purposes or revenge. One of the recurring U.S. explanations for the disorder was that the Iraqi people, angered by years of repression and deprivation under Saddam Hussein, were simply stealing back from the government what had been stolen from them. Asked to explain the reports of disorder in Baghdad, Secretary of Defense Donald Rumsfeld simply remarked "stuff happens."[31]

The result of this inaction and confusion over the nature of the looting and disorder was the emergence of a permissive opportunity structure for violence. Even with 150,000 troops, the United States did not have an effective force ratio to govern Iraq. According to a RAND estimate, a successful nation-building mission requires roughly twenty soldiers or peacekeepers per thousand persons in the population.[32] In 2003, Iraq had a force ration of only 6.1 soldiers per thousand persons. As a result, Iraq experienced a grave public security gap. This lack of troops was compounded by a lack of instructions for U.S. and allied soldiers for how to engage in policing tasks once Saddam Hussein's regime was overthrown, as well as cultural resistance within the military toward engaging in domestic law and order tasks. Iraq was also a permissive security environment because of the collapse of existing institutions, such as the judiciary and police, and widespread uncertainty about the future of those institutions and the extent to which they would be open to all of the ethnic and sectarian communities. This rising disorder of post-conflict Iraq and uncertainty over the future of these government institutions made those who were supportive of Saddam Hussein's government, such as Baathist party members, collaborators, and informers, particularly vulnerable for predatory violence. All of these factors—a public security gap, the collapse of existing institutions, and the vulnerability of Sunnis who supported Saddam Hussein in the population—combined to create an almost perfect opportunity structure for violence.

By late April 2003, it was increasingly clear that the United States had an effective plan for the war, but none for the post-conflict period. The post-conflict planning had begun under the auspices of the Office of Reconstruction and Humanitarian Assistance at the Pentagon, led by retired General Jay M. Garner. Appointed in January 2003, only three months before the invasion, Garner believed that the mission must quickly transfer authority to Iraqis and that his deployment should be completed by August.[33] His mission, weakened by significant infighting between the State Department and the Pentagon before the invasion, was woefully underprepared for the scale of the chaos engulfing Iraq. Many of his senior officers lacked translators and a basic knowledge of Iraqi society, including knowledge of who the chief political players were.[34] As U.S. officials found themselves grappling with the problems of restoring order and restoring services such as electricity, water, and sewage, Garner and his aides pushed forward with plans to create an interim government in order to transfer power more quickly to Iraq.

Alarmed by the scale of the disorder in Iraq, the Bush administration pushed Garner aside and on May 1 appointed former Ambassador L. Paul Bremer as the president's special envoy in Iraq. Bremer reversed Garner's plans for the rapid formation of an interim government and asserted that the United States and its allies would retain all effective powers of government under the auspices of the newly formed Coalition Provisional Authority (CPA).[35] In Bremer's view, the reconstruction of Iraq would be a bottom-up state-building exercise, as the CPA would need to start from scratch to rebuild basic institutions of government and to establish a free-market economy.[36] The CPA's shock therapy for Iraq began with dismantling some of the existing institutions that had supported the Hussein regime, most prominently the Iraqi army and Baath party. CPA Order No. 1 abolished the Baath party, effectively removing much of the top layer of officials from a range of public institutions, such as government ministries, and quasi-public institutions such as universities, hospitals, and state-run corporations. The order also required CPA officials to vet lower-ranking officials for their connections to the Baath Party before allowing them to keep their job.[37] The original plan for de-Baathification was to ban only senior Baathists, approximately 0.1 percent of the population, from government jobs while allowing many other nominal members of the Baath party to rehabilitate themselves through a government-led process of review.[38] Bremer anticipated that this order would lead to "temporary inefficiency" but believed that it would prove popular with ordinary Iraqis who had suffered under the regime.[39] But the order—which affected between thirty thousand and fifty thousand individuals—was criticized for fueling a backlash and for depriving the barely functioning government ministries of those officials who had the education and experience needed to run them.[40] These individuals were particularly dangerous because many were well connected and wealthy, and therefore could be easily mobilized if their exclusion from the government gave them cause to join the insurgency.[41] Moreover, the order committed the CPA to an arduous process of reviewing each candidate for a job for their Baathist credentials, which in turn slowed down the restaffing of the ministries needed to get the government on its feet. The Iraqi Governing Council (IGC), dominated by Shiite and Kurdish politicians, also pushed to extend the order further and to exclude more Sunnis from government service.[42] As Allawi has noted, this order underestimated the deep roots that the Baath party had within Iraqi society and was seen by Sunnis as an attempt to bar them from high offices in the new Iraq, to the advantage of Shi'a and Kurds.[43]

On 23 May 2003, Bremer announced CPA Order No. 2, which abolished the Defense Ministry, the Iraqi army, and many of the elite members of Saddam Hussein's army, including the Republican Guard, Baath Militia, and Fedayeen Saddam.[44] The order effectively terminated the service of all members of the former military and announced the creation of a new Iraqi army that would be representative of all Iraqis.[45] This order affected numerous Iraqis, including 385,000 people in the military; 285,000 people in the Ministry of the Interior, including the police and domestic security forces; and presidential security units, including the Republican Guard, which numbered 50,000.[46] CPA Order No. 2 also clarified the de-Baathification order, meaning that anyone with a rank above a colonel would be treated as a Baath party member and therefore be ineligible for membership in the new Iraqi army or pension payments.⁴⁷

In his memoirs, Bremer justified this decision on two grounds: (1) the Iraqi population, particularly Shi'a and Kurds, would not tolerate the restoration of a Sunni-dominated army populated with officers involved in repression and torture during Saddam Hussein's rule; and (2) the Iraqi army had effectively melted away and collapsed during the invasion, leaving no army that one could reconstitute if needed.⁴⁸ Some observers argued that both the military and the police had effectively dissolved when the regime was overthrown and that the existing barracks and bases had been stripped bare and left unusable.⁴⁹ As compensation to disgruntled soldiers, Bremer ordered that the United States make monthly payments, estimated to be sixty dollars a month, to all officers not excluded as part of de-Baathification until June 2004, and a one-time payment was made to conscripts.⁵⁰ Yet the funds were slow in coming from Washington, leaving many of these military officials without pay for the first months of the occupation. The effect was to leave thousands of former Iraqi officers unemployed, and facing dismal job prospects in a country with unemployment over 50 percent. As one U.S. official remarked later, "That week we made 450,000 enemies on the ground in Iraq."⁵¹ The consequences of this decision were magnified by the fact that many of their dependents were left with little to support themselves, thus making them an easy pool of young recruits for the insurgency.⁵² Moreover, many officers in Saddam Hussein's top-heavy army—which by one count had eleven thousand people at the general and colonel levels—were enraged by their dismissal, their loss of their privileges, and the prospect of being rehired only at a reduced rank.⁵³ By destroying the Baath party and the Iraqi army, Bremer had eliminated two of the few unifying national institutions, thereby leaving Iraq vulnerable to sectarian and ethnic political claims.⁵⁴ This order also released into a chaotic environment thousands of trained people with military experience who were resentful of the CPA. More seriously, this decision threw U.S. plans into doubt, as many of the contingency plans for the post-conflict period were premised on recalling the Iraqi army to restore order and stop the looting.⁵⁵ The United States quickly set in motion plans to form a new Iraqi army, comprised of 400,000 personnel, but this would take over three years to develop.⁵⁶

By May 2003, there was increasing evidence that the insurgency was not entirely sporadic and uncoordinated, but was organized and growing in strength. From the early days of the occupation, there were recurring rumors that cells of ex-intelligence officers (Mukhabarat) and Baathists had orders to wage an insurgency against U.S. forces in the event that Saddam Hussein's forces lost the conventional battle.⁵⁷ A memorandum discovered after the invasion suggested that cells of former Baath officials, Mukhabarat officers, and Fedeayeen units would burn the existing government buildings and files, destroy electric power stations and water conduits, and infiltrate Shi'a mosques.[58] Yet despite evidence that the insurgency was gaining momentum and growing more lethal, senior American officials kept arguing that no insurgency existed, and that the violence was attributed to expressive attacks (such as revenge killings) and instrumental (such as criminal violence). There was no doubt that much of this violence matched this description: revenge killings, particularly against former Baath members, skyrocketed, reaching hundreds killed in May 2003 alone.[59] Yet beneath this cover of expressive and instrumental attacks, more organized forms of strategic violence—such as bombings and assassinations—were increasingly apparent. But Bremer was reluctant to acknowledge the extent of the insurgency and kept insisting that "this is not a country in chaos."[60]

Determined to find a suitable interlocutor within Iraqi society, the United States sponsored the creation of an Iraqi Leadership Council, comprised of seven prominent Iraqi politicians, to coordinate with the CPA. But Bremer soon concluded that a wider cross section of Iraqi society would be needed in order to boost the legitimacy of the occupation, and on 13 July 2003, created the Iraqi Governing Council (IGC), comprising twenty-five members, including some prominent Sunnis. The Iraqi Governing Council agreed to a rotating presidency on a monthly basis and was broadly more representative of Iraqi society, including the disaffected Sunnis and ethnic minorities. It also had the political support of the UN's Special Representative to Iraq, Sergio Vieira de Mello, who had served in a similar capacity in East Timor.[61] But the IGC was criticized within Iraq for being composed of too many exiles, many of whom were distrusted by those Iraqis who had lived and suffered under Saddam Hussein.[62] Moreover, Bremer's government was at the mercy of the Ayatollah Ali Sistani, a prominent Shi'a cleric who was enormously popular but refused to meet with the United States or its allies. Sistani objected that the IGC was handpicked by the United States rather than subject to democratic vote and insisted that the UN should conduct an election.[63] The United States had won an outright victory over Saddam Hussein, but it found itself isolated in the post-conflict period and lacked a local partner who could help to enforce the terms of the settlement.

While the United States concentrated on finding reliable interlocutors for the various political factions within Iraq, the ground was moving beneath its feet. One of the important consequences of the invasion was the reversal of the traditional social and political hierarchy of Iraq, which had always put the Sunnis (roughly 20% of the population) in the dominant position over Shi'a (60%) and Kurds (20%). For the Sunnis, the invasion of Iraq was a disaster, for the overthrow of Saddam Hussein meant the end of their traditional privileges and their assumption of the right to rule over the Kurds and Shi'a communities. Many Sunnis were fearful of reprisals from Kurds and Shi'a for the years of repression under Saddam Hussein and were disaffected by CPA decisions—such as disbanding the Iraqi army—which appeared to disproportionately harm their interests. The absence of an effective government and the growing number of revenge killings of Baathists loyalists exacerbated the sense of vulnerability in the Sunni community. This collection of factors laid the groundwork for a Sunni-dominated insurgency, composed of both nationalist and Islamist forces, in Iraq.

This reversal of fortune worked to the advantage of the Kurds and Shi'a. The Kurds, who welcomed the overthrow of Saddam Hussein by the United States, were more determined to affirm their political and cultural autonomy within Iraq than to lead opposition to the United States and its allies. Kurdish peshmerga forces aligned to the two major Kurdish parties, the Patriotic Union of Kurdistan (PUK) and Kurdistan Democratic Party (KDP), asserted control over Kurdish territory and ensured that the insurgency could not take root there. For the Shi'a, this shift in Iraqi politics was particularly significant, for their leaders began to insist upon their rights as a majority in the newly democratic Iraq.[64] A range of Shi'a political parties emerged, most prominently the Da'awa party and the Supreme Council for the Islamic Revolution in Iraq (SCIRI). While Da'awa did not have its own militia, other parties followed the Hezbollah model, fielding their own militias. For example, the SCIRI fielded the Badr Brigades, which numbered nearly ten thousand troops who were trained by Iran.

Among the most important of these political parties/militias was the new Sadrist faction, led by the firebrand cleric Moqtada al-Sadr, who seized control of a vast slum in Baghdad (called Sadr City) while U.S. forces were otherwise engaged trying to reestablish basic public order. From 2003 onward, Sadr wielded his growing Mahdi Army (Jaish al-Mahdi or JAM) as leverage in his bargaining with both the U.S. and the Iraqi government. Sadr decreed that the IGC members were "non-believers" and called upon his followers to resist U.S. and British forces, though he often shied away from directly endorsing violence.[65] Though they were less well-trained than the peshmerga and the Badr Brigades, the JAM forces proved to be an energetic source of resistance to the United States and by mid-2004 were engaging in running battles against U.S. troops. By 2006, the JAM forces were estimated to have a total strength of 60,000 fighters.[66]

By summer 2003, the insurgency had begun to pick up steam. A truck bomb on 19 August 2003, destroyed the UN headquarters in Baghdad and killed UN representative Sergio Vieria de Mello, along with 14 others.[67] On 29 August 2003, a suicide bomb killed Mohammed Bakir al-Hakim, founder of SCIRI, along with 125 others. This attack, initially attributed to the Sadrists, was in fact launched by Abu Musab al-Zarqawi, a radical Islamist fighter who became the leader of the newly formed al Qaeda in Iraq.[68] With this attack, and as gang warfare began to spread, the new sectarian fault lines of the conflict were becoming increasingly clear. In March 2004, another massive suicide attack occurred, when Sunni insurgents attacked religious festivals in Karbala and Baghdad, killing 270 and wounding 570. This led to protests from the Shi'a that the CPA and IGC could not protect and them a rapid increase in the numbers joining Shi'a self-defense forces, including the Sadrists.[69] In December 2003, Saddam Hussein was caught by U.S. forces in Tikrit and handed over to Iraqi officials for trial.

Increasingly concerned about the potential threat posed by the Sadrists, U.S. forces began to move against Sadr and shut down his newspaper in March 2004. This led to a massive uprising across Shi'a areas, as JAM militias asserted control of the regions and tried to test the resolve of U.S. troops. Soon, the situation escalated with new unrest in the Sunni areas. On 31 March 2004, four U.S. contractors were attacked in Sunni-dominated Fallujah. The contractors were killed, hacked apart and burned, and their bodies were hung from a bridge over the Euphrates. The United States became concerned that the Sunni insurgents were beginning to hold territory and control cities, such as Fallujah, and soon moved against them. On April 3, Bremer ordered the arrest of one of Sadr's deputies. Seizing the moment, Sadr ordered an uprising across the Shi'a areas, focusing mainly on Najaf, so the United States and its allies faced essentially a dual uprising: a Sunni insurgency that was rooted in Fallujah and elsewhere, and a Shi'a uprising based mainly in the holy cities of Najaf and Karbala.[70] Even more alarmingly, there was growing evidence of coordination between Sunni and Shi'a fighters, as they made common cause against the United States.

The United States launched the first siege of Fallujah, evacuating thousands from the city and hunting the Sunni insurgents inside. The United States attacked the city with air strikes and ground operations in an attempt to pacify it, and found themselves confronted by gangs of insurgents who holed up in the city to force American troops into urban combat. The contest waged on and off for a month, but Washington was reluctant to commit to a full military effort to retake the city for fear of civilian casualties. The standoff was resolved only by a compromise to send a brigade of Sunni army officers—the Fallujah Brigade—in May 2004. This solution turned out to be misleading, for many members of the Fallujah Brigade joined the insurgency and the city was left un-policed, to become a source of violent resistance against the United States.[71] By October 2004, U.S. officials estimated that Fallujah was overrun with insurgents, including one thousand foreign fighters and five thousand Iraqi extremists.[72] The United States found itself launching a second major offensive against Sunni insurgents in Fallujah in November 2004, having concluded that leaving the city full of insurgents was weakening their case elsewhere.[73]

The Shi'a revolt followed a different logic, as Sadrist forces quickly gathered control over key cities, such as Karbala and Najaf, and engaged in running firefights with U.S. troops. The Sadrists later accepted a tense cease-fire brokered by Ayatollah Sistani in exchange for the release of prisoners, amnesty for Sadr himself, and reconstruction aid. The Sadrist movement returned to its strongholds, but the event dramatized the weakness of the U.S. position in Iraq. CPA officials recognized that the uprising had demonstrated the muscle of the Sadrist movement, even if many of its forces were poorly trained and could not hold onto territory.[74] Sadrist forces would continue to become more assertive in Shi'a held territories and engaged in regular insurgent attacks against British forces in Basra.[75]

Eager to signal the end of American occupation, the United States arranged for the transfer of sovereignty to the Iraqis by 30 June 2004. In 2004, the United States pushed for the passage of a Transitional Administrative Law (TAL), which would allow for a transfer of authority to a caretaker government, called the Iraqi Interim Government (IIG).[76] Fearful of attacks during the handover of power, the transfer was actually conducted two days early, and Bremer quickly exited the country. Yet the CPA still existed, and though a formal Iraqi government existed, it had relatively little independent power. On 30 January 2005, 8 million Iraqis voted for an Iraqi National Assembly. Despite threats from Abu Musab al-Zarqawi and al Qaeda, turnout was high in Shi'a and Kurdish areas, though the Sunnis continued their boycott.[77] The winner of the elections was the United Iraqi Alliance, dominated by Shi'a parties. In April 2005, the Transitional National Assembly selected Jalal Talabani as its president and Ibrahim Jaafari as prime minister. The effect of these elections was to confirm the reversal of the traditional social and political hierarchy of Iraq, now run by a government alliance of Shi'a and Kurdish parties. The Sunni population, which had boycotted the elections, joined the insurgency in greater numbers. As the violence increased, Iraqi voters approved a new constitution—again with a temporary Sunni boycott—which created a federal democracy.[78] The December 2005 parliamentary elections, which featured the end of the Sunni boycott and participation by some Sunni parties, produced the first permanent Iraqi government, again dominated by the United Iraqi Alliance. Yet the party failed to gain a majority, and the Iraqi politics fell back into deadlock amid escalating violence.

The bombing attack on the al-Askari shrine in Samarra marked a new phase in the insurgency, as Shi'a reacted in horror and began unleashing violent reprisals attacks on Sunni across Iraq. The scale and tempo of attacks against U.S. forces increased, and within cities like Baghdad the fighting began to increasingly resemble sectarian gang warfare. At this point, the shift in the fault lines of violence toward sectarianism became clear. Desperate to control the violence, President Talabani asked a Shi'a compromise candidate, Nouri al-Maliki, to form a government. At the time, Maliki was a reasonably obscure figure, but had some support within the Sadrist movement and could keep them from creating further unrest, at least temporarily.[79] While the United States scored some successes in its counterinsurgency campaign, including the death of al Qaeda in Iraq's leader Abu Musab al-Zarqawi on 7 June 2006, the situation was spinning out of control. By December 2006, the Iraq Study Group, a panel of experts appointed by President Bush to reconsider its strategy in Iraq, noted that the situation in Iraq was "grave and deteriorating."[80]

In January 2007, President Bush approved what was later described as the surge: an infusion of 20,000 extra troops to Baghdad and other largely Sunni-dominated troubled areas. Initially, the violence continued to spiral out of control, with more than two hundred killed in one day of bombing in Baghdad in April 2007.[81] A similar attack against the Kurdish Yazidi minority killed more than two hundred people.[82] In August 2007, the main Sunni party, the Iraqi Accordance Front, withdrew from the government under protest over a failed power sharing arrangement. But the United States kept insisting that a national unity government and the restoration of security would turn the tide in Iraq. One of the most important developments in this period was the emergence of what would be called "Awakening" movements, largely Sunni self-defense volunteers who offered to work with the United States to protect their own regions.[83] These Awakening movements—also called "Sons of Iraq" (SOI) under U.S. sponsorship—eventually numbered between sixty-five thousand and eighty thousand troops.[84] Yet they were also accused by Shi'a of being a sectarian militia, and of abusing their power by treating Shi'a civilians poorly. The concern among Shi'a and Kurds was that the United States was forming a tactical alliance with former Sunni insurgents in order to craft an exit strategy out of Iraq. But these forces—which patrolled their home regions and had higher levels of information about the loyalties of the local population—were effective and, in tandem with the surge of U.S. forces, significantly reduced the number of attacks against U.S. forces by late 2007.[85]

By early 2008, the al-Maliki government began to seize the initiative of a decline of in the violence and assert its control over the territory. In January 2008, the Iraqi Parliament passed legislation to allow former Baathists to return to government service. In March 2008, Prime Minister Maliki ordered a crackdown on the militias in Basra, which led to the retreat of the JAM and the withdrawal of Moqtada al-Sadr to Iran. By July 2008, the Sunni Iraqi Accordance Front rejoined the government, ending the sectarian boycott that had undermined its legitimacy. In September 2008, the United States transferred control over Anbar to the Iraqi government, in a symbolic move that recognized a turning point in the insurgency. In November 2008, the Iraqi Parliament approved a security pact with the United States and all U.S. troops withdrew from Iraq by the end of 2011.

The Evolution of the Insurgency (2003–2006)

Amid this political deadlock, the insurgency in Iraq developed slowly. By summer 2003, there was sporadic evidence of violent opposition to U.S. occupation and growing evidence of an organized insurgency. But by February 2006, the situation had evolved, with dozens of competing armed groups employing strategic violence for a wide range of goals beyond simply expelling U.S. forces. What emerged gradually in Iraq was not a single, coherent insurgency, but rather a multiplicity of armed actors fighting across and within ethnic and sectarian fault lines for a greater share of the power and resources of the state. The organizations that employed strategic violence or claimed to lead the resistance to the U.S. occupation rarely had identifiable or public political leadership.[86] Many of the Sunni insurgent organizations were small, comprising only a few cells and without any clear leadership. There was no single Sunni, Shi'a, or Kurdish armed force or militia, but rather multiple actors competed for market share within those populations.[87] To speak of the "insurgency" in this case is to use a shorthand for a disparate range of actors, often with conflicting objectives, sectarian and ethnic loyalties, and strategic and tactical preferences, that began to engage in strategic violence against U.S. forces and each other in summer 2003.

For this reason, much of the strategic violence in post-conflict Iraq bore a resemblance to gang-based warfare, where dozens of competing armed actors used the murder and expulsion of civilians as a means of competition.[88] By 2004, there were at least twenty different violent actors in Iraq, ranging from ex-Baathists, Iraqi Sunni nationalists (1920 Revolution Brigades, Salah-al-Din al-Ayoubi Brigades), Islamic jihadi groups (al Qaeda in Iraq, Ansar-al-Sunna Army), Iraqi Shi'a militias (Mahdi Army, Badr Brigades), the freelancing units of the Kurdish peshmerga, and a range of smaller tribal and criminal actors. No single actor was behind all or even most of the insurgent attacks, though some groups (such as the radical Islamic groups and Baathist/Sunni nationalists) were more responsible for certain types of acts (i.e., suicide attacks) than others.[89] The proximate motivations for individual attacks are also various, ranging from fear of political exclusion, concerns over the distribution of oil revenues, revenge, and profit. Many of these organizations had an underdeveloped political program or agenda. Moreover, not all of these organizations were involved in the "insurgency"; some of them sought to prop up the provisional Iraqi government, while many others hoped to tear it down.[90] Those Shiite and Kurdish forces that had a significant role in the government fought to preserve it, while other actors—including Sunni insurgents and jihadist groups such as al Qaeda in Iraq— were devoted to destroying it.

This complex environment—comprising both an insurgency against U.S. forces by Baathists and Sunni forces and sectarian gang warfare waged between competing militias, some of which operated on behalf of the Iraqi provisional government— came about during the period 2003–2006 through three steps: the emergence of the Baathist resistance, the expansion of the Sunni insurgency, and the countermobilization of Shi'a and Kurdish security forces. The result of these factors was the emergence of a security dilemma between the Sunni and Shi'a communities in the central and south part of the country and between Arabs and Kurds in the north. Amid these factors, the bombing of the al-Askari mosque in February 2006 proved to be a catalytic event that transformed this hard post-conflict environment into a full-fledged civil war.

Emergence of Baathist Resistance

The origin of the insurgency against the U.S. occupation of Iraq lies in part with the disbanding of the Iraqi army in May 2003. The U.S. military plan to occupy Iraq was premised on the assumption that U.S. officials could call Iraqi army units back into service to restore public order.[91] Their cooperation was needed in part because the United States had chosen to invade Iraq with a force of 150,000 troops, rather than the estimated 300,000–400,000 needed to occupy and administer the country on its own.[92] One U.S. military planner remarked that "we expected to be able to recall the Iraqi army. Once the CPA took the decision to disband the Iraqi Army and start again, our assumptions for the plan became invalid."[93] For many Iraqis officers, the decision constituted an act of betrayal. Before the invasion, the United States had been quietly sending messages to the Iraqi army that those who cooperated or at least did not fight would be rewarded with a place in the "new" Iraq.[94] The CPA decision appeared to break this promise, and despite the fact that Bremer and others later tried to keep Iraqi officers on the payroll the damage had been done. One senior Iraqi officer warned the United States that "all of us will become suicide bombers."[95] Others threatened ambushes and a sustained campaign of insurrection against U.S. forces.[96] Almost immediately, protests broke out in cities in Iraq, with army officers taking to the streets to demand a place in the new Iraqi security forces. The language of the protests made clear that to the Iraqi army a summary dismissal was considered an intolerable humiliation. Even in the relatively peaceful Mosul, the 101st airborne under the command of General David Petraeus confronted violent protests that wounded sixteen American troops.[97] Protests continued on and off until July 2003, until payments to senior Iraqi officers were restored, after Petraeus and others had warned the Pentagon about the extent of the risk these disgruntled officers posed.[98]

One of the chief reasons why the orders disbanding the Iraqi army and barring its senior officers from reinstatement were so disastrous is that it deprived U.S. officials of information on the loyalties of the Iraqi army members and of the mechanisms of domestic rewards and ingroup policing so necessary to controlling their actions in post-conflict Iraq. The original war plan had recognized the advantages of retaining both this information on loyalties and the mechanisms to reward Iraqi behavior. "We wanted to rapidly call the soldiers back," in the words of CENTCOM planner John Agoglia, "get them on our side, and then sort out who could and could not be trusted."[99] But disbanding the army meant that U.S. forces lost crucial information on the loyalties of key members of the Iraqi army in the early days of the post-conflict period. With the official institutions of the army in disarray, and with senior Iraqi military officers aware that they had little hope of reemployment because of the de-Baathification order, there were few regular channels of information for the United States or its allies to know whether army officers were joining the nascent Iraqi insurgency. To make matters worse, American military intelligence stopped its reporting on former Iraqi army officers once the protests ended in July 2003.[100] The behavior and sympathies of the Iraqi army became a matter for speculation rather than fact once the decision had been taken to dismiss them.

This absence of information on the loyalties of the Iraqi military was particularly damaging because the Iraqi military was already fragmented, with its leadership exercising variable levels of internal control over each unit. For example, as Marten has noted, Saddam Hussein

> intentionally splintered the ruling Baathist Party and his military and intelligence-gathering forces. By sowing distrust and discord he hoped to leave these forces unable to plan and execute a successful overthrow of his regime. He ensured that other high-ranking individuals within his regular forces spied on each other, explicitly borrowing from Hitler and Stalin, and sometimes forced his closest associates to personally kill those accused of betrayal in order to put blood on their hands.[101]

Recognizing that the greatest threat to his power came from his own Republican Guard, Hussein subdivided the elite force and created a Special Republican Guard loyal to him to protect against a coup.[102] Beyond this coup-proofing of the elite portions of the Iraqi military, Saddam Hussein developed private paramilitary and regional units that were not under the full control of the Defense Ministry.[103] Many of these units were trained to use small arms, sabotage, and bombing, all tactics that would be useful in the insurgency, though there is no evidence of a concerted Baathist plan for the insurgency.[104] The low levels of internal control meant that Saddam Hussein's army crumbled more quickly than expected in the U.S. invasion, but it also meant that its scattered elements could serve as the seeds of the insurgency that would bloom in the post-conflict period.

Even if this information on loyalties of Iraqi military officials could be determined, the CPA lacked efficient mechanisms of reward and punishment to influence their behavior. Throughout its tenure, the CPA was derided as incapable of delivering on basic social services.[105] More importantly, it lacked a regular budgeting authority and process by which it could pay the salaries of Iraqi officials. By early May 2003, senior Iraqi army officials presented themselves to U.S. officials and claimed to represent over 137,000 members of the armed forces. They requested payment of salaries in exchange for information about their numbers, but U.S. officials did not have money set aside to offer members of the Iraqi military even the twenty-dollar emergency payment given to all other government employees.[106] Without an ability to pay them, U.S. officials had little leverage over what members of the Iraqi army did in the post-conflict period; there was no way to pay off those who would reliably cooperate, and no way to sanction or coerce those willing to attack U.S. forces except for brute force. As a result, the United States was forced into a defensive position. It could capture or kill those who it witnessed doing harm to U.S. forces or the provisional Iraqi government, but it had no leverage with the mass of Iraqi officers whose sympathies were unknown. Many of the high-ranking Iraqi officer class, including some of those who offered information on the identities and loyalties of those in their ranks, simply disappeared. The underlying hope of U.S. policy was that political progress toward drafting a constitution and establishing a provisional government would take the wind out of the insurgency, but there was little inherent in this process that would allow them to restore leverage over the former members of the Iraqi army. Once the United States switched course and began to pay salaries for the Iraqi army officers in an attempt to restore this leverage, it found that the damage was already done, because "it was paying money to a bitter, demobilized army but was getting nothing in return, and had created a situation in which the soldiers were unsupervised, had no stake in the new order, and were free to create mischief, or worse."[107]

The decision to disband the army, and the bureaucratic delay in restoring the pay of those dismissed by the CPA, had several consequences. The most important consequence was to force the Iraqi army officers to take their chances on finding employment in a grim economic climate. According to the Iraqi Ministry of Labor, approximately 70 percent of the labor force in the country was unemployed in 2003.[108] Many Iraqi army officers, used to a relatively comfortable life under Saddam Hussein's regime, now faced dismal job prospects, which affected not just themselves but their dependents as well. The onset of poverty had a ripple effect and thus affected not only the unemployed officer but also their dependent children, which in turn produced a pool of discontented young men who would turn toward the insurgency. To find the means to survive, many former Iraqi army members began also to work with the dense networks of organized crime and corruption that had developed in Iraq during the period of UN sanctions.

The summary dismissal of the Iraqi army affected its members in other, less obvious ways. Many Iraqi army officers felt humiliated by the experience of watching Iraq being occupied by its enemy and having that enemy casually dismiss them from their jobs. Ibrahim al-Marashi reports that "the notion of humiliation after the disbandment of the Iraqi military emerged on numerous occasions and often in different contexts.... In a nation where honor (*sharaf*) often serves as a commodity more valuable than money itself, the disbandment decree was viewed as an insult to the honor of the oldest institution in Iraq and by extension to the Iraqi population at large, and finally as a violation of the honor of the individual Iraqi soldier."[109] This sense of outrage and humiliation over occupation, echoing the Iraqi experience of occupation under the British, contributed to making some members of the army sympathetic toward emerging groups within the insurgency.

Despite the fact that unemployment and a sense of insulted honor made many Iraqi army members sympathetic to the insurgency, the involvement of the Iraqi army in the insurgency was not wholesale. Initially, as Ahmed Hashim noted, many "waited to see whether the Americans were going to be liberators or occupiers."[110] After it was officially disbanded, the Iraqi army declined dramatically in the degree of its internal control, as latent factions within their ranks began to reorient themselves toward criminal and insurgent networks. As a result, the already fractionalized Iraqi army did not join the insurgency in its preexisting units but fragmented into smaller subunits and classes of members, with different loyalties, incentives, and willingness to assume risks in opposing U.S. forces. Their goals were diverse and could not be reduced only to the return of Saddam Hussein and his forces. Some former Baathists sought to draw the United States into an asymmetric conflict that would be to their advantage; others may have wanted to press the CPA into allowing for the return of the Baath party or its members to government service. In this respect, the strategic violence employed by what was called former regime elements (FRE) could be explained in terms of the direct pathway, as an attempt by Baath party members and Iraqi army members to renegotiate the terms of a conflict settlement that had excluded them.

There is only scattered evidence of their direct involvement of Baathist cells in strategic violence after 2003. From the early days of the occupation, there were recurring rumors that cells of ex-intelligence officers (Mukhabarat) and Baathists had orders to wage an insurgency against U.S. forces in the event that Saddam Hussein's forces lost the conventional battle.[111] A memorandum discovered by the CPA in August 2003 instructed members of the Mukhabarat on how to create an insurgency, specifically instructing members to engage in sabotage and looting, sniper attacks, ambushes, and assassinations.[112] In some cases, preexisting units of the Fedayeen Saddam, a paramilitary organization established by Saddam Hussein, began to attack U.S. forces in the so-called "Sunni Triangle" by late 2003. The sophistication of attacks and the weaponry used offered clear indication that members of the Baath party and the Iraqi army were leading attacks against Coalition forces, but it was unclear how much this was following a preexisting plan.[113] As later as 2005, U.S. intelligence officials estimated some thirty-four Baath party leaders were coordinating the insurgency via regional cells.[114] But the Baathists lacked a coherent leadership structure or a long-term plan.

In the words of a senior U.S. defense official, "There's no Saddam-like figure to whom they have allegiance and who is in overall charge of the insurgency."[115]

Beyond their direct involvement in attacks, the former Iraqi army provided a supply of trained officers, weapons, and personnel into the ranks of various Sunni insurgent groups. It appeared to the International Crisis Group that "these cells developed gradually, initially drawing individuals angered by dim prospects and resentful of the occupation and its indignities, and building on pre-existing party, professional, tribal, familial and geographic—including neighbourhood—networks."[116] The decomposition of the Iraqi army allowed elements within it the freedom of action to join the insurgency on their own terms, or to act as force multipliers to insurgent groups by providing weapons and training. These so-called former regime elements were valuable for at least two reasons. First, they had access to funds that the rest of the Sunni insurgency did not, particularly from assets and accounts pilfered from the regime and secret bank accounts abroad.[117] In this respect, they were able to provide "start up" funds to subsidize other Sunni organizations that lacked access to funds. Second, the former regime elements were also well trained and armed. Not only did they retain their personal weapons, but these units were effective in stripping the regime's armaments stockpiles during its collapse and the subsequent looting. To other Sunni insurgent organizations, these former regime elements were a useful source of funding and training that aided the effectiveness of their less well-trained operatives.

Expansion of Sunni Insurgency

But the Baathist resistance, as it was known in the early days of the occupation, merely provided the seeds of the Sunni-led insurgency. Their involvement—both as a direct attempt to renegotiate the peace settlement through the direct use of strategic violence and as a source of soldiers and materials for the insurgency—merely amplified the emergence of broader forms of resistance, involving a panoply of Sunni groups—some nationalist, some Islamist, some tribal, and some with combined nationalist-Islamist agendas—that emerged to oppose the U.S. occupation. In other words, the emergence of a Baathist insurgency against the United States (direct pathway) fed directly into the proliferation of new groups, which began to engage in violent bargaining for their own purposes (indirect pathway). As Mohammed Hafez notes, a range of other factors—including fear of Shi'a and Kurdish mobilization, the collapse of patronage networks to tribes, the decline of social services, and the heavy-handed approach of U.S. forces in dealing with the first signs of resistance—spurred a wider Sunni mobilization, particularly in Baghdad, Anbar, and other Sunni-dominated provinces.[118] Among the most important Sunni insurgent groups to emerge at this time were the Islamic Army in Iraq (IAI), 1920 Revolution Brigades of the Islamic and

National Resistance Movement, Mujahadeen Army of Iraq, Jaysh-al-Rashidin, Jaysh al-Taifa al-Mansoura, Jaysh Mohammed, and the Salah-al-Din al-Ayoubi Brigades of the Islamic Front for Iraqi Resistance, among other smaller groups.[119] While many of these organizations involved former Baathists and Iraqi army officers, they were not determined to restore the Baath party to power but instead saw themselves as the leading a nationalist-Islamist resistance against foreign occupiers. Some members of the Sunni insurgency were determined to put distance between themselves and the worst elements of the Baathists, emphasizing that many honorable Sunni Baathists and army officers were also victimized by Saddam Hussein for resisting his orders.[120] Most of these organizations had a relatively small membership, often comprised of Iraqi civilians with a mix of former Baath officials and sometimes jihadi actors, and adopted a mixture of nationalist and Islamist language to make their case.[121] Some organizations were so small as to comprise no more than a few individuals; others claimed to have as many as twelve brigades. Initially, these groups were deeply competitive, seeking to claim the mantle of Sunni resistance against the hated occupying forces. According to the International Crisis Group:

> In this phase, multiple groups, generally small and highly localized, vied for exposure and recognition to attract recruits and financial backing. Their initiatives were uncoordinated, their claims often wildly exaggerated, and their logic that of one upmanship. To heighten their profile, they distributed crude leaflets by pre-existing social networks (family, tribe, etc) and in mosques. They also filmed short, low-quality videos depicting armed operations; these were typically dropped off for the foreign press corps at the reception desk of major hotels. . . . By early 2004, videos had become highly professional, used by insurgent groups to make their case and highlight their deeds.[122]

Taking advantage of the permissive opportunity structure for violence, groups within the Sunni insurgency concentrated initially on terrorist violence and other shocking acts, such as summary executions and beheadings of hostages, while seeking to spread their message through websites and statements issued to major media outlets. By 2004, Sunni insurgent groups began to develop a rough division of labor and to issue joint communiqués, indicating a degree of coherence that was absent in the first few months of the occupation.[123] There was also a degree of competition, as various groups sought to outbid one another for a greater share of the Sunni popular support. But the insurgency remained scattered and without a coherent leader or program, resembling a latticework of disparate groups united around broad nationalist, antioccupation, and religious themes but divided in objectives, strategy, and tactics.

Among the most important developments during the expansion of the Sunni insurgency was the emergence of jihadist groups, including Ansar al-Sunna, al Qaeda in Iraq and Mujahadeen Army of Iraq. Some of these organizations had deep roots within Iraq, such as Ansar al-Sunna (which had operated for years in Kurdish territory) while al Qaeda in Iraq (and its forerunner, al-Tawhid wal-Jihad (TWJ)) were dominated by foreign fighters. These organizations had varying goals, with some aiming merely to restore Iraq to an Islamic government and others committed to al Qaeda's global jihad against the United States and its allies.[124] Despite these differences, each of these organizations is motivated by a Salafi ideology that holds that it is an inviolable responsibility of any good Muslim to rebel against any government not based on Islam.[125] In the service of this rebellion, these groups argued that they could treat Muslims (especially Shi'a) who disagree with this vision as *takfirs* (infidels) and attack them as they are outside the bounds of their faith. Despite the fact that they are relatively small in number, these jihadi organizations have claimed responsibility for many of the most indiscriminate acts of violence in post-conflict Iraq.[126] Groups such as TwJ/AQI were also responsible for multiple kidnappings, executions, and beheadings during 2004–2005.[127] These groups are also fluid, forming tactical alliances with one another and then splitting apart when needed. For example, al Qaeda in Iraq (AQI) introduced the Mujahadeen Shura Council in January 2005, which included smaller jihadi groups; in late 2006, the Mujahadeen Shura Council made alliances with Sunni insurgent groups and became the Islamic State of Iraq (ISI). These organizations operated like a wildcard within the normal transactional violence between Sunni and Shi'a, launching spectacular terrorist attacks—including suicide attacks—and engaging in brutal acts (such as kidnappings and beheadings) designed to amplify sectarian tensions and push Iraq toward a civil war. Abu Musab al-Zarqawi, the leader of AQI, laid out his strategy in a letter discovered in 2004 that these jihadi groups sought to attack Shi'a civilians to encourage Shiite reprisals, to draw the Sunnis into the war, and to create Sunni-jihadi alliance that would prove victorious.[128]

Reflecting these pressures, there was a distinct shift in the types and targets of violence as the number of groups within the Sunni insurgency expanded, as predicted by the indirect pathway. While the focus of many Sunni insurgent and jihadist organizations was on attacking U.S. forces, an increasing number of attacks began to target Shi'a and Kurdish civilians, often with more low-grade attacks such as murders and expulsions. There was a steady increase in intersectarian killings throughout this period, often totaling roughly 200 dead per month. Among the most significant attacks during this period was the killing of 270 Shi'a pilgrims by Sunni insurgents in Khadamiyah and Kerbala in March 2004.[129] By 2005, former Iraqi prime minister Ayad Allawi had concluded that a civil war had already begun, because of the tempo and scale of assassinations and expulsions and the emergence of sectarian militias on both sides.[130]

Countermobilization of Shi'a and Kurdish Forces

The third factor that drove the emergence of a complex insurgency in Iraq was the countermobilization of preexisting Shi'a and Kurdish armed groups. This process began in the early days of the occupation, as many of these organizations existed for decades before the U.S. invasion and had significant battle experience in opposing Saddam Hussein. Some of these organizations had supported the U.S. decision to invade Iraq, while others remained on the sidelines. But they began to adopt a variety of new roles as the protectors as the Sunni insurgency began to grow more powerful. In some cases, they also began to fragment as internal control over factions within their ranks declined, as competition for the loyalties of their constituent populations reoriented their incentive structures and produced a new range of targets for attack.

The countermobilization of the preexisting networks operated differently for the Shi'a and Kurds. Throughout 2003–2004, prominent Shi'a religious figures such as Ayatollah Sistani had counseled restraint among the Shi'a population. The Sadrist faction, representing the Shi'a urban underclass and loyal to Moqtada al-Sadr rather than the Shi'a religious establishment, was the first to ignore this advice and called for immediate resistance against U.S. occupation. While much of the Shi'a establishment was willing to give the Iraqi provisional government a chance, the Sadrist movement set up a shadow government and began to train the Jaysh al-Mahdi militia. Following the Hezbollah model, Sadr sought to give the Sadrist movement control over political offices, while using mass protests and the threat of force in order to force the Iraqi government to accede to its demands.[131] Most of the Shiite population did not follow this call to arms until the uprisings in Najaf and Kerbala from April and August 2004 transformed Sadr and his Mahdi Army into visible symbols of resistance to occupation. Once this uprising had finished, the Sadrist movement fragmented, as key lieutenants of Sadr broke ranks with the JAM mainstream and began to command their own fighters.[132] Despite repeated efforts by Sadr to rein in factions within his ranks in 2005–2006, the Sadrists became a movement, comprising multiple competing claimants, rather than a single coherent organization. A progressive sense of disenchantment with leadership of Sadr led other factions to emerge. In Basra, the JAM faction under the leadership of Ahmed al-Fartousi operated as a law unto itself, conducting attacks on British forces without Sadr's approval.[133] Among the most powerful of the Sadrist factions were the so-called Special Groups, which were trained by the Iranian military and intelligence networks. The three most prominent Shi'a special groups were Ketaib Hezbollah, Asaib Ahl al-Haq (League of the Righteous), and the Promise Day Brigade. These Shi'a militias periodically attacked U.S. forces and also participated in the killings and expulsions of Sunnis in southern Iraq.

Other Shi'a armed groups undertook a more complicated strategy, remaining political parties vying for power within government while at the same time having a private militia for their own purposes. The Supreme Council for Islamic Revolution in Iraq (SCIRI) offers an instructive case in point. SCIRI had a long history of opposition to Saddam Hussein, and through its armed wing, the Badr Brigades, it waged an insurgency against the Baathists for more than twenty years, while officially remaining in exile in Iran. Yet SCIRI remained an ambiguous organization: it had failed to back uprisings by the Shi'a in the south during the 1990s, and many Iraqis believed it to be controlled by Iranian intelligence.[134] In the early days of the U.S. occupation, SCIRI returned to Iraq and its forces began to assert some control over southern Iraq. Its leader, Mohammed Bakir al-Hakim, was killed in a terrorist attack in 2003, and the leadership passed to his brother, Abdel Aziz al-Hakim. Despite concerns that SCIRI was backed by Iran, its leadership proved willing to work with the United States from the late 1990s onward and after the war it proved willing to participate in the Iraqi Governing Council. At the same time, SCIRI controlled the Badr Brigades, a private militia force trained by Iran and numbering between four thousand and ten thousand troops.

SCIRI played a complex and often violent game remaining simultaneously inside and outside Iraqi politics. It allied with some smaller parties to form the United Iraqi Alliance, which won the most votes in the December 2005 legislative election. Once the government was formed, a significant portion of the membership of the Badr Brigades went into the police and Interior Ministry. The remainder of the organization was rebranded as the Badr Organization for Reconstruction and Development, but this was a cosmetic change as they did not fully disarm. Once in government, SCIRI was alleged to operate death squads from within the Interior Ministry. There were also persistent rumors that the Badr Organization operated death squads against Sunnis, including the infamous Wolf Brigade, which has been accused of torture and reprisals against ex-Baathists, Sunni clerics, and Palestinians living in Iraq.[135] The return of the Badr forces to Iraq, and the appointment of SCIRI official Bayan Jaber to the Interior Ministry in 2005, appeared to confirm to Sunni insurgents that Shiite forces were determined to control the government while conducting a dirty war of murder and expulsion against them. The behavior of SCIRI and the Badr Brigades also infuriated the Sadrists, who distrusted them for fighting on the side of Iran during the Iran-Iraq war and believed them to be puppets of the United States, Iran, and even Israel.[136]

The mobilization of the Shi'a forces was matched by the mobilization of the Kurdish peshmerga forces in Kurdistan in late 2003–2004.[137] The peshmerga forces were a powerful standing army, comprising 100,000 troops under arms. They had fought numerous campaigns against the Iraqi army under Saddam Hussein and Turkey and featured well-armed and well-trained units, with their own array of paramilitary and intelligence organizations. The peshmerga cooperated and even fought with United States during the invasion of Iraq, yet they were fundamentally interested in asserting control over disputed territories such as Kirkuk. The legal status of the peshmerga was recognized under the Transitional Administrative Law (TAL) in 2004, which granted the Kurdish Regional Government (KRG) the right to exercise control over security and policing functions in the territory. Yet the peshmerga's loyalties were divided among the Kurdistan Democratic Party of Iraq (KDP) and the Patriotic Union of Kurdistan (PUK), both of which were given substantial roles in the provisional Iraqi government.[138] The delegation of substantial autonomy to the Kurdish region, as well as the involvement at high levels of senior Kurdish politicians within the Iraqi government, induced a degree of restraint on behalf of the peshmerga forces, which largely stood by during the escalation of sectarian violence. Yet their presence—and the view among Sunnis and Shi'a that Kurdish parties sought independence for Kurdistan and would do whatever was necessary, inside and outside of government, to achieve it—convinced many Sunnis that no accommodation with the Kurdish parties was ever possible. This was particularly the case in cities such as Kirkuk, where the substantial minority populations of Sunni Arabs and Turkomen distrusted the peshmerga, leading to a security dilemma between Arabs, Kurdish, and Turkomen citizens in these territories.

The hard post-conflict environment in Iraq was marked by its diversity and complexity. There were two main tiers of violence: a Sunni-led insurgency against U.S. forces (direct pathway), and a sectarian and ethnic struggle between factions within the Sunni, Shi'a, and Kurdish populations (indirect pathway). Both pathways were coexistent within the same case at the same time, and attacks launched by one pathway sometimes fueled further attacks along the other pathway. No single ethnic or sectarian community featured a single, consistent representative, but rather all were divided between factions that had often had goals that diverged from the parent movement. The jihadi forces allied with the nationalist Sunnis could find common cause by attacking U.S. forces, but they had different visions for what Iraq would become. The peshmerga were committed to protecting Kurdish interests in Iraq, but the parties that controlled them defined those interests very differently. The Shi'a factions were among the most heterogeneous. Some were located partially inside a U.S.-backed government, while their own forces conducted death squads and campaigns of expulsion against the population. The Sadrists were opposed to U.S. occupation, yet willing to cut deals with the Iraqi government when needed. Despite their nominal opposition to Saddam Hussein, Sadrist forces included well-known Baathists within their ranks, and tactical coordination with Sunni insurgents was common, especially during the uprising in 2004.[139] Like all of the players, the Sadrists were divided among themselves and exercised less internal control than conventional armies. Table 8.1 identifies all of the powerful factions that emerged from 2003 to 2006.

By February 2006, Iraq had witnessed an explosion of new or resurgent armed

TABLE 8.1.
Competing Armed Actors in Iraq by Sectarian or National Community

Sunni	Shi'a	Kurdish	Salafi
Baathists / Former Regime Elements	Badr Organization	PUK Peshmerga	Ansar al-Sunna
Islamic Army in Iraq (IAI)	Mahdi Army / JAM	KDP Peshmerga	Al Qaeda in Iraq / Mujahadeen Shura Council
Salah-al-Din-Ayoubi	Ketaib Hezbollah		Mujahadeen Army of Iraq
1920 Revolution Brigades	Asaib Ahl al-Haq		
Jaysh-al-Rashidin	Promise Day Brigade		
Jaysh al-Taifa al-Mansoura Jaysh Mohammed Salah-al-Din al-Ayoubi Brigades of the Islamic Front for Iraqi Resistance Local Sunni militias	Local Shia militias		

Sources: Inventory of groups adapted from Hafez (2007) and al-Khaldi and Tanner (2006).

groups operating across the country. Not all of these groups were entirely new to Iraq; many mapped onto preexisting social networks and tribal ties that had existed well before the Saddam Hussein regime was in place. But the proliferation of groups amid the chaos of a post-conflict Iraq generated a security dilemma in intermixed areas. The gradual increase in strategic violence from 2003 to 2006 pushed the Iraqi people into the arms of alternative security providers, such as sectarian militias and tribal leaders, that offered security in a trade for political support in their home regions. Fearful of being unable to protect themselves, the Iraqi people began to pledge their loyalties to militias within their sectarian communities. In the words of a Mahdi Army fighter in Basra, "No one can remain independent. You have to belong to a party to enjoy its support and protection from others."[140] These hard choices produced a spiral of armament and mobilization that reinforced the security dilemma.[141] It also weakened the central government by transferring the loyalties of the population to smaller units, such as tribes, sectarian militias or political parties. In this combustible environment, the bombing of the al-Askari mosque became a catalytic event that pushed the society to a brutal war fought along dimensions that differed significantly from the U.S. invasion in 2003.

Violence in Iraq (2003–2008)

Compared to other cases here, post-conflict Iraq remains an outlier in terms the levels of violence that it experienced. Between March 2003 and December 2008, 83,262 Iraqis

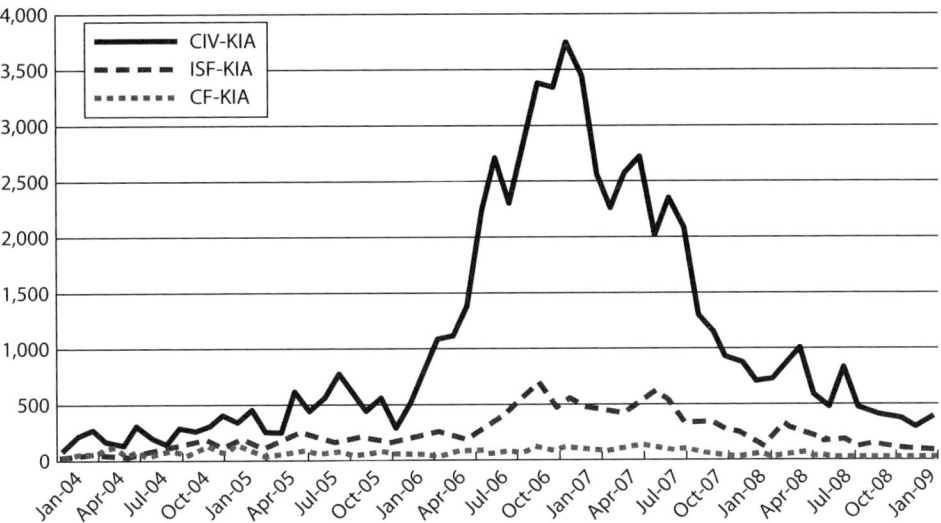

Figure 8.1. Casualties in Iraq, January 2004–July 2009. CF-KIA = Coalition forces killed in action; ISF-KIA = Iraqi security forces killed in action; CIV-KIA = civilians killed in action.

were killed in violent action of all types.[142] The sheer scale of the violence—especially after the bombing of the al-Askari mosque in February 2006—would classify it as an armed conflict from 2006 to 2008 rather than a hard post-conflict environment. Using previously unreleased data on violent attacks collected by CENTCOM, figure 8.1 illustrates the dramatic increase in violence after the al-Askari attack, as the situation morphed from a hard post-conflict environment to a sectarian civil war. The levels of violence against all three categories of victims—Coalition forces, Iraqi security forces, and civilians—increased dramatically after the February 2006 attack. Until that point, civilian casualties had peaked at 762 killed in one month in August 2005, and had declined thereafter. By March 2006, 1,077 civilians were being killed per month in reprisals across the country. By December 2006, nearly 3,718 people were being killed per month. Iraq would not return to the level of civilian casualties that it had in January 2006—nearly 500 killed per month—until May 2008. There was a more modest increase in attacks against Iraqi security forces during this period as well. During the height of the violence in 2006–2007, nearly 500 Iraqi security forces (ISF) members were being killed in attacks per month, often in suicide attacks on police stations and recruitment bureaus.

Across the period 2003–2008, the level of U.S. casualties remained high, with 4,216 killed. It experienced less variation than the civilian killings, though the number of Coalition casualties per month peaked with 961 killed during the height of the

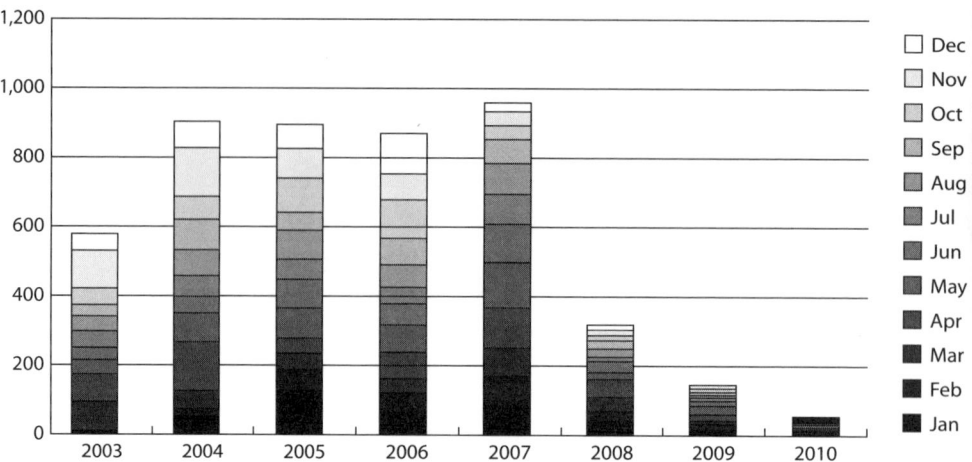

Figure 8.2. Coalition Casualties in Iraq, 2003–2010. *Source:* Unreleased CENTCOM data.

TABLE 8.2.
Total Killed and Wounded by Category,
January 2004–August 2008

	Killed	Wounded
Coalition Forces	3,592	30,068
Iraqi Security Forces	13,754	34,692
Civilians	63,185	86,957

Source: CENTCOM data released to author.

sectarian killing in 2007. There were also significant variations in the numbers killed per month, with high casualties often associated with events such as the new U.S. operations against insurgent forces. Figure 8.2 tracks the month-to-month rate of Coalition casualties within each year from 2003 to 2010.

According to unreleased CENTCOM data, the numbers wounded in Iraq are often significantly more than the number killed. Table 8.2 presents totals of killed and wounded across the period January 2004–August 2008. The total figures here are striking, especially considering the size of the population of Iraq. By this standard, 150,142 Iraqi civilians had been either wounded or killed out of a population of 31 million (0.004%). Similarly, 48,446 members of the Iraqi security forces had been wounded or killed out of a total population of 650,000 (0.074%).

Perhaps even more striking than these figures is the number of attacks launched by insurgents on all three categories of victims. According to statistics released by CENTCOM in October 2008, there had been a total of 118,246 attacks launched against these three categories of victims between June 2004 and August 2007. Of

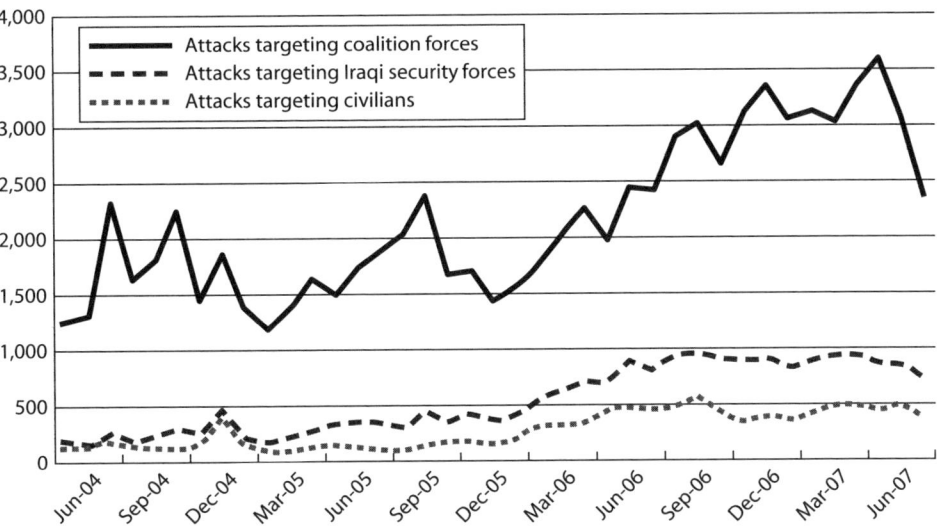

Figure 8.3. Attacks by Type of Victim, June 2004–August 2007.

these, most attacks (85,284) were directed against Coalition forces, compared with 21,725 attacks launched against Iraqi security forces and 11,237 attacks launched against civilians. Figure 8.3 suggests that even during the height of the intersectarian warfare in 2007–2008 most attacks were consistently directed against Coalition forces rather than civilians, though many of these attacks were probably minor, nonlethal incidents.

Attacks by Type of Victim, June 2004–August 2007

Regional variations in the levels of attacks were stark. Data collected by CENTCOM on attacks between January 2004 and August 2008 indicate that of a total 162,932 attacks that more than a third (37.42%) occurred in Baghdad itself. Table 8.3 indicates the extent of the attacks on the sectarian communities within each region.[143]

The regional variation in attacks indicates that Iraq was unevenly violent, even during the worst of the sectarian bloodletting (figure 8.4). Most regions in Iraq had less than 500 attacks per month, and some had significantly fewer attacks. Kurdish regions were by far the least violent. The three northernmost Kurdish regions—Arbil, Dahuk, and Sulamaniyah—together were the location of only 0.25 percent of the total attacks. The mixed Kurdish-Sunni regions, such as Diyala, Ninewa, and Ta'mim, were significantly more violent, with 24.19 percent of the overall attacks. Baghdad was by far the most violent region, comprising 37.4% of all attacks within this period. Regions within the Sunni triangle, including Anbar (16.11%) and Salah al Din (11.56%),

TABLE 8.3.
Attacks by Region, January 2004–August 2008

	Composition	Total Attacks	Percentage of Total
Anbar	Sunni	26,255	16.11
Arbil	Kurd	148	0.09
Babil	Sunni, Shi'a	3,470	2.13
Baghdad	Sunni, Shi'a	60,972	37.42
Basra	Sunni, Shi'a	7,185	4.41
Dahuk	Kurd	80	0.05
Dhi Qar	Shi'a	1,140	0.70
Diyala	Sunni, Kurd, Shi'a	14,257	8.75
Kerbala	Shi'a	423	0.26
Maysan	Shi'a	1,640	1.01
Muthanna	Sunni, Shi'a	372	0.23
Najaf	Shi'a	433	0.27
Ninawa	Sunni, Kurd	18,580	11.40
Qadisyah	Shi'a	1,335	0.82
Salah ad Din	Sunni, Kurd, Shi'a	18,334	11.56
Sulaymaniyah	Kurd	170	0.10
Ta'mim	Sunni, Kurd	6,581	4.04
Wasit	Shi'a	1,057	0.65

Source: CENTCOM data released to author.

had higher than average rates of attack as well. Shi'a dominated regions tended to be less violent, unless they were in fault-line regions with significant Sunni populations, such as Babil (2.13%) and Basra (4.41%). The regional variation indicates that the attacks lay on the fault lines between the sectarian and ethnic groupings and that, where one group was entirely dominant, the number of attacks was almost negligible. Figure 8.4 shows that there was significant temporal and geographic variation in the number of attacks per month, subject to population movements and shifts in the fault lines of the war.

The casualty totals per region indicate a similar level of variation. Using a sample of data from January 2004 to August 2008, table 8.4 breaks down the totals of killed and wounded per region. The casualties per region indicate the extent of the regional variation in the types of attacks. Most of the attacks against Coalition forces were in Baghdad (35.72%) and the western Sunni regions, such as Anbar (30.46%), Salah al Din (8.16%), and Diyala (6.29%). Attacks against the ISF are more evenly distributed, with higher levels in mixed regions, such as Diyala (15.62%) and Ninewa (14.25%). Casualties among civilians are more concentrated, with Baghdad accounting for 56.98 percent of the deaths among civilians and 46.30 percent of the reported wounded civilians. Civilian casualties remain high in Diyala (11.11%) and Ninewa (7.56%). The contrast here between locations of the deaths of Coalition forces and civilians is stark; for example, Anbar accounts for 30.46 percent of all Coalition casualties but only 3.45 percent of the civilian casualties.

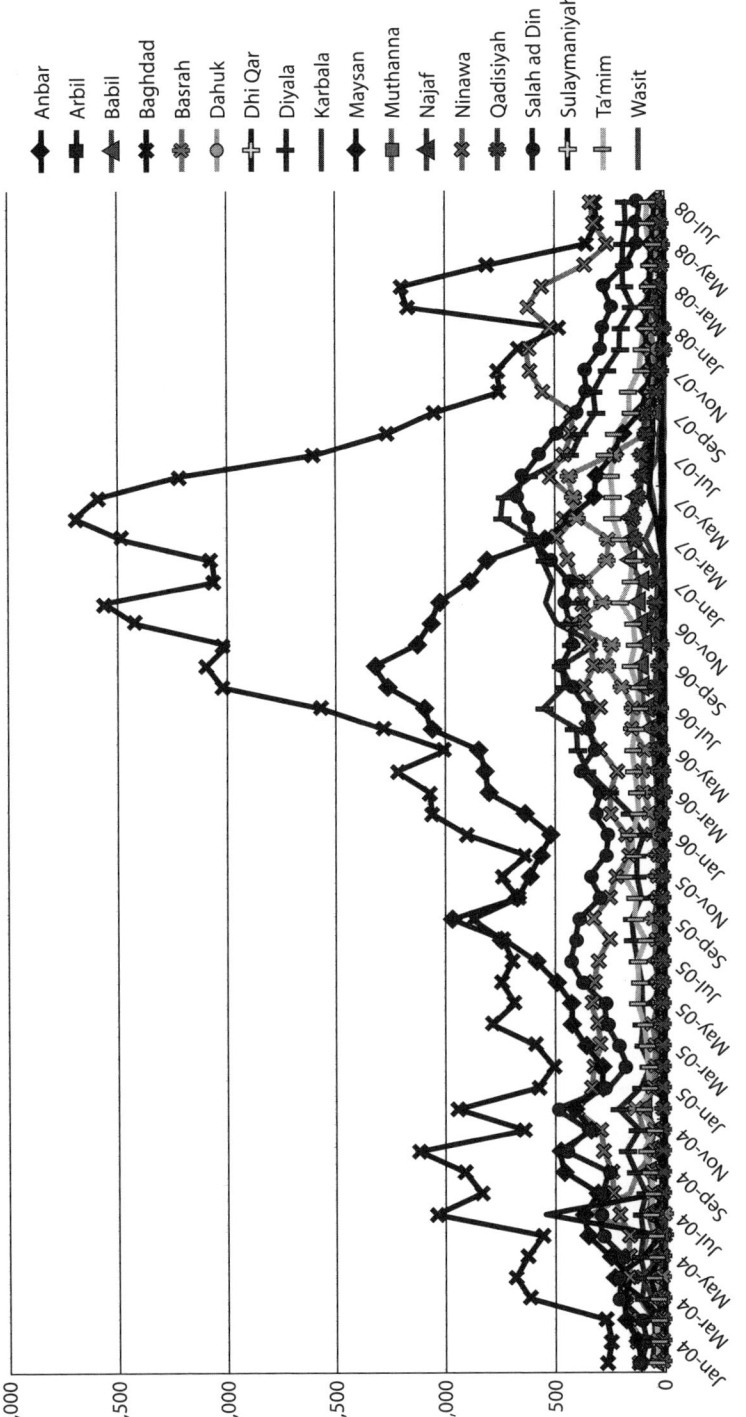

Figure 8.4. Regional Attack Trend Lines, January 2004–August 2008.

TABLE 8.4.
Casualties per Region, January 2004–August 2008, n (%)

	CF WIA		CF KIA		ISF WIA		ISF KIA		CIV WIA		CIV KIA	
Anbar	8,758	(29.13)	1,094	(30.46)	3,241	(9.34)	1,043	(7.58)	4,384	(5.04)	2,183	(3.45)
Arbil	24	(0.08)	0	(0.00)	188	(0.54)	66	(0.48)	700	(0.80)	242	(0.38)
Babil	891	(2.96)	93	(2.59)	1,094	(3.15)	412	(3.00)	4,115	(4.73)	2,173	(3.44)
Baghdad	10,248	(34.08)	1,283	(35.72)	12,255	(35.33)	4,729	(34.38)	40259	(46.30)	36,001	(56.98)
Basra	1,163	(3.87)	150	(4.18)	625	(1.80)	360	(2.62)	3,227	(3.71)	2,695	(4.27)
Dahuk	26	(0.09)	0	(0.00)	39	(0.11)	4	(0.03)	166	(0.19)	36	(0.06)
Dhi Qar	281	(0.93)	42	(1.17)	505	(1.46)	152	(1.11)	882	(1.01)	344	(0.54)
Diyala	1,639	(5.45)	226	(6.29)	4,785	(13.79)	2,148	(15.62)	8,656	(9.95)	7,019	(11.11)
Kabala	107	(0.36)	24	(0.67)	171	(0.49)	56	(0.41)	2,077	(2.39)	797	(1.26)
Maysan	247	(0.82)	21	(0.58)	41	(0.12)	31	(0.23)	291	(0.33)	115	(0.18)
Muthanna	70	(0.23)	3	(0.08)	138	(0.40)	28	(0.20)	187	(0.22)	74	(0.12)
Najaf	134	(0.45)	20	(0.56)	96	(0.28)	46	(0.33)	559	(0.64)	368	(0.58)
Ninewa	2,432	(8.09)	182	(5.07)	5,132	(14.79)	1,960	(14.25)	9,160	(10.53)	4,779	(7.56)
Qadisyah	214	(0.71)	35	(0.97)	539	(1.55)	299	(2.17)	1,045	(1.20)	676	(1.07)
Salah al Din	2,934	(9.76)	293	(8.16)	3,266	(9.41)	1,480	(10.76)	5,733	(6.59)	3,197	(5.06)
Sulaymaniyah	5	(0.02)	0	(0.00)	136	(0.39)	36	(0.26)	254	(0.29)	125	(0.20)
Ta'mim	753	(2.50)	90	(2.51)	1,870	(5.39)	665	(4.83)	4,447	(5.11)	1,504	(2.38)
Wasit	142	(0.47)	36	(1.00)	571	(1.65)	239	(1.74)	815	(0.94)	857	(1.36)
Total	30,068	(100.00)	3,592	(100.00)	34,692	(100.00)	13,754	(100.00)	86,957	(100.00)	63,185	(100.00)

Note: CF = Coalition Forces; ISF = Iraqi Security Forces; and CIV = civilians.

There is similar evidence of regional variation in sectarian attacks as well. Figure 8.5, employing a classification scheme based on the location of the Multinational Brigade for Coalition forces in Iraq, indicates that there were 11,712 sectarian incidents between January 2006 and August 2008, with 8,676 (74%) occurring within Baghdad. This trend remains consistent over time, with only two other regions (North, comprising the Kurdish regions, and Central, the regions around Baghdad) featuring high levels of sectarian incidents. The Shi'a dominated south did not experience the same level of sectarian incidents, despite the fact that it featured significant levels of violence against British forces and between Shiite militias.

The lethality of attacks varies significantly, in part because of the types of tactics employed (table 8.5). Across Iraq, attacks have a 72.21 percent lethality rate, meaning that on average fewer than one person are killed per attack. Yet some regions, such as the Shi'a regions of Arbil, Kerbala, Najaf, and Wasit, have higher rates of lethality for attacks. This is likely due to the fact that many of their recorded attacks occurred during the Sadrist uprisings in 2004. Some regions that featured a significant number of attacks on U.S. forces such as Anbar had a lower lethality rate than areas where the sectarian killing was more prevalent.

Data on the actual tactics of the violence employed are not available in the CENTCOM statistics. A study conducted with the Iraqi Body Count (IBC) data with a different date range (from 20 March 2003 to 19 March 2008) suggests that 92,614 Iraqis died from acts of violence over this period and that the tactic of violence varied significantly by perpetrator.[144] According to the IBC, 65 percent of the civilian deaths occurred during short-duration events (defined here as less than two days), while 35 percent occurred from long-duration events, such as the battles of Fallujah or the uprisings in Najaf. Most (73.9%) of the short-duration attacks were carried out by unknown perpetrators, with 12.4 percent attributed to the Coalition and 10.7 percent attributed to anti-Coalition forces.[145] Attacks by unknown perpetrators tended to be done by execution (31.9%), small-arms gunfire (13.4%), and suicide bomber (8.9%), and torture was evident in 29 percent of the victims.[146] Deaths attributed to anti-Coalition forces were from suicide bombers (5.5%), vehicle bombs (2.7%), and roadside bombs (2.1%). Deaths attributed to the Coalition were from air attacks (3.9%) and small-arms gunfire (1.6%).[147] By contrast, according to the Brookings Institute, U.S. and Coalition soldiers were killed by different tactics such as improvised explosive devices (39.%) and other hostile fire (29.2%) but were rarely killed by car bombs and executions, as many Iraqi civilians were.[148]

This analysis suggests that from the vantage point of the victims there were at least two side-by-side conflicts in Iraq during this period. From the perspective of U.S. and Coalition forces, this was an insurgency war waged by IEDs, snipers, and car bombs, as insurgents tried to disrupt the U.S. mission and the formation of an Iraqi state.

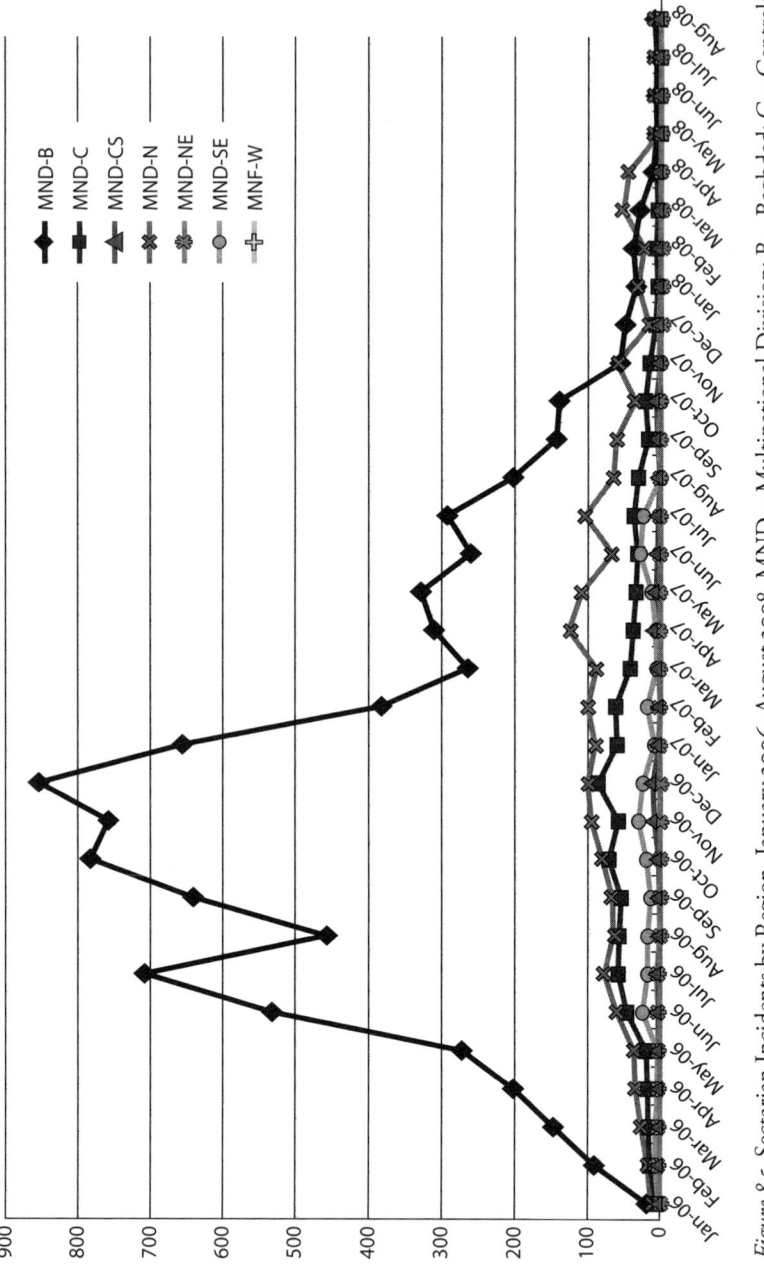

Figure 8.5. Sectarian Incidents by Region, January 2006–August 2008. MND = Multinational Division: B = Baghdad; C = Central; CS = Central South; N = North; NE = North East; SE = South East; W = West.

TABLE 8.5.
Lethality by Region, January 2004–August 2008

	Total Attacks	Total KIA	Lethality
Anbar	26,255	4,320	16.45%
Arbil	148	308	208.11%
Babil	3,470	2,678	77.18%
Baghdad	60,972	42,013	68.91%
Basra	7,185	3,205	44.61%
Dahuk	80	40	50.00%
Dhi Qar	1,140	538	47.19%
Diyala	14,257	9,393	65.88%
Kerbala	423	877	207.33%
Maysan	1,640	167	10.18%
Muthanna	372	105	28.23%
Najaf	433	434	100.23%
Ninawa	18,580	6,921	37.25%
Qadisyah	1,335	1,010	75.66%
Salah ad Din	18,834	4,970	26.39%
Sulaymaniyah	170	161	94.71%
Ta'mim	6,581	2,259	34.33%
Wasit	1,057	1,132	107.10%
Total	162,932	80,531	

From the perspective of the Iraqi civilians, the war was one of random and unpredictable violence, including sporadic terrorist attacks, all conducted over a surface of low-intensity murder, brutality, and expulsion. Though mass bombings and suicide attacks have garnered most of the headlines, most of the casualties from strategic violence have been created through low-casualty attacks, often with gunfire or other low-technology implements like car bombs. Murder, kidnapping, rape, torture, and expulsion were the most common tactics in the sectarian warfare that ran beneath the Sunni insurgency against U.S. forces.[149] The hard post-conflict environment, with escalating sectarian tensions and a growing insurgency against U.S. forces, became a dirty war in which Iraqis turned on each other with surprisingly brutality in the aftermath of the al-Askari attack.

Multiple Pathways

The complex environment—with two concurrent tiers of violence, including an insurgency against U.S. forces and a sectarian dirty war—cannot be explained by a single causal pathway. While U.S. mismanagement of the post-conflict period was a contributing factor to the chaotic environment, the drivers of strategic violence were more varied. Moreover, the high levels of strategic violence in this case were embedded in an environment with a substantial level of expressive and instrumental violence. The absence of public order in the days following the U.S. invasion created a permissive opportunity structure for waves of revenge killings to take place, especially against Baathists who had been complicit in the repression and torture of the Saddam Hussein regime. Within weeks of the de-Baathification order was put into place, there was evidence that "several hundred" former Baathists had been killed in Baghdad alone.[150] By 22 May, officials within Sadr city had reported between sixty and seventy deaths of Baathists and their informants, with significant evidence of torture and execution.[151] In Najaf, forty-two bodies were found executed but not a single arrest was made.[152] In Basra, more than a dozen Baathists were gunned down in the streets in waves of revenge killings during November 2003.[153] Especially in Shiite towns that were victimized by Saddam Hussein's regime, revenge killings of former Baath officials, Mukhabarat officers, and neighborhood informants were so common that the Iraqi police struggled to cope with the volume of cases. By December 2003, police officials with the CPA estimated that revenge killings were the fastest-growing crime in Baghdad and other Iraqi cities.[154] Revenge killings came from a variety of sources—personal vendettas, tribal justice, and organized hit operations—but were viewed sympathetically by much of the population. While noting that many of the attacks were organized and may have been professional hits, a senior Baghdad police officer remarked, "Iraqi blood runs very hot . . . and revenge killing is a crime of passion. People are tempted because they were so abused. Wouldn't you kill your child's torturer if you didn't see law and order on the street?"[155]

What remained unclear was the extent to which the violence in post-conflict Iraq involved reprisals organized for strategic gain. Much of the revenge violence was clearly expressive, as those who suffered greatly under Saddam Hussein's regime sought out vengeance on those that they blamed for turning them over to the regime. Newspaper accounts at the time emphasize that most of the dead bodies that appeared in morgues at the time were known to be former Baathists with strong links to the regime.[156] Many of the attacks had the appearances of professional hits and left relatively little evidence behind that would be traceable to a perpetrator. But there was also some evidence that armed groups emerged to purposefully target ex-Baathists, perhaps for strategic rather than expressive purposes. An organization called Islamic Tharallah (God's Revenge) emerged in 2003 to seek out former Baathists and conduct interviews to turn them over to local police, though it officially disavowed the use of reprisal violence.[157] Other militia organizations, many of which were attached to political parties, were also alleged to be involved in the "incidents of liquidations against senior members of the previous regime who had committed crimes against the people."[158] An organization called the Retribution Committee put posters around Baghdad announcing that it had given itself the authority to search, detain, and punish former allies of the regime.[159] Some of the organization of the reprisals was more ad hoc but very effective. Using documents looted from the offices of the Mukhabarat, Shiite hit squads began hunting down those who tortured or murdered civilians under Saddam's orders.[160] Such violence was typically met by a wall of silence. In Kut, more than thirty homes of former regime officials were burned down, often on a nightly basis, with no claim of responsibility and no witnesses coming forward.[161] In this case, revenge violence and its strategic variant, reprisal violence, were intertwined, making it difficult to assess, especially with the assassinations of key Baathists, which motive took precedence.[162]

The chaos of the early post-conflict period also provided an opportunity for instrumental violence, both criminal violence and denunciations, to flourish. To some extent, this was part of Saddam Hussein's plan. In October 2002, with the U.S. invasion looming, Hussein opened Iraq's jails, releasing thousands of prisoners and offering them an unconditional amnesty.[163] These newly released criminals arrived into an environment where criminal activity had been on the rise, as the UN sanctions regime forced many actors, including tribes, to circumvent the regime through crime in order to protect their populations.[164] Criminals found the permissive opportunity structure of the Iraqi state appealing, because it lowered their risks of getting caught and the absence of government left civilians vulnerable to predation and extortion. The growing criminalization of Iraqi society in the post-conflict period can be noted in the explosion of the kidnapping market. Small bands of criminals have taken advantage of the proliferation of armed actors in Iraq to run kidnapping networks, in which ordinary Iraqi civilians were abducted and ransomed back to their family for profit.[165] By some estimates between five and thirty people per day were abducted for ransom payments that averaged as high as $30,000 per person.[166] Similar criminal enterprises led to a flourishing black market, especially in petrol, and in protection rackets whereby citizens are "taxed" in return for security provided by the local mafia against potential predators.[167]

These criminal networks were often deeply intertwined with the insurgency, making a clear division of political and criminal violence nearly impossible to determine.[168] Similarly, Coalition officials found that separating the personal from the political was nearly impossible; aspiring Iraqi politicians denounced their rivals as former Baathists or supporters of the insurgency on a regular basis.[169] Efforts to get the Iraqi population to turn in members of the insurgency via a national tip line were challenging, as many civilians denounced others for personal grievances. U.S. forces found consistently that their efforts to turn to the Iraqi population for information were met by misdirection and dead ends.[170] Throughout the post-conflict period, these waves of expressive and instrumental violence produced a kind of cover that for a brief period of time masked the true extent of the strategic violence in post-conflict Iraq.

Yet ultimately the levels of strategic violence increased from summer 2003 to early 2006 to the point where the al-Askari attack would kick off waves of sectarian reprisals that pushed Iraq decisively into a civil war.[171] This is due to the operation of both direct and indirect pathways in producing strategic violence. As noted, former regime elements (sometimes known by their acronym FRE) were engaged in strategic violence, either as direct participants in insurgent activity or as contributors of soldiers and material to insurgent groups. These Baathist-led or assisted attacks were an attempt to renegotiate the terms of the peace settlement to produce terms favorable to them. Consistent with the predictions of the direct pathway, the type and targets of attack (particularly U.S. forces and representatives of the Coalition) mirrored that of the invasion in 2003. The violence that came from ex-Baathist and Iraqi army officials more closely resembled the kind of asymmetrical conflict that U.S. planners feared Saddam Hussein might wage. While the regime was overthrown, elements within the regime never gave up the fight in the post-conflict period, though they did so without a strong hierarchical organization or single leadership.

The evidence for the indirect pathway in the production of strategic violence is apparent, especially after 2006, in the emergence of multiple new claimants for power, the production of violence through bargaining among these factions, and the corresponding shifts in the type and target of violent attacks. Post-conflict Iraq was driven into chaos by multiple groups, some emerging from the ashes of the Iraqi army and from existing factions (like the Shiite parties and Sadrist movement) and others arising through a countermobilization of new Sunni, Shi'a, and Kurdish factions, which began to war with one another. Some of these organizations (like the Badr Brigade and the peshmerga) were strongly hierarchical and disciplined, whereas others (like many Sunni groups and the Sadrists) found that they had only weak internal control over their factions. The proliferation of factions and different wings within factions meant that strategic violence in Iraq was highly localized and reflected the microfoundational goals, strategies, and alliances of these factions rather than any overarching narrative about sectarian dominance. For example, different factions of the Mahdi Army alternatively attacked or tolerated Sunni civilians within their area of control on the basis of prior relations between Sunni and Shi'a within that city or region and their local leader's long-term goals.[172] This variation demonstrates that strategic violence in Iraq was often a product of preexisting tribal and social relations, and that regional or local politics could not always be reduced to sectarian or ethnic prejudice.[173] It also meant that some of the violence was internecine, as organizations occasionally employed violence against their own factions as a form of ingroup policing.

Distinct from the insurgency against U.S. forces, the strategic violence that tore much of the country apart can best be explained as a bargaining process between a series of armed groups, drawn from overlapping, often competitive, sectarian groupings.[174] These armed groups and their factions employed strategic violence as a means of contestation over territory, resources and the spoils of war. The strategic violence was largely transactional: it emerged in a bargaining process as a kind of chip that players could use to signal their strength in local political contests. In many cases, this was done to create defensible borders and to consolidate the control of one community over disputed territory; the violence that tore apart Baghdad, for example, reflected this competition for control of territory between Shiite and Sunni militias. In this kind of environment, strategic violence also has an organizational value, as such violence is a way of demonstrating strength and ensuring that political momentum is maintained by the perpetrator group.[175] This helps generate more recruits and funding in a competitive environment and convince the population to transfer their loyalties to that particular armed group. Much of the strategic violence evident in Iraq after 2006 had less to do with sectarian fault lines than with powerful local and tribal figures using attacks to maintain their fiefdoms and to protect their control over local economic resources.

In some cases, intersectarian bargaining drove strategic violence, particularly in intermixed areas, where some of the worst levels of brutality were evident. In areas where a single ethnic group was dominant (such as some Kurdish regions) or where the competitors for the loyalties of a sect were nonexistent (such as some Shiite regions), the levels of strategic violence in these regions were relatively low. But in regions where potential contestants for state power were multiple or evenly matched or had unknown or untested capabilities to inflict harm, the use of strategic violence—against each other or civilians from the "wrong" group—became a powerful way for an ambitious armed group to signal its political strength. For this reason, strategic violence was often concentrated in intermixed regions (such as Baghdad, Diyala, and Salah al Din) of intense contestation between sectarian communities. This regional concentration of violence became particularly apparent in 2006 when U.S. officials estimated that those three regions—comprising only 37 percent of the Iraqi population but also known to be a hotbed of the insurgency—were responsible for 81 percent of the attacks since 2003.[176]

The use of some types of strategic violence—murder, kidnapping, expulsion, and reprisal killings—as a form of intersectarian bargaining dynamic became particularly apparent after the al-Askari bombing. After this attack, there were waves of revenge attacks that spread across mixed areas, as rival Sunni and Shiite militias sought to murder and expel Iraqis from the other sect in order to "cleanse" those areas and make them more defensible. Some of the violence in the immediate aftermath of the bombing was driven be expressive motivations, such as anger and grief, but over time a growing portion was clearly strategic in orientation. After this attack, the Baghdad morgue reported between 569 and 591 bodies delivered to its offices, most of which were Sunni civilians killed in reprisal for the destruction of the Golden Dome.[177] Much of the intermixed areas around Baghdad exploded in violence, with militias conducting public executions and street clashes between sectarian militias emerging all across the city. By some estimates, as many as ninety-six Sunni mosques were damaged in Baghdad and twenty imams and sheiks were killed.[178] Dozens of bodies, many of which bore signs of torture, began to appear all around the city; Iraqi security forces and militias conducted mass arrests without warrants, and many of those arrested were later found with a gunshot to the head.[179]

This explosion of strategic violence affected both Sunni and Shi'a communities as both sides began to engage in a dirty war for control of Baghdad. Fearing Shiite militias and believing that the Iraqi security forces were infested with their agents, Sunnis began to form "watch patrols" and local militias to protect themselves. The result was a proliferation of gruesome attacks. As a UNAMI Human Rights report in 2006 described the scenario:

> However, hundreds of civilians are reported killed or wounded weekly, including women and children, as targeted or unintended victims of violent attacks. Dozens of bodies bearing signs of torture and showing execution style killings have continued to appear daily in and around Baghdad, as well as other parts of the country. As an illustration, on 7 March 18 bodies were found in an abandoned minibus, blinded, shot or strangled. The following day 23 bodies, many of them strangled, were found dumped in parts of Baghdad. 81 people were reported killed on 26–27 March, including 30 bodies found decapitated near Baquba. The Medico Legal Institute in Baghdad issued 1,294 death certificates in March and 1,155 in April. Many of these bodies, who include only individuals who have not been identified and whose death is violent or suspect, died as a result of shot wounds.[180]

One of the difficulties in analyzing this escalation in intersectarian bargaining has to do with collective attribution of responsibility for the attacks. The deaths of so many civilians around Baghdad were clearly strategic and designed to forcibly desegregate mixed neighborhoods, but there was little evidence of what specific organization was responsible for each attack, even if it was clear that the killings of many civilians from one sect were likely done by the other. This problem is also compounded by the fact that multiple armed groups often claimed credit for the same violent act.[181] Moreover, jihadi groups like al Qaeda in Iraq intervened in this intersectarian bargaining, often launching mass-casualty attacks designed to produce reprisals and further the polarization of the communities. Finally, some of the violence during this period was opportunistic, with individuals, criminal gangs, and would-be insurgents taking advantage of the chaos for their own ends. The result was that much of the intersectarian bargaining between Sunni and Shiite militias that drove much of the strategic violence was partially obscured by the presence of other actors, functioning almost as "noise" in the data and blurring attributions of responsibility.

The crime patterns clearly indicate a steady increase in intersectarian killing until

2006 and an explosion thereafter, amplified by the direct involvement of jihadi groups in attacks against Shiite targets. Especially after February 2006, the "pattern became one of attack and counter-attack, with Sunni militants staging what commanders call 'spectacular' strikes against Shiite targets and Shiite militias retaliating with abductions and murders of Sunnis."[182] On balance, this meant that more Shi'a civilians were killed in multiple fatality bombings than Sunnis, but Sunnis were more often killed in reprisals, many of which were not reported. By one estimate, 41 percent of the victims of multiple fatality bombings from 2007 to January 2011 were Shi'a, but for many victims, particularly from intermixed areas, their identities were unknown.[183] Much of the violence here began to assume a tit-for-tat pattern and involved multiple players from both the Sunni and Shi'a sides. On 12 March 2006, after 54 people were killed and hundreds wounded in car bombs in Sadr city, the 4 individuals accused of involvement in the attack were found summarily executed and hung from lampposts in the neighborhood.[184] For example, after a bloody weekend in October 2006 where a series of al Qaeda led mass-casualty bombings killed 110 Shiites, the Badr Organization unleashed their wrath in a series of calculated reprisals on Sunni targets around the mixed city of Balad, killing more than 80 in one day.[185] Attacks against mosques, religious leaders, or groups of pilgrims were particularly flash points, and often encouraged reprisals on the other community elsewhere in the country. The dramatic increase in civilian deaths in Iraq in 2006–2007 can be attributed to this cycle of escalation and reprisal that drove much of the worst violence.

This intersectarian bargaining constituted a dirty but undeclared war conducted for control of cities like Baghdad that lay on the fault lines between the sectarian and ethnic communities. The expulsions were conducted with strategic violence, but also with softer forms of intimidation such as "blackmail, seizure of property, raids on homes and businesses, use of checkpoints to push other factions out, kidnappings and extortion, misuse of government offices and police, and disappearances."[186] For example, many Sunnis in mixed areas around Baghdad reported receiving a DVD showing an exploding house, which they clearly interpreted as a warning to leave.[187] Because of the dense networks of information in local areas, the population will learn—through rumor campaigns or quiet warnings—which group was responsible for a murder.[188] As was the case in Kosovo, the sectarian cleansing campaigns were also conducted with signals. In this case, the signal was the delivery of "threat letters" or the kidnapping and torture of Iraqi males, who would live to communicate a message that the family must flee or suffer a worse fate.[189] As a result of this sectarian unmixing of neighborhoods, Iraqis became more entrenched in their sectarian identities and more wary of traveling to areas in which the other sect was dominant.[190] By the end of 2006, the UN estimated that there were 1.7 million internally displaced Iraqis, with an estimated 45,000 fleeing their homes per month.[191]

During this period, the Sunni and Shi'a insurgents were locked in an intense competition not only with each other but also with the multiple armed groups on each side that vied for control over the political direction of their sectarian community. In other words, the violent bargaining between groups occurred in two directions, both across sectarian lines and within a range of sectarian stakeholders from their community. The sheer number of competing armed actors within Iraq suggests that the leaders of major sectarian armed groups needed to be concerned not only with each other but also with new or emerging internal power centers within their own movement. A Shiite sectarian militia such as the Badr Organization, for example, was concerned with maintaining the relative balance of power with Sunni militias that can inflict harm on its own community but also with potential Shi'a competitors in its area of influence. Such intrasectarian politics is even more intense among the Sunnis, for whom there is a greater range of armed actors with more disparate goals. Because none of these actors have achieved full political control over their sectarian constituency, none can afford to be outflanked by letting their rivals appear more deadly.

For this reason, the Mahdi Army engaged in score-settling murders both with Sunnis who live near its base of operations in Sadr City and with Shiite groups like the Badr Organization and powerful Shiite tribes in the south of the country. In Basra, the major competition for power was between Shi'a sectarian militias, not between the major sectarian groups.[192] In the words of the International Crisis Group, the British withdrawal from Basra in September 2007 provided "a case study of Iraq's multiple and multiplying forms of violence. These have little to do with a sectarianism or anti-occupation resistance. Instead, they involve the systematic misuse of official institutions, political assassinations, tribal vendettas, neighborhood vigilantism and enforcement of social mores, together with the rise of criminal mafias that increasingly mingle with political actors."[193] An internal RAND analysis also suggested that looking exclusively as sectarian violence misses between 30 and 60 percent of the violence in Iraq and excludes a lot of violent attacks (such as nonexecution-style murders, IEDs, and small-arms fire) that tend to be employed in intrasectarian contests more than in intersectarian contests.[194]

Amid this bargaining—both intersectarian and intrasectarian—the logic of outbidding was also apparent. Outbidding occurs when organizations employ violence to signal their strength to a local constituency and to claim a greater share of the popular support in that community.[195] In other words, the logic of outbidding suggests that these armed groups compete for popular loyalties by flexing their political muscle and by demonstrating that they have the capacity to employ strategic violence. In an environment in which sect or ethnic group has multiple claimants aiming to represent them, the use of violence becomes an important signal of capacity and a way to force civilians to choose sides. This dynamic became particularly apparent in Shi'a regions, where multiple armed groups competed for market share of the loyalties of the population. In Basra, for example, there was an escalation of political and criminal violence after British troops withdrew, with much of the violence driven by intrasectarian competition in a fluid political environment.[196] With the population confronting choices to pledge their loyalty between SCIRI and the Sadrist movement, violence became "a routine means of social interaction utilized by political actors doubling as militiamen who seek to increase their share of power and resources."[197] A similar logic of outbidding was also apparent among Sunnis, who faced demands for loyalty from both Sunni nationalists and jihadi groups that were competing for the loyalties of that community.

Consistent with the indirect pathway, the strategic violence that emerged as a result of bargaining among factions within each community produced shifts in the types and targets of attack. The U.S. invasion to overthrow Saddam was a war directed at military targets, although by some estimates 7,958 Iraqi civilians died as a result of the fighting.[198] Yet the violence in the post-conflict period was predominantly directed at civilian targets and was sectarian and ethnic. The contrast here is stark: the war was a relatively clean one, conducted with surgical precision, while the post-conflict period descended into campaigns of intrasectarian bloodletting never anticipated by U.S. policy makers. This was in part because attacks on civilian targets became a substitute form of communication between the parties. In post-conflict Iraq, when armed factions engaged in open combat, the Iraqi security forces and U.S. forces intervened to bring hostilities to an end. Open attacks on Iraqi government targets and American forces were regularly launched, but for these groups a strategy premised on open confrontation would be prohibitively costly and unlikely to succeed. Because their ability to fight openly is limited, the armed actors face uncertainty about capabilities, particularly about which would win in an open contest for power. In other words, because of the size of the American and allied forces and the rapid build-up of Iraqi security forces, the strategic position of insurgents—particularly the asymmetry of power they faced and their vulnerability to a crushing blow by U.S. forces—precluded open violence as a means of signaling their ability to fight. In the words of an Iraqi journalist, "Sunnis and Shiites are not yet in an all-out fight because the Americans are still there."[199] When information on relative capabilities is uncertain and cannot be tested in open combat, leaders of armed groups face a serious dilemma: how can they signal their strength, and willingness to fight, to their opponents across sectarian lines and within their own sectarian group, without assuming unacceptable levels of risks?

As was the case in Kosovo, armed actors in Iraq sought to signal their capacity to fight by attacking civilians who cannot defend themselves. It has been long noted that terrorism can act as a form of signaling, as groups that lack the ability to impose their will by force resort to attacks on softer targets to show that they can impose costs on their enemies.[200] Jihadi groups in particular sought to demonstrate their staying power to Sunni and Shi'a by launching mass-casualty attacks on Iraq's minorities. Iraqi small minority groups, including Armenians, Turkomen, Palestinians, Chaldo-Assyrian Christians, Mandeans, Jews, and Yazidis, make up approximately 10 percent of the population. Too small to matter politically, these minorities are nevertheless victimized regularly by Islamist terrorist cells.[201] They were particularly subject to mass-casualty attacks that appear almost at random, without prior demands for concessions before or afterward. For example, a marketplace bomb on 7 July 2007 killed more than one hundred Shi'a Turkomen civilians in Armili, a village near Kirkuk.[202] This indiscriminate attack was quickly attributed to al Qaeda in Iraq and was based on sectarian grounds, yet there was no demands made by al Qaeda before the attack, and the Turkomen—who constitute only a small proportion of the population—had no power to concede substantial demands by al Qaeda. Similarly, a massive attack on 14 August 2007 against the Yazidi community in Kahtaniya killed more than five hundred and was attributed to al Qaeda in Iraq.[203] Like the attack against the Turkomen community, this attack was based on sectarian rationale but was not linked to any specific bargaining demands by al Qaeda in Iraq. Attacking these groups—which were in small in number and without a capacity to defend themselves—served little strategic purpose other than demonstrating their political staying power in an uncertain environment. Yet the demonstration effect of these attacks convinced many Sunnis that they needed to pledge their loyalty to a militia, as even these minorities began to arm themselves for their own protection.[204]

Similarly, repeated strategic attacks on civilians such as murders, kidnappings, and terrorist attacks served as a substitute communicative act that signals credibly to enemies across sectarian lines that a particular armed group has the ability to inflict harm. For example, attacks such as murders, expulsions, and car bombs can be way of demonstrating capabilities and of signaling strength for future contests. In this respect, militias can use highly discriminate forms of violence—such as executions, kidnappings, and arsons—as a form of tacit bargaining to allow them to signal their capability and to test the resolve of their rivals. The permissive opportunity structure of post-conflict Iraq—which allowed armed groups to compete and attack the U.S. and Iraqi government, but which made direct combat inadvisable because of the power asymmetry between U.S. forces and the insurgents— favored a shift in tactics to attacks hard to stop (such as terrorist bombings) or detect and monitor (such as murder and expulsions), and a shift toward softer targets like civilians.

Conclusion

The U.S. invasion in Iraq produced a post-conflict environment that could best be described as a "strategic surprise."[205] The post-conflict environment was dominated by an insurgency against U.S. forces and complex bargaining games between and among sectarian and ethnic forces. A war predicated on the assumption of relatively few casualties wound up producing a death toll of nearly 82,682, as a hard post-conflict environment rife with strategic violence gradually transformed into a full-blown sectarian war. In this respect, the post-conflict environment in Iraq is an object lesson in the dangers of underplaying the significance of strategic violence. The reluctance of U.S. and Iraqi officials to admit that the insurgency extended beyond regime "dead-enders," and to acknowledge the impact of a steady increase in intersectarian killings in creating the conditions for a security dilemma, proved decisive.[206] By the time the al-Askari bombing occurred, Iraq was essentially primed for violence and needed only a spark for the entire country to be engulfed in sectarian war.

Many lessons can be drawn from U.S. mismanagement of the occupation, but among the most important was that those fighting the war can remain wedded to a static image of victims and perpetrators long after the war finishes. The U.S. war plan was predominantly focused on Saddam Hussein and his loyalists and worked under the assumption that if these "bad apples" were removed that Iraq would become stable and democratic. This meant that U.S. planners remained focused on removing former Baathists who were involved in the resistance, while failing to grasp how the ground was shifting beneath their feet as new actors rose to prominence in post-conflict Iraq. For example, U.S. officials underestimated the strength of the Sadrist movement until the uprisings in Kerbala and Najaf; similarly, the role of Shiite death squads associated with the Badr Brigades and located in the Interior Ministry was underplayed by U.S. forces until late 2007. More generally, U.S. officials were slow to come to grips with the fact that their decision to invade Iraq had radically transformed the politics of Iraq, to the advantage of some (but not all) Shi'a and Kurdish parties and to the significant disadvantage of some of the Sunni community.

Second, the decision to disband the Iraqi military was a crucial mistake because it deprived U.S. and Iraqi forces of the ability to effectively reward and police factions within its ranks. To some extent, the Bremer regime was following a standard practice in reconstituting the security forces of a post-conflict regime by not automatically allowing combatants to serve and by insisting that no one with serious violations of human rights in their records be permitted to join. The goal was to produce nonsectarian, professional armed forces for the "new Iraq," but the unintended consequences were to shatter an institution that retained at best modest levels of internal control over its members and to turn those dismissed officers toward the insurgency. The cycles of mobilization that produced the insurgency in Iraq—where the former regime elements provided the Sunni national insurgency with well-trained personnel and materials, which improved their effectiveness and produced a countermobilization of Shi'a and Kurdish forces—are traceable to this decision. By sacrificing the ability to effectively reward or punish those actors, the United States found itself without leverage over those with the means of employing strategic violence. In seeking justice for those who suffered under Saddam Hussein's regime, the United States inadvertently created the conditions for the unraveling of the post-conflict order. The concluding chapter suggests that this painful trade-off between order and justice is more common in post-conflict states than is commonly realized.

PART THREE

PRODUCING PEACE
AFTER WARS

CHAPTER NINE

Controlling Violence
Implications and Policy Recommendations

All wars may end, but the end of a war rarely means the end of violence in a post-conflict state. On the contrary, these states are rife with violent acts of various form and purposes, and the peace that is produced by the settlement of the conflict is often fragile.[1] As chapter 2 discussed, post-conflict states feature some mix of expressive, instrumental, and strategic violence, interspersed with acts of opportunistic violence. Each post-conflict state will feature a unique combination of violent acts, and almost no case will be a straight replay of the violence during the war. The reasons why experts so often get it wrong when predicting violence in post-conflict states is that they underestimate the changes in the incentives and organizational structures of the combatants, which can alter the character of the violence in subtle and unexpected ways. As chapter 3 demonstrated, strategic violence is strikingly common in post-conflict states even when the peace settlement remains intact. Within the dataset of fifty-two post-conflict states, only four cases experienced a cessation of strategic violence when the war ended. Most post-conflict states experience some types of strategic violence—ranging from assassinations, reprisals, assaults against minorities or refugees, to terrorist attacks—which continue in some form for months or even years afterward. In some cases, this strategic violence bears a distinct resemblance to the violence that occurred during the war, featuring similar types and targets and revolving around the same fault lines that drove the war. In other cases, strategic violence is driven by local rivalries, grievances, and power struggles, and there is a corresponding shift in the types and targets of attack in the post-conflict period. In these cases, strategic violence is qualitatively different from the violence of the war and reflects the changes brought about by the peace settlement as well as the evolving political and intraorganizational relationships between the parties and new claimants to power.

The purpose of this book has been to explain the variations of violence in post-conflict states. In each of the case studies, it has described the post-conflict environment and described the patterns of violence for the five years following the peace settlement. It has emphasized that the three categories of violent activity (expressive, instrumental, and strategic) are empirically intertwined and that ascertaining motives for violent action under conditions of limited information is challenging. With due attention to this limitation, this book has undertaken a contextual analysis of the crime statistics and narrative reports to track variations in the type, target, and magnitude of strategic violence across cases. It has explained the source of those variations by highlighting two pathways—the direct pathway and the indirect pathway—both of which can produce the onset of strategic violence. Under the direct pathway, strategic violence emerges as a function of dissatisfaction with the peace settlement. In these cases, there continues to be violent bargaining between the original parties of the war, as they continue to wrestle with each other over the terms of the settlement or the division of the spoils. Under this pathway, the parties continue to fight along the same lines that they did during the war, hoping to overturn the peace settlement or to change its effective terms. As a result, the type and targets of violence are similar to the violence experienced under the war. Under the indirect pathway, the original combatants find that they cannot enforce the terms of the peace and fragment into smaller splinter groups due to an inability to reward and police their own factions. These splinter groups, some of which are involved in organized crime, will begin to employ violence for their own political, criminal, or idiosyncratic purposes. These highly localized bargaining games between splinter groups or factions are often detached from the macro-narrative of the conflict and revolve around local fault lines that were often negligible during the war itself. Consequently, strategic violence via the indirect pathway is markedly different from the wartime violence, featuring a new host of types and targets, as well as actors that have emerged out of the remnants of the original combatant group.

This conclusion first highlights some of the insights that arose from the case studies, emphasizing the diversity of motives for violent action, the roles of the pathways and opportunity structure in jointly determining the levels of strategic violence, and the importance of countermobilization in generating extreme levels of violence and a return to armed conflict. It then turns to two policy implications that have emerged in the case studies. First, it addresses the differences in perception between local actors and international custodians of peace that allow post-conflict violence to have an undetected but often substantial political effect.[2] The argument here is that strategic violence in post-conflict states is often an inside game, conducted between players within the society itself and embedded in social practices and codes of meaning unavailable to outside observers. In part because acts of strategic violence are conducted in covert or sublimated ways, these acts are dismissed as expressive or instrumental violence by peacekeepers or NGO officials, thus allowing their perpetrators to engage in violent bargaining with impunity. Second, it calls attention to the difficult moral choices that arise when an armed group has low levels of internal control in the post-conflict period. Contrary to the conventional wisdom, it argues the rapid demobilization, disarmament, and reintegration (DDR) of combatants into civilian life should not always be undertaken when the armed groups are little more than loose alliances of factions. In these cases, DDR programs may increase the risk of violence by unleashing discontented factions that will begin to fight for their own purposes in local bargaining games. For this reason, DDR programs should be implemented selectively depending on the levels of internal control that the combatants have. In cases where the combatants are internally divided or highly factionalized, peacekeepers may be better off helping armed groups maintain their organizational cohesion to allow them to enforce the settlement and to control the risks of factional violence, rather than forcing them to disband to participate in normal politics. The chapter closes with policy recommendations for how custodians of peace can prevent or manage violence in post-conflict states and shape the incentives of those who would act violently.

Implications of Case Studies

The case studies of violence in post-conflict states have demonstrated the diversity of motives for violent action in post-conflict states and, in some cases, the interdependence between strategic and criminal violence. In most of the cases surveyed here, the collapse of state institutions produced a window of opportunity for individuals to pursue personal vendettas and seek otherwise illicit goals as the post-conflict period began. Especially in cases where peacekeeping forces were slow to arrive or ill-equipped to handle disorder, the emergence of a public security gap created a ripe environment for predatory violence.[3] The widespread looting that followed the collapse of the Saddam Hussein regime in Iraq is a case in point, though it is perhaps an extreme example relative to what was observed elsewhere. Each case study noted that some of the violence was a result of the opportunity structure of the state, with factors such as the vulnerability of minority populations, the flexibility of institutions, and the presence of peacekeeping missions exerting either an amplifying or diminishing effect on the levels of strategic violence. Moreover, the case studies have emphasized that strategic attacks are typically enmeshed within waves of expressive and instrumental violence that can obscure their origin and purpose.[4] Because of this fact, assessing responsibility for the strategic violence was difficult in each case, because many strategic attacks (such as assassinations and reprisals) are conducted covertly. Further, as the behavior of the RPF in Rwanda revealed, actors will deny responsibility for attacks even when much of the available evidence points to them. To detect strategic violence requires connecting evidence of strategic intent—itself detectable only by the markers of style, tactics, and location of the act itself—to the goals of the original combatants and their splinters.

The case studies also confirm that there is substantial variation in the magnitude, type, and target of strategic attacks in those cases where it occurs. Table 9.1 tracks the variations in all three indicators across the five case studies and highlights not only the scope of variation across but also the differences in the number of deaths between cases classed at the same overall magnitude, the variation in the types and targets of violence between cases with the same magnitude, and the different magnitudes of violence evident in cases with similar initial starting conditions. The first difference is relatively straightforward. Although both Rwanda and Iraq qualify as having a mass magnitude of strategic violence, the number of people killed was more than twice as high in Iraq (7,300) than Rwanda (3,345) for their first year of the post-conflict period. This comparison indicates the differences in the levels of strategic violence between cases in which the settlement is stable yet violence continues (Rwanda) and those where an armed conflict has arguably resumed along different lines from the original war (Iraq). Second, there are stark differences in the types and targets of violence between cases of the same magnitude. While both cases featured indiscriminate assaults on civilians, Rwanda featured much more low-technology attacks (such as assaults with small arms or even machetes), whereas Iraq featured innovative technological devices, such as IEDs and car bombs. Similarly, while the overall levels of magnitude were similar in Kosovo and East Timor, the types of violent activity that occurred was very different, as the attacks against minorities in Kosovo employed tactics and technology (such as grenades, arsons, and remote-detonated bombs) that were more sophisticated and lethal than those employed in East Timor. Finally, a focused-paired comparison of cases reveals how different the magnitude of violence can be between cases with similar initial conditions. For example, Bosnia and Rwanda were both ethnic wars with high death tolls, yet Rwanda had a much greater level of violence in the post-conflict period. Kosovo and East Timor also had similar conditions and levels of violence, but target, type, and style of killing varied between them. Although post-conflict environments can be broadly categorized as hard or soft, there are important qualitative differences between cases within those categories.

The case studies also demonstrated that all levels of strategic violence could be produced via both the direct and indirect pathways. As argued in chapter 3, strategic violence at all levels is subject to equifinality, as both causal pathways may produce the same magnitude of violence.[5] There is no simple correlation between pathways and the overall level of violence because of the intervening role of the opportunity structure. Either of these pathways can equally generate a hard or soft post-conflict environment, depending on how the determination of the actors to continue the war (i.e., direct pathway) or the intensity of the microlevel bargaining games present (i.e., indirect pathway) interacts with the features of the opportunity structure in the state. Moreover, many of the cases demonstrated the greatest risks of a conflict spreading

TABLE 9.1.
Strategic Violence in the Case Studies

	Total Casualties from Strategic Violence	Magnitude	Types	Targets
Bosnia	42	Residual	Nonlethal attacks, harassment, intimidation, expulsion	Ethnic minorities, returnees, local political officials
Rwanda	3,345 (1995) 8,439 (1995–1999)	Mass	Reprisals, insurgent attacks, assassinations	Civilians, refugees, ex-FAR guerrilla members, RPF dissidents
Kosovo	213	Occasional	Reprisals, assassinations, bombings, grenade attacks, evictions, arsons	Serb, Roma and other minority civilians, Albanian party loyalists, dissidents, journalists
East Timor	322	Occasional	Assassinations, arsons, expulsions	Civilians, rival factions within the Fretilin forces
Iraq	7,300 (in 2003 alone) 82,682 (2003–2008)	Mass	Insurgent attacks, terrorism, assassinations, reprisals, expulsions	Sunni and Shi'a civilians, political officials, Coalition peacekeepers, NGOs and humanitarian aid officials

occur when a dynamic of countermobilization is present. In such cases, the levels of strategic violence are determined not only by the pathways and opportunity structure on their own but also by the reactions of their targets.

As chapter 3 argues, the direct pathway produces strategic violence that is broadly along the same fault lines and features the same types and targets that occurred during the war. This is clearly the case in both Bosnia and Rwanda. Although these cases had very different levels of strategic violence, the ethnic fault lines of both conflicts remained intact in the post-conflict period. Moreover, in both cases, much of the violence was conducted against civilians, just as the violence during the wars had been. Under the indirect pathway, there is some shift in the type and targets of violence, as the post-conflict attacks often derive from regional or local bargaining games rather than the original cause of the war. Such a dynamic was clearly the case in East Timor, which featured factional warfare among remnants of the Fretilin coalition and the emergence of a new regional fault line. In Kosovo, this shift was somewhat less clear cut. In this case, hard-line remnants of the KLA initially sought to expel Kosovo Serbs out of the country to guarantee its independence in spite of the ambivalence of the

TABLE 9.2.
Pathways in the Case Studies

	Level of Strategic Violence	Pathway(s)	Opportunity Structure	Post-Conflict Environment	Counter-mobilization
Bosnia	Residual	Direct	Nonpermissive	Soft	Limited
Rwanda	Mass	Direct	Permissive	Hard	Extensive
Kosovo	Occasional	Indirect	Permissive (1999–2000) Nonpermissive (2001–2004)	Soft	Limited
East Timor	Occasional	Indirect	Permissive	Soft	Extensive
Iraq	Mass	Direct and Indirect	Permissive	Hard	Extensive

UN Security Council Resolution 1244. Later, while parts of the KLA went legitimate and transformed themselves into the PDK party, much of the rest of KLA turned into political-criminal gangs that engaged in an internecine violent struggle. Some of these KLA splinters also conducted a low-grade or dirty war against Serb and Roma civilians as a way of demonstrating their capacity to UNMIK, KFOR and peer competitors in their environment. Finally, in Iraq both the direct and indirect pathways were at work, as cells of former Baathists fought U.S. troops while much of the rest of the Iraqi army unfolded into insurgent organizations and criminal groups engaged in what can best be described as large-scale gang warfare in the streets of Baghdad and other Iraqi cities.

Countermobilization was an important dimension of the production of strategic violence in most of these cases, though it had a variable effect on the levels of violence. In most cases, some limited amount of countermobilization took place, as the victims tried to arm themselves for self-protection. In Bosnia, the opportunity structure—specifically the reductions in vulnerability of the population because of ethnic flight and the presence of NATO peacekeeping forces—precluded significant countermobilization despite frequent attacks on minority returnees. In Kosovo, Serbian militia groups (such as the Bridge Watchers in Mitrovica) emerged in response to KLA-sponsored attacks, although the situation did not spiral out of control because of the presence of French peacekeepers in the northern region. In Iraq, the countermobilization drove much of the violence, as the demobilization of the Iraqi army produced conflict spirals that led to the arming of multiple factions among the Sunni and Shi'a communities.[6] Such countermobilization was uneven in Iraq, however, as the degree of internal control wielded by Kurdish authorities over their peshmerga prevented conflict spirals from taking place in much of their region.[7] In some cases, like East Timor, countermobilization was tiered, with multiple groups mobilizing and responding to violence at different stages. In others, the very question of who mobilized first is difficult to answer. In Rwanda, for example, the Hutu government fled to Zaire after the genocide and almost immediately began launching insurgent attacks into Rwanda itself. RPF reprisals against Hutu civilians and the subsequent invasion of Zaire led to the emergence of proxy forces, such as the AFDL, which in turn produced a countermobilization of local Congolese forces. The dynamic interaction between armed groups employing strategic violence and their targets in this case contributed to the vast increase in casualties and the spread of Africa's first intercontinental war.

Another key implication of the case studies is that the predominant scholarly depiction of most conflicts as a dyadic relationship between two unified actors is often misleading.[8] The case studies demonstrate that unified actors are rare, especially in civil or irregular wars. Armed groups vary significantly in terms of their organizational endowments, with some actors operating as a coalition of competing forces (CNRT in East Timor, the KLA in Kosovo), some maintaining organizational cohesion through external sponsorship (nationalist militias in Bosnia), and some have an extraordinary degree of internal control and cohesion owing to years of fighting experience (the RPF in Rwanda). In Iraq, for example, some of the insurgent organizations were relatively diffuse, cellular organizations without a stable organizational core, while others were semihierarchical and disciplined. Of all of rebel groups surveyed, only the RPF had the levels of internal control that traditionally marks a government or an organized military.

The analysis in the case studies suggests that there will be a significant risk of post-conflict violence via the indirect pathway in cases where the combatant group is organized horizontally as a loose alliance of interested parties. This risk was clearly demonstrated during the overthrow of the Gaddafi regime in Libya in 2011. NATO supported the "rebels," many of whom were allied under the banner of the National Transitional Council (NTC) in their effort to overthrow the Gaddafi regime. But the rebels were actually composed of disparate factions, including secular liberals, Islamists, and tribes, and the NTC exercised relatively little control over their wartime activities. Once the Gaddafi regime was overthrown, the rebel alliance fractured and turned on each other in intense factional violence.[9] The NTC became the face of the movement, much in the way that the PDK did in Kosovo, but the rest of rebels pursued their own ambitions in regional power struggles throughout the country. The aftermath of the war saw revenge attacks against Gaddafi supporters, reprisals against Africans (seen as mercenaries and loyal to Gaddafi), clan and tribal violence, and high levels of factional violence. A UN estimate suggests that various rebel factions "disappeared" more than seven thousand people after Gaddafi's rule to secret jails, some of which were outside the control of the political leadership of the NTC.[10] Consistent with the indirect pathway, the NTC unfolded in dozens of militias engaged in intense local or regional power struggles, all while claiming to be "guardians of the revolution."[11] A similar dynamic could emerge in post-conflict Syria, where the insurgency against the regime of Hafez al-Assad is currently composed of a diverse collection of Islamist and nationalist groups, only some of which cooperate under the auspices of the Free Syrian Army. If we assume that Assad does not crush the rebellion and restore full control over the country, post-conflict Syria is likely to experience intense factional violence for years, as these small, often internally divided factions will further fragment and battle each other over the spoils of war.

This portrayal of actors in post-conflict states—as heterogeneous organizations, beset by demands from their internal factions and struggling to maintain some discipline over their ranks—suggests that it is also wrong to always view their lack of compliance with a settlement or use of violence as evidence of spoiling.[12] As the case studies demonstrate, strategic violence was put to a much wider variety of purposes in four out of five of the cases. Only in Bosnia—which featured highly choreographed forms of violent activity, designed not to cause many casualties but to block minorities from returning to their homes—were the strategic attacks driven chiefly by spoiling, as it is conventionally understood. In this case, hard-line nationalist elements in the Republika Srpska and Croat-dominated regions were determined to stop the return to multiethnicity promised in the Dayton Accords. In this respect, they functioned as "inside spoilers," as they were parties to the peace settlement but never-theless tried to block the implementation of one of its key terms.[13] In the other four cases, strategic violence was directed by multiple parties to wide range of sometimes conflicting purposes, some of which had very little to do with the terms of the peace settlement. In Kosovo, some elements within the victorious KLA sought to expel the remaining Serbs from the territory in an attempt to stop the return to multiethnicity promised in UNSCR 1244. Yet many others were content to engage in predatory violence and intrafactional bargaining for much more local gains. This case is particularly complex because many of the attacks on Serbs could be attributed to outbidding, as ex-KLA factions competed with one another by attacking minorities as a signal of their strength and capacity to harm.[14] In East Timor, much of the violence revolved around elections, regional enmities, and local contests to power rather than an attempt to undo East Timor's long campaign for independence. In Rwanda, the purpose of the strategic violence varied by actor and time period. The ex-FAR rebels almost immediately began attacks as a way of waging an insurgency, while the RPF attempted through its repression of Hutu civilians to impose a victor's peace.[15] Yet as chapter 5 documented, the goals of the RPF subtly expanded to regional dominance during its post-conflict period. Similarly, in Iraq, the violence was put to so many purposes at once that conflict looked like a Hobbesian nightmare, with an insurgency conducted against U.S. troops conducted over the top of gang warfare by dozens of armed political and criminal groups.[16] In none of these cases was the violence an exact replay of what occurred during the war. Even in those cases where the fault lines and targets of violence remained broadly similar, the logic of the violence in the post-conflict period was subtly different, often inverting categories of victims and perpetrators and featuring tactics that were either unseen or marginal during the war itself. This analysis confirms that violence in post-conflict states is qualitatively different from the violence of the war that preceded it, and that its purposes are sometimes detached or distantly related from the fault line of that war.[17]

International Expectations and the Inside Game of Violence

Recognizing the diversity of purposes behind violence in post-conflict states is important for analytic clarity, but it is also important for developing a more sophisticated international policy response to violence in post-conflict states. One theme that emerges from the case studies is that the international response to strategic violence in post-conflict states has often been delayed, inconsistent, and hobbled by internal disagreements over how to interpret acts of strategic violence. More generally, despite the resources and expertise at their disposal, peacekeepers and international officials often seem behind the curve in interpreting violent acts and responding to them. To some extent, this is natural and inevitable: strategic attacks are often waged in a covert fashion, by actors using criminal gangs as proxies and then denying responsibility or even knowledge of violent activities carried out on their behalf. But even in cases where a steady drumbeat of attacks makes the purpose of the violence clear—for example, the concerted effort to murder and expel Serbs from Kosovo Albanian-majority territory in the first wave of violence in the post-conflict period, or the RPF's violent repression of dissidents and Hutu civilians—there was confusion and resistance among international officials toward acknowledging that actors were resuming strategic violence for their own purposes.

To some extent, this is due to a gap in perception between international officials and locals on the ground, who are much quicker to understand and acknowledge the purpose of these attacks than their international counterparts.[18] Many of those working in peacekeeping operations or NGOs try to draw a line under the conflict when peace settlement comes into force and insist that all parties have a fresh start in the post-conflict period. They expect locals to quickly put the horrors of armed conflict behind them and to suppress the desire for revenge in favor of reconciliation and justice.[19] International officials also come to post-conflict states with well-established notions about what is needed for reconstruction and political development and sometimes seek to apply these models without full attention to historical and cultural context.²⁰ They tend to overestimate their capacity to produce widespread social change and inadvertently create expectations of reform and development that they cannot match. Further, many are wedded to fixed notions of "good guys" and "bad guys" and consequently adopt a simplified view of victims and perpetrators that does not apply to the post-conflict period. The result of these perceptual biases is that insiders and outsiders to society have very different perceptions of the same political environment. While outsiders come to a post-conflict period with a determination to start anew and a belief that the past is behind them, many locals are able to identify the continuities and discontinuities in the objectives and strategies of armed actors between the war and post-conflict period that are lost on their international counterparts.

Moreover, many international officials have strong organizational incentives to downplay threats to the peace and to dismiss claims that strategic violence has a significant impact. The very success of the international peacekeeping operations hinges on the maintenance of the peace, so international organizations and NGOs alike have an incentive to portray strategic violence as inconsequential criminal acts rather than acknowledge its political purpose. International officials may also face pressure from their superiors to keep concerns over the problems posed by strategic violence out of the public domain, for fear of endangering cooperation with their partner governments or key funders. Combined with their perceptual biases, these organizational blinders make it particularly difficult for international officials to navigate what Stephen John Stedman has described as the "the fog of peacemaking," in which they must assess whether and why an actor is challenging the peace settlement or failing to enforce its terms under conditions of limited information and develop a coherent response.²¹ The vested organizational interests of the NGOs and international organizations in producing some kind of success in a post-conflict state can produce a reluctance to acknowledge how strategic violence may be changing, or undermining, the terms of the peace.

This strong desire to realize the peace in post-conflict states has two consequences for the interpretation of strategic violence. First, international officials often fall back on arguments about bitter historical experience or long-standing ethnic hatreds to dismiss all violence in the post-conflict period as revenge.²² This was particularly prevalent in the Balkans, where the notion that ethnic groups were continuing their long-standing historical grievances provided a cover for all manner of sins in the post-conflict period. For example, even after there was significant evidence of KLA-led strategic attacks on Serbian civilians in Kosovo in 1999–2000, leading actors in the international community pointed to ethnic hatred as the chief explanation for the violence.²³ UNMIK SRSG Bernard Kouchner remarked that "here I discovered hatred deeper than anywhere in the world, more than in Cambodia or Vietnam or Bosnia."²⁴ This explanation—which effectively confuses strategic violence for expressive violence—also serves a subtle justification for its continuance. Drawing a direct connection between wartime and postwar atrocities also implies a moral equivalence that subtly justified reprisal killings as a natural response to what had happened during the war. When confronted with growing violence in Kosovo following its war, Secretary of State Madeleine Albright remarked that "after all that has happened, we do not expect rival communities in Kosovo to immediately join hands and start singing folk songs."[25]

A second consequence is that the international officials will dismiss much of the remaining violent activity as criminal or merely predatory, without significance for the wider political settlement. International officials will often point to economic incentives for predation on the local population, organized crime, or the presence of natural resources as explanations for "local" violence.[26] This portrayal overstates the role of instrumental forms of violence—such as criminal activity—and implies that a technocratic solution, such as strengthening the local police force, can be an effective remedy.[27] As an overall explanation for the violence, this account is at least superficially plausible, as politics and crime are interdependent in some post-conflict environments and many political actors have extensive criminal ties. But it also offers a narrow and partial view of the motives of the violence, stripping it of its political character and reducing it to a nuisance activity attributable only to actors at the margins of the political system. The truth is more complex: some criminal activity has a political impact, and the waves of criminal activity that occur in post-conflict states can serve as an effective cover for strategic violence. Dismissing violence in post-conflict states as either revenge or crime underplays the significant levels of strategic violence even in cases where the peace settlement has held and more often reflects the biases and preferences of the international officials than the situation on the ground.

In part, the tendency of international officials to underestimate the impact of strategic violence derives from the fact that it is an inside game, conducted by local actors operating against others in a competitive environment. While some acts of strategic violence are obvious in purpose and form, many other attacks are conducted with subtle codes that send signals or nonverbal messages to others from that political and cultural environment but remain unavailable to outsiders. As chapter 2 argues, the communicative scope of strategic violence is one of its distinguishing characteristics and one of the reasons that it so effective. The custodians of peace—for example, peacekeepers, NGO officials, and others involved in the administration and reconstruction of post-conflict states—often come from different cultural contexts and have an inadequate understanding of the country in which they now operate. Without a substantial understanding of the politics, history, and culture of that society, they are ill-equipped to identify the meaning and impact of acts of strategic violence, especially amid all of the "noise" created by expressive and instrumental violence. The result is that international officials can underestimate the impact of low-level or covert forms of strategic violence in dramatically altering the peace. In Kosovo and East Timor, for example, international officials pushed for elections and the return of normal politics and downplayed steadily mounting evidence of factional violence that was effectively reordering political alliances on the ground. The true impact of the inside game of this strategic violence was lost on many UN peacekeepers and international officials, who tended to fall back on convenient explanations about revenge or crime because of their perceptual and organizational biases.

Hard Choices

One recurring theme throughout the case studies is that armed groups face demobilization dilemmas in the post-conflict period that are underappreciated by most international officials. The end of the war often means that these groups lose their raison d'être and experience a series of internal pressures, as various factions compete for leadership of the organization and a greater share of the spoils of war. Despite these pressures, many international actors (such as the UN, often supported by regional organizations or foreign states) have supported the implementation of comprehensive demobilization, disarmament, and reintegration (DDR) programs, even in cases where such programs would place additional strain on the already tenuous internal control wielded by the leaders of armed groups.[28] These DDR programs are designed to reintroduce combatants into civilian life by offering them training, job opportunities, and welfare benefits. The logic behind such programs is clear: unemployed ex-fighters are a potential source of instability in post-conflict states and finding a productive outlet for their labors is a way to mitigate the risks that they may return to violence.[29] Further, these groups have a particular set of psychological characteristics because of their experience in war that may make them vulnerable to antisocial behavior and involvement in ordinary crime.[30] Across cases as wide-ranging as Bosnia, East Timor, and Iraq, the instinct among international organizations and foreign donors alike is to sponsor comprehensive DDR programs designed to dissolve existing armed groups and to encourage some of their members to join institutions such as the police, army, and civilian defense corps.[31]

The analysis presented in the case studies suggests two reasons why proceeding with DDR programs may be unwise in cases where the combatants have low levels of internal control. First, as chapter 3 discussed, it is a mistake to assume that all rebel groups have comparable organizational endowments, as some resemble hierarchical militaries and others are little more than collections of allied factions. Yet advocates of DDR programs can sometimes "mirror image" the combatants, assuming that most, if not all, function like militaries and have high degrees of internal control. This implicit assumption is important because some DDR programs rely on leaders to demobilize their followers. But the case studies suggest that only in a subset of armed groups do leaders retain the level of internal control needed to effectively demobilize their followers and manage the risks of factional violence. Especially when wars are waged by a loose coalitions of factional interests (e.g., the Northern Alliance in Afghanistan or the NTC in Libya), it is highly unlikely that the nominal leaders of the organization would have the capacity or political will to order their disbandment. Moreover, even if they could, these leaders would sacrifice whatever control they had over their factions and possibly increase the risk of individual members freelancing in violence after the organization demobilized. In cases where the combatants have low levels of internal control, a drive toward demobilizing the rank and file of the organization may effectively increase the risk of violence via the indirect pathway by further weakening the level of control exercised by the leadership and allowing splinters to flourish.

Second, enforcing a DDR model that precludes the domestic rewards or ingroup policing for groups with weak levels of internal control may exacerbate the risks of violence. One of the chief demobilization dilemmas faced by the leaders of armed groups in post-conflict states is that they need to pay off rival factions with spoils, such as ministerial positions, jobs in the security services, or pensions, and punish those who would challenge them for control of the group. Yet in Bosnia, Kosovo, East Timor, and Iraq, international officials pressured local leaders not to engage in patronage and not to use force against factions outside the context of the law.[32] This pressure was applied to make sure that their behavior met standards of good governance promoted by foreign donors and did not engage in corruption. Yet enforcing a strict ban on the use of patronage and prohibiting the use of ingroup policing among factions restricts the ability of leaders to control their factions and may advance organizational decay, particularly in cases where internal control was already low. Restrictions on the ability of actors to exercise domestic reward and in-group policing may also lead to more widespread freelancing in violence. For example, in Kosovo, the international pressure on the KLA to transform itself into a political party and to compete in free elections prevented it from controlling hard-line factions within its ranks. A paradoxical effect of the KLA's "going legitimate" as a political party was that it further fractured its organizational cohesion and weakened its already tenuous levels of internal control. The result was an increase in factional bargaining and more attacks on Serbs and other minorities as a form of outbidding. This dynamic might have been inevitable with the KLA, given that it was a rebel organization with a horizontal structure and a low level of internal control over its members, but it is hard to believe that the constraints imposed by UNMIK and others assisted its wartime leadership in enforcing the terms of the settlement among its somewhat dissatisfied rank and file.

Similarly, international support for the development of a professional and democratic military and police force may paradoxically undermine efforts to control violence in cases where armed groups have low internal control. The process of "weeding out" the worst elements of armed groups from the ranks of the new police and military effectively expels the most dangerous members of the organization and leaves them disgruntled with the terms of the peace. As the East Timor case demonstrates, some of these actors will begin to develop their own power bases and use violence for their own purposes in regional or local power-games. Seen with hindsight, the decision to establish a small and lightly armed Timorese military had unintended consequences for the peace because it left hundreds of disgruntled Falintil veterans unemployed and encouraged some of the most violent members of the Fretilin organization to look for alternative options for employment and political power. Another unintended consequence of "cleaning house" in the ranks of the combatants is that the international custodian of peace may lose information on the loyalties and behavior of former combatants. U.S. officials later regretted not keeping large parts of the Iraqi army under the command and payroll of the Iraqi military leadership, as doing so would have allowed them to have knowledge of their activities and an ability to influence them.[33] The conventional wisdom of the DDR approach—that armed groups need to be disbanded and a professional set of security institutions must be created from scratch—must be challenged in cases where proceeding along this lines may produce high levels of factional violence. Instead, international donors may want to consider subsidizing organizations with low levels of internal control so that they retain internal control and improve their ability to police splinters or factions in their ranks, rather than simply assuming that their ranks must be demobilized and returned to civilian life. In other words, there may be post-conflict states where strategic violence will be reduced not by demobilizing the combatants but by helping their leaders to improve their capacity to monitor and control factions with inducements and the threat of nonviolent punishment.

This critique of DDR programs in cases where armed groups have low levels of internal control illustrates the kind of hard choices that custodians of peace face in post-conflict states. In many instances, all of their options are unpalatable: allowing patronage networks to remain intact often implies that that the international community is legitimizing corruption or rewarding individuals or factions that have committed war crimes or human rights abuses. It also may mean having to work with actors with questionable criminal ties. But the alternative may be much worse if disbanding these armed groups leads to the emergence of factional bargaining games and an increase in strategic violence. The decision to disband the Iraqi army provided a stark example of the consequences of this choice. American officials were concerned not to ally themselves with Baathist forces and parts of the Iraqi military that had supported the Saddam Hussein regime for fear of linking the United States to actors that had blood on their hands. The United States also was concerned to bring some justice to the victims of Saddam Hussein's crimes by prosecuting the worst offenders. Yet the decision to disband the Iraqi army ultimately left thousands of Iraqi army officers unemployed and eager to join an insurgency that would lead to the deaths of thousands. In post-conflict states, order and justice are often competing priorities, and the decisions made in favor of one can have disastrous consequences for the other.

Policy Recommendations

This book has emphasized the diversity of purposes of strategic violence in post-conflict states and has argued against interpretations of this violence that frame it narrowly as spoiling the peace. As such, there are no "best practices" associated with dealing with post-conflict violence, for each case has to be analyzed on the basis of the actual patterns of violence, the organizational makeup of the combatants, and the contextual details of the case itself. If anything, the analysis here calls for a close examination of the organizational structures and political dilemmas faced by combatants when crafting peace settlements and enforcing their terms. Moreover, this book has emphasized that international organizations are often bystanders to the conflict and fail to understand the inside game of the conflict itself. For this reason, they should operate with a degree of skepticism about their ability to influence the decisions of the parties or the factions within them. That said, there are at least three general policy recommendations that may help to understand and manage the threat posed by strategic violence in post-conflict states.

First, in cases where the risks of violence are significant, the preventive deployments of peacekeepers and police (such as CIVPOL units) may be needed. A coherent response to strategic violence requires a well-equipped peacekeeping force with a police capacity and, perhaps more importantly, an understanding of the scope of the problem.[34] However, having military and police forces with the capacity and will to reestablish public order is a necessary but insufficient condition for putting an end to strategic violence. The speed and location of deployment is important. Peacekeepers and qualified police should be deployed rapidly to strategically contested or otherwise "hot" regions in advance of the return of combatants and refugees. If their numbers are low, deployments would be concentrated over small geographic regions where the targeted groups reside in order to provide a signal to those considering violence that it will not be tolerated. Whenever possible, they should be deployed even before the peace settlement is in force to prevent a public security gap from emerging. As the United States learned to its peril in Iraq, locals will form impressions about the peacekeepers—and their willingness to use force to maintain order and prevent indiscriminate killing—in the early days of a post-conflict period. In this respect, the theatrical element of a peacekeeping deployment—how it arrives and assumes control and wields its authority—is significant, for a well-equipped and aggressive preventive deployment functions like a signal of a credible commitment to the peace.

Second, peacekeeping missions need to be equipped with greater capacity to collect data on violent crime in post-conflict states and analyze it for rapid policy response. The UN policing missions in Bosnia, Kosovo, and East Timor often had a relatively chaotic start and had little capacity to collect or analyze data on violent crime, especially in the first few months of the mission. In Kosovo, a data analysis capacity was eventually established within CIVPOL, but no data were collected for the first three months of the mission. Moreover, the UN headquarters has no standing capacity to collect data on violence from its various peacekeeping missions and analyze it to apply lessons learned from its experiences to new missions. One of the most striking aspects of the firsthand research for this project has been discovering that only fragmentary and incomplete data on violence exist even among these comparatively well-equipped peacekeeping missions. Crime data were often stored in hard copy, without adequate records or filing, so that future members of the peacekeeping missions would have no idea where to locate it. In East Timor, all of the crime records for 1999–2003 were left on the laptops of personnel from the peacekeeping mission or kept in hard copy in boxes, with no coherent filing system.[35] In Bosnia, there was no single collection of violent crime data available, and the existing data (presented in chapter 4) were scattered through the archives in the UN headquarters.[36] The development of a standing data repository and analysis capacity in UN headquarters would be an important first step toward remedying this problem. Additionally, the UN and donor governments should consider developing relatively simple statistical packages that can be used for the collection and interpretation of crime statistics in post-conflict states. These programs can be sent at the outset of future peacekeeping mission to ensure that there are no gaps in the crime data and allow a quicker and more carefully tailored response to the patterns of violent crime. Having information on hand about violent crime patterns is also essential for developing effective policy responses and for holding actors that may be sponsoring or endorsing this violence responsible for their activities.

Finally, there needs to be a greater link between the political development of the post-conflict state and the policy responses to violence. Partially because of their organizational biases, international officials tend to focus on political milestones (like elections) instead of the problem of violence, which they often treat as epiphenomenal to the political and economic reconstruction of the society. But much of the violence—especially strategic violence—is ineluctably political and cannot be dismissed as merely "noise" as the society moves toward a stable political order. In the first instance, peacekeepers and those working in post-conflict states need to be sensitive to the ways in which the arrival of the post-conflict period has reordered the incentives and organizational structures of combatants and produced new motives for violence unheard of before the war. But they also need to recognize that as outsiders they will generally have less of an ability to influence this violence than those from within the society itself. Given this fact, they must craft peace settlements and enforcement strategies that create incentives for local actors to engage in ingroup policing against the factions in their ranks. One way to do this is to carefully tie political concessions and benefits to the ability of local leaders to control those within their ranks who would use strategic violence, while penalizing or marginalizing those who claim to be unable to stop the attacks coming from their ranks. Only by recognizing the central role played by violence in post-conflict states, and by deliberately shaping the incentive structures of local actors to prevent factional violence and make violent action costly, can international officials help to bring about a lasting resolution to a war.

NOTES

Chapter 1 • The Challenge of Violence in Post-Conflict States

1. On false optimism, see Blainey, *The Causes of War*, and Johnson, *Overconfidence and War*.
2. Iklé, *Every War Must End*; Rose, *How Wars End*.
3. On war duration, see Blainey, *The Causes of War*, 186–227; Bennett and Stam, "The Duration of Interstate Wars, 1816–1985." On the duration of civil wars, see Collier et al., "On the Duration of Civil War," and DeRouen and Sobek, "The Dynamics of Civil War."
4. Woodward, *Plan of Attack*. According to Woodward, the top secret intelligence order for regime change was approved on 16 February 2002. For a discussion of when members of the administration perceived that war was inevitable, see Boyle, "A War in Search of a Rationale."
5. Woodward, *Plan of Attack*; Bremer, *My Year in Iraq*.
6. Shinseki, Testimony to the Senate Armed Services Committee, 25 February 2003; *USA Today*, "Army Chief: War to Occupy Iraq Massive."
7. Shanker, "New Strategy Vindicates Ex-Army Chief Shinseki."
8. Wolfowitz, Testimony to the House Budget Committee, 27 February 2003. For a critique, see Kaplan, *Daydream Believers*.
9. The State Department actually did warn senior Bush administration officials that there were deficiencies in CENTCOM's planning for public security in the aftermath of the Hussein regime. This view was revealed in a declassified memorandum to Under Secretary of State Paula Dobriansky, 7 February 2003 at www.gwu.edu/~nsarchiv/NSAEBB/NSAEBB163/iraq-state-03.pdf.
10. The casualty figures for direct combat operations are drawn from the minimum estimates of the Iraq Body Count, as of 25 March 2009. The numbers of Iraqi civilian deaths are drawn directly from CENTCOM data released to the author, which are presented in chapter 8.
11. O'Bryant and Waterhouse, "U.S. Forces in Iraq."
12. Bearden, "Afghanistan, Graveyard of Empires." For a critique of the notion that Afghans never tolerate foreign rulers, see Barfield, *Afghanistan*.
13. Apple, "A Military Quagmire Remembered."
14. Silverstein, "Our Scary New Best Friends."
15. This fear came true, as there was significant yet underreported evidence of ethnic cleansing in southern Afghanistan after the defeat of the Taliban. See Harris, "Warlords Bring New Terrors."

16. For praise of the Afghan model, see O'Hanlon, "A Flawed Masterpiece." For a critique, see Biddle, "Afghanistan and the Future of Warfare."

17. Biddle, "Allies, Airpower, and Modern Warfare."

18. Barfield, *Afghanistan*, 318–319.

19. Human Rights Watch, "Killing You Is a Very Easy Thing."

20. Bergen, "The Taliban, Regrouped and Rearmed"; Jones, *In the Graveyard of Empires*.

21. Jones, "The Rise of Afghanistan's Insurgency."

22. As is discussed in chapter 3, a *hard security environment* is one defined by a prevalence of strategic violence, while a *soft security environment* has a mix of expressive and instrumental violence but relatively little strategic violence.

23. The phrase "out of control" comes from an ISAF report commissioned in 2008. Reported in Sengupta, "Afghanistan: Slipping Out of Control."

24. Tenet, *At the Centre of the Storm*, 318; Feith, *War and Decision*, 515–516. Additionally some informed observers—such as General Anthony Zinni—predicted the potentially disastrous effects of an intervention on public order in Iraq. See CDI Terrorism Project, "A General Speaks on the War in Iraq," available at www.cdi.org/terrorism/zinni-iraq-conditions-pr.cfm, accessed 21 January 2010.

25. See Blainey, *The Causes of War*; Jervis, *Perception and Misperception*; Johnson, *Overconfidence and War*.

26. See Johnson, *Overconfidence and War*.

27. The original formulation of groupthink is Janis, *Victims of Groupthink*.

28. On the military's reluctance to learn from insurgencies, see Shafer, "The Unlearned Lessons of Counter-Insurgency," and Nagl, *Learning How to Eat Soup*.

29. Petersen, *Understanding Ethnic Violence*, 40–61.

30. De Zayas *A Terrible Revenge*; Frommer, *National Cleansing*; Deak et al., *The Politics of Retribution*.

31. See the case studies in Spector, *In the Ruins of Empire*.

32. Ibid., 81.

33. See Stedman, "Spoiler Problems in Peace Processes." For contrasting accounts on the decision to exclude actors from the settlement, see Cunningham, "Veto Players and Civil War Duration," and Nilsson, "Partial Peace."

34. On splintering in conflict and post-conflict environments, see McCormick and Owen, "Factionalism, Violence and Bargaining in Civil Wars"; Nilsson, *Dangerous Liaisons*; Kreutz, "Navigating the Fog of Peace"; Kreutz, "Uncertainty and Civil War Recurrence"; Cunningham et al., "Shirts Today, Skins Tomorrow"; Bakke et al., "A Plague of Initials"; Findley and Rudloff, "Combatant Fragmentation and the Dynamics of Civil Wars."

35. Kalyvas, *The Logic of Violence in Civil Wars*.

36. For an account of Reconstruction violence, see Foner, *A Short History of the Reconstruction*. On the violence, see Rable, *But There Was No Peace*, and Shapiro, *White Violence and Black Response*, 5–92.

37. Shapiro, *White Violence and Black Response*, 5–6.

38. Rable, *But There Was No Peace*, 20.

39. Crouch, "A Spirit of Lawlessness," 222–223.

40. Rable, *But There Was No Peace*, 25.

41. Ibid., 28.

42. Ibid., 12.

43. Ibid., 132–142; Long, "Knights of the White Camellia," *The Handbook of Texas Online*, www.tshaonline.org/handbook/online/articles/vek01, accessed 25 March 2011.

44. Foner, *A Short History of the Reconstruction*, 186–187.

45. Crouch, "A Spirit of Lawlessness"; Rable, *But There Was No Peace*. Shapiro notes also that the violence can be described as an "informal civil war" between those supporting an egalitarian political order and those opposed, but documents a number of forms of violence that are not reducible to a conflict fought along racial lines. See Shapiro, *White Violence and Black Response*, 8.

46. Crouch, "A Spirit of Lawlessness," 9.

47. Rable, *But There Was No Peace*, 6.

48. Foner, *A Short History of the Reconstruction*, 190.

49. For an illustrative example, see Woolfolk Higgins *The Scalawag in Alabama Politics*; Wetta, "Bulldozing the Scalawags."

50. Rable, *But There Was No Peace*, 36–37.

51. Ibid., 29.

52. On revenge violence, see Boyle, "Revenge and Reprisal Violence in Kosovo." On instrumental and criminal violence in post-conflict states, see Nitzschke and Studdard "The Legacies of War Economies; Reno, "Understanding Criminality in West African Conflicts"; Zinecker, "From Exodus to Exitus; Hume, "Armed Violence and Poverty in El Salvador"; Gavigan, "Organized Crime"; Limbach, "Oligopolies of Violence"; Wantchekon and Yehoue, "Crime in New Democracies"; Williams, "Organized Crime and Corruption in Iraq"; Steenkamp, "The Legacy of War."

53. This book uses the concept of *strategic violence* as opposed to discriminate versus indiscriminate violence, which is used more widely in the literature. Examples of this approach include Kalyvas, *The Logic of Violence in Civil Wars*; Balcells, "Rivalry and Revenge"; Lyall, "Does Indiscriminate Violence Incite Insurgent Attacks?" Similarly, the literature on civilian victimization deals with strategic violence, though it does not use that term. Examples include Valentino, *Final Solutions*; Downes, *Targeting Civilians in War*. Finally, the literature on spoiling often (though not exclusively) deals with strategic violence. See Stedman, "Spoiler Problems in Peace Processes"; Greenhill and Major, "The Perils of Profiling."

54. Kalyvas, *The Logic of Violence in Civil Wars*, 173–209.

55. For a similar argument on decoupling, see ibid., 16–31.

56. The literature on counterinsurgency in Afghanistan and Iraq is vast. On Iraq, see Hoffman, *Insurgency and Counterinsurgency in Iraq*; Allawi, *The Occupation of Iraq*; and Diamond, "What Went Wrong in Iraq." On Afghanistan, see Jones, *Counterinsurgency in Afghanistan*; Cassidy, *Counterinsurgency and the Global War on Terror*; Giustozzi, *Koran, Klashnikov and Laptop*; and Ucko, *The New Counterinsurgency Era*. An exception to this exclusive focus on high-casualty insurgencies within this literature is Kilcullen's *The Accidental Guerrilla*, which does provide an account of COIN efforts in East Timor and explicitly asks why so little violence emerged there.

57. On spoilers, see Stedman, "Spoiler Problems in Peace Processes," and Greenhill and Major, "The Perils of Profiling." For a critical discussion of this literature, see Nilsson and Söderberg, "Revisiting an Elusive Concept."

58. On conflict termination, see Pillar, *Negotiating Peace*; Goemans, *War and Punishment*;

Hartzell et al., "Stabilizing the Peace after Civil"; Werner and Yuen, "Making and Keeping Peace"; Werner, "The Precarious Nature of Peace"; Downes, "The Problem with Negotiated Settlements"; Walter, "The Critical Barrier to Civil War Settlement"; Toft, *Securing the Peace*.

59. Nicholas Sambanis refers to such violence as "residual violence" if it does not mean the war has resumed. See Sambanis, "Partition as a Solution to Ethnic War." See also Johnson, "Partitioning to Peace."

60. Moreover, this book does not assume that such local actors, or splinter groups, are motivated solely by greed. For a critique of this prevalent view, see Autesserre, "Hobbes and the Congo" 268.

61. This is the critique of those who work on the "liberal peace." See Paris, *At War's End*; MacGinty and Richmond, *The Liberal Peace and Post-War Reconstruction*. See also Fortna, *Does Peacekeeping Work?*, 3–4.

62. See Walter, "The Critical Barrier to Civil War Settlement."

63. The term *custodians of peace*, which comes from Stedman's "Spoiler Problems in Peace Processes," reflects an assumption that external actors are somehow responsible for the peace. This article also has a good discussion of the organizational blinders experienced by these custodians and the difficulties involved in detecting the intention behind spoiling in peace processes.

64. Some recent exceptions include Nilsson, *Dangerous Liaisons*; Autesserre, *The Trouble with Congo*; Berdal and Suhrke, *The Peace In-Between*; and Themner, *Violence in Post-Conflict Societies*.

65. Some of the spoiling literature interprets substantial levels of violence after a peace settlement as necessarily an attempt to spoil the peace, when the reality may be much different. An exception to the general rule that treats all violence as a referendum on the peace settlement (either its terms or whom it excludes) is Newman and Richmond, "Peace Building and Spoilers."

66. This borrows from the notion of *dirty bargaining*, or bargaining with violence, and comes from Schelling, *Arms and Influence*.

67. Example of the somewhat stylized accounts of government and rebel interaction predominant in the conflict termination literature are Mason and Fett, "How Civil Wars End"; Walter, "The Critical Barrier to Civil War Settlement"; and Toft, *Securing the Peace*.

68. Bakke et al., "A Plague of Initials."

69. Zartman, *Elusive Peace*.

70. Werner and Yuen, "Making and Keeping Peace."

71. This book defines *splinters* as groups that break off from the main ranks of an organization, while *factions* often remain inside the confines of a group's membership and can become splinters only if they exit.

72. The increase in the number of intrastate and extrastate wars, and the corresponding decrease in international war, is reported in Human Security Report (2009/2010), www.hsrgroup.org/human-security-reports/20092010/overview.aspx, accessed 13 June 2012.

73. The literature on opportunity structures with respect to violence is vast. See particularly Tilly, *The Politics of Collective Violence*; Della Porta, *Social Movements, Political Violence and the State*; McAdam et al., *Dynamics of Contention*. It should be noted that this definition of an opportunity structure differs from others in the literature and has been adapted, and somewhat simplified, for post-conflict states. For a similar application, see Greenhill and Major "The Perils of Profiling."

74. The insight of flexible institutions affecting the opportunity structure of those who

might act violently derives from Charles Tilly and Sidney Tarrow's concept of a political opportunity structure. For a concise statement, see Tilly and Tarrow, *Contentious Politics*.

75. Kreutz, "How and When Armed Conflicts End." The Uppsala Conflict Termination dataset is available at www.pcr.uu.se/research/ucdp/datasets/ucdp_conflict_termination_data set/, accessed 11 November 2011.

76. The full definition of strategic violence and the coding criteria used to determine whether an act is "strategic" or not are discussed in chapter 2.

77. There are fifty-one separate source datasets, as Badme, Ethiopia, has no entries of violence. Some of the source datasets do not have five full years of data collected because the war relapsed before that the post-conflict period elapsed.

78. On how source selection influences violence statistics, see Davenport and Ball, "Views to a Kill."

79. On the dangers of underreporting, see Archer and Gartner, *Violence and Crime in Cross-National Perspective*, 30–35. On crime levels in post-conflict states, see Archer and Gartner, 63–97.

80. The exception here is the Rwanda case study, for which no summary statistics from the UN or the Rwandan government have been made publicly available.

81. George and Bennett, *Case Studies and Theory Development*, 81.

Chapter 2 · Understanding Violence after Wars: Concepts and Contexts

1. Woollacott, "Iraq's Insurgents"; Hashim, *Insurgency and Counterinsurgency in Iraq*, 123; and Metz, "The 'New' Iraq Insurgency," available at www.project-syndicate.org/commentary/metz1/English, accessed 11 November 2011.

2. Kalyvas, "The Ontology of 'Political Violence'"; Kalyvas, *The Logic of Violence in Civil War*.

3. Kalyvas, *The Logic of Violence in Civil War*.

4. In some post-conflict states, including Kosovo, East Timor, and Northern Ireland, the police have made some efforts to classify crimes as political, ethnic, or sectarian. But these cases are the exceptions, not the rule.

5. This is remarkably close to the *Oxford English Dictionary* definition of violence: "The exercise of physical force so as to inflict injury on, or cause damage to, persons or property; action or conduct characterized by this; treatment or usage tending to cause bodily injury or forcibly interfering with personal freedom." See the *Oxford English Dictionary*, 12:221.

6. Definitions of violence that focus on the direct and excessive use of force are called the "Minimalist Conception of Violence" by Bufacchi, "Two Concepts of Violence." This approach is defined as "observational" in Grundy and Weinstein, *The Ideologies of Violence*, 9–10. The quote is from Nieburg, *Political Violence*, 11–12.

7. Nieburg, *Political Violence*, 11.

8. For example, Michael Hechter has noted that no one has been able to disentangle expressive and instrumental violence at the aggregate level for empirical analysis. Consequently, he recommends ignoring expressive motives entirely as a driver of nationalist violence. See Hechter, "Explaining Nationalist Violence."

9. This book shares the assumption with much of the civil war termination literature that strategic violence from conventional spoiling behavior is risky because it raises the prospect

of war recurrence. However, it parts company with this literature on the assumption that all strategic violence after wars is necessarily a referendum on the settlement in some way. As it is conceptualized here, it is motivated by dissatisfaction with the settlement under the direct pathway, but under the indirect pathway it is more of a function of the dissolution of the original combatants. Moreover, strategic violence can be put to a range of proximate purposes detached from the peace settlement itself.

10. This distinction is widely used across the fields of political science, criminology, and psychology. This distinction was deployed to describe different types of protest events in Gurr, *Why Men Rebel*, 304–316. See also Hechter, "Explaining Nationalist Violence."

11. This study does not tackle the issue of rational versus irrational sources of violence, in part because such distinctions imply an understanding of not only the goals of an action (i.e., whether they are rational or not) but a judgment about the means used for taking them. Such an approach runs into considerable empirical difficulties, for it is hard for an outside observer to adduce based on contextual details whether an individual acted "rationally" in achieving a given goal. For a discussion of rational choice and "irrationalist" perspectives on violence, see Rule, *Theories of Civil Violence*, 32–41 and 91–94.

12. Kalyvas, *The Logic of Violence in Civil War*, 24.

13. Within criminology, illustrative examples include Mieth and Drass, "Exploring the Social Context," and Cohn and Rotton, "Even Criminals Take a Holiday" and references therein. In psychology, this distinction has also been widely applied. See particularly Berkowitz, *Aggression*.

14. On sadism and brutality in warfare, see Mueller, *Remnants of War*, and Bourke, *An Intimate History of Killing*. On torture and mutilations in the context of a rioting episode, see Horowitz, *The Deadly Ethnic Riot*, 111–123. The counterargument of the psychological accounts of barbarism is that the technology of certain kinds of warfare (such as counterinsurgencies) encourages actors to engage in barbarism to establish control over, and extract information from, contested regions. See Kalyvas, *The Logic of Violence in Civil War*.

15. Kalyvas, *The Logic of Violence in Civil War*.

16. Le Bon, *The Crowd*.

17. On expressive rioting outstripping its original purpose and giving rise to organizations preparing for rebellion, see Gurr, *Why Men Rebel*, 304–316.

18. Eric Hoffer noted that emotions such as hatred constitute "unifying agents" for individuals, as they link their objectives with that of the collective. See his *The True Believer*, 91–126.

19. Horowitz, *The Deadly Ethnic Riot*, 117.

20. This book deploys a conception of revenge violence—as an individual and expressive act—that is different from reprisals, understood here as both categorical and strategic. The original distinction was developed in Boyle, "The Prevention and Management of Reprisal Violence in Post-Conflict States," later published in a shorter form in Boyle, "Revenge and Reprisal Violence in Kosovo."

21. Kalyvas, *The Logic of Violence in Civil War*, 25.

22. On cultural scripts for violence, see Brubaker and Laitin, "Ethnic and Nationalist Violence"; Waldmann, "Revenge without Rules"; Stewart and Strathern, *Violence*, particularly 1–14; Boehm, *Blood Revenge*.

23. Kalyvas, *The Logic of Violence in Civil War*, 25.

24. Ibid.; see also Balcells, "Rivalry and Revenge."

25. On this motive, see Horowitz, *Ethnic Groups in Conflict*, 95–228.

26. This is clearly referring to rationality of means rather than of ends. The problem with this is that such a calculation must take into account individual-specific knowledge (i.e., what did the actor know, and when did he or she know it). See Hardin, *One for All*, 16.

27. Stuart and Stuart, "Instrumental Violence," *Encyclopedia of Interpersonal Violence*, available at http://dbproxy.lasalle.edu:2592/entry/sageiv/instrumental_violence, accessed 10 November 2011.

28. Petersen, *Understanding Ethnic Violence*.

29. Kalyvas, "The Ontology of 'Political Violence.'"

30. This is well discussed in Gurr, "Psychological Factors in Civil Violence."

31. Kalyvas, "The Ontology of 'Political Violence,'" 479.

32. This chapter avoids the use of the term *political violence* because it is often cast so broadly that virtually any form of action can be termed a form of political violence. Especially in post-conflict states, many forms of violent action have political effect but have a criminal or expressive purpose. For this reason, this study sets aside the traditional concept of political violence, though in practice much of what is termed here as strategic violence is functionally equivalent to political violence.

33. For riots in urban areas, see Horowitz, *The Deadly Ethnic Riot*, 381–384. For denunciations, see Kalyvas, *The Logic of Violence in Civil War*.

34. See Kalyvas, "Wanton and Senseless."

35. On the instrumental use of terrorist violence, see Byman, "The Logic of Ethnic Terrorism," and Neumann and Smith, "Strategic Terrorism."

36. For violence as a way of signaling political claims, see Tilly, *The Politics of Collective Violence*, 26–54. On the symbolic dimension of violence, see Kaufman, *Modern Hatreds*.

37. This is similar to "polyvalent performance" in Tilly's terminology. See Tilly, *The Politics of Collective Violence*, 176.

38. Hoffman and McCormick, "Terrorism, Signaling and Suicide Attack," 246.

39. Ibid.

40. It is not conclusive because criminal groups may employ some seemingly strategic tactics (e.g., grenade attacks) to strategic ends.

41. See Midlarsky, "Nihilism in Political Chaos," and Kalyvas, "Wanton and Senseless." For how collective violence is used to control defection, see Gould, "Collective Violence and Group Solidarity."

42. Obviously there will be debate within each case about which acts cross the threshold of aiming to transform the balance of power and resources in a state. Interpreting violence for this purpose is based on contextual details of the violent act itself so no a priori categorization is useful.

43. Elsewhere in the literature this is described as a distinction between discriminate (selective) and indiscriminate (nonselective) violence. See Kalyvas, *The Logic of Violence in Civil War*; Weinstein, *Inside Rebellion*; and Downes, *Targeting Civilians in War*.

44. Much of the literature on political violence and terrorism sidesteps intentions and asserts without evidence that an actor meant to do X or Y by acting violently. In fact, the issue of intention is much more complex, particularly when examining individual acts.

45. This point—extensively addressed in philosophy—raises the question of whether an external observer can ever detect the intention behind a written text or, indeed, an action (such

as a crime). To do so implies that one may conclusively identify an intention in the mind of another actor and interpret it. This is particularly problematic with speech acts, which convey thoughts or ideas imperfectly and run up against the limits and constraints that humans face when employing imprecise language. The seminal treatment of intention (though not uncontested) is Anscombe, *Intention*. Much of the argument developed here is based on insights developed by Quentin Skinner (though applied to a different context, the written word) on the possibility of recovering intention (or some approximation thereof) on the basis of contextual analysis. See Skinner, *Visions of Politics*, 90–144.

46. Hollis and Smith, *Explaining and Understanding International Relations*, 171–176. More generally the distinction between understanding and explaining a phenomenon is borrowed from Hollis and Smith to organize the inquiry into strategic violence after wars in chapters 2 and 3.

47. This account was given to me by a number of interviewees during my fieldwork in Kosovo in 2002 and 2003.

48. For example, advocates of a "relational" account of (collective) violence sidestep the role of ideas in motivating violence, in part because it is difficult to trace the precise causal effect of ideas and relies instead on causal mechanisms. See Tilly, *The Politics of Collective Violence*, and McAdam et al., *Dynamics of Contention*.

49. See Tilly, *The Politics of Collective Violence*.

50. While this is generally the case, there is some evidence of organized football hooliganism in Europe. See, for instance, Armstrong, *Football Hooligans*.

51. The literature on spoilers rarely confronts the problem, in part because this is not its focus. Generally, the spoiling literature treats violence as just one of many ways that an actor may try to influence the settlement and does not study violence in its own right. For an exception, see MacGinty, "Northern Ireland."

52. This was a point that was well recognized by Stedman, "Spoiler Problems in Peace Processes," but has fallen out of much of the literature subsequently.

53. Even this method, however, is probabilistic. With imperfect information, the outside observer can always misinterpret the intention of a violent act. The claim made in this study is merely that in most cases the intention of an act can be reasonably accurately ascertained from the contextual details of the act.

54. On police method, see Bayley, *Police for the Future*.

55. Interview with John Avery, Crime Analysis Unit, UNMIK CIVPOL, Pristina, Kosovo, 24 March 2003.

56. The Federal Bureau of Investigation, for example, has developed a checklist of contextual details that must be analyzed by their agents in the course of any investigation. The British system, by contrast, relies primarily on the victim's statement and secondarily on contextual details.

57. Confirmed during author's interviews with CIVPOL and UNPOL officials in field visits.

58. Kalyvas has pointed out that whenever possible scholars should use microlevel data to detect the patterns of violence that lie beneath the master narrative of the conflict. The problem with this argument is that many cases do not have microlevel data available to the public. In the post-conflict states studied here, for instance, the individual incident reports were deemed unsuitable for public release because they were internal UN documents and contained sensitive

information about the names of victims, alleged perpetrators, and witnesses. Unfortunately such data limitations are the rule rather than the exception.

59. Ecological inference was first identified as a problem in Robinson, "Ecological Correlations and the Behaviour of Individuals."

60. Reporting bias can be a serious problem in this instance. The sources used and the criteria for reporting the incident vary widely by source, thus complicating efforts to have a representative sample across the state in question. On the implications of sources for data collection, see Davenport and Ball, "Views to a Kill." One particular source of bias in reporting has to do with overreporting the violence that occurs within cities (known as the urban bias). This is particularly important in the case of data drawn from media sources, as journalists tend to be located in the major cities and thus overreport these incidents relative to what occurs in the countryside. See Kalyvas, "The Urban Bias in Research on Civil Wars."

61. Bob, *The Marketing of Rebellion*.

62. King, *A Solution to the Ecological Inference Problem*, 21.

63. Violence is understood as "transactional" when it emerges in tit-for-tat patterns.

64. Boyle, "Revenge and Reprisal Violence in Kosovo."

65. For an account of how drugs can impede state building, see Felbab Brown, "Peacekeepers among Poppies." On interdependence, see McMullin, "Organized Criminal Groups and Conflict"; Andreas "Symbiosis." For an account on how involvement in criminality can open up new channels for political participation, see Reno, "Understanding Criminality in West African Conflicts."

66. On "war economies," see Nitzschke and Studdard, "The Legacies of War Economies."

67. For an overview, see Keen, *The Economic Benefits of Civil War*, and Andreas, "Criminalizing Consequences of Sanctions"; Andreas, *Blue Helmets and Black Markets*; and Glenny, *McMafia*, 33–59.

68. Glenny, *McMafia*, 44.

69. On violent specialists, see Tilly, *The Politics of Collective Violence*, 40. On the recruitment problem, see Weinstein, *Inside Rebellion*.

70. See particularly Weinstein, *Inside Rebellion*. On "greed vs. grievance," see Collier and Hoeffler, "On the Economic Causes of Civil War," and Collier and Hoeffler, "Greed and Grievance in Civil War." For additional testing, see De Soysa, "Paradise Is a Bazaar?"; Azam and Hoeffler, "Violence against Civilians." For a critical overview, see Berdal and Malone, *Greed and Grievance*.

71. Steenkamp, "The Legacy of War."

72. See particularly Andreas, "Criminalizing Consequences of Sanctions: Embargo Busting and Its Legacy." 336.

73. See Andreas, "Criminalizing Consequences of Sanctions."

74. Glenny, *McMafia*.

75. Quoted in Kalyvas, *The Logic of Violence in Civil War*, 57.

76. Mueller, "The Banality of 'Ethnic War'" and the extended argument in *Remnants of War*.

77. Gavigan, "Organized Crime, Illicit Power."

78. Lister and O'Neill, "IRA plc."

79. MacGinty, "Looting in the Context of Violent Conflict."

80. On violence against the Roma, see O'Neill, *Kosovo*, 55–57.

81. Report of the OSCE/ODHIR/Council of Europe Field Mission on the situation of the Roma in Kosovo (27 July–6 August 1999), available at www.coe.int/t/dg3/romatravellers/archive/documentation/fieldvisits/missionkosovo99_en.asp, accessed 11 March 2011.

82. See Horowitz, *The Deadly Ethnic Riot*, 162–165, on how opposition in war can transform targeting afterward.

83. International Crisis Group, *What Happened to the KLA?*

84. Glenny, *McMafia*, 33–59.

85. See the discussion of former warlords and criminals running for office in Collier, *War, Guns and Votes*.

Chapter 3 • Explaining Violence after Wars: Patterns and Pathways

1. In other words, strategic violence is subject to equifinality, in that there are more than one plausible causal pathways that can explain its incidence. On this concept, see George and Bennett, *Case Studies and Theory Development*, 161–162. For a similar application to war termination, see Stanley and Sawyer, "The Equifinality of War Termination."

2. It is not possible to construct a single general theory that explains all of the varying forms of expressive, instrumental, and strategic violence within a post-conflict state because much of the sources of expressive and instrumental violence will be proximate and microfoundational (e.g., personalized grievances, predation, and business rivalries). These often inscrutable motives are difficult to test systematically in the absence of microlevel data (e.g., the direct testimony from the witnesses and victims). On the role of such motives in war, see Kalyvas, "The Ontology of 'Political Violence'"; Kalyvas, "Wanton and Senseless."

3. This pathway follows a long tradition of studies that address the role of organizational structure, recruitment, and dynamics in motivating rebellion. See Popkin, *The Rational Peasant*; Lichbach, *The Rebel's Dilemma*; Taylor, "Rational and Revolutionary Collective Action"; Gates, "Recruitment and Allegiance"; Wood, *Insurgent Collective Action in El Salvador*; Weinstein, *Inside Rebellion*.

4. The dynamics of patronage and punishment are familiar to many organizations and also traditional societies. For a classic account, see Wilson, "The Economy of Patronage." On the role that patronage plays within the state, see Migdal, *Strong Societies and Weak States*, 238–258; Scott, "Patron-Client Politics and Political Change in Southeast Asia," 91–113; and Eisenstadt and Roniger, "Patron-Client Relations as a Model for Social Change."

5. This chapter relaxes the assumption of homogeneity among rebel groups and argues that their original organizational endowments—for example, leadership, organizational structure, and ability to control violence—have an important impact on their behavior in the post-conflict period. Similarly, it draws from Kalyvas the insight that information about wartime loyalties of members of the population plays an important role in influencing violence. Here it is argued that informational asymmetries—what the "insiders" to a conflict know that outsiders do not—matters in controlling the emergence of factions. See Kalyvas, *The Logic of Violence in Civil Wars*.

6. This definition is adapted with some modifications from the definitions in the Uppsala Conflict Data Program Conflict Termination dataset. The UCDP data are designed to capture data on the ending of different types of wars (interstate, intrastate, extrastate) but do not include data on violence for the post-conflict period. The UCDP Conflict Termination

dataset served as the basis for the dataset developed here. See Kreutz, "How and When Armed Conflicts End " and associated codebook and data.

7. On cease-fires and the return to conflict, see Fortna, *Peace Time*.

8. The issue of what constitutes a cease-fire and a negotiated settlement is complex. There was an explicit effort in this dataset to include only cease-fires that were seen as an immediate precursor to a negotiated settlement between the parties.

9. Some of the excluded conflicts include Myanmar's battles with KIO, KNU, and Mong Tai Army; India's battles with Sikh insurgents, NLFT, MCC/PWG, and Pakistan-backed Kashmiri fighters; Israel's ongoing battles with the Palestine Liberation Organization (PLO) and Hamas, Somalia's battles against the SNM, SPM, USC, and SICS; and Pakistan's battles with the TNSM.

10. On power sharing, Hartzell and Hoddie, "Institutionalizing Peace"; Hoddie and Hartzell, "Civil War Settlements."

11. On the stability of military victories, see Toft, *Securing the Peace*. On the victor's peace, see Berdal and Suhrke, *The Peace In-Between*.

12. This study does not limit its focus to cases with third-party or UN involvement but includes all post-conflict states whether they had a mission or not. The role of external actors or peacekeepers in shaping the incidence of violence is discussed through the analysis of the opportunity structures.

13. See, for illustrative examples, Walter, "The Critical Barrier to Civil War Settlement"; Hartzell et al., "Stabilizing the Peace after Civil War"; and Hartzell and Hoddie, "Institutionalizing Peace."

14. This distinction is used particularly in the Correlates of War dataset and related literature. See www.correlatesofwar.org/, accessed 11 February 2011.

15. This chapter uses the term *internal* or *intrastate* war broadly to encompass wars fought on ethnic, political, and sectarian grounds. The risks of contagion for the spread of ethnic conflict are well known, but see particularly Lake and Rothschild, *The International Spread of Ethnic Conflict*.

16. The United Kingdom is an interesting case to consider here. The number of civilians killed in the Blitz (1940–1941) has been estimated to be 30,000, with 50,000 injured. See Robinson, "The Blitz," at www.bbc.co.uk/history/worldwars/wwtwo/ff3_blitz.shtml, accessed 16 July 2012. Because the United Kingdom experienced casualties on its territory, it would qualify as a post-conflict state, even though German forces never launched a ground invasion of Britain. The United States is a borderline case here, as it experienced one serious attack (Pearl Harbor) in which 2,400 U.S. personnel were killed. This is a particularly tricky case, because Hawaii did not declare statehood until 1959 so the territoriality criterion could arguably not apply.

17. The territoriality requirement explains why Israel is not a post-conflict state in this case. Approximately 43 Israeli civilians and 121 Israeli Defense Force personnel were killed in the 2006 war, though the majority of the civilian casualties came from sporadic rocket attacks from Hezbollah forces in South Lebanon.

18. For the sake of simplicity, many of these cases will be treated as a single conflict in the dataset.

19. This argument mirrors some of that from the "new wars" literature, which sees fluid fronts featuring irregular armed forces as a recurring feature of contemporary conflicts. See Kaldor, *New and Old Wars*. For a critique, see Kalyvas, "New and Old Wars: A Valid Distinction?"

20. On the long term effects of war, see Ghobarah et al., "Civil Wars Kill People."
21. See Hartzell et al., "Stabilizing the Peace after Civil War."
22. Denyer, "Drift towards Repression."
23. Bosleigh and Page, "Tamil Tigers Admit Defeat."
24. Kepel, *Jihad*, 297.
25. It is important to be careful in this assessment. In many cases, the formal conclusion of a war is only a nominal point in a longer struggle between two actors. As Séverine Autesserre has noted, outsiders may label environments as post-conflict depending on their perception of the status of the war itself, which may or may not correspond to how the combatants view it. The term itself is infused with a degree of subjective labeling, as what outsiders may consider post-conflict may just be yet another phase of fighting between long-standing adversaries to insiders. See Autesserre, *The Trouble with the Congo*, 65.
26. The literature on the impact of conflict is vast, but see particularly Ghobarah et al., "Civil Wars Kill People." On the impact of war on the state, see Tilly, *Coercion, Capital and European States*, and Tilly, "Warmaking and State-Making as Organized Crime."
27. On the Weberian aspect of post-conflict states, see Boyle, "Policing the Neo-Imperial Frontier."
28. For a skeptical discussion of Hobbesian environments, see Kalyvas, *The Logic of Violence in Civil War*, 52–62.
29. See Allawi, *The Occupation of Iraq*.
30. Such refugees are often claimed to produce a contagion effect on conflict. See Salehyan and Gleditsch, "Refugees and the Spread of Civil War."
31. Ghobarah et al., "Civil Wars Kill People," and Collier et al., *Breaking the Conflict Trap*, 13–50.
32. Steenkamp, "The Legacy of War."
33. The classic exposition is Scott, *Weapons of the Weak*.
34. Tilly, *The Politics of Collective Violence*, 40.
35. Andreas, *Blue Helmets and Black Markets*.
36. Kalyvas, *The Logic of Violence in Civil War*, 87–110.
37. Horowitz, *The Deadly Ethnic Riot*, 128–131.
38. For example, Linda Melvern reports that perpetrators of the Rwandan genocide often checked ethnic identity cards before killing Tutsis, for fear that they would kill someone they considered a loyal Hutu. See Melvern, *A Conspiracy to Murder*, 186.
39. Beevor, *The Battle for Spain*, 405.
40. A similar dynamic was in play during the war. See Balcells, "Rivalry and Revenge."
41. Lottman, *The People's Anger*.
42. Petersen, *Understanding Ethnic Violence*, 40–61.
43. Boyle, "Revenge and Reprisal Violence in Kosovo."
44. De Zayas, *A Terrible Revenge*.
45. See Boyle, "Revenge and Reprisal Violence in Kosovo."
46. Zartman, *Elusive Peace*; Werner and Yuen, "Making and Keeping Peace"; Werner, "The Precarious Nature of Peace"; Downes, "The Problem with Negotiated Settlements"; Walter, "The Critical Barrier to Civil War Settlement"; Toft, *Securing the Peace*.
47. Fearon, "Iraq's Civil War."
48. Autesserre, *Trouble with Congo*.

49. The concept of *dirty bargaining*—that is, bargaining involving the infliction of harm as part of the bargaining process—comes from Schelling, *Arms and Influence*.

50. Introduction, Report of the Commission for Historical Clarification, 1999, available at: http://shr.aaas.org/guatemala/ceh/report/english/toc.html, accessed 13 April 2010.

51. Statistics quoted in Rosenberg, "Witness."

52. Seelke, "Gangs in Central America."

53. This time period was selected for two reasons: time effectiveness, given that it would be unduly costly in time and effort to track every conflict since 1945 or before; and increasing quality in the available data on specific violent incidents in the post-1990 era, as more newspaper reporting became available through databases such as Lexus Nexus.

54. This chapter employs the criteria for these used by the Uppsala Conflict program. See Kreutz, "How and When Armed Conflicts End" and associated codebooks and data.

55. See Toft, *Securing the Peace*, for a similar comparison between the outcomes and stability of peace in military victories and negotiated settlements.

56. Kreutz, "How and When Armed Conflicts End" and associated codebooks and data.

57. One partial exception here is South Lebanon (PC 31). The Uppsala tally of battle-related deaths suggests that 821 people died during the war in 2006. However, an independent UN Human Rights Council assessment accepted a Lebanese estimate that 1,121 people died during the war. See www2.ohchr.org/english/bodies/hrcouncil/docs/specialsession/A.HRC.3.2.pdf, accessed 16 July 2012. I have erred on the side of including South Lebanon in the case selection due to this dispute, though I have kept the 821-casualty estimate to be consistent with the other battle casualty statistics drawn from the same source. This is why it is "approximately" 1,000 casualties.

58. The case selection was done as follows. Using the Uppsala Conflict Termination dataset as a starting point, I extracted all cases that ended before 1989. I excluded cases with fewer than 1,000 battle deaths as a way of eliminating those cases that did not experience major war in their territory, with the exception of South Lebanon (2007–2009) due to the controversies over the total casualties from the war. The following cases (along with their entry numbers) were relabeled for descriptive accuracy from the UCDP Conflict Termination dataset: Indonesia (PC 250) was recoded as East Timor; Morocco (253) was recoded as Western Sahara; Bangladesh (PC 234) was recoded as Chittagong Hills secession; Bosnia and Herzegovina (376) recoded as running between 1991 and 1995 (rather than as separate years); Azerbaijan (361) recoded in Nagorno-Karbakh; Russia (380) recoded as Chechnya; Israel (420) recorded as South Lebanon; Yugoslavia (398) recoded as Kosovo; Australia, US, and UK-Iraq (413) recoded as Iraq; Indonesia (320) recoded as Aceh; Israel (421) recoded as South Lebanon. The following overlapping cases—listed as two wars in the UCDP dataset—were merged as one case (and hence are considered one post-conflict period here): Congo (424 and 163); Iraq (115 and 147); Ethiopia (136 and 402); Yugoslavia (353 and 376); Iraq (115 and 147). Dropped cases (with Uppsala entry number) include Myanmar (63, 38,131); India (297, 55, 56, 33, 264); Israel (70); Somalia (269, 271); Al Qaeda-USA (410), and Pakistan (386). The multiple wars in India and Myanmar cases were dropped because they were long-running secessionist wars without precise end points.

59. The searches were conducted by looking for key terms, such as *violence, attack, murder*, and *kill* in the key terms of the article, while limiting the search to the country of interest and to the time period of the post-conflict state. The search was designed to take advantage of local newspaper sources, if included as part of the Nexus U.K. package, but in many cases this

was not available, and the results were compiled from major wire sources (Reuters, Associated Press, BBC World Service) and international newspapers, such as the *New York Times*, *The Times* (London), and similar newspapers. This search normally returned newspaper accounts of violent activity, though sometimes with stories unrelated to the country in question. In some cases, there would be as many as three thousand separate news articles per case, which often involved multiple stories on the same violent event. When conflicting casualty reports appeared, the dataset errs on the side of the last casualty total reported, as this is usually the corrected and more reliable figure.

60. It is important to note here that in light of the difficulty in assessing intentions under conditions of limited information (as described in chapter 2) that there is a possibility that some of these types of attacks were unintentionally included in the strategic violence totals.

61. There was no independent data collection for Northern Ireland, because the Police Service of Northern Ireland collected "deaths from the security situation"—in other words deaths from strategic violence—on its own. Its tallies included casualties in the police, security forces, and civilians. Full data are available at www.psni.police.uk/deaths_cy.pdf, accessed 17 July 2012.

62. Documents on this dispute can be found at the Permanent Court of Arbitration website, www.pca-cpa.org/showpage.asp?pag_id=1150, accessed 10 July 2012.

63. It is important to remember in this case that government's war against the Tamil Tigers continued throughout this period.

64. For a fascinating comparative analysis of this case, see Nilsson, *Dangerous Liaisons*.

65. BBC News, "Congo's 'Ninja' Leader to Disarm."

66. See particularly Sambanis, "Partition as a Solution to Ethnic War"; Johnson, "Partitioning to Peace"; and Toft, *Securing the Peace*.

67. This figure taken from the Brookings Institute, Iraq Index, July 2012, available at www.brookings.edu/~/media/Centers/saban/iraq%20index/index201207.pdf, accessed 11 July 2012.

68. A Wilcoxon signed ranks test found that only the difference in means for relapsed and non-relapsed cases was statistically significant at 0.05 level.

69. This corresponds with a finding by Licklider, "The Consequences of Negotiated Settlements," and Toft, *Securing the Peace*.

70. Fortna, in *Does Peacekeeping Work?*, found that there is no evidence that peacekeepers only go to easy cases, and that generally they are sent to what is assumed to be tough post-conflict environments.

71. The calculations for population are drawn from the Penn World Tables and are calculated as a simple average across the post-conflict period. Version 6.3 was employed. See Heston, Summers, and Aten, Penn World Table Version 6.3, available at http://pwt.econ.upenn.edu/php_site/pwt_index.php.

72. The twenty-five-casualty threshold was selected because this is the median number of casualties per year in the dataset.

73. Hume, "Armed Violence and Poverty in El Salvador."

74. This is possibly due to underreporting of strategic attacks in newspaper accounts, and it is likely that the actual number of deaths from strategic violence is higher.

75. See Hume, "Armed Violence and Poverty in El Salvador"; Zinecker, "From Exodus to Exitus"; McIlwaine and Moser, "Violence and Social Capital in Urban Poor Communities."

76. This corresponds with what Horowitz calls a "target group." See Horowitz, *The Deadly Ethnic Riot*, 17–27.

77. Another four cases had truncated data collection because their post-conflict period stretched past the 2009 cutoff point.

78. This comparison holds up when comparing the medians as well (259 for relapsed cases, compared to nonrelapsed cases).

79. In other words, there is a clear risk of an endogenous relationship between the levels of strategic violence and relapse. I am grateful to Joakim Kreutz for this point.

80. Strategic violence is measured by the deaths from attacks, while this dataset employs the Uppsala Conflict Program's estimates for when wars have occurred to measure relapses.

81. Connable and Libicki, *How Insurgencies End*, appendix A.

82. Jones, *In the Graveyard of Empires*.

83. On riots, see Horowitz, *The Deadly Ethnic Riot*. On assassinations, see Bell, *The Assassin*, and Lotrione, "When to Target Leaders." For an overview of risk factors for insurgency, see Fearon and Laitin, "Ethnicity, Insurgency and Civil War."

84. On spoiling, see Stedman, "Spoiler Problems in Peace Processes"; Greenhill and Major, "The Perils of Profiling"; Pearlman, "Spoiling Inside and Out"; and Nilsson and Kovacs, "Revisiting an Elusive Concept."

85. On civilian victimization in irregular wars, see Valentino et al., "Draining the Sea," and Humpfreys and Weinstein, "Handling and Mishandling Civilians in War." On the duration of peace, see Downes, "The Problem with Negotiated Settlements"; Fortna, "Scraps of Paper"; and Werner and Yuen, "Making and Keeping Peace."

86. For example, this violence is often referred to as residual violence if the peace settlement remains intact, without inquiring as to any other purposes attached to it. See Sambanis, "Partition as a Solution to Ethnic War," 437–483.

87. This is a key point made by Kalyvas, *The Logic of Violence in Civil War*.

88. Fearon has pointed out that the lack of reliable data on low-intensity violence makes it difficult to pinpoint a precise end of a conflict. See Fearon, "Why Do Some Civil Wars Last So Much Longer than Others?," 278–280.

89. Greenhill and Major, "The Perils of Profiling," 10.

90. On spoilers, see Stedman, "Spoiler Problems in Peace Processes."

91. On war termination, see Walter, "The Critical Barrier to Civil War Settlement"; Walter, "Designing Transitions from Civil War"; Fortna, "Scraps of Paper"; Werner and Yuen, "Making and Keeping Peace"; and Toft, *Securing the Peace*.

92. On credible commitments, see Walter, "The Critical Barrier to Civil War Settlement"; Walter, "Designing Transitions from Civil War"; Fearon, "Commitment Problems and the Spread of Ethnic Conflict."

93. See, among others, Bensahel, "Preventing Insurgencies."

94. Human Rights Watch, *Angola Unravels*.

95. Salehyan and Gleditsch, "Refugees and the Spread of Civil War"; Greenhill, *Weapons of Mass Migration*.

96. See Lémarchand, *The Dynamics of Violence in Central Africa*.

97. For a similar argument in favor of decoupling violence from spoiling, see Zahar, "Political Violence in Peace Processes."

98. Richmond, *The Transformation of Peace*; Goodhand, "Stabilizing a Victor's Peace?"

99. Human Rights Watch, *Paying for the Taliban's Crimes*.

100. In some cases, the parties may calculate that they have more to gain by continuing to

fight. See Mason and Fett, "How Civil Wars End." On timing, see Zartman, *Elusive Peace*. On stalling, see Walter, "Designing Transitions from Civil War," 130–131.

101. Zartman, *Elusive Peace*, 5. On two-level games, see Putnam, "Diplomacy and Domestic Politics."

102. Werner, "Negotiating the Terms of the Settlement."

103. Werner and Yeun, "Making and Keeping Peace."

104. For arguments about letting the war burn itself out, see Luttwak, "Give War a Chance," and on the mutually hurting stalemate, see Zartman, *Elusive Peace* (1995).

105. A conventional assumption of much of the bargaining literature is that there will be a clear variation in gains between winners and losers. There are some who argue that settlements can be constructed without clear losers if an external actor is willing to provide side payments to actors who would otherwise lose. See Zartman, *Elusive Peace*.

106. See Nilsson, "Partial Peace."

107. See Stedman, "Spoiler Problems in Peace Processes," for a discussion.

108. See Snidal, "Relative Gains," and Licklider, *Stopping the Killing*.

109. Collier et al., "Post-Conflict Risks," 462. This figure was calculated in Collier et al., *Breaking the Conflict Trap*.

110. The term *custodians of peace* come from Stedman, "Spoiler Problems in Peace Processes."

111. Knox, "See No Evil, Hear No Evil."

112. On latent spoilers, see Greenhill and Major, "The Perils of Profiling."

113. See particularly Walter, "The Critical Barrier to Civil War Settlement"; Walter, "Designing Transitions from Civil War."

114. There is a wide literature on the importance of third-party monitoring and support for peace settlements, and a conventional argument for the failure of agreements points to inadequate third-party management and enforcement. For some examples, see Hampson, *Nurturing Peace*, and Stedman et al., *Ending Civil Wars*. For a critique, see Paris, *At War's End*.

115. Werner, "The Precarious Nature of Peace."

116. This concept is also addressed in Staniland, "Organizing Insurgency."

117. This is an insight developed at length in Weinstein, *Inside Rebellion*.

118. This does not always mean that professional militaries or hierarchical organizations will obey; many militaries have participated in coups, particularly when there is not a strong tradition of civilian control over the military. But all other things being equal, developed hierarchical groups are less likely to suffer defection from a peace agreement than comparable horizontal or cellular groups.

119. This notion of information advantages affecting the ability to use violence efficiently comes from Kalyvas, *The Logic of Violence in Civil War*.

120. Staniland makes a convincing case that the social foundations of rebel organizations matter and that this social basis matters in shaping their effectiveness. See Staniland, "Organizing Insurgency."

121. A similar argument is made in Sinno, "Armed Groups' Organizational Structure."

122. International Crisis Group, *Security Sector Reform in the Congo*.

123. The employment of patronage implies a store of resources with which the leadership of an organization can maximize support, produce collective action, and cement its political base in order to be competitive with other rival organizations in its environment. See Wilson, "The Economy of Patronage," and Scott, "Patron-Client Politics and Political Change in Southeast Asia."

124. Weinstein, *Inside Rebellion*, and Staniland, "Organizing Insurgency."

125. Weinstein, *Inside Rebellion*, and Beardsley and McQuinn, "Rebel Groups as Predatory Organizations."

126. Weinstein, *Inside Rebellion*.

127. Weber, *Theory of Social and Economic Organization*.

128. Tucker, "The Theory of Charismatic Leadership."

129. For a recent discussion, see Patir, "The Israeli-Palestinian Conflict," available at www.icsr.info/publications/papers/1319713960ICSR_AtkinPaperSeries_YaelPatir.pdf, accessed 22 July 2012.

130. Zartman, *Elusive Peace*, 5.

131. On ingroup policing, see Laitin, "Marginality," 49–53; Brubaker and Laitin, "Ethnic and Nationalist Violence," 433; and Byman, "The Logic of Ethnic Terrorism," 162–166.

132. Internal unity is also essential for enforcing implementation of the agreement. See Pearlman, "Spoiling Inside and Out."

133. Recent studies have begun to relax the assumption that combatants are unitary actors and consider the effects of factionalism on their ability to strike a bargain. See McCormick and Owen, "Factionalism, Violence and Bargaining in Civil Wars"; Lake, "Rational Extremism"; Cunningham et al., "Shirts Today, Skins Tomorrow"; Bakke et al., "A Plague of Initials."

134. For a good discussion of the necessity of mechanisms to inflict harm, see Toft, *Securing the Peace*.

135. This can be particularly difficult given that peer monitoring is less effective in nonhierarchical rebel groups. See Weinstein, *Inside Rebellion*, 134.

136. Here this accepts the insight from Kalyvas, *The Logic of Violence in Civil War*, that information about wartime loyalties and interests is an important input in determining rates of violence.

137. This argument borrows significantly from the discussion in Kalyvas, *The Logic of Violence in Civil War*, about the risks associated with indiscriminate punishment.

138. Atlas and Licklider, "Conflict among Former Allies."

139. Walter, "Designing Transitions from Civil War"; Toft, *Securing the Peace*.

140. On organizing for rebellion before the war, see Lichbach, *The Rebel's Dilemma*.

141. See the discussion in Toft, *Securing the Peace*.

142. On the outbidding dynamic that drives this violence, see Bloom, *Dying to Kill*.

143. See especially Byman, "The Logic of Ethnic Terrorism."

144. The full set of these reports is available in an online archive at http://onlinebooks.library.upenn.edu/webbin/serial?id=crhrp, accessed 11 June 2012. To code each case, I consulted the narrative sections on "Arbitrary or Unlawful Deprivation of Life," which provided a short narrative summary of the deaths from political or strategic violence for each year of the post-conflict period and made a judgment about the coding for the entire period.

145. This is calculated by dividing the number of cases that have the predicted levels of violence based on the pathway in evidence. It assumes any case where the direct or indirect pathway can be associated with scattered or occasional levels of violence.

146. The concept of an opportunity structure is widely used in the literature on contentious politics and has been applied to collective violence. Much of this discussion owes a debt to Tilly, *From Mobilization to Revolution* and *The Politics of Collective Violence*.

147. A political opportunity structure can have a formal (institutional) aspect and an infor-

mal, cultural one. See Della Porta, "Research on Social Movements and Political Violence." For a recent application, see Gleditsch and Ruggeri, "Political Opportunity Structures, Democracy, and Civil Wars."

148. Posen, "The Security Dilemma and Ethnic Conflict"; Kaufman, "Possible and Impossible Solutions to Ethnic Civil Wars"; and Toft, *The Geography of Ethnic Conflict*.

149. Posen, "The Security Dilemma and Ethnic Conflict," 32.

150. Kaufmann, "Possible and Impossible Solutions to Ethnic Civil Wars," 148.

151. Ibid., 145.

152. Huntington, *Political Order in Changing Societies*. For a critique, see Tilly, "Does Modernization Breed Revolution?"

153. Horowitz, "Conciliatory Institutions and Constitutional Processes in Post-Conflict States."

154. Simonsen, "Addressing Ethnic Divisions in Post-Conflict Statebuilding."

155. On the incentives for violence provided by elections, see Snyder, *From Voting to Violence*.

156. Doyle and Sambanis, *Making War and Building Peace*; Collier et al., "Post-Conflict Risks"; and Fortna, *Does Peacekeeping Work?*

157. Quinlivan, "Burden of Victory," available at www.rand.org/publications/randreview/issues/summer2003/burden.html, accessed 19 July 2012.

158. See Quinlivan, "Burden of Victory."

159. See Bensahel et al., "Improving Capacity for Stability and Reconstruction Operations."

160. See Jett, *Why Peacekeeping Fails*.

161. A good survey is available in Findlay, *The Use of Force in UN Peace Operations*.

162. This was clearly apparent in Afghanistan. See Jones, *In the Graveyard of Empires*.

163. It is also possible that countermobilization could affect not just their former enemies, but also of groups that were outside the original conflict, thus producing the introduction of new groups into the conflict.

164. Posen, "The Security Dilemma and Ethnic Conflict."

165. On the spiral model, see Jervis, "Cooperation under the Security Dilemma."

166. Walter and Snyder, *Civil Wars, Insecurity and Intervention*, 23.

167. See MacGinty, "Looting in the Context of Violent Conflict."

Chapter 4 · Bosnia-Herzegovina

1. Secretary of State Warren Christopher made this statement to the House Foreign Affairs committee. See "Statement of Warren Christopher, Secretary of State," 94.

2. It has been described as a "symmetric non-conventional" war. See Kalyvas and Sambanis, "Bosnia's Civil War," 212.

3. For historical overviews, see Cigar, *Genocide in Bosnia*; Friedman, *The Bosnian Muslims*; Glenny, *The Balkans*; Gow, *The Serbian Project and Its Adversaries*; Hoare, *How Bosnia Armed*; Kaplan, *Balkan Ghosts*; Malcolm, *Bosnia*; Mazower, *The Balkans*; O'Ballance, *Civil War in Bosnia*; Rieff, *Slaughterhouse*; Silber and Little, *Yugoslavia*; Woodward, *Balkan Tragedy*; Zimmerman, *Origins of a Catastrophe*.

4. The UCDP conflict termination dataset figures estimate that 87,400 people were killed

in conflict. Subsequent work by the Sarajevo-based Investigation and Documentation Center (IDC) have put the figure closer to 100,000, far less than the 200,000 to 250,000 total that was often used during and after the war. See Reuters, "Research Halves Bosnia Death Toll." For a critique of this estimate that raises some questions on methodology and data collection, see Ball et al., "The Bosnian Book of the Dead." The refugee and internally displaced statistics come from early estimates produced by the CIA and are quoted in Burg and Shoup, *The War in Bosnia-Herzegovina*, 171.

5. Burg and Shoup, *The War in Bosnia-Herzegovina*, 171.

6. For an overview of these efforts, see Daalder, *Getting to Dayton*, 5–36, and Goodby, "When War Won Out."

7. McMahon and Western, "The Death of Dayton."

8. Cousens, "The Dayton Agreement on Bosnia," 543.

9. Holbrooke, *To End A War*, 363.

10. McMahon and Western, "The Death of Dayton."

11. Bosnia (3.7 million) also has a larger population than Kosovo (1 million), so this difference is applicable at a per capita level as well. The death toll for Serbia's strategic violence between 1995 and 2000 is somewhat misleading, as it captures some of the violence that led to the Kosovo war in 1999.

12. Noted Balkans expert Susan Woodward, for example, predicted a breakdown in law and order given the chaotic demobilization of the soldiers and the economic stresses that Bosnia was under at the onset of the post-conflict period. See Woodward, *Implementing Peace in Bosnia and Herzegovina*, 89.

13. International Crisis Group, *The Wages of Sin*, 33–35.

14. Berdal et al., "Post-War Violence in Bosnia and Herzegovina," 76.

15. See Weller and Wolff, "Bosnia and Herzegovina Ten Years after Dayton," and Berdal et al., "Post-War Violence in Bosnia and Herzegovina," 75–94.

16. Burg and Shoup, *The War in Bosnia-Herzegovina*, 171.

17. See particularly Ó Tuathail and Dahlman, "The Effort to Reverse Ethnic Cleansing in Bosnia-Herzegovina." On the Bosnian Serb policy of ethnic cleansing, see Gow, *The Serbian Project and Its Adversaries*.

18. The Dayton Accords have been referred to as a "coerced compromise." See Cousens, "The Dayton Agreement on Bosnia," 538.

19. See Ibid., 546.

20. Special arrangements were also made for two cities trapped in or near majorities of other ethnic groups, Gorazde and Brcko, which have been subject to high levels of international supervision.

21. See particularly Malik, "The Dayton Agreement and Elections in Bosnia."

22. Bose, *Bosnia after Dayton*, 65.

23. Cited in Cousens, "The Dayton Agreement on Bosnia," 547.

24. Ó Tuathail and Dahlman, "The Effort to Reverse Ethnic Cleansing in Bosnia-Herzegovina," 441.

25. Quoted in ibid.

26. See Woodward, "Bosnia-Herzegovina," 105.

27. The constitution also recognizes "Others" as constituent peoples but does not accord them the same rights in the House of Peoples.

28. Chandler, *Faking Democracy after Dayton*, 69.
29. Bose, *Bosnia after Dayton*, 63.
30. McMahon and Western, "The Death of Dayton."
31. For a full text of the Dayton Accords, see www1.umn.edu/humanrts/icty/dayton/dayton accord.html, accessed 12 June 2011.
32. Cousens, "The Dayton Agreement on Bosnia," 552.
33. Ibid.
34. Bose, *Bosnia after Dayton*, 81.
35. Cousens, "The Dayton Agreement on Bosnia," 552.
36. OSCE, Office of Democratic Institutions and Human Rights, "Bosnia and Herzegovina Elections, 1998."
37. Ibid., 4.
38. Divjak and Pugh, "The Political Economy of Corruption in Bosnia-Herzegovina," 374.
39. Ibid.
40. Figures quoted in Robinson and Sucic, "Two Decades from War."
41. Divjak and Pugh, "The Political Economy of Corruption in Bosnia-Herzegovina," 374.
42. Ibid.
43. Ibid., 374–375.
44. Woherl, *Bosnia: Current Issues and U.S. Policy*, 5.
45. Cousens, "The Dayton Agreement on Bosnia," 540.
46. As Marc Weller and Stefan Wolff point out, the legal authority of the PIC remains questionable. See Weller and Wolff, "Bosnia and Herzegovina Ten Years after Dayton," 5.
47. For a critique on this point, see Chandler, *Faking Democracy after Dayton*.
48. Holbrooke, *To End a War*, 337.
49. See particularly Clark, *Waging Modern War*, 77–106.
50. Holbrooke, *To End a War*, 324.
51. Schear, "Bosnia's Post-Dayton Traumas," 93.
52. As an example of these irregularities, independent tallies of turnout recorded that this election had turnouts of 106% or 120%. See Soloway, "Fair or Not, Results of Bosnia."
53. There was considerable debate over whether this election was held too early, and whether U.S. pressure for this election was due to the Clinton administration's desire to have a foreign policy success on the eve of the presidential elections. See Rieff, "Abandoning Bosnia—Again."
54. OSCE Chairman in Office Flavio Cotti, quoted in International Crisis Group, *Doing Democracy a Disservice*.
55. The election results are available in Government Accounting Office, "Bosnia Peace Operation."
56. The data here are drawn from the OSCE and are cited in ibid.
57. To some extent, the RS position was due to its relationship with Belgrade, which opposed much of the efforts of NATO to rebuild Bosnia when Slobodan Milosevic was in power.
58. On the consociational features, see Bose, *Bosnia after Dayton*, 63.
59. For a discussion of the calls to partition Bosnia, see Kumar, *Divide and Fall*, and Bose, *Bosnia after Dayton*, 149–203.
60. Jahić and Kalamujić, "Reporter's Notebook."
61. DeVine and Mathison, "Corruption in Bosnia-Herzegovina, 2005," 13.
62. Larise, "Corrupted Political Elites or Mafiotic State Structures?"

63. Ibid., 5.
64. Pugh, "Postwar Political Economy," 470–471.
65. The Deutschmark (DM) was used by some Balkan states, including Croatia, and other foreign donors as a stable base currency for aid transfers in the early post-conflict period.
66. Donais, *The Political Economy of Peacebuilding*, 76.
67. Ibid., 77.
68. Divjak and Pugh, "The Political Economy of Corruption in Bosnia-Herzegovina," 378.
69. Festić and Rausche, "War by Other Means," 27–30.
70. Holbrooke, *To End a War*, 352.
71. Quoted in Chandler, *Faking Democracy after Dayton*, 71.
72. International Crisis Group, *Doing Democracy a Disservice*.
73. For details on this election, see General Accounting Office, "Bosnia Peace Operations," 63.
74. International Crisis Group, *Is Dayton Failing?*, 14.
75. Chandler, *Faking Democracy after Dayton*, 54–55.
76. Ibid., 201–202.
77. International Crisis Group, *Is Dayton Failing*, 15.
78. Election results, reported at www.ipu.org/parline-e/reports/arc/2039_98.htm, accessed 15 July 2011.
79. Bose, *Bosnia after Dayton*, 24.
80. International Crisis Group, *Is Dayton Failing*, 18.
81. Office of the High Representative, Decision Removing Ante Jelavic from His Position as the Croat member of the Joint Presidency, Sarajevo, 7 March 2001.
82. Kroeger, "SDS Ejects Founder Karadzic."
83. Bose, *Bosnia after Dayton*, 277.
84. On the predatory violence, see Mueller, *Remnants of War*.
85. Kalyvas and Sambanis, "Bosnia's Civil War," 213.
86. Ibid., 215.
87. Ibid., 215–216.
88. Ibid., 216.
89. Ibid., 212.
90. Shanty and Mishra, *Organized Crime*, 86.
91. Gow, *The Serbian Project and Its Adversaries*, 80–84.
92. Ibid., 77. The original Yugoslavian army under Tito was called the Yugoslav People's Army (Jugoslovenska Narodna Armija). Its successor forces were the Army of Yugoslavia (Vojska Jugoslavije) and the Bosnian Serb military (Vojska Republike Srpske).
93. Nettlefield, *Courting Democracy in Bosnia and Herzegovina*, 70.
94. Gow, *The Serbian Project and Its Adversaries*, 233–235. The Croatian force was the Hrvatska Vijeće Odbrane (HVO).
95. See Hoare, *How Bosnia Armed*, 50–59.
96. Nettlefield, *Courting Democracy in Bosnia and Herzegovina*, 71.
97. The ARBiH (also known as the ABiH) was the Army of Bosnia and Herzegovina (Armija Bosne i Hercegovine).
98. Moratti and El-Rayess, "Transitional Justice and DDR," 12.
99. Cox, "Bosnia and Herzegovina," 250–251.
100. Gaub, *Military Integrations after Civil Wars*, 102.

101. Ibid.

102. International Crisis Group, *Ensuring Bosnia's Future*, 14.

103. The RS police forces also remained populated with war criminals. Ibid.

104. See the respective discussions of SDS and HDZ involvement in violence in two International Crisis Group reports: *The Wages of Sin* and *Impunity in Drvar*.

105. Statistic cited in Moratti and El-Rayess, "Transitional Justice and DDR," 12.

106. Ibid., 13.

107. Bojicic-Dzelilovic, "Peace on Whose Terms?"

108. Ibid.

109. Cited in Woodward, "Bosnia-Herzegovina," 95.

110. The statistic on housing damage comes from Ministry for Human Rights and Refugees (BiH), *Housing and Urban Profile*, 6.

111. This is particularly notable in light of calls by nationalist RS officials to reject the "occupation" of NATO.

112. There were reported problems with the systems in place with IPTF statistics, including "double-counting" some statistics, as well as incorrect classification. Source: Interoffice Memorandum, to Stephen Bowen from Anna Korula, Reporting by Human Rights Office, 7 October 1998, UMMIBH Archives, New York, 2005 0118 box 2.

113. For example, in a UN Office of Drugs and Crime analysis conducted in 2004, Bosnia's homicide rate per 100,000 members of the population (1.8) is the same as Croatia, which has a similar population and demographic profile. No direct comparative data is available for the years in question. See UNDOC, International Homicide Rate per 100,000 persons Fact Sheet, 2004, available at www.unodc.org/documents/data-and-analysis/IHS-rates-05012009.pdf, accessed 20 July 2011.

114. Human Rights Watch, "A Failure in the Making," www.unhcr.org/refworld/country ,,HRW,,BIH,,3ae6a8570,0.html, accessed19 July 2011.

115. Reuters, "NATO Chief Raps Bosnia Factions."

116. Associated Press, "Muslim Farmer Killed Cutting Hay in Serb Zone."

117. Reuters, "Attack on Serbs Followed Disappearance of Moslems."

118. Human Rights Watch, "Politics of Revenge," available at www.hrw.org/en/news/1997/08/07/politics-revenge-bosnias-una-sana-canton-systematically-violate-dayton-accords-and-i, accessed 22 July 2011.

119. U.S. AID, Bosnia and Herzegovina: Conflict Assessment, 13.

120. Cited in Woodward, "Bosnia-Herzegovina," 96.

121. O' Connor, "Violence Flares."

122. Hedges, "Outbreaks of Violence Continue in Bosnia."

123. Stephen, "Serbs Attacks Moslems in Disputed Bosnian Village."

124. Agence France Presse, "Two Attacked after Crossing Mostar Border."

125. O' Connor, "Violence Flares."

126. Agence France Presse, "NATO Commander to Protest Serb Attack on Refugees."

127. See the description of this incident in Dempsey, "Rethinking the Dayton Agreement," 11.

128. International Crisis Group, *Impunity in Drvar*, 5–6.

129. Human Rights Watch, "Update: Non-Compliance with the Dayton Accords."

130. Ibid.

131. Ibid.

132. Hedges, "On Bosnia's Ethnic Fault Line."

133. Andreas, *Blue Helmets and Black Markets*, 121–126.

134. Many of these criminal networks would cooperate across ethnic lines even at the height of the war. See Glenny, *McMafia*, 38–39.

135. Andreas, *Blue Helmets and Black Markets*, 124.

136. Divjak and Pugh, "The Political Economy of Corruption in Bosnia-Herzegovina," 373–386.

137. Hedges, "Gangs Descend."

138. General Accounting Office, Crime and Corruption, 19.

139. Cited in Pugh, "Postwar Political Economy in Bosnia and Herzegovina," 468.

140. Discussion paper attached to fax scheduling a meeting by Ambassador Donald Hays, Principal Deputy High Representative for Bosnia-Herzegovina, 14 March 2002, Subject: Confirmation of a Meeting. Source: UNMIBH archives, UN headquarters, New York City, box 2003 002 1, transcript in the possession of author.

141. Festić and Rausche, "War by Other Means," 28–29.

142. Interoffice Memorandum, to Eric Morris D/SRSG from Vinod Kapur, Chief, Trust Fund, 31 May 1999, UNMIBH archives, UN headquarters, New York City, box 2005 0120 box 34, transcript in the possession of author.

143. Discussion paper to Hays, UNMIBH archives.

144. Ibid.

145. Pugh, "Postwar Political Economy in Bosnia and Herzegovina," 474.

146. Cited in Andreas, *Blue Helmets and Black Markets*, 123.

147. World Bank, *Bosnia and Herzegovina: Diagnostic Surveys of Corruption*, 2, available at www1.worldbank.org/publicsector/anticorrupt/Bosnianticorruption.pdf, accessed 21 July 2011.

148. It is well acknowledged that certain types of illicit activity are more likely to lead to violence and conflict than others, though the reasons why remain somewhat unclear. See Andreas and Wallman, "Illicit Markets and Violence."

149. Hedges, "A War Bred Underworld Threatens Bosnia Peace."

150. Griffiths, "Investigation."

151. This estimate was produced by the Bosnian newspaper *Nezavisne Novine*, which did a comprehensive survey in its black book of the drugs and human trafficking routes in the Western Balkans. Its numbers are disputed by RS officials. See B92 News, "Heroin Trafficking Route Passes through Bosnia," 10 February 2011, available at www.b92.net/eng/news/region-article.php?yyyy=2011&mm=02&dd=10&nav_id=72641, accessed 21 July 2011.

152. Hedges, "Gangs Descend."

153. Cited in Mavris, "Human Smugglers and Social Networks," 1.

154. Andreas, *Blue Helmets and Black Markets*, 126–127.

155. Border Service Project (BSP)/C Input to November 2000 SF Report, File #4, UNMIBH archives, UN headquarters, New York City, box 2005 0120 box 34, transcript in the possession of author.

156. Cited in Andreas, *Blue Helmets and Black Markets*, 128.

157. For example, the Chinese "Snakehead" gangs often charge up to $60,000 per person for transit into Western Europe, usually organized via Belgrade and then the RS, but often insist that the refugee repay the debt through forced labor in sweatshops or restaurants.

158. Mavris, "Human Smugglers and Social Networks," 7.

159. BBC News, "Victims of Bosnia's Sex Trade," available at http://news.bbc.co.uk/2/hi/europe/1807189.stm, accessed 22 July 2011.

160. Crossette, "Peacekeeping's Unsavory Side"; see also Andreas, *Blue Helmets and Black Markets*, 128–129.

161. Source: Internal UNMIBH records.

162. Andreas, *Blue Helmets and Black Markets*, 131–132.

163. Schork, "UN Plays Down Serbs Sarajevo Truce Violations"; Reuters, "Bosnia Fetes Christmas Peace Despite Air Attack."

164. Latal, "Man Injured by Sniper Fire"; Reuters, "Sniper Attack on Sarajevo Tram Breaks Peace."

165. McDowall, "Grenade Hits Sarajevo Streetcar."

166. Schork, "UN Plays Down Serbs Sarajevo Truce Violations."

167. Reuters, "NATO Chief Raps Bosnia Factions on Peace Breaches."

168. Agence France Presse, "Serbs Threaten to Down U.S. Helicopter."

169. Maguire, "Croat Arson Campaign Omen of NATO's Future Woes."

170. Human Rights Watch, "Northwestern Bosnia," available at www.unhcr.org/refworld/country,,HRW,,BIH,,3ae6a7de0,0.html, accessed 22 July 2011.

171. International Crisis Group, *Grave Situation in Mostar*.

172. The casualty estimate of the siege of Sarajevo comes from Schork, "Peace Puts Down Roots in Bosnia."

173. Holbrooke, *To End a War*, 335–336.

174. Woodward, "Bosnia-Herzegovina," 101.

175. Holbrooke, *To End a War*, 336.

176. Ibid.

177. Woodward, "Bosnia-Herzegovina," 101.

178. Schear, "Bosnia's Post-Dayton Traumas," 93.

179. CNN, "Bosnian Serbs Frantically Flee Sarajevo." CNN reports that fifty thousand Serbs were present in the suburbs at that time. Holbrooke estimates that there were sixty thousand evacuees of a total population of seventy thousand. Holbrooke, *To End a War*, 335.

180. Woodward, "Bosnia-Herzegovina," 101.

181. Holbrooke, *To End a War*, 336–337; Woodward, "Bosnia-Herzegovina," 101.

182. UNHCR, Returns Summary to Bosnia-Herzegovina, from 1 January 1996 to 31 January 2001, given to author in Sarajevo in July 2008.

183. While the UNHCR has gradually grown more professional in measuring refugee statistics, there is still considerable definitional ambiguity and methodological ambiguity in counting refugees. See particularly Crisp, "Who Has Counted the Refugees?"

184. See also Ó Tuathail and Dahlman, "The Effort to Reverse Ethnic Cleansing in Bosnia-Herzegovina," 451.

185. Subsequent data released by UNHCR suggest that 457,194 minority returns had occurred by 2006, with 102,111 occurring in 2002 alone.

186. See particularly UNHCR, Target Area Initiative: Facilitating the Return and Reintegration of Refugees and Displaced Persons in Bosnia and Herzegovina, December 1996 (unpublished paper), and UNHCR, Bosnia and Herzegovina: Repatriation and Return Operation 1998, Document HIWG/97/7, 10 December 1997, 17–18. For a full discussion, see Ó Tuathail and Dahlman, "The Effort to Reverse Ethnic Cleansing in Bosnia-Herzegovina," 439–461.

187. International Crisis Group, *The Continuing Challenge of Refugee Returns*, 1–2.
188. Berdal et al., "Post-War Violence in Bosnia and Herzegovina," 83–84.
189. UNHCR, Extremely Vulnerable Individuals: The Need for Continuing International Support in Light of the Difficulties to Reintegration upon Return, Sarajevo, November 1999.
190. International Crisis Group, *The Continuing Challenge of Refugee Return*, 18.
191. Internal SFOR study, cited in ibid.
192. BBC News, "Bosnian Serbs Attack Croats Returning to Northern Bosnia."
193. Dempsey, "Rethinking the Dayton Agreement," 10.
194. International Crisis Group, "Return of Displaced Persons to Jajce and Travnik," 3 June 1998, available at www.unhcr.org/refworld/country,,ICG,,BIH,,3ae6a6f08,0.html, accessed 21 July 2011.
195. Dempsey, "Rethinking the Dayton Agreement," 12.
196. Geitner, "Bosnian Serb Police Attack Muslim Returnees."
197. Agence France Presse, "NATO Commander to Protest Serb Attack on Refugees."
198. Agence France Presse, "Moslems Attack Bus Carrying Serbs in Eastern Bosnia."
199. See the tactics described in O'Connor, "Muslim Rioters in Bosnia Attack on a U.S. Army Column."
200. International Crisis Group, *The Continuing Challenge of Refugee Returns*, 19.
201. IPTF, Office of the Commissioner, UN IPTF Status Report, 21 August 1997.
202. UN ECOSOC, UN Commission on Human Rights, Statement of Human Rights Watch, Rights of Persons Belonging to National, Ethnic, Religious or Linguistic Minorities, 17 March 1998. See also Agence France Presse, "SFOR Confirms Attackers Were Serbs."
203. Arnaut, "Moslems Say Serb Mortar Bombs Drove Them from Village."
204. International Crisis Group, *The Continuing Challenge of Refugee Returns*, 18.
205. UNHCR, Returnee Monitoring Study, 9.
206. Ibid.
207. Cosic, "NATO Takes Tough Stance on Bosnia's Bombings."
208. U.S. Department of State, Bosnia and Herzegovina Country Report on Human Rights Practices for 1998; Reuters, "Bosnian Croat Leader Condemns Mosque Attack."
209. U.S. State Department, *Patterns of Global Terrorism, 1997*.
210. UNHCR, Update on Conditions for Return to Bosnia and Herzegovina, Geneva, 4–5.
211. As noted earlier, it is more likely that events causing deaths would be reported in the press, while nonlethal events would not. This would suggest that the number of nonlethal incidents is likely to be larger than reported here, and the rate of lethality even lower.
212. The average casualty rate for Bosnia from 1995 to 1999 was 8.40 deaths per year, which is below the threshold of 25 deaths per year for residual violence.
213. See particularly Woodward, "Bosnia-Herzegovina."
214. On the calming effect of IFOR in the immediate post-conflict period, see Schear, "Bosnia's Post-Dayton Traumas," 91–93.
215. Quinlivan, "Burden of Victory."
216. Berdal et al., "Post-War Violence in Bosnia and Herzegovina," 89.
217. See Dahlman and Ó Tuathail, "The Legacy of Ethnic Cleansing," 572.
218. Cited in Berdal et al., "Post-War Violence in Bosnia and Herzegovina," 87.
219. For a summary, see Osland, "The EU Police Mission in Bosnia and Herzegovina"; see also Berdal et al., "Post-War Violence in Bosnia and Herzegovina," 87.

220. The concept of repertoires of contentious action comes predominantly from the social movement literature. This argument draws particularly on that of Tilly, *The Politics of Collective Violence*, and Tarrow, *Power in Movement*.

221. For how crowds participate in the collective protest events, see Tarrow, "Cycles of Collective Action."

222. Ó Tuathail and Dahlman, "The Effort to Reverse Ethnic Cleansing in Bosnia-Herzegovina," 455.

223. See particularly Bose, *Bosnia after Dayton*, and Chandler, *Faking Democracy after Dayton*.

224. For example, the International Crisis Group (ICG) concluded that the attacks in Drvar were approved, if not supported, by the top levels of the HDZ in Mostar and Zagreb. See International Crisis Group, *Impunity in Drvar*, 10. Similar conclusions were reached about the SDS leadership.

225. Human Rights Watch, "The Continuing Influence of Bosnia's Warlords."

226. International Crisis Group, *Minority Return or Mass Relocation*, Report No. 33, 14 May 1998, p. i.

227. Quoted in International Crisis Group, *Impunity in Drvar*, 10.

228. Michel, "Opposition under No Holds Barred Attack in Northwest Bosnia."

229. Special Police memorandum, "Note concerning the Structure and Activities of the Secret Police Organization AID in Bihac Area," 10 December 1997, UNMIBH archives, UN headquarters, New York City, box 2005 0120 box 34, transcript in the possession of author.

230. Latin, "Sarajevo Trial May Lift Lid on Assassinations," available at http://iwpr.net/report-news/sarajevo-trial-may-lift-lid-assassinations, accessed 25 July 2011.

231. Agence France Presse, "Bosnian Croat Opposition Figure Wounded in Machine Gun Attack"; Human Rights Watch, "The Continuing Influence of Bosnia's Warlords."

232. Quoted in Zakaria, "The Rise of Illiberal Democracy."

Chapter 5 · Rwanda

1. There is considerable debate over the total number killed due to uncertainties over census data in Rwanda and the speed and scale of the killing across the country. Among the most systematic treatments was Allison Des Forges's account, which estimated that 500,000 people were killed. See Des Forges, *Leave None to Tell the Story*, 15–16. The UN's independent inquiry into the genocide places the total killed at 800,000, though the official estimate from the RPF-controlled Rwandan government estimates it to be as high as 1 million. For a discussion, see Straus, *The Order of Genocide*, 51–52, and Prunier, *The Rwanda Crisis*, 263–265.

2. The question of participation in the violence is too complex to be dealt with here. See particularly Straus, *The Order of Genocide*; Fuji, *Killing Neighbors*; and McDoom, "Rwanda's Ordinary Killers," available at http://eprints.lse.ac.uk/28153/1/wp77.pdf, accessed 19 August 2011. For narrative accounts of participation, see the reporting by Hatzfield in *Machete Season* and *Life Laid Bare*.

3. See Verwimp, "Machetes and Firearms."

4. Prunier, *The Rwanda Crisis*, 247.

5. On the history of the crisis, see Prunier, *The Rwanda Crisis*; Mamdani, *When Victims Become Killers*; Melvern, *Conspiracy to Murder*; and Kakwenzire and Kamukama, "The Devel-

opment and Consolidation of Extremists Forces"; Powers, *"A Problem from Hell"*; Dallaire with Beardsley, *Shake Hands with the Devil*; Lemarchand, *The Dynamics of Violence in Central Africa*.

6. For examples, see Jones, *Peacemaking in Rwanda*; Khadigala, "Implementing the Arusha Peace Agreement on Rwanda"; Clapham, "Rwanda"; Kuperman, "The Other Lesson of Rwanda"; Adelman and Suhrke, *The Path of Genocide*. It is important to stress that only some accounts emphasize that the genocide was an unstoppable consequence of the breakdown of the Arusha Accords, while others (such as Dallaire) emphasize that steps could have been taken by the UN or others to stop the genocide in its infancy.

7. One open question was whether these ethnic antipathies were deeply rooted in the society or were contingent and manufactured by political parties for their own short-term gain. For the latter view, see Straus, *The Order of Genocide*, 18–23.

8. Prunier, *The Rwanda Crisis*, 173.

9. Ibid., 268, and 321–328. For a systematic analysis of this point, which suggests that a "double genocide" did not take place, see Verwimp, "Testing the Double Genocide Thesis." This claim, as would be expected, has been strongly rejected by the Rwandan government, which called for a decisive rejection of the "double genocide" hypothesis in its response to the UN report on atrocities in the Congo. See Government of Rwanda, "Rwanda's Comments on the Draft UN Mapping Report on the DRC."

10. On the latter observation, see particularly Mamdani, *When Victims Become Killers*, 234–264.

11. Prunier, *From Genocide to Continental War*, 3.

12. Ibid., 5.

13. Reyntjens, "Rwanda, Ten Years On."

14. Terry points out that much of the looted assets in Rwanda were sold for personal gain by opportunistic officials. See Terry, *Condemned to Repeat*, 160.

15. This estimate is from Human Rights Watch but is confirmed by others. See Hintjens, "Post-Genocide Identity Politics in Rwanda," 22. Some of these cases were forwarded to the International Criminal Tribunal for Rwanda (ICTR), while others were handled through traditional justice, specifically in *gacaca* courts.

16. Cited in Reyntjens, *The Great African War*, 181.

17. Figures are from the U.S. Committee on Refugees, cited in Prunier, *The Rwanda Crisis*, 312.

18. The CIA World Factbook reports that 84 percent of the Rwandan population is Hutu, though this is difficult to confirm due to the lack of a reliable census in the post-conflict period. See www.cia.gov/library/publications/the-world-factbook/geos/rw.html, accessed 9 September 2012.

19. Reyntjens, "Rwanda, Ten Years On," 178.

20. Prunier, *The Rwanda Crisis*, 329.

21. For the former, see ibid., 324; for the latter, see Reyntjens, "Rwanda, Ten Years On," 194.

22. Kinzer, *A Thousand Hill*, 190. This book is broadly sympathetic to the RPF and to Kagame particularly.

23. Reyntjens, *The Great African War*, 28.

24. Terry, *Condemned to Repeat*, 159.

25. Orth, "Rwanda's Hutu Extremist Genocidal Insurgency: An Eyewitness Perspective," 83. Gourevitch maintains that the RDR was a paramilitary organization with links to the former FAR. See Gourevitch, *We Wish to Inform You*.

26. Former CDR official Jean-Bosco Barayagwiza, quoted in Prunier, *The Rwanda Crisis*, 314.
27. Orth, "Rwanda's Hutu Extremist Genocidal Insurgency," 86.
28. Gourevitch, *We Wish to Inform You*, 268–269.
29. UNAMIR Mandate, available at www.un.org/en/peacekeeping/missions/past/unamirM.htm, accessed 11 August 2011.
30. Reyntjens, "Rwanda, Ten Years On," 179.
31. Ibid.
32. Prunier, *The Rwanda Crisis*, 334.
33. See Terry, *Condemned to Repeat*, 185–186.
34. Prunier, *The Rwanda Crisis*, 363.
35. Hintjens, "Post-Genocide Identity Politics in Rwanda," 26.
36. Eltringham, *Accounting for Horror*, 109.
37. Reyntjens, *The Great African War*, 47.
38. Ibid., 48–49.
39. Ibid., 80.
40. Pomfret, "Rwandans Led the Revolt in Congo."
41. Ibid.
42. Cited in Reyntjens, *The Great African War*, 141.
43. Amnesty International, *Rwanda: Ending the Silence*, available at www.amnesty.org/en/library/asset/AFR47/032/1997/en/0f834c89-e9b8-11dd-935f-7f9f204ae31f/afr470321997en.html, accessed 11 August 2011.
44. Reyntjens, "Rwanda, Ten Years On," 195.
45. Presidential adviser Claude Dusaidi, quoted in Reyntjens, "Rwanda, Ten Years On," 195.
46. Ibid., 180.
47. These numbers are from the CIA World Factbook, though there are some suggestions that Tutsi numbers may be even lower, perhaps as low as 10 percent, following the genocide. The Twa constitute 1 percent of the population. See the CIA World Factbook 2013 at www.cia.gov/library/publications/the-world-factbook/geos/rw.html, accessed 29 January 2013.
48. See particularly Hintjens, "Post-Genocide Identity Politics in Rwanda."
49. Reyntjens, "Rwanda, Ten Years On," 188.
50. Cohen, *Global Diasporas*.
51. Reported by Amnesty International, cited by Reyntjens, *The Great African War*, 189.
52. See International Crisis Group, *Rwanda at the End of the Transition*. Developments after the post-conflict period have confirmed this drift toward authoritarianism. In 2001, the first local elections in Rwanda were held since the genocide, but the RPF carefully controlled the process by banning parties from campaigning and pressuring voters to select the "right" candidates. This process was followed by the presidential and parliamentary elections, in which the opposition party the MDR was banned and a law was passed which permitted parties to campaign only if they could "reflect the unity of the Rwandan people." The 2003 elections, which were marked by disappearances, voting irregularities, and outright fraud, nonetheless gave Kagame the presidency with 95 percent of the vote.
53. Reyntjens, *The Great African War*, 145.
54. Ibid., 194–196.
55. MONUC stands for Mission de l'Organisation des Nations-Unies au Congo.

56. Quoted in Reyntjens, *The Great African War*, 198. This number has been subsequently challenged by the International Rescue Committee for being too high and based on questionable assumptions. See the discussion in the Human Security Report (2009/2010), 123–131. Full report available at www.hsrgroup.org/docs/Publications/HSR20092010/20092010HumanSecurityReport-Part2-ShrinkingCostsOfWar.pdf, accessed 29 January 2013.

57. Mamdani, *When Victims Become Killers*, 164. MDR eventually discarded the "Parmehutu" from its name because of its ethnocentric implications.

58. Kuperman, "Provoking the Genocide," 63.

59. Ibid., 66.

60. Reed, "The Rwandan Patriotic Front."

61. Reed, "Exile, Reform and the Rise of the Rwandan Patriotic Front."

62. Reed "The Rwandan Patriotic Front," 49.

63. Kuperman, "Provoking the Genocide," 65.

64. Watson, "War and Waiting," 53.

65. Reed, "Exile, Reform and the Rise of the Rwandan Patriotic Front," 484.

66. Kuperman, "Provoking the Genocide," 65.

67. Reed, "Exile, Reform and the Rise of the Rwandan Patriotic Front," 484.

68. Ibid., 486.

69. Reed, "The Rwandan Patriotic Front," 49.

70. Prunier, *The Rwanda Crisis*, 70.

71. Cited in Reed, "The Rwandan Patriotic Front," 49.

72. Prunier, *The Rwanda Crisis*, 71. Watson argues that the number of Rwandan Tutsis in the ranks of the Ugandan army was smaller than other estimate. See Watson, "War and Waiting," 54. Not all of the fourteen thousand recruits were RPF, with some estimates of the ranks of RPF at four thousand soldiers.

73. This was admitted by Kagame after the fact. See Watson, "War and Waiting," 54.

74. Kuperman, "Provoking the Genocide," 69–70.

75. Reed, "Exile, Reform and the Rise of the Rwandan Patriotic Front," 488.

76. Ibid.

77. Kuperman, "Provoking the Genocide," 70.

78. There is some doubt about whether Rwigyema was killed by enemy fire or by his own troops. See Prunier, *The Rwanda Crisis*, 94–96.

79. Kuperman, "Provoking the Genocide," 70.

80. Watson, "War and Waiting," 54.

81. Ibid.

82. The figure of $1 million comes from Kuperman, "Provoking the Genocide," 67.

83. Reed, "Exile, Reform and the Rise of the Rwandan Patriotic Front" 496.

84. National Intelligence Council Memorandum, 13 May 1994, NIC 00270/94, in possession of author through Freedom of Information Act request F-2009–00120 (22 December 2008).

85. Reed, "The Rwandan Patriotic Front," 50.

86. Central Intelligence Agency, *Memorandum: The Massacres in Rwanda*, 28 April 1994, in possession of the author through Freedom of Information Act request F-2009-00120 (22 December 2008).

87. For an unsympathetic account of its strategy, see Kuperman, "Provoking the Genocide," 79.

88. Ibid., 78.

89. There is some criticism of the RPF for its unwillingness to prioritize protecting its own ethnic kin over achieving its strategic goals, such as the conquest of the country. See Kuperman, "Provoking the Genocide," 79–82.

90. Odom, "Guerrillas in the Mist," 5–6.

91. Lemarchand, *The Dynamics of Violence in Central Africa*, 96–97.

92. Reyntjens, *The Great African War*, 33.

93. Reyntjens, "Rwanda, Ten Years On," 183.

94. Reed, "Exile, Reform and the Rise of the Rwandan Patriotic Front," 498.

95. Watson, "War and Waiting," 54.

96. Reyntjens, *The Great African War*, 28.

97. Ibid., 29.

98. Prunier, *From Genocide to Continental War*, 11.

99. Prunier, *The Rwanda Crisis*, 360.

100. Ibid., 360.

101. Prunier, *From Genocide to Continental War*, 17.

102. Des Forges, *Leave None to Tell the Story*, 16. Note that this is the page for the printout rather than the original Des Forges piece, which is not available in hard copy. The subsequent references follow suit with this pattern.

103. These trend lines are broadly consistent with Prunier's analysis, which suggested that the high levels of killings in the immediate post-genocide period abated for some time and resumed in March 1996. See Prunier, *The Rwanda Crisis*, 361.

104. Reuters News, "Rwandan Troops Taking Law into Own Hands—Amnesty."

105. The quote is from Amnesty International, "Rwanda: Reports of Killings and Abductions by the Rwandese Patriotic Army, April–August 1994," 3.

106. Ibid., 3–4.

107. Ibid., 4.

108. Ibid.

109. Ibid., 6.

110. Ibid., 8.

111. Ibid., 9.

112. Reyntjens, *From Genocide to Continental War*, 20.

113. Ibid., 19–20.

114. Reuters News, "Rwandan Troops Kill 16—Civilians."

115. Amnesty International, "Rwanda: Alarming Resurgence of Killings."

116. Reuters, "Amnesty Getting Daily Reports of Rwanda Massacres."

117. BBC Monitoring Service, "Another Soldier Executed in Public for Murder."

118. Reyntjens, *Great African War*, 176.

119. Dow Jones International News, "Army Commander Says Rwandan Rebels Kill at Least 110 People"; Dow Jones News Service, "Grenade Explosion, Crash Kill at Least 20 on Bus to Rwanda."

120. Dodd, "Rwandan President Says 1,000 Infiltrators Detained."

121. McKinley, "Machete Returns to Rwanda, Rekindling a Genocidal War."

122. Reuters, "Seven Rwandan Soldiers Killed in Attack—Radio"; Associated Press Newswires, "Rwandan Rebels Reportedly Kill 11 Children in School Attack."

123. Dow Jones News Service, "Rwandan Hutu Rebels Kill 58 in Northwestern Village."
124. BBC News, "'Infiltrators' Kill 24 in the Center of the Country."
125. Hranjski, "Rwandan Rebels Kill 94 Civilians."
126. Kaban, "Rwanda Says over 40 Prisoners Killed by Rebels."
127. Lauras, "Rwandan Rebels Strategically Target Jails, Seek Recruits."
128. Mseteka, "Hutu Rebels Kill Mayor, 11 Others in Northwest Rwanda." In some cases, the freed prisoners would voluntarily return to the jail rather than be caught between the ex-FAR rebels and the RPF. See Agence France-Presse, "Rebels Kill 12 in Northwest Rwanda."
129. BBC Monitoring Service, "Militia Kills 20 Civilians, 80 Prisoners in Northwest—Agency Report."
130. McKinley, "In Pastoral Western Rwanda, Ethnic Foes Engage in Murderous Tit-for-Tat."
131. BBC Monitoring Service, "Government Forces Kill 70 'Infiltrators.'"
132. Reuters, "Rwandan Villagers Kill 27 Hutu Rebels."
133. BBC News, "'Armed Criminals' Kill Seven Civilians in Gitarama Province"; BBC News, "'Infiltrators' Kill 24 in the Center of the Country."
134. *New York Times*, "Rwanda and Zaire Units Exchange Fire on Border."
135. For some illustrative attacks, see the *New York Times*, "At Least Twelve Shot Dead Inside Rwandan Camp."
136. McKinley, "Rwanda's Paralyzing Wound: Hutu-Tutsi Killings."
137. See Terry, *Condemned to Repeat*, 166–168.
138. Kaban, "Rwanda Genocide Killers Uproot Tutsis in Zaire."
139. Antonie, "Rwandan Refugees Flood towards Tanzania."
140. McKinley, "Stoked by Rwandans, Tribal Violence Spreads in Zaire."
141. McKinley, "Machete Returns to Rwanda, Rekindling a Genocidal War."
142. Kaban, "62 Dead in Sweep against Rwandan Rebels-Aid Workers."
143. Reuters, "UN Workers Say over 100 Killed in Rwanda Operation."
144. BBC News, "UN Says 148 Killed in Rwanda Massacre of Tutsis."
145. See Reyntjens, *The Great African War*, 80–101.
146. Quoted in McKinley, ""Machete Returns to Rwanda, Rekindling a Genocidal War."
147. The events here, and debates over the levels of casualties, are in Prunier, *From Genocide to Continental War*, 38–42.
148. Reuters, "Two Local Officials Assassinated in Southern Rwanda."; Reuters, "Gunmen Kill Local Official in Rwanda—Radio."
149. Reuters, "At Least 43 Killed in Fresh Rwanda Violence."
150. BBC News, "Rebels Kill Prosecutors and Colleague"; Reuters, "Gunmen Kill Rwandan Judge."
151. Smerdon, "Rwandan Genocide Survivors Being Hunted Down—Report."
152. Reuters, "UN Says 162 People Killed in Rwanda in May."
153. Reuters, "Fifteen Rwandan Genocide Survivors Killed in Attack."
154. McKinley, "In Pastoral Western Rwanda, Ethnic Foes Engage in Murderous Tit-for-Tat."
155. BBC News, "Editor of Publication Critical of Government in Coma after Being Attacked."
156. Human Rights Watch, *Rwanda: The Crisis Continues*, 14.
157. *New York Times*, "Hutu Militiamen Kill 3 Spanish Aid Workers in Rwanda."

158. Bedford, "Gunmen Assassinate Top Hutu Official in Rwanda."

159. BBC Monitoring Service, "Criminals Kill 25 in Separate Incidents."

160. Mseteka, "Former Rwandan Minister Wounded in Attack."

161. The Kenyan police arrested three suspects and linked the murder to an alleged theft by Sendashonga. See AP Online, "Rwanda Cops Hold 3 in Pols Murder." For a discussion of whether these suspects were guilty, and the extent of possible RPF responsibility, see Prunier, *From Genocide to Continental War*, 365–368.

162. Kagame admitted that Rwanda led the effort to overthrow Zairean president Mobutu Sese Seko in 1996–1997. See Pomfret, "Rwandans Led Revolt in Congo." See particularly the discussion of Rwanda's role in generating the scramble for the Congo's resources in Reyntjens, *The Great African War*.

163. See the discussion of Odom, "Guerrillas in the Mist," 6–7.

164. As an example, see Human Rights Watch, *Rwanda: The Crisis Continues*.

165. The casualty range is from Reyntjens, *Great African War*, 27. The geographic location is from Prunier, *The Rwanda Crisis*, 360, n. 10.

166. Des Forges, *Leave None to Tell the Story*, 18.

167. Ibid.

168. There is some debate about whether the report was ever completed. Des Forges suggests that the Gersony was ordered by UN Secretary General Boutros Boutros Ghali to never produce a written report and to speak to no one about its findings. Others such as Reyntjens have suggested that the report was written but merely embargoed or suppressed.

169. The report is entitled "Summary of UNHCR Presentation before Commission of Experts, 10 October 1994, Prospects for Early Repatriation of Rwandan Refugees Currently in Burundi, Tanzania and Zaire." It was leaked with a covering note written by François Fouinat to Mrs. B. Molina-Abram, Secretary of the Commission of Experts on Rwanda, on 11 October 1994. Hard copy is in the author's possession. The actual text of the summary is hereafter referred to as Gersony summary.

170. Gersony summary, 4.

171. Ibid.

172. Reported in a leaked situation report from Refugee International. See SITEP #10, Rwandan Refugees in Tanzania, New Arrivals Report, 17 May 1994.

173. Gersony summary, 5.

174. Ibid., 6.

175. Quote of the Gersony report is from Des Forges, *Leave None to Tell the Story*, 18. This quote is not in the Gersony summary quoted above and presumably comes from some version of the original report.

176. Interoffice Memorandum, to the Secretary, from Assistant Secretary (Africa) George E. Moose, subject: New Human Rights Abuses in Rwanda, no date listed, in the possession of author.

177. Prunier, *From Genocide to Continental War*, 31.

178. Interoffice Memorandum, to the Secretary, from Assistant Secretary (Africa) George E. Moose.

179. Des Forges, *Leave None to Tell the Story*, 19.

180. Interoffice Memorandum, to the Secretary, from Assistant Secretary (Africa) George E. Moose.

181. Des Forges, *Leave None to Tell the Story*, 20.

182. Amnesty International, "Rwanda: Reports of Killings and Abductions by the Rwandan Patriotic Army, April–August 1994," 2.

183. Ibid., 1.

184. Ibid., 2–4.

185. Des Forges, *Leave None to Tell the Story*, 6.

186. Ibid., 15.

187. Ibid., 22.

188. Reyntjens, *The Great African War*, 31.

189. Ibid., 28.

190. Prunier, *From Genocide to Continental War*, 3.

191. Ibid., 11.

192. Quoted in ibid., 366.

193. One of the arguments deployed by those defending Hutu genocidaires is that Kagame and his allies always had a master plan for invading Zaire and overthrowing Mobutu. To this point, Christopher Black, lead counsel for Hutu former general Augustin Ndindiliyiamana at the ICTR, has introduced as evidence a letter allegedly sent by Kagame to Jean Baptiste Bagaza in Burundi on 10 August 1994, which spells out his goal to occupy all of Zaire. This letter was introduced as oral evidence in the ICTR on 18 November 2008, and no hard copy has ever surfaced. Due to its source, this claim must be treated with some suspicion and would need to be carefully verified and supported by evidence before treated as accurate or reliable. For his account, see Black, "The Rwandan Patriotic Front's Bloody Record and the History of U.N. Cover-Ups," available at http://sfbayview.com/2010/the-rwandan-patriotic-fronts-bloody-record-and-the-history-of-u-n-cover-ups/, accessed 31 August 2011.

194. Reyntjens, *The Great African War*, 47.

195. French, "Kagame's Hidden War in the Congo."

196. Prunier, *From Genocide to Continental War*, 69.

197. Reyntjens, *The Great African War*, 48.

198. Quoted in ibid., 57.

199. Prunier, *From Genocide to Continental War*, 71–72.

200. There is some evidence to suggest that the RPF, as a regime founded in exile, was always inclined to think regionally in its approach, so it is not surprising that they would think this way during the post-conflict period.

201. These fixed notions of the problem and the "good" and "bad" guys in post-conflict states are surprisingly durable. For example, Assistant Secretary of State Susan Rice declared after visiting the Great Lakes that the problem there was the danger of another genocide and that Museveni and Kagame were determined to stop it. See French, "Kagame's Hidden War in the Congo."

Chapter 6 · *Kosovo*

1. Michael Ignatieff has even gone so far as to call the 1990s the "era of humanitarian intervention." See Ignatieff, "Is the Human Rights Era Ending?" See also Woodward, "Humanitarian War: A New Consensus?," and Roberts, "NATO's 'Humanitarian War' over Kosovo."

2. These numbers are from the newspaper-generated datasets, which are the most broadly

comparable, and are both for comparable five-year periods. In Kosovo, the comparison with East Timor is for the period 2000–2004 and excludes some of the reported violence in 1999, a portion of which may include atrocities committed within wartime but only reported in the post-conflict period.

3. Interview with Gentile, 15 April 2003.

4. Many of the other minority groups in Kosovo—Roma, Ashkali, Gorani, Egyptians, and Turks—were also threatened by Albanian groups as a result of their perceived sympathy or collaboration with the Yugoslav security forces before and during the war.

5. This chapter uses the estimate from Cocozzelli, *War and Social Welfare: Reconstruction after Conflict*. Other estimates, including from the UNHCR, have put the number of Kosovo Serb refugees as high as 230,000. See "UNHCR Condemns Violence against Serb Returnee in Kosovo."

6. On the Kanun code, see Schwander-Sievers, "The Enactment of 'Tradition,'" 114–116.

7. Montgomery, "Horrors of the KLA Prison Camp."

8. Human Rights Watch, "Abuses against Serbs and Roma in the New Kosovo."

9. The number of CIVPOL was expanded from its initial allotment of 3,110 to 4,450 in 2000. See Dobbins et al., *America's Role in Nation-Building*, 119. As chapter 3 noted, the force ratio (23.6) for NATO peacekeeping mission in Kosovo was among the highest in the post–Cold War period.

10. See Boyle, "Explaining Strategic Violence after Wars."

11. Estimates vary slightly, but Serbs constituted approximately 10 percent of the overall population by 1999–2000.

12. On the history of Kosovo and the war, see Booth, *The Kosovo Tragedy*; Chomsky, *The New Military Humanism*; Chomsky, *A New Generation Draws the Line*; Clark, *Waging Modern War*; Fromkin, *Kosovo Crossing*; Ignatieff, *Virtual War*; Judah, *Kosovo: War and Revenge*; Parenti, *To Kill a Nation*; Waller et al., *Kosovo: The Politics of Delusion*; Weymouth and Henis, *The Kosovo Crisis*. For a recent ten-year retrospective of the conflict, see Mertus, "Operation Allied Force."

13. *Kosovo Report*, 90.

14. Ibid.

15. The casualty figures in Kosovo have been controversial because of the propaganda claims of both NATO and the Yugoslav authorities. This study adopts the estimate produced by the American Association for the Advancement of Science, which conducted a study for the International Criminal Tribunal for Yugoslavia (ICTY), which counted exhumations and interviewed more than three thousand Albanians and Serbs to produce an estimate. See AAAS, *Political Killings in Kosova/Kosovo, March–June 1999*.

16. The Serb casualty estimates have never been verified, and the Yugoslav government generally used the higher numbers. Human Rights Watch produced the estimate of five hundred civilian deaths and later complained that the Pentagon underestimated the number of civilian deaths and refused to provide details on their casualty estimates. See Human Rights Watch, "New Figures on Civilian Deaths in Kosovo War."

17. It is still an open question why the Milošević government capitulated when it did. Some suggest that a Russian decision to declare its full support for NATO's nonnegotiable demands led Milošević to seek a settlement. See Bellamy, *Kosovo and International Society*, 197–199. Others have said that a decision within NATO to leak to the press the fact that NATO was now

contemplating a ground invasion of Yugoslavia was decisive in convincing Milošević to give in to NATO demands. Source: Interview with Gen. Klaus Naumann. Others have suggested that air power alone was sufficient to force his capitulation. See Stigler, "A Clear Victory for Air Power."

18. *Kosovo Report,* 100.

19. Interview with Naumann. See also *Kosovo Report,* 103. One controversial incident during KFOR's arrival in Kosovo was the Russian seizure of the Pristina airport and the subsequent controversy over Russian participation in KFOR. For more on this, see Clark, *Waging Modern War,* and Shawcross, *Deliver Us from Evil.*

20. See particularly Mertus, *Kosovo: How Myths and Truths Started a War.*

21. The KLA was more aggressive than the LDK in attempting to win control over the province. KFOR forces found KLA "commanders" in each city and province, and the KLA was already providing basic social services, including security, by the time KFOR arrived.

22. *Kosovo Report,* 105, and also *Newsweek International,* "The Fire This Time."

23. O'Neill, *Kosovo: An Unfinished Peace,* 45–46.

24. *Kosovo Report,* 110–111.

25. Judah, *Kosovo: War and Revenge,* 286.

26. Cited in Cocozzelli, *War and Social Welfare,* 58.

27. International Crisis Group, *Violence in Kosovo,* 3.

28. This chapter attempts, as much as it is possible, to use proper accents for personal names in a way that the individual themselves would. For place names, however, this chapter defaults to an Anglicized version of the place name, as is used frequently in narrative accounts of the conflict and the violence in the post-conflict period. This is because all towns, villages, and other geographic locations in Kosovo are described differently in the Albanian or Serbian language, and to use one name might be interpreted as bias implying the "ownership" of the town. No such bias is intended here.

29. *Kosovo Report,* 118.

30. Ibid., 115.

31. His full name is Bishop Artemije Radosavljević, but he is widely known only as Bishop Artemije.

32. UNSCR 1244 allows for the appointment of a special representative to the secretary general who is directly responsible for all UN activities in the province and reports directly to the UN secretary general.

33. According to UNMIK regulation 2001/19, the PISG would consist of a 120-member Assembly, a president, prime minister, and nine ministries. They are Ministry of Finance and Economy; Ministry of Trade and Industry; Ministry of Education, Science and Technology; Ministry of Culture, Youth and Sports; Ministry of Health, Environment and Spatial Planning; Ministry of Labor and Social Welfare; Ministry of Transport and Communication; Ministry of Public Services; and Ministry of Agriculture, Forests and Rural Development.

34. For example, after a Serb teenager was shot in Lipljan in January 2004, Serb villagers blockaded a road, cutting off Albanian villages, and attacked those who passed by. International Crisis Group, *Collapse in Kosovo,* 11.

35. On the Bridge Watchers, see International Crisis Group, *UNMIK's Kosovo Albatross.*

36. BBC News, "Timeline: Kosovo," 12 May 2009.

37. One of the most controversial aspects of the March 2004 riots involves allegations that

no Serbs were involved in the death of the Albanian boys. One of the surviving boys was interviewed on television, and it was implied by the newscasters– though never directly stated by the boy—that Serbs had been responsible. Investigations by the UN and a respected Albanian judge have questioned this story because of inconsistencies with the boy's account and a lack of corroboration with other victims and witnesses. See Human Rights Watch, *Failure to Protect*, 19–21. The role of Kosovo's media in inflaming ethnic tensions has come under particular scrutiny after this event. See the OSCE, *The Role of the Media*, 7–11.

38. This initial estimate was reported by UNMIK spokesperson Derek Chappell. See Reuters, "Scores Arrested in Wake of Kosovo Violence." The most comprehensive analyses published are International Crisis Group, *Collapse in Kosovo*, and Human Rights Watch, *Failure to Protect*.

39. International Crisis Group, *Collapse in Kosovo*, i.

40. Human Rights Watch, *Failure to Protect*, 26. A report from the European Centre for Minority Issues says that one KFOR soldier died but this is unconfirmed. See Schenker, "Violence in Kosovo and the Way Ahead."

41. UCK is short for Ushtria Clirimtare E Kosoves, the Albanian name for the Kosovo Liberation Army (KLA). See International Crisis Group, *Collapse in Kosovo*, 45.

42. Ashkali are members of the Roma group who claim descent from Persia. Most speak Albanian, and some identify themselves as Albanians.

43. International Crisis Group, *Collapse in Kosovo*, 45.

44. Wood, "Kosovo War-Crimes Trial Splits West and Prosecutors."

45. Haradinaj was arrested again on appeal from the ICTY on the grounds that his first trial was marred by witness intimidation, but the charges were dropped in 2012. See BBC News, "New War Crimes Trial for Former Kosovo PM Haradinaj."

46. BBC News, "UN Plans for Kosovo Independence."

47. Judah, *War and Revenge*, 117–120.

48. Ibid., 137.

49. O'Neill, *Kosovo: An Unfinished Peace*, 23.

50. Many members of the KLA, among others, blamed Rugova for failing to get the Kosovo question resolved during the Dayton Peace Accords that ended the Bosnian war.

51. Judah, *War and Revenge*, 282.

52. International Crisis Group, *What Happened to the KLA?*, 20.

53. Hedges, "Kosovo's Next Masters," 40.

54. BBC News, "Police Seize Former Kosovo Rebel." Remi was named a "threat to peace" by the United States and was arrested by UNMIK on suspicion of murder and torture for his wartime activities during 1998–1999.

55. Hedges, "Kosovo's Next Masters," 37.

56. Ibid.

57. Ibid., 39–40.

58. See Hockenos, *Homeland Calling*. However, it should be noted that among most well-funded local NGOs, the Mother Theresa Society, was deeply linked to LDK, not KLA, structures. See Cocozzelli, *War and Social Welfare*, 49–55.

59. While there have been a number of discoveries of small-arms caches around Kosovo, the single largest discovery of weapons occurred in Klecka, in the Drenica region, in June 2000. Tripod-mounted heavy machine guns, rifles, mortars, rocket-propelled grenade launchers, antitank

and antipersonnel mines, flak jackets and large amounts of ammunition, and communication equipment were discovered. See BBC News, "Kosovo Arms Caches 'Was KLA's.'"

60. CNN, "Kosovo Liberation Army Disarms to Meet Midnight Deadline."
61. International Crisis Group, *What Happened to the KLA?*, 1.
62. International Crisis Group, *Who's Who in Kosovo*.
63. International Crisis Group, *What Happened to the KLA?*, 2. The International Crisis Group commented that the PDK presidency looked more like a class reunion of the old People's Movement of Kosovo (LPK) party, the original exiled Kosovo independence party that operated in Switzerland and Germany in the mid-1990s, than a new political party. Fourteen of the twenty-one members of the presidency of the PDK came directly from the old LPK party and the rest, like Mahmuti, came from the LPK-aligned PBD.
64. Hedges, "Crisis in the Balkans."
65. The OSCE election results are available at www.osce.org/kosovo/20464.
66. These OSCE election results are available at www.osce.org/kosovo/20466.
67. Simons, "Former Leader in Kosovo Acquitted of War Crimes."
68. Sofalia, "Kosovo Parliament to Investigate Illegal Intelligence Service SHIK."
69. Pozhidaev and Andzhelich, "Beating Swords into Ploughshares," 30.
70. Interview with Siebentritt.
71. International Crisis Group, *What Happened to the KLA?*, 11. Confirmed in interview with Siebentritt.
72. Interview with Siebentritt.
73. Interview on background with a senior U.S. Department of State official C, Washington, DC, 28 March 2001.
74. See Clewlow, "The Kosovo Protection Corps."
75. Wood, "Kosovo Gripped by Racketeers."
76. Pozhidaev and Andzhelich, "Beating Swords into Ploughshares," 31.
77. Ibid.
78. Hedges, "Kosovo Rebel Force Will Be Serbian Province's New Power Broker."
79. Judah, "The Kosovo Liberation Army," 71–72.
80. Ibid., 72. See also Hockenos, *Homeland Calling*, 258–259.
81. See the discussion of the feud between Haradinaj and the Musaj family, formerly part of the FARK, in Barnett, "Intra-KLA Blood Feuds Wrack Kosovo."
82. International Institute for Strategic Studies, "The Kosovo Liberation Army."
83. UNMIK, Division of Public Information, 11 May 2003.
84. International Crisis Group, *Kosovo after Haradinaj*, 6.
85. Immigration and Refugee Board of Canada, "Kosovo/Albania."
86. International Crisis Group, *Kosovo after Haradinaj*, 7.
87. B92 News, "Kosovo Terror Group Issues Fresh Threats." For the designation of this group as a terrorist group by UNMIK, see UNMIK Order 2003/9, available at www.unmikonline.org/regulations/admdirect/2003/ADE2003_09.pdf.
88. Pozhidaev and Andzhelich, "Beating Swords into Ploughshares," 31.
89. B92 News, "Kosovo Terror Group Issues Fresh Threats."
90. International Crisis Group, *Kosovo after Haradinaj*, 5.
91. Ibid., 7.
92. BBC News, "Who Are the Rebels?"

93. International Crisis Group, *What Happened to the KLA?*, 13.
94. Ibid., 11.
95. O'Neill, *Kosovo: An Unfinished Peace*, 29.
96. Priest, *The Mission*, 316.
97. International Crisis Group, *What Happened to the KLA?*, 13.
98. *Zeri* Weekly, 22 January 2000, quoted in International Crisis Group, *What Happened to the KLA?*, 13.
99. Ibid.
100. A leaked KFOR intelligence report on Xhavit Haliti suggested that the SHIK worked directly for the PDK leadership, had ties to the Albanian intelligence services, and was also embedded within the KPC information and intelligence divisions. Document in possession of the author.
101. Aliu, "Kosovo's LDK Asks for Full Report on Assassinations."
102. International Crisis Group, *An Army for Kosovo?*, 6–7.
103. International Crisis Group, *What Happened to the KLA?*, 8.
104. Ibid.
105. Ibid.
106. International Crisis Group, *Collapse in Kosovo*, 17.
107. International Crisis Group, *What Happened to the KLA?*, 15.
108. International Crisis Group, *Kosovo after Haradinaj*, 5–6.
109. International Crisis Group, *An Army for Kosovo?*, 6.
110. Ibid., 7.
111. International Crisis Group, *What Happened to the KLA?*, 15.
112. Aliu, "Ex-KLA Chief Too Busy to Count Veterans."
113. Reuters, "Kosovo Guerrilla Veterans Warn of New War."
114. BBC News, "KLA War Veterans Warn Official's Arrest Will Affect Kosovo Peace Process."
115. Human Rights Watch, *Failure to Protect*.
116. Hedges, "As U.N. Organizes, Rebels Are Taking Charge of Kosovo."
117. Priest, *The Mission*, 317.
118. Ibid.
119. Ibid., 312.
120. Ibid., 317.
121. Ibid., 311.
122. International Crisis Group, *Serbia: Maintaining Peace in Presevo Valley*, 1.
123. Ibid., 11–12.
124. Pozhidaev and Andzhelich, "Beating Swords into Ploughshares," 31.
125. Reuters, "Powell Tells Kosovo Leaders to Act against Violence."
126. Reuters, "Update 1: Kosovo Leaders Tell Macedonia Rebels to Stop Fight."
127. International Crisis Group, *Serbia: Maintaining Peace in Presevo Valley*, 1.
128. See Boyle, "Revenge and Reprisal Violence in Kosovo."
129. Human Rights Watch, "Federal Republic of Yugoslavia: Abuses against Serbs and Roma in the New Kosovo."
130. This phenomenon was called a *strategic sale* and involved Albanians forcing Serbs to sell their homes to Albanians, often at gunpoint and with the support of the KLA.
131. International Crisis Group, *Violence in Kosovo: Who's Killing Whom?*, 3.

132. Quoted in Schwander-Sievers, "The Enactment of 'Tradition': Albanian Constructions of Identity, Violence and Power in Times of Crisis," 114.

133. International Crisis Group, *Violence in Kosovo: Who's Killing Whom?*, 3. KFOR reports that the breakdown of murder victims is as follows: 145 ethnic Albanian, 135 Serb, and 99 others. Amnesty International reported a KFOR-recorded murder total of 414 by 10 December 1999, with 150 ethnic Albanian victims, 140 Serbs, and 124 people of unknown ethnicity. See Amnesty International, *Prisoners in Our Own Homes*, 3. The Kosovo Serb National Council disputed these statistics and claims that 400 Serbs have been murdered, but never provided any evidence.

134. There is a considerable amount of "noise" in these data, as UNMIK crime records often differ slightly depending on their publication. For example, many of the annual crime totals for 1999 differ slightly with the regional totals provided by UNMIK CIVPOL. Anything listed as "N/A" in this or subsequent tables was not available.

135. The Northern Ireland population total is from the 2001 census. See Northern Ireland Statistics and Research Agency, "Census 2001 Population Report." An interesting counterpoint for Kosovo is Albania, which has a reputation for lawlessness and a weak government and only reported 5,612 crimes in 1999. However, the data may suffer from underreporting and not reflect the true extent of criminality in Albania. Source: Interpol, Crime Statistics, Albania.

136. Human Rights Watch, "Abuses against Serbs and Roma in the New Kosovo."

137. Internal UNMIK Crime Presentation, February 2001, in the possession of author.

138. The UNMIK Crime Motive database records were provided to author by John Avery, UNMIK Serious Crimes Analysis Division.

139. The motive classification has some difficulties, in part because what constituted a "political" or "ethnic" crime was never specified. This left some CIVPOL officers classifying crimes in a haphazard fashion and may have led to an undercounting of the political and ethnic motives behind crimes in 2000–2001.

140. While the 2000 UNMIK data represent a considerable improvement in scope and detail over the 1999 data, both datasets are imperfect. The reliability of some tallies, particularly in 2000, is questionable and may be affected by undercounting or double counting. Also, some of the data may either be double-reported or excluded from the police files because they were handled by KFOR.

141. UN Mission in Kosovo CIVPOL, "Offence Statistics by Motive."

142. Pristina had the largest population of any region of Kosovo, estimated to be 1 million, or 50 percent of the population of Kosovo. It is therefore unsurprising that it should have the highest crime rates.

143. European Commission, Emergency Assessment of Damaged House and Local/Village Infrastructure, 21.

144. Human Rights Watch, "Abuses against Serbs and Roma in the New Kosovo."

145. Source: Phil Kaplan, Political Officer, U.S. Department of State, Washington, DC, 28 March 2001.

146. Internal OSCE population estimates, provided to the author.

147. The data are drawn from OSCE municipal profiles for 2000–2001 at www.osce.org/kosovo/documents/reports/municipal_profiles/, accessed 26 May 2003, calculated by author. Hard copy in possession of author.

148. OSCE Municipal Profiles, 2000–2001, at www.osce.org/kosovo/documents/reports/municipal_profiles/.

149. Pec kept a steady rate of "other minorities," approximately 4.8 percent for both years. Prizren's population of "other minorities" decreased in relative terms from 13.14 to 9.87 percent. Source: OSCE population records, calculated by author.

150. Calculated by the author from OSCE internal records.

151. International Crisis Group, *UNMIK's Bridging Kosovo's Mitrovica Divide*

152. The French role in Mitrovica attracted considerable controversy, as some accused them of being too favorable to the Serbs and willing to turn a blind eye to the activities of the Bridge Watchers. See ibid.

153. One concern here must be whether the data reported here—that is, those that made it into major English-language wire reports—are representative of the universe of violent events. It may be more likely that certain kinds of violent activity—for instance, attacks on peacekeepers or international officials, or interethnic attacks—are overrepresented in this sample, relative to other ordinary expressive or instrumental acts of violence.

154. Boyle, "Revenge and Reprisal Violence in Kosovo."

155. International Crisis Group, *Kosovo after Haradinaj*, 6.

156. One exception here was the assassination of a Bulgarian UNMIK employee in October 1999. He was reported killed after speaking Serbian in Pristina, which suggest that he was mistaken for a Serb. He was killed by an angry crowd in the middle of the street. See Gray, "Bulgarian UN Employee Shot Dead in Kosovo." Attacks on Serbian interpreters working for UNMIK were more common.

157. There is some difficulty in deciding how to delineate the time period here. As chapter 3 specified, post-conflict status lasts five years, and accordingly the lower estimate (213) for the full five-year period (2000–2004) is used here. This is also because 37 of the 71 deaths recorded in 1999 for the newspaper-generated dataset reflect some killings that may have occurred during the war but were discovered afterward, and some events that occurred right at the onset of the post-conflict period. In order to use the most careful, conservative estimate, I chose to use the lower estimate for 2000–2004 in chapter 3, though both are reported here.

158. This sample is a testament to the extent of underreporting of violent crime in post-conflict states. This sample draws from a comprehensive survey of major English-language newspapers. Yet the actual UNMIK records—which themselves have a substantial underreporting problem—include far more crimes than appear in English-language newspapers.

159. Quoted in Muja, "Ethnic Albanians Burn Down Serb Houses in Kosovo."

160. Quoted in Reuters, "Ancient Kosovo City Hit by Arson, Serbs Terrified."

161. Human Rights Watch, "Abuses against Serbs and Roma in the New Kosovo."

162. Ibid. and Heinrich, "Serbs Shot Dead in Kosovo Field, NATO Says."

163. Gall, "In Rebound of Rage, a Serb Dies in Kosovo"; BBC News, "Five Dead Following Celebration of Albania's State Holiday."

164. Agence France Presse, "Two Serbs, Child Shot Dead in Kosovo."

165. Reuters News, "Four Bosnians Killed in Kosovo Attack."

166. Agence France Presse, "Elderly Kosovo Serb Murdered, Wife Badly Injured."

167. Associated Press, "Two Serbs Found Axed to Death."

168. Agence France Presse, "Three Serbs Murdered in Kosovo—UN."

169. Human Rights Watch, "Abuses against Serbs and Roma in the New Kosovo."

170. Ibid.

171. Ibid.
172. Reuters News, "Kosovo Guerrillas Execute Three Serbs—Beta Agency."
173. Agence France Presse, "Five Albanians Slain in Kosovo Attack."
174. Associated Press, "Serb Refugees Attacked in a Visit to Their Homes in Kosovo."
175. Agence France Presse, "One Serb Killed, Four Injured in Spate of Kosovo Attacks."
176. Agence France Presse, "Serbian Man Killed in Drive-By Shooting."
177. Reuters, "Leading Kosovo Serb Politician Wounded—KFOR."
178. Reuters News, "Gunmen Pin Down Kosovo Peacekeepers for Two Hours."
179. Gray, "Sniper Dead, French Wounded in Kosovo Battle."
180. Agence France Presse, "Three Serbs Injured in Kosovo Shooting."
181. OSCE, *Second Assessment of the Situation of Ethnic Minorities in Kosovo*, 8.
182. Agence France Presse, "Kosovo Serb Shot Dead in Front of Home."
183. Agence France Presse, "Dozens Injured by Car Bomb in Kosovo."
184. BBC News. "Mortar Bomb Attacks Reported on Three Serb Homes in Kosovo."
185. Reuters "Over 10 Wounded in Grenade Attacks on Kosovo's Serbs"; Reuters, "Grenade Attack on Kosovo Café Injures Three"; Reuters, "Kosovo Serb Killed, Several Hurt in Attack on Café"; BBC News, "Six Serbs Injured in Grenade Attack on Village Shop."
186. Agence France Presse, "Kosovo Serb Shot Dead in Front of Home."
187. Reuters, "Grenades Kill Two Kosovo Serbs, U.N. Alarmed."
188. Vermeylan, "Two Serb Teenagers Killed in Kosovo Mortar Attack."; BBC News, "Group of 20 Ethnic Albanians Attack Two Serbs in Central Town."
189. Reuters, "Serious Attacks Mar Kosovo Peace."
190. Gray, "Mortar Attacks Kills Two in Kosovo Own."
191. Reuters, "Serb Killed in Kosovo Mortar Attack."
192. Vasovic, "Shots, Grenades, Blast on Serb Side of Divided City Leaves Wounded."
193. Amnesty International, *Federal Republic of Yugoslavia (Kosovo): Update from the Field*, 3.
194. OSCE, *Preliminary Assessment on the Situation of Ethnic Minorities in Kosovo*, 6.
195. Ibid.
196. Agence France Presse, "Serbs Shot Dead in Flashpoint Kosovo Region."
197. Buza, "Two U.S. Soldiers Injured in Kosovo Explosion."
198. Reuters, "Blast Hurts Kosovo Serbs—UN."
199. OSCE, *Preliminary Assessment on the Situation of Ethnic Minorities in Kosovo*, 3.
200. OSCE, *Third Assessment of the Situation of Ethnic Minorities in Kosovo*, 5.
201. Buza, "Kosovo Serbs Die in Rocket Attack on UN Bus."
202. Amnesty International, *Prisoners in Our Own Homes*, 12.
203. Dhimgjoka, "Seven Serbs Killed, 43 Injured in Kosovo Bomb Blast."
204. Amnesty International, *Prisoners in Our Own Homes*, 17.
205. OSCE, *Second Assessment on the Situation of Ethnic Minorities in Kosovo*, 8.
206. OSCE, *Third Overview of the Situation of Ethnic Minorities in Kosovo*, 4.
207. Pain, "Kosovo Mine Blast Kills Two Serbs."
208. Abrashi, "Ethnic Albanian Killed in Kosovo Grenade Attack, UN Calls Meeting."
209. Agence France Presse, "Ethnic Albanian Former Guerilla Leader Wounded."
210. Agence France Presse, "Bomb Caused Kosovo Political Centre Blast."
211. Associated Press, "Car Explosion Kills One, Injures Two."

212. Agence France Presse, "Two Explosions Hit Police, Court Building in Kosovo Capital."
213. OSCE/UNHCR, *Assessment of the Situation of Ethnic Minorities in Kosovo* (November 1999–January 2000), para. 14.
214. Roddy, "Kosovo Woman Killed, Agencies Warn on Minorities."
215. Becatoros, "Leading Serb Doctor Shot Dead in a Street in Kosovo."
216. Reuters, "Serb Working for UN Killed in Kosovo."
217. Agence France Presse, "One Killed in 'Terrorist' Bomb at the Home of Yugoslav Official in Kosovo"; Peyrille, "Car Bomb Kills One Serb, Injures Four in Pristina: KFOR."
218. Associated Press, "Gunmen Murder Ethnic Albanian Politician with Ties to Yugoslavia."
219. Agence France Presse, "High-Ranking Officer of the Kosovo Protection Corps Slain."
220. Reuters, "Man Shot Dead at Kosovo Guerrilla Headquarters"; Associated Press, "Four Kosovo Serbs Are Wounded in Attack."
221. Agence France Presse, "Senior Politician Killed in Kosovo."
222. Reuters, "Local Albanian Official Wounded in Shooting Daily"; Agence France Presse, "Member of Kosovo Protection Corps Murdered."
223. Agence France Presse, "Grenade Attack against Moderate Kosovo Candidate."
224. Agence France Presse, "Four Shot Dead, One Body Found in a Kosovo Day of Violence"; Agence France Presse, "Bomb Attack Tarnishes Success of Kosovo Poll."
225. Reuters News, "Masked Gunmen Wound New Kosovo Councilor."
226. Agence France Presse, "Ibrahim Rugova's Right Hand Man Shot Dead in Kosovo."
227. Agence France Presse, "Bomb Destroys the Offices of Moderate Kosovo Leader"; Reuters, "Two Kosovo Albanian Moderates Shot Dead"; BBC News, "Arson Attack Damages Ethnic Albanian Party Office."
228. Agence France Presse, "Two Dead in Shooting after Kosovo Assembly's Inaugural Session."
229. Reuters News, "Kosovo Albanian Politician Shot Dead."
230. Reuters, "Bomb Injures Ex-Kosovo Guerrilla and Family."
231. Agence France Presse, "Eight Injured in Western Kosovo Shooting."
232. Associated Press, "Three Killed in Post-Election Violence in Kosovo."
233. BBC News, "Kosovo President's Close Associate Heavily Injured in Planted Car Bomb Incident."
234. Associated Press, "Grenade Thrown at Kosovo President's Home."
235. Agence France Presse, "Vehicle Blast Injures Kosovo Minister, Four Others."
236. Associated Press, "Kosovo Journalist Wounded in Shooting"; Associated Press, "Prominent Kosovo Businessman Wounded in an Ambush."
237. Reuters, "Three Shot Dead in Kosovo Revenge Ambush."
238. Associated Press, "Key Witness in Trial of Ex-rebels Killed in Roadside Ambush in Kosovo."
239. Agence France Presse, "Kosovo Trial Witness Narrowly Escapes Death."
240. Reuters, "Three Killed in Gangland-Style Kosovo Shooting."
241. Reuters, "One Policeman Shot Dead in Kosovo—UN Official"; Associated Press, "One Policeman Killed, Two Wounded in Ambush in Kosovo."
242. Kirka, "Attackers Ambush Police Patrol in Northern Kosovo."
243. Institute for War and Peace Reporting, "Serbia: LDK Takes Stand on Kosovo Violence."
244. Ibid.

245. B92 News, "Kosovo Intelligence Service Killed 450 People."
246. Aliu, "Kosovo's LDK Asks for Full Report on Assassinations."
247. Agence France Presse, "New Clashes in Kosovo Town after Five Killed in Sectarian Upsurge."
248. Agence France Presse, "Three Kosovo Albanians Killed, Dozens Hurt in Unrest."
249. Agence France Presse, "Ethnic Albanians Attack Peacekeepers after Killings in Kosovo."
250. Agence France Presse, "More than 900 Kosovo Albanians Displaced in Divided Town."
251. Vasovic, "Fight in Divided Town Sparks Violence, Dozens Wounded."
252. Buza, "Sixteen UN Police Hurt in Clash with Kosovo Serbs."
253. Mutler, "Peacekeepers Clash with Serbs in Kosovo"; Agence France Presse, "Kosovo Serbs Attack UN Police Station, KFOR Peacekeepers"; Reuters, "Kosovo Peacekeepers and Protesters Clash, Many Hurt."
254. Agence France Presse, "Thirteen Peacekeepers Injured in Clashes with Kosovo Albanians."
255. Kirka, "Serb Woman and Child Injured in Grenade Attack."
256. Associated Press, "NATO, UN Police Clash with Ethnic Albanians in Kosovo."
257. Human Rights Watch, "Evidence of KLA Secret Prisons in Kosovo and Albania."
258. Human Rights Watch, "Abuses against Serbs and Roma in the New Kosovo," 11.
259. This tactic may explain why the kidnapping statistics for highly contested regions (like Pristina and Gnjilane) were disproportionately high in 2000.
260. Human Rights Watch, "Abuses against Serbs and Roma in the New Kosovo."
261. Ibid.
262. Ibid.
263. Ibid.
264. BBC News, "Serbian Policeman Wounded in Kosovo 'Buffer Zone' Attack."
265. Associated Press, "Two Dead, Three Wounded in Reported Serb-Albanian Clash in Southern Serbia."
266. Agence France Presse, "Two Serb Policemen Injured in Shooting near Kosovo Border."
267. Agence France Presse, "Mortar Attack against Serb Police near Kosovo: Judge." Agence France Presse, "Serb Policeman Injured in Ethnic Albanian Mortar Attack near Kosovo."
268. Abrashi, "Serbs Shot At, One Injured in Tense Serbian Region Bordering on Kosovo."
269. Associated Press, "Four Yugoslav Soldiers Injured in Contested Border Zone."
270. Abrashi, "Russian Peacekeeper Killed along Kosovo Border."
271. Reuters, "Kosovo Peacekeepers Shot at near Serbian Boundary."
272. Ilic, "Serb Policeman Killed, Three Wounded in Ethnic Albanian Attacks."
273. Agence France Presse, "Ethnic Albanians Kidnap Four Serbs in Southern Serbia."
274. Ilic, "Albanian Insurgents Attack Serbian Police inside Buffer Zone."
275. Agence France Presse, "Two Policeman Killed, One Wounded along Serbia-Kosovo Border."
276. Agence France Presse, "Serbian Children Targeted in Kosovo Attack."
277. Agence France Presse, "Three Macedonian Soldiers Killed in Heavy Fighting on Kosovo Border."
278. Abrashi, "U.S. Soldiers Wound Two Men in Kosovo Gunfight."
279. Agence France Presse, "Three Killed as Macedonia Conflict Spills into Kosovo."
280. Potter, "Newsman, Villager Killed in Kosovo Border Shelling."
281. Abrashi, "British Peacekeeper Killed, Two Wounded in Kosovo."

282. Reuters, "Eight Macedonian Soldiers Killed near Border."
283. Buza, "15 Injured in Attack on Serb Refugee Convoy."
284. Human Rights Watch, "Abuses against Serbs and Roma in the New Kosovo."
285. Ibid.
286. Ibid.
287. Amnesty International, *Prisoners in Our Own Homes*, 11.
288. See Tilly, *The Politics of Collective Violence*, 176. This study uses "polyvalent communication" in place of Tilly's "polyvalent gestures" to signal that it need not be the gesture of an individual (but in fact could be a written or broadcast message) which communicates a polyvalent signal.
289. See Scott, *Domination and the Arts of Resistance*.
290. Human Rights Watch, "Abuses against Serbs and Roma in the New Kosovo."
291. OSCE, *Assessment of the Situation of Ethnic Minorities in Kosovo* (November 1999–January 2000), para. 78. The OSCE Assessments were published and updated periodically with new information as the situation evolved. This means that the numbering of the reports is haphazard. This full report is sometimes referred to as the Fourth Assessment of the Situation of Ethnic Minorities in Kosovo and is available at http://www.unhcr.org/3c3c18cf2.html, accessed 21 July 2013.
292. Reuters, "Serious attacks Mar Kosovo Peace."
293. OSCE, *Assessment of the Situation of Ethnic Minorities in Kosovo* (November 1999–January 2000), para. 78.
294. Agence France Presse, "Kosovo Attacks Wound Serb Woman, Ethnic Albanian Men."
295. Associated Press, "Serbian Orthodox Church Blown Up in Kosovo."
296. Amnesty International, *Prisoners in Our Own Homes*, 14.
297. Ibid.
298. Ibid.
299. Associated Press, "Two Serb Orthodox Churches Attacked in Kosovo."
300. Human Rights Watch, *Kosovo: Human Rights Developments*.
301. Interview with Siebentritt.
302. Watson, "Report Details Cycle of Violence in Kosovo."
303. OSCE, *Third Assessment of the Situation of Ethnic Minorities in Kosovo*, Executive Summary, 1; CNN, "Kosovo Bus Bombing Condemned."
304. Human Rights Watch, *Under Orders: War Crimes in Kosovo*, 2.
305. International Crisis Group, *What Happened to the KLA?*, 14.
306. Quoted in Die Welt Online, "BND Kosovo Affair: German Spy Affair Might Have Been Revenge."
307. Associated Press, "Kosovo PM to Be Investigated for Alleged Organ Trafficking."
308. Lewis, "Report Identifies Hashim Thaci as 'Big Fish' in Organized Crime."
309. Hedges, "Leaders of Kosovo Rebels Tied to Deadly Power Play."
310. Lewis, "Report Identifies Hashim Thaci as 'Big Fish' in Organized Crime."
311. Reuters, "More Killings Reported in Kosovo."
312. Die Welt Online, "BND Kosovo Affair: German Spy Affair Might Have Been Revenge."
313. Quoted in International Crisis Group, *Collapse in Kosovo*, 15. This echoes a comment by Serbian prime minister Vojislav Kostunica that the attacks were "planned in advance and

coordinated . . . an attempted pogrom and ethnic cleansing." See BBC News, "Kosovo Clashes 'Ethnic Cleansing.'"

314. International Crisis Group, *Collapse In Kosovo*, 15. Holkeri later noted that it was "utterly disappointing" that ethnic Albanian political leaders had failed to condemn the attacks. See BBC News, "NATO Condemns Kosovo Extremists."

315. See UN Security Council, "Report of the Secretary General of the United Nations Interim Administration in Kosovo," para 2.

316. Agence France Presse, "NATO Chief says Kosovo Violence Was 'Orchestrated.'"

317. International Crisis Group, *Collapse in Kosovo*, 15.

318. Another explanation for why Lipljan was spared violence was that Finnish KFOR protected a church housing Serb IDPs. See BBC News, "Kosovo Rioters Burn Serb Churches."

319. International Crisis Group, *Collapse in Kosovo*, 16. The International Crisis Group notes that the simultaneous appearance of mobs in three major Serb settlements in Pristina—Kosovo Polije, Lipljan, and Obilic—suggests "premeditation and reserve-planning by extremist and criminal groups."

320. Admiral Gregory Johnson, commander of NATO forces in Southern Europe, said that there was a "modicum of organization" behind the violence and that it amounted to "ethnic cleansing." See Agence France Presse, "Kosovo Violence Could Have Been Organized—Top NATO official." Veton Surroi, a prominent political analyst, argued after riots that violence in Kosovo had entered a "second phase, when this kind of violence is clearly conducted and organized." Surroi argues that the violence was organized with the intention of "frightening the Serb population—to expel it from parts of central Kosovo by destroying Serb religious buildings" and "of directing the accumulated anger of the population against UNMIK and KFOR, things that until now were never possible." See Hayton, "'Sinister Purpose' to Kosovo Clashes?"

321. Human Rights Watch, *Failure to Protect*, 17.

322. Ibid., 60.

323. Ibid., 27.

Chapter 7 · East Timor

1. The original name for the Indonesian military was Angkatan Bersenjata Republik Indonesia (ABRI), which was later changed to Tentara Nasional Indonesia (TNI) in 1998.

2. East Timor's Commission for Reception, Truth and Reconciliation (CAVR) estimated that 180,000 people were killed in the Indonesian occupation between 1975 and 1999. See CAVR, "Responsibility and Accountability," 6.

3. For more on the history of East Timor, see Dunn, *East Timor*; Fox and Babo Soares, *Out of Ashes*; Greenlees and Garran, *Deliverance*; Hainsworth and McCloskey, *The East Timor Question*; Martin, *Self-Determination in East Timor*; Fernandes, *Reluctant Saviour*.

4. Lord, "The Diplomacy on East," 74–98. For more on the ambivalent relationship of Australia to East Timor, see Fernandes, *Reluctant Saviour*.

5. Greenlees and Garran, *Deliverance*, 28.

6. Vatikiotis, *Indonesian Politics under Suharto*, 204–232.

7. Greenlees and Garran, *Deliverance*, 77–78.

8. The official account of this communication is available at Department of Foreign Af-

fairs and Trade (DFAT), *East Timor in Transition, 1998–2000*, 29–37. For a critical view, see Fernandes, *Reluctant Savior*, 38–46.

9. Greenlees and Garran, *Deliverance*, 94.
10. BBC News, "East Timor Chooses Independence."
11. Crouch, "The TNI and East Timor Policy," 155.
12. Ibid., 156.
13. The report by the UN representative James Dunn pointed out a degree of wanton discrimination toward the family of pro-independence forces. See Greenlees and Garran, *Deliverance*, 214.
14. McDonald et al., *Masters of Terror*, 24.
15. Ibid., 36.
16. Greenlees and Garran, *Deliverance*, 214–215.
17. Fernandes, *Reluctant Saviour*, 76.
18. Crouch, "The TNI and East Timor Policy," 159. For a discussion of the extent to which General Wiranto and Habibie were in charge of events in East Timor, see Greenlees and Garran, *Deliverance*, 248–254.
19. Horowitz, *The Deadly Ethnic Riot*, 102–109. This argument is implicitly applied to East Timor in Crouch's arguments about vengeance, "The TNI and East Timor Policy," 162.
20. McDonald et al., *Masters of Terror*, 70.
21. Crouch, "The TNI and East Timor Policy," 160. There is also some evidence that the TNI planned for an exodus of presumably pro-independence refugees, numbering roughly 200,000 people. See ibid., 159.
22. Nevins, *A Not-So-Distant Horror*, 102.
23. Crouch, "The TNI and East Timor Policy," 157–158.
24. Martin, *Self-Determination in East Timor*, 125.
25. Greenlees and Garran, *Deliverance*, 270. Some estimates put Falintil's true numbers as even smaller, numbering only two hundred fighters. See Kilcullen, *The Accidental Guerrilla*, 207.
26. Greenlees and Garran, *Deliverance*, 270.
27. Ibid., 270–271.
28. For a skeptical take on this pressure, see Fernandes, *Reluctant Saviour*. There is also some evidence that Australia hoped to delay East Timor's independence from Indonesia, but this has not been confirmed. See Agence France Presse, "Australia Resisted ETimor Independence."
29. DFAT, *East Timor in Transition, 1998–2000*, 138, 142. Despite this fact, it is not clear that this intervention sets a precedent within Asia, for many other Asian countries do not see supporting the East Timor mission as indicative of a high level of support for humanitarian intervention. See Cotton, "Against the Grain: The East Timor Intervention."
30. DFAT, *East Timor in Transition 1998–2000*, 146.
31. Ibid., 157.
32. Londey, *Other People's Wars*, 245–246.
33. The initial UN mission was UNAMET (United Nations Assistance Mission for East Timor), which was designed to help facilitate the ballot on independence. Following the violence after the results were announced, the UN announced a follow-on mission titled UNTAET (UN Transitional Administration in East Timor), authorized in UN Security Council Resolution 1272 on 25 October 1999. See DFAT, *East Timor in Transition, 1998–2000*, 156–157.

34. See especially Martin, *Self-Determination in East Timor*.
35. DFAT, *East Timor in Transition, 1998–2000*, 148.
36. Londey, *Other People's Wars*, 249.
37. DFAT, *East Timor in Transition, 1998–2000*, 148.
38. Smith and Dee, *Peacekeeping in East Timor*, 69.
39. Londey, *Other People's Wars*, 257.
40. UN Security Council Resolution 1272, authorized 25 October 1999.
41. Smith and Dee, *Peacekeeping in East Timor*, 160.
42. Ibid., 59.
43. Ibid., 63.
44. Ibid., 65.
45. The quote comes from Chopra, "The UN's Kingdom of East Timor," 29. See also Smith and Dee, *Peacekeeping in East Timor*, 65.
46. See particularly Chopra, "The UN's Kingdom of East Timor."
47. Governo Republica Democratica de Timor Leste, *Timor Leste*, 26.
48. Ibid., 27.
49. Ministry of Planning and Finance, Timor Leste, *Poverty in a New Nation*, xv.
50. Traub, "Inventing East Timor." For a criticism of Traub's reading of the country, see Wedgewood, "Trouble in Timor."
51. Smith and Dee, *Peacekeeping in East Timor*, 66.
52. UN Security Council, "Report of the Secretary-General on the United Nations Transitional Administration in East Timor," 17 April 2002, para. 4.
53. BBC News, "Australia Rapped over E Timor Oil."
54. Ball, "The Defence of East Timor: A Recipe for Disaster?," 176.
55. Quoted in ibid., 176.
56. *Independent Study on the Security Force Options and Security Sector Reform for East Timor*.
57. Ball, "The Defence of East Timor: A Recipe for Disaster?," 178.
58. BBC News, "Indonesia and E Timor Heal Wounds."
59. UN News Centre, "UN Peacekeeping Mission in East Timor Comes to an End."
60. BBC News, "E Timor Rally for School Religion."
61. BBC News, "E Timor Troops Riot over Sacking."
62. International Crisis Group, *Resolving Timor-Leste's Crisis*, 6.
63. Ibid., 6–7.
64. Ibid., 8.
65. Associated Press, "Ex-Soldiers Burn Cars, Shops in East Timor."
66. International Crisis Group, *Resolving Timor-Leste's Crisis*, 9.
67. Ibid., 11.
68. Ibid., 11–12.
69. Ibid., 15.
70. The UNMIT Mandate is available at www.un.org/en/peacekeeping/missions/unmit/mandate.shtml, accessed 11 April 2011.
71. ABC News Online, "East Timor PM Calls Off Hunt for Rebel Leader."
72. Fitzpatrick, "Fretilin Sidelined in Timorese Cabinet."
73. O'Brien, "East Timor Rioters Attack UN Convoy as Violence Expands East."
74. Joliffe, "Ramos-Horta Shot Twice."

75. Greenlees, "Hundreds Mourn at Burial of East Timor Rebel."
76. Murdoch, "President Pardons Rebels Who Shot Him."
77. Traub, "Inventing East Timor."
78. Kilcullen, *The Accidental Guerrilla*, 208.
79. International Crisis Group, *Resolving Timor-Leste's Crisis*, 1.
80. Traub, "Inventing East Timor."
81. Shoesmith, "Divided Leadership in a Semi-Presidential System," 231–252.
82. Ibid., 238.
83. Ibid., 240.
84. Greenlees and Garran, *Deliverance*, 19.
85. Babo Soares, "Political Developments Leading to the Referendum," 57–58.
86. Shoesmith, "Divided Leadership in a Semi-Presidential System," 235.
87. International Crisis Group, *Resolving Timor-Leste's Crisis*, 3.
88. Ibid., 4.
89. Shoesmith, "Divided Leadership in a Semi-Presidential System," 241.
90. International Crisis Group, *Resolving Timor-Leste's Crisis*, 4.
91. Ibid., 5.
92. Rees, "The UN's Failure to Integrate Falintil Veterans May Cause East Timor to Fail." Also quoted in full in International Crisis Group, "Timor-Leste Security Sector Reform," n. 27.
93. Internal UN Report, quoted on International Crisis Group, *Resolving Timor-Leste's Crisis*, 5–6.
94. Scambray, "Anatomy of a Conflict," 268.
95. International Crisis Group, *Resolving Timor-Leste's Crisis*, 5.
96. Scambray, "Anatomy of a Conflict," 270.
97. Ibid.
98. International Crisis Group, *Resolving Timor-Leste's Crisis*, 5.
99. International Crisis Group, *Timor-Leste Security Sector Reform*, 14–15.
100. Scambray, "Anatomy of a Conflict," 270.
101. Australian Broadcasting Corporation, "Alkatiri Denies Arming Own Security Force."
102. International Crisis Group, *Resolving Timor-Leste's Crisis*, 6.
103. Ibid., 12.
104. Scambray, "Anatomy of a Conflict," 269.
105. Fogarty, "Who Are the Rebels?"
106. Scambray, "A Survey of Gangs and Youth Groups in Dili, Timor-Leste," 12.
107. Smith, "Timor Leste: Strong Government, Weak State," 286.
108. Scambray, "Anatomy of a Conflict," 268.
109. Scambray, "A Survey of Gangs and Youth Groups in Dili, Timor-Leste," 13.
110. International Crisis Group, *Resolving Timor-Leste's Crisis*, 3.
111. Scambray, "A Survey of Gangs and Youth Groups in Dili, Timor-Leste," 13.
112. Scambray, "Anatomy of a Conflict," 269.
113. Scambray, "A Survey of Gangs and Youth Groups in Dili, Timor-Leste," 14.
114. Radio Australia, "UN Steps Up Security Ahead of Elections."
115. *Sydney Morning Herald*, "East Timor Tense as Soldiers Desert Barracks."
116. Scambray, "A Survey of Gangs and Youth Groups in Dili, Timor-Leste," 13.
117. Scambray, "Anatomy of a Conflict," 269.

118. Ibid., 271.

119. Scambray, "A Survey of Gangs and Youth Groups in Dili, Timor-Leste," 6.

120. Ibid., Annex 02, 22–23.

121. McDonald et al., *Masters of Terror*, 72.

122. Modvig et al., "Torture and Trauma in Post-Conflict East Timor," 1763.

123. Dunn, *East Timor*, 375.

124. Ibid., 375.

125. Ibid., 375–376.

126. Traub, "Inventing East Timor," 81.

127. This number is disputed by some observers who consider it inflated for the purposes of attaining more international assistance. See Human Rights Watch, "Indonesia/East Timor: Forced Expulsions to West Timor and the Refugee Crisis."

128. Ibid. See also Londey, *Other People's Wars*, 249.

129. Human Rights Watch, "Indonesia/East Timor: Forced Expulsions to West Timor and the Refugee Crisis."

130. Interview with General Smith.

131. Interview with Candeias.

132. Interview with Clark, UNPOL officer in Liquicia.

133. UN Security Council, "Report of the Secretary-General on the United Nations Transitional Administration in East Timor," 17 April 2002, para. 39.

134. U.S. Department of State Cable, Ref 27 State 230264, February 2001, para 2.

135. Ibid., para 3.

136. Ibid., para 5.3.

137. A 2009 estimate suggests that one-third of all women in East Timor had been victims of domestic violence. See Hodal, "Timor-Leste Strives to Overcome Culture of Domestic Violence." Both NGO officials and the police remarked to the author that domestic violence played a significant role in the assault totals during this period, but no hard data were available.

138. This point was made to the author in repeated interactions with UN and PNTL officials in field visits to East Timor in April–May 2005.

139. These crime statistics were obtained in hard copy from the PNTL headquarters. There are no reliable crime statistics from before this period, and no other public source of crime statistics for East Timor exists. The table of violent crime is exactly as they had calculated it and excludes some crimes—such as rape and sexual assault—normally classified as violent crime.

140. Interview with two senior Serious Crimes Unit UNPOL officers.

141. PNTL Crime Statistics 2003, provided directly to author.

142. Ibid.

143. Ibid.

144. UNPOL statistics, U.S. Department of State Cable, entitled East Timor Criminal Activities for the Week Ending October 30, 2004, para 8.

145. Ibid.

146. Ibid., para 9.

147. Internal PNTL crime statistics, provided to author in Dili, May 2005. The definition of violent crimes is somewhat idiosyncratic here, as the PNTL includes suicides and child abuse as violent crimes but counts rapes and sexual assaults in a separate category.

148. Ibid.

149. Most of the events of strategic violence were clustered in 1999–2000, with only four events in 2001, two each in 2002 and 2003, and none in 2004.

150. Interview with Clark, UNPOL/ICITAP.

151. McDonald et al., *Masters of Terror*, 70.

152. Ibid.

153. Crouch, "The TNI and East Timor Policy," 160. The "willing" members of the population who would prefer to be transferred by the TNI to West Timor was estimated to be 200,000.

154. Ball, "Silent Witness: Australian Intelligence and East Timor," in McDonald et al. *Masters of Terror*, 246.

155. According to a defector, Tomas Goncalves, the governor of Timor, Abilio Osorio Soares, issued this order at a meeting in Dili on 26 March 1999. See McDonald et al., *Masters of Terror*, 250.

156. Dunn, quoted in ibid., 73.

157. Ibid.

158. Interview with Major General Smith.

159. Ibid. See also Smith and Dee, *Peacekeeping in East Timor*, 86.

160. Interview with Clark.

161. On lisan, see Senier, "Traditional Justice as Transitional Justice," 67–88. See also interview with Dos Santos.

162. International Crisis Group, *Resolving Timor-Leste's Crisis*, 4.

163. Ibid.

164. Ibid., 4–5.

165. BBC News, "East Timor Declares State of Alert."

166. UNMISET, "Executive Summary of Investigations of Police Response to the Riots of 4 December 2002," para 18.

167. International Crisis Group, *Resolving Timor-Leste's Crisis*, 5.

168. BBC News, "East Timor Declares State of Alert."

169. Quoted in UNMISET, "Executive Summary of Investigations of Police Response to the Riots of 4 December 2002," para 6.

170. Head, "E Timor's 'Wrong Kind of Leader.'"

171. McCall, "Timor Fighter Turns His Venom on Its Leaders."

172. Donnan, "East Timor's Ethnic Violence Puzzles Analysts."

173. International Crisis Group, *Resolving Timor-Leste's Crisis*, 6.

174. Interview with Clark. This point was also made to the author by numerous observers when the author was present in Dili for the April–May 2005 riots.

175. Report of the United Nations Special Commission of Inquiry for Timor Leste, 2 October 2006, quoted in USAID, "The Crisis in Timor-Leste," n. 34.

176. Quoted in Sahin, "Building the State in Timor-Leste," 258.

177. Ibid., 259.

178. Ibid.

179. International Crisis Group, *Resolving Timor-Leste's Crisis*, 7.

180. Ibid., 7–8.

181. See particularly Horowitz, *The Deadly Ethnic Riot*.

182. Scambray, "Anatomy of a Conflict," 273.

183. Ibid.
184. Ibid., 277.
185. International Crisis Group, *Resolving Timor-Leste's Crisis*, 8.
186. Ibid., 9.
187. Ibid., 11.
188. Ibid., 12.
189. Scambray, "Anatomy of a Conflict," 275.
190. Ibid., 273.
191. BBC News, "E Timor PM Accused of Unrest."
192. United Nations, "Report of the United Nations Independent Commission of Inquiry," 5–7, chronology quoted in Scambray, "Anatomy of a Conflict," 272.
193. Scambray, "Anatomy of a Conflict," 274.
194. Gusmao, "CNRT Was Born to Serve Our Nation and People."

Chapter 8 · Iraq

1. On the multiple rationales for the Iraq war, see Boyle, "A War in Search of a Rationale."
2. This was known as the 1 percent doctrine, which held that any substantial risk of possible cooperation between states having weapons of mass destruction program and terrorist organizations must be treated as a certainty and dealt with as an existing, rather than potential, threat. See Suskind, *The One Percent Doctrine*.
3. This assumption was revealed in the Army's War Plan, called Eclipse II, which was discussed in an Army War College internal summary document. See Ricks, *Fiasco*, 110.
4. The oft-repeated argument that the United States had no plan for postwar Iraq is not true. The Office of Reconstruction and Humanitarian Assistance, led by Jay Garner, had developed reasonably sophisticated plans for a refugee crisis and humanitarian relief but was stymied by others within the administration, notably Donald Rumsfeld, from developing and funding a coherent reconstruction plan. See Packer, *The Assassin's Gate*, 120–124.
5. In October 2002, Secretary of Defense Donald Rumsfeld did compose a memorandum that identified the types of problems that the United States could face in Iraq and mentioned an unconventional struggle by Iraqi intelligence forces and ethnic strife between Sunnis, Shiites, and Kurds, but his note did not receive wide circulation. See Woodward, *Plan of Attack*, 205–206.
6. Vice President Cheney made this comment in a *Meet the Press* interview on 16 March 2003. See Woodward, *State of Denial*, 151.
7. This comment was drawn from a *60 Minutes* interview in 2007. See CNN, "Bush: Congress Can't Stop Troop Increase."
8. As noted in chapter 3, this chapter presents all of the data from 2003 to 2008, despite the fact that only 2003 clearly qualifies as a post-conflict year.
9. See Fearon, "Iraq's Civil War."
10. Biddle and Friedman, "The Iraq Data Debate."
11. Donald Horowitz defines a precipitant act broadly, as one that is sufficient to generate future violence. The precipitant event and the violence that follows may sometimes have the same social or political causes. See Horowitz, *The Deadly Ethnic Riot*, 1–42.
12. CNN, "Gunmen Strikes at 27 Baghdad Mosques, Kill Imams."

13. Fearon, "Iraq's Civil War."

14. As will be revealed in the data analysis section, Iraq reached the first month with more than 1,000 people killed in June 2004, by which point the annual total of civilians killed was 1,255. If this total includes the totals of coalition and Iraqi security forces, it would be reached even earlier.

15. Woodward, *State of Denial*.

16. On al Qaeda in Iraq, see Marten, *Warlords*, 148–152.

17. These data were collected by the author via a Freedom of Information Request and delivered directly by CENTCOM on 10 May 2010.

18. For the history of Iraq, and an account of why the nuclear, chemical, and biological weapons program became such a concern for the United States following the Persian Gulf War in 1991, see Butler, *Saddam Defiant*; Adeed Dawisha, *Iraq*; Dodge, *Inventing Iraq*; Polk, *Understanding Iraq*; Simons, *Iraq*; Sluglett, *Britain in Iraq*; Stansfield, *Iraq*; Tripp, *A History of Iraq*.

19. See particularly the account in Clarke, *Against All Enemies*. President Bush is quoted as saying that the United States will go after Iraq at a time of its choosing as early as 15 September 2001. See Gordon and Trainor, *Cobra II*, 19.

20. The quote is from an address given by President Bush in Cincinnati. CNN, "Bush: Don't Wait for Mushroom Cloud." It is well known today that there was no large scale WMD program in Iraq. See the full discussion in Circincione et al., *WMD in Iraq*.

21. Radio Free Europe, "FBI Reports: Saddam's Weapons Bluff Aimed at Iran."

22. UN Security Council Resolution 1441, 8 November 2002.

23. Benedetto, "Poll: Most Back War, but Want UN Support."

24. Carter, "Iraq: Summary of Forces," 2.

25. See Woodward, *Plan of Attack*. By some unconfirmed estimates, between thirty thousand and sixty thousand Iraqis were killed in the invasion. See ibid., 407–408.

26. This decision was taken largely by Secretary of Defense Donald Rumsfeld, who objected to estimates that approximately 300,000–400,000 troops would be needed.

27. BBC News, "Saddam Hussein Arrested in Iraq."

28. Allawi, *The Occupation of Iraq*, 94.

29. Direct quote from Robert Giffords, U.S. adviser to the Interior Ministry, quoted in Bremer, *My Year in Iraq*, 19.

30. Allawi, *The Occupation of Iraq*, 116–117.

31. Loughlan, "Rumsfeld on Looting in Iraq: Stuff Happens."

32. Quinlivan, "Burden of Victory."

33. Larry Diamond, *Squandered Victory*, 32.

34. Ibid., 35.

35. Ibid., 37.

36. Bremer, *My Year in Iraq*, 63.

37. Ibid., 40–41.

38. Dobbins et al., *Occupying Iraq*, xxvii.

39. Bremer, *My Year in Iraq*, 45.

40. Diamond, *Squandered Victory*, 39.

41. Woodward, *State of Denial*, 194.

42. Dobbins et al., *Occupying Iraq*, xxvii.

43. Allawi, *The Occupation of Iraq*, 151–152.

44. Bremer, *My Year in Iraq*, 57.
45. Ibid.
46. Ricks, *Fiasco*, 162.
47. Ibid., 162–163.
48. Bremer, *My Year in Iraq*, 55. See also Woodward, *State of Denial*, 154. This argument is a somewhat simplistic reading of how the Shi'a and Kurds saw the Iraqi army. See Allawi, *The Occupation of Iraq*, 156–157.
49. Dobbins et al., *Occupying Iraq*, 53–55.
50. Bremer, *My Year in Iraq*, 58. On the payment for the initial, see Bensahel et al., *After Saddam*, 144.
51. Quoted in Diamond, *Squandered Victory*, 39.
52. Ibid., 39–40.
53. Estimate is from Dobbins et al., *Occupying Iraq*, 55.
54. Ricks, *Fiasco*, 163.
55. Ibid.
56. Allawi, *The Occupation of Iraq*, 158.
57. Klein, "Saddam's Revenge."
58. Woodward, *State of Denial*, 184.
59. Allawi, *The Occupation of Iraq*, 144–145.
60. Quoted in Diamond, *Squandered Victory*, 42.
61. Bremer, *My Year in Iraq*, 82.
62. Diamond, *Squandered Victory*, 43.
63. Stansfield, *Iraq*, 171–172.
64. Allawi, *The Occupation of Iraq*, 137.
65. Cockburn, *Moqtada al-Sadr*, 135.
66. See *The Iraq Study Group Report*.
67. CNN, "Truck Bomb Kills Chief UN Envoy to Iraq."
68. Cockburn, *Moqtada al-Sadr*, 136.
69. Ibid., 144.
70. This account borrows significantly from ibid., 144–145.
71. Diamond, *Squandered Victory*, 239.
72. U.S. Department of State, Cable from Political-Military Action Team No. 1986, 10 October 2004, FOIA request Case 200702866 PM2, in the possession of author.
73. Ricks, *Fiasco*, 392–404.
74. Cockburn, *Moqtada al-Sadr*, 146–147.
75. Katzman, *Iraq*, 34.
76. Stansfield, *Iraq*, 175.
77. Ibid., 182–183.
78. BBC News, "Iraq Constitution Boycott Is Over."
79. Cockburn, *Moqtada al-Sadr*, 188.
80. *Iraq Study Group Report*, xiii.
81. BBC News, "Up to 200 Killed in Baghdad Bombs."
82. Graff, "Yazidis Fear Annihilation after Iraq Bombings."
83. There is no consensus on why the Awakening/SOI movements emerged and took hold as they did at that point. Marc Lynch emphasizes the role of dialogue and engagement among

Sunnis to form a consensus to oppose AQI, while Marten emphasizes that U.S. support was the glue that made the SOI movements stick together. See Lynch, "Explaining the Awakening," and Marten, *Warlords*, 139–186.

84. *International Herald Tribune*, "A Dark Side to Iraq 'Awakening' Groups."

85. A recent analysis found that the "surge" was effective, but only in tandem with changes on the ground, including the arrival of Awakening/SOI movements, in reducing violence. See Biddle et al., "Testing the Surge," 7–40.

86. Metz, "Insurgency and Counterinsurgency in Iraq," 28.

87. See Beckett, "Insurgency in Iraq," 6, and Metz, "Insurgency and Counter-Insurgency in Iraq," 28–29.

88. Fearon, "Iraq's Civil War," 5.

89. Moore and Roug, "Deaths across Iraq Shows."

90. Hafez calls this system integration (where Sunni nationalist groups sought inclusion in the government), as opposed to system collapse. See Hafez, "Suicide Terrorism in Iraq," 599.

91. See the discussion in Kaplan, "Who Disbanded the Iraqi Army?"

92. See particularly Woodward, *Plan of Attack*.

93. Colonel Kevin Benson, quoted in Ricks, *Fiasco*, 163.

94. Ibid., 164. For a full discussion of the impact of the psyops campaign, see Hosmer, *Iraqi Resistance*, 104–108.

95. Khairi Jassim, quoted in Ricks, *Fiasco*, 164.

96. Ibid.

97. Gordon and Trainor, *Cobra II*, 556.

98. Ricks, *Fiasco*, 164–165.

99. Gordon and Trainor, *Cobra II*, 555.

100. Ricks, *Fiasco*, 165.

101. Marten, *Warlords*, 145.

102. Quinlivan, "Coup-Proofing."

103. Marten, *Warlords*, 145.

104. Ibid., 145, n. 28.

105. Those on the ground in Iraq often wryly noted that CPA stood for "Can't Produce Anything." See Chandrasekaran, *Imperial Life in the Emerald City*.

106. Woodward, *State of Denial*, 188–189.

107. Gordon and Trainor, *Cobra II*, 556.

108. Cockburn, *The Occupation*, 71.

109. al-Marashi, "Disbanding and Rebuilding the Iraqi Army," 46–47.

110. Hashim, *Insurgency and Counterinsurgency in Iraq*, 19.

111. Klein, "Saddam's Revenge."

112. Bremer, *My Year in Iraq*, 127.

113. See, for instance, an interview with Izzat al-Douri, a former Saddam Hussein lieutenant who was an active force in the insurgency during this period and after. See Ghosh, "Exclusive: Insurgent Ba'athist in His Own Words."

114. Hendren, "Ex-Baathists Play Crucial Insurgent Role, U.S. Says."

115. Ibid.

116. International Crisis Group, *In their Own Words*.

117. Testimony of Daniel L. Glaser, Acting Assistant Secretary for Terrorist Financing and

Financial Crimes, U.S. Department of the Treasury, before the House Financial Services Subcommittee on Oversight and Investigations and House Armed Services Subcommittee on Terrorism, 28 July 2005, 2.

118. Hafez, *Suicide Bombers in Iraq*, 40–44.

119. Ibid., 37.

120. Ibid., 39. ICG, *In their Own Words*, 1–3.

121. Ibid.

122. Ibid., 7.

123. Ibid., 8.

124. Hafez, *Suicide Bombers in Iraq*, 63–64.

125. Ibid., 64–70.

126. Hafez, *Suicide Bombers in Iraq*, 71. See also Tilghman, "The Myth of AQI."

127. U.S. Department of State, Cable from Political-Military Action Team No. 1902, 29 July 2004, FOIA request Case 200702866 PM2, in the possession of author.

128. Hafez, *Suicide Bombers in Iraq*, 76–77.

129. Cockburn, *Moqtada al-Sadr*, 179.

130. Ricks, *Fiasco*, 436.

131. Cochrane, *Iraq Report 12*, 13.

132. Ibid., 15.

133. Ibid., 21.

134. Cockburn, *Moqtada al-Sadr*, 132.

135. Beeher, *Iraq's Militia Groups*; Knickmeyer, "Official: Guard Force Is Behind Death Squads."

136. Cockburn, *Moqtada al- Sadr*, 132.

137. On the history of the Kurds, see Bulloch, *No Friends but the Mountains*; McDowall, *A Modern History of the Kurds*; Romano, *The Kurdish Nationalist Movement*.

138. See Katzman, *Iraq*, 33.

139. U.S. Department of State, Cable from Political-Military Action Team No. 1798, 27 April 2004, in the possession of author.

140. Quoted in International Crisis Group, *Where Is Iraq Heading?*, 10.

141. Posen, "The Security Dilemma and Ethnic Conflict." For a recent application to Iraq, see Kaufmann, "What Have We Learned about Ethnic Conflict?"

142. There are numerous sources for data on violence against civilians in Iraq. This chapter uses previously unreleased data collected by the U.S. Central Command. This is a possibly low estimate, for some studies have suggested that the military may undercount the total number killed. For an overview of this debate, see Fischer, "Iraqi Civilian Death Estimates." Unofficial data also vary significantly in the estimated numbers killed. The Iraq Index, introduced by the Brookings Institute, culls official statistics released by the Department of Defense and other sources to generate a single composite source and is updated on a biweekly basis. Other unofficial sources include the Iraqi Body Count (www.iraqbodycount.org/) and the Iraq Coalition Casualty Count (http://icasualties.org/oif/IraqiDeaths.aspx). Finally, and most controversially, two *Lancet* studies—one produced in 2004 and a second, more detailed study in 2006—have estimated the numbers killed as high as 655,000. These studies have come under criticism for their methodology. See Roberts et al., "Mortality before and after the 2003 Invasion of Iraq," and Burnham et al., "Mortality after the 2003 Invasion of Iraq." For a good discussion of the

controversy, see Brown, "Study Claims Iraq's 'Excess' Death Toll Has Reached 655,000." For a critique of the *Lancet* studies, see Kane, "The Lancet Surveys of Mortality in Iraq."

143. The sectarian composition of each region is derived from a CIA ethnographic mapping done in 2003. See www.lib.utexas.edu/maps/middle_east_and_asia/iraq_ethno_2003.jpg.

144. Hsiao-Rei Hicks et al., "Violent Deaths of Iraqi Civilians, 2003–2008," 3.

145. Ibid., 4, table 1.

146. Ibid., 3.

147. Ibid., 5, table 2.

148. Brookings Institute, Iraq Index (29 May 2011), 11.

149. See particularly International Crisis Group, *The Next Iraqi War*.

150. *Washington Post*, "Iraqis Hunting, Killing Former Baathists."

151. Carnegie, "Wave of Baghdad Killings."

152. Fisk, "Hooded Men Executing Saddam Officials."

153. Brinkley, "Revenge Killings Thin Ex-Baathists Ranks."

154. Coker, "Revenge Killings Are Soaring in Iraq."

155. Ibid.

156. See particularly Fisk, "Hooded Men Executing Saddam Officials," and Coker, "Revenge Killings Are Soaring in Iraq."

157. Hasan, "Hardline Group Denies Involvement in 'Revenge Killings' in Basra."

158. Quote is from a senior Iraqi police officer interviewed in ibid.

159. Immigration and Refugee Board of Canada, "Iraq: Reports of violence and acts of revenge against the general population against the officials and their families of Saddam Hussein's regime following Hussein's fall," 15 January 2004, IRQ42228.E.

160. Ratnesar et al., "Vengeance Has Its Day."

161. BBC News, "Revenge Attacks Target Former Regime."

162. For a similar dynamic, see Boyle, "Revenge and Reprisal Violence in Kosovo."

163. Blair, "Saddam Empties Iraq's Jails."

164. Williams, "Criminals, Militias and Insurgents," 26.

165. Siperco, "Subversive Markets."

166. Semple, "Kidnapped in Iraq: Victim's Tale of Clockwork Death and Ransom."

167. Glanz and Worth, "Attacks on Iraq Oil Industry Aid Vast Smuggling Scheme."

168. Semple, "Kidnapped in Iraq,"

169. See particularly the account in Stewart, *Occupational Hazards*.

170. Cave, "Hunt for 3 G.I.s in Iraq Slowed by False Trails."

171. On this dynamic, see Boyle, "Bargaining, Fear and Denial."

172. The Mahdi Army behaves differently from region to region in part because it is inchoate and high-factionalized, which has led Moqtada al-Sadr to call a six-month freeze in activity in 2007 so that he can "reorganize" it. See BBC News, "Sadr 'Freezes' Militia Activities."

173. This echoes a distinction drawn by Stathis Kalyvas, when he speaks of the gap between the macro-level explanation for a conflict and its microfoundations. See Kalyvas, *The Logic of Violence in Civil Wars*, 388–392.

174. See, for instance, McCormick and Owen, "Factionalism, Violence and Bargaining in Civil Wars," 361–390.

175. Crenshaw, "The Causes of Terrorism," 387.

176. Cited in Hafez, *Suicide Bombers in Iraq*, 94.

177. Bodies reported in the IBC dataset (October 2007).
178. Unconfirmed estimate from the Iraqi Islamic Party, cited in UN Assistant Mission for Iraq (UNAMI), Human Rights Report, 1 January–28 February 2006.
179. UN Assistant Mission for Iraq (UNAMI), Human Rights Report, 1 January–28 February 2006, para 11.
180. UN Assistant Mission for Iraq (UNAMI), Human Rights Report, 1 March–30 April 2006, 1–2.
181. Hafez, "Suicide Terrorism in Iraq," 608–611.
182. Tavernise, "Cycle of Revenge Fuels a Pattern in Iraqi Killings."
183. The Brookings Institute, Iraq Index (29 May 2011), 7. The Iraq Index estimates that during this period Shi'a constituted 4,785 victims of the 11,632 killed in multiple fatality bombings.
184. UN Assistant Mission for Iraq (UNAMI), Human Rights Report, 1 March–30 April 2006, 2.
185. Knickmeyer and Saif Aldin, "Dozens of Iraqis Killed in Reprisals."
186. Cordesman, *Iraq's Evolving Insurgency*, 93.
187. Kukis, "Ethnic Cleansing in a Baghdad Neighbourhood."
188. See in particular al-Khalidi and Tanner, "Sectarian Violence."
189. See Kukis, "Ethnic Cleansing in a Baghdad Neighbourhood."
190. Cockburn, "Destruction of Holiest Shia Shrine Brings Iraq to the Brink of Civil War."
191. Cordesman, *Iraq's Evolving Insurgency*, 93.
192. ICG, *Where Is Iraq Heading?*
193. Ibid., i.
194. Johnson, "Seeing with One Eye Open." On average, 48.7 percent of all violent incidents between August 2006 and August 2007 were classified as nonsectarian. In a three month sample (May–August 2007), 2,667 murders were classified as sectarian.
195. See Bloom, *Dying to Kill*.
196. International Crisis Group, *Where Is Iraq Heading?*
197. Ibid., 18.
198. This number is drawn from the Iraq Body Count estimate, for March–May 2003.
199. Unnamed Iraqi journalist quoted in International Crisis Group, *The Next Iraqi War*, 23.
200. See particularly Kydd and Walter, "The Strategies of Terrorism."
201. Taneja, "Assimilation, Exodus and Eradication."
202. Jackson, "Crushing Iraq's Human Mosaic."
203. Reuters, "Iraqi Red Crescent Says 500 Killed in Yazidi Attack."
204. *USA Today*, "Iraqis Told to Arm for Self-Defense after 220 Killed"; and Howard, "They Won't Stop until We Are All Wiped Out."
205. The term has been developed by Williams, "Organized Crime in Iraq."
206. *USA Today*, "Rumsfeld Blames Iraq Problems on 'Pockets of Dead Enders.'"

Chapter 9 • Controlling Violence: Implications and Policy Recommendations

1. MacGinty, *No War, No Peace*, and Berdal and Suhrke, *The Peace In-Between*.
2. The term custodians of peace comes from Stedman, "Spoiler Problems in Peace Processes."
3. The public security gap has been discussed in various sources. See particularly Oakley et al., *Policing the New World Disorder*, and Call and Barnett, "Looking for a Few Good Cops."

4. This is described in Boyle, "Revenge and Reprisal Violence in Kosovo."

5. George and Bennett, *Case Studies and Theory Development*.

6. The concept of the spiral model is from Jervis, *Perception and Misperception*, 58–113. This has been explicitly applied to Iraq in Kaufmann, "What Have We Learned about Ethnic Conflict?"

7. One exception here would be Kirkuk, where significant violence occurred and conflict spirals were present.

8. As noted earlier, this insight on the heterogeneity of armed groups has recently been explored in Weinstein, *Inside Rebellion*; Nilsson, *Dangerous Liaisons*; Kreutz, "Navigating the Fog of Peace"; Cunningham, "Divide and Conquer or Divide and Concede"; Bakke et al., "A Plague of Initials"; Cunningham et al., "Shirts Today, Skins Tomorrow."

9. Chivers and Krauss, "Six Dead as Libyan Militias Clash Near Tripoli."

10. Sengupta and Hughes, "Leaked UN Report Reveals Torture, Lynching and Abuse in Post-Gaddafi Libya."

11. Kirkpatrick, "In Libya, the Fighting May Outlast the Revolution."

12. This point was recognized in Stedman, "Spoiler Problems in Peace Processes."

13. See Stedman's description of inside spoilers in ibid., 8–9.

14. Bloom, *Dying to Kill*.

15. On the victor's peace, see Berdal and Suhrke, *The Peace In-Between*.

16. The term *Hobbesian nightmare* was used by Dodge in his "Staticide in Iraq," available at http://mondediplo.com/2007/02/04iran, accessed 10 November 2011.

17. This second observation is also made in Kalyvas, *The Logic of Violence in Civil War*.

18. A similar argument is developed at length in Autesserre, *The Trouble with Congo*.

19. Similarly, there is a vast amount of literature on the post-conflict reconciliation and judicial programs that dwarfs the relatively few studies on violence in post-conflict states. This reflects the overall bias toward considering reconciliation and prosecution of war crimes as effective remedies in post-conflict states and overlooks the central role played by violence within them. It is also interesting to note that such assumptions about the capacity of people to forgive in post-conflict states are relatively new. Even leaders like Charles DeGaulle acknowledged that his followers would need some time to seek vengeance and gave his followers forty-eight hours for *régler les comptes* (settling accounts).

20. See particularly Oliver Richmond's argument that such peacekeeping missions produce a virtual peace. See Richmond, "UN Peace Operations and the Dilemmas of the Peacebuilding Consensus." For a similar application that makes the point about how this can ignore local forms of peace, see MacGinty, "Indigenous Peacemaking versus Liberal Peace."

21. Stedman, "Spoiler Problems in Peace Processes," 17–18.

22. This is often, though not always, derived from the view that ancient ethnic hatreds cause conflict. The seminal statement of this view is Kaplan, *Balkan Ghosts*.

23. O'Neill, *Kosovo*, 62.

24. Quoted in ibid., 52.

25. Quoted in ibid., 53.

26. Autesserre, *The Trouble with Congo*, 72.

27. Boyle, "Policing the Neo-Imperial Frontier."

28. The literature on DDR is vast and largely consists of case studies and lessons learned, often sponsored by international organizations. For an introduction and overview, see Berdal,

Disarmament and Demobilization after Civil Wars. For an empirical analysis that suggests that UN sponsored DDR programs are less effective than assumed, see Humpfreys and Weinstein, "Demobilization and Reintegration." For a conceptual critique, see Muggah, "No Magic Bullet."

29. More generally, the number of young men in a society is related to its risk of civil conflict. See Collier and Hoeffler, "Greed and Grievance in Civil War."

30. On the trauma of fighters, see Humphreys and Weinstein, "What the Fighters Say." Interestingly, the common assumption that ex-combatants will get involved in petty crime may not be warranted. A study by Paul Collier in 2004 found no evidence that ex-combatants were more involved in petty crime than others in the population. See Collier, "Demobilization and Insecurity."

31. It is not fair to suggest that the international organizations push DDR programs that are one-size-fits-all models. One of the recurring themes in this academic and policy literature is that DDR programs must be holistic and suited to local needs, and existing programs have gone to great lengths to be tailored to individual's needs.

32. In many of these cases, this is seen as corruption and runs against the grain of the rule-of-law initiatives favored by foreign donors.

33. Mulrine, "Marine Chief: Disbanding Iraqi Army Was a Big Mistake." This was a view widely held within the U.S. government after 2004 and a debate over who was responsible for this mistake carried on for years. For a discussion, see Kaplan, "Who Disbanded the Iraqi Army?," available at www.slate.com/articles/news_and_politics/war_stories/2007/09/who_disbanded_the_iraqi_army.html, accessed 12 July 2012.

34. See Perito, *Where Is the Lone Ranger?*, and Perito and Bayley, *The Police in War*.

35. This fact was conveyed to the author by UNTAET officials during his visit to Dili in May 2005.

36. The author negotiated this access with the UN and searched through dozens of boxes to find crime statistics, which were kept in hard copies scattered throughout the files. This research was conducted in September 2008.

BIBLIOGRAPHY

Cited Interviews

Avery, John, Crime Analysis Unit, UNMIK CIVPOL, Pristina, Kosovo, 24 March 2003.
Candeias, Sophia, Legal Office, Serious Crimes Unit, Dili, East Timor, 24 April 2005.
Clark, Karl, former UNPOL officer in Liquicia and current ICITAP officer, Dili, East Timor, 24 April 2005.
Dos Santos, Casmiro, Judicial System Monitoring Program, Dili, East Timor, 25 April 2005.
Gentile, Andrea, Mission Management Division, CIVPOL Office, Department of Peacekeeping Operations, UN Secretariat, New York, 15 April 2003.
Kaplan, Phil, Political Officer, U.S. Department of State, Washington, DC, 28 March 2001.
Nauman, General Klaus (Germany), London, 13 September 2002.
Senior officers (interview with two officers on background), Serious Crimes Unit UNPOL, Dili, 28 April 2005.
Senior official (interview on background), U.S. State Department, Washington, DC, 28 March 2001.
Siebentritt, Carl, former Political Officer at U.S. Office Pristina, Amalfi Restaurant, Pristina, Kosovo, 25 June 2002.
Smith, General Mike, Canberra, Australia, 9 May 2005.

Original Sources

American Bar Association, Central and Eastern Europe Law Initiative, and the American Association for the Advancement of Science. *Political Killings in Kosova/Kosovo, March–June 1999*. June 2002.
Bosnia Election Results (1998), reported at http://www.ipu.org/parline-e/reports/arc/2039_98.htm, accessed 15 July 2011.
Brookings Institute. Iraq Index, 29 May 2011. Hard copy.
———. Iraq Index, 12 July 2012, available at http://www.brookings.edu/~/media/Centers/saban/iraq%20index/index201207.pdf, accessed 11 July 2012.
CENTCOM. Iraq violence statistics, 2004–2008. Released to the author via Freedom of Information Act request. Case No. 200702866 PM2.
Central Intelligence Agency. *Memorandum: The Massacres in Rwanda*, 28 April 1994, in possession of author through Freedom of Information Act request F-2009-00120.

Christopher, Warren. "Statement of Warren Christopher, Secretary of State," Foreign Assistance Legislation for Fiscal Year 1994 (Parts 1 and 8), Hearings and markup before the House Foreign Affairs committee, 103 Congress, session 1. Washington, DC: Government Printing Office, 1993.

CIA Ethnographic Mapping, 2003, available at http://www.lib.utexas.edu/maps/middle_east_and_asia/iraq_ethno_2003.jpg.

CIA World Factbook, "Rwanda" https://www.cia.gov/library/publications/the-world-factbook/geos/rw.html, accessed 9 September 2012.

Commission for Reception, Truth and Reconciliation (CAVR). "Responsibility and Accountability," in *Chega! The Report of the Commission for Reception, Truth and Reconciliation* (Dili, 2005).

Correlates of War dataset, available at http://www.correlatesofwar.org/, accessed 11 February 2011.

Dayton Accords, 1995, available at http://www1.umn.edu/humanrts/icty/dayton/daytonaccord.html, accessed 12 June 2011.

Department of Foreign Affairs and Trade (Australia). *East Timor in Transition, 1998–2000: An Australian Policy Challenge.* Canberra, 2001.

Department of State Memorandum Addressed to Undersecretary of State Paula Dobriansky, Subject: Iraq Contingency Planning, 7 February 2003 at http://www.gwu.edu/~nsarchiv/NSAEBB/NSAEBB163/iraq-state-03.pdf accessed 11 July 2012.

European Commission, Emergency Assessment of Damaged House and Local/Village Infrastructure, Kosovo Damage Assessment, July 1999.

General Accounting Office. "Bosnia Peace Operation: Progress toward Achieving the Dayton Agreement's Goals," February 1997, available at http://www.gpo.gov/fdsys/pkg/GAOREPORTS-NSIAD-97-132/pdf/GAOREPORTS-NSIAD-97-132.pdf, accessed 11 June 2012.

———. "Bosnia Peace Operations." Washington, DC, June 1998, available at http://www.gao.gov/archive/1998/ns98138.pdf, accessed 15 July 2011.

———. Crime and Corruption Threaten Successful Implementation of Dayton Peace Agreement. Washington, DC, 2000, GAO/NSIAD-00-156.

Gersony Report Summary, "Summary of UNHCR Presentation Before Commission of Experts, 10 October 1994, Prospects for Early Repatriation of Rwandan refugees currently in Burundi, Tanzania and Zaire." Covering note written by Francois Fouinat to Mrs. B. Molina-Abram, Secretary of the Commission of Experts on Rwanda, on 11 October 1994. Hard copy is in the author's possession.

Government of Rwanda. "Rwanda's Comments on the Draft UN Mapping Report on the DRC," available at http://www.ohchr.org/Documents/Countries/ZR/DRC_Report_Comments_Rwanda.pdf, accessed 22 January 2013.

Governo Republica Democratica de Timor Leste. *Timor Leste: Ita Iha Nebe Ona Ohin Loron.* Dili: February 2003.

President Xanana Gusmao. "CNRT Was Born to Serve Our Nation and People," 29 June 2007, available at http://www.prnewswire.co.uk/news-releases/cnrt-was-born-to-serve-our-nation-and-its-people-153580585.html, accessed 6 July 2011.

Heston, Alan, Robert Summers, and Bettina Aten. Penn World Table Version 6.3, Center for International Comparisons of Production, Income and Prices at the University of Pennsylvania, August 2009. The full source and codebook is available at http://pwt.econ.upenn.edu/php_site/pwt_index.php, accessed 11 July 2012.

Immigration and Refugee Board of Canada. "Iraq: Reports of Violence and Acts of Revenge against the General Population against the Officials and Their Families of Saddam Hussein's Regime Following Hussein's Fall." 15 January 2004, IRQ42228.E.

———. "Kosovo/Albania: The Albanian National Army (Armata Kombetare Shqiptare, AKSh)." Profile, 27 August 2008.

Independent Study on the Security Force Options and Security Sector Reform for East Timor. Centre for Defence Studies, King's College London, August 2000.

Interoffice Memorandum, to the Secretary, from Assistant Secretary (Africa) George E. Moose, subject: New Human Rights Abuses in Rwanda, no date listed, in the possession of author.

Interpol. Crime Statistics: Albania, available at http://www.interpol.int/Public/Statistics/ICS/1999/Albania1999.pdf, accessed 13 March 2003.

Introduction. Report of the Commission for Historical Clarification, 1999, available at http://shr.aaas.org/guatemala/ceh/report/english/toc.html, accessed 13 April 2010.

IPTF, Office of the Commissioner. UN IPTF Status Report, 21 August 1997.

Iraq Body Count statistics. http://www.iraqbodycount.org/, accessed 25 March 2009.

Iraq Coalition Casualty Count. http://icasualties.org/oif/IraqiDeaths.aspx, accessed 2 August 2011.

KFOR Intelligence Report, Xhavit Haliti, undated. Hard copy in possession of author.

Ministry for Human Rights and Refugees (BiH). Housing and Urban Profile of Bosnia and Herzegovina: An Outline of Devastations, Recovery and Development Perspectives, Sarajevo, May 2006.

Ministry of Planning and Finance, Timor Leste. *Poverty in a New Nation: Analysis for Action.* Dili: November 2003.

National Intelligence Council Memorandum. 13 May 1994, NIC 00270/94, in possession of author through Freedom of Information Act request F-2009-00120 (22 December 2008).

Northern Ireland Statistics and Research Agency. "Census 2001 Population Report," 2001, available at http://www.nisra.gov.uk/census/pdf/Census2001PopRep.pdf, accessed 13 July 2004.

Office of the High Representative. Decision Removing Ante Jelavic from his position as the Croat member of the Joint Presidency, Sarajevo, 7 March 2001.

OSCE. *Assessment of the Situation of Ethnic Minorities in Kosovo.* 15 February 2000.

———. *Assessment of the Situation of Ethnic Minorities in Kosovo.* 10 October 2000.

———. *Assessment of the Situation of Ethnic Minorities in Kosovo.* 28 July 2001.

———. *Assessment on the Situation of Ethnic Minorities in Kosovo.* 1 October 2001.

———. *Assessment of the Situation of Ethnic Minorities in Kosovo.* 27 May 2002.

———. *Assessment of the Situation of Ethnic Minorities in Kosovo.* 12 March 2003.

———. Election results for the Kosovo Assembly, 2001, available at http://www.osce.org/kosovo/20466.

———. Internal population estimates, 1999–2000. Hard copy provided to the author.

———. Municipal election results for Kosovo, 2000, available at http://www.osce.org/kosovo/20464.

———. Municipal profiles at http://www.osce.org/kosovo/documents/reports/municipal_profiles/, accessed 26 May 2003, hard copies given to author.

———. *Overview of the Situation of Ethnic Minorities in Kosovo.* 3 November 1999.

———. *Preliminary Assessment on the Situation of Minorities in Kosovo.* 10 July 1999.
———. *The Role of the Media in the March 2004 Events in Kosovo.* Vienna, 2004.
———. *Second Assessment of the Situation of Ethnic Mino in Kosovo.* 26 July 1999.
——— *Third Assessment of the Situation of Ethnic Minorities in Kosovo.* 3 November 1999.
OSCE. Office of Democratic Institutions and Human Rights. "Bosnia and Herzegovina Elections, 1998," 12–13 September 1998, available at http://www.osce.org/odihr/elections/bih/14045, accessed 12 June 2011.
———. "Bosnia and Herzegovina Municipal Elections, 13–14 September 1997," available at http://www.osce.org/odihr/elections/bih/14025, accessed 12 June 2011.
OSCE/UNHCR. Assessment on the Situation of Ethnic Minorities in Kosovo, November 1999–January 2000, available at http://www.unhcr.org/3c3c18cf2.html, accessed 21 July 2013.
———. *Update on the Situation of Ethnic Minorities in Kosovo.* 10 June 2000.
Permanent Court of Arbitration website, http://www.pca-cpa.org/showpage.asp?pag_id=1150, accessed 10 July 2012.
PNTL Crime Statistics. 2003. Dili, East Timor. Hard copy given to author.
Police Service of Northern Ireland. Crime Statistics, available at http://www.psni.police.uk/deaths_cy.pdf, accessed 17 July 2012.
Refugee International. SITEP #10, Rwandan Refugees in Tanzania, New Arrivals Report, 17 May 1994.
Report of the OSCE/ODHIR/Council of Europe Field Mission on the situation of the Roma in Kosovo, (27 July–6 August 1999), available at http://www.coe.int/t/dg3/roma travellers/archive/documentation/fieldvisits/missionkosovo99_en.asp, accessed 11 March 2011.
State Department Human Rights Reports, on-line archive, available at http://onlinebooks.library.upenn.edu/webbin/serial?id=crhrp, accessed 11 June 2012.
Testimony of General Eric Shinseki, Senate Armed Services Committee. 25 February 2003.
Testimony of Daniel L. Glaser, Acting Assistant Secretary for Terrorist Financing and Financial Crimes, U.S. Department of the Treasury, before the House Financial Services Subcommittee on Oversight and Investigations and House Armed Services Subcommittee on Terrorism, 28 July 2005.
UNAMIR Mandate. Available at http://www.un.org/en/peacekeeping/missions/past/unamir M.htm, accessed 11 August 2011.
UN Assistant Mission for Iraq (UNAMI). Human Rights Report, 1 January–28 February 2006.
———. Human Rights Report, 1 March–30 April 2006.
UN ECOSOC. UN Commission on Human Rights, Statement of Human Rights Watch, Rights of Persons Belonging to National, Ethnic, Religious or Linguistic Minorities, 17 March 1998.
UNHCR. Bosnia and Herzegovina: Repatriation and Return Operation 1998, Document HIWG/97/7, 10 December 1997.
———. Extremely Vulnerable Individuals: The Need for Continuing International Support in Light of the Difficulties to Reintegration upon Return. Sarajevo, November 1999.
———. Returnee Monitoring Study, Minority Returns to Bosnia and Herzegovina, Geneva, 2000.

———. Returns Summary to Bosnia-Herzegovina, from 1/1/96–1/31/2001, given to author in Sarajevo in July 2008.

———. Target Area Initiative: Facilitating the Return and Reintegration of Refugees and Displaced Persons in Bosnia and Herzegovina. December 1996. Unpublished paper.

———. "UNHCR Condemns Violence against Serb Returnee in Kosovo," 7 October 2003, available at http://www.unhcr.org/3f82afa34.html, accessed 8 January 2012.

———. Update on Conditions for Return to Bosnia and Herzegovina. Geneva, January 2005.

UNMIBH archives

1. Interoffice Memorandum, to Stephen Bowen from Anna Korula, Reporting by Human Rights Office, 7 October 1998, UMMIBH Archives, New York, 2005 0118 box 2.

2. Discussion paper attached to fax scheduling a meeting by Ambassador Donald Hays, Principal Deputy High Representative for Bosnia-Herzegovina, 14 March 2002, Subject: Confirmation of a Meeting. Source: UNMIBH archives, UN headquarters, New York City, box 2003 002 1, transcript in the possession of author.

3. Interoffice Memorandum, to Eric Morris D/SRSG from Vinod Kapur, Chief, Trust Fund, 31 May 1999, UNMIBH archives, UN headquarters, New York City, box 2005 0120 box 34, transcript in the possession of author.

4. Border Service Project/C Input to November 2000 SF Report, File #4, UNMIBH archives, UN headquarters, New York City, box 2005 0120 box 34, transcript in the possession of author.

5. Special Police memorandum, "Note Concerning the Structure and Activities of the Secret Police Organization AID in Bihac Area," 10 December 1997, UNMIBH archives, UN headquarters, New York City, box 2005 0120 box 34, transcript in the possession of author.

UNMIK. Division of Public Information. "Press Release," 11 May 2003.

———. Crime Presentation. Internal Document, February 2001, obtained by author.

———. Crime Statistics. available at http://www.unmikonline.org/civpol/statistics.htm, accessed 28 October 2002, also in hard copy obtained by author.

———. Order 2003/9, available at http://www.unmikonline.org/regulations/adm direct/2003/ADE2003_09.pdf.

UNMISET. "Executive Summary of Investigations of Police Response to the Riots of 4 December 2002."

UN Mission in Kosovo CIVPOL. "Offence Statistics by Motive." Unpublished. 2001–2002.

UNMIT Mandate, available at http://www.un.org/en/peacekeeping/missions/unmit/man date.shtml, accessed 11 April 2011.

UN News Center. "UN Peacekeeping Mission in East Timor Comes to an End." 19 May 2005.

UN Office of Drugs and Crime. International Homicide Rate per 100,000 Persons Fact Sheet, 2004, available at http://www.unodc.org/documents/data-and-analysis/IHS-rates-05012009.pdf, accessed 20 July 2011.

UNPOL statistics. Dili, East Timor, provided in hard copy to author, 2005.

UN Security Council. "Report of the Secretary-General on the United Nations Transitional Administration in East Timor." 17 April 2002.

———. "Report of the Secretary General of the United Nations Interim Administration in Kosovo." 30 April 2005, UN Doc S/2004/348.

———. Resolution 1244, authorized 10 June 1999.

———. Resolution 1272, authorized 25 October 1999.

———. Resolution 1441, authorized 8 November 2002.

U.S. AID. Bosnia and Herzegovina: Conflict Assessment, Washington, DC, July 2005, 13, available at http://pdf.usaid.gov/pdf_docs/PNADD627.pdf, accessed 20 July 2011.

———. "The Crisis in Timor-Leste: Causes, Consequences and Options for Conflict Management and Mitigation." November 2006.

U.S. Department of State. Bosnia and Herzegovina Country Report on Human Rights Practices for 1998, 26 February 1998.

———. Cable, East Timor Criminal Activities for the Week Ending October 30, 2004, October 30, 2004. FOIA request 200600437.

———. Cable, Ref 27 State 230264, February 2001. FOIA request 200600437.

———. Cable from Political-Military Action Team No. 1798 (Iraq), 27 April 2004, FOIA request Case 200702866 PM2.

———. Cable from Political-Military Action Team No. 1902 (Iraq), 29 July 2004, FOIA request Case 200702866 PM2.

———. Cable from Political-Military Action Team No. 1986, 10 October 2004, FOIA request Case 200702866 PM.

———. *Patterns of Global Terrorism 1997.* Washington, DC: April 1998.

Wolfowitz, Paul. Testimony to the House Budget Committee. 27 February 2003.

World Bank. *Bosnia and Herzegovina: Diagnostic Surveys of Corruption.* Washington, DC: 2000, 2, available at http://www1.worldbank.org/publicsector/anticorrupt/Bosnianticorruption.pdf, accessed 21 July 2011.

Secondary Sources

ABC News Online. "East Timor PM Calls Off Hunt for Rebel Leader." 18 April 2007.

Abrashi, Fisnik. "British Peacekeeper Killed, Two Wounded in Kosovo." Associated Press, 14 April 2001.

———. "Ethnic Albanian Killed in Kosovo Grenade Attack, UN Calls Meeting." Associated Press, 29 January 2001.

———. "Russian Peacekeeper Killed Along Kosovo Border." Associated Press, 11 April 2001.

———. "Serbs Shot At, One Injured in Tense Serbian Region Bordering on Kosovo." Associated Press, 16 December 2000.

———. "U.S. Soldiers Wound Two Men in Kosovo Gunfight." Associated Press, 7 March 2001.

Adelman, Howard, and Astri Suhrke. *The Path of Genocide: The Rwanda Crisis from Uganda to Zaire.* New Brunswick: Transaction, 2000.

Agence France Presse. "Australia Resisted ETimor Independence." 2 February 2006.

———. "Bomb Attack Tarnishes Success of Kosovo poll." 6 November 2000.

———. "Bomb Caused Kosovo Political Centre Blast." 19 August 2000.

———. "Bomb Destroys the Offices of Moderate Kosovo Leader." 16 October 2001.

———. "Bosnian Croat Opposition Figure Wounded in Machine Gun Attack." 1 October 1996.

———. "Dozens Injured by Car Bomb in Kosovo." 14 December 2002.

———. "Eight Injured in Western Kosovo Shooting." 4 April 2002.
———. "Elderly Kosovo Serb Murdered, Wife Badly Injured." 29 December 2000.
———. "Ethnic Albanian Former Guerilla Leader Wounded." 7 July 2000.
———. "Ethnic Albanians Attack Peacekeepers after Killings in Kosovo." 5 February 2000.
———. "Ethnic Albanians Kidnap Four Serbs in southern Serbia." 16 February 2001.
———. "Five Albanians Slain in Kosovo Attack." 21 August 2001.
———. "Four Shot Dead, One Body Found in a Kosovo day of Violence." 5 November 2000.
———. "Grenade Attack against Moderate Kosovo Candidate." 23 October 2000.
———. "High-Ranking Officer of the Kosovo Protection Corps Slain." 17 April 2000.
———. "Ibrahim Rugova's Right Hand Man Shot Dead in Kosovo." 23 November 2000.
———. "Kosovo Attacks Wound Serb Woman, Ethnic Albanian Men." 22 June 2000.
———. "Kosovo Serb Shot Dead." 27 August 2000.
———. "Kosovo Serb Shot Dead in Front of Home." 10 January 2000.
———. "Kosovo Serbs Attack UN Police Station, KFOR Peacekeepers." 14 March 2001.
———. "Kosovo Trial Witness Narrowly Escapes Death." 26 September 2003.
———. "Kosovo Violence Could Have Been Organized—Top NATO Official." 18 March 2004.
———. "Member of Kosovo Protection Corps Murdered." 1 October 2000.
———. "More than 900 Kosovo Albanians Displaced in Divided Town." 12 February 2000.
———. "Mortar Attack against Serb Police near Kosovo: Judge." 10 July 2000.
———. "Moslems Attack Bus Carrying Serbs in Eastern Bosnia." 7 August 1996.
———. "NATO Chief Says Kosovo Violence Was 'Orchestrated.'" 22 March 2004.
———. "NATO Commander to Protest Serb Attack on Refugees." 27 May 1996.
———. "New Clashes in Kosovo Town after Five Killed in Sectarian Upsurge." 4 February 2000.
———. "One Killed in 'Terrorist' Bomb at the Home of Yugoslav Official in Kosovo." 22 November 2000.
———. "One Serb Killed, Four Injured in Spate of Kosovo Attacks." 7 January 2000.
———. "Senior Politician Killed in Kosovo." 16 June 2000.
———. "Serb Policeman Injured in Ethnic Albanian Mortar Attack near Kosovo." 2 January 2001.
———. "Serbian Children Targeted in Kosovo Attack." 17 August 2003.
———. "Serbian Man Killed in Drive-By Shooting." 1 June 2000.
———. "Serbs Shot Dead in Flashpoint Kosovo Region." 6 August 2000.
———. "Serbs Threaten to Down U.S. Helicopter: U.S. General." 7 July 1996.
———. "SFOR Confirms Attackers Were Serbs, Used Petrol Bombs." 12 March 1997.
———. "Thirteen Peacekeepers Injured in Clashes with Kosovo Albanians." 21 January 2001.
———. "Three Killed as Macedonia Conflict Spills into Kosovo." 29 March 2001.
———. "Three Kosovo Albanians Killed, Dozens Hurt in Unrest." 4 February 2000.
———. "Three Macedonian Soldiers Killed in Heavy Fighting on Kosovo Border." 4 March 2001.
———. "Three Serbs Injured in Kosovo Shooting." 7 August 2001.
———. "Three Serbs Murdered in Kosovo—UN." 4 June 2003.
———. "Two Attacked after Crossing Mostar Border." 24 February 1996.

---. "Two Dead in Shooting after Kosovo Assembly's Inaugural Session." 11 December 2001.

---. "Two Explosions Hit Police, Court Building in Kosovo Capital." 20 July 2003.

---. "Two Policeman Killed, One Wounded along Serbia-Kosovo Border." 4 August 2001.

---. "Two Serb Policemen Injured in Shooting near Kosovo Border." 21 April 2000.

---. "Two Serbs, Child Shot Dead in Kosovo." 29 May 2000.

---. "Rebels Kill 12 in Northwest Rwanda." 10 December 1997.

---. "Vehicle Blast Injures Kosovo Minister, Four Others." 22 February 2004.

Aliu, Fatmir. "Ex-KLA Chief Too Busy to Count Veterans." *Balkans Insight*, 29 August 2012, available at http://www.balkaninsight.com/en/article/kla-s-supreme-commander-too-busy-to-count-veterans, accessed 30 January 2013.

---. "Kosovo's LDK Asks for Full Report on Assassinations." *Balkans Insight*, 31 July 2012.

al-Khalidi, Ashraf and Victor Tanner, "Sectarian Violence: Radical Groups Drive Internal Displacement in Iraq." Brookings Institute (Occasional Paper, October 2006).

Allawi, Ali. *The Occupation of Iraq: Winning the War, Losing the Peace*. New Haven: Yale University Press, 2007.

al-Marashi, Ibrahim. "Disbanding and Rebuilding the Iraqi Army: The Historical Perspective." *Middle East Review of International Affairs* 11:3 (September 2007), 42–53.

Amaut, Samir. "Moslems Say Serb Mortar Bombs Drove Them from Village." Reuters, 12 November 1996.

Amnesty International. *Federal Republic of Yugoslavia (Kosovo): Update from the Field*. January 2000.

---. *Prisoners in Our Own Homes: Amnesty International's Concerns for the Human Rights of Minorities in Kosovo/Kosova*. April 2003.

---. "Rwanda: Alarming Resurgence of Killings." 12 August 1996.

---. *Rwanda: Ending the Silence*. 25 September 1997, available at http://www.amnesty.org/en/library/asset/AFR47/032/1997/en/0f834c89-e9b8-11dd-935f-7f9f204ae31f/afr470321997en.html, accessed 11 August 2011.

---. "Rwanda: Reports of Killings and Abductions by the Rwandese Patriotic Army, April–August 1994." 14 October 1994.

Andreas, Peter. *Blue Helmets and Black Markets: The Business of Survival in the Siege of Sarajevo*. Ithaca, NY: Cornell University Press, 2008.

---. "Criminalizing Consequences of Sanctions: Embargo Busting and Its Legacy." *International Studies Quarterly* 49 (2005), 335–350.

---. "Symbiosis between Peace Operations and Illicit Business in Bosnia." *International Peacekeeping* 16:1 (February 2009), 33–46.

Andreas, Peter, and Joel Wallman. "Illicit Markets and Violence: What Is the Relationship?" *Crime, Law and Social Change* 52 (2009), 225–229.

Anscombe, G. E. M. *Intention*. 2nd edition. Cambridge, MA: Harvard University Press, 2000.

Antonie, Victor. "Rwandan Refugees Flood Towards Tanzania." Reuters, 31 March 1995.

AP Online. "Rwanda Cops Hold 3 in Pols Murder." 20 May 1998.

Apple, R. W., Jr. "A Military Quagmire Remembered: Afghanistan as Vietnam." *New York Times*, October 31, 2001.

Armstrong, Gary. *Football Hooligans: Knowing the Score*. Oxford: Oxford University Press, 1998.

Archer, Dane, and Rosemary Gartner, *Violence and Crime in Cross-National Perspective*. Yale: Yale University Press, 1984.
Associated Press. "Car Explosion Kills One, Injures Two." 26 December 2002.
———. "Ex-Soldiers Burn Cars, Shops in East Timor." 28 April 2006.
———. "Four Kosovo Serbs Are Wounded in Attack." 8 May 2000.
———. "Four Yugoslav Soldiers Injured in Contested Border Zone." 28 January 2001.
———. "Grenade Thrown at Kosovo President's Home." 12 March 2004.
———. "Gunmen Murder Ethnic Albanian Politician with Ties to Yugoslavia." 3 September 2001.
———. "Key Witness in Trial of Ex-Rebels Killed in Roadside Ambush in Kosovo." 15 April 2003.
———. "Kosovo Journalist Wounded in Shooting." 24 September 2004.
———. "Kosovo PM to Be Investigated for Alleged Organ Trafficking." 29 August 2011.
———. "Muslim Farmer Killed Cutting Hay in Serb Zone." 2 August 1996.
———. "NATO, UN Police Clash with Ethnic Albanians in Kosovo." 10 October 2002.
———. "One Policeman Killed, Two Wounded in Ambush in Kosovo." 24 November 2003.
———. "Prominent Kosovo Businessman Wounded in an Ambush." 27 November 2004.
———. "Rwandan Rebels Reportedly Kill 11 Children in School Attack." 18 May 1998.
———. "Serb Refugees Attacked in a Visit to their Homes in Kosovo." 13 November 2003.
———. "Serbian Orthodox Church Blown Up in Kosovo." 17 July 2000.
———. "Three Killed in Post-Election Violence in Kosovo." 27 October 2002.
———. "Two Dead, Three Wounded in Reported Serb-Albanian clash in Southern Serbia." 27 February 2000.
———. "Two Serb Orthodox Churches Attacked in Kosovo." 17 November 2002.
———. "Two Serbs Found Axed to Death." 28 February 2001.
Atlas, Pierre, and Roy Licklider. "Conflict among Former Allies after Civil War Settlement: Sudan, Zimbabwe, Chad and Lebanon." *Journal of Peace Research* 36:1 (January 1999), 35–54.
Australian Broadcasting Corporation. "Alkatiri Denies Arming Own Security Force." 8 June 2006.
Autesserre, Séverine. "Hobbes and the Congo: Frames, Local Violence, and International Intervention." *International Organization* 63 (Spring 2009), 249–280.
———. *The Trouble with the Congo: Local Violence and the Failure of International Peacebuilding*. Cambridge: Cambridge University Press, 2010.
Azam, Jean Paul, and Anke Hoeffler, "Violence against Civilians: Looting or Terror?" *Journal of Peace Research* 39:4 (2002), 461–485.
B92 News. "Heroin Trafficking Route Passes through Bosnia," 10 February 2011, available at http://www.b92.net/eng/news/region-article.php?yyyy=2011&mm=02&dd=10&nav_id=72641, accessed 21 July 2011.
———. "Kosovo Intelligence Service Killed 450 People." B92 News, 9 June 2011.
———. "Kosovo Terror Group Issues Fresh Threats." 21 January 2008.
Bakke, Kristen M., Kathleen Gallagher Cunningham, and Lee J. M. Seymour. "A Plague of Initials: Fragmentation, Cohesion and Infighting in Civil Wars." *Perspectives on Politics* 10:2 (June 2012), 265–283.
Babo Soares, Dionisio. "Political Developments Leading to the Referendum," in James J. Fox

and Dionisio Babo Soares (eds.), *Out of Ashes: The Destruction and Reconstruction of East Timor*. Canberra: ANU E Press, 2003, 53–73.

Balcells, Laia. "Rivalry and Revenge: Violence against Civilians in Conventional Civil Wars." *International Studies Quarterly* 54:2 (June 2010), 291–313.

Ball, Desmond. "The Defence of East Timor: A Recipe for Disaster?" *Pacifica Review* 14:3 (October 2002), 175–189.

Ball, Patrick, Ewa Tabeau, and Philip Verwimp. "The Bosnian Book of the Dead: Assessment of the Database." Unpublished paper. 14 June 2007.

Barfield, Thomas. *Afghanistan: A Cultural and Political History*. Princeton: Princeton University Press, 2010.

Barnett, Neil. "Intra-KLA Blood Feuds Wrack Kosovo." *Budapest Times.* 25 July 2005.

Bayley, David. *Police for the Future*. Oxford: Oxford University Press, 1994.

BBC Monitoring Service. "Another Soldier Executed in Public for Murder." 2 February 1998.

———. "Criminals Kill 25 in Separate Incidents." 3 January 1998.

———. "Government Forces Kill 70 'Infiltrators.'" 20 April 1998.

———. "Militia Kills 20 Civilians, 80 Prisoners in Northwest—Agency Report." 21 November 1997.

BBC News. "'Armed Criminals' Kill Seven Civilians in Gitarama Province." 29 November 1997.

———. "Arson Attack Damages Ethnic Albanian Party Office." 24 October 2001.

———. "Australia Rapped over E Timor Oil." 19 May 2004.

———. "Bosnian Serbs Attack Croats Returning to Northern Bosnia." 29 April 1996.

———. "Congo's 'Ninja' Leader to Disarm." 6 June 2007.

———. "E Timor PM Accused of Unrest." 17 October 2006.

———. "E Timor Rally for School Religion." 20 April 2005.

———. "E Timor Troops Riot over Sacking." 26 April 2006.

———. "East Timor Chooses Independence." 4 September 1999.

———. "East Timor Declares State of Alert." 4 December 2002.

———. "Editor of Publication Critical of Government in Coma after Being Attacked." 2 February 1995.

———. "Five Dead Following Celebration of Albania's State Holiday." 30 November 1999.

———. "Group of 20 Ethnic Albanians Attack Two Serbs in Central Town." 25 October 1999.

———. "Indonesia and E Timor Heal Wounds." 9 April 2005.

———. "'Infiltrators' Kill 24 in the Center of the Country." 10 November 1997.

———. "Iraq Constitution Boycott Is Over." 25 July 2005.

———. "KLA War Veterans Warn Official's Arrest Will Affect Kosovo Peace Process." 12 April 2004.

———. "Kosovo Arms Caches 'Was KLA's.'" 23 June 2000, available at http://news.bbc.co.uk/1/hi/world/europe/803159.stm, accessed 4 July 2004.

———. "Kosovo Clashes 'Ethnic Cleansing.'" 20 March 2004.

———. "Kosovo President's Close Associated Heavily Injured in Planted Car Bomb Incident." 26 September 2003.

———. "Kosovo Rioters Burn Serb Churches." 18 March 2004.

———. "Mortar Bomb Attacks Reported on Three Serb Homes in Kosovo." 13 July 1999.

———. "NATO Condemns Kosovo Extremists." 22 March 2004.
———. "New War Crimes Trial for Former Kosovo PM Haradinaj." 21 June 2010, available at http://www.bbc.co.uk/news/world-europe-10709093, accessed 28 December 2012.
———. "Police Seize Former Kosovo Rebel." 11 August 2002.
———. "Rebels Kill Prosecutors and Colleague." 25 March 1996.
———. "Revenge Attacks Target Former Regime." 20 June 2003.
———. "Saddam Hussein Arrested in Iraq." 14 December 2003.
———. "Sadr 'Freezes' Militia Activities." 29 August 2007.
———. "Serbian Policeman Wounded in Kosovo 'Buffer Zone' Attack." 24 November 1999.
———. "Six Serbs Injured in Grenade Attack on Village Shop." 12 May 2000.
———. "Timeline: Kosovo." 12 May 2009, available at http://news.bbc.co.uk/1/hi/world/europe/country_profiles/3550401.stm, accessed 15 May 2009.
———. "UN Plans for Kosovo Independence." 27 March, 2007.
———. "UN Says 148 Killed in Rwanda Massacre of Tutsis." 25 August 1997.
———. "Up to 200 Killed in Baghdad Bombs." 18 April 2007.
———. "Victims of Bosnia's Sex Trade." 22 March 2002, available at http://news.bbc.co.uk/2/hi/europe/1807189.stm, accessed 22 July 2011.
———. "Who Are the Rebels?" 20 March 2001, available at http://news.bbc.co.uk/2/hi/europe/1231596.stm, accessed 29 January 2013.
Bearden, Milton. "Afghanistan, Graveyard of Empires." *Foreign Affairs*, November/December 2001, 17–30.
Beardsley, Kyle, and Brian McQuinn. "Rebel Groups as Predatory Organizations: The Political Effects of the 2004 Tsunami in Indonesia and Sri Lanka." *Journal of Conflict Resolution* 53:4 (2009), 629–645.
Becatoros, Elena. "Leading Serb Doctor Shot Dead in a Street in Kosovo." Associated Press, 27 February 2000.
Beckett, Ian F. W. "Insurgency in Iraq: An Historical Perspective." January 2005. Strategic Studies Institute. Carlisle, PA.
Bedford, Julian. "Gunmen Assassinate top Hutu Official in Rwanda." Reuters News, 5 March 1995.
Beeher, Lionel. *Iraq's Militia Groups*. Council on Foreign Relations, 2005, available at http://www.cfr.org/publication/8175/#4, accessed 8 August 2011.
Beevor, Anthony. *The Battle for Spain: The Spanish Civil War, 1936–1939*. London: Penguin, 2006.
Bell, J. Bowyer. *The Assassin: Theory and Practice of Political Violence*. New Brunswick: Transaction Publishers, 2005.
Bellamy, Alex J. *Kosovo and International Society*. Hampshire: Palgrave, 2002.
Benedetto, Richard. "Poll: Most Back War, but Want UN Support." *USA Today*, March 16, 2003.
Bennett, D. Scott, and Allan C. Stam. "The Duration of Interstate Wars, 1816–1985." *American Political Science Review* 90 (1996), 239–257.
Bensahel, Nora. "Preventing Insurgencies after Major Combat Operations." Washington, DC: RAND, 2006.
Bensahel, Nora, Olga Oliker, Keith Crane, Richard R. Brennan Jr., Heather S. Gregg, Thomas Sullivan, and Andrew Rathnell. *After Saddam: Prewar Planning and the Occupation of Iraq*. Washington, DC: RAND, 2008.

Bensahel, Nora, Olga Oilker, and Heather Petersen. *Improving Capacity for Stability and Reconstruction Operations*. Santa Monica: RAND, 2009.

Berdal, Mats. *Disarmament and Demobilization after Civil Wars: Arms, Soldiers and the Termination of Armed Conflict*. Adelphi Paper No. 303. Oxford: Oxford University Press, 1996.

Berdal, Mats, Gemma Collantes-Celador, and Merima Zupcevic Buzadzic. "Post-War Violence in Bosnia and Herzegovina," in Mats Berdal and Astri Suhrke (eds.), *The Peace In-Between: Post-War Violence and Peacebuilding*. London: Routledge, 2012, 75–94.

Berdal, Mats, and David Malone. *Greed and Grievance: Economic Agendas in Civil War*. Boulder, CO: Lynne Reiner, 2000.

Berdal, Mats, and Astri Suhrke (eds.). *The Peace In-Between: Post-War Violence and Peacebuilding*. London: Routledge, 2011.

Bergen, Peter. "The Taliban, Regrouped and Rearmed." *Washington Post*, 10 September 2006.

Berkowitz, Leonard. *Aggression: Causes, Consequences and Controls*. New York: McGraw Hill, 1993.

Biddle, Stephen. "Afghanistan and the Future of Warfare." *Foreign Affairs* 82:2 (March/April 2003), 31–46.

———. "Allies, Airpower, and Modern Warfare: The Afghan Model in Afghanistan and Iraq." *International Security* 30:3 (Winter 2005/2006), 161–176.

Biddle, Stephen, and Jeffrey Friedman. "The Iraq Data Debate: Civilian Casualties from 2006–2007." *Council on Foreign Relations Backgrounder* (28 September 2007).

Biddle, Stephen, Jeffrey A. Friedman, and Jacob Shapiro, "Testing the Surge: Why Did Violence Decline in Iraq in 2007." *International Security* 37:1 (Summer 2012), 7–40.

Black, Christopher. "The Rwandan Patriotic Front's bloody record and the history of U.N. Cover-Ups." *San Francisco Bay View*, September 15, 2010, available at http://sfbayview.com/2010/the-rwandan-patriotic-fronts-bloody-record-and-the-history-of-u-n-cover-ups/, accessed 31 August 2011.

Blainey, Geoffrey. *The Causes of War*. 3rd edition. New York: Free Press, 1988.

Blair, David. "Saddam Empties Iraq's Jails." *The Telegraph*, 21 October 2002.

Bloom, Mia. *Dying to Kill: The Allure of Suicide Terror*. New York: Columbia University Press, 2005.

Bob, Clifford. *The Marketing of Rebellion: Insurgents, Media and International Activism*. Cambridge: Cambridge University Press, 2005.

Boehm, Christopher. *Blood Revenge: The Enactment and Management of Conflict in Montenegro and Other Tribal Societies*. Philadelphia: University of Pennsylvania Press, 1984.

Bojicic-Dzelilovic, Vesna. "Peace on Whose Terms? Veteran's Associations in Bosnia and Herzegovina," in Edward Newman and Oliver Richmond (eds.), *Challenges to Peacebuilding: Managing Spoilers During Conflict Resolution*. Tokyo: United Nations Press, 2006, 200–219.

Booth, Ken (ed.). *The Kosovo Tragedy: The Human Rights Dimensions*. London: Frank Cass, 2001.

Bose, Sumantra. *Bosnia after Dayton: Nationalist Partition and International Intervention*. London: Hurst, 2002.

Bosleigh, Robert, and Jeremy Page. "Tamil Tigers Admit Defeat as Battle Reaches Its Bitter End." *The Times* (UK), 18 May 2009.

Bourke, Joanna. *An Intimate History of Killing: Face to Face Killing in Twentieth Century Warfare*. London: Granta, 1999.

Boyle, Michael J. "Bargaining, Fear and Denial: Explaining Violence against Civilians in Iraq, 2004–2007." *Terrorism and Political Violence* 21:2 (2009), 261–287.

———. "Explaining Strategic Violence after Wars." *Studies in Conflict and Terrorism* 32:3 (2009), 209–236.

———. "Policing the Neo-Imperial Frontier: CIVPOL Policing in the New Protectorates," in Ricardo Soares de Oliveria and James Mayall, *The New Protectorates: International Tutelage and the Making of Liberal States*. London: Hurst, 2011, 197–220.

———. "Revenge and Reprisal Violence in Kosovo." *Conflict, Security and Development* 10:2 (2010), 186–216.

———. "The Prevention and Management of Reprisal Violence in Post-Conflict States." Ph.D. dissertation, University of Cambridge, 2005.

———. "A War in Search of a Rationale." *International Affairs* 84:5 (2008), 1009–1023.

Bremer, L. Paul. *My Year in Iraq*. New York: Simon and Schuster, 2006.

Brinkley, Joel. "Revenge Killings Thin Ex-Baathists Ranks." *New York Times*, 1 November 2003.

Brown, David. "Study Claims Iraq's 'Excess' Death Toll Has Reached 655,000." *Washington Post*, 11 October 2006.

Brubaker, Rogers, and David D. Laitin. "Ethnic and Nationalist Violence." *Annual Review of Sociology* 24 (1998), 423–452.

Bufacchi, Vittorio. "Two Concepts of Violence." *Political Studies Review* 3:2 (April 2005), 193–204.

Bulloch, John. *No Friends but the Mountains: The Tragic History of the Kurds*. London: Viking, 1992.

Burg, Steven L., and Paul K. Shoup. *The War in Bosnia-Herzegovina: Ethnic Conflict and International Intervention*. New York: M. E. Sharpe, 2000.

Burnham, G. et al, "Mortality after the 2003 Invasion of Iraq: A Cross-Sectional Cluster Sample Survey." *Lancet* 368:9545 (2006), 1421–1428.

Butler, Richard. *Saddam Defiant: The Threat of Weapons of Mass Destruction and the Crisis of Global Security*. London: Phoenix, 2000.

Buza, Shaban, "15 Injured in Attack on Serb Refugee Convoy." Reuters, 27 October 1999.

———. "Kosovo Serbs Die in Rocket Attack on UN Bus." Reuters, 2 February 2000.

———. "Sixteen UN Police Hurt in Clash with Kosovo Serbs." Reuters, 8 April 2002.

———. "Two U.S. Soldiers Injured in Kosovo Explosion." Reuters, 31 July 2002.

Byman, Daniel. "The Logic of Ethnic Terrorism." *Studies in Conflict and Terrorism* 21:2 (1998), 149–169.

Call, Chuck, and Michael Barnett. "Looking for a Few Good Cops: Peacekeeping, Peacebuilding, and CIVPOL." *International Peacekeeping* 6:4 (1999), 43–68.

Carnegie, Marc. "Wave of Baghdad Killings as Iraqis Take Revenge on the Baath Party." Agence France Presse, 22 May 2003.

Carter, Lindwood B. "Iraq: Summary of Forces." *CRS Research Report*, 28 November 2005.

Cassidy, Robert M. *Counterinsurgency and the Global War on Terror: Military Culture and Irregular War*. Westport: Praeger, 2006.

Cave, Damien. "Hunt for 3 G.I.s in Iraq Slowed by False Trails." *New York Times*, 18 May 2007.

CDI Terrorism Project, "A General Speaks on the War in Iraq," 31 October 2002, available at www.cdi.org/terrorism/zinni-iraq-conditions-pr.cfm, accessed January 21, 2010.

Chandler, David. *Faking Democracy after Dayton*. London: Pluto Press, 1999.
Chandrasekaran, Rajiv. *Imperial Life in the Emerald City: Inside Iraq's Green Zone*. New York: Knopf, 2006.
Chivers, C. J., and Clifford Krauss. "Six Dead as Libyan Militias Clash Near Tripoli." *New York Times*, 13 November 2011.
Chomsky, Noam. *A New Generation Draws the Line: Kosovo, East Timor, and the Standards of the West*. London: Verso, 2000.
———. *The New Military Humanism*. Monroe, ME: Common Courage Press, 1999.
Chopra, Jarat. "The UN's Kingdom of East Timor." *Survival* 42:3 (Autumn 2000), 27–39.
Cigar, Norman. *Genocide in Bosnia: The Policy of "Ethnic Cleansing."* College Station: Texas A&M Press, 1995.
Circincione, Joseph D., Jessica Tuchman Mathews, George Perkovich, with Alexis Orton. *WMD in Iraq: Evidence and Implications*. Washington, DC: Carnegie Endowment, January 2004.
Clark, Wesley. *Waging Modern War*. New York: Public Affairs, 2001.
Clarke, Richard. *Against All Enemies: Inside America's War on Terror*. New York: Free Press, 2004.
Clapham, Christopher. "Rwanda: The Perils of Peacemaking." *Journal of Peace Research* 35:2 (1998), 193–210.
Clewlow, Ade. "The Kosovo Protection Corps: A Critical Study of Its De-activation as a Transition." Oslo: NUPI Report, January 2010.
CNN. "Bosnian Serbs Frantically Flee Sarajevo." 21 February 1996.
———. "Bush: Congress Can't Stop Troop Increase." 14 January 2007.
———. "Bush: Don't Wait for Mushroom Cloud." 8 October 2002.
———. "Gunmen Strikes at 27 Baghdad Mosques, kill imams." 22 February 2006, available at http://edition.cnn.com/2006/WORLD/meast/02/22/iraq.main/index.html, accessed 11 November 2008.
———. "Kosovo Bus Bombing Condemned." 16 February 2001, available at http://edition.cnn.com/2001/WORLD/europe/02/16/kosovo.attack.02/, accessed 22 July 2003.
———. "Kosovo Liberation Army Disarms to Meet Midnight Deadline." 21 July 1999.
———. "Truck Bomb Kills Chief UN Envoy to Iraq." 20 August 2003.
Cochrane, Marisa. *Iraq Report 12: The Fragmentation of the Sadrist Movement*. Institute for the Study of War, 2009.
Cockburn, Patrick. "Destruction of Holiest Shia Shrine Brings Iraq to the Brink of Civil War." *The Independent*, 23 February 2006.
———. *Moqtada al-Sadr and the Battle for the Future of Iraq*. New York: Scribner, 2008.
———. *The Occupation: War and Resistance in Iraq*. London: Verso, 2006.
Cocozzelli, Fred. *War and Social Welfare: Reconstruction after Conflict*. New York: Palgrave, 2010.
Cohen, Robin. *Global Diasporas*. London: University College London Press, 1997.
Cohn, Ellen G., and James Rotton. "Even Criminals Take a Holiday: Instrumental and Expressive Crimes on Major and Minor Holidays." *Journal of Criminal Justice* 31:4 (July-August 2003), 351–360.
Coker, Margaret. "Revenge Killings Are Soaring in Iraq." *Cox News Service*, 28 December 2003.

Collier, Paul. "Demobilization and Insecurity: A Study in the Economics of the Transition from War to Peace." *Journal of International Development* 6 (1994), 343–351.

———. *War, Guns and Votes: Democracy in Dangerous Places*. New York: Harper Perennial, 2010.

Collier, Paul, Lani Elliot, Havard Hegre, Anke Hoeffler, Marta Reynal-Querol, and Nicholas Sambanis (eds.). *Breaking the Conflict Trap: Civil War and Development Policy, World Bank Policy Research Report*. Oxford: Oxford University Press, 2003.

Collier, Paul, and Anke Hoeffler. "On the Economic Causes of Civil War." *Oxford Economic Papers* 50 (1998), 563–573.

———. "Greed and Grievance in Civil War." Centre for the Study of African Economies, University of Oxford, March 2000.

Collier, Paul, Anke Hoeffler, and Måns Söderbom. "On the Duration of Civil War." World Bank Research Policy Paper No. 2681, September 2001.

———. "Post-Conflict Risks." *Journal of Peace Research* 45:4 (2008), 461–478.

Connable, Ben and Martin Libicki. *How Insurgencies End*. Washington, DC: RAND, 2010.

Cordesman, Anthony. *Iraq's Evolving Insurgency and the Risk of Civil War*. Washington, DC: Center for Strategic and International Studies, 26 January 2007.

Cosic, Sabina. "NATO Takes Tough Stance on Bosnia's Bombings." Reuters News, 22 October 1996.

Cotton, James. "Against the Grain: The East Timor Intervention." *Survival* 43:1. Spring 2001, 127–142.

Cousens, Elizabeth M. "The Dayton Agreement on Bosnia," in Stephen John Stedman, Donald Rothschild and Elizabeth M. Cousens (eds.), *Ending Civil Wars: The Implementation of Peace Agreements*. Boulder, CO: Lynne Rienner, 2002, 531–566.

Cox, Marcus. "Bosnia and Herzegovina: The Limits of Liberal Imperialism," in Charles T. Call (ed.), *Building States to Build Peace*. Boulder, CO: Lynne Rienner, 2008, 249–270.

Crenshaw, Martha. "The Causes of Terrorism." *Comparative Politics* 13:4 (July 1981), 379–399.

Crisp, Jeff. "Who Has Counted the Refugees? UNHCR and the Politics of Numbers." New Issues in Refugee Research, Working Paper No. 12, UNHCR, 12 June 1999.

Crossette, Barbara. "Peacekeeping's Unsavory Side." *The Atlantic*, 10 June 2003.

Crouch, Barry A. "A Spirit of Lawlessness: White Violence, Texas Blacks, 1865–1868." *Journal of Social History* 18:2 (Winter 1984), 217–232.

Crouch, Harold. "The TNI and East Timor Policy," in James J. Fox and Dionisio Babo Soares (eds.), *Out of Ashes: The Destruction and Reconstruction of East Timor*. Canberra: ANUE Press, 2003, 141–167.

Cunningham, David E. "Veto Players and Civil War Duration." *American Journal of Political Science* 50:4 (October 2006), 875–892.

Cunningham, Kathleen Gallagher. "Divide and Conquer or Divide and Concede: How Do States Respond to Internally Divided Separatists?" *American Political Science Review* 105:2 (May 2011), 275–297.

Cunningham, Kathleen Gallagher, Kristin M. Bakke, and Lee J. Seymour, "Shirts Today, Skins Tomorrow: Dual Contests and the Effects of Fragmentation in Self-Determination Disputes." *Journal of Conflict Resolution* 56:1 (2012), 67–93.

Daalder, Ivo. *Getting to Dayton: The Making of America's Bosnia Policy*. Washington. DC: Brookings Institute, 2000.

Dahlman, Carl, and Gearóid Ó Tuathail, "The Legacy of Ethnic Cleansing: The International Community and the Returns Process in Post-Dayton Bosnia-Herzegovina." *Political Geography* 24: (2005), 569–599.

Dallaire, Lt. General Romeo, with Major Brent Beardsley. *Shake Hands with the Devil: The Failure of Humanity in Rwanda.* London: Arrow, 2004.

Darby, John. *Violence and Reconstruction.* Notre Dame: University of Notre Dame Press, 2006.

Davenport, Christian, and Patrick Ball. "Views to a Kill: Exploring the Implications of Source Selection in the Case of Guatemalan State Terror, 1977–1995." *Journal of Conflict Resolution* 46:3 (June 2002), 427–450.

Dawisha, Adeed. *Iraq: A Political History from Independence to Occupation.* Princeton: Princeton University Press, 2009.

Deak, Istvan, Jan T. Gross, and Tony Judt. *The Politics of Retribution in Europe.* Princeton: Princeton University Press, 2000.

Della Porta, Donatella. "Research on Social Movements and Political Violence." *Qualitative Sociology* 31 (2008), 221–230.

———. *Social Movements, Political Violence and the State.* Cambridge: Cambridge University Press, 1995.

Dempsey, Gary. "Rethinking the Dayton Agreement." Policy Analysis 327. Washington, DC: CATO Institute, 14 December 1998.

Denyer, Simon. "Drift towards Repression Mars Peace in Sri Lanka." *The Guardian*, 17 July 2012.

DeRouen, Karl R., Jr., and David Sobek. "The Dynamics of Civil War Duration and Outcome." *Journal of Peace Research* 41: 3 (May 2004), 303–320.

Des Forges, Alison. *Leave None to Tell the Story: Genocide in Rwanda.* New York: Human Rights Watch, 1999.

De Soysa, Indra. "Paradise Is a Bazaar? Greed, Creed and Governance in Civil War, 1989–1999." *Journal of Peace Research* 39:4 (2002), 395–416.

DeVine, Vera, and Harald Mathison. "Corruption in Bosnia-Herzegovina, 2005." R. 2005.81. Bergen: Chr. Michelson Institute, 2005.

de Zayas, Alfred Maurice, *A Terrible Revenge: The Ethnic Cleansing of Eastern European Germans.* London: Palgrave Macmillan, 1994.

Dhimgjoka, Merita. "Seven Serbs Killed, 43 Injured in Kosovo Bomb Blast." Associated Press, 16 February 2001.

Diamond, Larry. *Squandered Victory: The American Occupation and the Bungled Effort to Bring Democracy to Iraq.* New York: Owl Books, 2005.

———. "What Went Wrong in Iraq." *Foreign Affairs* (September/October 2004), 34–56.

Die Welt Online. "BND Kosovo Affair: German Spy Affair Might Have Been Revenge," 30 November 2008, available at http://www.welt.de/english-news/article2806537/German-spy-affair-might-have-been-revenge.html, accessed 9 September 2009.

Divjak, Boris, and Michael Pugh. "The Political Economy of Corruption in Bosnia-Herzegovina." *International Peacekeeping* 15:3 (June 2008), 373–386.

Dobbins, James, Seth G. Jones, Benjamin Runkle, and Siddharth Mohandas. *Occupying Iraq: A History of the Coalition Provisional Authority.* Washington, DC: RAND, 2009.

Dobbins, James, John G. McGinn, Keith Crane, Seth G. Jones, Rollie Lal, Andrew Rathmell, Rachel Swanger, and Angela Timilsina, *America's Role in Nation-Building: From Germany to Iraq*. Washington, DC: RAND, 2003.

Dodd, Mark. "Rwandan President Says 1,000 Infiltrators Detained." Reuters, 1 January 1996.

Dodge, Toby. *Inventing Iraq*. New York: Columbia University Press, 2003.

———. "Staticide in Iraq." *Le Monde Diplomatique* (February 2007), available at http://mondediplo.com/2007/02/04iran, accessed 10 November 2011.

Donais, Tim. *The Political Economy of Peacebuilding in Post-Dayton Bosnia*. London: Routledge, 2005.

Donnan, Shawn. "East Timor's Ethnic Violence Puzzles Analysts." *Financial Times*, 10 June 2006.

Dow Jones International News. "Army Commander Says Rwandan Rebels Kill at Least 110 People." 2 August 1998.

Dow Jones News Service. "Grenade Explosion, Crash Kill at Least 20 on Bus to Rwanda." 25 August 1998.

———. "Rwandan Hutu Rebels Kill 58 in Northwestern Village." 10 February 1998.

Downes, Alexander B. "The Problem with Negotiated Settlements to Ethnic Civil Wars." *Security Studies* 13:4 (Summer 2004), 230–279.

———. *Targeting Civilians in War*. Ithaca: Cornell University Press, 2008.

Doyle, Michael W., and Nicholas Sambanis. *Making War and Building Peace: United Nations Peace Operations* Princeton: Princeton University Press, 2006.

Dunn, James. *East Timor: A Rough Passage to Independence*. 3rd edition. Double Bay, NSW: Longueville Books, 2003.

Eisenstadt, S. N., and Louis Roniger. "Patron-Client Relations as a Model for Social Change." *Comparative Studies in Society and History* 22:1 (January 1980), 42–77.

Eltringham, Nigel. *Accounting for Horror: Post-Genocide Debates in Rwanda*. Sterling, VA: Pluto Press, 2004.

Fearon, James D. "Commitment Problems and the Spread of Ethnic Conflict," in David A. Lake and Donald Rothschild (eds.), *The International Spread of Ethnic Conflict: Fear, Diffusion and Escalation*. Princeton: Princeton University Press, 1998, 107–126.

———. "Iraq's Civil War." *Foreign Affairs* (March/April 2007), 1–13.

———. "Why Do Some Civil Wars Last So Much Longer than Others?" *Journal of Peace Research* 41:3 (2004), 278–280.

Fearon, James D., and David Laitin, "Ethnicity, Insurgency and Civil War." *American Political Science Review* 97:1 (2003), 75–90.

Feith, Douglas J. *War and Decision: Inside the Pentagon at the Dawn of the War on Terrorism*. New York: Harper Collins, 2008.

Felbab Brown, Vanda. "Peacekeepers among Poppies: Afghanistan, Illicit Economies and Intervention." *International Peacekeeping* 16:1 (February 2009), 100–114.

Fernandes, Clinton. *Reluctant Saviour: Australia, Indonesia and the People of East Timor*. Victoria: Scribe Publications, 2004.

Festić, Amra, and Adrian Rausche. "War by Other Means: How Bosnia's Clandestine Political Economies Obstruct Peace and Statebuilding." *Problems of Post-Communism* 51:3 (May/June 2004), 27–34.

Findlay, Trevor. *The Use of Force in UN Peace Operations*. Oxford: Oxford University Press, 2002.

Findley, Michael, and Peter Rudloff. "Combatant Fragmentation and the Dynamics of Civil Wars." Unpublished Paper, 8 March 2011.

Fischer, Hannah. "Iraqi Civilian Death Estimates." *Congressional Research Service*, 22 November 2006.

Fisk, Robert. "Hooded Men Executing Saddam Officials." *The Independent*, 28 December 2003.

Fitzpatrick, Stephen. "Fretilin Sidelined in Timorese Cabinet." *The Australian*, 9 August 2007.

Fogarty, Philippa. "Who Are the Rebels?" BBC News, 11 February 2008.

Foner, Eric. *A Short History of the Reconstruction, 1863–1877*. New York: Harper Perennial, 1990.

Fortna, Virginia Page. *Does Peacekeeping Work?* Princeton: Princeton University Press, 2008.

———. *Peace Time: Cease-Fire Agreements and the Durability of Peace*. Princeton: Princeton University Press, 2004.

———. "Scraps of Paper: Agreements and the Durability of Peace." *International Organization* 57:2 (Spring 2003), 337–372.

Fox, James J. "Tracing the Path, Recounting the Past: Historical Perspective on Timor," in James J. Fox and Dionisio Babo Soares (eds.), *Out of Ashes: The Destruction and Reconstruction of East Timor*. Canberra: ANU E Press, 2003, 1–27.

Fox, James J., and Dionisio Babo Soares (eds.). *Out of Ashes: The Destruction and Reconstruction of East Timor*. Canberra: ANU E Press, 2003.

French, Howard W. "Kagame's Hidden War in the Congo." *New York Review of Books* 56:14 (24 September 2009), available at http://www.nybooks.com/articles/archives/2009/sep/24/kagames-hidden-war-in-the-congo/?pagination=false, accessed 21 September 2011.

Friedman, Francine. *The Bosnian Muslims: Denial of a Nation*. Boulder, CO: Westview, 1996.

Fromkin, David. *Kosovo Crossing: American Ideals Meet Reality on the Balkans Battlefields*. New York: Free Press, 1999.

Frommer, Benjamin. *National Cleansing: Retribution against Nazi Collaborators in Post-War Czechoslovakia*. Cambridge: Cambridge University Press, 2004.

Fuji, Lee Ann. *Killing Neighbors: Webs of Violence in Rwanda*. Ithaca: Cornell University Press, 2009.

Gall, Carlotta. "In Rebound of Rage, a Serb Dies in Kosovo." *New York Times*, 3 December 1999.

Gates, Scott. "Recruitment and Allegiance: The Microfoundations of Rebellion." *Journal of Conflict Resolution* 46:1 (2002), 111–130.

Gaub, Florence. *Military Integrations after Civil Wars: Multiethnic Armies, Identity and Post-Conflict Reconstruction*. London: Routledge, 2011.

Gavigan, Patrick. "Organized Crime, Illicit Power Structures and Guatemala's Peace Process." *International Peacekeeping* 16:1 (2009), 62–76.

Geitner, Paul. "Bosnian Serb Police Attack Muslim Returnees." Associated Press, 29 August 1996.

George, Alexander L., and Andrew Bennett. *Case Studies and Theory Development in the Social Sciences*. Cambridge, MA: MIT Press, 2005.

Ghobarah, Hazem Adam Paul Huth, and Bruce Russett. "Civil Wars Kill People—Long after the Shooting Stops." *American Political Science Review* 97:2 (May 2003), 189–202.

Ghosh, Bobby. "Exclusive: Insurgent Ba'athist in His Own Words." *Time Magazine*, 24 July 2006.

Giustozzi, Antonio. *Koran, Klashnikov and Laptop: The Neo-Taliban Insurgency in Afghanistan*. London: Hurst, 2009.
Glanz, James, and Robert F. Worth. "Attacks on Iraq Oil Industry Aid Vast Smuggling Scheme." *New York Times*, 4 June 2006.
Gleditsch, Kristian Skrede, and Andrea Ruggeri. "Political Opportunity Structures, Democracy, and Civil Wars." *Journal of Peace Research* 47:3 (2010), 299–310.
Glenny, Misha. *The Balkans*. New York: Viking, 2000.
———. *McMafia: Seriously Organized Crime*. London: Vintage, 2009.
Goemans, Hein. *War and Punishment: The Causes of War Termination and the First World War*. Princeton: Princeton University Press, 2000.
Goodby, James E. "When War Won Out: Bosnian Peace Plans before Dayton." *International Negotiation* 1:3 (1996), 501–523.
Goodhand, Jonathan. "Stabilizing a Victor's Peace? Humanitarian Action and Reconstruction in Eastern Sri Lanka." *Disasters* 34:3 (October 2010), 342–367.
Gordon, Michael R., and General Bernard E. Trainor. *Cobra II: The Inside Story of the Invasion and Occupation of Iraq*. New York: Vintage, 2007.
Gould, Roger V. "Collective Violence and Group Solidarity: Evidence from a Feuding Society." *American Sociological Review* 64:3 (1999), 356–380.
Gourevitch, Philip. *We Wish to Inform You that Tomorrow We Will Be Killed with Our Families*. London: Picador, 1999.
Gow, James. *The Serbian Project and Its Adversaries: A Strategy of War Crimes*. Montreal: McGill-Queen's University Press, 2003.
Graff, Peter. "Yazidis Fear Annihilation after IRAQ Bombings." Reuters, 16 August 2007.
Gray, Andrew. "Bulgarian UN Employee Shot Dead in Kosovo." Reuters News, 12 October 1999.
———. "Mortar Attacks Kills Two in Kosovo Town." Reuters, 8 September 1999.
———. "Sniper Dead, French Wounded in Kosovo Battle." Reuters, 13 February 2000.
Greenhill, Kelly M. *Weapons of Mass Migration: Forced Displacement, Coercion and Foreign Policy*. Ithaca: Cornell University Press, 2010.
Greenhill, Kelly M., and Solomon Major. "The Perils of Profiling: Civil War Spoilers and the Collapse of Intrastate Peace Accords." *International Security* 31 (2007), 7–40.
Greenlees, Donald. "Hundreds Mourn at Burial of East Timor Rebel." *New York Times*, 15 February 2008.
Greenlees, Donald, and Robert Garran. *Deliverance: The Inside Story of East Timor's Fight for Freedom*. Crows Nest, NSW: Allan & Unwin, 2002.
Griffiths, Hugh. "Investigation: Will Europe Take on Bosnia's Mafia?" Institute for War and Peace Reporting, BCR 531, 21 February 2005.
Grundy, Kenneth W., and Michael A. Weinstein. *The Ideologies of Violence*. Columbus, Ohio: Charles E. Merrill Publishing Company, 1974.
Gurr, Ted Robert. "Psychological Factors in Civil Violence." *World Politics* 20:2 (January 1968), 245–278.
———. *Why Men Rebel*. Princeton: Princeton University Press, 1970.
Hafez, Mohammed. *Suicide Bombers in Iraq: The Strategy and Ideology of Martyrdom*. Washington, DC: USIP, 2007.
———. "Suicide Terrorism in Iraq: A Preliminary Assessment of the Quantitative Data and Documentary Evidence." *Studies in Conflict and Terrorism* 29:6 (2006), 591–619.

Hainsworth, Paul, and Stephen McCloskey. *The East Timor Question*. London: I. B. Tauris, 2000.
Hardin, Russell. *One for All: The Logic of Group Conflict*. Princeton: Princeton University Press, 1995.
Hashim, Ahmed. *Insurgency and Counterinsurgency in Iraq*. Ithaca: Cornell University Press, 2006.
Harris, Paul. "Warlords Bring New Terrors." *The Observer*, 2 December 2001.
Hartzell, Caroline, and Matthew Hoddie. "Institutionalizing Peace: Power Sharing and Post Civil War Conflict Management." *American Journal of Political Science* 47:2 (April 2003), 318–332.
Hartzell, Caroline, Matthew Hoddie, and Donald Rothschild, "Stabilizing the Peace after Civil War: An Investigation of Some Key Variables." *International Organization* 55:1 (Winter 2001), 183–208.
Hasan, Omar. "Hardline Group Denies Involvement in 'Revenge Killings' in Basra." Agence France Presse, 11 November 2003.
Hashim, Ahmed. *Insurgency and Counterinsurgency in Iraq*. Ithaca: Cornell University Press, 2006.
Hatzfield, Jean. *Life Laid Bare: The Survivors in Rwanda Speak*. New York: Other Press, 2000.
———. *Machete Season: The Killers in Rwanda Speak*. New York: Farrar, Straus and Giroux, 2003.
Hayton, Bill. "'Sinister Purpose' to Kosovo Clashes?" BBC News, 19 March 2004.
Head, Jonathan. "E Timor's 'Wrong Kind of Leader.'" BBC News, 26 June 2006.
Hechter, Michael. "Explaining Nationalist Violence." *Nations and Nationalism* 1:1 (1995), 53–68.
Hedges, Chris, "As U.N. Organizes, Rebels Are Taking Charge of Kosovo." *New York Times*, 29 July 1999.
———. "Crisis in the Balkans: The Separatists: Leaders of Kosovo Rebels Tied to Deadly Power Play." *New York Times*, 25 June 1999.
———. "Gangs Descend, to Pick Bosnia's Carcass Clean." *New York Times*, 7 October 1996.
———. "Kosovo Rebel Force Will Be Serbian Province's New Power Broker." *New York Times*, 6 June 1999.
———. "Kosovo's Next Masters." *Foreign Affairs* 78:3 (May/June 1999), 24–42.
———. "Leaders of Kosovo Rebels Tied to Deadly Power Play." *New York Times*, 25 June 1999.
———. "On Bosnia's Ethnic Fault Line, It's Still Tense but the World Is Silent." *New York Times*, 28 February 1997.
———. "Outbreaks of Violence Continue in Bosnia." *New York Times*, 30 August 1997.
———. "A War Bred Underworld Threatens Bosnia Peace." *New York Times*, 1 May 1996.
Hendren, John. "Ex-Baathists Play Crucial Insurgent Role, U.S. Says." *Los Angeles Times*, 11 January 2005.
Heinrich, Mark. "Serbs Shot Dead in Kosovo Field, NATO Says." Reuters, 24 July 1999.
Hintjens, Helen. "Post-Genocide Identity Politics in Rwanda." *Ethnicities* 8:1 (2008), 5–41.
Hoare, Mark Attila. *How Bosnia Armed*. London: Saqi Books, 2004.
Hodal, Kate. "Timor-Leste Strives to Overcome Culture of Domestic Violence." *The Guardian*, 24 August 2012.

Hockenos, Peter. *Homeland Calling: Exile Patriotism and the Balkan Wars.* Ithaca: Cornell University Press, 2003.
Hoddie, Matthew, and Carolyn Hartzell. "Civil War Settlements and the Implementation of Military Power-Sharing Agreements." *Journal of Peace Research* 40:3 (May 2003), 303–320.
Hoffer, Eric. *The True Believer: Thoughts on the Nature of Mass Movements.* New York: Harper Perennial, 2002.
Hoffman, Bruce. *Insurgency and Counterinsurgency in Iraq.* Washington, DC: RAND, 2004.
Hoffman, Bruce, and Gordon McCormick, "Terrorism, Signaling and Suicide Attack." *Studies in Conflict and Terrorism* 27 (2004), 243–281.
Holbrooke, Richard. *To End A War.* New York: Modern Library, 1999.
Hollis, Martin, and Steve Smith. *Explaining and Understanding International Relations.* Oxford: Clarendon, 1991.
Horowitz, Donald. "Conciliatory Institutions and Constitutional Processes in Post-Conflict States." *William and Mary Law Review* 49:4 (2008), 1213–1248.
———. *The Deadly Ethnic Riot.* Berkeley: University of California Press, 2001.
———. *Ethnic Groups in Conflict.* Berkeley: University of California Press, 1985.
Hosmer, Stephen T. *Why the Iraqi Resistance to the Coalition Invasion Was So Weak.* Santa Monica, CA: RAND, 2007.
Howard, Michael. "They Won't Stop until We Are All Wiped Out. Among the Yezidi, a people in Mourning." *The Guardian.* 18 August 2007.
Hranjski, Hrvoje. "Rwandan Rebels Kill 94 Civilians." *AP Online*, 28 May 1998.
Hsiao-Rei Hicks, Madelyn, Hamit Dardagan, Gabriela Guerrero, Serdan, Peter M. Bagnall, John M. Sloboda, and Michael Spagat, "Violent Deaths of Iraqi Civilians, 2003–2008: Analysis by Perpetrator, Weapon, Time and Location." *PLoS Medicine*, 8:2 (February 2011), 1–15.
Human Rights Watch. *Angola Unravels: The Rise and Fall of the Lusaka Peace Process.* New York: Human Rights Watch, 1999.
———. "The Continuing Influence of Bosnia's Warlords." 1 December 1996.
———. "Evidence of KLA Secret Prisons in Kosovo and Albania." 9 April 2009.
———. "A Failure in the Making: Human Rights and the Dayton Agreement," 1 June 1996, available at http://www.unhcr.org/refworld/country,,HRW,,BIH,,3ae6a8570,0.html, accessed 19 July 2011.
———. *Failure to Protect: Anti-Minority Violence in Kosovo, March 2004.* 26 July 2004.
———. "Federal Republic of Yugoslavia: Abuses against Serbs and Roma in the New Kosovo," *Human Rights Watch Report* 11:10 (August 1999).
———. "Indonesia/East Timor: Forced Expulsions to West Timor and the Refugee Crisis," 11:7 (December 1999), available at http://www.hrw.org/reports/1999/wtimor/, accessed 11 January 2005.
———. *"Killing You Is a Very Easy Thing for Us."* New York: Human Rights Watch, 2003.
———. *Kosovo: Human Rights Developments* (2000), available at http://www.hrw.org/wr2k1/europe/yugoslavia-kosovo.html, accessed 23 August 2004.
———. "New Figures on Civilian Deaths in Kosovo War," 8 February 2000, http://www.hrw.org/news/2000/02/07/new-figures-civilian-deaths-kosovo-war, accessed 7 October 2003.
———. "Northwestern Bosnia: Human Rights Abuses during the Cease-Fire and

Peace Negotiations," 1 February 1996, available at http://www.unhcr.org/refworld/country,,HRW,,BIH,,3ae6a7de0,0.html, accessed 22 July 2011.

———. *Paying for the Taliban's Crimes: Abuses against Ethnic Pashtuns in Northern Afghanistan* 14:2. New York: Human Rights Watch, April 2002.

———. "Politics of Revenge in Bosnia's Una Sana Canton Systematically Violate the Dayton Accords and International Law," 7 August 1997, available at http://www.hrw.org/en/news/1997/08/07/politics-revenge-bosnias-una-sana-canton-systematically-violate-dayton-accords-and-i, accessed 22 July 2011.

———. *Rwanda: The Crisis Continues* 7:1 (April 1995).

———. *Under Orders: War Crimes in Kosovo; Abuses after June 12, 1999.* 2001. http://www.hrw.org/reports/2001/kosovo/undword2c.html, accessed July 31, 2002.

———. "Update: Non-Compliance with the Dayton Accords: Ongoing Ethnically-Motivated Expulsions and Harassment in Bosnia." 1 August 1996.

Human Security Report Project. Human Security Report (2009/2010), available at http://www.hsrgroup.org/human-security-reports/20092010/overview.aspx, accessed 13 June 2012.

Hume, Mo. "Armed Violence and Poverty in El Salvador: A Mini-Case Study for the Armed Violence and Poverty Initiative." University of Bradford, 2004.

Humpfreys, Maccartan, and Jeremy M. Weinstein. "Demobilization and Reintegration." *Journal of Conflict Resolution* 51:4 (August 2007), 531–567.

———. "Handling and Mishandling Civilians in War." *American Political Science Review* 100:3 (August 2006), 429–447.

———. "What the Fighters Say: A Survey of Ex-Combatants in Sierra Leone June–August 2003." Working Paper. Conducted in partnership with PRIDE. Interim Report (July 2004), available at http://www.columbia.edu/~mh2245/Report1_BW.pdf, accessed 11 July 2012.

Huntington, Samuel P. *Political Order and Changing Societies.* New Haven: Yale University Press, 2006.

Ignatieff, Michael. "Is the Human Rights Era Ending?" *New York Times*, 5 February 2002.

———. *Virtual War: Kosovo and Beyond.* New York: Metropolitan Books, 2000.

Iklé, Fred Charles. *Every War Must End.* Revised Edition. New York: Columbia University Press, 1991.

Ilic, Dragan. "Serb Policeman Killed, Three Wounded in Ethnic Albanian Attacks." Associated Press, 9 March 2001.

———. "Albanian Insurgents Attack Serbian Police inside Buffer Zone." Associated Press, 27 March 2001.

Independent International Commission on Kosovo. *The Kosovo Report.* Oxford: Oxford University Press, 2000.

Institute for War and Peace Reporting. "Serbia: LDK Takes Stand on Kosovo Violence," 24 January 2003.

International Crisis Group. *An Army for Kosovo?* Europe Report No. 174, 28 July 2006.

———. *Bridging Kosovo's Mitrovica Divide.* Europe Report No. 165, 13 September 2005.

———. *Collapse in Kosovo.* ICG Europe Report No. 155. 22 April 2004.

———. *The Continuing Challenge of Refugee Returns in Bosnia and Herzegovina.* Balkans Report No. 137, 13 December 2002.

———. *Doing Democracy a Disservice: 1998 Elections in Bosnia and Herzegovina*. 9 September 1998.

———. *Ensuring Bosnia's Future: A New International Engagement Strategy*. Europe Report No. 180, 15 February 2007, 14.

———. *Grave Situation in Mostar: Robust Response Required*. ICG Bosnia Report No. 19, 13 February 1997.

———. *Impunity in Drvar*. Balkans Report, No. 40, 20 August 1998.

———. *In their Own Words: Reading the Iraqi Insurgency*. Middle East Report No. 50, 15 February 2006.

———. *Is Dayton Failing? Bosnia Four Years after the Peace Agreement*. Balkans Report 80, 28 October 1999, 14.

———. *Kosovo after Haradinaj*. Europe Report No. 163, 26 May 2005.

———. *Kosovo's Linchpin: Overcoming Division in Mitrovica*. 31 May 2000.

———. *Minority Return or Mass Relocation*. Report No. 33, 14 May 1998.

———. *The Next Iraqi War: Sectarianism and Civil Conflict*. Middle East Report No. 52, 27 February 2006.

———. *Resolving Timor-Leste's Crisis*. Asia Report No. 120, 10 October 2006.

———. "Return of Displaced Persons to Jajce and Travnik," 3 June 1998, available at http://www.unhcr.org/refworld/country,,ICG,,BIH,,3ae6a6f08,0.html, accessed 21 July 2011.

———. *Rwanda at the End of the Transition: A Necessary Liberalization*. Brussels: 13 November 2002.

———. *Security Sector Reform in the Congo*. Africa Report No. 104, 13 February 2006.

———. *Serbia: Maintaining Peace in Presevo Valley*. Europe Report No. 198, 16 October 2007.

———. *Timor-Leste Security Sector Reform*. Asia Report No. 143. 17 January 2008.

———. *UNMIK's Kosovo Albatross: Tackling Division in Mitrovica*. ICG Balkans Report No. 131. June 2002.

———. *Violence in Kosovo: Who's Killing Whom?* Balkans Report No. 78. 2 November 1999.

———. *The Wages of Sin: Confronting Bosnia's Republika Srpska*. Balkans Report No. 118. 8 October 2001.

———. *What Happened to the KLA?* Europe Report No. 88. 3 March 2000.

———. *Where Is Iraq Heading? Lessons from Basra*. Middle East Report No. 67. 25 June 2007.

———. *Who's Who in Kosovo*. ICG Balkans Report, No. 76. 31 August 1999.

International Herald Tribune. "A Dark Side to Iraq 'Awakening' Groups." 4 January 2008.

International Institute for Strategic Studies, "The Kosovo Liberation Army," 5:4 (May 1999), available at http://www.iiss.org/publications/strategic-comments/past-issues/volume-5—1999/volume-5—issue-4/the-kosovo-liberation-army/, accessed 2 May 2002.

Iraq Study Group Report: A Way Forward, a New Approach. New York: Vintage, 2006.

Jackson, Patrick. "Crushing Iraq's Human Mosaic." BBC News, 13 July 2007.

Jahić, Dino, and Azhar Kalamujić. "Reporter's Notebook: Bosnia-Herzegovina, the Rules of Patronage." Global Integrity Project, 2009, available at http://report.globalintegrity.org/Bosnia%20and%20Herzegovina/2009/notebook, accessed 11 June 2011.

Janis, Irving. *Victims of Groupthink*. New York: Houghton Mifflin, 1972.

Jervis, Robert. "Cooperation under the Security Dilemma." *World Politics* 30:2 (January 1978), 167–213.

———. *Perception and Misperception in International Politics.* Princeton, NJ: Princeton University Press, 1976.
Jett, Dennis C. *Why Peacekeeping Fails.* New York: Palgrave, 1999.
Johnson, Carter. "Partitioning to Peace: Sovereignty, Demography and Ethnic Civil Wars." *International Security* 32:4 (Spring 2008), 140–170.
Johnson, Dominic. *Overconfidence and War: The Havoc and Glory of Positive Illusions.* Cambridge, MA: Harvard University Press, 2004.
Johnson, Kirk A. "Seeing with One Eye Open: Why Sectarian Violence Measures Create an Incomplete Picture of Civilian Casualties in Iraq." Unpublished, August 28, 2007.
Joliffe, Jill. "Ramos-Horta Shot Twice." *Sydney Morning Herald*, 11 February 2008.
Jones, Bruce D. *Peacemaking in Rwanda: The Dynamics of Failure.* Boulder, CO: Lynne Rienner, 2001.
Jones, Seth G. *Counterinsurgency in Afghanistan.* Washington, DC: RAND, 2008.
———. *In the Graveyard of Empires: America's War in Afghanistan.* New York: W. W. Norton, 2009.
———. "The Rise of Afghanistan's Insurgency: State Failure and Jihad." *International Security* 32:4 (2008), 7–40.
Judah, Tim. "The Kosovo Liberation Army" Perceptions (September–November 2000), 61–77.
———. *Kosovo: War and Revenge.* New Haven: Yale University Press, 2000.
Kaban, Elif. "Rwanda Says over 40 Prisoners Killed by Rebels." Reuters News, 21 May 1996.
———. "Rwanda Genocide Killers Uproot Tutsis in Zaire." Reuters News, 28 May 1996.
———. "62 Dead in Sweep against Rwandan Rebels-Aid Workers." Reuters News, 14 July 1996.
Kakwenzire, Joan, and Dixon Kamukama, "The Development and Consolidation of Extremists Forces in Rwanda, 1990–1994," in Howard Adelman and Astri Suhrke (eds.), *The Path of Genocide: The Rwanda Crisis From Uganda to Zaire.* New Brunswick, NJ: Transaction, 2000, 61–92.
Kaldor, Mary. *New and Old Wars: Organized Violence in a Global Era.* Cambridge: Polity, 2001.
Kalyvas, Stathis. *The Logic of Violence in Civil Wars.* Cambridge: Cambridge University Press, 2006.
———. "New and Old Wars: A Valid Distinction?" *World Politics* 54:1 (October 2001), 99–118.
———. "The Ontology of 'Political Violence': Action and Identity in Civil Wars." *Perspectives on Politics* 1:3 (September 2003), 475–494.
———. "The Urban Bias in Research on Civil Wars." *Security Studies* 13:3 (Spring 2004), 160–190.
———. "Wanton and Senseless: The Logic of Massacres in Algeria." *Rationality and Society* 11:3 (1999), 243–285.
Kalyvas, Stathis N., and Nicholas M. Sambanis. "Bosnia's Civil War: Origins and Violence Dynamics," in Paul Collier and Nicholas Sambanis (eds.), *Understanding Civil War: Evidence and Analysis,* volume II. Washington, DC: World Bank, 2005, 191–229.
Kane, David. "The Lancet Surveys of Mortality in Iraq." Working Paper, Unpublished (2007).

Kaplan, Fred. *Daydream Believers: How a Few Grand Ideas Wrecked American Power.* New Jersey: John Wiley, 2008.

———. "Who Disbanded the Iraqi Army?" *Slate.com* (7 September 2007), available at http://www.slate.com/articles/news_and_politics/war_stories/2007/09/who_disbanded_the_iraqi_army.html, accessed 12 July 2012.

Kaplan, Robert. *Balkan Ghosts: A Journey Through History.* New York: Vintage, 1994.

Katzman, Kenneth. *Iraq: Post-Saddam Governance and Security.* CRS Report for Congress, 27 March 2007.

Kaufmann, Chaim. "Possible and Impossible Solutions to Ethnic Civil Wars." *International Security* 20:4 (Spring 1996), 136–175.

———. "What have we learned about Ethnic Conflict? What Can We Do in Iraq?" *Harvard International Review* 28:4 (2007), 44–50.

Kaufman, Stuart J. *Modern Hatreds: The Symbolic Politics of Ethnic War.* Ithaca: Cornell University Press, 2001.

Keen, David. *The Economic Benefits of Civil War.* London: Adelphi Papers, 1998.

Kepel, Gilles. *Jihad: The Trail of Political Islam.* London: I. B. Tauris 2008.

Khadigala, Gilbert M. "Implementing the Arusha Peace Agreement on Rwanda," in Stephen John Stedman, Donald Rothschild, and Elizabeth M. Cousens (eds.), *Ending Civil Wars: The Implementation of Peace Agreements.* Boulder, CO: Lynne Rienner, 2002, 463–498.

Kilcullen, David. *The Accidental Guerrilla.* London: Hurst, 2009.

King, Gary. *A Solution to the Ecological Inference Problem: Reconstructing Individual Behavior from Aggregate Data.* Princeton, NJ: Princeton University Press, 1997.

Kinzer, Stephen. *A Thousand Hills: Rwanda's Rebirth and the Man Who Dreamed It.* New York: John Wiley, 2008.

Kirka, Danica. "Attackers Ambush police patrol in northern Kosovo." Associated Press, 25 March 2004.

———. "Serb Woman and Child Injured in Grenade Attack." Associated Press, 6 June 2000.

Kirkpatrick, David D. "In Libya, the Fighting May Outlast the Revolution." *New York Times*, 1 November 2011.

Klein, Joe. "Saddam's Revenge." *Time Magazine*, 18 September 2005.

Knickmeyer, Ellen. "Official: Guard Force Is Behind Death Squads." *Washington Post*, 14 October 2006.

Knickmeyer, Ellen, and Muhammed Saif Aldin, "Dozens of Iraqis Killed in Reprisals" *Washington Post*, 16 October 2006.

Knox, Colin. "See No Evil, Hear No Evil: Insidious Paramilitary Violence in Northern Ireland." *British Journal of Criminology* 42:1 (2002), 164–185.

Kreutz, Joakim. "Navigating the Fog of Peace." Paper presented at the SGIR 7th Pan-European International Relations Conference, 9–11 September 2010, Stockholm.

———. "How and When Armed Conflicts End: Introducing the UCDP Conflict Termination Dataset." *Journal of Peace Research* 47:2 (2010), 243–250.

———. "Uncertainty and Civil War Recurrence." Presentation at the Jan Tinbergen Peace Science Society Conference, Amsterdam, 27–30 June 2009.

Kroeger, Alix. "SDS Ejects Founder Karadzic." BBC News, 24 December 2001.

Kukis, Mark. "Ethnic Cleansing in a Baghdad Neighbourhood." *Time Magazine.* 25 October 2006.

Kumar, Radha. *Divide and Fall: Bosnia in the Annals of Partition.* London: Verso, 1997.

Kuperman, Alan J. "The Other Lesson of Rwanda: Mediators Sometimes Do More Harm than Good." *SAIS Review* 16:1 (1996), 221–240.

———. "Provoking the Genocide: A Revised History of the Rwandan Patriotic Front." *Journal of Genocide Research* 6:1 (2004), 61–84.

Kydd, Andrew, and Barbara Walter. "Strategies of Terrorism." *International Security* 31:1 (2006), 49–80.

Laitin, David D. "Marginality." *Rationality and Society* 7:1 (1995), 49–53.

Lake, David. "Rational Extremism: Understanding Terrorism in the Twenty-First Century." *Dialog-IO* (Spring 2002), 15–29.

Lake, David, and Donald Rothschild (eds.). *The International Spread of Ethnic Conflict: Fear, Diffusion and Escalation.* Princeton: Princeton University Press, 1998.

Larise, Dunja. "Corrupted Political Elites or Mafiotic State Structures? The Case of the Federation of Bosnia-Herzegovina." *HUMSEC Journal*, no. 3 (2009), 5. Full text available at http://www.humsec.eu/cms/fileadmin/user_upload/humsec/Journal/dunnja_larise_final_version.pdf, accessed 11 June 2011.

Latal, Srecko. "Man Injured by Sniper Fire; Tension High in Sarajevo." Associated Press, 1 December 1996.

Latin, Ena. "Sarajevo Trial May Lift Lid on Assassinations," BCR Issue 338, Institute for War and Peace Reporting, 22 May 2002, available at http://iwpr.net/report-news/sarajevo-trial-may-lift-lid-assassinations, accessed 25 July 2011.

Lauras, Didier. "Rwandan Rebels Strategically Target Jails, Seek Recruits." Agence France Presse, 4 December 1997.

Le Bon, Gustave. *The Crowd: A Study of the Popular Mind.* London: Filiquarian Publishing, 2005.

Lemarchand, René. *The Dynamics of Violence in Central Africa.* Philadelphia: University of Pennsylvania Press, 2009.

Lewis, Paul. "Report Identifies Hashim Thaci as 'Big Fish' in Organized Crime." *The Guardian*, 24 January 2011.

Lichbach, Mark Irving. *The Rebel's Dilemma.* Ann Arbor: University of Michigan Press, 1998.

Licklider, Roy. "The Consequences of Negotiated Settlements in Civil Wars, 1945–1993." *American Political Science Review* 89:3 (September 1995), 681–690.

———. *Stopping the Killing: How Civil Wars End.* New York: New York University Press, 1993.

Limbach, Daniel. "Oligopolies of Violence in Post-Conflict Societies." Institute for Global and Area Studies, Hamburg, November 2007.

Lister, David, and Sean O'Neill. "IRA plc Turns from Terror into Biggest Crime Gang in Europe." *The Times*, 25 February 2005.

Londey, Peter. *Other People's Wars: A History of Australian Peacekeeping.* Crow's Nest, NSW: Allan and Unwin, 2004.

Long, Christopher. "Knights of the White Camellia," *The Handbook of Texas Online* (http://www.tshaonline.org/handbook/online/articles/vek01), accessed March 25, 2011. Published by the Texas State Historical Association.

Lord, Grayson S. "The Diplomacy on East Timor: Indonesia, the United Nations and the International Community," in James J. Fox and Dionisio Babo Soares (eds.), *Out of Ashes: The Destruction and Reconstruction of East Timor.* Canberra: ANU E Press, 2003, 74–98.

Lotrione, Catherine. "When to Target Leaders." *Washington Quarterly* 26:3 (2003), 73–86.

Lottman, Herbert. *The People's Anger: Justice and Revenge in Post-Liberation France*. London: Hutchinson Press, 1986.

Loughlan, Sean. "Rumsfeld on Looting in Iraq: Stuff Happens." CNN.com, 11 April 2003.

Luttwak, Edward. "Give War a Chance." *Foreign Affairs* 78:4 (July/August 1999), 36–44.

Lyall, Jason. "Does Indiscriminate Violence Incite Insurgent Attacks? Evidence from Chechnya." *Journal of Conflict Resolution* 53:3 (June 2009), 331–362.

Lynch, Mark. "Explaining the Awakening: Engagement, Publicity, and the Transformation of Iraqi Sunni Political Attitudes." *Security Studies* 20:1 (2011), 36–72.

MacGinty, Roger. "Indigenous Peacemaking Versus Liberal Peace." *Cooperation and Conflict* 43:2 (June 2008), 139–163.

———. "Looting in the Context of Violent Conflict: A Conceptualization and Typology." *Third World Quarterly* 25:5 (2004), 857–870.

———. "Northern Ireland: A Peace Process Thwarted by Accidental Spoiling," in Edward Newman and Oliver Richmond, *Challenges to Peacebuilding: Managing Spoilers during Conflict Resolution*. New York: United Nations University Press, 2006, 153–172.

———. *No War, No Peace: The Rejuvenation of Stalled Peace Processes and Peace Accords*. London: Palgrave, 2006.

MacGinty, Roger, and Oliver Richmond. *The Liberal Peace and Post-War Reconstruction*. London: Routledge, 2009.

Maguire, Sean. "Croat Arson Campaign Omen of NATO's Future Woes." Reuters News, 4 December 1995.

Malcolm, Noel. *Bosnia: A Short History*. New York: New York University Press, 1996.

Malik, John. "The Dayton Agreement and Elections in Bosnia: Entrenching Ethnic Cleansing through Democracy." *Stanford Journal of International Law* 32:2 (2000), 303–355.

Mamdani, Mahmood. *When Victims Become Killers*. Princeton, NJ: Princeton University Press, 2001.

Marten, Kimberly. *Warlords: Strong-Arm Brokers in Weak States*. Ithaca: Cornell University Press, 2012.

Martin, Ian. *Self-Determination in East Timor: The United Nations, the Ballot and International Intervention*. Boulder, CO: Lynne Reiner, 2001.

Mason, T. David, and Patrick J. Fett, "How Civil Wars End: A Rational Choice Approach" *Journal of Conflict Resolution* 40:4 (December 1996), 546–568.

Mavris, Lejla. "Human Smugglers and Social Networks: Transit Migration through the States of Former Yugoslavia." UNHCR Evaluation and Policy Unit, Working Paper No. 72, December 2002.

Mazower, Mark. *The Balkans: A Short History*. New York: Modern Library, 2002.

McAdam, Doug, Sidney Tarrow, and Charles Tilly. *Dynamics of Contention*. Cambridge: Cambridge University Press, 2001.

McCall, Chris. "Timor Fighter Turns His Venom on Its Leaders." *South China Morning Post*, 6 March 2003.

McCormick, Gordon, and Guillermo Owen. "Factionalism, Violence and Bargaining in Civil Wars." *Homo Oeconomicus* XX:4 (March 2004), 361–390.

McDonald, Hamish, Desmond Ball, James Dunn, Gerry van Klinken, David Bourchier, Douglas Kammen, and Richard Tanter (eds.). *Masters of Terror: Indonesia's Military and Violence in East Timor in 1999*. Canberra, Australia: Strategic and Defence Center, 2002.

McDoom, Omar. "Rwanda's Ordinary Killers: Interpreting Popular Participation in the Rwandan Genocide," Crisis States Programme, London School of Economics and Political Science, December 2005, available at http://eprints.lse.ac.uk/28153/1/wp77.pdf, accessed 19 August 2011.

McDowall, David. *A Modern History of the Kurds*. New York: I. B. Tauris, 1996.

McDowall, Liam. "Grenade Hits Sarajevo Streetcar; U.S. Helicopters Protect Airport." Associated Press, 9 January 1996.

McIlwaine, Cathy, and Carol Moser. "Violence and Social Capital in Urban Poor Communities: Perspectives from Colombia and Guatemala." *International Journal of Development* 13 (2001), 965–984.

McKinley, James C. "In Pastoral Western Rwanda, Ethnic Foes Engage in Murderous Tit-for-Tat." *New York Times*, 6 October 1996.

———. "Machete Returns to Rwanda, Rekindling a Genocidal War." *New York Times*, 15 December 1997.

———. "Rwanda's Paralyzing Wound: Hutu-Tutsi Killings." *New York Times*, 22 December 1997.

———. "Stoked by Rwandans, Tribal Violence Spreads in Zaire." *New York Times*, 16 June 1996.

McMahon, Patrice C., and Jon Western. "The Death of Dayton." *Foreign Affairs* (September/October 2009), 69–83.

McMullin, Jaremy. "Organized Criminal Groups and Conflict: The Nature and Consequence of Interdependence." *Civil Wars* 11:1 (March 2009), 75–102.

Melvern, Linda. *A Conspiracy to Murder: The Rwandan Genocide*. London: Verso, 2004.

Mertus, Julie. *Kosovo: How Myths and Truths Started a War*. Berkeley: University of California Press, 1999.

———. "Operation Allied Force: Handmaiden of an Independent Kosovo." *International Affairs* 85:3 (2009), 461–476.

Metz, Steven F. "Insurgency and Counterinsurgency in Iraq." *Washington Quarterly* (Winter 2003–2004), 25–36.

———. "The 'New' Iraq Insurgency." Project Syndicate (2005). Available at http://www.project-syndicate.org/commentary/metz1/English, accessed 11 November 2011.

Michel, Francoise. "Opposition under No Holds Barred Attack in Northwest Bosnia." Agence France Presse, 25 August 1996.

Midlarsky, Manus I. "Nihilism in Political Chaos: Himmler, Bin Laden and Altruistic Punishment." *Studies in Conflict and Terrorism* 27 (2004), 187–296.

Mieth, Terance D., and Kriss A. Drass. "Exploring the Social Context of Instrumental and Expressive Homicides: An Application of Qualitative Comparative Analysis." *Journal of Quantitative Criminology* 15:1 (1999), 1–21.

Migdal, Joel S. *Strong Societies and Weak States: State-Society Relations and the State in the Third World*. Princeton: Princeton University Press, 1988.

Modvig, J., J. Pagaduan-Lopez, J. Rodenberg, CMD Salud, et al. "Torture and Trauma in Post-Conflict East Timor." *The Lancet* 356 (18 November 2000), 1763.

Montgomery, Michael. "Horrors of the KLA Prison Camp." BBC News, 10 April 2009, available at http://news.bbc.co.uk/2/hi/europe/7990984.stm accessed 10 April 2009.

Moore, Solomon, and Louise Roug. "Deaths across Iraq Shows It Is a Nation of Many Wars, with U.S. in the Middle." *Los Angeles Times*, 7 October 2006.

Moratti, Massimo, and Amra Sabic El-Rayess. "Transitional Justice and DDR: The Case of Bosnia-Herzegovina." International Center for Transitional Justice, June 2009.

Mseteka, Buchizya. "Former Rwandan Minister Wounded in Attack." Reuters News, 27 February 1996.

———. "Hutu Rebels Kill Mayor, 11 Others in Northwest Rwanda." Reuters News, 11 December 1997.

Mueller, John. "The Banality of 'Ethnic War.'" *International Security* 25:1 (Summer 2000), 42–70.

———. *Remnants of War*. 2nd edition. Ithaca: Cornell University Press, 2007.

Muggah, Robert. "No Magic Bullet: A Critical Perspective on Disarmament, Demobilization and Reintegration (DDR) and Weapons Reductions in Post-Conflict Contexts." *Round Table* 94:379 (April 2005), 239–252.

Muja, Aferdita. "Ethnic Albanians Burn Down Serb Houses in Kosovo." Reuters News, 20 June 1999.

Mulrine, Anna. "Marine Chief: Disbanding Iraqi Army Was a Big Mistake." *US News and World Report*, 14 March 2007.

Murdoch, Lindsay. "President Pardons Rebels Who Shot Him." *Sydney Morning Herald*. 25 August 2010.

Mutler, Alison. "Peacekeepers Clash with Serbs in Kosovo." Associated Press, 5 April 2000.

Nagl, John. *Learning How to Eat Soup with a Knife*. Chicago: University of Chicago Press, 2005.

Nettlefield, Lara J. *Courting Democracy in Bosnia and Herzegovina: The Hague Tribunal's Impact in a Post-War State*. Cambridge: Cambridge University Press, 2010.

Neumann, Peter R., and M. L. R. Smith. "Strategic Terrorism: The Framework and Its Fallacies." *Journal of Strategic Studies* 28:4 (2005), 571–595.

Nevins, Joseph. *A Not-So-Distant Horror: Mass Violence in East Timor*. Ithaca: Cornell University Press, 2005.

New York Times. "At Least Twelve Shot Dead Inside Rwandan Camp." 8 January 1995.

———. "Hutu Militiamen Kill 3 Spanish Aid Workers in Rwanda." 20 January 1997.

———. "Rwanda and Zaire Units Exchange Fire on Border." 25 September 1996.

Newman, Edward, and Oliver Richmond. "Peace Building and Spoilers." *Conflict, Security and Development* 6 (2006), 101–110.

Newsweek International. "The Fire This Time: A New Round of Balkan Revenge and Bloodletting Begins. But This Time the Targets Are Kosovo's Serbs." 5 July 1999.

Nieburg, H. L. *Political Violence*. New York: St. Martin's Press, 1969.

Nilsson, Desirée. "Partial Peace: Rebel Groups Inside and Outside of Civil War Settlements." *Journal of Peace Research* 45:4 (2008), 479–495.

Nilsson, Desirée, and Mimmi Söderberg. "Revisiting an Elusive Concept: A Review of the Debate on Spoilers in Peace Processes." *International Studies Review* 13 (2011), 606–626.

Nilsson, R. Anders. *Dangerous Liaisons: Why Ex-Combatants Return to Violence; Cases from the Republic of Congo and Sierra Leone*. Report/Uppsala University, 2008.

Nitzschke, Heiko, and Kaysie Studdard. "The Legacies of War Economies: Challenges and Options for Peacemaking and Peacebuilding." *International Peacekeeping* 12:2 (2005), 222–239.

Oakley, Robert B., Michael J. Dziedzic, and Eliot M. Goldberg (eds.). *Policing the New World Disorder: Peace Operations and Public Security*. Washington, DC: National Defense University, 1998.

O'Ballance, Edgar. *Civil War in Bosnia, 1992–1994*. New York: St. Martin's 1995.

O'Brien, Emma. "East Timor Rioters Attack UN Convoy as Violence Expands East." Bloomburg, 13 August 2007.

O'Bryant, JoAnne, and Michael Waterhouse. "U.S. Forces in Iraq." *CRS Report for Congress*, 24 July 2008.

O'Connor, Mike. "Muslim Rioters in Bosnia Attack on a U.S. Army Column." *New York Times*, 15 November 1996.

———. "Violence Flares as Bosnians Try to Regain Their Prewar Homes." *New York Times*, 22 April 1996.

Odom, Lt. Colonel Thomas P. "Guerrillas in the Mist: A Defense Attaché Watches the Rwandan Patriotic Front Transform from Insurgent to Counterinsurgent." *Small Wars Journal* (July 2006), 1–14.

O'Hanlon, Michael. "A Flawed Masterpiece." *Foreign Affairs* 81:3 (May/June 2002), 47–63.

O'Neill, William G. *Kosovo: An Unfinished Peace*. London: Lynne Reiner, 2002.

Orth, Rick. "Rwanda's Hutu Extremist Genocidal Insurgency: An Eyewitness Perspective." *Small Wars and Insurgencies* 12:1 (Spring 2001), 76–109.

Osland, Kari M. "The EU Police Mission in Bosnia and Herzegovina." *International Peacekeeping* 11:3 (2004), 544–560.

Osler Hampson, Fen. *Nurturing Peace: Why Peace Settlements Succeed or Fail*. Washington, DC: USIP Press, 1996.

Ó Tuathail, Gearóid, and Carl Dahlman. "The Effort to Reverse Ethnic Cleansing in Bosnia-Herzegovina: The Limits of Return." *Eurasian Geography and Economics* 45:6 (2004), 439–464.

Oxford English Dictionary. Volume 12. Oxford: Clarendon Press, 1978.

Packer, George. *The Assassin's Gate*. New York: Farrar, Straus and Giroux, 2005.

Pain, Hugh. "Kosovo Mine Blast Kills Two Serbs." Reuters, 15 June 2000.

Parenti, Michael. *To Kill a Nation: The Attack on Yugoslavia*. London: Verso, 2000.

Paris, Roland. *At War's End*. Cambridge: Cambridge University Press, 2004.

Patir, Yael. "The Israeli-Palestinian Conflict and the Israeli Perception of 'No Partner' for Peace: An Insight into the Israeli Mindset." Atkins Paper Series, International Center for the Study of Radicalization, October 2011, available at http://www.icsr.info/publications/papers/1319713960ICSR_AtkinPaperSeries_YaelPatir.pdf, accessed 22 July 2012.

Pearlman, Wendy. "Spoiling Inside and Out: Internal Political Contestation and the Middle East Peace Process." *International Security* 33:3 (Winter 2008–2009), 79–109.

Perito, Robert M. *Where Is the Lone Ranger When We Need Him? America's Search for a Post-Conflict Stability Force*. Washington, DC: USIP, 2004.

Perito, Robert M., and David Bayley (eds.). *The Police in War: Fighting, Insurgency and Violent Crime*. Boulder, CO: Lynne Rienner, 2010.

Petersen, Roger. *Understanding Ethnic Violence: Fear, Hatred and Resentment in Twentieth Century Eastern Europe*. Cambridge: Cambridge University Press, 2002.

Peyrille, Alexandre. "Car Bomb Kills One Serb, Injures Four in Pristina: KFOR." Agence France Presse, 18 April 2001.

Pillar, Paul. *Negotiating Peace: War Termination as a Bargaining Process.* Princeton: Princeton University Press, 1983.
Polk, William R. *Understanding Iraq.* New York: Harper Collins, 2005.
Pomfret, John. "Rwandans Led the Revolt in Congo." *Washington Post*, 9 July 1997.
Popkin, Samuel. *The Rational Peasant: The Political Economy of Rural Society in Vietnam.* Berkeley: University of California Press, 1979.
Posen, Barry. "The Security Dilemma and Ethnic Conflict." *Survival* 35:1 (Spring 1993), 27–47.
Potter, Beth. "Newsman, Villager Killed in Kosovo Border Shelling." Reuters, 29 March 2001.
Power, Samantha. *"A Problem from Hell": America and the Age of Genocide.* New York: Harper Perennial, 2002.
Pozhidaev, Dmitry, and Razva Andzhelich. "Beating Swords into Ploughshares: Reintegration of Former Combatants in Kosovo." Pristina: February 2005, available at http://unddr.org/docs/Beating%20Swords%20Into%20Plowshares.pdf, accessed 10 November 2011.
Priest, Dana. *The Mission: Waging War and Keeping Peace with America's Military.* New York: W. W. Norton, 2004.
Prunier, Gerard. *From Genocide to Continental War: The "Congolese" Conflict and the Crisis of Contemporary Africa.* London: Hurst and Company, 2009.
———. *The Rwanda Crisis: History of a Genocide.* 6th edition. London: Hurst and Company, 2008.
Pugh, Michael. "Postwar Political Economy in Bosnia and Herzegovina: The Spoils of Peace." *Global Governance* 8:4 (October/December 2002), 467–482.
Putnam, Robert. "Diplomacy and Domestic Politics: The Logic of Two Level Games." *International Organization* 42:3 (Summer 1988), 427–460.
Quinlivan, James T. "Burden of Victory: The Painful Arithmetic of Stability Operations." *RAND Review* (Summer 2003), available at http://www.rand.org/publications/randreview/issues/summer2003/burden.html, accessed on 19 July 2012.
———. "Coup-Proofing: Its Practice and Consequence in the Middle East." *International Security* 24:2 (Fall 1999), 131–165.
Rable, George C. *But There Was No Peace: The Role of Violence in the Politics of the Reconstruction.* Athens: University of Georgia Press, 2007.
Radio Australia, "UN Steps Up Security Ahead of Elections," 8 February 2007, available at http://www.radioaustralia.net.au/international/radio/onairhighlights/451068, accessed 11 January 2013.
Radio Free Europe. "FBI Reports: Saddam's Weapons Bluff Aimed at Iran." 2 July 2009.
Ratnesar, Romesh, Brian Bennett, Simon Robinson, Vivienne Walt, and Hassan Fattah. "Vengeance Has Its Day." *Time Magazine*, 1 December 2003.
Reno, William. "Understanding Criminality in West African Conflicts." *International Peacekeeping* 16:1 (2009), 47–61.
Rees, Edward. "The UN's Failure to Integrate Falintil Veterans May Cause East Timor to Fail." *Online Opinion Australia*, 2 September 2003.
Reuters. "Amnesty Getting Daily Reports of Rwanda Massacres." 19 December 1997.
———. "Ancient Kosovo City Hit by Arson, Serbs Terrified." 13 July 1999.
———. "At Least 43 Killed in Fresh Rwanda Violence." 11 July 1996.
———. "Attack on Serbs Followed Disappearance of Moslems." 7 September 1996.

———. "Blast Hurts Kosovo Serbs—UN." 31 August 2003.
———. "Bomb Injures Ex-Kosovo Guerrilla and Family." 21 January 2002.
———. "Bosnia Fetes Christmas Peace Despite Air Attack." 25 December 1995.
———. "Bosnian Croat Leader Condemns Mosque Attack." 17 March 1997.
———. "Eight Macedonian Soldiers Killed near Border." 28 April 2001.
———. "Fifteen Rwandan Genocide Survivors Killed in Attack." 21 June 1996.
———. "Four Bosnians Killed in Kosovo Attack." 12 January 2000.
———. "Grenade attack on Kosovo Café Injures Three." 14 September 1999.
———. "Grenades Kill Two Kosovo Serbs, U.N. Alarmed." 28 September 1999.
———. "Gunmen Kill Local Official in Rwanda—Radio." 5 March 1996.
———. "Gunmen Kill Rwandan Judge." 31 August 1995.
———. "Gunmen Pin Down Kosovo Peacekeepers for Two Hours." 29 August 2002.
———. "Iraqi Red Crescent Says 500 Killed in Yazidi Attack." 22 August 2007.
———. "Kosovo Albanian Politician Shot Dead." 17 January 2002.
———. "Kosovo Guerrilla Veterans Warn of New War." 8 July 2007.
———. "Kosovo Guerrillas Execute Three Serbs—Beta Agency." 14 June 1999.
———. "Kosovo Peacekeepers and Protesters Clash, Many Hurt." 15 August 2002.
———. "Kosovo Peacekeepers Shot at Near Serbian Boundary." 4 May 2001.
———. "Kosovo Serb Killed, Several Hurt in Attack on Café." 18 December 1999.
———. "Leading Kosovo Serb Politician Wounded—KFOR." 1 November 1999.
———. "Local Albanian Official Wounded in Shooting Daily." 3 August 2000.
———. "Man Shot Dead at Kosovo Guerrilla Headquarters." 26 September 1999.
———. "Masked Gunmen Wound New Kosovo Councilor." 16 November 2000.
———. "More Killings Reported in Kosovo." 14 December 1999.
———. "NATO Chief Raps Bosnia Factions on Peace Breaches." 4 January 1996.
———. "One Policeman Shot Dead in Kosovo—UN Official." 7 September 2003.
———. "Over 10 Wounded in Grenade Attacks on Kosovo's Serbs." 8 August 1999.
———. "Powell Tells Kosovo Leaders to Act against Violence." 13 April 2001.
———. "Research Halves Bosnia Death Toll." 24 November 2005.
———. "Rwandan Troops Kill 16—Civilians." 19 April 1995.
———. "Rwandan Troops Taking Law into Own Hands—Amnesty." 6 April 1995.
———. "Rwandan Villagers Kill 27 Hutu Rebels." 2 November 1998.
———. "Scores Arrested in Wake of Kosovo Violence." 22 March 2004.
———. "Serb Killed in Kosovo Mortar Attack." 8 November 1999.
———. "Serb Working for UN Killed in Kosovo." 16 May 2000.
———. "Serious Attacks Mar Kosovo Peace." 5 September 1999.
———. "Seven Rwandan Soldiers Killed in Attack—Radio." 4 February 1996.
———. "Sniper Attack on Sarajevo Tram Breaks Peace." 18 December 1996.
———. "Three Killed in Gangland-Style Kosovo Shooting." 3 April 2003.
———. "Three Shot Dead in Kosovo Revenge Ambush." 4 January 2003.
———. "Two Kosovo Albanian Moderates Shot Dead." 20 October 2001.
———. "Two Local Officials Assassinated in Southern Rwanda." 28 February 1996.
———. "UN Says 162 People Killed in Rwanda in May." 13 June 1996.
———. "UN Workers Say Over 100 Killed in Rwanda Operation." 25 July 1996.
———. "Update 1: Kosovo Leaders Tell Macedonia Rebels to Stop Fight." 22 March 2001.

Reed, Wm. Cyrus. "Exile, Reform and the Rise of the Rwandan Patriotic Front." *Journal of Modern African Studies* 34:3 (September 1996), 479–501.

———. "The Rwandan Patriotic Front: Politics and Development in Rwanda." *Issue: A Journal of Opinion* 23:2 (1995), 48–53.

Reyntjens, Filip. *The Great African War: Congo and Regional Geopolitics, 1996–2006.* Cambridge: Cambridge University Press, 2009.

———. "Rwanda, Ten Years On: From Genocide to Dictatorship." *African Affairs* 103 (2004), 177–210.

Richmond, Oliver P. *The Transformation of Peace*. London: Palgrave, 2005.

———. "UN Peace Operations and the Dilemmas of the Peacebuilding Consensus." *International Peacekeeping* 11:1 (Spring 2004), 83–101.

Ricks, Thomas. *Fiasco: The American Military Adventure in Iraq*. New York: Penguin, 2006.

Rieff, David. "Abandoning Bosnia—Again." *Newsweek*, 16 September 1996.

———. *Slaughterhouse: Bosnia and the Failure of the West*. New York: Touchstone, 1996.

Roberts, Adam. "NATO's 'Humanitarian War' over Kosovo." *Survival* 41:3 (Autumn 1999), 102–123.

Roberts, L., et al, "Mortality Before and After the 2003 Invasion of Iraq: Cluster Sample Survey." *Lancet* 364:9448 (2004), 1857–1864.

Robinson, Bruce. "The Blitz," 30 March 2011, available at http://www.bbc.co.uk/history/worldwars/wwtwo/ff3_blitz.shtml, accessed 16 July 2012.

Robinson, Matt, and Daria Sito Sucic. "Two Decades from War, a New Fight to Save Bosnia." *Chicago Tribune*, 4 April 2012.

Robinson, W. S. "Ecological Correlations and the Behaviour of Individuals." *American Sociological Review* 15 (June 1950), 351–357.

Roddy, Michael. "Kosovo Woman Killed, Agencies Warn on Minorities." Reuters, 9 September 1999.

Romano, David. *The Kurdish Nationalist Movement: Opportunity, Mobilization and Identity.* Cambridge: Cambridge University Press, 2006.

Rose, Gideon. *How Wars End: Why We Always Fight the Last Battle*. New York: Simon and Schuster, 2010.

Rosenberg, Mica. "Witness—In Guatemala, Violence Is Always Near." Reuters, 3 February 2008.

Rule, James B. *Theories of Civil Violence*. Berkeley: University of California Press, 1988.

Sahin, Selver B. "Building the State in Timor-Leste." *Asian Survey* 47:2 (March/April 2007), 250–267.

Salehyan, Idean, and Kristian Skedre Gleditsch. "Refugees and the Spread of Civil War." *International Organization* 60 (Spring 2006), 335–366.

Sambanis, Nicholas. "Partition as a Solution to Ethnic War: An Empirical Critique of the Theoretical Literature." *World Politics* 52 (July 2000), 437–483.

Scambray, James. "Anatomy of a Conflict: The 2006–2007 Communal Violence in East Timor." *Conflict, Security and Development* 9:2 (2009), 265–288.

———. "A Survey of Gangs and Youth Groups in Dili, Timor-Leste," a Report Commissioned by Australia's Agency for International Development, AUSAID. 15 September 2006.

Schear, James A. "Bosnia's Post-Dayton Traumas." *Foreign Policy* 104 (Autumn 1996), 86–101.

Schelling, Thomas. *Arms and Influence*. New Haven: Yale University Press, 1966.
Schenker, Harald. "Violence in Kosovo and the Way Ahead." *ECMI Brief* #10. March 2004.
Schork, Kurt. "Peace Puts Down Roots in Bosnia—before NATO Comes." Reuters News, 15 December 1996.
———. "UN Plays Down Serbs Sarajevo Truce Violations." Reuters News, 15 December 1996.
Schwander-Sievers, Stephanie. "The Enactment of 'Tradition': Albanian Constructions of Identity, Violence and Power in Times of Crisis," in Bettina E. Schmidt and Ingo W. Schroeder (eds.), *Anthropology of Violence and Conflict*. London: Routledge, 2001, 97–120.
Scott, James C. *Domination and the Arts of Resistance: Hidden Transcripts*. New Haven: Yale University Press, 1990.
———. "Patron-Client Politics and Political Change in Southeast Asia." *American Political Science Review* 66:1 (1972), 91–113.
———. *Weapons of the Weak: Everyday Forms of Peasant Resistance*. New Haven: Yale University Press, 1985.
Seelke, Clare Ribando. "Gangs in Central America." Congressional Research Service Report. 26 November 2012.
Semple, Kirk. "Kidnapped in Iraq: Victim's Tale of Clockwork Death and Ransom." *New York Times*. 7 May 2006.
Sengupta, Kim. "Afghanistan: Slipping Out of Control." *The Independent*, 19 February 2009.
Sengupta, Kim, and Solomon Hughes. "Leaked UN Report Reveals Torture, Lynching and Abuse in Post-Gaddafi Libya." *The Independent*, 24 November 2011.
Senier, Amy. "Traditional Justice as Transitional Justice: A Comparative Case Study of Rwanda and East Timor." *Praxis: The Fletcher Journal of Human Security* 13 (2008), 67–88.
Shafer, D. Michael. "The Unlearned Lessons of Counter-Insurgency." *Political Science Quarterly* 103 (Spring 1988), 57–80.
Shanker, Thom. "New Strategy Vindicates Ex-Army Chief Shinseki." *New York Times*, 12 January 2007.
Shanty, Frank G., and Patit Paban Mishra. *Organized Crime: An International Encyclopedia* (Santa Barbara: ABC-CLIO, 2008).
Shapiro, Herbert. *White Violence and Black Response*. Amherst: University of Massachusetts Press, 1988.
Shawcross, William. *Deliver Us From Evil: Warlords and Peacekeepers in a World of Endless Conflict*. London: Bloomsbury, 2000.
Shoesmith, Dennis. "Divided Leadership in a Semi-Presidential System." *Asian Survey* 43: 2 (2003), 231–252.
Silber, Laura, and Allan Little. *Yugoslavia: Death of a Nation*. New York: TV Books, 1996.
Silverstein, Ken. "Our Scary New Best Friends." *Salon*, 25 September 2001.
Simons, Geoff. *Iraq: From Sumer to Saddam*. New York: St. Martin's Press, 2004.
Simons, Marlise. "Former Leader in Kosovo Acquitted of War Crimes." *New York Times*. 4 April 2008.
Simonsen, Sven Gunmar. "Addressing Ethnic Divisions in Post-Conflict State-Building: Lessons from Recent Cases." *Security Dialogue* 36:3 (2005), 297–318.
Sinno, Abdulkader H. "Armed Groups' Organizational Structure and Their Strategic Options." *International Review of the Red Cross* 9:882 (June 2011), 311–332.

Siperco, Ian. "Subversive Markets: The Economic Roots of the Iraq Insurgency." RUSI Papers (2007).

Skinner, Quentin. *Visions of Politics*. Volume I: *Regarding Method*. Cambridge: Cambridge University Press, 2002.

Sluglett, Peter. *Britain in Iraq: Contriving King and Country.* New York: Columbia University Press, 2007.

Smerdon, Peter. "Rwandan Genocide Survivors Being Hunted Down—Report." Reuters News, 3 April 1996.

Smith, Anthony. "Timor Leste: Strong Government, Weak State." *Southeast Asian Affairs* (2004), 279–294. Singapore: ISEAS Publications.

Smith, Michael G., and Moreen Dee. *Peacekeeping in East Timor: The Path to Independence*. Boulder: Lynne Reiner, 2003.

Snidal, Duncan. "Relative Gains and the Problem of International Cooperation." *American Political Science Review* 85:3 (1991), 701–726.

Snyder, Jack. *From Voting to Violence: Democratization and Nationalist Conflict*. New York: W. W. Norton, 2000.

Sofalia, Korik. "Kosovo Parliament to Investigate Illegal Intelligence Service SHIK." Technorati, 24 April 2011, available at http://technorati.com/politics/article/kosovo-parliament-to-investigate-on-illegal/, accessed 11 November 2011.

Soloway, Colin. "Fair or Not, Results of Bosnia Elections Are Now Certified." *Chicago Tribune*, 30 September 1996.

Spector, Ronald H. *In the Ruins of Empire: The Japanese Surrender and the Battle for Postwar Asia*. New York: Random House, 2008.

Staniland, Paul. "Organizing Insurgency: Networks, Resources and Rebellion in South Asia." *International Security* 37:1 (Summer 2012), 142–177.

Stanley, Elizabeth A., and John P. Sawyer. "The Equifinality of War Termination: Multiple Paths to Ending War." *Journal of Conflict Resolution* 53 (2009), 651–676.

Stansfield, Gareth. *Iraq*. Cambridge: Polity, 2007.

Stedman, Stephen John. "Spoiler Problems in Peace Processes." *International Security* 22:2 (1997), 5–53.

Stedman, Stephen, Donald Rothschild, and Elizabeth M. Cousens (eds.). *Ending Civil Wars: The Implementation of Peace Agreements*. Boulder, CO: Lynne Rienner, 2002.

Steenkamp, Chrissie. "The Legacy of War: Conceptualizing a 'Culture of Violence' to Explain Violence after Peace Accords." *Round Table* 94 (2005), 253–267.

Stephen, Chris. "Serbs Attacks Moslems in Disputed Bosnian Village." Agence France Presse, 26 January 1997.

Stewart, Pamela J., and Andrew Strathern. *Violence: Theory and Ethnography*. London: Continuum Press, 2002.

Stewart, Rory. *Occupational Hazards*. London: Picador, 2006.

Stigler, Andrew L. "A Clear Victory for Air Power: NATO's Empty Threat to Invade Kosovo." *International Security* 27:3 (Winter 2002–2003), 124–157.

Straus, Scott. *The Order of Genocide: Race, Power and War in Rwanda*. Ithaca: Cornell University Press, 2006.

Stuart, Gregory L., and Richard B. Stuart, "Instrumental Violence." *Encyclopedia of Interper-*

sonal Violence (2008), available at http://dbproxy.lasalle.edu:2592/entry/sageiv/instrumental_violence, accessed 10 November 2011.

Suskind, Ron. *The One Percent Doctrine: Deep Inside America's Pursuit of Its Enemies Since 9/11.* New York: Simon and Schuster, 2006.

Sydney Morning Herald. "East Timor Tense as Soldiers Desert Barracks." 30 March 2006.

Taneja, Preti. "Assimilation, Exodus and Eradication: Iraq's Minority Communities since 2003." Minority Rights Group International (2007), available at http://www.minorityrights.org/?lid=2805, accessed 22 July 2013.

Tarrow, Sidney. "Cycles of Collective Action: Between Moments of Madness and the Repertoire of Contention." *Social Science History* 17:2 (Summer 1993), 281–307.

———. *Power in Movement: Social Movements and Contentious Politics.* Cambridge: Cambridge University Press, 1998.

Tavernise, Sabrina. "Cycle of Revenge Fuels a Pattern in Iraqi Killings." *New York Times*, 20 November 2006.

Taylor, Michael. "Rational and Revolutionary Collective Action," in Michael Hechter (ed.), *Rationality and Revolution.* Cambridge: Cambridge University Press, 1988, 63–97.

Tenet, George. *At the Centre of the Storm: My Years at the CIA.* New York: Harper Collins, 2007.

Terry, Fiona. *Condemned to Repeat: The Paradox of Humanitarian Action.* Ithaca: Cornell University Press, 2002.

Themner, Anders. *Violence in Post-Conflict Societies: Remobilizers and Relationships.* London: Routledge, 2011.

Tilghman, Andrew. "The Myth of AQI." *Washington Monthly*, October 2007, available at http://www.washingtonmonthly.com/features/2007/0710.tilghman.html, accessed 8 August 2011.

Tilly, Charles. *Coercion, Capital and European States, AD 990–1992.* London: Blackwell, 1992.

———. "Does Modernization Breed Revolution?" *Comparative Politics* 5:3 (April 1973), 425–477.

———. *From Mobilization to Revolution.* Reading, MA: Addison-Wesley, 1978.

———. *The Politics of Collective Violence.* Cambridge: Cambridge University Press, 2003.

———. "Warmaking and State-Making as Organized Crime," in Peter Evans, Dietrich Ruschemeyer, and Theda Skocpol, *Bringing the State Back in.* Cambridge: Cambridge University Press, 1985, 169–187.

Tilly, Charles, and Sidney Tarrow. *Contentious Politics.* Boulder: Paradigm, 2006.

Toft, Monica Duffy. *The Geography of Ethnic Conflict: Identity, Interests and the Indivisibility of Territory.* Princeton: Princeton University Press, 2005.

———. *Securing the Peace: The Durable Settlement of Civil Wars.* Princeton: Princeton University Press, 2010.

Traub, James. "Inventing East Timor." *Foreign Affairs* 79 (July/August 2000), 74–89.

Tripp, Charles. *A History of Iraq.* Cambridge: Cambridge University Press, 2007.

Tucker, Robert C. "The Theory of Charismatic Leadership." *Daedalus* 97:3 (Summer 1968), 731–756.

Ucko, David H. *The New Counterinsurgency Era: Transforming the U.S. Military for Modern Wars.* Washington, DC: Georgetown University Press, 2009.

USA Today. "Army Chief: War to Occupy Iraq Massive." 25 February 2003.
———. "Iraqis Told to Arm for Self-Defense after 220 Killed." July 8, 2007.
———. "Rumsfeld Blames Iraq Problems on 'Pockets of Dead Enders.'" 18 June 2003.
Valentino, Benjamin A. *Final Solutions: Mass Killing and Genocide in the 20th Century.* Ithaca: Cornell University Press, 2004.
Valentino, Benjamin, Paul Huth, and Dylan Balch Lindsay. "Draining the Sea: Mass Killing and Guerrilla Warfare." *International Organization* 58 (Spring 2004), 375–407.
Vasovic, Alexander. "Fight in Divided Town Sparks Violence, Dozens Wounded." Associated Press, 7 March 2000.
———. "Shots, Grenades, Blast on Serb Side of Divided City Leaves Wounded." Associated Press, 7 March 2000.
Vatikiotis, Michael R. J. *Indonesian Politics under Suharto: The Rise and Fall of the New Order.* 3rd edition. London: Routledge, 1998.
Vermeylan, Jan. "Two Serb Teenagers Killed in Kosovo Mortar Attack." Reuters News, 17 August 1999.
Verwimp, Philip. "Machetes and Firearms: The Organization of Massacres in Rwanda." *Journal of Peace Research* 43:5 (2006), 5–22.
———. "Testing the Double Genocide Thesis for Central and Southern Rwanda." *Journal of Conflict Resolution* 47:4 (August 2003), 423–442.
Waldmann, Peter. "Revenge without Rules: On the Renaissance of an Archaic Motif of Violence." *Studies in Conflict and Terrorism* 24 (2001), 435–450.
Waller, Michael, Kyril Drezov, and Bulent Gokay. *Kosovo: The Politics of Delusion.* London: Frank Cass, 2001.
Walter, Barbara. "The Critical Barrier to Civil War Settlement." *International Organization.* 51:3 (Summer 1997), 335–364.
———. "Designing Transitions from Civil War: Demobilization, Democratization and Commitments to Peace." *International Security* 24:1 (1999), 127–155.
Walter, Barbara, and Jack Snyder (eds.). *Civil Wars, Insecurity and Intervention.* New York: Columbia University Press, 1999.
Wantchekon, Leonard, and Etienne Yehoue. "Crime in New Democracies." Draft paper, 8 November 2002.
Washington Post. "Iraqis Hunting, Killing Former Baathists." 20 May 2003.
Watson, Catherine. "War and Waiting." *Africa Report* (November/December 1992), 51–55.
Watson, Paul. "Report Details Cycle of Violence in Kosovo." *Los Angeles Times*, 7 December 1999.
Weber, Max. *Theory of Social and Economic Organization.* New York: Free Press, 1997.
Wedgewood, Ruth. "Trouble in Timor." *Foreign Affairs* 79:6 (November/December 2000), 197–199.
Weinstein, Jeremy M. *Inside Rebellion: The Politics of Insurgent Violence.* Cambridge: Cambridge University Press, 2007.
Weller, Marc, and Stefan Wolff. "Bosnia and Herzegovina Ten Years after Dayton: Lessons for Internationalized Statebuilding." *Ethnopolitics* 5:1 (March 2006), 1–13.
Werner, Suzanne. "Negotiating the Terms of the Settlement: War Aims and Bargaining Leverage." *Journal of Conflict Resolution* 42:3 (June 1998), 321–343.

———. "The Precarious Nature of Peace: Resolving the Issues, Enforcing the Settlement, and Renegotiating the Terms." *American Journal of Political Science* 43:3 (July 1999), 912–934.

Werner, Suzanne, and Amy Yuen, "Making and Keeping Peace." *International Organization* 59 (Spring 2005), 261–292.

Wetta, Frank J. "Bulldozing the Scalawags: Some Examples of the Persecution of Southern White Republicans in Louisiana During Reconstruction." *Louisiana History* 21:1 (Winter 1980), 43–58.

Weymouth, Anthony, and Stanley Henis (eds.). *The Kosovo Crisis: The Last American War in Europe?* London: Pearson Education, 2001.

Williams, Phil. "Criminals, Militias and Insurgents: Organized Crime in Iraq." Carlisle, PA: Strategic Studies Institute, June 2009.

———. "Organized Crime and Corruption in Iraq." *International Peacekeeping* 16:1 (2009), 115–135.

———. "Organized Crime in Iraq: Strategic Surprise and Lessons for Future Contingencies." *Prism* 1:2 (2010), 47–68.

Wilson, James Q. "The Economy of Patronage." *Journal of Political Economy* 69:4 (August 1961), 369–380.

Woherl, Steven. *Bosnia: Current Issues and U.S. Policy*. Washington, DC: Congressional Research Service, 27 February 2012..

Wood, Elizabeth Jean. *Insurgent Collective Action in El Salvador*. New York: Cambridge University Press, 2004.

Wood, Nicholas. "Kosovo Gripped by Racketeers." BBC News, 5 April 2000.

———. "Kosovo War-Crimes Trial Splits West and Prosecutors." *New York Times*, 8 April 2007.

Woodward, Bob. *Plan of Attack*. New York: Simon and Schuster, 2004.

———. *State of Denial*. New York: Simon and Schuster, 2006.

Woodward, Susan L. *Balkan Tragedy: Chaos and Dissolution after the Cold War*. Washington, DC: Brookings Institute, 1995.

———. "Bosnia-Herzegovina: How Not to End a Civil War," in Barbara F. Walter and Jack Snyder (eds.), *Civil War, Insecurity and Intervention*. New York: Columbia University Press, 1999, 73–115.

———. "Humanitarian War: A New Consensus?" *Disasters* 25:4 (2001), 331–344.

———. *Implementing Peace in Bosnia and Herzegovina: A Post-Dayton Primer and a Memorandum of Warning*. Washington, DC: Brookings Institute, 1996.

Woolfolk Higgins, Sarah. *The Scalawag in Alabama Politics, 1865–1881*. Tuscaloosa: University of Alabama Press, 1977.

Woollacott, Martin. "Iraq's Insurgents Are More Nihilist than Nationalist." *The Guardian*, 6 February 2004.

Zahar, Marie Joelle. "Political Violence in Peace Processes: Voice, Exit, and Loyalty in the Post-Accord Period," in John Darby (ed.), *Violence and Reconstruction*. Notre Dame: University of Notre Dame Press, 2006, 33–53.

Zakaria, Fareed. "The Rise of Illiberal Democracy." *Foreign Affairs* (November/December 1997), 22–43.

Zartman, William (ed.). *Elusive Peace: Negotiating an End to Civil War.* Washington, DC: Brookings Institute, 1995.

Zeri Weekly, 22 January 2000.

Zimmerman, Warren. *Origins of a Catastrophe.* New York: Times Books, 1996.

Zinecker, Heidrum. "From Exodus to Exitus: Causes of Post-War Violence in El Salvador." Peace Research Institute Frankfurt, Report No. 80 (2007).

INDEX

Note: Page numbers in *italics* indicate figures and tables.

AAK (Alliance for the Future of Kosovo), 188–89, 212
ABRI/TNI (Indonesian military), 227, 229–31, 236, 247–48
actors: in case studies, 311; custodians of peace, 326n63; in post-conflict states, 8, 54, 75–76; signing of peace settlements by, 12–14, 76–77; static images of, 174, 301, 314. *See also* insurgencies; international organizations; military services; police services; targets of attacks
ADFL (Alliance of Democratic Forces for the Liberation of Congo-Zaire), 150, 152, 173
Afghanistan: ethnic cleansing in, 323n15; fears of quagmire in, 2–3; geographic variation in violence in, 71–72; as hard security environment, 55; motives for violence in, 34–35; as post-conflict state, 50, 51
Agoglia, John, 273
Ahtisaari, Martti, 184
Albania, 361n135
Albanian Liberation Army (ALA), 191
Albanian National Army (ANA/AKSh), 190–91, 216
Albright, Madeleine, 315
Alkatiri, Mari: as Chief Minister, 233; compromises and, 236; Gusmao and, 237–38; patronage and, 249; Petitioners and, 253; as prime minister, 234, 250; resignation of, 255
Allawi, Ali A., 262, 264
Allawi, Ayad, 278
Alliance for the Future of Kosovo (AAK), 188–89, 212

Alliance of Democratic Forces for the Liberation of Congo-Zaire (ADFL), 150, 152, 173
al Qaeda in Iraq, 258, 260, 267, 277–78, 296, 300
Amin, Idi, 154
Amnesty International report on Rwanda, 169–70
ANA/AKSh (Albanian National Army), 190–91, 216
Andreas, Peter, 40–41, 126
Angola, 67, 75
Annan, Kofi, 169, 222
armed conflict: experience of, as shaping post-conflict states, 52–55; in Iraq, 282–83, *283*. *See also* civil wars; relapse into armed conflict; wars
Armed Forces of the Republic of Kosovo (FARK), 190
armed groups: distributional (reward) and policing activities of, 83–84; horizontal alliance of, 311–12; splintering of, 84–87. *See also* demobilization, disarmament, and reintegration (DDR) of armed groups; *specific armed groups*
arsons: in Bosnia, 125, 130, 135; in Kosovo, 177, 198, 217
Arusha Accords, 143, 147, 151
al-Askari mosque, bombing of, 259, 269, 283, *283*, 295–96
Assad, Hafez al-, 312
assassinations: in Kosovo, 211–13; in Rwanda, 166; as strategic violence, 29, *32*
attacks on international forces: in Bosnia, 129–30; in Kosovo, 214, 216

Australia, 231–32, 235
Awakening movements, 270

Baath party: dismantling of, 264–65, 273; resistance of, 272–76, 292–93. *See also* Iraqi army, dissolution of
Badme, Ethiopia, 59, 62
Badr Brigades, 280, 301
bargaining: "dirty bargaining," 56–57; gains between winners and losers in, 338n105; in Iraq, 294–99
Bashota, Sokol, 187
Bildt, Carl, 108
Bizimungu, Pasteur, 147
Bllaca, Nazim, 213
bombings: in Bosnia, 135; in Iraq, 259, 269, 283, *283*, 295–96; in Kosovo, 209–11, 218–19
booby-traps in Kosovo, 210
Bose, Sumantra, 105
Bosnia-Herzegovina: as case study, 17; civil war in, 1; crime networks in, 40, 102, 110; criminal violence in, 126–29; Dayton Accords and, 104–8; DDR in, 85, 117–18; direct pathway in, 101–3; ethnic cleansing in, 104, 114, 130–31; explanations for violence in, 136–42; flexibility of institutions in, 92, 103, 106–7, 110, 138; opportunistic violence in, 125–26; opportunity structure in, 103, 137–38; overview of, 99–103; policing resources in, 92, 129–30; post-conflict period in, 100, 108–14; revenge violence in, 122, 124; riots in, 101, 117, 124–25; Rwanda compared to, 18; spoiling strategy in, 312; strategic violence in, 118–19, *120, 121*, 122, *123*, 136–42. *See also* Dayton Peace Accords
Bremer, L. Paul, 263–65, 266, 268, 272, 301
Bukosi, Bujar, 190
Bush, George W., 1, 257, 270

case studies: datasets for, 16–17; implications of, 307–13, *309, 310*; selection of, 17–19, *18*. *See also* Bosnia-Herzegovina; East Timor; Iraq; Kosovo; Rwanda
categorical victimization: in Bosnia, 126; in Kosovo, 207, 219; in Rwanda, 163; strategic violence and, 31, *32*; types of, 69
Çeku, Agim, 184
charismatic leadership, 82
Cheney, Dick, 257

Christopher, Warren, 99
civil wars: in Bosnia-Herzegovina, 1; in Iraq, 259; as relapsed post-conflict states, 78; in Spain, 49–50, 54. *See also* Reconstruction era
CIVPOL (Civilian Police of UNMIK), 176, 183
CNRT (Conselho Nacional de Reconstrução de Timor), 228, 235, 236–37, 238, 240, 249–50
Coalition Provisional Authority (CPA), 263, 269, 272, 273–74
Cohen, Robin, 151
Colimau 2000, 241, 254, 255
collective intent, 34–36
collective level, expressive violence at, 27–28
combatants, mobilization of, 40
Committee for Popular Defense of Democratic Republic of East Timor (CPD-RDTL), 240–41, 251, 253
communication of messages: in Kosovo, 215, 217–18; polyvalent communication with violence, 30, 217–18; understanding, 315–16. *See also* signaling political claims with violence
Congo Brazzaville, 59, 62, 64
Conselho Nacional de Reconstrução de Timor (CNRT), 228, 235, 236–37, 238, 240, 249–50
contagion effects, 75–76, 334n30
contextual details of violence and intention, 35–36
control over violence, 38–39
countermobilization: indirect pathway and, 87; in Iraq, 94, 279–82, *282*; in Kosovo, 182; levels of violence and, 308–9, 310–11; overview of, 93–94; as reaction to strategic violence, 15; against Rwanda, 173
CPA (Coalition Provisional Authority), 263, 269, 272, 273–74
CPD-RDTL (Committee for Popular Defense of Democratic Republic of East Timor), 240–41, 251, 253
criminal networks: in Bosnia, 40, 102, 110; in East Timor, 241; Hussein regime and, 42–43; imposition of sanctions and, 40–41; in Kosovo, 177, 203; opportunistic violence of, 41, 42; PDK and, 220–21; in post-conflict states, 54
criminal violence: in Bosnia, 126–29; dismissing strategic violence as, 315; in East Timor, 244–45; in Iraq, 293; in Kosovo, 178; low-intensity, 9–10; political violence and,

40–44; in Reconstruction era, 6–7; in soft security environments, 57. *See also* criminal networks; gang warfare
cross-border strategic violence: in East Timor, 232; in Kosovo, 215–16. *See also* Rwanda
cross-national dataset, 15–17, 58–59, *60–61, 62, 63*
custodians of peace, 326n63

data collection capacity, 320
dataset, 15–17
Dayton Peace Accords: flexibility of institutions of, 103, 106–7, 110, 138; military, police, and intelligence structures and, 116; overview of, 99–101, 104–8, 142; support for, 118, 139–40
DDR. *See* demobilization, disarmament, and reintegration (DDR) of armed groups
de Amaral, Xavier, 237
deaths from strategic violence. *See* cross-national dataset
deindividuation within mass movements, 27
demobilization, disarmament, and reintegration (DDR) of armed groups: in Bosnia, 85, 117–18; in East Timor, 85–86; implications of, 316–19; internal control and, 85–86; in Iraq, 260, 264–65; in Kosovo, 181, 184–96; patronage and, 83–84
Democratic League of Kosovo (LDK), 180, 212–13
Democratic Republic of Congo (DRC), 50–51, 56, 81, 150, 152. *See also* Zaire
demonstrative violence in Kosovo, 216–18, 225–26
dependent variable: strategic violence as, 44, 74; in studies, 10, 72–74
Des Forges, Allison, 167–68, 170
diasporic nationalism, 151–52
direct pathway to strategic violence: in case studies, 308–10, *310*; hypotheses about, 89–90, *90*; indirect pathway and, 88; in Iraq, 76, 275, 281; in Kosovo, 178–79, 224–25; overview of, 11, 46–47, 75–79; variables in, 88, *88*. *See also* Bosnia-Herzegovina; Rwanda
"dirty bargaining," 56–57
discriminate violence, 325n53, 329n43
distributional (reward) activities of armed groups, 83–84. *See also* patronage, exercise of
Divjak, Boris, 107
Djukanovic, Milo, 42
Dodik, Milorad, 110, 112

domestic reward. *See* patronage, exercise of
domestic violence in East Timor, 244
double genocide hypothesis, 144
DRC (Democratic Republic of Congo), 50–51, 56, 81, 150, 152. *See also* Zaire
Dreshaj, Alil, 212
drive-by shootings in Kosovo, 208, 213, 219
drug traffic through Bosnia, 128

East Timor: aftermath period in, 250–55, *251*; as case study, 18; DDR in, 85–86; factionalism in, 236–42, 250–55; flexibility of institutions in, 92, 237; Kosovo compared to, 18–19, 256; leadership of, 82; opportunity structure in, 233; overview of, 227–28, 255–56; post-conflict period in, 228–35, 242–50, *244, 245, 246, 247*; targets of attack in, 69, 247–48; violence in, 242–55
ecological inference problem, 37
Egypt, 52
elections: in Bosnia, 109–10, 111–13; in East Timor, 229, 233, 235, 238; in Iraq, 269; in Kosovo, 181–82; in Rwanda, 157
elites, criminal activities of, 42–43
El Salvador, 57, 68
Ethiopian-Eritrean war, 62
ethnic cleansing: in Afghanistan, 323n15; in Bosnia, 104, 114, 130–31; in Iraq, 259, 297; as strategic violence, 30, 32
ethnic divisions: in Bosnia, 100, 102, 104–5, 110, 112–13, 124, 137; in East Timor, 230, 242–43, 247, 253; in Kosovo, 177–78, 182, 201–3. *See also* ethnic cleansing
expressive violence: in Bosnia, 136; in Iraq, 266; in Kosovo, 177, 196–97; overview of, 25, 26–28; in Reconstruction era, 6–7; in Rwanda, 147, 174; typology of, *32*. *See also* revenge violence; riots

factionalism: in Bosnia, 141–42; DDR programs and, 316–19; in East Timor, 236–42, 250–55; internal control and, 84–87; in Iraq, 281–82, *282*; KLA and, 186–87, 188–96, *196*; in Kosovo, 178, 204, 212–13, 221–22, 223–24
factions, definition of, 326n71
Falintil, 228, 230–31, 237, 249. *See also* F-FDTL
false positive problem, 36–37
FARK (Armed Forces of the Republic of Kosovo), 190

Fartousi, Ahmed al-, 279
FAR (Rwandan Armed Forces) units, ex-members of, 148, 149, 150, 163–64, 165, 170–71
Fearon, James D., 259
Fedayeen Saddam, 275
Federation of Bosnia-Herzegovina, 104
F-FDTL (Falintil-Forças de Defesa de Timor Leste), 234–35, 237, 239, 240, 253, 254
former regime elements (FRE) in Iraq, 275, 276, 294
France, Nazi sympathizers in, 54–55
Fretilin: coalition government and, 235; in elections, 233; Gusmao and, 237–38; internal control of, 249–50; as pro-independence, 227, 228; Sagrada Familia and, 255. *See also* Falintil

Gaddafi regime, 311
Gama, Cornelio, 241, 250–51
gang warfare: in East Timor, 247, 252; in Iraq, 258, 271; in Kosovo, 213, 225
Garner, Jay M., 263, 373n4
genocide: in Rwanda, 76, 143–44, 166; as strategic violence, 30, *32*
geographic variation in post-conflict violence: in East Timor, 245–46; in Iraq, 258, 285–86, *286, 287, 288,* 289, *290,* 295; in Kosovo, 200–201, *201,* 204, *204,* 225; overview of, 71–72
Germany, reprisals in and expulsions from, 55
Gersony, Robert, 167
Gersony report, 167–69
government: in Bosnia, 105–7, 128; disposition of population toward, 53–54; in East Timor, 232–33; of Iraq, 264, 266, 269, 280; in Kosovo, 182; in Rwanda, 151, 350n52. *See also* elections
Government of the Republic of Kosova, 180
grenade attacks: in Bosnia, 130, 135; in Kosovo, 209–11
groupthink, problem of, 4
Guatemala, 41, 57, 68
Gusmao, Xanana: Alkatiri and, 235; as charismatic leader, 82, 228; CNRT and, 236; factionalism and, 251; Falintil and, 231, 238, 239, 249; F-FDTL and, 234; Petitioners and, 253–54; philosophy of, 237; as president, 233, 250; return of, 232
Gutteres, Francisco, 249, 251

Habibie, B. J., 229, 231
Habyarimana regime, 156
Haekkerup, Hans, 182
Hafez, Mohammed, 276
Hakim, Abdel Aziz al-, 280
Hakim, Mohammed Bakir al-, 267, 280
Haliti, Xhavit, 187
Haradinaj, Daut, 190, 211
Haradinaj, Ramush, 183–84, 185, 188–89, 193, 211
hard security environments: Afghanistan as, 55; Iraq as, 55, 56, 260, 281, 291; magnitude of violence in, 66, *67*; overview of, 55–57; Rwanda as, 56, 150–51, 159
Hashim, Ahmed, 275
hierarchical organizations and internal control, 80
Hintjens, Helen, 151
Holbrooke, Richard, 100, 105, 131, 142
Holkeri, Harri, 222
horizontal organizations and internal control, 80–81, 311–12
Horowitz, Donald, 27
Howard, John, 229
Human Rights Report, U.S. State Department, 89
Human Rights Watch, 219–20, 223
human trafficking through Bosnia, 128–29
Huntington, Samuel, 91
Hussein, Saddam, 42–43, 257, 261, 268, 275, 293
hypotheses about strategic violence, 13–14, 89

identity, ethnic or religious, targets selected based on, 69. *See also* categorical victimization
IFOR/SFOR in Bosnia, 104, 107–8, 126, 131, 137–38
indirect pathway to strategic violence: in case studies, 308–10, *310*; direct pathway and, 88; hypotheses about, 89–90, *90*; internal control and, 80–84; in Iraq, 276, 278, 281, 294–300; in Kosovo, 178–79, 225–26; overview of, 11–12, 47, 79–80, 86, 87–88; splintering, factionalism, and, 84–87; targeting of groups and, 86–87; variables in, 88, *88*. *See also* East Timor
indiscriminate violence, 325n53, 329n43
individual intent, 34–36

individual victimization, 69
Indonesia, 243–44, 247–49
Indonesian military (ABRI/TNI), 227, 229–31, 236, 247–48
inference of intention from effect, 37
informational asymmetries and internal control, 119, 272–73, 332n5
ingroup policing: DDR programs and, 317–18; by Gusmao, 231; by KLA, 84, 220–21; of pro-independence coalition in East Timor, 249–50; by RPF, 157
institutions of settlement, flexibility of: in Bosnia, 92, 103, 106–7, 110, 138; in East Timor, 92, 237; overview of, 91–92
instrumental violence: in Bosnia, 118, 136; in East Timor, 244, 244–46, 245; in Iraq, 266, 293; in Kosovo, 177, 197; overview of, 25, 28–29; in Rwanda, 174; strategic violence as type of, 30; typology of, 32. *See also* criminal violence
insurgencies: in Afghanistan, 3; in Iraq, 2, 265–66, 270–82, 282, 293, 299–300; in post-conflict period, 70–71, 71; reasons for, 75; in Rwanda, 147–51, 155; as strategic violence, 29–30, 32
intention and violence, 32–38, 74
Interahamwe members, 148, 163
INTERFET, 231–32
internal control: countermobilization and, 94; DDR programs and, 85–86, 316–19; definition of, 80; enforcement of compliance with peace settlements and, 12–13; factors in level of, 80–82; informational asymmetries and, 272–73, 332n5; KLA and, 184–85, 221; of nationalist parties in Bosnia, 114–18; PDK and, 221; process of splintering and, 84–87; of pro-independence coalition in East Timor, 249–50; RPF and, 152, 153–58, 163; as variable, 13–14; variations in level of, and prospects for violence, 83–84
International Crisis Group, 277
international organizations: in Bosnia, 100, 107–8, 129–30; in East Timor, 231–32, 234, 235; inside game of violence and, 313–16; in Kosovo, 175, 176; perceptions of "good guys" and "bad guys" of, 174, 301, 314; in Rwanda, 148, 149. *See also* NATO; OSCE; UN
IRA (Irish Republican Army), 42

Iraq: Baathist resistance in, 272–76; Bush administration and, 1; as case study, 18, 259–60; countermobilization in, 94, 279–82, 282; dataset for, 16; direct pathway in, 76, 275, 281; as hard security environment, 55, 56, 260, 281, 291; indirect pathway in, 276, 278, 281, 294–300; insurgency in, 2, 265–66, 270–82, 282, 293, 299–300; magnitude of violence in, 65, 66; opportunity structure in, 263, 277, 292–93, 300; as outlier, 19, 64; overview of, 257–61, 301–2; pathways in, 281, 291–300; planning for, 323n9; policing functions in, 93; post-conflict period in, 2, 4–5, 261–70; as post-conflict state, 49, 51, 259; public security gap in, 53, 263; Sunni insurgency in, 268, 276–78; targets of violence in, 14, 183–85, 278, 284, 289, 290, 291, 299–300; U.S. invasion of, 257–58, 261–62, 291–92; U.S. surge in, 270; violence in, 282–91, 283, 284, 285, 286, 287, 288, 290
Iraqi army, dissolution of, 264–65, 272–73, 274–75, 301–2
Iraqi Governing Council, 264, 266, 280
Iraqi Interim Government, 269
Iraqi National Assembly, 269
Irish Republican Army (IRA), 42
Israel, 83
Ivanovic, Oliver, 182
Izetbegović, Alija, 109, 110, 113

Jaafari, Ibrahim, 269
Jaber, Bayan, 280
Jackson, Michael, 186, 189
JAM (Jaish al-Mahdi/Mahdi Army), 267, 268, 279, 294, 298
Jelavic, Ante, 113
jihadi groups, 260, 277–78, 296, 300. *See also* al Qaeda in Iraq

Kabila, Laurent Désiré, 150, 152, 173
Kagame, Paul: genocide and, 170; in government, 157; insurgency and, 155; invasion of Zaire and, 150; RPF and, 147, 153, 156, 172, 173
Kahn, Shaharyar, 169
Kalyvas, Stathis, 27, 28, 114
Karadzic, Radovan, 104, 108, 111, 113, 127
Karzai, Hamid, 3
KFOR in Kosovo, 176, 180, 183, 214, 216
kidnappings: in Iraq, 293; in Kosovo, 214–15

KLA (Kosovo Liberation Army): assassinations and, 212; assets of, 185–86; dissolution of, 181, 184–96; domestic rewards and, 187–88; drug trade and, 41; ex-members of, 176; factions in, 186–87, 188–96, *196*; former agencies of, 191–93; in-group policing of, 84; internal control of, 184–85, 221; kidnappings by, 215; motives for violence within, 178–79; political wing of, 180; regional units of, 193–94; reprisals by, 207–8; responsibility for violence of, 219–24; revenge attacks and, 38–39; Thaçi and, 42, 185
Klickovic, Gojko, 131
Kodra, Fadil, 193
Kosovo: assassinations in, 211–13; border incidents and, 215–16; as case study, 18; church bombings in, 218–19; DDR in, 85–86; demonstrative violence in, 216–18; direct pathway in, 178–79, 224–25; East Timor compared to, 18–19, 256; first wave of violence in, 196–203, *198, 199, 200, 201*, 224–25; grenade, mortar, and bomb attacks in, 209–11; indirect pathway in, 178–79, 225–26; kidnappings in, 214–15; motives for killings in, 32; opportunity structure in, 176–77, 196–97; overview of, 175–79, 224–26; policing resources in, 92, 183, 216; post-conflict period in, 180–84; revenge and reprisal attacks in, 207–8; riots in, 214; Roma in, 42; second wave of violence in, 203–4, *204, 205*, 206, 225–26; sniper fire in, 208–9. *See also* KLA
Kosovo Liberation Army. *See* KLA
Koštunica, Vojislav, 182
Kouchner, Bernard, 181, 314
KPC (Kosovo Protection Corps), 181, 189–90
KPS (Kosovo Police Service), 183
Krajisnik, Momcilo, 109, 111
Krasniqi, Ahmet, 190
Krasniqi, Beqir, 192
Krasniqi, Jakup, 187
Kurds in Iraq, 266, 267, 279, 280–82
Kuwait, 59, 62

landmines: in Bosnia, 135; in Kosovo, 211
LDK (Democratic League of Kosovo), 180, 212–13
leadership, nature of, and internal control, 82
Lebanon, 50, 59, 67
Lemarchand, René, 157

Lequi, Osorio Mau, 255
Leutar, Jozo, 128
levels of strategic violence: in case studies, 308–9; collective, 27–28; countermobilization and, 308–9, 310–11; opportunity structure and, 14–15, 47–48, 90–91; underestimating, 313–16. *See also* magnitude of violence
Liberation Army of Presevo, Medvedja, and Bujanovac (UCPMB), 195–96, 216
Libya, 311–12
Lincoln, Abraham, 41
Lobato, Rogerio, 238–40, 249, 250, 251
local cleavages, 28–29
local dynamics and strategic violence, 10
looting: in Iraq, 258, 262, 276, 307; in Kosovo, 200–201; as reward, 40, 42

Macedonia, 191, 216
magnitude of violence, 64–67, *65, 66, 67*, 308, *309*. *See also* levels of strategic violence
Mahdi Army (JAM), 267, 268, 279, 294, 298
Mala, Besim, 212
Maliki, Nouri al-, 269, 270
Marashi, Ibrahim al-, 274–75
Marten, Kimberly, 273
martial arts gangs, 241, 255
mass-scale violence: in Iraq, 258, 300; overview of, 66–67, *67*; in Rwanda, 160, 161
methodology, 15–17, 37–38
military planners: Iraq invasion and, 257; post-conflict period in Iraq and, 263, 272–73; security threat and, 4; static image of actors and, 301
military services: of Bosnia, 114–18; for East Timor, 233–35; pensions and disability benefits for ex-soldiers, 117, 194, 265, 272. *See also* demobilization, disarmament, and reintegration (DDR) of armed groups; *specific armed groups*
military victories and post-conflict states, 49, 64
Milošević, Slobodan, 175, 180, 182
minimalist definition of violence, 25
Ministry of Public Order (MRP), 194–95
misperception of security threat, 4
Mladic, Ratko, 104, 111
mobilization of combatants, 40
Moose, George E., 168
mortar attacks: in Bosnia, 130, 135; in Kosovo, 209–11

motives: in Afghanistan, 34–35; in Bosnia, 136–42; of KLA, 178–79; in Kosovo, 32, 198–99, *199*; of RPF, 170–73; in Rwanda, 170–73; for signing peace settlements, 12–14, 76–77; for violence, 32–38
Mozambique, 67
MRP (Ministry of Public Order), 194–95
Mueller, John, 41
MUNJ (National Movement for Unity and Justice), 241, 254
Murici, Ramiz, 212–13
Museveni, Yoweri, 154, 155
Mustafa, Rustem, 185, 211
Mutsinzi, Edouard, 166
Myanmar, 49

nationalist parties: in Bosnia, 109–11, 112–13, 114–18, 127–28, 133, 134, 136–37, 139–41; Serbian, 182
National Liberation Army (NLA), 191, 216
National Movement for Unity and Justice (MUNJ), 241, 254
NATO: in Bosnia, 100, 104, 107–8, 112, 129–30; in Kosovo, 175; Libya and, 311. *See also* IFOR/SFOR in Bosnia; KFOR in Kosovo
negative cases, 59, 62, *63*, 64
negotiated settlements and post-conflict states, 49, 56, 64
NLA (National Liberation Army), 191, 216
nonlethal strategic violence in Bosnia, 138–39
Northern Alliance in Afghanistan, 2, 76
Northern Ireland: Good Friday agreement in, 79; Irish Republican Army, 42; Kosovo compared to, 197–98, *199*

Obote, Milton, 154, 155
observational definition of violence, 25
occasional violence: in East Timor, 247; in Kosovo, 175–76; overview of, 66–67, *67*
OHR (Office of the High Representative) in Bosnia, 100, 108, 112, 113, 138
opportunistic violence: analysis of crime statistics and, 38–39; in Bosnia, 125–26; of criminal networks, 41, 42; in Iraq, 296; reversal of fortune and, 55; in Rwanda, 147
opportunity structure: in Bosnia, 103, 137–38; in East Timor, 233; for expressive violence, 26–27; factors in, 91–93; in Iraq, 263, 277, 292–93, 300; in Kosovo, 176–77, 196–97;

levels of strategic violence and, 14–15, 47–48, 90–91; in Rwanda, 146–47
organizational endowments and internal control, 80–81
Orsnaco, 241
OSCE (Organization for Security and Cooperation in Europe): in Bosnia, 100, 108, 112, 113; in Kosovo, 180, 219
outbidding, 298–99
overconfidence in prediction of security threat, 4

Palestinians, internal control of, 83
Party for Democratic Progress of Kosovo (PDK), 186, 187–88, 193–94, 195, 219–24
pathways/patterns of strategic violence. *See* direct pathway to strategic violence; indirect pathway to strategic violence
patronage, exercise of: in Bosnia, 105–6, 107, 110–11, 138; by CPA, 273–74; DDR programs and, 317–18; in East Timor, 249–50; in Kosovo, 187–88; overview of, 81–82, 83–84; by RPF, 157
PDK (Party for Democratic Progress of Kosovo), 186, 187–88, 193–94, 195, 219–24
peacekeeping missions: in Bosnia, 137–38; data collection capacity of, 320; in East Timor, 232, 235; in Kosovo, 356n9; preventive deployment of, 319–20; recognition of threats to peace by, 313–15; in Rwanda, 146. *See also* IFOR/SFOR in Bosnia; KFOR in Kosovo; *specific UN missions*
peace settlements: actors signing, 12–14, 76–77; Arusha Accords, 143, 147, 151; dissatisfaction with, and direct pathway, 75–79; enforcement of terms of, 12–13, 79–80, 321; failure of, 56; flexibility of institutions of, 91–92; incentive structures and, 77, 321; magnitude of violence and, 66–67; repression after, 76. *See also* Dayton Peace Accords; peacekeeping missions
pensions and disability benefits for ex-soldiers: in Bosnia, 117; in Iraq, 265, 272; in Kosovo, 194
Persian Gulf War, 62
Petersen, Roger D., 28
Petitioners, 240, 250, 252–53, 254
Petraeus, David, 272
Petritsch, Wolfgang, 112, 113
Philippines, 75

PNTL (Policia Nacional de Timor-Leste): disintegration of, 255; F-FDTL and, 235, 254; human rights violations of, 245; inflexibility of, 237; regional divide and, 253; riots and, 250; selection process for, 239–40
police services: in Bosnia, 92, 116–17, 129–30, 138; in East Timor, 238–39; in Iraq, 93, 262; in Kosovo, 92, 183, 216; preventive deployment of, 319–20. *See also* PNTL
Policia Nacional de Timor-Leste. *See* PNTL
Policia Ushtarake (PU), 191–92, 195
policing activities of armed groups, 83–84. *See also* in-group policing
policy recommendations, 319–21
Polisi, Denis, 150
political development of post-conflict states and policy responses to violence, 320–21
political violence and criminal violence, 40–44. *See also* strategic violence
polyvalent communication with violence, 30, 217–18
Poplasen, Nikola, 112–13
population: preferences and wartime behavior of, 54–55; traumatized, after armed conflict, 53–54; vulnerability of groups in, 91. *See also* refugees
population flight, 37
post-conflict period: in Afghanistan, 3; in American South, 5–8; in Bosnia, 100, 108–14; dataset, 58–59, *60–61, 62, 63*; in East Timor, 228–35, 242–50, *244, 245, 246, 247*; geographic variation within states in, 71–72; insurgencies in, 70–71, *71*; in Iraq, 2, 4–5, 261–70; in Kosovo, 180–84; magnitude of violence in, 64–67, *65, 66*; problems in prediction of, 4–5, 305; relapse into armed conflict in, 69–70, *70*; in Rwanda, 145–53; strategic violence in, 305–7; targets of violence in, 69; temporal variation in violence in, 72, *73*; transformation of actors in, 8; types of violence in, 67–69, *68*
post-conflict states: Afghanistan as, 50, 51; categories of violence in, 8–9; definition of, 48–51; Iraq as, 49, 51, 259; local dynamics of, 10; negotiated settlements and, 49, 56, 64; opportunity structures in, 14–15; Rwanda as, 50–51; as *sui generis* cases, 11; transitory status as, 56; types of, 55–58; weak states compared to, 51–55. *See also* post-conflict period

precipitant acts, 373n11
prison raids in Rwanda, 164
protection rackets: in Bosnia, 128; in Iraq, 293; in Kosovo, 189, 197; macro-cleavages and, 40
Provisional Government of Kosova, 180
Prunier, Gérard, 143, 159
PU (Policia Ushtarake), 191–92, 195
public security gap: after armed conflict, 52–53; in East Timor, 233, 243; in Iraq, 53, 263; in Kosovo, 176; opportunistic expressive violence and, 26–27; prevention of, 319–20
Pugh, Michael, 107

Radisic, Zivko, 113
Ramos-Horta, Jose, 235, 236, 237, 238, 250, 251, 255
RANU (Rwandese Alliance for National Unity), 153–55. *See also* RPF
rational choice literature, 74
Reconstruction era, 5–8, 10, 29
Reed, Wm. Cyrus, 157
Rees, Edward, 239
refugees: from East Timor, 243–44; flows of, in Kosovo, 180; from Rwanda, 146, 148–50. *See also* refugees, attacks on; refugees, return of
refugees, attacks on: in Bosnia, 131–35, *132, 134*; in East Timor, 247; in Kosovo, 208; in Rwanda, 164–66
refugees, return of: to Bosnia, 105, 118, 131–35, *132, 134*; to Kosovo, 181
regional division in East Timor, 252–55, 256
regional variation in post-conflict violence. *See* geographic variation in post-conflict violence
Reinado, Alfredo, 235, 240, 241, 254–55
relapse into armed conflict: dataset, 69–70, *70*; as dependent variable in studies, 10, 73–74; hard security environment compared to, 56; magnitude of violence and, 65. *See also* direct pathway to strategic violence; indirect pathway to strategic violence
religious targets: in Bosnia, 135; in Iraq, 259, 269, 283, *283*, 295–96, 297; in Kosovo, 218–19; as symbolic attacks, 29, *32*
reporting bias problem, 37
reprisals: described, 29, *32;* in Iraq, 292–93; in Kosovo, 207–8; revenge violence compared to, 328n20; in Rwanda, 161, 163
Republika Srpska (RS), 104
residual violence: in Bosnia, 101; defined, 66–67, *67*, 326n59, 337n86

resources: internal control and, 81–82; for policing and peacekeeping, 92–93. *See also* patronage, exercise of

revenge violence: in Bosnia, 122, 124; capacity to forgive and, 380n19; dismissing all violence as, 314–15; as expressive violence, 26, *32*; in Iraq, 266, 292; in Kosovo, 177, 197, 200, 207–8; reprisals compared to, 328n20; in Rwanda, 147

reversal of fortune, violence after: armed conflict as priming for, 55; examples of, 4–5; in Iraq, 266–67, 269; in Kosovo, 176–77

Rexhepi, Bajram, 223

Reyntjens, Filip, 148, 151, 163, 171

Rice, Susan, 153

riots: in Bosnia, 101, 117, 124–25; in East Timor, 247, 250, 252, 253–55; as expressive violence, 27; in Kosovo, 183, 214, 222–23; as strategic violence, 29, *32*

Rodriguez, Roque, 236, 249

RPA (Rwandan Patriotic Army), 150

RPF (Rwandan Patriotic Front): Arusha Accords and, 147; DRC and, 152–53; expansion of goals of, 172–73; internal control of, 152, 156–58, 163; invasion of Rwanda by, 155–56; motives for violence of, 170–72; origin of, 153–54; overview of, 143–44; refugee camps and, 148, 149–50; responsibility for violence of, 167–70

Ruak, Taur Matan, 231, 234, 236, 238, 253

Rugova, Ibrahim, 180, 183, 184, 213

Rumsfeld, Donald, 1, 262, 373n4, 373n5, 374n26

Rwanda: assassinations in, 166; Bosnia compared to, 18; as case study, 17–18; dataset for, 16; direct pathway in, 75–76; explanations for violence in, 170–73; genocide in, 76, 143–44, 166; as hard security environment, 56, 150–51, 159; magnitude of violence in, 65, *66*; opportunity structure in, 146–47; overview of, 143–45, 173–74; post-conflict period in, 145–53; as post-conflict state, 50–51; raids by ex-FAR forces in, 163–64; reprisals in, 161, 163; RPF in, 153–58; violence in, 158–61, *160*, *161*, *162*, 163–66, 170–73. *See also* RPF

Rwandan Armed Forces (FAR) units, ex-members of, 148, 149, 150, 163–64, 165, 170–71

Rwandan Patriotic Army (RPA), 150

Rwandan Patriotic Front. *See* RPF

Rwandese Alliance for National Unity (RANU), 153–55. *See also* RPF

Rwangabo, Pierre Clever, 166

Rwigyema, Fred, 155, 156

Sadr, Muqtada al-, 267, 268, 270, 279

Sadrists, 268–69, 279, 281, 299, 301

Saembilan, Samb, 241

Sagrada Familia, 241, 250–51, 255

Salafi ideology, 278

Salsinha, Gustão, 241

Sambanis, Nicholas, 114

sanctions, imposition of, and criminal networks, 40–41

Scambray, James, 239, 254

scattered violence, 66–67, *67*

Scheffer, Jaap de Hoop, 222

SCIRI (Supreme Council for the Islamic Revolution in Iraq), 267, 280, 299

sectarian cleansing. *See* ethnic cleansing

security threats, prediction of, 1–3, 305

Sendashonga, Seth, 166

Serbia, 184, 215–16

sex trafficking in Bosnia, 129

shadow governments in Kosovo, 180–81, 196

Sherbimi Informativ I Kosoves (SHIK), 191, 192, 213

Shi'a Muslims in Iraq, 266, 267, 268–69, 279–82

Shinseki, Eric, 1, 2

Shoesmith, Dennis, 237–38

signaling political claims with violence, 30, 297, 298–300

Silajdzic, Haris, 141

Sistani, Ali, 266, 268, 279

Smith, Leighton, 108

sniper fire: in Bosnia, 130; in Kosovo, 208–9

soft security environments: Bosnia as, 101, 118; East Timor as, 228, 233; magnitude of violence in, 66, *67*; overview of, 57–58

Spanish Civil War, 49–50, 54

splintering of armed groups, 84–87. *See also* factionalism

splinters, definition of, 326n71

spoiling strategy: in case studies, 312–13; literature on, 325n53, 326n65, 330n51; pathways and, 72–73, 75; strategic violence from, 327–28n9

Sri Lanka, 52, 59, 62

Stedman, Stephen John, 314
Steiner, Michael, 191
strategic sales in Kosovo, 360n130
strategic violence: armed conflict as priming states for, 52–55; in Bosnia, 118–19, *120, 121, 122, 123,* 136–42; characteristics of, 30–31; conception of, 9–11; definition of, 29, 31, 33; as dependent variable of study, 44, 74; in East Timor, 242–55; first wave of, in Kosovo, 196–203, *198, 199, 200, 201,* 224–25; as focus of study, 24; in Iraq, 282–91, *283, 284, 285, 286, 287, 288, 290;* low-intensity, 9–10, 56–57; overview of, 25; patterns of, 45; in post-conflict states, 8–9, 52–55, 305–7; in Rwanda, 158–61, *160, 161, 162,* 163–66, 170–73; second wave of, in Kosovo, 203–4, *204, 205,* 206, 225–26; spoiling strategy and, 327–28n9; theoretical framework for, 11–15; types of, 29–30; typology of, 32. *See also* direct pathway to strategic violence; indirect pathway to strategic violence; opportunity structure; *specific types of violence*
Sunni Muslims in Iraq, 264–65, *266–67,* 268, 269, 276–78
support for peace settlements, as variable, 13–14
Supreme Council for the Islamic Revolution in Iraq (SCIRI), 267, 280, 299
Syla, Azem, 187
symbolic attacks, 29, 32. *See also* religious targets
Syria, 312

Talabani, Jalal, 269
Taliban, 2–3, 76
targeted killings, 29, 32. *See also* assassinations
targets of attacks: after armed conflicts, 54–55; in Bosnia, 129–30; categorization of, 31; countermobilization of, 15, 87, 93–94; in East Timor, 69, 247–48; indirect pathway and, 86–87; in Iraq, 14, 278, 283–85, *284,* 289, *290,* 291, 299–300; in Kosovo, 199–200, *200, 204, 205,* 206, 207, 209, 216–18, 225–26; opportunity structure and, 91; overview of, 308, *309;* pathways and, 14; in post-conflict period, 69; in Reconstruction era, 6–7; returnees to Bosnia, 131–35, *132, 134;* in Rwanda, 143; stability of, over time, 74; strategic violence and, 30. *See also* categorical victimization; refugees, attacks on; religious targets
temporal criterion for post-conflict states, 51
temporal variation in violence in post-conflict period, 72, *73,* 258. *See also* Kosovo, first wave of violence in; Kosovo, second wave of violence in
territoriality criterion for post-conflict states, 50
terrorist attacks, 30, *32*
Thaçi, Hashim: criminal activities of, 220–21; government headed by, 180; independence and, 224; KLA and, 42, 185; PDK and, 187, 188; as prime minister, 42, 184; riots and, 223; on rogue elements, 193
Tilly, Charles, 217
tit-for-tat patterns of killings: in Bosnia, 124, 134; in Iraq, 297; in Rwanda, 165
TNI. *See* Indonesian military
Traub, James, 236
Twagiramungu, Faustin, 147
types of violence, 29–30, 67–69, *68,* 308, *309.* *See also specific types of violence*

UCPMB (Liberation Army of Presevo, Medvedja, and Bujanovac), 195–96, 216
Uganda, 153, 154
UN (United Nations): International Police Task Force in Bosnia, 108, 112, 116, 119, 129–30, 137; Kosovo and, 181; peacekeeping missions of, 64–65, 92–93; in Rwanda, 153; standards before status policy of, 183. *See also* UNHCR; *specific missions*
UNAMET (United Nations Mission in East Timor), 232, 368n33
UNAMIR (United Nations Assistance Mission to Rwanda), 148, 169
UNHCR (United Nations High Commissioner for Refugees): in Bosnia, 108, 133; Gersony report and, 167–69; in Rwanda, 148, 149
UNMIK (UN Mission in Kosovo), 176, 181, 183
UNMISET (United Nations Mission of Support in East Timor), 234
UNMIT (United National Integrated Mission in Timor Leste), 235
UNOTIL (United Nations Office in East Timor), 234
UNTAET (United Nations Transitional Administration in East Timor), 232, 368n33
Uppsala Conflict Termination Dataset, 58

Vasic, Josif, 212
verbal threats, 25

Veseli, Kadri, 192
veterans' associations in Kosovo, 186, 194, 223
victims. *See* targets of attacks
Vieira de Mello, Sergio, 232, 233, 266, 267
Vietnam War, 2
violence: definition of, 25–26; forms of, 23; intention and, 32–38; interpretations of, 313–16; limited information on, 23–24, 44; opportunistic, and analysis of crime statistics, 38–39; policy responses to, and political development of post-conflict states, 320–21; typology of, 31–32, *32*. *See also* motives; strategic violence; *specific types of violence*
"violent specialists," 54

WANRA groups in East Timor, 229, 248
warnings by perpetrators of strategic violence, 30
wars: as gamble, 1; overlapping, 50–51; resumption of, as dependent variable in studies, 10. *See also* armed conflict; civil wars
wartime behavior, targets selected based on, 54–55, 69

weak states compared to post-conflict states, 51–55
Weber, Max, 82
Westendorp, Carlos, 111, 112
West Timor, 243–44
winners, dissatisfaction of: in Kosovo, 178; in Rwanda, 144–45, 171
Wirth, Tim, 168
Wolfowitz, Paul, 2
World Health Organization homicide statistics, 68

Yudhoyono, Susilo Bambang, 234
Yugoslavia, 99, 115, 175, 180

Zaire: Mobutu regime in, 150; motives for RPF to attack, 172–73; refugees from Rwanda in, 146, 148–50; RPF in, 144. *See also* Democratic Republic of Congo
Zarqawi, Abu Musab al-, 267, 269, 278
Zbulim-Kinderzbulim (ZKZ), 191, 192–93, 195
Zemaj, Tahir, 213
Zubak, Kresimir, 109